WORLD POLITICS
94/95

Fifteenth Edition

Editor

Helen E. Purkitt
United States Naval Academy

Dr. Helen E. Purkitt obtained her Ph.D. in International Relations from the University of Southern California. She is Professor of Political Science at the U.S. Naval Academy. Her research and teaching interests include political decision-making, the politics of southern Africa, foreign policy, international relations, and national security issues. Recent publications include "Political Decision-Making in the Context of Small Groups: The Cuban Missile Crisis Revisited—One More Time," in E. Singer and V. Hudson (Eds.), *Political Psychology and Foreign Policy* (Westview, 1992), and "Artificial Intelligence and Intuitive Foreign Policy Decisionmakers Viewed as Limited Information Processors: Some Conceptual Issues and Practical Concerns for the Future," in V. Hudson (Ed.), *Artificial Intelligence and International Politics* (Westview, 1991).

Annual Editions
A Library of Information from the Public Press

Cover illustration by Mike Eagle

The Dushkin Publishing Group, Inc.
Sluice Dock, Guilford, Connecticut 06437

This map has been developed to give you a graphic picture of where the countries of the world are located, the relationship they have with their region and neighbors, and their positions relative to the superpowers and power blocs. We have focused on certain areas to more clearly illustrate these crowded regions.

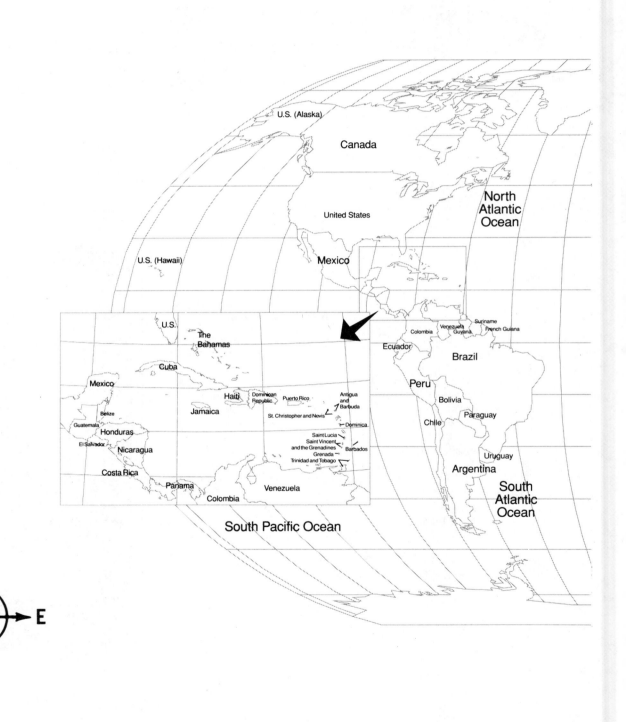

The Annual Editions Series

Annual Editions is a series of over 60 volumes designed to provide the reader with convenient, low-cost access to a wide range of current, carefully selected articles from some of the most important magazines, newspapers, and journals published today. Annual Editions are updated on an annual basis through a continuous monitoring of over 300 periodical sources. All Annual Editions have a number of features designed to make them particularly useful, including topic guides, annotated tables of contents, unit overviews, and indexes. For the teacher using Annual Editions in the classroom, an Instructor's Resource Guide with test questions is available for each volume.

VOLUMES AVAILABLE

Africa
Aging
American Foreign Policy
American Government
American History, Pre-Civil War
American History, Post-Civil War
Anthropology
Biology
Business Ethics
Canadian Politics
Child Growth and Development
China
Comparative Politics
Computers in Education
Computers in Business
Computers in Society
Criminal Justice
Drugs, Society, and Behavior
Dying, Death, and Bereavement
Early Childhood Education
Economics
Educating Exceptional Children
Education
Educational Psychology
Environment
Geography
Global Issues
Health
Human Development
Human Resources
Human Sexuality
India and South Asia
International Business
Japan and the Pacific Rim

Latin America
Life Management
Macroeconomics
Management
Marketing
Marriage and Family
Mass Media
Microeconomics
Middle East and the Islamic World
Money and Banking
Multicultural Education
Nutrition
Personal Growth and Behavior
Physical Anthropology
Psychology
Public Administration
Race and Ethnic Relations
Russia, Eurasia, and Central/Eastern Europe
Social Problems
Sociology
State and Local Government
Third World
Urban Society
Violence and Terrorism
Western Civilization, Pre-Reformation
Western Civilization, Post-Reformation
Western Europe
World History, Pre-Modern
World History, Modern
World Politics

Library of Congress Cataloging in Publication Data
Main entry under title: Annual Editions: World Politics. 1994/95.
1. International relations. 2. United States—Foreign relations. I. Purkitt, Helen E., comp.
II. Title: World Politics.
ISBN 1–56134–290–4   327″.05

Fifteenth Edition

Printed in the United States of America

Printed on Recycled Paper

To the Reader

In publishing ANNUAL EDITIONS we recognize the enormous role played by the magazines, newspapers, and journals of the *public press* in providing current, first-rate educational information in a broad spectrum of interest areas. Within the articles, the best scientists, practitioners, researchers, and commentators draw issues into new perspective as accepted theories and viewpoints are called into account by new events, recent discoveries change old facts, and fresh debate breaks out over important controversies.

Many of the articles resulting from this enormous editorial effort are appropriate for students, researchers, and professionals seeking accurate, current material to help bridge the gap between principles and theories and the real world. These articles, however, become more useful for study when those of lasting value are carefully *collected, organized, indexed,* and *reproduced* in a *low-cost format,* which provides easy and permanent access when the material is needed. That is the role played by *Annual Editions.* Under the direction of each volume's *Editor,* who is an expert in the subject area, and with the guidance of an *Advisory Board,* we seek each year to provide in each *ANNUAL EDITION* a current, well-balanced, carefully selected collection of the best of the public press for your study and enjoyment. We think you'll find this volume useful, and we hope you'll take a moment to let us know what you think.

Annual Editions: World Politics 94/95 is aimed at filling a void in materials for learning about world politics and foreign policy. Among the dozens of textbooks and anthologies available today, this comprehensive and timely compilation of readings brings together summaries of the major problems concerning relations among nations and other international actors in an easily understandable language.

The articles are chosen for those who are new to the study of world politics. The objective of this compilation is to stimulate interest in learning about issues that often seem foreign, remote, and irrelevant, but that actually have profound consequences for economic well-being, security, and even survival.

International relations can be viewed as a complex and dynamic system of actions and reactions by a diverse set of actors that produce new situations that require further actions. The readings in this volume convey the complexities and the dynamic interdependence of international relations in the world today. The interdependence of relationships means that events in places as far away as Japan, the Middle East, South Africa, and Latin America affect the United States, just as America's actions, and inactions, have significant repercussions for other states. Interdependence also refers to the increased role of non-state actors such as international corporations, the United Nations, and CNN. These non-state actors increasingly influence the scope, nature, and pace of change in the international system. International events proceed at such a rapid pace, however, that often what is said about international affairs today may be outdated tomorrow.

This focus on the immediate issues of the day is why it is important for readers to begin to develop a mental framework or image of the international system as a complex system that loosely connects a diverse set of actors who interact about an ever-changing agenda of international issues. This collection of articles about international events provides up-to-date information and commentaries about the current set of issues on the world agenda. Some of the readings also analyze the significance of emerging trends in the types of actors and processes that define the structure of the post–cold war international system.

This fifteenth edition of *Annual Editions: World Politics 94/95* is divided into eight units. The collapse of communist regimes throughout the world means that we can no longer view international relations through the prism of a bipolar system. Instead, national, regional, and subregional issues are increasingly important aspects of international relations in the emerging multipolar system.

The first five units reflect this changing reality by focusing on the major actors and trends in five geographical areas or "subsystems": (1) the Western Hemisphere; (2) the independent nation-states of the former Soviet Union; (3) the countries of West and Central Europe; (4) the Pacific Basin region, which encompasses a diverse set of countries including Japan, China, the newly industrialized countries (NICs) and communist regimes of South East Asia, and countries located on the Indian subcontinent or along the rim of the Pacific Ocean; and (5) the Middle East and Africa. After discussing the policy issues and concerns of major actors and the analyses of key issues and trends in each of these regions, the book turns to three broad areas of concern to international relations: the international political economy; arms issues—proliferation, regional arms races, arms control, and disarmament; and the role of international entities and emerging issues related to collective security and the management of global issues in a New World Order. In each unit, a variety of political perspectives is offered to make readers more aware of the complexities of the problems in international relations, and to stimulate their consideration of alternative perspectives about the world.

I wish to thank my colleagues and the previous users of *Annual Editions: World Politics* who have taken time to contribute articles or comments on this collection of readings. Please continue to provide feedback to guide the annual revision of this anthology by filling out the article rating form on the last page of this book.

Helen E. Purkitt

Helen E. Purkitt
Editor

Contents

Unit
1

The Western Hemisphere

Eight selections discuss current and future United States foreign policy, North American free trade, and the role Latin America plays in the Western Hemisphere.

The concepts in bold italics are developed in the article. For further expansion please refer to the Topic Guide, the Index, and the Glossary.

Unit 2

The Former Soviet Union

Four articles examine the events that contributed to the unraveling of the Soviet Union. Internal strife, Boris Yeltsin, new Russian foreign policy, and the future of Russia are discussed.

Unit 3

Europe

Eight selections review some of the historic events that will alter Western and Central Europe. Topics include the future of NATO, the turmoil in the former Yugoslavia, and Central/Eastern Europe's strivings toward democracy.

The concepts in bold italics are developed in the article. For further expansion please refer to the Topic Guide, the Index, and the Glossary.

Unit 4

The Pacific Basin

Five articles examine some of the countries instrumental in the economic evolution of the Pacific Basin. Japan, China, and North Korea are considered.

The concepts in bold italics are developed in the article. For further expansion please refer to the Topic Guide, the Index, and the Glossary.

Unit 5

The Middle East and Africa

Seven articles review the current state of the Middle East and Africa. The quest for democracy in Africa, the force of Islam, turmoil in the Horn of Africa, and South Africa's future foreign policy are among the topics discussed.

Unit 6

The International Political Economy

Five articles examine the global marketplace as politics redefine the rules of the economic game.

The concepts in bold italics are developed in the article. For further expansion please refer to the Topic Guide, the Index, and the Glossary.

Unit 7

The Politics of Arms, Arms Proliferation, and Arms Control

Five selections discuss the current state of the arms race by considering the future of deterrence, world military expenditures, and a new nuclear order.

Unit 8

Collective Security and Emerging Global Issues in the New World Order

Six articles discuss the influence that international organizations have on world peace, defense in the twenty-first century, and world poverty and pollution.

The concepts in bold italics are developed in the article. For further expansion please refer to the Topic Guide, the Index, and the Glossary.

The concepts in bold italics are developed in the article. For further expansion please refer to the Topic Guide, the Index, and the Glossary.

Topic Guide

This topic guide suggests how the selections in this book relate to topics of traditional concern to students and professionals involved with the study of world politics. It is useful for locating articles that relate to each other for reading and research. The guide is arranged alphabetically according to topic. Articles may, of course, treat topics that do not appear in the topic guide. In turn, entries in the topic guide do not necessarily constitute a comprehensive listing of all the contents of each selection.

TOPIC AREA	TREATED IN:	TOPIC AREA	TREATED IN:
Africa	29. Radicals Gain Strength in Horn of Africa 30. From Peace-keeping to Peace Enforcement 31. Africa's 'New Wind of Change' 32. South Africa's Future Foreign Policy	**Democracy**	1. Clash of Civilizations? 22. Japan: The End of One-Party Dominance 30. From Peace-keeping to Peace Enforcement 31. Africa's 'New Wind of Change' 43. Jihad vs. McWorld
Arms Control and Proliferation	24. North Korea: The Dangerous Outsider 38. Five Minutes Past Midnight 39. Dismantling the Arsenals 40. Fighting Off Doomsday 41. Shifting Battle Lines in Arms Race 42. The Bomb or Peace	**Economic Reforms**	17. Great Transformation 22. Japan: The End of One-Party Dominance 35. Beyond Conditionality 37. In Beijing and Moscow, Starkly Different Policies and Results
Asia	3. Evaluating Foreign Policy Relationships 21. Rivals or Partners? 22. Japan: The End of One-Party Dominance 23. Rise of China 24. North Korea: The Dangerous Outsider 25. What Is an Economy For? 37. In Beijing and Moscow, Starkly Different Policies and Results	**Ethnic Conflict**	1. Clash of Civilizations? 12. Will Russia Disintegrate into Bantustans? 15. Searching for Identity, Germany Struggles with Its History 16. Europe Slams the Door 19. Why Yugoslavia Fell Apart 20. The Answer 26. Can It Really Be Peace? 48. Deceptive Stereotypes about 'Tribal Warfare'
Balkans	19. Why Yugoslavia Fell Apart 20. The Answer 48. Deceptive Stereotypes about 'Tribal Warfare'	**Europe (Central)**	17. Great Transformation 18. In a New Slovakia, Fears Are Both New and Old 19. Why Yugoslavia Fell Apart 20. The Answer
China	23. Rise of China 37. In Beijing and Moscow, Starkly Different Policies and Results	**Europe (Western)**	4. Renewed Security Partnership? 13. Redefined NATO Faces Growing Pains 14. Reinventing the Politics of Europe 15. Searching for Identity, Germany Struggles with Its History 16. Europe Slams the Door 39. Dismantling the Arsenals 44. Defence in the 21st Century
Commonwealth of Independent States (former Soviet Union)	5. Ten Issues in Search of a Policy 9. Real Coup 10. New Russian Foreign Policy 11. Security Issues and the Eastern Slavic States 12. Will Russia Disintegrate into Bantustans?	**European Union (European Community)**	14. Reinventing the Politics of Europe
Communism's Collapse	1. Clash of Civilizations? 9. Real Coup 12. Will Russia Disintegrate into Bantustans? 18. In a New Slovakia, Fears Are Both New and Old 19. Why Yugoslavia Fell Apart 23. Rise of China 43. Jihad vs. McWorld	**Germany**	14. Reinventing the Politics of Europe 15. Searching for Identity, Germany Struggles with Its History 16. Europe Slams the Door
		IMF and the World Bank	35. Beyond Conditionality

The Western Hemisphere

The main theme to emerge from the articles in this unit is that continuing conflicts among members of the foreign policy establishment in the United States has led to a failure to articulate a set of goals or ideas capable of guiding the national security policies of the United States in response to the dramatic and sweeping changes of the 1990s. The collapse of communism in Eastern Europe and the Soviet Union altered the face of Europe and the fundamental pattern of international relations worldwide. But turbulence and change characterized the end of bipolarity, as a resurgence of ethnic tensions surfaced throughout Europe. "Ethnic cleansing" spread from Croatia to Bosnia-Herzegovina and threatened to escalate into a more generalized Balkans conflict. Similar disintegrative tendencies emerged throughout the world. Mass starvation and ethnic conflict in Somalia were only two of the more publicized human tragedies occurring in the world today. As it became apparent that the breakup of multiethnic states, rather than the demise of communism, was the profound trend of the early post–cold war era, the euphoria over the dawn of a new era waned.

Throughout the 1990s, Americans have focused only intermittently on international events and trends. Once the troops from Desert Storm came home in 1991, events in Iraq and throughout the Middle East were dropped from America's agenda. Since 1992, public opinion polls show that the majority of Americans support putting domestic and social problems ahead of international affairs. Most recent polls indicate that the majority of Americans are supportive of President Clinton's emphasis on domestic rather than foreign affairs. Americans are more concerned about health care, jobs, and crime than foreign affairs. Intractable domestic issues are the top priority of most Americans.

Given the domestic political environment, the Clinton administration did not articulate a detailed national security strategy beyond general commitments to promoting democratic and free-market economic reforms and promises to use foreign policy to promote U.S. economic interests worldwide. Ad hoc decisions in response to highly visible international events served as a stimulus for major changes in foreign policies. This pattern perhaps developed from a desire on the part of the administration and a majority of Americans to limit U.S. military involvement abroad. The announcement of the withdrawal of U.S. troops from operations in Somalia after U.S. soldiers were killed in clashes with Somali militiamen in 1993 was supported by the majority of Americans. Similarly, while Americans were disturbed by the atrocities against civilians in the Bosnian conflict, little support for increased U.S. involvement in this conflict was generated until a highly publicized incident in which over 60 civilians were killed by a mortar shell in the marketplace in the besieged capital of Sarajevo, Bosnia. This led to a series of bold new initiatives by the Clinton administration to obtain a negotiated settlement.

Despite the back-seat priority accorded foreign policy issues on the American political agenda, the Clinton administration racked up a number of dramatic foreign policy successes during its first years in office, including Senate approval of the North American Free Trade Agreement (NAFTA), the September 1993 Israeli–Palestinian Liberation Organization (PLO) accord on the future of the occupied territories, the Ukrainian-Russian agreement designed to eliminate long-range missiles from Ukraine in exchange for U.S. economic and security guarantees, and an agreement after a year of waffling by North Korean leaders to permit international inspections of most nuclear facilities. After the marketplace tragedy of Sarajevo, the Clinton administration quickly threw its weight behind a number of UN/NATO-sponsored initiatives in the Balkans. Beginning in February 1994, U.S. support was critical for the success of the negotiated cease-fire in Sarajevo, backed by the threat of NATO force. Next, the Clinton administration sponsored the signing of a Croat-Muslim accord designed to be the first step in an international effort to compel a new political status quo in Bosnia reflecting Serb control of over 70 percent of the territory.

Despite these successes, and public approval for limiting U.S. military involvement abroad, the foreign policy agenda of the Clinton administration remains a subject of intense criticism, particularly from members of the foreign policy elite. While such critics disagree among themselves on the details of an optimal foreign policy agenda, they are united in the view that America must give more attention to its role as the last remaining superpower, both to protect U.S. interests abroad and to promote peace and prosperity worldwide. For example, in "The Conceptual Poverty of U.S. Foreign Policy," Jonathan Clarke argues that the most serious foreign policy problem facing the Clinton administration is the need to construct a new concept of America's place in the world. This conceptualization, Clarke maintains, should replace the current reactive, seat-of-the-pants management of foreign affairs practiced by the administration.

Policy disagreements about U.S. foreign policy are tied to a lack of a bipartisan consensus on the nature of future international threats to U.S. interests. While most agree that international relations are still characterized by threats to world peace, a clear conception of the nature of these threats is lacking. During the cold war, there were often clearly identifiable adversaries operating in conflicts against a background of stable global alliances. Cold war experiences do not seem relevant for understanding contemporary conflicts—there is a lack of "good guys/bad guys" or "good solutions." Consequently, debates center on the appropriate role for the United States.

Many observers who stress the importance of promoting U.S. economic interests abroad recognize the increased strategic importance of the Asia-Pacific region—the world's leading area in rate of economic growth. Other observers emphasize that the United States and Europe are at a critical turning point in their security partnership. Thus, the choices made in the United States, in European capitals, and in organizations like NATO over the next few years may determine the shape of international relations for decades. Catherine McArdle Kelleher, in "A Renewed Security Partnership? The United States and the European Community in the 1990s," outlines some reasons why now is the time to establish a new vision for a renewed security partnership with our European allies. Such an agreement aims to ensure the continuation of collective action by the West. In a non–zero-sum world, foreign policy success may depend on the willingness of the United States to help others to succeed, to engage in new forms of multilateralism, and to forge new forms of international cooperation. Unless the United States learns how to deal with Europeans on equal terms and in novel ways, NATO may succumb to its cold war success. Recent experiences in the Gulf War, Operation Restore Hope in Somalia, and the conflict in the Balkans underscore the need for international norms to provide multilateral preventive diplomacy and peacekeeping.

Nowhere is the need for new diplomatic, economic, political, and security arrangements to ensure continuing international peace and prosperity more evident than among the United States, Japan, Europe, and the newly independent republics of the former Soviet Union. Promoting economic and political reform in Russia and securing denuclearization in Ukraine have been major national security priorities of recent U.S. administrations. However, after Boris Yeltsin had to resort to force to crush political opponents in October 1993 and encountered an electoral backlash against rapid Western-style economic reforms, there has been increased concern in the United States about the wisdom of tying U.S. policies too closely to Yeltsin's ability to retain control of the Russian government.

While the resignation of Mikhail Gorbachev on December 25, 1991, and the formation of the Commonwealth of Independent States, hastily formed in 1992 as an alternate framework to guide relations among the former republics, marked the formal end of the Soviet Union, the more enduring patterns of international relations among the independent states remain highly fluid. There is a re-

surgence of support for former communist politicians and institutions, along with anti-Western biases created by economic dislocations, rising inflation, plummeting standards of living, a heightened sense of nationalism, and crime, as the controls of national governments have weakened.

Since the collapse of the Soviet Union, the United States has not formulated a policy to address the multitude of challenges created by the demise of the former empire. The complexity of these international relationships is evident in Paul Goble's article, which outlines 10 key issues that the United States must address to develop a coherent and comprehensive policy approach with the post-Soviet states.

The importance of multilateralism, especially in the realm of international economics, and the importance of cooperation with hemispheric neighbors was underscored in 1992 with the signing of NAFTA by leaders of Canada, the United States, and Mexico. While leaders agreed to reduce regional trade barriers to promote future hemispheric prosperity, the accord faced formidable opposition in each country.

Reducing national trade barriers greatly expanded the amount of intraregional trade among countries in Latin America. Expansion of hemispheric trade underscores the importance of U.S. trade relations with these neighbors. For nearly two centuries, the United States has viewed Latin America as within its exclusive sphere of influence to be protected from hostile foreign intrusions. As G. Pope Atkins reminds us in "Latin America's International Relations in the Post–Cold War Era," this America-centric focus was never particularly effective.

Looking Ahead: Challenge Questions

Given the changes in the world, what will be the most important national security threats to the United States?

Is there a need to maintain NATO forces in Europe? For what purposes?

Should the United States encourage the formation of an all-European security force?

Should the United States provide more aid to prevent economic and political disintegration in the republics of the former Soviet Union?

What advice would you give the president or the Congress about downsizing the military while promoting U.S. interests abroad?

Is it in the U.S. economic interest to pursue hard-line policies in trade disputes with Japan or regarding human rights violations in China?

What principles might guide U.S. policy toward Latin America now that the cold war is over?

The Clash of Civilizations?

Samuel P. Huntington

Samuel P. Huntington is the Eaton Professor of the Science of Government and Director of the John M. Olin Institute for Strategic Studies at Harvard University. This article is the product of the Olin Institute's project on "The Changing Security Environment and American National Interests."

THE NEXT PATTERN OF CONFLICT

World politics is entering a new phase, and intellectuals have not hesitated to proliferate visions of what it will be—the end of history, the return of traditional rivalries between nation states, and the decline of the nation state from the conflicting pulls of tribalism and globalism, among others. Each of these visions catches aspects of the emerging reality. Yet they all miss a crucial, indeed a central, aspect of what global politics is likely to be in the coming years.

It is my hypothesis that the fundamental source of conflict in this new world will not be primarily ideological or primarily economic. The great divisions among humankind and the dominating source of conflict will be cultural. Nation states will remain the most powerful actors in world affairs, but the principal conflicts of global politics will occur between nations and groups of different civilizations. The clash of civilizations will dominate global politics. The fault lines between civilizations will be the battle lines of the future.

Conflict between civilizations will be the latest phase in the evolution of conflict in the modern world. For a century and a half after the emergence of the modern international system with the Peace of Westphalia, the conflicts of the Western world were largely among princes—emperors, absolute monarchs and constitutional monarchs attempting to expand their bureaucracies, their armies, their mercantilist economic strength and, most important, the territory they ruled. In the process they created nation states, and beginning with the French Revolution the principal lines of conflict were between nations rather than princes. In 1793, as R. R. Palmer put it, "The wars of kings were over; the wars of peoples had begun." This nineteenth-century pattern lasted until the end of World War I. Then, as a result of the Russian Revolution and the reaction against it, the conflict of nations yielded to the conflict of ideologies, first among communism, fascism-Nazism and liberal democracy, and then between communism and liberal democracy. During the Cold War, this latter conflict became embodied in the struggle between the two superpowers, neither of which was a nation state in the classical European sense and each of which defined its identity in terms of its ideology.

These conflicts between princes, nation states and ideologies were primarily conflicts within Western civilization, "Western civil wars," as William Lind has labeled them. This was as true of the Cold War as it was of the world wars and the earlier wars of the seventeenth, eighteenth and nineteenth centuries. With the end of the Cold War, international politics moves out of its Western phase, and its centerpiece becomes the interaction between the West and non-Western civilizations and among non-Western civilizations. In the politics of civilizations, the peoples and governments of non-Western civilizations no longer remain the objects of history as targets of Western colonialism but join the West as movers and shapers of history.

THE NATURE OF CIVILIZATIONS

During the Cold War the world was divided into the First, Second and Third Worlds. Those divisions are no longer relevant. It is far more meaningful now to group countries not in terms of their political or economic systems or in terms of their level of economic development but rather in terms of their culture and civilization.

What do we mean when we talk of a civilization? A civilization is a cultural entity. Villages, regions, ethnic groups, nationalities, religious groups, all have distinct cultures at different levels of cultural heterogeneity. The culture of a village in southern Italy may be different from that of a village in northern Italy, but both will share in a common Italian culture that distinguishes them from German villages. European communities, in turn, will share cultural features that distinguish them from Arab or Chinese communities.

Arabs, Chinese and Westerners, however, are not part of any broader cultural entity. They constitute civilizations. A civilization is thus the highest cultural grouping of people and the broadest level of cultural identity people have short of that which distinguishes humans from other species. It is defined both by common objective elements, such as language, history, religion, customs, institutions, and by the subjective self-identification of people. People have levels of identity: a resident of Rome may define himself with varying degrees of intensity as a Roman, an Italian, a Catholic, a Christian, a European, a Westerner. The civilization to which he belongs is the broadest level of identification with which he intensely identifies. People can and do redefine their identities and, as a result, the composition and boundaries of civilizations change.

Civilizations may involve a large number of people, as with China ("a civilization pretending to be a state," as Lucian Pye put it), or a very small number of people, such as the Anglophone Caribbean. A civilization may include several nation states, as is the case with Western, Latin American and Arab civilizations, or only one, as is the case with Japanese civilization. Civilizations obviously blend and overlap, and may include subcivilizations. Western civilization has two major variants, European and North American, and Islam has its Arab, Turkic and Malay subdivisions. Civilizations are nonetheless meaningful entities, and while the lines between them are seldom sharp, they are real. Civilizations are dynamic; they rise and fall; they divide and merge. And, as any student of history knows, civilizations disappear and are buried in the sands of time.

Westerners tend to think of nation states as the principal actors in global affairs. They have been that, however, for only a few centuries. The broader reaches of human history have been the history of civilizations. In *A Study of History*, Arnold Toynbee identified 21 major civilizations; only six of them exist in the contemporary world.

WHY CIVILIZATIONS WILL CLASH

Civilization identity will be increasingly important in the future, and the world will be shaped in large measure by the interactions among seven or eight major civilizations. These include Western, Confucian, Japanese, Islamic, Hindu, Slavic-Orthodox, Latin American and possibly African civilization. The most important conflicts of the future will occur along the cultural fault lines separating these civilizations from one another.

Why will this be the case?

First, differences among civilizations are not only real; they are basic. Civilizations are differentiated from each other by history, language, culture, tradition and, most important, religion. The people of different civilizations have different views on the relations between God and man, the individual and the group, the citizen and the state, parents and children, husband and wife, as well as differing views of the relative importance of rights and responsibilities, liberty and authority, equality and hierarchy. These differences are the product of centuries. They will not soon disappear. They are far more fundamental than differences among political ideologies and political regimes. Differences do not necessarily mean conflict, and conflict does not necessarily mean violence. Over the centuries, however, differences among civilizations have generated the most prolonged and the most violent conflicts.

The conflicts of the future will occur along the cultural fault lines separating civilizations.

Second, the world is becoming a smaller place. The interactions between peoples of different civilizations are increasing; these increasing interactions intensify civilization consciousness and awareness of differences between civilizations and commonalities within civilizations. North African immigration to France generates hostility among Frenchmen and at the same time increased receptivity to immigration by "good" European Catholic Poles. Americans react far more negatively to Japanese investment than to larger investments from Canada and European countries. Similarly, as Donald Horowitz has pointed out, "An Ibo may be . . . an Owerri Ibo or an Onitsha Ibo in what was the Eastern region of Nigeria. In Lagos, he is simply an Ibo. In London, he is a Nigerian. In New York, he is an African." The interactions among peoples of different civilizations enhance the civilization-consciousness of people that, in turn, invigorates differences and animosities stretching or thought to stretch back deep into history.

Third, the processes of economic modernization and social change throughout the world are separating people from longstanding local identities. They also weaken the nation state as a source of identity. In much of the world religion has moved in to fill this gap, often in the form of movements that are labeled "fundamentalist." Such movements are found in Western Christianity, Judaism, Buddhism and Hinduism, as well as in Islam. In most countries and most religions the people active in fundamentalist movements are young, college-educated, middle-class technicians, professionals and business persons. The "unsecularization of the world," George Weigel has remarked, "is one of the dominant social facts of life in the late twentieth century." The revival of religion, "la revanche de

Dieu," as Gilles Kepel labeled it, provides a basis for identity and commitment that transcends national boundaries and unites civilizations.

Fourth, the growth of civilization-consciousness is enhanced by the dual role of the West. On the one hand, the West is at a peak of power. At the same time, however, and perhaps as a result, a return to the roots phenomenon is occurring among non-Western civilizations. Increasingly one hears references to trends toward a turning inward and "Asianization" in Japan, the end of the Nehru legacy and the "Hinduization" of India, the failure of Western ideas of socialism and nationalism and hence "re-Islamization" of the Middle East, and now a debate over Westernization versus Russianization in Boris Yeltsin's country. A West at the peak of its power confronts non-Wests that increasingly have the desire, the will and the resources to shape the world in non-Western ways.

In the past, the elites of non-Western societies were usually the people who were most involved with the West, had been educated at Oxford, the Sorbonne or Sandhurst, and had absorbed Western attitudes and values. At the same time, the populace in non-Western countries often remained deeply imbued with the indigenous culture. Now, however, these relationships are being reversed. A de-Westernization and indigenization of elites is occurring in many non-Western countries at the same time that Western, usually American, cultures, styles and habits become more popular among the mass of the people.

Fifth, cultural characteristics and differences are less mutable and hence less easily compromised and resolved than political and economic ones. In the former Soviet Union, communists can become democrats, the rich can become poor and the poor rich, but Russians cannot become Estonians and Azeris cannot become Armenians. In class and ideological conflicts, the key question was "Which side are you on?" and people could and did choose sides and change sides. In conflicts between civilizations, the question is "What are you?" That is a given that cannot be changed. And as we know, from Bosnia to the Caucasus to the Sudan, the wrong answer to that question can mean a bullet in the head. Even more than ethnicity, religion discriminates sharply and exclusively among people. A person can be half-French and half-Arab and simultaneously even a citizen of two countries. It is more difficult to be half-Catholic and half-Muslim.

Finally, economic regionalism is increasing. The proportions of total trade that were intraregional rose between 1980 and 1989 from 51 percent to 59 percent in Europe, 33 percent to 37 percent in East Asia, and 32 percent to 36 percent in North America. The importance of regional economic blocs is likely to continue to increase in the future. On the one hand, successful economic regionalism will reinforce civilization-consciousness. On the other hand, economic regionalism

may succeed only when it is rooted in a common civilization. The European Community rests on the shared foundation of European culture and Western Christianity. The success of the North American Free Trade Area depends on the convergence now underway of Mexican, Canadian and American cultures. Japan, in contrast, faces difficulties in creating a comparable economic entity in East Asia because Japan is a society and civilization unique to itself. However strong the trade and investment links Japan may develop with other East Asian countries, its cultural differences with those countries inhibit and perhaps preclude its promoting regional economic integration like that in Europe and North America.

Common culture, in contrast, is clearly facilitating the rapid expansion of the economic relations between the People's Republic of China and Hong Kong, Taiwan, Singapore and the overseas Chinese communities in other Asian countries. With the Cold War over, cultural commonalities increasingly overcome ideological differences, and mainland China and Taiwan move closer together. If cultural commonality is a prerequisite for economic integration, the principal East Asian economic bloc of the future is likely to be centered on China. This bloc is, in fact, already coming into existence. As Murray Weidenbaum has observed,

> Despite the current Japanese dominance of the region, the Chinese-based economy of Asia is rapidly emerging as a new epicenter for industry, commerce and finance. This strategic area contains substantial amounts of technology and manufacturing capability (Taiwan), outstanding entrepreneurial, marketing and services acumen (Hong Kong), a fine communications network (Singapore), a tremendous pool of financial capital (all three), and very large endowments of land, resources and labor (mainland China).... From Guangzhou to Singapore, from Kuala Lumpur to Manila, this influential network—often based on extensions of the traditional clans—has been described as the backbone of the East Asian economy.[1]

Culture and religion also form the basis of the Economic Cooperation Organization, which brings together ten non-Arab Muslim countries: Iran, Pakistan, Turkey, Azerbaijan, Kazakhstan, Kyrgyzstan, Turkmenistan, Tadjikistan, Uzbekistan and Afghanistan. One impetus to the revival and expansion of this organization, founded originally in the 1960s by Turkey, Pakistan and Iran, is the realization by the leaders of several of these countries that they had no chance of admission to the European Community. Similarly, Caricom, the Central American Common Market and Mercosur rest on common cultural foundations. Efforts to build a broader Caribbean-Central American economic entity bridging the Anglo-Latin divide, however, have to date failed.

As people define their identity in ethnic and religious terms, they are likely to see an "us" versus "them" relation existing between themselves and people of different ethnicity or religion. The end of ideologically defined states in Eastern Europe and the former Soviet Union permits traditional ethnic identities and animosities to come to the fore. Differences in culture and religion create differences over policy issues, ranging from human rights to immigration to trade and commerce to the environment. Geographical propinquity gives rise to conflicting territorial claims from Bosnia to Mindanao. Most important, the efforts of the West to promote its values of democracy and liberalism as universal values, to maintain its military predominance and to advance its economic interests engender countering responses from other civilizations. Decreasingly able to mobilize support and form coalitions on the basis of ideology, governments and groups will increasingly attempt to mobilize support by appealing to common religion and civilization identity.

The clash of civilizations thus occurs at two levels. At the micro-level, adjacent groups along the fault lines between civilizations struggle, often violently, over the control of territory and each other. At the macro-level, states from different civilizations compete for relative military and economic power, struggle over the control of international institutions and third parties, and competitively promote their particular political and religious values.

THE FAULT LINES BETWEEN CIVILIZATIONS

The fault lines between civilizations are replacing the political and ideological boundaries of the Cold War as the flash points for crisis and bloodshed. The Cold War began when the Iron Curtain divided Europe politically and ideologically. The Cold War ended with the end of the Iron Curtain. As the ideological division of Europe has disappeared, the cultural division of Europe between Western Christianity, on the one hand, and Orthodox Christianity and Islam, on the other, has reemerged. The most significant dividing line in Europe, as William Wallace has suggested, may well be the eastern boundary of Western Christianity in the year 1500. This line runs along what are now the boundaries between Finland and Russia and between the Baltic states and Russia, cuts through Belarus and Ukraine separating the more Catholic western Ukraine from Orthodox eastern Ukraine, swings westward separating Transylvania from the rest of Romania, and then goes through Yugoslavia almost exactly along the line now separating Croatia and Slovenia from the rest of Yugoslavia. In the Balkans this line, of course, coincides with the historic boundary between the Hapsburg and Ottoman empires. The peoples to the north and west of this line are Protestant or Catholic; they shared the common experiences of European history—feudalism, the Renaissance, the Reformation, the Enlightenment, the French Revolution, the Indus-

trial Revolution; they are generally economically better off than the peoples to the east; and they may now look forward to increasing involvement in a common European economy and to the consolidation of democratic political systems. The peoples to the east and south of this line are Orthodox or Muslim; they historically belonged to the Ottoman or Tsarist empires and were only lightly touched by the shaping events in the rest of Europe; they are generally less advanced economically; they seem much less likely to develop stable democratic political systems. The Velvet Curtain of culture has replaced the Iron Curtain of ideology as the most significant dividing line in Europe. As the events in Yugoslavia show, it is not only a line of difference; it is also at times a line of bloody conflict.

Conflict along the fault line between Western and Islamic civilizations has been going on for 1,300 years. After the founding of Islam, the Arab and Moorish surge west and north only ended at Tours in 732. From the eleventh to the thirteenth century the Crusaders attempted with temporary success to bring Christianity and Christian rule to the Holy Land. From the fourteenth to the seventeenth century, the Ottoman Turks reversed the balance, extended their sway over the Middle East and the Balkans, captured Constantinople, and twice laid siege to Vienna. In the nineteenth and early twentieth centuries as Ottoman power declined Britain, France, and Italy established Western control over most of North Africa and the Middle East.

After World War II, the West, in turn, began to retreat; the colonial empires disappeared; first Arab nationalism and then Islamic fundamentalism manifested themselves; the West became heavily dependent on the Persian Gulf countries for its energy; the oil-rich Muslim countries became money-rich and, when they wished to, weapons-rich. Several wars occurred between Arabs and Israel (created by the West). France fought a bloody and ruthless war in Algeria for most of the 1950s; British and French forces invaded Egypt in 1956; American forces went into Lebanon in 1958; subsequently American forces returned to Lebanon, attacked Libya, and engaged in various military encounters with Iran; Arab and Islamic terrorists, supported by at least three Middle Eastern governments, employed the weapon of the weak and bombed Western planes and installations and seized Western hostages. This warfare between Arabs and the West culminated in 1990, when the United States sent a massive army to the Persian Gulf to defend some Arab countries against aggression by another. In its aftermath NATO planning is increasingly directed to potential threats and instability along its "southern tier."

This centuries-old military interaction between the West and Islam is unlikely to decline. It could become more virulent. The Gulf War left some Arabs feeling proud that Saddam Hussein had attacked Israel and

Western Christianity circa 1500

Orthodox Christianity and Islam

RUSSIA

FINLAND

SWEDEN

ESTONIA

LATVIA

LITHUANIA

BELA-RUSSIA

POLAND

CZECH REP.

SLOVAKIA

UKRAINE

SLOVENIA

HUNG.

MOLD.

CROATIA

ROMANIA

BOSNIA

SERBIA

MONTE-NEGRO

MACEDONIA

BULGARIA

ALB.

ITALY

GREECE

TURKEY

Black Sea

N

0 — 200 MILES

Source: W. Wallace, THE TRANSFORMATION OF WESTERN EUROPE. London: Pinter, 1990.
Map by Ib Ohlsson for FOREIGN AFFAIRS.

stood up to the West. It also left many feeling humiliated and resentful of the West's military presence in the Persian Gulf, the West's overwhelming military dominance, and their apparent inability to shape their own destiny. Many Arab countries, in addition to the oil exporters, are reaching levels of economic and social development where autocratic forms of government become inappropriate and efforts to introduce democracy become stronger. Some openings in Arab political systems have already occurred. The principal beneficiaries of these openings have been Islamist movements. In the Arab world, in short, Western democracy strengthens anti-Western political forces. This may be a passing phenomenon, but it surely complicates relations between Islamic countries and the West.

Those relations are also complicated by demography. The spectacular population growth in Arab countries, particularly in North Africa, has led to increased migration to Western Europe. The movement within Western Europe toward minimizing internal boundaries has sharpened political sensitivities with respect to this development. In Italy, France and Germany, racism is increasingly open, and political reactions and violence against Arab and Turkish migrants have become more intense and more widespread since 1990.

On both sides the interaction between Islam and the West is seen as a clash of civilizations. The West's "next confrontation," observes M. J. Akbar, an Indian Muslim author, "is definitely going to come from the Muslim world. It is in the sweep of the Islamic nations from the Maghreb to Pakistan that the struggle for a new world order will begin." Bernard Lewis comes to a similar conclusion:

> We are facing a mood and a movement far transcending the level of issues and policies and the governments that pursue them. This is no less than a clash of civilizations—the perhaps irrational but surely historic reaction of an ancient rival against our Judeo-Christian heritage, our secular present, and the worldwide expansion of both.[2]

Historically, the other great antagonistic interaction of Arab Islamic civilization has been with the pagan, animist, and now increasingly Christian black peoples to the south. In the past, this antagonism was epitomized in the image of Arab slave dealers and black slaves. It has been reflected in the on-going civil war in the Sudan between Arabs and blacks, the fighting in Chad between Libyan-supported insurgents and the government, the tensions between Orthodox Christians and Muslims in the Horn of Africa, and the political conflicts, recurring riots and communal violence between Muslims and Christians in Nigeria. The modernization of Africa and the spread of Christianity are likely to enhance the probability of violence along this fault line. Symptomatic of the intensification of this conflict was the Pope John Paul II's speech in

Khartoum in February 1993 attacking the actions of the Sudan's Islamist government against the Christian minority there.

On the northern border of Islam, conflict has increasingly erupted between Orthodox and Muslim peoples, including the carnage of Bosnia and Sarajevo, the simmering violence between Serb and Albanian, the tenuous relations between Bulgarians and their Turkish minority, the violence between Ossetians and Ingush, the unremitting slaughter of each other by Armenians and Azeris, the tense relations between Russians and Muslims in Central Asia, and the deployment of Russian troops to protect Russian interests in the Caucasus and Central Asia. Religion reinforces the revival of ethnic identities and restimulates Russian fears about the security of their southern borders. This concern is well captured by Archie Roosevelt:

> Much of Russian history concerns the struggle between the Slavs and the Turkic peoples on their borders, which dates back to the foundation of the Russian state more than a thousand years ago. In the Slavs' millennium-long confrontation with their eastern neighbors lies the key to an understanding not only of Russian history, but Russian character. To understand Russian realities today one has to have a concept of the great Turkic ethnic group that has preoccupied Russians through the centuries.[3]

The conflict of civilizations is deeply rooted elsewhere in Asia. The historic clash between Muslim and Hindu in the subcontinent manifests itself now not only in the rivalry between Pakistan and India but

---

The crescent-shaped Islamic bloc, from the bulge of Africa to central Asia, has bloody borders.

---

also in intensifying religious strife within India between increasingly militant Hindu groups and India's substantial Muslim minority. The destruction of the Ayodhya mosque in December 1992 brought to the fore the issue of whether India will remain a secular democratic state or become a Hindu one. In East Asia, China has outstanding territorial disputes with most of its neighbors. It has pursued a ruthless policy toward the Buddhist people of Tibet, and it is pursuing an increasingly ruthless policy toward its Turkic-Muslim minority. With the Cold War over, the underlying differences between China and the United States have reasserted themselves in areas such as human rights, trade and weapons proliferation. These differences are unlikely to moderate. A "new cold war," Deng Xaioping reportedly asserted in 1991, is under way between China and America.

The same phrase has been applied to the increasingly difficult relations between Japan and the United States. Here cultural difference exacerbates economic conflict. People on each side allege racism on the other, but at least on the American side the antipathies are not racial but cultural. The basic values, attitudes, behavioral patterns of the two societies could hardly be more different. The economic issues between the United States and Europe are no less serious than those between the United States and Japan, but they do not have the same political salience and emotional intensity because the differences between American culture and European culture are so much less than those between American civilization and Japanese civilization.

The interactions between civilizations vary greatly in the extent to which they are likely to be characterized by violence. Economic competition clearly predominates between the American and European subcivilizations of the West and between both of them and Japan. On the Eurasian continent, however, the proliferation of ethnic conflict, epitomized at the extreme in "ethnic cleansing," has not been totally random. It has been most frequent and most violent between groups belonging to different civilizations. In Eurasia the great historic fault lines between civilizations are once more aflame. This is particularly true along the boundaries of the crescent-shaped Islamic bloc of nations from the bulge of Africa to central Asia. Violence also occurs between Muslims, on the one hand, and Orthodox Serbs in the Balkans, Jews in Israel, Hindus in India, Buddhists in Burma and Catholics in the Philippines. Islam has bloody borders.

CIVILIZATION RALLYING: THE KIN-COUNTRY SYNDROME

Groups or states belonging to one civilization that become involved in war with people from a different civilization naturally try to rally support from other members of their own civilization. As the post–Cold War world evolves, civilization commonality, what H. D. S. Greenway has termed the "kin-country" syndrome, is replacing political ideology and traditional balance of power considerations as the principal basis for cooperation and coalitions. It can be seen gradually emerging in the post–Cold War conflicts in the Persian Gulf, the Caucasus and Bosnia. None of these was a full-scale war between civilizations, but each involved some elements of civilizational rallying, which seemed to become more important as the conflict continued and which may provide a foretaste of the future.

First, in the Gulf War one Arab state invaded another and then fought a coalition of Arab, Western and other states. While only a few Muslim governments overtly supported Saddam Hussein, many Arab elites privately cheered him on, and he was highly popular among large sections of the Arab publics. Islamic fundamentalist movements universally supported Iraq rather than the Western-backed governments of Kuwait and Saudi Arabia. Forswearing Arab nationalism, Saddam Hussein explicitly invoked an Islamic appeal. He and his supporters attempted to define the war as a war between civilizations. "It is not the world against Iraq," as Safar Al-Hawali, dean of Islamic Studies at the Umm Al-Qura University in Mecca, put it in a widely circulated tape. "It is the West against Islam." Ignoring the rivalry between Iran and Iraq, the chief Iranian religious leader, Ayatollah Ali Khamenei, called for a holy war against the West: "The struggle against American aggression, greed, plans and policies will be counted as a jihad, and anybody who is killed on that path is a martyr." "This is a war," King Hussein of Jordan argued, "against all Arabs and all Muslims and not against Iraq alone."

The rallying of substantial sections of Arab elites and publics behind Saddam Hussein caused those Arab governments in the anti-Iraq coalition to moderate their activities and temper their public statements. Arab governments opposed or distanced themselves from subsequent Western efforts to apply pressure on Iraq, including enforcement of a no-fly zone in the summer of 1992 and the bombing of Iraq in January 1993. The Western-Soviet-Turkish-Arab anti-Iraq coalition of 1990 had by 1993 become a coalition of almost only the West and Kuwait against Iraq.

Muslims contrasted Western actions against Iraq with the West's failure to protect Bosnians against Serbs and to impose sanctions on Israel for violating U.N. resolutions. The West, they alleged, was using a double standard. A world of clashing civilizations, however, is inevitably a world of double standards: people apply one standard to their kin-countries and a different standard to others.

Second, the kin-country syndrome also appeared in conflicts in the former Soviet Union. Armenian military successes in 1992 and 1993 stimulated Turkey to become increasingly supportive of its religious, ethnic and linguistic brethren in Azerbaijan. "We have a Turkish nation feeling the same sentiments as the Azerbaijanis," said one Turkish official in 1992. "We are under pressure. Our newspapers are full of the photos of atrocities and are asking us if we are still serious about pursuing our neutral policy. Maybe we should show Armenia that there's a big Turkey in the region." President Turgut Özal agreed, remarking that Turkey should at least "scare the Armenians a little bit." Turkey, Özal threatened again in 1993, would "show its fangs." Turkish Air Force jets flew reconnaissance flights along the Armenian border; Turkey suspended food shipments and air flights to Armenia; and Turkey and Iran announced they would not accept dismemberment of Azerbaijan. In the last years of its existence, the Soviet government supported Azerbaijan because its government was dominated by former

communists. With the end of the Soviet Union, however, political considerations gave way to religious ones. Russian troops fought on the side of the Armenians, and Azerbaijan accused the "Russian government of turning 180 degrees" toward support for Christian Armenia.

Third, with respect to the fighting in the former Yugoslavia, Western publics manifested sympathy and support for the Bosnian Muslims and the horrors they suffered at the hands of the Serbs. Relatively little concern was expressed, however, over Croatian attacks on Muslims and participation in the dismemberment of Bosnia-Herzegovina. In the early stages of the Yugoslav breakup, Germany, in an unusual display of diplomatic initiative and muscle, induced the other 11 members of the European Community to follow its lead in recognizing Slovenia and Croatia. As a result of the pope's determination to provide strong backing to the two Catholic countries, the Vatican extended recognition even before the Community did. The United States followed the European lead. Thus the leading actors in Western civilization rallied behind their coreligionists. Subsequently Croatia was reported to be receiving substantial quantities of arms from Central European and other Western countries. Boris Yeltsin's government, on the other hand, attempted to pursue a middle course that would be sympathetic to the Orthodox Serbs but not alienate Russia from the West. Russian conservative and nationalist groups, however, including many legislators, attacked the government for not being more forthcoming in its support for the Serbs. By early 1993 several hundred Russians apparently were serving with the Serbian forces, and reports circulated of Russian arms being supplied to Serbia.

Islamic governments and groups, on the other hand, castigated the West for not coming to the defense of the Bosnians. Iranian leaders urged Muslims from all countries to provide help to Bosnia; in violation of the U.N. arms embargo, Iran supplied weapons and men for the Bosnians; Iranian-supported Lebanese groups sent guerrillas to train and organize the Bosnian forces. In 1993 up to 4,000 Muslims from over two dozen Islamic countries were reported to be fighting in Bosnia. The governments of Saudi Arabia and other countries felt under increasing pressure from fundamentalist groups in their own societies to provide more vigorous support for the Bosnians. By the end of 1992, Saudi Arabia had reportedly supplied substantial funding for weapons and supplies for the Bosnians, which significantly increased their military capabilities vis-à-vis the Serbs.

In the 1930s the Spanish Civil War provoked intervention from countries that politically were fascist, communist and democratic. In the 1990s the Yugoslav conflict is provoking intervention from countries that are Muslim, Orthodox and Western Christian. The parallel has not gone unnoticed. "The war in Bosnia-

Herzegovina has become the emotional equivalent of the fight against fascism in the Spanish Civil War," one Saudi editor observed. "Those who died there are regarded as martyrs who tried to save their fellow Muslims."

Conflicts and violence will also occur between states and groups within the same civilization. Such conflicts, however, are likely to be less intense and less likely to expand than conflicts between civilizations. Common membership in a civilization reduces the probability of violence in situations where it might otherwise occur. In 1991 and 1992 many people were alarmed by the possibility of violent conflict between Russia and Ukraine over territory, particularly Crimea, the Black Sea fleet, nuclear weapons and economic issues. If civilization is what counts, however, the likelihood of violence between Ukrainians and Russians should be low. They are two Slavic, primarily Orthodox peoples who have had close relationships with each other for centuries. As of early 1993, despite all the reasons for conflict, the leaders of the two countries were effectively negotiating and defusing the issues between the two countries. While there has been serious fighting between Muslims and Christians elsewhere in the former Soviet Union and much tension and some fighting between Western and Orthodox Christians in the Baltic states, there has been virtually no violence between Russians and Ukrainians.

Civilization rallying to date has been limited, but it has been growing, and it clearly has the potential to spread much further. As the conflicts in the Persian Gulf, the Caucasus and Bosnia continued, the positions of nations and the cleavages between them increasingly were along civilizational lines. Populist politicians, religious leaders and the media have found it a potent means of arousing mass support and of pressuring hesitant governments. In the coming years, the local conflicts most likely to escalate into major wars will be those, as in Bosnia and the Caucasus, along the fault lines between civilizations. The next world war, if there is one, will be a war between civilizations.

THE WEST VERSUS THE REST

The West is now at an extraordinary peak of power in relation to other civilizations. Its superpower opponent has disappeared from the map. Military conflict among Western states is unthinkable, and Western military power is unrivaled. Apart from Japan, the West faces no economic challenge. It dominates international political and security institutions and with Japan international economic institutions. Global political and security issues are effectively settled by a directorate of the United States, Britain and France, world economic issues by a directorate of the United States, Germany and Japan, all of which maintain extraordi-

narily close relations with each other to the exclusion of lesser and largely non-Western countries. Decisions made at the U.N. Security Council or in the International Monetary Fund that reflect the interests of the West are presented to the world as reflecting the desires of the world community. The very phrase "the world community" has become the euphemistic collective noun (replacing "the Free World") to give global legitimacy to actions reflecting the interests of the United States and other Western powers.[4] Through the IMF and other international economic institutions, the West promotes its economic interests and imposes on other nations the economic policies it thinks appropriate. In any poll of non-Western peoples, the IMF undoubtedly would win the support of finance ministers and a few others, but get an overwhelmingly unfavorable rating from just about everyone else, who would agree with Georgy Arbatov's characterization of IMF officials as "neo-Bolsheviks who love expropriating other people's money, imposing undemocratic and alien rules of economic and political conduct and stifling economic freedom."

The very phrase "world community" has become a euphemism to give legitimacy to the actions of the West.

Western domination of the U.N. Security Council and its decisions, tempered only by occasional abstention by China, produced U.N. legitimation of the West's use of force to drive Iraq out of Kuwait and its elimination of Iraq's sophisticated weapons and capacity to produce such weapons. It also produced the quite unprecedented action by the United States, Britain and France in getting the Security Council to demand that Libya hand over the Pan Am 103 bombing suspects and then to impose sanctions when Libya refused. After defeating the largest Arab army, the West did not hesitate to throw its weight around in the Arab world. The West in effect is using international institutions, military power and economic resources to run the world in ways that will maintain Western predominance, protect Western interests and promote Western political and economic values.

That at least is the way in which non-Westerners see the new world, and there is a significant element of truth in their view. Differences in power and struggles for military, economic and institutional power are thus one source of conflict between the West and other civilizations. Differences in culture, that is basic values and beliefs, are a second source of conflict. V. S. Naipaul has argued that Western civilization is the "universal civilization" that "fits all men." At a superficial level much of Western culture has indeed permeated the rest of the world. At a more basic level, however, Western concepts differ fundamentally from those prevalent in other civilizations. Western ideas of individualism, liberalism, constitutionalism, human rights, equality, liberty, the rule of law, democracy, free markets, the separation of church and state, often have little resonance in Islamic, Confucian, Japanese, Hindu, Buddhist or Orthodox cultures. Western efforts to propagate such ideas produce instead a reaction against "human rights imperialism" and a reaffirmation of indigenous values, as can be seen in the support for religious fundamentalism by the younger generation in non-Western cultures. The very notion that there could be a "universal civilization" is a Western idea, directly at odds with the particularism of most Asian societies and their emphasis on what distinguishes one people from another. Indeed, the author of a review of 100 comparative studies of values in different societies concluded that "the values that are most important in the West are least important worldwide."[5] In the political realm, of course, these differences are most manifest in the efforts of the United States and other Western powers to induce other peoples to adopt Western ideas concerning democracy and human rights. Modern democratic government originated in the West. When it has developed in non-Western societies it has usually been the product of Western colonialism or imposition.

The central axis of world politics in the future is likely to be, in Kishore Mahbubani's phrase, the conflict between "the West and the Rest" and the responses of non-Western civilizations to Western power and values.[6] Those responses generally take one or a combination of three forms. At one extreme, non-Western states can, like Burma and North Korea, attempt to pursue a course of isolation, to insulate their societies from penetration or "corruption" by the West, and, in effect, to opt out of participation in the Western-dominated global community. The costs of this course, however, are high, and few states have pursued it exclusively. A second alternative, the equivalent of "band-wagoning" in international relations theory, is to attempt to join the West and accept its values and institutions. The third alternative is to attempt to "balance" the West by developing economic and military power and cooperating with other non-Western societies against the West, while preserving indigenous values and institutions; in short, to modernize but not to Westernize.

THE TORN COUNTRIES

In the future, as people differentiate themselves by civilization, countries with large numbers of peoples of different civilizations, such as the Soviet Union and Yugoslavia, are candidates for dismemberment. Some other countries have a fair degree of cultural homogeneity but are divided over whether their society belongs to one civilization or another. These are torn countries. Their leaders typically wish to pursue a bandwagoning strategy and to make their countries members of the West, but the history, culture and traditions of their countries are non-Western. The most obvious and prototypical torn country is Turkey. The late twentieth-century leaders of Turkey have followed in the Attatürk tradition and defined Turkey as a modern, secular, Western nation state. They allied Turkey with the West in NATO and in the Gulf War; they applied for membership in the European Community. At the same time, however, elements in Turkish society have supported an Islamic revival and have argued that Turkey is basically a Middle Eastern Muslim society. In addition, while the elite of Turkey has defined Turkey as a Western society, the elite of the West refuses to accept Turkey as such. Turkey will not become a member of the European Community, and the real reason, as President Özal said, "is that we are Muslim and they are Christian and they don't say that." Having rejected Mecca, and then being rejected by Brussels, where does Turkey look? Tashkent may be the answer. The end of the Soviet Union gives Turkey the opportunity to become the leader of a revived Turkic civilization involving seven countries from the borders of Greece to those of China. Encouraged by the West, Turkey is making strenuous efforts to carve out this new identity for itself.

During the past decade Mexico has assumed a position somewhat similar to that of Turkey. Just as Turkey abandoned its historic opposition to Europe and attempted to join Europe, Mexico has stopped defining itself by its opposition to the United States and is instead attempting to imitate the United States and to join it in the North American Free Trade Area. Mexican leaders are engaged in the great task of redefining Mexican identity and have introduced fundamental economic reforms that eventually will lead to fundamental political change. In 1991 a top adviser to President Carlos Salinas de Gortari described at length to me all the changes the Salinas government was making. When he finished, I remarked: "That's most impressive. It seems to me that basically you want to change Mexico from a Latin American country into a North American country." He looked at me with surprise and exclaimed: "Exactly! That's precisely what we are trying to do, but of course we could never say so publicly." As his remark indicates, in Mexico as in Turkey, significant elements in society resist the redefinition of their country's identity. In Turkey, European-oriented leaders have to make gestures to Islam (Özal's pilgrimage to Mecca); so also Mexico's North American-oriented leaders have to make gestures to those who hold Mexico to be a Latin American country (Salinas' Ibero-American Guadalajara summit).

Historically Turkey has been the most profoundly torn country. For the United States, Mexico is the most immediate torn country. Globally the most important torn country is Russia. The question of whether Russia is part of the West or the leader of a distinct Slavic-Orthodox civilization has been a recurring one in Russian history. That issue was obscured by the communist victory in Russia, which imported a Western ideology, adapted it to Russian conditions and then challenged the West in the name of that ideology. The dominance of communism shut off the historic debate over Westernization versus Russification. With communism discredited Russians once again face that question.

President Yeltsin is adopting Western principles and goals and seeking to make Russia a "normal" country and a part of the West. Yet both the Russian elite and the Russian public are divided on this issue. Among the more moderate dissenters, Sergei Stankevich argues that Russia should reject the "Atlanticist" course, which would lead it "to become European, to become a part of the world economy in rapid and organized fashion, to become the eighth member of the Seven, and to put particular emphasis on Germany and the United States as the two dominant members of the Atlantic alliance." While also rejecting an exclusively Eurasian policy, Stankevich nonetheless argues that Russia should give priority to the protection of Russians in other countries, emphasize its Turkic and Muslim connections, and promote "an appreciable redistribution of our resources, our options, our ties, and our interests in favor of Asia, of the eastern direction." People of this persuasion criticize Yeltsin for subordinating Russia's interests to those of the West, for reducing Russian military strength, for failing to support traditional friends such as Serbia, and for pushing economic and political reform in ways injurious to the Russian people. Indicative of this trend is the new popularity of the ideas of Petr Savitsky, who in the 1920s argued that Russia was a unique Eurasian civilization.[7] More extreme dissidents voice much more blatantly nationalist, anti-Western and anti-Semitic views, and urge Russia to redevelop its military strength and to establish closer ties with China and Muslim countries. The people of Russia are as divided as the elite. An opinion survey in European Russia in the spring of 1992 revealed that 40 percent of the public had positive attitudes toward the West and 36 percent had negative attitudes. As it has been for much of its history, Russia in the early 1990s is truly a torn country.

To redefine its civilization identity, a torn country must meet three requirements. First, its political and economic elite has to be generally supportive of and enthusiastic about this move. Second, its public has to be willing to acquiesce in the redefinition. Third, the dominant groups in the recipient civilization have to be willing to embrace the convert. All three requirements in large part exist with respect to Mexico. The first two in large part exist with respect to Turkey. It is not clear that any of them exist with respect to Russia's joining the West. The conflict between liberal democracy and Marxism-Leninism was between ideologies which, despite their major differences, ostensibly shared ultimate goals of freedom, equality and prosperity. A traditional, authoritarian, nationalist Russia could have quite different goals. A Western democrat could carry on an intellectual debate with a Soviet Marxist. It would be virtually impossible for him to do that with a Russian traditionalist. If, as the Russians stop behaving like Marxists, they reject liberal democracy and begin behaving like Russians but not like Westerners, the relations between Russia and the West could again become distant and conflictual.[8]

THE CONFUCIAN-ISLAMIC CONNECTION

The obstacles to non-Western countries joining the West vary considerably. They are least for Latin American and East European countries. They are greater for the Orthodox countries of the former Soviet Union. They are still greater for Muslim, Confucian, Hindu and Buddhist societies. Japan has established a unique position for itself as an associate member of the West: it is in the West in some respects but clearly not of the West in important dimensions. Those countries that for reason of culture and power do not wish to, or cannot, join the West compete with the West by developing their own economic, military and political power. They do this by promoting their internal development and by cooperating with other non-Western countries. The most prominent form of this cooperation is the Confucian-Islamic connection that has emerged to challenge Western interests, values and power.

Almost without exception, Western countries are reducing their military power; under Yeltsin's leadership so also is Russia. China, North Korea and several Middle Eastern states, however, are significantly expanding their military capabilities. They are doing this by the import of arms from Western and non-Western sources and by the development of indigenous arms industries. One result is the emergence of what Charles Krauthammer has called "Weapon States," and the Weapon States are not Western states. Another result is the redefinition of arms control, which is a Western concept and a Western goal. During the Cold War the primary purpose of arms control was to establish a stable military balance between the United States and its allies and the Soviet Union and its allies. In the post–Cold War world the primary objective of arms control is to prevent the development by non-Western societies of military capabilities that could threaten Western interests. The West attempts to do this through international agreements, economic pressure and controls on the transfer of arms and weapons technologies.

A Confucian-Islamic connection has emerged to challenge Western interests, values and power.

The conflict between the West and the Confucian-Islamic states focuses largely, although not exclusively, on nuclear, chemical and biological weapons, ballistic missiles and other sophisticated means for delivering them, and the guidance, intelligence and other electronic capabilities for achieving that goal. The West promotes nonproliferation as a universal norm and nonproliferation treaties and inspections as means of realizing that norm. It also threatens a variety of sanctions against those who promote the spread of sophisticated weapons and proposes some benefits for those who do not. The attention of the West focuses, naturally, on nations that are actually or potentially hostile to the West.

The non-Western nations, on the other hand, assert their right to acquire and to deploy whatever weapons they think necessary for their security. They also have absorbed, to the full, the truth of the response of the Indian defense minister when asked what lesson he learned from the Gulf War: "Don't fight the United States unless you have nuclear weapons." Nuclear weapons, chemical weapons and missiles are viewed, probably erroneously, as the potential equalizer of superior Western conventional power. China, of course, already has nuclear weapons; Pakistan and India have the capability to deploy them. North Korea, Iran, Iraq, Libya and Algeria appear to be attempting to acquire them. A top Iranian official has declared that all Muslim states should acquire nuclear weapons, and in 1988 the president of Iran reportedly issued a directive calling for development of "offensive and defensive chemical, biological and radiological weapons."

Centrally important to the development of counter-West military capabilities is the sustained expansion of China's military power and its means to create military power. Buoyed by spectacular economic development, China is rapidly increasing its military spending and vigorously moving forward with the modernization of its armed forces. It is purchasing weapons from the former Soviet states; it is developing long-range missiles; in 1992 it tested a one-megaton nuclear device. It is developing power-projection capabilities, acquiring aerial refueling technology, and trying to purchase an aircraft carrier. Its military buildup and assertion of sovereignty over the South China Sea are provoking a multilateral regional arms race in East

Asia. China is also a major exporter of arms and weapons technology. It has exported materials to Libya and Iraq that could be used to manufacture nuclear weapons and nerve gas. It has helped Algeria build a reactor suitable for nuclear weapons research and production. China has sold to Iran nuclear technology that American officials believe could only be used to create weapons and apparently has shipped components of 300-mile-range missiles to Pakistan. North Korea has had a nuclear weapons program under way for some while and has sold advanced missiles and missile technology to Syria and Iran. The flow of weapons and weapons technology is generally from East Asia to the Middle East. There is, however, some movement in the reverse direction; China has received Stinger missiles from Pakistan.

A Confucian-Islamic military connection has thus come into being, designed to promote acquisition by its members of the weapons and weapons technologies needed to counter the military power of the West. It may or may not last. At present, however, it is, as Dave McCurdy has said, "a renegades' mutual support pact, run by the proliferators and their backers." A new form of arms competition is thus occurring between Islamic-Confucian states and the West. In an old-fashioned arms race, each side developed its own arms to balance or to achieve superiority against the other side. In this new form of arms competition, one side is developing its arms and the other side is attempting not to balance but to limit and prevent that arms build-up while at the same time reducing its own military capabilities.

IMPLICATIONS FOR THE WEST

This article does not argue that civilization identities will replace all other identities, that nation states will disappear, that each civilization will become a single coherent political entity, that groups within a civilization will not conflict with and even fight each other. This paper does set forth the hypotheses that differences between civilizations are real and important; civilization-consciousness is increasing; conflict between civilizations will supplant ideological and other forms of conflict as the dominant global form of conflict; international relations, historically a game played out within Western civilization, will increasingly be de-Westernized and become a game in which non-Western civilizations are actors and not simply objects; successful political, security and economic international institutions are more likely to develop within civilizations than across civilizations; conflicts between groups in different civilizations will be more frequent, more sustained and more violent than conflicts between groups in the same civilization; violent conflicts between groups in different civilizations are the most likely and most dangerous source of escalation that could lead to global wars; the paramount axis of world politics will be the relations between "the West and the Rest"; the elites in some torn non-Western countries will try to make their countries part of the West, but in most cases face major obstacles to accomplishing this; a central focus of conflict for the immediate future will be between the West and several Islamic-Confucian states.

This is not to advocate the desirability of conflicts between civilizations. It is to set forth descriptive hypotheses as to what the future may be like. If these are plausible hypotheses, however, it is necessary to consider their implications for Western policy. These implications should be divided between short-term advantage and long-term accommodation. In the short term it is clearly in the interest of the West to promote greater cooperation and unity within its own civilization, particularly between its European and North American components; to incorporate into the West societies in Eastern Europe and Latin America whose cultures are close to those of the West; to promote and maintain cooperative relations with Russia and Japan; to prevent escalation of local inter-civilization conflicts into major inter-civilization wars; to limit the expansion of the military strength of Confucian and Islamic states; to moderate the reduction of Western military capabilities and maintain military superiority in East and Southwest Asia; to exploit differences and conflicts among Confucian and Islamic states; to support in other civilizations groups sympathetic to Western values and interests; to strengthen international institutions that reflect and legitimate Western interests and values and to promote the involvement of non-Western states in those institutions.

In the longer term other measures would be called for. Western civilization is both Western and modern. Non-Western civilizations have attempted to become modern without becoming Western. To date only Japan has fully succeeded in this quest. Non-Western civilizations will continue to attempt to acquire the wealth, technology, skills, machines and weapons that are part of being modern. They will also attempt to reconcile this modernity with their traditional culture and values. Their economic and military strength relative to the West will increase. Hence the West will increasingly have to accommodate these non-Western modern civilizations whose power approaches that of the West but whose values and interests differ significantly from those of the West. This will require the West to maintain the economic and military power necessary to protect its interests in relation to these civilizations. It will also, however, require the West to develop a more profound understanding of the basic religious and philosophical assumptions underlying other civilizations and the ways in which people in those civilizations see their interests. It will require an effort to identify elements of commonality between Western and other civilizations. For the relevant future, there will be no universal civilization, but instead a world of different civilizations, each of which will have to learn to coexist with the others.

NOTES

1. Murray Weidenbaum, *Greater China: The Next Economic Superpower?*, St. Louis: Washington University Center for the Study of American Business, Contemporary Issues, Series 57, February 1993, pp. 2–3.
2. Bernard Lewis, "The Roots of Muslim Rage," *The Atlantic Monthly,* vol. 266, September 1990, p. 60; *Time,* June 15, 1992, pp. 24–28.
3. Archie Roosevelt, *For Lust of Knowing,* Boston: Little, Brown, 1988, pp. 332–333.
4. Almost invariably Western leaders claim they are acting on behalf of "the world community." One minor lapse occurred during the run-up to the Gulf War. In an interview on "Good Morning America," Dec. 21, 1990, British Prime Minister John Major referred to the actions "the West" was taking against Saddam Hussein. He quickly corrected himself and subsequently referred to "the world community." He was, however, right when he erred.
5. Harry C. Triandis, *The New York Times,* Dec. 25, 1990, p. 41, and "Cross-Cultural Studies of Individualism and Collectivism," Nebraska Symposium on Motivation, vol. 37, 1989, pp. 41–133.
6. Kishore Mahbubani, "The West and the Rest," *The National Interest,* Summer 1992, pp. 3–13.
7. Sergei Stankevich, "Russia in Search of Itself," *The National Interest,* Summer 1992, pp. 47–51; Daniel Schneider, "A Russian Movement Rejects Western Tilt," *Christian Science Monitor,* Feb. 5, 1993, pp. 5–7.
8. Owen Harries has pointed out that Australia is trying (unwisely in his view) to become a torn country in reverse. Although it has been a full member not only of the West but also of the ABCA military and intelligence core of the West, its current leaders are in effect proposing that it defect from the West, redefine itself as an Asian country and cultivate close ties with its neighbors. Australia's future, they argue, is with the dynamic economies of East Asia. But, as I have suggested, close economic cooperation normally requires a common cultural base. In addition, none of the three conditions necessary for a torn country to join another civilization is likely to exist in Australia's case.

*We have heard it now from two Administrations, two
parties, in a row: yes, the Cold War is over, but the world is more dangerous,
because less predictable, than it was while the Cold War
was still on. The world is indeed dangerous, the author argues, but
not more dangerous to the United States*

THE CONCEPTUAL POVERTY OF U.S. FOREIGN POLICY

JONATHAN CLARKE

IN CONGRESSIONAL TESTIMONY AND public statements Secretary of State Warren Christopher has described the Bosnian crisis as a "problem from hell." His predecessors in office may be forgiven for thinking that he overstates his case. They would grant that the problem would have been more tractable had the Serbs been Communist-inspired Soviet surrogates, and therefore subject to immediate Western retaliation with scant regard paid to the ancient ethnic animosities that give us pause today. But, those predecessors might argue, the problems they themselves encountered and mastered on their watches—the rebuilding of Europe and Japan, the containment of communism, the removal of Soviet forces from Afghanistan, to name but a few examples from the past generation—were not necessarily any less complex and demanding than those that are now facing the Clinton Administration.

They would further say that their success in these areas did not come by chance but derived from their rigorous efforts to clarify where the American interest lay and then to pursue it vigorously. They would fault the Administration for an inadequate intellectual performance in defining both for itself and for the American people what it is that America stands for in the post–Cold War era.

Curiously, the Clinton Administration, bristling as it is with academic talent, has been content to live hand to mouth on foreign policy, embracing stale concepts from the bygone era of the Cold War. Despite Clinton's cam-paign criticism of President George Bush's lack of vision, and despite promises of "a fresh assessment" of U.S. foreign policy, the President, it seems, either doesn't comprehend or doesn't wish to grapple with the fact that in foreign policy he stands at a historic crossroads.

Unlike all his predecessors since the First World War, Bill Clinton does not face the inevitability of armed struggle against a global enemy. Military threats against the United States and its allies are at an all-time low. Compare Bosnia, a country where neither American lives nor American possessions are at stake (and which Clinton has described as his "most difficult foreign-policy problem"), with some of the lethal challenges of the recent past. Against these comparatively happy circumstances abroad, public finances at home are in terminal distress, struggling to satisfy conflicting demands.

To get away from reactive, seat-of-the-pants management of foreign affairs, Clinton badly needs to construct a new concept of America's place in the world which will allow him to protect the interests and project the values of the United States while simultaneously finding significant savings in those sections of the budget devoted to defense and international discretionary spending. To suc-

Jonathan Clarke is the author of a foreign-policy paper published by the Cato Institute last March. From 1973 to 1992 he was a member of the British Diplomatic Service. Clarke is at work on a book about Anglo-American relations.

ceed in this task he will, as Hercule Poirot says, have to exercise his "gray cells." Otherwise a relentless combination of global events, CNN film crews, and syndicated columnists will imprison him and leave him and his presidency floundering.

The Neo–Cold War Orthodoxy

PROFESSIONAL DIPLOMATS OFTEN SAY THAT TRYing to think strategically about foreign policy is a waste of time. Each and every problem is different, and the best one can hope for is to muddle through—"pasted-together diplomacy," in former Secretary of State Lawrence Eagleburger's colorful phrase. Unfortunately, the Bosnian experience has demonstrated what happens when foreign policy is made on the fly: directionless vacillation between cowboy and wimp. In point of fact, a successful foreign policy requires an intellectual underpinning or mooring in a vision of the country's mission in the world. The lesson from Bosnia is that this is not merely an academic exercise but an important practical necessity. As yet there is no sign that anyone at the top of the Administration is ready to step back from all-night caucusing and take on the calm, deliberative task that would produce the required new strategic concept.

Clinton's foreign-policy team needs a fresh source of energy. To date it has failed to deliver any of the "bold new thinking" of which Christopher improbably spoke at the time of his nomination. (Quite to the contrary, in perhaps the most decisive action thus far of his tenure as Secretary of State, Christopher moved swiftly to silence the one senior State Department official, Under Secretary of State for Political Affairs Peter Tarnoff, who dared to speak, albeit tentatively and off the record, of the need to close the gap between U.S. foreign-policy aspirations and resources.) Instead, what has emerged is a defensive rehash of warmed-over ideas adding up to what might be called "neo-Cold War orthodoxy" or "sole-remaining-superpower syndrome."

The central contention of this traditionalist school is that, a few ritual genuflections in the direction of new thinking aside, it is business as usual. The United States must remain "activist" in foreign policy and prepared to intervene in any of the world's problems. To this end it must retain a large military and, in the words of Secretary of Defense Les Aspin, the readiness to "fight every day." Advocates of reform who suggest that in today's much improved security environment there is less need for American interventionism, or that military solutions are less applicable to contemporary problems, are stigmatized as isolationists or 1930s-style appeasers.

Proponents of this no-change approach have hardly been prolific writers or speakers about the fundamentals underlying their ideas, but the evidence at hand indicates that their views draw on four main theses:
• The end of the Cold War has not reduced the level of international threat. New dangers have replaced the old ones.
• The collapse of the Soviet-American superpower bipolarity

has made the world a more unstable and complex place.
• Only the United States has the power to solve the problems of the world.
• The United States has a unique moral responsibility to protect humanitarian values.

These assumptions freeze U.S. foreign policy in a Cold War time warp. If they are accepted and followed, the United States will remain the world's policeman, military spending will remain high, the peace dividend will be meager, and U.S. diplomacy will too readily reach for military solutions.

Others will ask whether there are not alternative options. So far press and academic commentators, while acknowledging the need for review, have been slow to make the case for a substantively new strategic doctrine. Too many members of the foreign-policy elite have been concerned, in the words of *Foreign Policy* editor Charles William Maynes, to find "a new rationale for its continued relevance in high policy circles," rather than seeing that the time has come for a fresh intellectual start. Mainstream opinion has coalesced around the view of James Hoge, the editor of *Foreign Affairs*, that the world remains an "unsettling" and "dangerous" place. Luminaries of the Bush foreign-policy team, including Eagleburger and Bush's national security adviser, Brent Scowcroft, are banding together to advocate maintaining the Cold War establishment. The search for alternatives will therefore have to begin with a critical examination of the claims of the neo–Cold War orthodoxy.

A Discretionary Jungle

THE FIRST THESIS ASSERTS THAT DESPITE THE cessation of the Soviet threat, the United States still faces a hostile world. CIA Director James Woolsey has won the accolade of a cartoon in *The Economist* for his vivid image of the world as a "jungle filled with a bewildering variety of poisonous snakes." In the same vein Chester A. Crocker, a former assistant secretary of state, has written that "historic changes since 1989 have profoundly destabilized the previously existing order without replacing it with any recognizable or legitimate system. New vacuums are setting off new conflicts. Old problems are being solved, begetting new ones."

Before going on to look at these new problems, recall the ultimate threat that hung over the United States every day of the Cold War: total national annihilation through the doctrine of "mutual assured destruction." Now that this threat is, in the words of Senators Sam Nunn and Richard Lugar, "at an all time low," it requires a major effort of imagination to recollect that twenty-four months ago nuclear submarines roamed the ocean depths, strategic bombers were on twenty-four-hour-alert active duty, and hardened silos were on active maintenance, all to prevent the destruction of the United States in a thermonuclear holocaust.

The secondary threat from the Soviet Union during

THE CENTRAL CONTENTION OF THE PREVAILING TRADITION-ALIST SCHOOL IS THAT IT IS BUSINESS AS USUAL. THE UNITED STATES MUST REMAIN "ACTIVIST" IN FOREIGN POLICY AND PREPARED TO INTERVENE IN ANY OF THE WORLD'S PROBLEMS.

the Cold War was global opposition to American interests and values. This took the form of both armed aggression and clandestine subversion. In effect the Soviets were standing on the other side of the school yard saying, "We repudiate all that America stands for. We represent a better system, a better way of organizing society. Follow us —or else." In the face of this across-the-board challenge, the Cold War arms buildup and the containment policy were an inevitable and logical reaction.

What are the new threats to which the foreign-policy establishment has been drawing our attention so urgently? Nuclear proliferation, anti-democratic movements, Islamic fundamentalism, narcotics, ethnic tumult, international terrorism: these are real problems, real dangers, and should not be underestimated.

Close analysis, however, shows that they share an interesting element: not one carries with it the immediate physical threat of annihilation of the United States which was present every second of the Cold War. There is a discretionary quality about them. A direct Soviet attack on Germany or South Korea would have activated the treaty-defined obligation of a U.S. military response. Today we can pick and choose. The "principals committee" (consisting of the President's top national-security advisers) can discuss options for weeks, while the Secretary of State can embark on a week-long tour of European capitals to seek allied support. The leisurely six months of unopposed buildup between Desert Shield (August of 1990) and Desert Storm (January of 1991) makes the point. This is not to deny the reality of the new threats; it is simply to note that they are of a different quality. Today's threats do not present a *systemic* challenge to American interests. The very existence of Soviet communism was predicated on global opposition to the United States; today's world holds no such enemy. The attempts of Charles Krauthammer and other syndicated columnists to construct a new Comintern out of Iranian-inspired Islamic fundamentalism, or of the Harvard professor Samuel Huntington and other academics to detect a new source of global conflict in a form of Bismarckian *Kulturkampf* between "the West and the rest," collapse under the weight of their internal contradictions.

To be sure, today's threats are not entirely toothless. The introduction of nuclear weapons to the Korean peninsula, for example, provoking as it might a copycat reaction in Japan and Indonesia, would be of great con-cern. But this is very different from the situation that prevailed during the Cold War. We now have no adversary who possesses the ballistic missiles, massed armor, and industrial base of the Warsaw Pact countries. The challenge to American interests is tangential or by extension. Today's discretionary problems simply do not carry the same weight as yesterday's life-threatening dangers. To argue that they do undermines the credibility of the traditionalists as architects of U.S. foreign policy for the next century.

In terms of the threat to the United States itself or its allies, the world environment is far more benign today than it was formerly. Contrary to Christopher's assertions, America's foreign-policy agenda is very far from "overflowing with crises and potential disasters." The United States does not face the rise of a dominant, hegemonic power. There is therefore much less threat-based need for the United States to become actively involved in regional conflicts. Management of these can safely be delegated to nations nearer the action, with the United States playing a supporting role.

Belgrade Is Not Munich

THE SECOND THESIS CONCERNS THE CONCEPT of stability or order in a bipolar world and a multipolar one. Implicit in it is a remarkable reinterpretation of history. Foreign-policy experts from the Cold War era, even including such a forward-thinking writer as the former Secretary of Defense James Schlesinger, would have us believe that the Cold War was a period of "unique disciplines" inasmuch as each side recognized the constraints implicit in the other's capacity for massive retaliation.

The theory goes that during this period the superpowers contented themselves with playing, through surrogates, a bloodless and painless version of the "great game" by a mutually agreed set of Marquis of Queensberry rules that imposed limits on the potential spread of conflict. The theorists now argue that the dissolution of the fear of nuclear holocaust "has made the world safe for conventional war," and that such a war, for example in the Balkans or the Caucasus, could ignite conflict across a continent.

This analysis calls upon us to indulge in collective amnesia about the Cold War. Unfortunately, the facts cannot be forgotten so readily. The list is long and unappetizing. The Soviet Union really did try to blockade Berlin and draw Greece behind the Iron Curtain; children really did hide under their desks during the Cuban missile crisis; Soviet tanks really did roll into Prague, Budapest, and Kabul; on Soviet orders, refugees really were shot and allowed to bleed to death under the Berlin Wall; dictatorships in Cuba, Ethiopia, Angola, and Mozambique really did rise on the backs of Soviet-equipped and -trained security services; state sponsors of anti-American terrorism really were fêted in Moscow; the Soviet Union really did bankroll the Communist parties of Western Europe and Latin America. None of this was a dream. To combat all this, the West really did live on the nuclear high wire. And as for conventional war during the Cold War, the history books burgeon with the records of major conflagrations: Vietnam, Biafra, Chad, the Iran-Iraq war, successive Arab-Israel wars, the India-Pakistan war, Nicaragua, El Salvador, the Indonesian confrontation, the Chinese annexation of Tibet, the ethnic massacres in Sri Lanka, the Turkish invasion of Cyprus.

The hard reality is that the Cold War was a period of sustained global instability, not one of blissful Soviet-American condominium between consenting adult partners. At the global level a change of vast significance has since taken place. The threat of nuclear self-destruction no longer hangs over the world. The disappearance of this threat has removed a huge source of instability. What people find confusing, however, is that at the sub-global or local level the world gives the appearance of being wildly unstable. Across the map more red lights seem to be blinking in such hitherto unfamiliar places as Bosnia, Armenia, Georgia, Abkhazia, Tajikistan, South Ossetia, and the Trans-Dniester Republic, among other trouble spots.

Adherents of the neo–Cold War orthodoxy misinterpret these developments as well, regarding them as denoting a more anarchic world. They seek to present these conflicts as outgrowths of a new chaos that will be deepened if Washington adopts what President Bush called a "passive and aloof" policy. In fact, though their names are exotic, these conflicts are no different in intensity from many others that have disfigured this century and, it is certain, will continue into the next. The end of the Cold War has not ended history. Rather, the breakup of the Soviet empire has stranded many population groups on the wrong side of borders that themselves emerged from the breakup in 1917–1918 of the earlier Hohenzollern, Romanoff, Hapsburg, and Ottoman empires. Sometimes border adjustment will take place without bloodshed (for example, the fusion of East and West Germany and the divorce between the Czech Republic and Slovakia), but, as often as not, conflicts will occur as people attempt to right perceived wrongs or assert ancient irredentist claims.

In assessing how to react to these problems, note that in one crucial respect they are significantly different from

their Cold War predecessors. None of them—not even Bosnia or the Hindu-Muslim confrontation in India, each of which has the potential to spill across borders—threatens to become a global crisis of the sort that would necessarily embroil the United States. Strategic rocket forces are not going to move to a higher state of readiness as a result of any of these current disputes. None of them is a forerunner of the emergence of an expansionist hegemonic power, Jefferson's "force . . . wielded by a single hand," the threat of which—be it in Europe, Korea, or Kuwait—has traditionally motivated large-scale American intervention.

Unlike such powers as Napoleonic France and Nazi Germany, Serbia, for example, has no territorial ambitions beyond the borders of the former Yugoslavia; the Khmer Rouge does not covet the rest of Indochina. It is bad analysis to conflate minor, regionally containable problems with global threats to world peace. That sort of bloated language may belong to UN resolutions; it should find no place in American thinking. Belgrade is not Munich.

Is the World "More Complex"?

THE OTHER ASPECT OF THIS SECOND THESIS IS the claim that the world is a more complex place. Superficially this, too, may appear to be so. For example, instead of one nuclear power, the Soviet Union, the United States now has to deal with four: Russia, Ukraine, Belarus, and Kazakhstan. But the West is not dealing with four separate nuclear-use doctrines. Clearly, the last three former Soviet republics are using their nuclear weapons as bargaining chips in their dealings with the Western financial community. No increase in the complexity of the threat to the United States is implied.

Further, the end of the superpower rivalry has simplified the diplomacy involved in international issues. Whereas once the Middle East peace negotiations, Bosnia, or Iraq would have had to be approached through an infinitely complex minefield of Soviet-American competitiveness, now a broad international collegiality exists. This does not mean that differences of opinion will never arise (they manifestly have done so over Bosnia), but the search for solutions is no longer subordinate to superpower rivalries. The United States is comfortable with Russia's taking a leading role in the matter of Bosnia, whereas once it would have labored mightily to prevent Soviet meddling.

This means that problems can be approached much more on their merits. For example, would Syria have been willing to sit down with Israel had it not seen the collapse of its Cold War sponsor? True enough, the problems themselves remain complex—and now American policymakers have to take account of parliamentary opinion in the former Soviet republics rather than dealing with one monolithic government. In an increasingly interdependent and multilateral world many of the problems are fantastically complicated (the Stockholm International Peace Research Institute has, for example, identified thirty current territorial disputes in the Caucasus region alone), but the passing of the Cold War has stripped away one thick layer of complexity: superpower rivalry is no longer involved. Regarding national security, it is not the case that the world is more complex. Complex, yes—but not more so.

In one respect it is fair to concede that an additional level of complexity exists. This is in the field of analysis. No longer do analysts have the luxury of a single lens through which they can scrutinize the world's problems. Rather than being one-dimensional in an anti-communist or Soviet-containment context, problems have now become multifaceted and individual. As we have seen in Bosnia, this has brought into the foreground complexities that hitherto would have been little noticed.

But this returns us to the core problem facing the Administration's foreign-policy makers: how to define American interests in a world where there is no longer a monolithic challenge to them but where the Administration is daily called upon to address disparate regional problems of uncertain relevance to American security. To say that the diagnosis is more complex does not mean that the illness is too.

The Sole-Remaining-Superpower Syndrome

THE THIRD AND FOURTH THESES—THAT ONLY the United States has the power to solve the world's problems, and that the United States has a unique moral responsibility to protect humanitarian values—both derive from the sole-remaining-superpower syndrome. Underlying both is the thought that, as George Bush said, "there is no one else." National Security Adviser Anthony Lake has spoken in a similar vein of the United States' "monopoly on power."

This outlook has resulted in an important conceptual error in our status quo foreign policy. It assumes that the mere identification of problems is enough to trigger American involvement. While paying lip service to the view that the United States cannot be the world's policeman, it blithely calls for the United States to prevent Europe from dissolving into "chaos," to offer security guarantees to Ukraine, to interpose American forces in any possible conflict between China and Japan, and to guard the Golan Heights—to name a diverse list of actual or potential commitments that were under discussion in the first six months of this year.

This approach is thorny with difficulties. The most important of these is the implicit assumption that some form of U.S. intervention, most often military, is the best or indeed a viable route toward a solution of the problem under consideration. During the Cold War, when the challenges faced by the United States or its allies were often

of a military nature, recourse to arms was often necessary. The Soviets would not have left Afghanistan had not the United States armed the *mujahideen*. Grenada and the Caribbean generally would not be the sleepy, democratic backwater it is today if the United States had not intervened to throw out Bernard Coard and his Communist bully boys.

The world has, however, moved on. Even if for argument's sake one concedes that the United States has vital interests in every corner of the globe, today's problems are still far less susceptible to military solutions than the earlier ones were. The reason for the lack of consensus on Bosnia was not that the U.S. military could not do the job of repelling Serbian aggression but that this was only part of the job. We wanted also to persuade Serbs, Croats, and Muslims to live side by side in peace. For this purpose high-level bombing seems as inappropriate across the Atlantic as it would be in Los Angeles in mediating the feuds of the Bloods and the Crips.

American policy analysts who suffer from the sole-remaining-superpower syndrome are not alone in placing too high a value on military might. Brian Urquhart, the former UN undersecretary-general for special political affairs, advocated in *The New York Review of Books* the creation of a UN force to be globally deployed with rules of engagement that, unlike today's, would allow the UN troops to shoot before they were shot at. This sounds fine; it is always tempting to imagine that the man with the badge and the gun can sort things out. The scheme might even have worked in the set-piece confrontations of the Cold War, but the "internal security" character of today's problems—even those, such as Bosnia or Nagorno-Karabakh, that have a pseudo-international format but are in all essentials civil wars—makes the U.S.-marshall approach much less promising. Changing the color of the helmets or relabeling the approach as "assertive multilateralism" will not render the application of military power to civilian problems any more successful. After all, we do not argue that a firepower deficit is what keeps us from solving the problems of our inner cities.

A further example of the inapplicability of the military option may be found in connection with Islamic fundamentalism. Even if one accepts the fanciful proposition that Iranian-driven fundamentalism is the new problematic "ism" of the post–Cold War era, it is extremely doubtful that U.S. military intervention can provide any sort of solution. The West has a dismal track record in understanding Islam. Ill-considered Western support for the repressive policies of Shah Reza Pahlavi is in part responsible for the anti-Western virulence of today's regime in Tehran. A policy that offers more of the same in, say, Egypt or Saudi Arabia is courting disaster—all the more so if it risks delivering enormous stocks of state-of-the-art military equipment into the hands of fanatics.

Alas, Martin Indyk, the new director of Near East and South Asian affairs at the National Security Council, is leading policy in this direction. Indyk and, under his tutelage, Christopher even use the Cold War language of "containment" and "balance of power" to characterize the Administration's policy. There are undoubtedly many ugly aspects of Iran. But to base U.S. policy in the region on a partnership with inherently unstable conservative Arab states and to conduct a campaign of Cold War-style military confrontation against Iran is to risk replicating the Ayatollah's revolution throughout the Arab world.

A better alternative to confronting Islam as a potential military threat might be to put more resources into understanding the forces that drive the religion's advance. Perhaps they are not so different from what underlies the revival of Christian fundamentalism in the United States—namely, a search for stable values amid alienation from the harsh economic realities and materialism of the late twentieth century.

The new problems will place a premium on detailed knowledge. In the 1960s and 1970s the Ford Foundation poured a great deal of money into Chinese studies, and there emerged a generation of students who understood China. This knowledge promises to be of great benefit to relations between the United States and China, which looks to be the potential superpower of the next century. A similar program aimed at understanding Islam promises equal benefits.

More Will Than Wallet

A FURTHER PROBLEM WITH THE STATUS QUO APproach is that the sole-remaining-superpower syndrome betrays a curiously old-fashioned mindset deriving from the 1950s, when the United States produced more than 40 percent of world GDP. With the U.S. share now about 20 percent, one does not need to be a believer in Paul Kennedy's theory of "imperial overstretch" to see that the American comparative advantage is not at all what it was. The European Community, for example, now has a larger economy than the United States does. Of course, in the strictly military sphere the United States remains pre-eminent. In a stand-up fight, if the enemy does us the favor of running across an open field and up a hill into our artillery, as in Pickett's charge on the third day at Gettysburg, the United States is more than a match for anyone. But one theme of post–Cold War analysis is that stand-up fights will be few and far between. The radio-controlled land mine and the sniper's rifle will be the weapons of choice. Talk of a monopoly of power fails to take account of something Clinton himself has said: "The currency of national strength in this new era will be denominated not only in ships and tanks and planes, but in diplomas and patents and paychecks."

To accept responsibility for all the world's problems is to ignore the necessity for economic trade-offs. Foreign policy can no longer be formulated in a resource vacuum. In his inaugural address in 1989 President Bush said that America had "more will than wallet." Four years and a trillion dollars of additional debt later, the time has come to align policy aspirations with resource realities.

Defense spending in the United States, as in any other country, is a public-policy choice that has a very direct impact on domestic welfare. It is normally predicated on real or anticipated threats to the *salus populi*, not on open-ended commitments to accept responsibilities that might better fall to others. It is blindingly obvious that if the United States is willing to tax itself to take unpleasant and dangerous action that benefits other nations, regardless of whether they share in the costs, it is in the economic interest of those other nations to prolong that (for them) happy situation as long as possible.

Foreign nations are only too happy to see the United States as the protector of last resort—but too often this becomes the first resort. The willingness of the United States to assume their burdens saves them money, which they can spend on a domestic priority such as raising educational standards, an advantage that comes back to haunt the United States on the trade front. Clinton's statement that "it is time for our friends to bear more of the burden" will have little impact until America's allies see GIs leaving Europe, Japan, and Korea.

An undifferentiated list of the world's problems is not therefore a valid argument for maintaining the status quo in the foreign-policy and national-security apparatus. A rigorous effort is needed to relate the problems to U.S. interests and resources. Policy analysts have realized this. They know full well that in the absence of the Soviet threat many of the world's conflicts generate little public interest.

To compensate for this, these analysts are reviving that unlamented analytic casualty of the Vietnam War, the domino theory. State Department officials have joined forces with the columnists of *The New York Times* to project a seamless escalation of fighting from Bosnia into Kosovo, Macedonia, and Albania and on into a general Balkan war involving Greece, Turkey, Hungary, Bulgaria, and Romania, with Iranian *mujahideen* thrown in for good measure. All too soon we are back in the Sarajevo of 1914. The fact that the analysts have produced little real evidence that this progression is likely or that American involvement would be helpful rather than prejudicial to a solution has not prevented them from having an effect on policy. Clinton himself spoke of the dangers of a wider Balkan war to support his decision to install American troops in Macedonia.

Just as there are domestic problems that fall outside the purview of the federal government, so there are foreign problems that are better addressed by local or regional entities than by outsiders, who, however pure their motives, may have neither the depth of knowledge nor the commitment to the long haul to solve the problem. Indeed, they may even complicate matters. Somalia is a case in point. What started out as a humanitarian mission to feed the starving all too soon involved bombing sorties by U.S. helicopter gunships, and Madeleine Albright, the U.S. ambassador to the UN, had to defend the killing of Somali children by the very troops who had been dispatched to protect them. This style of "peacemaking" recalls Tacitus' description of the Roman approach in first-century Britain: "*Ubi solitudinem faciunt pacem appellant*" —"Where they make a desert, they call it peace."

Before active U.S. engagement or intervention is justified, a vital next stage, going beyond mere problem identification, is necessary. This is a rigorous demonstration that the problem could usefully be addressed by the U.S. military.

Why Morality Is Not Enough

THE FOURTH THESIS IN SUPPORT OF THE STATUS quo has to do with morality. This appears under many guises, such as humanitarian relief, resistance to genocide, human rights, and support for democracy. It includes new rationales for international activism, such as the ideas of UN Secretary-General Boutros Boutros Ghali on limited sovereignty, which would facilitate outside intervention in the previously sacrosanct area of domestic affairs.

These ideas have great appeal in the United States, where the proposition that America has a special moral duty to right the wrongs of the world has been a resonant theme ever since Woodrow Wilson, in introducing his Fourteen Points to govern the Armistice settlement of the First World War, consciously repudiated the traditional but, in his view, amoral European and American practices of balance-of-power politics and pursuit of national interest. Whereas John Adams could write in 1783, "There is a Ballance of Power in Europe. Nature has formed it. Practice and Habit have confirmed it, and it must exist forever," and John Quincy Adams in his famous July 4, 1821, address could say of America that "She goes not abroad in search of monsters to destroy," Wilson took the United States into the Great War not to restore the equilibrium of Europe but to "vindicate the principles of peace and justice."

The loss of the Soviet Union as the leitmotif of American interventionism has brought morality to prominence as proponents of the Cold War orthodoxy seek to resist change. The issue for the Clinton Administration is not whether morality belongs in the foreign-policy realm but the practical choices that derive from its presence there. This is not going to be an easy circle to square. Previous Administrations have tried and come up short. Jeane Kirkpatrick's ingenious but specious distinction between different sorts of dictatorships—"ours," who are "authoritarian," and "theirs," who are "totalitarian"—comes to mind.

Alas, unless morality is anchored in some coherent concept of national interest, it is likely to prove an erratic compass. The reasons are familiar: Morality is indivisible. It does not apply selectively. If it is right to support democracy in the former Soviet republics, then it must be wrong to neglect encroachments on it in Algeria and Peru. If we demand that Hong Kong accept Vietnamese boat people, we ourselves must do the same for Haitian

ones. If it was our duty to provide succor to Somalia, we should do likewise for Sudan.

Morality demands total commitment. Half measures are not allowed. If we are called upon to counter genocide in Bosnia, we must deliver, even if that means ground troops, casualties, and tremendous expenditures. Morality is also timeless. If on moral grounds Warren Christopher rejects the concept of Muslim safe havens in Bosnia one week, he cannot credibly or logically withdraw his objection a month later.

Advocates of placing morality at the center of foreign policy dismiss these issues as irrelevant to anything except a "petty consistency." They assert that, in the manner of a hospital emergency room, it is possible to perform triage on international problems and come up with a list of priorities. This, of course, goes to the crux of the question, Where do morality and practicality meet? Morality, as a long-standing motivator in U.S. foreign policy, will necessarily point the way to areas where American values and public opinion demand activity. This is as it should be. But two things are clear:

First, triage can take place only on the basis of American national interest. If the civil war in Bosnia attracts our interest while that in Angola does not, this cannot be because killing is less morally repugnant in Africa than in Europe. It must be because the United States has a greater national-interest stake in Bosnia than in Angola. Of course, this dilutes the moral message. It is well to bear in mind Churchill's words: "The Sermon on the Mount is the last word in Christian ethics. . . . Still, it is not on those terms that Ministers assume their responsibilities of guiding states."

Second, as discussed above in connection with military intervention, even if morality appears to make an overwhelming case for activism, it must still be balanced by considerations of effectiveness. Where is the morality if U.S. arms supplied to the Bosnian Muslims do no more than, in the words of the British Foreign Secretary, Douglas Hurd, "greatly increase the killing and the length of the war"? How are American values enhanced if, in support of human rights, trade sanctions are applied against China which bring political liberalization to a halt, snuff out the fledgling democratic movement in Hong Kong, and ultimately strengthen the Communist old guard's grip on power?

The Limits of Force

THE CENTRAL ERROR THE TRADITIONALISTS make is to try to freeze in place the traditional politico-military approach to international problem-solving. According to this approach, although political means come first, military force is never far behind. For the reasons given above, the passing of the Cold War has rendered this thinking obsolete. The United States will be making a critical mistake if, as Albright is urging, it gives this old approach a new lease on life under UN auspices.

The major consequence of the persistence of this thinking will be to saddle the United States with continued excessive military costs. Although the defense establishment would have us believe that costs have been cut to the bone and that, in the words of Admiral Frank Kelso, the chief of naval operations, the military is "on the ragged edge of readiness," the reality is otherwise. Despite promised reductions in spending, the military budget will still consume more than $1.3 *trillion* over the next five years, and a further $150 billion will go for intelligence. It will take until 1998, nearly ten years after the Berlin Wall came down, before spending in terms of constant dollars returns to the levels of the late 1950s and mid-1970s. This is more than 150 percent of the combined expenditures of all the other members of NATO; in 1991 the United States spent $850 more per capita on defense than Japan. Our NATO allies are more than matching the U.S. defense reductions. Something is out of balance here.

Since units in the U.S. military have multiple tasks, it is not easy to match lines in the budget with possible scenarios. Forces in Europe, for example, can also be deployed to the Middle East. However, a generally accepted rule of thumb during the Cold War was that some 50 percent of defense expenditures was intended to deter Soviet advances in Europe. This threat has disappeared once and for all. But instead of accepting the logic of the situation, the neo–Cold War orthodoxy cleaves to its image of an unstable world bristling with new dangers and threats that only the United States is able to resist.

During the election campaign Clinton rightly decried those who wish to raid the foreign-aid and defense budgets for the sake of "domestic wish lists." It is axiomatic that security is a first charge on resources: if the nation is endangered, money must be found. But the obverse is also true. To sustain a bloated budget on the basis of an outmoded and flawed doctrine (not to mention some downright incredible scenarios, including opposing a Russian invasion of the Baltic states, penned by the Pentagon's more imaginative scribes) is equally unpatriotic.

If nothing else, Bosnia has shown the limits, both military and political, of power in the post–Cold War era. By ignoring this lesson and failing to order a *de novo* review of the resources devoted to foreign policy—something from which our European allies have not shied despite their much closer proximity to the zone of instability—the traditionalists are robbing the nation of a unique opportunity to make healthy, safe, and much-needed adjustments to America's role in the world. The reductions in foreign-policy spending that have taken place or are planned are real indeed but, compared with the opportunity, do not go far enough. It is not too much to look for reductions in intelligence and defense spending of 50 percent or more.

Toward a New Strategy

WHERE DOES THIS ANALYSIS LEAD ON THE more creative side of the equation? What are the implications for practical policy formation?

The first priority must be to adjust expectations to reality. Foreign policy is no longer where the action is. Those used to the daily red meat of the Cold War and looking for fresh sources of provender will be disappointed. Today's wars (Bosnia, Angola, Armenia-Azerbaijan, the anti-narcotics battle, among others) and today's problems (ethnic upheaval, religious intolerance, terrorism, economic imbalances, fragile democracies) do not provide the all-encompassing challenge that was inherent in totalitarian fascism and communism. The era of the crusader has passed away. The holy places are no longer in the hands of infidels. At the end of the twelfth century the warrior king Richard the Lion Heart faced a similar letdown. On his return to England, having performed dazzling feats of arms outside Jerusalem, he found the tasks of peacetime governance prosaic and unfulfilling. Preferring to search for military glory in France, he neglected his royal duties. The kingdom he bequeathed to his successor soon dissolved among the fractious baronies.

So it is today. With American ideas and values commanding unparalleled acceptance, there is simply less need for the United States to guard the frontiers against the forces of darkness. There is no evil empire. The level of threat does not call for the forward deployment of heavy-infantry divisions, which are, in any case, ill equipped to answer the more subtle questions posed by the contemporary world. Furthermore, problems at home cast an ever-lengthening shadow.

As a consequence, U.S. policymakers need to accustom domestic and international public opinion to the idea that U.S. intervention is no longer either sound policy or a first-resort option. Instead, the United States will adopt a "cooperative security" approach, in which leadership will not necessarily be in U.S. hands and responsibility will be devolved down the line to the parties or regional organizations most directly concerned.

This doctrine needs to be articulated clearly and publicly. Present policy, which asserts the leadership of the United States, as Christopher did repeatedly in repudiating Tarnoff, but which the Administration's actions cause foreign nations to suspect is weakly founded, produces two negative results: it stunts the growth of regional organizations—for example, the fledgling European Community "Eurocorps"—and thereby delays the day when they might be able to exercise real responsibility; and it saps American credibility, causing both potential aggressors and potential victims to behave unreliably.

Second, the United States needs to focus on fundamentals, not symptoms, around the world. This means paying more attention to economics. The success, for example, of the democratic experiment in Russia and else-where in Eastern Europe depends not on politico-military artifices such as the Conference on Security and Cooperation in Europe and the North Atlantic Cooperation Council (modestly useful though these organizations are) but on whether people are able to put bread on the table. The essential kind of support is thus less glamorous than shipping Stinger missiles over the Khyber Pass, but the consequences of failure in terms of a relapse into authoritarianism are just as great.

Islamic fundamentalism, terrorism, nuclear proliferation, ethnic and religious conflict, all fish in the pond of economic disequilibrium. In Egypt fundamentalism is propagating itself primarily among the poor and dispossessed, who reach out to religion to make sense of their blighted lives. Infiltrators from Tehran may exploit this sense of deprivation—but to focus exclusively on them, as President Hosni Mubarak would have us do in his quest for aid and arms, is to treat the symptom, not the disease. In Peru an indigenous terrorist movement is taking advantage of a population alienated from the political process. Ukraine flaunts its nuclear weapons partly out of resentment over inattention from the G7 aid donors. In India chronic economic underperformance prompts Hindus to seek scapegoats in the Muslim population.

Without a successful world economy, none of these problems is soluble. Unfortunately, no agreement exists about the best path along which to ascend to general prosperity. There are as many views as there are economists. This is not the place to adjudicate their views—that must await a separate study. All that needs to be said in the foreign-policy context is that economic decisions have assumed a greater-than-ever geostrategic importance, and must be coordinated at the highest level. To take a small example, an obvious bureaucratic disconnect exists in a policy whereby with one hand the Administration dispatches ground troops to shore up Macedonia's security while with the other, at the behest of the textile industry, it applies trade sanctions that imperil that country's viability.

Third, the concept of American interests must be returned to the heart of the foreign-policy decision-making process. Reformists and conservatives can probably agree that the only sustainable basis for placing American forces in harm's way is that American national interests are at stake. There will be dispute about what these interests are. One man's genocide is another man's quagmire. In a forest of conflicting claims and counterclaims, national interests will provide a sure compass. Once again, this demands a rigorous intellectual process and will involve the

jettisoning of much Cold War baggage. Where once American interests seemed under global threat and public opinion stood ready to pay the necessary price in lives and treasure, today direct threats to the United States are few indeed.

Fourth, no U.S. foreign policy can stray far from American values. But any attempt by the United States to impose its interpretation of human rights on foreign countries is likely to be fruitless. Instead, the United States should put the world on notice that the degree of cooperation between itself and foreign countries will depend crucially on their observance of normally accepted humanitarian values.

Cooperative security, the cold logic of national interest, and economics may taste like thin gruel, even if seasoned with human rights. These themes do not "stiffen the sinews" or "summon up the blood." But that is the nature of today's foreign policy. It is better to recognize this fact than to base policy on a windy rhetoric that makes unredeemable promises.

Consolation for the absence of stirring inspiration may be found in the good policy decisions that flow from these guidelines. For example, nonintervention in Bosnia would have been the obvious option from the start. If it had been clear that we were not going to intervene, this might have prompted the belligerent parties into dealing more realistically with one another, or goaded the Europeans into earlier, more decisive action. The economic theme would invigorate policy toward the lands of the former Soviet empire and assuage some of the fears about religious extremism. Concern for human rights would signal to a transgressor like China that so long as its violations continue, it will face yearly battles to retain its access to American investment and markets.

Before his inauguration in 1913, President-elect Woodrow Wilson told his friends, "It would be an irony of fate if my administration had to deal chiefly with foreign affairs." There is little doubt that President Clinton would echo this sentiment. But as Bosnia, Somalia, and Russia show, there is no escape. To enable him to bring stability and consistency to this aspect of his job, the President needs a new strategic model. At present he is receiving backward-looking advice that, because it fails to take account of the dramatic changes in the world and the deterioration of domestic finances, opens a gap between rhetoric and performance. This damages American credibility. The nation is entitled to something better. The President should have the courage of his convictions and demand the real changes that he was elected to bring about.

Evaluating Foreign Policy Relationships: America and Post–Cold War Asia

Michel Oksenberg and Hongying Wang

East-West Center

In January, a group of leading U.S. non-governmental organizations specializing in Asia met to discuss U.S. interests in the Asia-Pacific area and to suggest policy implications for the new American administration. The meeting was convened in Washington by The Asia Society, the East-West Center, the National Committee on U.S.–China Relations, and The Johnson Foundation. Co-conveners were The Asia Foundation, the Carnegie Endowment, and The Japan Society. This was the first time these organizations have jointly co-sponsored an event.

In the last two decades, the Asia-Pacific region, the vast area from Pakistan to Japan and from Australia to Siberia, has led the world in economic growth. Although unevenness exists both among and within countries in the region, the average GNP growth for the region as a whole is around 6 percent, in contrast to about 2 percent elsewhere in the world. With living standards rising rapidly here, for more than half the world's population, a vast market is in the making. Meanwhile, because of the successful export-oriented development strategies and the high savings rate of its countries, the region—led by Japan, Taiwan, and Hong Kong—has become an important source of capital in the world economy.

The fate of the United States is intertwined with the Asia-Pacific region. It has become the largest export market for the United States and is a major source of

Great powers secure their destinies not only by bringing peace and prosperity to problem areas but also by nurturing ties with regions of growing importance.

capital to finance American indebtedness. It is the native place of millions of new immigrants, many of whom remain engaged in the politics of their native lands and remit earnings to their kin. The political stability and economic opportunities in this region are vital to American security and prosperity.

In recent years, the U.S. government has not paid sufficient attention to the Asia-Pacific region. Many Asian leaders wonder whether the United States intends dramatically to reduce its involvement in Asia and foster a North- and South-American trading bloc. These fears are fed not only by the creation of athe North America Free Trade Agreement (NAFTA) and reductions in the military presence, but also symbols and time commitments of U.S. leaders.

發展
Development

The [...] reign policy has been on [...] former Soviet Union and Easte[...] rope, peace talks in the Middle East and the negotiation for NAFTA. These concerns are understandable. But whether the balance in national attention—the slighting of Asia and Pacific—is wise is a different matter. Just as a business must invest in growth areas to protect its future, great powers secure their destinies not only by bringing peace and prosperity to problem areas but also by nurturing ties with regions of growing importance.

改變
Change

America's relative neglect of Asia could imperil the nation's future. It could trigger preemptive Asian moves, for example, to form its own regional trading bloc. Or, believing the United States will not remain militarily engaged, some Asian nations may initiate a rapid arms build-up to compensate for the anticipated withdrawal of U.S. forces.

Increasingly, local trends shape the future of the Asia-Pacific region. The success of American policy toward Asia and the Pacific will depend on understanding and responding to these indigenous forces, adjusting to them and influencing them on the margin in favor of U.S. interests.

From *Wingspread Journal,* Vol. 15, Issue 2, Summer 1993, pp. 1, 10-11. © 1993 by The Johnson Foundation, Inc. Reprinted by permission.

STRATEGIC DEVELOPMENTS IN THE ASIA-PACIFIC REGION

協力

Partnership

Four major interrelated developments are sweeping the entire region: (1) strategically, the emergence of a multi-polar international structure; (2) economically, rapid growth and its strategic consequences; (3) cultural and social change brought on especially by the telecommunications transformation; and (4) generational political succession and its implications. These developments, occurring unevenly across the region, elicit different responses from governments in the region. For example, Thailand is confronting its AIDS epidemic more rapidly than India. Malaysia and Indonesia contrast sharply in their telecommunications policies. Even Hong Kong, Singapore, Taiwan, and Korea—often lumped together as the "Four Dragons"—differ significantly in their economic development strategies. The vast variances among the Asia-Pacific countries stem from differences in their natural conditions, historical backgrounds, the effectiveness of their political systems and so on.

Yet, this region is increasingly interdependent, and all countries—to varying degrees—are being challenged by a common set of problems and changes. It pays, therefore, to take a region-wide look at the broad trends. Extensive American involvement is necessary both to sustain the current, favorable situation and to enable the United States to seize the opportunities that Asia and the Pacific offer.

POTENTIAL PROBLEMS

Post–Cold War Asia appears, on the surface, to be peaceful and increasingly prosperous. A multi-polar system has emerged that offers increased stability. The prospects for continued, rapid growth are bright. A discernible trend exists toward liberalization. Most countries in the region are not burdened by intolerable debt loads, chronically high rates of inflation, or ineffective govern-

ments. The region stands in sharp contrast to Latin America, Africa, and the lands of the former Soviet Union.

But it is worth briefly mentioning what could go wrong. The region is vulnerable to a number of potential problems:

- The failure of the Uruguay Round and the breakdown of the GATT (General Agreement on Tariffs and Trade) system would imperil the export-led development strategies of many Asian countries. Growing protectionism could impel formation of an exclusive Asian trading bloc.
- The Japanese-American partnership remains crucial to the security and growth of the entire region. Were the alliance to deteriorate and become animosity-ridden, the consequences would be profound. Yet the continued wise management of Japanese-American relations cannot be taken for granted.
- Mainland China's future is uncertain. Its political system confronts the challenge of having an orderly succession to Deng Xiaoping.

Meanwhile, other aspects of China promote troubling thoughts about its long-term prospects. Its military budget is increasing rapidly; it is purchasing advanced weaponry from the former Soviet states. It is becoming a major arms supplier, and its commitment to non-proliferation of weapons of mass destruction is suspect.

- Chinese foreign policy gives some indication of becoming more muscular or assertive. The Asian equilibrium depends on a unified and effectively governed mainland China that lives at peace with its neighbors. It is by no means obvious that such a China will continue to exist. Specifically, Beijing's relations with Hong Kong and Taiwan could easily go awry.
- The future of the Korean peninsula is also uncertain. North Korea remains isolated; its prospects after Kim Il-song are unknown. Its nuclearization or collapse would pose severe challenges.
- Regional tensions in South and Southeast Asia persist. The Cambodian tragedy has not yet ended. Despite progress, Indo-Pakistani relations remain acrimonious.
- New problems loom on the horizon. In particular, AIDS is spreading rapidly and will reach epidemic proportions throughout the region by the decade's end. Narcotics production and use is also rising. And, severe environmental

problems are affecting health, quality of life, and growth rates.

IMPLICATIONS FOR THE FOREIGN POLICIES OF THE GREAT POWERS

The major trends and potential problems have made the strategic calculus for each of the great powers more complex. China no longer derives strategic benefit from being a balancer between the two superpowers. China's diminished security value to the United States in its global confrontation with the former Soviet Union means that Washington no longer downplays its differences with Beijing on such issues as trade, human rights, and arms sales.

The fate of the United States is intertwined with this region.

China's leaders have had to cultivate other means for advancing their interests as a result of the more acrimonious Sino-American relationship. Thus, they have developed constructive ties with their neighbors. They have become quite active diplomatically on the world scene, and they have adopted a somewhat more assertive and muscular approach to such issues as territorial integrity and claims to islands in coastal waters.

Without the anti-Soviet underpinnings of the Japanese-American alliance, neither Japan nor the United States is as willing as in the past to accommodate the needs of its partner. With American economic difficulties at home, Washington is more willing to press Tokyo to share the burden of global and regional security with the United States. Tokyo, however, often seems more willing to pursue its own interests.

The removal of a common external threat has weakened the previous sense of urgency to resolve Japanese-American tensions. Even as it retains its identity as a leading industrialized democracy, with a permanent membership on the UN Security Council in its future, Japan is also re-emphasizing its identity as an Asian country.

In Asia, as elsewhere, Russian influence is now in eclipse. But that country will not remain dormant for long. When Russia revives, how will it act? Questions abound. Will it regain economic vitality

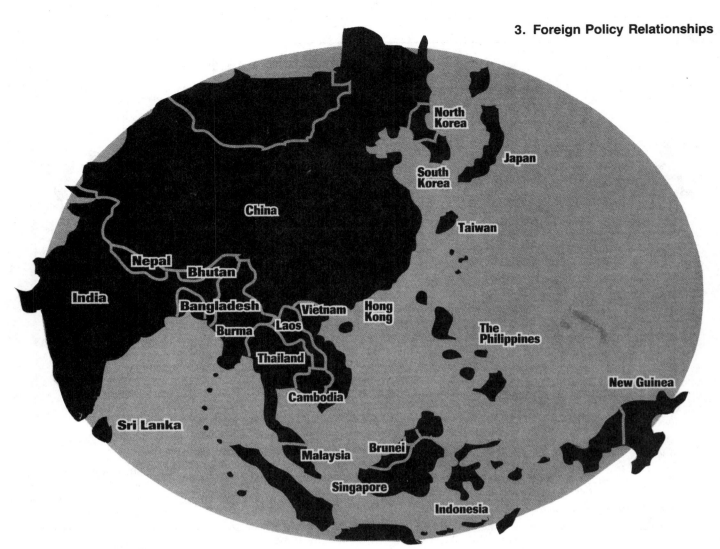

but retain the same expansionist tradition that shaped Russian history from Ivan the Terrible through Peter the Great and in the Soviet era as well? Or, will Russia's nature be so fundamentally transformed that it will join the "zone of peace" that is said to exist among democratic countries?

Further, Russia now no longer borders on Central Europe. Will these developments require Moscow to concentrate more attention on the Asian portion of its periphery? And how much control will Moscow exercise over its Siberian and Far Eastern territories? If these regions acquire greater autonomy, what are the implications for Northeast Asian security arrangements?

With the demise of the Soviet Union, India can no longer draw upon Soviet support in its pursuit for regional ambitions in the sub-continent. The collapse of the ruble and the drastic reduction of oil resources and technology supplied by Russia compel India to look West.

Of all the powers, perhaps the United States faces the greatest challenge in adjusting to Asia's new realities. The dis-

appearance of the Soviet Union has undermined a basic reason for American political and military involvement in the Asia-Pacific for the past 45 years. To sustain the American presence requires a new rationale to replace the old one of containment. American policy-makers are still in the process of developing a coherent and persuasive rationale for Asian engagement. America's new approach will have to take into account the adjustments other powers have made in their foreign policies.

均衡
Balance

The United States faces some very tough choices in Asia. How much priority should it attach to Asia? Will its leaders

devote time to the region and nurture personal ties with all the major countries? How should the United States respond to impulses emanating in Asia toward multilateralism? Should the United States welcome proposals for multilateralism that include the United States or should it continue its emphasis on bilateral ties? How should it pursue its human rights agenda? What level of military presence should it retain? How should it advance its economic interests?

選擇
Choices

Providing new answers to these old questions will be at the core of American debate on Asia policy in the months and years ahead.

31

A Renewed Security Partnership?

THE UNITED STATES AND THE EUROPEAN COMMUNITY IN THE 1990S

Catherine McArdle Kelleher

Catherine McArdle Kelleher is a senior fellow in the Brookings Foreign Policy Studies program and draws on this essay in her contribution to Global Engagement, *edited by Janne A. Nolan (Brookings, forthcoming).*

The United States and Europe are at a critical turning point in the definition of their security partnership. After the fall of the Berlin Wall, most Americans assumed that the existing transatlantic security system could—and should— meet any challenges offered by the emerging world order. After all, since the mid-1960s NATO had become in effect the permanent diplomatic conference for the North Atlantic region. To many Europeans, however, the dramatically changing world situation breathed new life into efforts, admittedly sporadic and futile, since the end of World War II, to fashion a common European defense identity and to go beyond Europe's past dependence on the United States for security. The crisis in Yugoslavia has shaken both beliefs. What is now the common conception of security? What is the commitment on both sides of the Atlantic to multilateral action in the interests of peace and security?

The run-up to the NATO Summit now set for next January will be a critical time for policy choice but also for American leadership. European elites are distracted by deep recession, weak governments, the failures to meet the Maastricht milestones toward political and economic union, and the continuing adjustment to a united Germany. The Clinton administration has its own distractions—the pressing domestic agenda of health care and economic revitalization, a people awaiting a long-postponed peace dividend, and a Congress increasingly turning inward. But the time to establish a new vision for a renewed European-American security partnership, to define the parameters for a renewed cooperative security system that limits offensive forces, ensures transparency, and provides for collective action, is now.

The Twin Requirements for Security

The first task will be to rediscover the interrelationship of economic and military security. Much of the recent debate over European-American security, for example, has tended to cast NATO and the European Community as alternative security systems. In fact, as originally conceived (and as they have functioned practically for decades), they were actually interdependent institutions within a common security vision. From the outset, Americans and Europeans viewed security as having both military and economic requirements. The direct threats, especially in the first decade after World War II, were seen as Soviet expansionism and a German military renewal. But the most fundamental fear was of a return to the dangers of the 1930s: the lack of economic security eroding political allegiance to democratic values and the lack of military security allowing a looming totalitarian threat to overwhelm weak national militaries. The European Community and NATO were thus intertwined answers to the same question: how to preserve peace in Europe against internal and external threat.

From its first days, the EC (then the European Coal and Steel Community) created new ways of doing business across borders and new sources of

From *The Brookings Review*, Fall 1993, pp. 30-35. © 1993 by The Brookings Institute. Reprinted by permission.

confidence and mutual reassurance. Its successes nurtured a perception of the inevitability of a European "zone of peace," for the time limited to Western Europe but eventually to embrace all of Europe.

Meanwhile NATO evolved into a fully fledged cooperative security organization. In no other region of the world was there more progress toward the mutual coordination and regulation of military capabilities and operations. NATO also developed initiatives on economic security, in particular taking into account the impact of defense cooperation on national economies in burdensharing formulas.

A telling success of the broadly complementary approach of the EC and NATO came in their treatment of Germany. Both NATO and the EC recognized that security was most easily achieved by making Germany a partner and by enmeshing all member states cooperatively in its containment and its economic prosperity. Avoiding an isolated Germany, vulnerable, as after World War I, to demagogic legends, meant developing mutual security structures. Guarding against German "singularization"—and therefore promoting the extension to all Western European states of mutual arms regulation and transparency in military defense decisionmaking—became the political foundation for European cooperation in all fields.

The fall of the wall allowed the expansion of this regime into a Europe-wide system. National equipment and personnel ceilings are set and regularly inspected under the Conventional forces in Europe (CFE) treaty; there are enhanced confidence-building and stabilizing measures under the Conference on Security and Cooperation in Europe (CSCE); and greater transparency is assured under both CFE and the emerging Open Skies regime. In operational terms, the total regime sets a new standard for openness and mutual constraint among the 40-plus participating states.

Yet both the Yugoslav crisis and the recent debate over U.S.-European security challenge the common vision, both of the security threats and of the means to combat them. For most Europeans, the greatest present threat is economic chaos and political collapse in the former Soviet Union and Eastern Europe. Many Americans also see the risks of new economic and ethnic instability but so far have failed to find a strategy that would parallel the stabilizing effects of the postwar Marshall Plan. Moreover, most Americans (and perhaps too few Europeans) also focus on military security both in Europe and in the new global order for which European cooperation is essential. Their challenge to all critics has been to find an organization other than NATO that can meet its military security standards.

Adapting to the New Security Order

Much of the debate so far has been mired in theological concerns about "security architecture." The first shot was the Berlin speech of U.S. Secretary of State James Baker a month after the wall fell. In U.S. eyes, it was a call for cooperative change—for adapting to the unfolding new world order while continuing the European-American partnership in NATO. Europeans, however, saw Baker's speech as simply the latest in recurring U.S. attempts to forestall the emergence of common European foreign and security policy.

In the debate that followed, France and a somewhat ambivalent Germany lined up on one side and the United States, Britain, and several smaller European states on the other. President François Mitterrand and Chancellor Helmut Kohl took initiative after initiative to establish European union and a clear European defense identity, one not dependent on the survival of NATO or a particular U.S. presence in Europe. One decision was to establish, under the authority of the Western European Union (WEU), a 35,000-man Franco-German corps as the nucleus of a Eurocorps, eventually perhaps a European army.

U.S. reaction was strong. Despite German reassurance, the Bush administration saw the proposals as steps to undermine NATO and the U.S. security role in Europe. The British, Dutch, and Italians also sought to preserve existing Atlantic structures and opposed strengthening WEU at the cost of weakening NATO.

The compromises finally reached stressed mutual political adjustment, both in the EC and in NATO. The EC's December 1991 Maastricht Treaty on European Union foresaw only the "eventual framing of a common defense policy, which might in time lead to a common defense." WEU was to serve as the defense "component" of the European Union *and* to constitute NATO's "European pillar."

NATO for its part recognized that it shares responsibility for security with WEU and CSCE and pledged to provide for the "necessary mutual transparency and complementarity" to make cooperation possible. It also agreed to allow forces assigned to NATO—German and eventually Belgian and Spanish as well—to be assigned simultaneously to the Eurocorps.

Both NATO and WEU forces will also respond to peacekeeping tasking by the CSCE and the United Nations. WEU will form a rapid reaction force but not an independent standing force. Units assigned to it by NATO member states will wear two hats—one NATO, one WEU—and will be subject first to tasking from the NATO command. In some areas, such as traditional arms control negotiations and conflict prevention, primary responsibility is assigned to the CSCE. The result is a rather untidy but robust organizational chart with overlapping responsibilities and memberships that can but need not be used. But the Yugoslav crisis demonstrated once again that the key is not architecture but political choice and the willingness to undertake the risks and burdens of joint action. The consensus in both NATO and WEU extends only to the defense of national borders, not to joint crisis management or peacekeeping even in NATO's near abroad.

Turning Down the Volume

For now the decibel level of the debate is fairly moderate. President Clinton, unlike Bush, seems to recognize the value of more equal partnership. And the EC's political setbacks after Maastricht—the delays in ratification, Europe's slide into recession, and the collapse of the Exchange Rate Mechanism (ERM)— have convinced many Americans that Europe's evolution will be far slower and more congruent with mutual American-European interests. But, as before, many Americans underestimate the strength of Europe's drive for closer union in all its aspects and what, for Europeans, is the self-evident connection between economic and military security policies.

More important, NATO's transformation is far from complete. Most of NATO's military changes are still geared only to updated border defense. Its political changes do not go to the heart of the post–Cold War challenge: how to define a new overarching purpose that will go beyond the alliance as an end in itself or as a defense against uncertainty. For many in Europe, especially Eastern Europe, NATO's sole function is to frame U.S. involvement in Europe and to structure its leadership role. But Americans in increasing numbers are questioning the costs of and the need for such a role without a transformed rationale and new instruments. Is NATO really necessary, they ask? Would America's bedrock interest in Europe not be served equally well by a European security pillar linked loosely to a North American pillar?

At this stage in Europe's political evolution, there is and probably can be no fixed institutional hierarchy. But the political drift at present is worrisome, as is the failure to agree on a new overarching European-American security concept, let alone a new transatlantic division of labor. Overlapping organizational responsibilities in a transitional period can be a source of weakness as well as of flexibility and strength. Bosnia shows they can allow confusion and delay if the tasking priorities are not clear or provide excuses for inaction.

Moreover, absent a new effective forum for regular high-level political consultation, neither the United States nor the EC states may be able to pursue the transparency and complementarity needed to sustain security partnership. NATO has no political analog to the close military cooperation and joint planning under SHAPE; CSCE still barely exists in institutional terms. The CFE-CSCE-Open Skies regime needs political deepening and military extension particularly in light of growing Russian military concerns about regional balances. And U.S.-EC consultations under the Transatlantic Declaration of November 1990 are still less frequent and more constrained in scope than is appropriate.

Outreach to the East

The biggest challenge facing Europe and the United States is whether, how, and when to incorporate the new states of the East into the evolving security order. Initially, France and Germany backed making the CSCE a pan-European security system, an eventual NATO replacement or at least a link to the United States and Canada that would forge a European "peace system." In parallel, the EC focused on the immediate problems of economic assistance. The United States, pleading deficit woes, readily ceded that role to Europe. It gave CSCE its usual half-hearted support and insisted that the restructuring not compromise NATO's role.

Rhetorically, at least, CSCE has provided for comprehensive outreach to the East. More than 50 states, including all the former Soviet republics, have signed on to its principles. But its achievements so far are limited though it now has a permanent secretary-general and has taken on expanded roles in dispute resolution and conflict prevention.

Since August 1991, CSCE has faced direct competition from the North Atlantic Cooperation Council (NACC), a German-American initiative undertaken in the aftermath of the Soviet coup attempt. The aim was to involve Eastern European states as limited partners in the NATO security dialogue—without granting them full or even associate alliance membership. Now extended to the former Soviet republics as well, NACC has notched some real achievements, including persuading the former Soviet states to agree to an equitable division of the Soviet CFE arms limitations and implementing military exchanges and joint training planning. The long-term impact of NACC is still unclear; it has limited formal standing, and the French government has already proposed the Balladur alternative to NACC (and CSCE as well) that would in effect exclude a number of former Soviet republics from any European security community. What *is* clear is that NACC will succeed only if it is either a training stage toward membership or an organization with significant operational tasks—as in peacekeeping or humanitarian assistance.

What most East European states want is full membership in the EC for economic security and in NATO for military security. But admitting these states as members presents formidable problems. All existing European and transatlantic institutions presuppose that their member states can provide for the basic security and human rights of their populations, ensure minimal political order, and implement the democratic rule of law with general public compliance within clear state boundaries. Accommodating states in decline, states not yet emergent, and states that may never exercise effective democratic political control would stretch the present institutions beyond their limits.

For the EC, although it has long recognized the security-related need to redistribute resources within Europe (heretofore North to South), admitting Russia and the former Soviet republics to Europe seems an unmanageable challenge. The EC has extended a promise of eventual membership only to the six Central and Southeastern European states—and that without specifying a date. Europeans agree that the primary long-term security task must be economic restructuring in the East, but they see the task as global in scope, beyond Europe's own capacity.

Expansion of NATO's formal membership is similarly constrained but is less important than extending and expanding operational cooperation. The goal is to "normalize" interaction and joint action with those NACC states that commit to NATO's basic principles, including democratic control of military forces and decisionmaking, the sharing of burdens and risks, and commitment to the peaceful resolution of disputes under the UN Charter. Intense dialogue and growing common experience will be at least short-term surrogates for, and incentives toward, the behavioral tests for eventual membership.

Joint Action outside the Alliance Territory

Practically speaking, how has the evolving European-American security system been working outside the traditional NATO area? In the Gulf War and Somalia, the United States took the initiative to organize and lead an ad hoc coalition involving European states but outside either NATO or the WEU-EC framework. In Yugoslavia the EC took the initiative at the outset, but without great success and with increasing dependence on the UN, CSCE, and NATO.

The test the EC set for itself in Yugoslavia was not that traditionally foreseen under collective security regimes: an international assessment of blame and the imposition, by force if necessary, of a collective solution. Rather the standard was that set by the EC states over the past decades—early conflict resolution, early protection of human rights, the timely imposition of sanctions, and the commitment to use all efforts to ensure a war-free Europe.

During the first years of crisis in former Yugoslavia, in the face of deafening silence from the Bush administration and the United States, the EC tried an expanding array of approaches. But there were no lasting successes—only greater divisions, frustration, and indecision. Even now, there is no consensus on what to do once the fighting stops.

The Community's failure is hardly singular. The CSCE has engaged mostly at the formal level (for example, by suspending Serbia's membership). Since the summer of 1992, and certainly since the Clinton administration took office, NATO has become far more energized, and the planning for peacekeeping by SHAPE together with some NACC members has been pathbreaking. But as the August debate over air strikes demonstrated, NATO does not have the critical consensus to use its own command structure, let alone to decide independently on use of force.

The explanations for failure are myriad. The Yugoslav crisis happened before Europe was ready; Yugoslavia's ethnic politics hinder outsiders' attempts to act; the physical terrain makes intervention risky and potentially expensive in lives and equipment; the multilateral instruments for coping with civil war are still too rudimentary.

But the critical factor appears to be the lack of political will. Member governments and their populations, in the EC as in the United States, are unwilling to risk the lives of their military forces in direct intervention. Air strikes were threatened only in the end game of the Bosnian negotiations, and then only grudgingly. And the use of force, even to defend the supply of humanitarian aid, was deemed too risky.

The Yugoslav crisis demonstrates the limits of European and transatlantic commitment to cooperative security action beyond the defense of their own borders—a challenge that seems destined to recur under present international conditions. Democracies require popular support for action—whatever is needed for the present and whatever may be needed if the conflict worsens and the political or military costs mount. European-American cooperation is achieved only through negotiation, often subject to the delays that dog democracies and sometimes disrupted by the intransigencies of powerful states.

What that means in the short run is that action will be taken by individual states who decide to act, often led by the United States or with U.S. logistical support and political approval. That will certainly be true as long as European states are not able or willing to invest in the hardware, the power projection capabilities, and the training needed for peacekeeping. But even a European commitment to eventual joint action will not necessarily ensure timely crisis intervention or effective peacekeeping without renewed political cooperation. And U.S. support for European operations without prior consultation and planning seems questionable—which brings the argument back to a NATO or NATO-like framework for joint action.

Options for the Future

Of two things regarding the transatlantic alliance we can be sure. Europe and the United States will not undergo a dramatic fracture nor will they lose interest in each other. Two broad options remain. The American and European security systems could merge under an umbrella organization called NATO. Or they could evolve separately into two systems bound to cooperation only in circumstances of mutual interest or under direct threat.

The worst possible eventuality would be two weakened systems unable to meet their goals because of high costs and lack of political will, with the EC endorsing the rhetoric of a European defense identity but doing little to make it work, and the United States unwilling and unable either to maintain forces in Europe or to join with or support European forces.

What of the NATO option? One possibility, a simple reduction of past NATO structures to more "cost-effective" levels, is not only unlikely, but probably undesirable given the new international demands. Also to be avoided is a simple division of labor occasionally espoused by advocates of the "two pillar" approach. With variations, the argument recurs: NATO in its transatlantic form becomes activated if and only if the United States is involved or the conflict involves nuclear weapons or Europe's own security institutions have not resolved the conflict or restored the status quo ante. This relegates the United States to the role of expeditionary fire brigade, one not easily played in the face of declining public or congressional support or even defense cuts.

What is needed is a fundamental transformation of the alliance, involving agreement on broad goals and eventual membership or scope, as well as on a specific division of labor and a significant overlap of missions and capabilities. If the NATO umbrella is to work, commitments cannot be à la carte or simply the result of decisions made on a case-by-case basis. But that does not rule out organizational transformation or selective participation in certain tasks, separate as well as common priorities for each pillar, and national, regional, or cooperative funding of key projects and activities. Indeed, viewed broadly, these have been the tools with which the United States has worked for the past 40 years to ensure cooperation in NATO—among nuclear and non-nuclear states, states in NATO's tightly integrated central front and on its loosely tied southern and northern flanks, states rich and poor.

One attractive alternative is to give NATO and the NACC primary responsibility for the security dialogue with Central Europe and the former Soviet republics. NATO would be the decisionmaking forum for both Americans and Europeans on three key issues: preparation for involving the East in peacekeeping and peacemaking; assistance to the East on the democratization of security and on defense restructuring; and crisis management tasking from the CSCE and the UN. Carrying out these responsibilities would require regular transatlantic political consultation and a permanent policy forum, as well as maintenance of key levels of NATO's present integrated command. Probably it would also involve some cross-Atlantic deployments and training as well as a continued U.S. presence on the continent.

But this must be an organization that assumes an engaged, internationalist EC. There is no need to exclude European military integration, EC support for the East, or even direct EC-East ties for security cooperation in specified areas or for particular missions. The EC might indeed be charged explicitly as a "subcontractor" on issues like defense conversion and export controls. It would, however, remove from contention the issue of first responsibility, something that several EC members would indeed appreciate.

The EC could be given primary responsibility for building economic security in the East, through direct aid or channeling private-public humanitarian ventures. The charge to the EC might well be to develop a plan for broad trade and credit agreements to promote imports from the East or to arrange for favorable lending to the East for investment and for building infrastructure. Clearly the joint military-economic security burden would have to be redefined. Most important would be EC-U.S. agreement on calculating a new metric to acknowledge the contributions and the obligations of all participating states in the interrelated economic and military spheres.

The greatest change would have to be in the behavior of the United States—a pattern already somewhat practiced by the Clinton administration. The United States would have to take far more seriously the question of sharing responsibility—of not subjecting its allies to unilateral decisions or commitments that bind them to U.S. decisions. It would have to be prepared to hear and accept the EC speaking with one equal voice in security issues as in trade. It would have to be willing to be subject on some issues to joint decisions—as would its European partners. The United States would thereby give up a major bargaining threat—precipitous congressional or executive action on cuts or withdrawal. It would have to downgrade some useful bilateral channels of influence and pressure. It would probably have to accede on specific joint EC-U.S. procedures for agreement (not just notification) about the temporary withdrawal of forces for other missions out of area. But it would gain a stronger framework for its own efforts to transform security policy, for planning purposes as well as at least limited efforts toward force specialization between pillars.

It has been suggested, most recently by Chancellor Kohl, that this transformation requires a new transatlantic treaty. Treaty supporters argue that it would complement the North Atlantic Treaty, not replace it, and add the keystone to the range of treaties the EC is concluding with critical nation states. It would emphasize the EC-U.S. relationship in all its facets, not just military security or even an expanded definition of military and economic security.

U.S. officials to date have supported the idea of intensifying and expanding U.S.-EC relations, but have been less enthusiastic about a treaty as the means to do so. They point out that the real question is political commitment, the decision on both sides of the Atlantic to proceed to new forms of cooperation. They also note the recent failure of the EC states to arrive at common positions of critical importance to the United States, most particularly on the Uruguay Round of GATT talks and the plans for the "no-fly zones" and air strikes in Bosnia. Treaty or not, they argue, the key questions in the post–Cold War era will be the basis for cooperative action and the equitable sharing of burden and benefit.

In sum, neither side of the U.S.-EC dialogue has been as willing to explore new options jointly or to build on what has already been achieved together as the post–Cold War security challenge demands. The guilt of joint inaction in Bosnia may spur greater agreement; domestic budget pressures and needs for electoral justifications for national military establishments may speed the process. But the NATO Summit in January provides the decision-forcing deadline to begin the significant transformations required.

From Vladivostock to Vancouver

The security regimes that have evolved in Europe and in the Atlantic relationship offer a complex, interwoven system of institutions adequate to most security requirements in the present era of relative peace in Europe. Short of massive civil unrest in Russia or unlikely global conflict, the pieces now in place could provide the building blocks for a new security cooperation whose potential reach is, as the CSCE motto proclaims, from Vladivostock to Vancouver, from the borders of Florida to those of Anatolia. What is lacking is the political decision to take on this task and to rally weary publics behind it.

The choices facing Europe and the United States today are remarkably like those they faced at the end of World War II. The arguments for action and inaction are the same; the political and military resources needed are of comparable magnitudes. The tools available for a cooperative solution are also alike—international and multilateral institution building, cooperation before competition, democratization and economic prosperity as the lodestones in the search for security. Few states have had the luxury of confronting the same choices twice, perhaps on even more favorable terms the second time.

The opportunities and risks are clear. The time for choice is at hand.

Ten Issues in Search of a Policy: America's Failed Approach to the Post-Soviet States

"At the beginning of perestroika, the Soviet Union's leading Americanist, Georgi Arbatov, predicted that Mikhail Gorbachev was going to do something far more threatening to the United States than any of his predecessors had done: he was going to take away its enemy. . . . The current policy difficulties in dealing with the post-Soviet states. . .testify to the fundamental wisdom of his observation."

PAUL A. GOBLE

PAUL A. GOBLE *is a senior associate at the Carnegie Endowment for International Peace in Washington, D.C. He previously served as special adviser on Soviet nationality problems at the State Department.*

Since the collapse of the Soviet Union, the United States has failed to articulate a coherent and comprehensive policy toward the 15 states that have taken its place. The reasons for this are both many and obvious, but the consequences are that opportunities have been missed to promote American interests, with the United States unwittingly generating new threats to its own security. Given the nature of the changes themselves, their implications for others, and the limitations both intellectually and politically of the United States, the emergence of an ideal policy anytime soon can hardly be expected. But because of the importance of this region, the United States needs to make a start.

Neither the Bush administration—which actively opposed the collapse of the Soviet Union and then took credit for its demise—nor the Clinton administration—which has been unwilling to focus on this most important of foreign policy issues—has been prepared for the multitude of challenges the end of the Soviet Union poses for the United States.

ONE COUNTRY OR FIFTEEN?

Perhaps more than any other nation, the United States was distressed to see the Soviet Union collapse. The Soviet Union had defined American foreign policy for a generation, had imposed a discipline on domestic arrangements in the United States, and in recent years had entered into a kind of partnership with it on key issues such as arms control. President George Bush spoke out against the union's demise most clearly in his August 1991 speech in Kiev; while many American officials disagreed with his words and their venue, they did accept the thrust of the argument.

As a result, the United States has tended to place more value on the institutions of the Commonwealth of Independent States than other countries have, and has dealt with the region as "Russia plus branch offices." No one can quibble with the notion that the United States has more business with Russia than with any other country. Nor can anyone object to Russia's continued centrality in the former Soviet Union. Yet it has led many to conclude that a single approach to the entire but much differentiated region will work. Unfortunately, the American tendency to continue to see this area as one region and the CIS as a significant entity has had consequences that the United States cannot possibly have wanted.

By supporting the CIS's military command structure, the United States undermined control of the Russian military and Russia's nuclear weapons. Also, by alienating many of the non-Russians, the United States has led them to be less amenable to American influence on key questions and has allowed nationalistic groups greater opportunity to attract support. The potentially dangerous flip side to Washington's treatment of ethnic issues has been the implicit aid and comfort given by the United States to the nearly one-third of the Russian population that would like to see the empire restored and the hard-line politicians in Moscow who would like to achieve that goal.

ACCEPTING A RUSSIAN MONROE DOCTRINE

Since February, Russian President Boris Yeltsin has demanded that the United States and the international community accept Russia's claim that it is the sole guarantor of stability and human rights in the 15 former Soviet republics and that it alone could use military force to guarantee that the rights of all groups were protected. In public at least, Washington has been silent, undoubtedly leading Yeltsin and others to conclude that the United States would acquiesce, especially since it had not responded to Serbian aggression in Bosnia and Herzegovina.

This failure to speak out forcefully also has given Yeltsin the signal that in his political struggles at home, the West will allow him to compromise with the very worst elements in his country rather than give him reason not to. It has led to a "go-it-alone" nationalist reaction in many other countries that will lead only to more conflicts. This indication that the West would accept a reconstituted empire based in Moscow has undermined Washington's credibility elsewhere in the world.

The sharp Russian reaction to press reports that the Clinton administration was considering the possibility of acting as a mediator between Russia and the other new countries underscores the difficulties and possible unintended consequences of any Western involvement. Moscow's harsh words on these reports also underscore just how committed virtually the entire Russian political class is to dominating Russia's neighbors, an attitude that will make American support for Russia more problematic.

"SUDDEN" MINORITIES AND POTENTIAL FIFTH COLUMNS

The demise of the Soviet Union did not "solve" that region's nationality problems: more than 25 million Russians were left in the 14 non-Russian countries; more than 18 million citizens of the other 14 countries were left outside their respective homes; and more than 17 million people were left without their own statehood. How these groups are treated matters profoundly, but to date, the United States has followed Moscow in being concerned only about ethnic Russians and only about their problems as Moscow has defined them.

Nearly 80 percent of the Russians living outside Russia live in just three places—Ukraine, Belarus, and Kazakhstan—where language and citizenship issues have been minimal. And the overwhelming majority of these are citizens of the countries where they reside: only 50,000 have chosen to become citizens of Russia and only some of the 1.6 million Russians in Estonia and Latvia are not yet citizens of some country. As in Central Asia, where many Russians have been forced to leave, the greatest human rights abuses are not perpetrated by the governments but rather by the population against the will of the government.

Russian complaints have been entirely disingenuous. They have focused exclusively on the rights of Russians and almost exclusively on regions—the Baltic states and Moldova (in the latter Moscow has dispatched the 14th

Army at the behest of the local Russian population)—where the problems can be solved if only Moscow is willing to negotiate. Instead, it has used force and the threat of force, making the situation more difficult for obvious reasons. The West's failure to speak out about this, to accept the depredations of the Russian military in Moldova and in Tajikistan and Azerbaijan and the threats to Estonia and Latvia only encourage extremists on both sides.

WILL RUSSIA GO THE WAY OF THE SOVIET UNION?

The American approach to these issues has been a mixture of denial ("it can't happen") and false analogy ("the demise of the Russian Federation would result from the same causes and have the same consequences as the end of the Soviet Union"). Both these perspectives are wrong. As Yeltsin said only four days after his April 25 referendum win, "it is no secret that the country is gripped by a feeling of anxiety about the integrity of the Russian state."

That Russia may collapse is a possibility. That it would collapse for the same reasons as did the Soviet Union or that its demise would have the same consequences for the West is not. The end of the Soviet Union was the end of an empire, and while Russia has some aspects of an empire, what is happening now is the death of a state. Moreover, the demise of the Russian state would not end the story: military assets would be loosed, regions would threaten each other and the other successor states, and the threat of nuclear war would increase dramatically.

The first thing Washington needs to recognize is that its denials and false analogies are leading policymakers to ask either no questions or the wrong ones, and that it can hardly be helped if good answers are not forthcoming. Unfortunately, at the present time, both despite and because of its focus on Moscow, the United States knows far less about the Russian Federation than it does about the other states.

THE FALSE PRIMACY OF ECONOMICS

Marxism may have died in the Soviet bloc, but a profound belief in economic determinism lurks behind much of America's approach to Russia and the other states of this region. There seems to be a notion that if we just get the economics right, everything else will follow. Implicit in this assumption is that Russia and the other countries are already democracies because they have had elections and are no longer "Communist." That is errant nonsense. Economic transformation is of course important, but it need not take place under or lead to democracy. There are too many examples where economic change has had just the opposite effect.

The United States needs to recognize that culture does matter and that democracy and free market capitalism are not necessarily normal conditions for most countries—even if they are the most desirable for the United States and others.

WHERE IS THE GREATEST DANGER OF PROLIFERATION?

Not surprisingly, the United States has been worried about the dangers of nuclear proliferation with the disintegration of the Soviet Union. Unfortunately, it has focused almost all of its attention on one issue—what will happen to nuclear weapons in the three non-Russian successor states—and neglected the more fundamental question of what will happen to nuclear weapons in the region as a whole. Russia watchers have badly mishandled the former, even as they have neglected the latter.

Nuclear weapons remain on the territory of Belarus, Ukraine, and Kazakhstan. Fortunately for everyone, these are three of the most anti-nuclear places on earth thanks to Soviet nuclear accidents and tests. The West's contribution was to make them think that going nuclear might be a good idea. Supporting the CIS and not insisting that these weapons belonged to only a single successor state (Russia) encouraged these regimes to think in nuclear terms. Also, viewing these countries as more important because they have nuclear weapons leads them to conclude that the West would neglect them even more if they did what it asked: namely, give the weapons back to Russia. Finally, by siding with Russia on all key issues and refusing to recognize that Ukraine and the others have legitimate security concerns, the United States has inadvertently convinced these governments that going nuclear is their only option.

A MARSHALL PLAN FOR RUSSIA?

One of the more amusing elements of American discussions about what to do for Russia and the other post-Soviet states concerns aid. Many believe that if the West gives enough, these countries will make a quick transition to democracy and free market capitalism; some have suggested that what is needed is a new Marshall Plan. This is the worst false analogy of all. The Marshall Plan was the perfect American foreign policy effort: it was short term, it was expensive, and it was directed at people who knew how to spend the money even better than the United States did because they had been both democratic and enjoyed free market economies only a few years earlier.

That is clearly not the situation in the post-Soviet states. With the exception of the Baltic countries, none of these countries has a tradition of either democracy or free market development, and none has the cultural supports of tolerance or the willingness to accept extreme income differentials. Moreover, they have just gone through the trauma of the Soviet system, and the transition out is extremely difficult. As one Polish wit put it, "Everyone can turn an aquarium into fish soup, but no one has yet figured out how to turn fish soup into an aquarium."

Clearly, United States policymakers need to think about long-term programs of technical assistance rather than "big bang," short-term efforts. Indeed, the latter are likely to be counterproductive because they will not be sustained and will thus breed resentment when what they hope to achieve does not materialize in two or three years. This is not to say that Washington should not provide massive humanitarian aid, but rather that it should not confuse it with political assistance. Moreover, to date, Western aid has gone overwhelmingly to Russia: the current United States foreign aid bill earmarked 76 percent of all assistance to Russia alone.

FUNDAMENTALISM

Nowhere is America's unwillingness to accept the former republics as countries greater than in the Muslim countries of the Caucasus and Central Asia. Having seen them slip out from under Russia's sphere of influence, many in the United States assume they must fall into the sphere of either Turkey or Iran, with a clear American preference for the former. Not only is this the height of arrogance, assuming that these are not real countries that naturally make their own choices, and not only does it ignore both geography and history, but it has led to a curious American policy whereby the United States has been unintentionally promoting the development of a fundamentalist Islamic movement in the region because of the misguided way in which it has chosen to promote secularism.

Curiously, the United States has already forgotten the way it set in place a similar course of action through its support of Iran's Shah Mohammed Reza Pahlavi. Failing to oppose his crackdown on all political opposition—a policy that left only the mosque as a channel for public opinion and that inevitably politicized Islam—produced what is now called Islamic fundamentalism. Having decided that a little temporary stability is more valuable than long-term development in Central Asia, Washington is now repeating the mistake. It is a shortsighted policy now just as it was in Iran. Moreover, by supporting some of the most retrograde and thuggish regimes in the region, the United States has discredited its own message of democratization and has reduced America's influence just when it could be most useful.

PEACE AT ANY PRICE

The most serious misreading of ethnic conflicts has been in the Caucasus, especially in the war between Armenia and Azerbaijan over Nagorno-Karabakh. United States policymakers have failed to understand what the war is about, what the parties want, and what the most important players in the region can and will do.

For its own reasons—the fear of another April Glaspie episode—the Bush administration chose to exclude Iran from talks about a settlement in Nagorno-Karabakh, even though in this area Iran was playing a very positive role. As a result, the war has expanded, the

Azerbaijani government has collapsed, and the regimes in both Baku and Tbilisi are increasingly authoritarian.

The desire to get an armistice rather than peace is noble but again shortsighted, for it guarantees that this region will explode again, leading either to the reimposition of Russian control—currently the most likely outcome now that Heydar Aliyev is back in power in Azerbaijan—or to the destruction at some point of the Armenian nation or at least the Armenian state.

THE STRENGTH OF WEAKNESS, THE WEAKNESS OF STRENGTH

Perhaps the most remarkable development in the region has been Yeltsin's discovery of a strategy that Mikhail Gorbachev exploited so successfully near the end of his stay in the Kremlin: namely, the incredible power of weakness. Yeltsin argues, and many in Washington accept, that the West must support him, no matter what he does, because he is so weak and any opposition would help topple him and bring to power hard-liners who do not favor his approach.

The argument is not without attraction, but it is extremely dangerous for several reasons. By conceding this point, the West allows—indeed, encourages—Yeltsin to oppose the West to demonstrate his independence and removes any incentive for good behavior. This acquiescence thus gives him the whip hand on all policies in the region. And this then may result in having "Yeltsin without Yeltsinism," just as there was Gorbachev without Gorbachevism at the end of perestroika. It is not clear that this *People* magazine approach to foreign policy is ever a good idea; it is certainly a dangerous one in a situation as unstable and uncertain as this one. And while international politics requires compromises, this kind of compromise, when the West is in a position of strength, is self-destructive.

FIVE GUIDING PRINCIPLES

This brief survey of issues the West has not handled well suggests five principles that should guide it in this region:

- First, the United States should always be clear about what its principles are. Although compromises may have to be made in particular cases, positions should be forcefully presented on all issues, such as human rights.
- Second, a policy of "tough love" must be adopted for all 15 countries alike, insisting especially on good behavior among them and not taking sides for the sake of convenience.
- Third, the importance of culture should be acknowledged, both the strength of cultural dispositions that will have to be changed if this region is going to make the desired transitions and the diversity that led to the region's disintegration in the first place.
- Fourth, a commitment should be made to help for the long term; this is the only way to integrate this area because short-term solutions will not work.
- Fifth, the United States must both admit its own limitations and recognize its responsibilities. American politicians have been lecturing Russians that they must cease to be a cause and become a country; so must Americans. And they must recognize that this new group of countries will require much on America's part, rather than assuming—as one pressure group in the United States says in its television advertising—that now that the cold war is over, everyone can relax. Instead, United States policymakers must recognize that the world we now live in is more dangerous and more demanding, but also more promising and more free than the one that we have mercifully escaped.

At the beginning of perestroika, the Soviet Union's leading Americanist, Georgi Arbatov, predicted that Mikhail Gorbachev was going to do something far more threatening to the United States than any of his predecessors had done: he was going to take away its enemy. It is virtually certain that Arbatov did not then know just how far Gorbachev would go in that direction, or just how disorienting the lack of a single enemy would be for the United States. The current policy difficulties in dealing with the post-Soviet states, however, testify to the fundamental wisdom of his observation.

Islam in the West's Sights: The Wrong Crusade?

David Ignatius

David Ignatius is foreign editor for the Washington Post.

The Cold War has barely ended, but already the search seems to be on for a new global, universal enemy—around which the United States can orient its foreign policy. Japan has been making an impressive bid. But topping the global-threat list in recent weeks has been our all-too-reliable nemesis: fundamentalist Islam.

Islam seems in many ways to fit the bill, enemy-wise: It's big; it's scary; it's anti-Western; it feeds on poverty and discontent; it spreads across vast swaths of the globe that can be colored green on the television maps in the same way that communist countries used to be colored red.

Already, strategists are invoking familiar Cold War concepts: "containment" of Iranian influence in Central Asia, which was the unspoken rationale for Secretary of State James A. Baker's trip there last month; the drawing of "red lines" for the Muslim fundamentalist leaders of Sudan by a U.S. emissary last November, warning them against any export of terrorism or revolution; an "iron fist" military coup in Algeria two months ago to prevent Muslims from winning elections there.

Even assassination seems to be a permissible weapon against the Islamic threat, as in Israel's killing of Hezbollah militia leader Abbas Musawi in Lebanon last month.

But before the United States and its allies embark on a new 40-year crusade to contain the global menace, it may be wise to reflect a moment. Does funda-mentalist Islam truly threaten the national security of the United States in the same way that Soviet communism did? Does a new cold war against Islam really make sense?

These questions don't have any easy or obvious answers. What follows are some tentative thoughts, drawn from conversations with senior British and French officials during a recent trip to Europe. The discussions focused on three key Arab countries—Algeria, Iraq and Saudi Arabia—which are moving haltingly toward modern political institutions but are also imperiled by Islamic fundamentalism. The question in each case is: What to do?

The underlying problem for the United States in each of these countries, and indeed across the Middle East, is that we are pulled in two directions at once. We favor democracy and want to extend to the Arabs the great democratic revolution that has swept the rest of the globe over the past decade. But we are also afraid of democracy in the Arab world, fearing that it will displace friendly despots and enfranchise our enemies, the fundamentalists. The outcome, in that case, might not be democracy, but theocracy.

Until the United States can resolve this contradiction—and decide whether it loves democracy more than it fears Islam—our response to political changes in the Arab world is likely to be incoherent.

The West also needs to be clearer about the basics: Islamic fundamentalism is not a disease that spreads willy-nilly to infect whole populations; it is (like Protestant fundamentalism) a religious response to the confusions and contradictions of the modern world. Fundamentalism in Sunni countries like Algeria won't necessarily have the same explosive character it assumed among Shiites in Iran and Lebanon. The Shiites themselves aren't all radical fundamentalists; in Iraq, some have been among the most passionate advocates of modernism and democracy. Fundamentalists aren't necessarily anti-democratic; some are serving as members of the Jordanian parliament. And finally, as much as fundamentalists seem to abhor the modern world, some also recognize that they must make an accommodation with it.

If the West really intends to confront radical Islam, it will need to learn considerably more about its enemy.

To appreciate the anxiety the French government is feeling these days about Algeria, it may help to recall the Carter administration's panic about Iran in late 1978, when U.S. analysts were first beginning to understand the depth of Islamic opposition to the shah. The essential questions are the same: Can the Islamic explosion be contained? Should the West encourage a military crackdown—or political reforms?

For now, the Algerian military has chosen the first option, and most Western governments seem to be praying that the crackdown will work. The army seized power on Jan. 11, just five days before elections in which the fundamentalist Islamic Salvation Front (FIS) was expected to win control of the assembly. The generals swept aside President Chadli Bendjedid, whose crime was that he had been prepared to share power with the fundamentalists. The army has banned the FIS and declared a state of emergency.

French officials stress that their dilemma in Algeria is, if anything, worse than what the Carter administration faced in Tehran. Algeria is poorer than Iran, and the modernizing elite there is smaller. Algeria's history with France is not simply a story of economic and political meddling, as was the case between America and Iran, but one of outright colonialism. And the distance between the angry Islamic masses and "Le Grand Satan" is not half a world, but just across the Mediterranean.

The best answer, when you don't have an answer, is to do nothing. And that has essentially been the French policy. The French have been trying to keep their heads down and stay in touch with all parties in Algeria.

French officials indicate that an ideal solution would be something like Egypt, which has maintained political stability in the face of a vast Islamic movement. But Egypt's success stems in part from its network of social control; its internal security service, the moukhabarat, is said to have an informer on every street corner in the country.

Algeria's problem, according to French analysts, is that its army is so isolated from its society these days that younger Algerians simply won't cooperate. The Egyptian approach of genial repression might make sense if it would work. But many French analysts seem skeptical that the military will succeed.

The most hopeful view I encountered came, paradoxically, from a French official who is convinced the Algerian army will fail and the fundamentalists will triumph. His optimism, if you can call it that, is drawn from a historical analogy.

It is possible, he said, that the fundamentalists will play the same purifying—and ultimately modernizing—role that the Protestant Reformation played in Europe. He cited Max Weber's famous argument, in "The Protestant Ethic and the Spirit of Capitalism," that the 17th-century Protestant fundamentalists paved the way for the development of modern political and economic institutions in Europe.

Perhaps, said the French official, the Muslim fundamentalists will play a similar role in sweeping away the corrupt old political culture of the Arab world and preparing the ground for something new. He noted that support for the fundamentalists in Algeria, as in Iran, has come in part from the bazaar, from the merchants and small businessmen who have been ignored by the statist regime.

"The Algerian people didn't vote for the FIS because they thought it would get them a place in heaven but because they thought it would develop the country," agrees Algerian political scientist Lahouari Addi, currently a visiting professor at Princeton. Addi argues that Algeria is at "the doorway of political modernity," but will pass through only after the Islamic utopia has been tried and has been seen to fail.

An interesting thought. Perhaps even true. But as Americans like to say, don't bet the farm on it.

The Iraqi opposition celebrated a sad anniversary in London a few days ago. It was one year after the Shiites of southern Iraq, encouraged by the allied victory in the Gulf War, rose up against Saddam—only to be crushed by Saddam's Republican Guards.

What happened a year ago is sad indeed, but it is not really a mystery. Iraqi exiles in London argue that it is part of the same broad dilemma the United States is facing across the Middle East. We are reluctant to tamper with the status quo—even in the case of a despotic regime like Saddam's—for fear that it will help the Muslim fundamentalists.

The rationale for America's status-quo policy was evident a year ago. The Bush administration allowed the Shiite uprising to be destroyed because it appeared to threaten the interests of our key ally in the Gulf, Saudi Arabia. The Saudis, as Sunni Moslems, favor continued rule by the Sunni minority in Baghdad. They have no use for a democratic Iraq, which would enfranchise the Shiite majority.

Washington has taken its lead from Riyadh. That is why the Bush administration has been so tongue-tied on Iraq, and why it never utters the word "democracy."

The result has been an awkward stalemate. Sanctions remain in place, but they seem to be hurting most the Iraqi civilian population. Meanwhile, Iraq is fragmenting. British officials say that Saddam's control is now limited to the Sunni heartland of central Iraq. The north is evolving into an autonomous Kurdish region; the south, at least at night, is said to be in the hands of Shiite irregulars. Emerging is the very thing the United States claims it fears most: a de facto partitioning of Iraq.

Even the Saudis are said to be getting uneasy with this status quo.

The question, now as a year ago, is whether the West can give Saddam's weakened, vulnerable regime the final push. U.S. and British officials want to impose even tighter sanctions, in the hope that the slow strangulation of the Iraqi military and economy will encourage one of Saddam's army colleagues to move against him. But is a military coup against Saddam—which would replace one Sunni dictator with another—really the best outcome we can hope for in Iraq?

A more aggressive strategy in Iraq would require the United States and Saudi Arabia to adjust their attitudes toward the Shiite groups they found so distasteful a year ago. "The Shiite groups on the whole are the most impressive," argues a British official. "They have the greatest interest in toppling the regime."

The danger, of course, is that a Shiite-led, post-Saddam government in Iraq—while starting life as a democracy—could quickly become an Islamic theocracy, ruled by the Koran and hostile to Western interests.

The Saudis, who have the most at stake, will be the key to any change in strategy. Explains a Western diplomat: "The Saudis are in a jam. They certainly want to see the back of Saddam. But they don't want it to be in a way that will lead to the splintering of Iraq and the creation of a Shiite entity."

But there seems to be a growing recognition in Riyadh that greater power for Iraqi Shiites wouldn't necessarily produce a mini-Iran. Many of the leading modernizers of Iraq have been Shiites; and the Iraqi Shiites didn't flock to Khomeini during the eight-year war with Iran. They remained loyal to the secular Iraqi state.

A sign that the Saudis may indeed be adjusting their policy came last month, when the leader of the Iranian-backed Shiite opposition group, Mohammed Bakr Hakim, was invited to Riyadh for talks. If the Saudis can overcome their fear of a Shiite-backed government in Baghdad, maybe Washington can too.

Let us turn finally to our fundamentalists, the Saudis. For they are in many ways the key to unraveling the policy knot described at the beginning.

For 50 years, the stability of Saudi Arabia (and its oil reserves) has been the cornerstone of U.S. policy in the Middle East. When the Saudis have sneezed, the State Department has gotten a cold.

Because the Saudis have wanted stable, Sunni-led rule in key countries of the Arab world, we have wanted stable, Sunni-led rule. Because the Saudis have been wary of Arab democracy, we have been wary. Because the Saudis have been a status-quo power, we have been a status-quo power. Because the Saudis have seemed comfortable with the political stalemate across the Arab world, we have been comfortable.

Thus the importance of King Fahd's announcement a week ago that he is embarking on a modest program of political reform. The changes will include a consultative assembly, more orderly procedures for political succession, some protection for individual rights, and the beginnings of a national constitution.

These changes hardly make Saudi Arabia a democracy. But they are not nothing. King Fahd has been talking about implementing these same reforms for a decade. The fact it took him so long suggests that the reforms matter.

What matters, too, is that the Saudi reforms were adopted despite growing concern about radical Islamic fundamentalism within the kingdom. In this sense, King Fahd has gone in a direction opposite to that of the Algerian military. He knows that the new reforms may provide a platform for fundamentalists who criticize the Saudi monarchy. But he is apparently willing to take the risk.

King Fahd makes an unlikely reformer. But if even a modest political change can take place in Saudi Arabia—traditionally the most frightened and reactionary power in the Middle East—then perhaps the political glacier that has frozen the region for a generation will begin to melt.

Latin America's International Relations in the Post-Cold War Era

G. Pope Atkins

INTRODUCTION

During the latter half of the 1980s, Latin America, along with the rest of the world, entered a new post-Cold War era. Some aspects of the new era's effects on the region's international relations were profound and obvious. East-West conflict, played out especially in Central America and the Caribbean, were no longer relevant. The United States abandoned its 180-year-old preoccupation in the Latin American region with minimizing what it saw as hostile foreign intrusions in the western hemisphere. Consequently, other issues rose to the top of everyone's agenda, including international trade and investment, external debt, democracy, human rights, immigration, refugees, drug trafficking, and the physical environment. Most Latin American states and the United States adopted a primarily (but not exclusively) economic foundation for inter-American relationships, concentrating on free trade agreements.

This article focuses on the current structure and conditions of Latin America's international relations. Such an exercise raises questions about the appropriate "levels of analysis" in contemporary world politics. Many specialists on Latin America are impatient with overall regional parameters and highlight the major countries and subregions. Others emphasize a larger regional level, the Inter-American System of all the states in the western hemisphere, and see inter-American cooperation as an important path to international problem-solving. Globalists say that the most important issues today are world-wide in scope and consequently analytic efforts should concentrate on that level, with a view to resolving current issues within global regimes. In my view, an accurate picture of the structure of Latin America's international relations requires that we acknowledge and link national, sub-regional, regional, hemispheric, and global levels of analysis. In addition, the compelling nature of the

issues and the high stakes involved for all cry out for action in all arenas. The following comments outline an overview of the structure of Latin America's international relations along these lines.

THE LATIN AMERICAN REGION

Some analysts argue that intra-Latin American differences and heterogeneity are so profound that generalizations are virtually impossible. While this level of interaction does have considerable limitations, the idea of Latin America as a unit in world affairs has in some respects actually increased in coherence in the post-Cold War world.

Latin America is defined in international relations as that portion of the western hemisphere south of the United States. It comprises an area roughly two-and-one-half times larger than the United States, is populated by over 420 million people, and is mostly occupied by thirty-three independent states exhibiting tremendous diversity in terms of culture, size, and other aspects. Spanish American states with widely varying stages of development and international capabilities comprise eighteen of them; huge Brazil is Portuguese in origin; tiny Haiti has maintained its West African culture to a remarkable degree. These twenty states, all but two of which (Cuba and Panama) gained their independence during the first third of the nineteenth century, together account for some 97 percent of Latin America's territory and population. An additional thirteen small countries may be classified as "new" states, gaining independence beginning in 1962. Twelve of them are former British colonies in the Caribbean area; the thirteenth is Suriname, a former colony of the Netherlands.

Despite the diversity, a Latin American regional subsystem has always exhibited to some degree an international life of its own. This has been revealed in Latin American self-perceptions. From the earliest days of statehood, Latin Americans have tended to band together when outsiders intervened or exerted other pressures. They have also formally organized among themselves, especially since World War II, to achieve common (usually developmental) purposes. A few examples, far from inclusive, illustrate the point. The eleven-member Latin American Free Trade Association, established in 1961 and reorganized in 1980 as the Latin American Integration Association, includes all of the large regional economies so that it represents an important transregional if not a total regional association. In 1975 the Latin American Economic System (SELA) was created and has near-universal regional membership. Latin American Groups have been created within or with reference to other international organizations, such as the United Nations, Third World associations, and the European Community, in order to caucus on a regional basis before confronting the outside world. Most recently, the Group of 15 has become preeminent as the leading Latin American organizational voice on the new agenda of issues; it represents at least 90 per cent of the region's population and GDP. Statements emanating from these and other Latin American inter-governmental organizations indicate a renewed impetus for regional cooperation.

Nevertheless, viewing Latin America only in terms of a single unit is insufficient. We also need to highlight those subregions where different conditions obtain.

MEXICO

Mexico stands apart for the combined reason that it is a large and important state and has intense special bilateral relations with the United States. It has become a cliche to say that here the First and Third Worlds directly confront each other as nowhere else in the world. The basic reality of the special and complicated Mexican–U.S. association, in sharp contrast to much of the historical relationship, is that a strong mutual dependency exists. While the United States is clearly the stronger partner, Mexico has considerable say. Much of the relationship is essentially bilateral and divorced from the broader Latin American arena. The issues have long been determined by territorial proximity and increasingly integrated economies and societies in terms of trade and investment, migration and tourism. With regard to the dominant inter-American issues during most of the 1980s—Central American conflict, Cuba, external debt, and the narcotics traffic—Mexico differed with and opposed the United States on all of them.

During the latter half of the 1980s, Mexico abandoned its historic protectionist investment and trade policies and pressed for a free trade agreement with the United States, by far its major trading partner; Mexico is the United States' third largest. The United States responded in 1990 and free trade negotiations

began; Canada joined the process, resulting in trilateral talks seeking a North American Free Trade Area (NAFTA). An agreement was signed by the three parties in December 1991 and each commenced its ratification procedures. Thus Mexico fundamentally reoriented its highly protectionist foreign economic policies that had grown out of the nationalist principles of the Mexican Revolution of 1910, and the creation of a NAFTA became the centerpiece of Mexican foreign policy.

THE CIRCUM-CARIBBEAN

The Circum-Caribbean is a complex geographic and political region that includes the islands of the Caribbean Sea and those nearby in the Atlantic Ocean, the Central American isthmus, and the north coast of South America extending to the Atlantic Ocean outside the Caribbean Sea, so that Venezuela, Colombia, and Suriname are included. It has its own further subregions, most notably Central America and the Commonwealth Caribbean Countries. During the twentieth century, the United States has pursued a hegemonic presence in the Circum-Caribbean, intervening militarily as late as in Grenada in 1983 and Panama 1989–1990. The Panama Canal has historically loomed large in U.S. calculations; it is still of concern, although the canal's strategic and commercial importance has sharply declined. After World War II the United States had a primary concern with deterring what it saw as the spread of communism and Soviet expansionism. A principal challenge arose when Cuba became the Soviet Union's first high-priority Latin American interest with their alignment after 1959; later, with the Nicaraguan Revolution of 1979, the Soviets supported the Sandinistas in Nicaragua and by extension the Farabundo Marti National Liberation Front (FMLN) insurgency in El Salvador.

Regional changes attendant to the post-Cold War era were especially dramatic in the Circum-Caribbean. Trends were apparent in the 1980s. One of the most striking was the assertiveness of local Latin American states challenging the United States with proposals for the negotiated settlement of Central American conflict. In 1983, Mexico, Venezuela, Colombia, and Panama organized the Contadora Group to offer a multilateral negotiating formula challenging U.S. unilateral and bilateral policies focusing on coercive measures; they were joined by the Contadora Support Group formed by the geographically-removed states of Argentina, Brazil, Peru, and Uruguay. This was followed in 1987 by the multilateral peace plan (the Esquipulus II accords) agreed to by all five Central American states on the initiative of President Oscar Arias of Costa Rica.

The Soviet role changed dramatically. While it is a matter of debate whether the Reagan administration in the 1980s exaggerated the Soviet threat (in my view it greatly did so), in the post-Cold War era the Soviet Union became a part of the Central American peace process. It ceased weapons transfers to Cuba and Nicaragua and pressured them to end arms deliveries to insurgents in El Salvador. The February 1990 elections in Nicaragua that ejected the Sandinista government also ended the by-then reluctant Soviet role. In the meantime, the Soviets joined the United States in the UN Security Council to create a peacekeeping force that was sent to Central America. With the decline of Soviet power and then the breakup of the Soviet Union itself, commitments to Cuba were reduced and then virtually canceled. Cuba itself became isolated, increasingly internationally inactive, and absorbed with its own severe economic and social problems.

Post-Cold War U.S. policies in the Circum-Caribbean are mixed. The military intervention in Panama indicated that the United States was still willing to use military compulsion in the area even in the post-Cold War era, although the Bush administration said it was a unique case; the evidence, in my view, suggests that it was. The United States subsequently entered into long-term negotiations for free trade agreements with the Central American countries, the members of the Caribbean Community (CARICOM) of former British dependencies (all but one now independent states), and some other Caribbean states. Mexico initiated negotiations with Central America with the view of establishing a free trade area between the five Central American countries and Mexico, implying the potential of their being a part of NAFTA.

THE SOUTHERN CONE OF SOUTH AMERICA

The third important subregion comprises most of South America beyond the Caribbean, the countries in what is often called the Southern Cone. The key states are Argentina, Brazil, and Chile, and the others are Uruguay, Paraguay, Bolivia, and Peru, with Ecuador sometimes drawn in. Brazil could, like Mexico, be singled out as forming its own subsystem; it stands apart from the rest of Latin America because of its Portuguese cultural heritage, large size, and potential to be a much more influential state in global politics.

The subregion has a number of special characteristics that make it dramatically different from the northern half of Latin America. South America beyond the Caribbean has not been a sphere of influence of the United States or anyone else; no outside great power has had the function of international policeman enforcing the peace. In addition, the South American states have a broad array of external relationships. It is a multilateralized trading area, with long-standing cultural and economic ties with Europe, and Japan an important economic actor. Brazil in particular devel-

oped a multilateral network of international trade and strong ties with its immediate neighbors, in Europe, the Middle East and Africa, and Japan, in addition to those with the United States. The United States has begun negotiations with the subregional states for free trade agreements, but South Americans have indicated a continuing interest in multilateralized international economic and other relationships.

Positive international trends are evident in South America, with which the United States had little to do. All of the governments moved away from military regimes to constitutional democracies—although democracy is under stress, as indicated in 1992 in Peru by the assumption of dictatorial powers by the elected president of Peru, and in Venezuela by two attempted coups d'etat by disaffected elements of the armed forces. The subregion's traditional international rivalries have been muted. A Brazilian rapprochement began in 1979 and was extended thereafter, to include extensive bilateral economic and other kinds of policy integration. Those two states joined with Uruguay and Paraguay to form the Southern Cone Common Market (MERCOSUR). Argentina and Chile definitively settled their contentious Beagle Channel dispute in 1983. In February 1990 Argentina and the United Kingdom reestablished relations, broken during their 1982 war over the Falkland/Malvinas islands; they now pursue their differences through diplomacy.

INTER-AMERICAN SYSTEM

The western hemispheric Inter-American System (IAS), founded in 1889, is today largely comprised of the separate but coordinated Organization of American States (OAS), Inter-American Treaty of Reciprocal Assistance (Rio Treaty) regime, and Inter-American Development Bank (IDB). The OAS is the predominant entity and in 1991 achieved universal membership of all thirty-five of the sovereign states of the Americas. (Cuba is a member since inter-American sanctions imposed in 1962 deny participation, not membership, to the Castro government.) IAS activities have developed over the past century to encompass cooperation along a broad economic front, peaceful settlement of disputes, promotion of nonintervention and sovereign equality, pursuit of mutual security, and encouragement of representative democracy and human rights. The IAS in the post-Cold War era has been revived as an appropriate organizational setting within which to encounter inter-American problems, overcoming much of the decline it experienced after the mid-1960s. Latin Americans were dissatisfied with U.S. efforts to transform the IAS into an anti-communist alliance, while the United States, emphasizing mutual security, was less than enthusiastic about Latin American preoccupation with economic matters. The IAS became virtually impotent in the field of mutual security; it did continue economic development activities but was not an important arena for addressing the external debt difficulties.

The possibilities for sustaining an increased role for the IAS are enhanced by the diminished propensity of the United States to dictate unilaterally combined with the emergence of Latin American positive nationalism. The matter of a hemispheric free trade agreement, if realized, would ultimately involve the need for some sort of inter-American organizational form. (President Bush's proposal in a speech on June 27, 1990 called for a Western Hemispheric Free Trade Area; as indicated above, it is being pursued on several fronts, albeit in fragmented form for the present.) Such an association would draw all Latin American states, including Brazil and those in the Southern Cone, closer to the U.S. economy. Some of the Latin American economies, however, are large—Brazil's is among the world's top ten in size, and those of Mexico and Argentina are significant; the economies of Chile and Venezuela are notable. Furthermore, in light of the Latin American desire to maintain and expand global relations, even with a hemispheric free trade agreement the region would not be an exclusive U.S. preserve.

THE GLOBAL SYSTEM

Latin American governments and regional intergovernmental organizations indicate keen interest in their involvement in the global international system. They are sorting out what the post-Cold War world will be and what roles they will play in it, with reference to the United Nations and to other actors in the outside world. Latin Americans had been instrumental in shaping the United Nations system from the beginning and took leadership roles in the New International Economic Order (NIEO), a formal Third World association pursued especially in the serial United Nations Conference on Trade and Development (UNCTAD) and in the General Assembly. Beginning in 1961, many of them also joined the Non-Aligned Movement. Latin American military regimes reduced their active interest in extra-regional affairs during the 1970s and into the 1980s, but the democratic governments since then have sought to reintegrate. The end of the Cold War challenged the identity of both the Non-Aligned Movement and the NIEO, since alignment became a non-issue in the former instance and the demise of the Soviet Union reduced the leverage of the latter; the Latin American interest in both movements has consequently declined. Nevertheless, as a general matter, Latin Americans seek to maintain and expand their relations with the European Community (although considerable tensions characterize the inter-regional relationships) and other international associations, Japan and other states, and transnational political parties and non-governmental organizations as part of their thrust to be active and important participants in whatever new global system finally emerges.

Global Village or
Global Pillage?

JEREMY BRECHER

Jeremy Brecher is a historian and co-editor of Global Visions: Beyond the New World Order *(South End).*

For most of the world's people, the "New World Economy" is a disaster that has already happened. Those it hurts can't escape it. But neither can they afford to accept it. So many are now seeking ways to reshape it.

When I first started writing about the destructive effects of globalization three years ago, The North American Free Trade Agreement was widely regarded as a done deal. The near defeat of NAFTA reveals pervasive popular doubt about the wisdom of an unregulated international market. The struggle against NAFTA represented the first major effort by Americans who have been hurt by global economic integration to do something about it. Like many mass movements, it included contradictory forces, such as the Mexico-bashing bigotry of Pat Buchanan, the populist grandstanding of Ross Perot and the nationalistic protectionism of some in the labor movement.

But other elements of the struggle against NAFTA prefigure a movement that could radically reshape the New World Economy. Out of their own experiences and observations, millions of Americans have constructed a new paradigm for understanding the global economy. Poor and working people in large numbers have recognized that NAFTA is not primarily about trade; it is about the ability of capital to move without regard to national borders. Capital mobility, not trade, is bringing about the "giant sucking sound" of jobs going south.

For the first time in many years, substantial numbers of people mobilized to act on broad class interests. I haven't seen a movement for years in which so many people at the grass roots took their own initiative. Typical was the unexpectedly large, predominantly blue-collar anti-NAFTA rally in New Haven, where a labor leader told me, "We didn't turn these people out."

The New Global Pillage

NAFTA became a symbol for an accumulation of fears and angers regarding the place of working people in the New World Economy. The North American economic integration that NAFTA was intended to facilitate is only one aspect of the rapid and momentous historical transformation from a system of national economies toward an integrated global economy. New information, communication, transportation and manufacturing technologies, combined with tariff reductions, have made it possible to coordinate production, commerce and finance on a world scale. Since 1983, the rate of

National governments have lost much of their power to direct their own economies.

world foreign direct investment has grown four times as fast as world output.

This transformation has had devastating consequences. They may be summarized as the "seven danger signals" of cancerous, out-of-control globalization:

Race to the bottom. The recent quantum leap in the ability of transnational corporations to relocate their facilities around the world in effect makes all workers, communities and countries competitors for these corporations' favor. The consequence is a "race to the bottom" in which wages and social and environmental conditions tend to fall to the level of the most desperate. This dynamic underlies U.S. deindustrialization, declining real wages, eradication of job security, and

From *The Nation*, December 6, 1993, pp. 685-688. © 1993 by The Nation Company, Inc. Reprinted by permission.

downward pressure on social spending and investment; it is also largely responsible for the migration of low-wage, environmentally destructive industries to poor countries like Mexico and China.

Global stagnation. As each work force, community or country seeks to become more competitive by reducing its wages and its social and environmental overheads, the result is a general downward spiral in incomes and social and material infrastructures. Lower wages and reduced public spending mean less buying power, leading to stagnation, recession and unemployment. This dynamic is aggravated by the accumulation of debt; national economies in poor countries and even in the United States become geared to debt repayment at the expense of consumption, investment and development. The downward fall is reflected in the slowing of global GNP growth from almost 5 percent per year in the period 1948-1973 to only half that in the period 1974-89 and to a mere crawl since then.

Polarization of haves and have-nots. As a result of globalization, the gap between rich and poor is increasing both within and between countries around the world. Poor U.S. communities boast world-class unemployment and infant mortality. Meanwhile, tens of billions of dollars a year flow from poor to rich regions of the world, in the form of debt repayment and capital flight.

Loss of democratic control. National governments have lost much of their power to direct their own economies. The ability of countries to apply socialist or even Keynesian techniques in pursuit of development, full employment or other national economic goals has been undermined by the power of capital to pick up and leave. Governmental economic power has been further weakened throughout the world by neoliberal political movements that have dismantled government institutions for regulating national economies. Globalization has reduced the power of individuals and communities to shape their destinies.

Walter Wriston, former chairman of Citicorp, recently boasted of how "200,000 monitors in trading rooms all over the world" now conduct "a kind of global plebiscite on the monetary and fiscal policies of the governments issuing currency. . . . There is no way for a nation to opt out." Wriston recalls the election of "ardent socialist" François Mitterrand as French President in 1981. "The market took one look at his policies and within six months the capital flight forced him to reverse course."

Unfettered transnational corporations. Transnationals have become the world's most powerful economic actors, yet there are no international equivalents to national antitrust, consumer protection and other laws that provide a degree of corporate accountability.

Unaccountable global institutions. The loss of national economic control has been accompanied by a growing concentration of unaccountable power in international institutions like the International Monetary Fund, the World Bank and the General Agreement on Tariffs and Trade (GATT). For poor countries, foreign control has been formalized in the World Bank's "structural adjustment plans," but I.M.F. decisions and GATT rules affect the economic growth rates of all countries. The decisions of these institutions also have an enormous impact on the global ecology.

Those harmed by the New World Economy need not be passive victims.

Global conflict. Economic globalization is producing chaotic and destructive rivalries. In a swirl of self-contradictory strategies, major powers and transnationals use global institutions like GATT to impose open markets on their rivals; they pursue trade wars against one another; and they try to construct competing regional blocs like the European Community and NAFTA. In past eras, such rivalries have ultimately led to world war.

In sum, the result of unregulated globalization has been the pillage of the planet and its peoples.

Transnational Economic Programs

What are the alternatives to destructive globalization? The right offers racism and nationalism. Conventional protectionism offers no solution. Globalization has also intellectually disarmed the left and rendered national left programs counterproductive. Jimmy Carter's sharp turn to the right in 1978; François Mitterrand's rapid abandonment of his radical program; the acceptance of deregulation, privatization and trade liberalization by poor countries from India to Mexico; and even the decision of Eastern European elites to abandon Communism—all reflect in part the failure of national left policies.

But the beginnings of a new approach emerged from the anti-NAFTA movement itself. Rather than advocate protectionism—keeping foreign products out—many NAFTA opponents urged policies that would raise environmental, labor and social standards in Mexico, so that those standards would not drag down those in the United States and Canada. This approach implied that people in different countries have common interests in raising the conditions of those at the bottom.

Indeed, the struggle against NAFTA generated new transnational networks based on such common interests. A North American Worker-to-Worker Network links grass-roots labor activists in Mexico, the United States and Canada via conferences, tours, solidarity support and a newsletter. Mujer a Mujer similarly links women's groups. The Highlander Center, Southerners for Economic Justice, the Tennessee Industrial Renewal Network and a number of unions have organized meetings and tours to bring together Mexican and U.S. workers. There are similar networks in other parts of the world, such as People's Plan 21 in the Asian-Pacific and Central American regions and the Third World Network in Malaysia.

These new networks are developing transnational programs to counter the effects of global economic restructuring. Representatives from environmental, labor, religious, consumer and farm groups from Mexico, the United States and Canada have drawn up "A Just and Sustainable Trade and Development Initiative for North America." A parallel synthesis, "From Global Pillage to Global Village," has been endorsed by more than sixty grass-roots organizations. Related proposals by the Third World Network have recently been published as "Towards a New North-South Economic Dialogue."

Differing in emphasis and details, these emerging alternative programs are important not only because of the solutions they propose but also because those solutions have emerged from a dialogue rooted in such a diversity of groups and experiences. Some require implementation by national policy; some by international agreement; some can be implemented by transnational citizen action. Taken together, they provide what might be described as "seven prescriptions" for the seven danger signals of the unregulated global economy:

International rights and standards. To prevent competition from resulting in a race to the bottom, several of these groups want to establish minimum human, labor and environmental rights and standards, as the European Community's "social charter" was designed to do. The International Metalworkers Federation recently proposed a ten-point "World Social Charter," which could be incorporated into GATT.

"A Just and Sustainable Trade and Development Initiative for North America" spells out in some detail an alternative to NAFTA that would protect human and worker rights, encourage workers' incomes to rise in step with productivity and establish continental environmental rights, such as the right to a toxics-free workplace and community. Enforcement agencies would be accessible to citizens and could levy fines against parties guilty of violations. The initiative especially emphasizes the rights of immigrants. Activists from nongovernmental organizations in all three countries have proposed a citizens' commission to monitor the human, labor and environmental effects of trade and investment.

Upward spiral. In the past, government monetary and fiscal policy, combined with minimum wages, welfare state programs, collective bargaining and other means of raising the purchasing power of have-nots, did much to counter recession and stagnation within national economies. Similar measures are now required at international levels to counter the tendency toward a downward spiral of inadequate demand in the global economy. The Third World Network calls on the I.M.F. and World Bank to replace their ruinous structural adjustment plans with policies that "meet the broad goals of development . . . rather than the narrower goal of satisfying the needs of the creditors." It also demands a reduction of developing country debt. "A Just and Sustainable Trade and Development Initiative" proposes that the remaining debt service be paid in local currency into a democratically administered development fund. Reversing the downward spiral also ultimately requires a "global Keynesianism" in which international institutions support, rather than discourage, national full-employment policies.

An upward spiral also requires rising income for those at the bottom—something that can be encouraged by international labor solidarity. Experiments in cross-border organizing

by U.S. unions like the Amalgamated Clothing and Textile Workers and the United Electrical Workers, in cooperation with independent unions in Mexico, aim to defeat transnationals' whipsawing by improving the wages and conditions of Mexican workers.

Redistribution from haves to have-nots. "A Just and Sustainable Trade and Development Initiative" calls for "compensatory financing" to correct growing gaps between rich and poor. A model would be the European Community funds that promote development in its poorer members. The Third World Network calls for commodity agreements to correct the inequities in the South's terms of trade. It also stresses the need to continue preferential treatment for the South in GATT and in intellectual property protection rules.

Strengthened democracy. NAFTA, GATT and similar agreements should not be used—as they now can be—to preempt the right of localities, states, provinces and countries to establish effective labor, health, safety and environmental standards that are higher than the guaranteed minimum in international agreements. Above all, democratization requires a new opportunity for people at the bottom to participate in shaping their destiny.

Codes of conduct for transnational corporations. Several transnational grass-roots groups call for codes of conduct that would, for example, require corporations to report investment intentions; disclose the hazardous materials they import; ban employment of children; forbid discharge of pollutants; require advance notification and severance pay when operations are terminated; and prohibit company interference with union organizing. United Nations discussions of such a code, long stymied by U.S. hostility, should be revived.

While the ultimate goal is to have such codes implemented by agreements among governments, global public pressure and cross-border organizing can begin to enforce them. The Coalition for Justice in the Maquiladoras, for example, a group of religious, environmental, labor, Latino and women's organizations in Mexico and the United States, has issued a code of conduct for U.S. corporations in Mexico and has used "corporate campaign" techniques to pressure them to abide by its labor and environmental provisions.

Reform of international institutions. Citizens should call on the U.N. to convene a second Earth Summit focusing on democratizing the I.M.F. and the World Bank, and consider formation of new institutions to promote equitable, sustainable and participatory development. International citizen campaigns, perhaps modeled on the Nestlé boycott and the campaign against World Bank–funded destruction of the Amazon, could spotlight these institutions.

Multiple-level regulation. In place of rivalry among countries and regions, such programs imply a system of democratically controlled public institutions at every level, from global to local.

After NAFTA: Globalization From Below

These proposals provide no short-term panacea; they are objectives to organize around. The New World Economy is not going to vanish from the political agenda. Neither will the passions and political forces aroused by the NAFTA debate. Many of the same issues will resurface in connection with the Asia-Pacific Economic Cooperation Forum and with GATT. As the fiftieth anniversaries of the I.M.F. and World Bank approach, calls for their reform are being sounded all over the world.

The struggle against NAFTA has shown that those harmed by the New World Economy need not be passive victims. So many politicians were so unprepared for the strength of the anti-NAFTA movement because it represented an eruption into the political arena of people who have long been demobilized. But to influence their economic destinies effectively, they need a movement that provides an alternative to the Ross Perots and Pat Buchanans. Such a movement must act on the understanding that the unregulated globalization of capital is really a worldwide attack of the haves on the have-nots. And it must bring that understanding to bear on every affected issue, from local layoffs to the world environment. "From Global Pillage to Global Village" suggests a vision to guide such a movement:

> The internationalization of capital, production and labor is now being followed by the internationalization of peoples' movements and organizations. Building peoples' international organizations and solidarity will be our revolution from within: a civil society without borders. This internationalism or "globalization from below" will be the foundation for turning the global pillage into a participatory and sustainable global village.

The organizations that have led the fight against NAFTA have a responsibility not to retreat to parochial concerns. They must regroup and begin addressing the broader impact of economic globalization on people and planet.

The Former Soviet Union

To outsiders the former Soviet Union appears to be a cauldron of contrasts—a complex region composed of 15 independent nation-states trying to define separate national interests. But ex-Soviet citizens share a sense of disorientation and "pocketbook" shock as they cope with a declining standard of living and the emergence of clusters of nouveau riche capitalists. Everywhere, former communist leaders, the military, and vocal nationalists prove adept at adjusting to Western-style capitalism. Nationalism fills the spiritual vacuum left by the end of communist ideology.

On December 25, 1991, President Mikhail Gorbachev resigned. This marked the end of the 75-year-old Union of Soviet Socialist Republics (USSR). Upon his leaving office, the Soviet Union went out of existence, the Communist Party was discredited, and the economy fell into shambles. Although the beginnings of this collapse started with Stalin's death and reactions to his reign of terror, Gorbachev played a key role in the demise of the Soviet empire. The reforms he instituted in the mid-1980s fostered the growth of aspects of democratic movements.

As chaos increased and the Baltic republics declared their independence, leaders of Russia, Ukraine, and Belarus (formerly Byelorussia) moved to establish a new Commonwealth of Independent States (CIS), which included 12 of the former 15 republics. Each state of the new commonwealth retained the right to exert national sovereignty while negotiating ways to cooperate and coordinate in specific areas with other members of the CIS. Although the CIS framework was more myth than reality, its formation was a recognition of the extensive interdependence that continued to bind these states. As Susan Clark notes in "Security Issues and the Eastern Slavic States," virtually all security issues have to be understood in the context of their interconnections. The most vital national security questions are not resolved: a search continues for ways to establish political, economic, and military relations, to train personnel, and to deal with arms sales.

In January 1994, the reform-minded leader of Belarus, Stanislav Shushkevich, was ousted by a Communist-dominated parliament supporting closer economic and security ties with Russia. A "creeping communist coup" completed a gradual shift in Belarus from an independent state to a protectorate of Russia. Russian control was cemented with the signing of a security treaty placing Belarus under Russia's military umbrella and forging a bilateral accord for a monetary union virtually surrendering Belarus's right to make its own monetary decisions in exchange for financial and other aid from Moscow.

The Ukraine, in contrast, attempted to move closer to the West's economic and strategic orbit as tensions with Russia increased. In 1994, Ukraine signed an agreement for a phased elimination of nuclear weapons in exchange for Western aid, bilateral U.S. security guarantees, and membership in NATO's Partnership for Peace program, which afforded a right to consult with NATO but no promise of military aid.

These recent agreements reflect the high priority the West places on international controls over the nuclear weapons arsenal of the former Soviet Union. In 1992, Kazakhstan and Belarus agreed to eliminate nuclear weapons on their territory, but a similar agreement between Russia and Ukraine required extensive outside intervention due to Ukraine's rising distrust of Russia's policy goals and the growing economic value in a collapsing economy of enriched uranium extracted from nuclear warheads.

Ukraine's agreement to denuclearize and its promise to sign the Nuclear Non-Proliferation Treaty (NPT), came only after a series of protracted three-way talks among Ukraine, Russia, and the United States. In the official agreement, signed in early 1994, Russia agreed to observe the "sovereignty" of Ukraine and to forgive large debts for past Russian energy imports; the United States promised nuclear fuel, economic and technical aid, and bilateral security guarantees. Economic interdependence between Russia and Ukraine guaranteed the two states would remain closely linked in an increasingly tense relationship. In fact, Ukrainian leaders warned that if Russia disrupted future fuel shipments to the Ukraine, the agreement would not be implemented.

Rising nationalism and increased ethnic tensions fuel demands for self-determination. Many observers believe that the struggle is unstoppable, no matter what state governments or international organizations do. Even in Russia itself, the prospect of fragmentation into smaller political units increases. Bogdan Szajkowski, in "Will Russia Disintegrate into Bantustans?" outlines the stages of disintegration and predicts further breakups as the Russian federation devolves into smaller entities.

Recent events in Russia are consistent with such pessimistic predictions. Russia has experienced increased domestic instability, rising crime, and the intensification of the political struggle between Yeltsin's supporters of free-market economic and political reforms and their opponents. The struggle for political control culminated in early October 1993 in an effort in Parliament to topple the Yeltsin government. Yeltsin crushed the uprising with the support of loyal military troops, who quickly retook control of the Russian Parliament building in a bloody battle. A temporary halt to the crisis was achieved after Yeltsin promised to support a new constitutional order and to hold parliamentary elections before the end of 1993.

The economic slide and the strong showing of communists and extreme nationalists in the parliamentary elections forced Boris Yeltsin to moderate the pace of reforms and to make adjustments in Russia's generally pro-Western foreign policy during 1994. After President Clinton departed Moscow in February 1994, the market reformers resigned from Yeltsin's cabinet. His new cabinet supported a slowdown in the pace of economic reforms and renewal of subsidies to large Soviet-style factories and farms, despite warnings that this would worsen Russia's high inflation rate.

The December 1993 parliamentary elections further affected the balance of power, as Yeltsin was forced by the new constitution to share formal executive powers with Parliament. Over Yeltsin's objections, the lower house, the Duma, quickly exercised its new power by granting amnesty to the leaders of the October 1993 upheaval.

In the area of foreign policy, representatives in the Duma moved to renounce Yeltsin's generally pro-Western foreign policies. Vladimir Zhirinovsky's extremist nationalist party, which placed first in these elections, had campaigned on a platform that included calls for the restoration of the borders of the former Soviet empire, the use of Russian troops to protect the 25 million ethnic Russians living outside Russia, and promises to protect Serbian brothers against foreign troops in former Yugoslavia.

In response to the strong showing of Zhirinovsky and widespread perceptions of him as a potential competitor in the 1996 presidential elections, the new Yeltsin government adopted a more nationalist tone, less conciliatory in its dealings with Western countries and more conciliatory towards opponents in Parliament, to search for a more lasting civil peace in Russia.

Yeltsin's political compromises reflected an erosion of support for his economic and political reforms. Economic "shock policies," aimed to shift Russia to a market economic system in the shortest possible time, failed. Throughout the land, economic reforms had painful consequences for workers and military conscripts. A horde of unemployed workers struggled to meet the higher prices demanded for the basic necessities of food and shelter. The conspicuous consumption and growing gap in the living standards between the emerging entrepreneurial class and the majority increased the pain for those trying to cope with a deteriorating economy. No one really knows how long millions of people would bear the high cost of transition if economic conditions worsen.

The situation is not encouraging: Only four republics, large Russia and Ukraine, and small Estonia and Lithuania, are heavily industrialized. Given the degree of interdependence among the ex-Soviet republics, it is difficult to foresee how they will recover from economic depression without extensive cooperation and forms of integration. Many of the democratic transformations are failing as communists and nationalists consolidate political power at the expense of democratic reformers. A situation may emerge in which inventing the "union of sovereign states" creates a cycle of lawlessness, anarchy, and arbitrary rule.

The West searches for ways to promote peaceful transitions in the region. A $24 billion package of economic aid promised by the United States and Germany took the form of debt deferrals, commercial export credits, and short-term loan guarantees; funds actually reaching citizens were minuscule. Critics of this kind of Western aid call for more aid, relaxed loan terms, and redirecting aid away from central government to regional "grass-roots" groups. As anti-American sentiment grows, former communists and nationalists exploit it by claiming that their societies have gone downhill since Western experts began advising governments. In America, critics call for a debate to discuss "who lost Russia?"

Looking Ahead: Challenge Questions

In a post-war era, should the republics of the former Soviet Union continue to occupy a central place in the foreign policy concerns of the United States and its NATO allies?

Should NATO members be willing to extend more specific security guarantees than those outlined in the Partnership for Peace Proposal to ex-Soviet republics? If so, which ones?

Should the United States provide more economic aid to Russia or other ex-Soviet states?

Does the United States need to be concerned about Russian reactions to future actions by NATO in Bosnia? Central Europe? Ukraine?

What do Europeans fear will happen if there is economic decline and growing unrest in the republics of the former Soviet Union?

THE REAL COUP

Melor Sturua

Melor Sturua, a columnist and former editor for the Soviet daily Izvestia, *is a visiting professor of political science at the University of Minnesota's Hubert H. Humphrey Institute of Public Affairs.*

The failed August 1991 coup in Moscow is being portrayed widely as an event that, virtually by itself, has brought on the collapse of the Soviet system. Indeed, in spite of then foreign minister Eduard Shevardnadze's famous warning in December 1990 that a dictatorship was approaching, the world was taken by surprise when it nearly happened. The announcement of *perestroika* six years ago was similarly unforeseen, even though the stagnation of the Brezhnev years dictated that any Soviet leader would have to implement major changes just to survive.

All along, Soviet-watchers in the West have tended to focus on dramatic moments like the coup attempt or the announcement of *perestroika*, neglecting the slower, subterranean transformations that make such events possible. The putsch and its aftermath have finally and fully revealed the crushing defeat of communism and the bankruptcy of Marxist-Leninist ideology, but the coup alone did not bring on the Soviet empire's dissolution: Rather, it was another dramatic sign of the gradual erosion of the Soviet regime's power, which began with Joseph Stalin's death in March 1953.

To date the beginning of the Soviet empire's collapse with Stalin's death seems paradoxical, because in the decades that followed Soviet power still appeared formidable. In the post-Stalin period, the communist empire outside the Soviet frontier expanded further; Soviet or Warsaw Pact forces invaded Hungary in 1956, Czechoslovakia in 1968, and Afghanistan in 1979; and Stalin's successors continued the persecution of dissidents inside the Soviet Union. But even as these events were taking place, the regime's power was eroding. Without Stalin, Stalinism was doomed, but it would only decline with time. Much as we see a star that no longer exists because its light must travel so far to reach Earth, we could see the effects of Stalin's rule long after his death.

Stalin's most important legacy to his successors was not the hydrogen bomb, the innumerable Soviet armed forces, or the all-powerful Communist party. Rather, it was the fear he instilled in the Soviet people through his indescribable reign of terror. His successors used this fear to govern the empire. But ultimately they could not increase or even preserve this fear, and it gradually dissipated, giving way to hatred and disrespect among the Soviet people. Their mocking anecdotes about ossified general secretaries were a sign of a serious lack of legitimacy. When Gorbachev came to power after the Soviet Union's shameful relay of aging leaders—Leonid Brezhnev, Yuri Andropov, Konstantin Chernenko—there was relatively little fear left among the people, and little wealth left in the regime's coffers. Gorbachev had to commence changes—*perestroika*—to survive.

In addition to overcoming fear, the Soviet people had to destroy a second legacy of Stalinism: the slave philosophy that has dominated Soviet thinking. The great Russian writer Anton Chekhov used to say that all his life he had tried to squeeze the slave out of himself, drop by drop. Likewise, the Soviet people needed to begin the slow and painstaking transformation into a free-thinking society, willing to challenge its leaders and its own previous assumptions. During the coup, Russian president Boris Yeltsin defied the coup plotters by standing courageously atop a tank. But this single act of heroism would have been impossible without the individual heroism of thousands of Soviet citizens. The pro-democracy Soviets who successfully defended the Russian "White House" during three unforgettable days in August were victorious because they had accomplished the seemingly impossible task of squeezing the slave out of their veins.

In explaining the coup's failure, observers have pointed to the indecision and unprofessionalism of its execution. The plotters made several costly errors. They failed to either arrest or kill Yeltsin, destroy his stronghold—the Russian Parliament building—seal the borders, and shut down the Western media. The junta's incompetence was so total that Gorbachev loyalists were reportedly able to continue their work in the Kremlin across the hall from where the coup's leaders were meeting.

This analysis is absolutely correct. But these errors were not the main cause of the coup's failure. The coup was doomed by the transformations that had taken place in the Soviet Union since Stalin's death. The plotters were veteran professionals of the system, including KGB chairman Vladimir Kryuchkov, Prime Minister Valentin Pavlov, Interior Minister Boris Pugo, Defense Minister Dmitri Yazov, and others. But they were no Stalins. And, more important, the country had ceased to be Stalinist. Three decades without Stalin made *perestroika* possible; six years with Gorbachev made the coup impossible.

When the plotters arrested Gorbachev at his dacha at Foros in the Crimea, almost nobody could resist the temptation to draw a parallel between this event and Nikita Khrushchev's ouster in 1964. Khrushchev had also been vacationing at the Black Sea before the coup. But Khrushchev's overthrow is not important for its similarity to the August coup, but for the profound differences between the two. Khrushchev's "thaw" did not shake the foundation of Stalinism. Although he denounced Stalin's crimes and cult of personality, Khrushchev failed to transform the essence of the Soviet regime. Indeed, even as he was being overthrown, Khrushchev himself played by its rules: He did not resist when the plotters in Moscow decided to oust him. The only visible effect of his "thaw" was that he was only dismissed, and not shot. He became a non-person. In contrast, Gorbachev's *perestroika* not only saved its architect physically, but also politically.

The plotters of this coup were accomplished Communist bureaucrats and apparatchiks. Living too long within the Kremlin's walls, they could not grasp the fundamental changes taking place outside. They seem to have believed that the Soviet regime was still as powerful and omnipresent as it had been under Stalin—when his word alone was more than enough to enforce any decision.

The plotters made another fatal mistake. They failed to realize that with the Soviet people no longer mesmerized by the fear of Stalin's rule, the regime's survival depended upon Gorbachev's legitimacy. By challenging that legitimacy they committed political suicide—bringing down the whole structure of the Soviet empire and Communist dictatorship with them.

The "Ninth Man"

In evaluating Gorbachev's part in the coup, we tend to view him as either a victim or a hero. But his role is perhaps better understood as that of the "ninth man" on the eight-man coup committee.[1] Gorbachev surrounded himself with the very hardliners who would try to overthrow him, believing, arrogantly, that his well-known political skills would be sufficient to keep these conservatives indefinitely at bay. He was chronically indecisive on pushing *perestroika* toward its logical conclusion; he attempted to pursue democracy without shaking off obsolete socialist dogmas; and he was inflexible in dealing with liberal forces like Yeltsin. Gorbachev himself made the putsch inevitable.

Even this description of Gorbachev's role captures only part of the truth. The main truth is that even during the coup, and immediately after it, Gorbachev was the last defender of the old regime. By undercutting Gorbachev's power and destroying his legitimacy, the plotters inadvertently delivered the final blow to the very structure they intended to save. Indeed, in the few weeks after the coup, the liberal and democratic forces of the disintegrating Soviet Union succeeded in accomplishing what *perestroika* could not during its six-year run.

It was only because of Gorbachev's powerful presence that nobody knew how rotten the two principal pillars of the Soviet regime—the Communist party and the KGB—truly were. Now, both within the Soviet Union and abroad, the coup is being thought of by many as a blessing in disguise, because its defeat accelerated the demise of the Soviet empire and of Communist dictatorship—the task that Gorbachev was unwilling or did not dare to complete. The 72 hours that Mikhail Gorbachev spent under house arrest were the finest hours of his career. Afterward, despite his astonishing survivability, he began to slide into oblivion. Though he survived the military coup, he could not survive the democratic revolution it spurred on.

---

[1] *Melor Sturua, "The Coup's Ninth Man,"* New York Times, *Thursday, 22 August 1991, Op-Ed section.*

During the May-June 1990 Soviet-American summit in Washington, one of the main architects of *perestroika*, who accompanied Gorbachev, told me something that stuck in my mind. "Yes," he said, "we made a colossal mistake with [Czechoslovak Communist party leader Alexander] Dubček. If we hadn't overthrown him in 1968 we wouldn't now have [Václav] Havel in the Prague Kremlin."

But even if Dubček had remained in power, the Soviet Union could not have maintained its control over Czechoslovakia. Nor could Dubček's reforms, like the reforms of *perestroika*, endure. They were simply too limited to prevent a democratic revolution. Both as a leader and as a symbol of liberal communism, Dubček could not have stopped the rise of a democratic Havel.

Had Moscow actively supported Dubček, he could only have postponed Havel's ultimate victory. Had Moscow not interfered at all, events might even have accelerated, as the rapid changes throughout Eastern Europe in 1989–90 confirm. Imre Pozsgay in Hungary, Hans Modrow in the German Democratic Republic, and Wojciech Jaruzelski in Poland—none of them could stop their domestic Havels. Dubček would have been only a transitional figure, his Prague Spring and "socialism with a human face" only transitional phenomena.

Yet it would be a grave mistake to imagine that the rule of a transitional character such as Dubček automatically gives rise to a Havel. To so imagine is to give history only an optimistic reading. If a Dubček held power too long, he might lose his human face in a struggle for survival. The Prague Spring would be replaced by a Moscow Winter. A Dubček would have been either transformed into or removed in favor of someone like his non-reformist successor, Gustáv Husák. Such a transformation took place in Poland, where Communist party leader Władysław Gomułka saw his popularity decline along with his reformist zeal. From every Dubček the trend runs either forward to a Havel or backward to a Husák—or even as far back as the Stalinist regime of Czechoslovakian president Klement Gottwald.

The same phenomenon also appears in the Soviet Union. In Czechoslovakia, Dubček's reforms signaled the beginning of a democratization process, but the arrival of true democracy would wait for Havel. Gorbachev's *perestroika*, like Dubček's Prague Spring, could have overcome counterrevolutionary forces only by passing from the democratization phase to true democracy. But the "socialist choice" proclaimed by Gorbachev—partial liberalization in politics and more efficiency in economics without changing the essence of the regime—had little to do with democracy.

The system of soviets formalized by V. I. Lenin was not democracy, but a camouflage for the unrestricted rule of the Communist party. Lenin promoted the idea that power should be wielded by these workers' councils throughout the country, calling for "All power to the soviets!" Yet he truly supported this slogan only when that power was held by Bolsheviks.

The amendment of Article VI of the Soviet Constitution, which in 1990 formally ended the Communist party's monopoly on political power, accelerated a Dubček-style democratization process, but it did not bring a Havel-style democracy: a real multiparty system. The Soviet Union lingered too long in this democratization phase, not only delaying true democracy but inviting a reactionary backlash. Witness the shift to the right and the stagnation in the (increasingly insignificant) Congress of Peoples Deputies and the Supreme Soviet. Although they initially appeared to be progressive bodies, they were ultimately reduced to rubber-stamping presidential decrees.

Similarly, Gorbachev personally lingered too long in the democratization phase. Without implementing further democratic reforms, Gorbachev risked being transformed into or replaced by a dictator. The developments in the Soviet Union before the coup demonstrated unmistakably that if *perestroika*, Gorbachev's own form of "socialism with a human face," did not evolve toward democracy, it would instead evolve toward dictatorship, as predicted by Shevardnadze. In the end, Soviet "socialism with a human face" was not so much a significant step toward democracy, but rather a limited deviation from dictatorship.

The failed coup signaled not only the end of Communism but the end of *perestroika* as well. When Gorbachev came back to Moscow from his captivity in the Crimea, he did not realize that in the 72 hours of his absence the country had changed more profoundly than during the entire six years of his rule. Clearly he had missed a crucial moment in his country's history: Upon his miraculous return to Moscow, some of his first remarks were, regrettably, about reforming the Communist party and the validity of the "socialist choice."

Dismantling Communism

Gorbachev was, of course, dead wrong. After the failure of the coup the choice was in the hands of the people, and they chose decisively. The destruction of Feliks Dzerzhinsky's statue in front of KGB headquarters in Lubyanka Square was as historic as the fall of the Berlin Wall. By pulling down the statue of the founding father of the state security system, Muscovites and all Soviet citizens showed that they had succeeded at last in exorcising fear and slavery. Gorbachev's attempt to simply replace the head of the KGB and preserve the institution was met with decisive resistance.

With Dzerzhinsky's statue fell the various statues of Lenin, the father of the Communist party and the Soviet state. Left without the KGB—its "sword of intimidation"—the Communist party was defenseless. Its power had no moral or legal justification whatsoever. In Gorbachev's presence, Yeltsin signed a decree that suspended the Communist party of Russia. Gorbachev tried to resist, but the following day he resigned as general secretary of the Communist party of the Soviet Union and appealed to the party's Central Committee to disband itself.

The appeal was long overdue. In sacrificing his general-secretaryship, Gorbachev hoped to save his presidency. In sacrificing the Communist party, he hoped to save the union. But his attempts were futile. The closing of the headquarters of the Central Committee of the Communist party in Staraya Ploshchad (Old Square) sealed the fate of the police state created by the Bolsheviks in October 1917. The party and the state had been defeated by freedom and independence: The quest of the Soviet people for freedom and the quest of the republics for independence had destroyed the socialist and imperial structure of the Soviet Union.

The botched coup also hastened the downfall of the old regime in another way: It identified the reactionaries in the government, facilitating their removal. Many upon whom the president had depended and whom he personally had selected, it seemed, had betrayed him. The coup even revealed that the seemingly loyal General Vadim Medvedev, who always followed on Gorbachev's heels clutching a mysterious briefcase under his arm, was not the president's aide-de-camp, but his warden; he did not serve Gorbachev, but the KGB.

Gorbachev was shocked by the turn of events. To most observers, his reaction revealed his phenomenal shortsightedness, his astonishing inability to judge people. Gorbachev had even forced his vice-presidential nominee—Gennadi Yanayev, the future titular head of the coup committee—upon the Parliament that had initially rejected him. His most trusted advisers were the chief masterminds of the coup: Yazov and Kryuchkov.

Attributing Gorbachev's selection of advisers to his "shortsightedness" obscures his true motivations. The men Gorbachev chose for the most powerful positions in the government and the party were not political unknowns, and Gorbachev selected them for a specific purpose with full knowledge of their backgrounds. He wanted to restructure, not destroy, the Communist dictatorship. And the people he chose were the best men available for the task. The commander-in-chief and his army were in step with one another; only when Gorbachev betrayed his advisers by preparing to sign a union treaty that would have loosened the Kremlin's control over the republics, seriously weakening the central party apparat, did his advisers strike. In this sense, they did not betray him. He betrayed them: In the last moment his positive human qualities outweighed his political conservatism and narrow-mindedness.

Shortsightedness did not dictate Gorbachev's choice of his entourage. Nor was it through shortsightedness that he pushed away his old liberal advisers. He felt a hostility toward the democrats and an attraction to conservatives and hardliners—the Stalinists of the *perestroika* mold. He was rude and unforgiving toward the former and forgiving toward the latter. There were massacres in Tbilisi, in Baku, in Vilnius, in Riga, and elsewhere, but Gorbachev punished nobody—though as president and commander-in-chief he should have been the first defender of law and order. He forgave Prime Minister Pavlov's July 1991 parliamentary move to directly challenge his presidential powers. He forgave the impudence of the party bosses and the disobedience of the military and security forces.

There are many reasons for Gorbachev's behavior, but perhaps one is most important: Gorbachev, being a political animal, cherishes power above everything. Gorbachev deeply believed that the real threat to his power was coming from the Left and not from the Right. And he was confident that he could control the conservatives while the liberals seemed unmanageable.

Seemingly, the August coup should have smashed his illusions about the Left and the Right—about the unmanageability of the former and the manageability of the latter. The trusted Right betrayed him, and the untrustworthy Left came to his rescue. But in fact the August coup, at least in Gorbachev's first instinct, reaffirmed his analysis. Even the enraged hard-liners could not depose him, but the democrats who saved him destroyed his real power bases: the central Communist party apparatus and the KGB. In the final analysis, the real coup was not undertaken by Gorbachev's advisers and staff, but by another group of plotters headed by Yeltsin: It was they who decisively transferred power from the old union to the republics and who hastened the demise of the Soviet Communist party. While Gorbachev's advisers tried to subvert developing democratic structures through their coup, Yeltsin's reformers sought to destroy the totalitarian structures already weakened by *perestroika*.

Gorbachev survived both coups and still wields some power, not because his 72-hour crash course in the Crimea transformed him into an enlightened liberal, but because the new democratic forces and structures cannot take hold without a rather weakened but legitimate transitional figure in the central power structure. So now his very powerlessness has now become the source of his remaining power.

How Gorbachev plays this last role of his political career will determine how he will go into the history books. What is clear now is that Gorbachev's dream of a "socialist choice" never materialized: Neither the Left nor the Right gave him this choice.

The new Russian foreign policy

Neil Malcolm

Neil Malcolm is Professor of Russian Politics and Head of the Russian and East European Research Centre at the University of Wolverhampton. Until September 1993 he was Head of the Russian and CIS Programme at the Royal Institute of International Affairs. His edited volume *Russia and Europe: an End to Confrontation* has recently been published by Pinter. His article in this issue is based on a talk he gave at Chatham House on 27 September 1993.

Unfamiliarity with Russia and its sheer size still colour Western perceptions of Russia's international behaviour. It tends to be pictured either as a sphinx (Winston Churchill's 'riddle wrapped in a mystery inside an enigma'), or as a bear – brutish, uncommunicative and unpredictably aggressive. Thus the good showing of Vladimir Zhirinovsky's Liberal Democratic Party (LDP) in the December 1993 elections to the Russian State Duma seems to have shocked many commentators out of post-Cold War complacency, only for them to relapse into old nightmares about Russian expansionism. Of course the present situation is unstable, and it is right to be concerned about potential dangers, but these can only be assessed properly by setting current developments in perspective, with a good understanding of how the internal setting of Russian foreign policy has changed in recent years. It might be as well to begin by recalling the second (and less frequently cited) part of Churchill's judgment: 'But perhaps there is a key. That key is Russian national interest.'[1] This article focuses on developments in thinking about foreign policy in Russia since 1991 and on changes in the national interest and foreign policy-making, and draws connections with recent changes in policy itself.

Policy debate

During the seven decades after 1917, discussion of international affairs in Moscow was confined within the constricting framework of an elaborate structure of myths concerning the Soviet Union's role in the world – as the champion of international progress and proletarian revolution. The crumbling of Communist rule was accompanied by the collapse of this whole structure of ideas. The shock-waves and reverberations generated by this collapse are still traversing the field of discussion of foreign policy in Russia. There is a tendency to swing from one extreme to another. Yet there is also a clear underlying trend, a flight from what is described as 'ideology', and a pragmatic concern with what writers refer to as the concrete national interests of the new Russian state.

The first phase, which got under way well before 1991, was dominated by a wholesale reaction against traditional Soviet foreign policy doctrine. It had two main aspects. The first was a rejection of Stalinist militarism and economic isolationism. It culminated in the endorsing of visions of a new, peaceful and increasingly economically integrated world order. One of the main spokesmen for this view was Vladimir Petrovsky, a Deputy Foreign Minister of the Soviet Union (now Deputy Secretary-General of the United Nations). In 1991, Petrovsky declared that the building of the 'common European home' was a putting into practice of Kantian principles of international relations. The new Europe, he said, is 'a component and a prototype of a new system of human relations built on the principles of non-violence, solidarity and cooperation'.[2] Such views underpinned the 'New Political Thinking' of Petrovsky's superior, Eduard Shevardnadze. They had a dramatic effect on the Soviet Union's international image, and they helped to ease Soviet acceptance of the international retreats and climb-downs of 1990 and 1991.

The second aspect of reaction against pre-existing Soviet doctrine was the swing towards an almost unconditional Westernism. This became most marked in statements which came from the Russian Foreign Ministry in the first months of Russian statehood, in early 1992. It was repeatedly declared that Russia intended 'to enter the club of the most dynamically developing democratic countries'; that it was 'the missing component of the democratic pole of the Northern Hemisphere'; that it was about to 'return to Europe'; and so on.[3] From the end of the 1980s, however, a reverse movement was already under way. Of course, those who began to argue against what they called 'excessive idealism' and uncritical Westernism did not do so in the language of Communist orthodoxy but rather by appealing to the 'national interest', conceived mainly in terms of short- and medium-term economic and security advantages.

While a minority of conservative-minded writers tended to emphasise the importance of military means (and of not letting down the country's guard in the face of the Western intrigues which were all around it), self-described 'realists' from the more numerous reformist camp contented themselves with calling for a more 'commonsense' approach to international affairs. They objected to Shevardnadze's high-minded language, making the point that increased interdependence in world affairs was in itself no guarantee of peace and cooperation. Yet they maintained that

From *The World Today*, Vol. 50, No. 2, February 1994, pp. 28-32. *The World Today*, published by The Royal Institute of International Affairs. Reprinted by permission.

Russia had no option but to throw in its lot with the West, whatever the underlying tensions and conflicts of interest. They were not calling for a strategic change in policy, they said, but simply for a more clear-eyed application of it. Criticism of particular aspects of the foreign policy of the new post-Communist Russian government was not slow in appearing, however.

During 1992, arguments tended to centre around the question of geographical priorities. Critics of the Foreign Ministry argued that too much attention had been paid to the 'far abroad', and not enough to the 'near abroad', that is, to the countries which had emerged from the former Soviet Union. Sergei Stankevich, a senior foreign policy adviser to President Yeltsin, declared in an important statement printed in March 1992 that Russian policy-makers should be focusing on the developing 'arc of crisis' in their own backyard. Russia should avoid being drawn into a North-South, anti-Islamic confrontation in which it would suffer disproportionately because of its location and because of its own substantial Moslem minority population. 'It is obvious,' he wrote, 'that we should seek a new balance appropriate to the present-day situation of Russia between Western and Eastern orientations. Meanwhile the first thing is to strengthen our position in the East, correcting the evident distortion created by the authors of the "common European home" conception.'[4]

Stankevich labelled his new policy orientation 'Eurasianism'. This has led to misunderstanding, because the term Eurasianism has been used in the past to describe extreme anti-Western trends in Russian thinking about international relations. Eurasianism as it evolved in Russia in 1992, however, was a mixture of quite varied tendencies.[5] The predominant one, and the one represented by Stankevich in his article, was what has been described as 'demo-patriotic'. This is an increasingly influential current which is fundamentally Westernist in its attitude but sees a pragmatic need for a more assertive foreign policy. As Sergei Karaganov, who is the organiser of the influential Council on Foreign and Defence Policy, a consultative group made up of politicians, officials, experts and industrial leaders, has written more recently:

'One could even argue that on the way to modernity Russia will have to live through a period of increased nationalism and statism.' And he continued: 'This period is already starting. It is not only inevitable, it is also necessary in order to resurrect a country so badly damaged by totalitarianism and mismanagement.'[6]

This assertiveness was seen by 'demo-patriots', then, as something quite natural after the upheavals of 1988 to 1991, as a way of restoring morale and as a way of filling the international power vacuum, especially in the area of the former Soviet Union. It was also necessary, of course, to guard the modernisers' flanks against the extreme right, who already in 1992 were using xenophobia as a weapon in the internal political battle. A characteristic statement in the conservative newspaper *Sovetskaya Rossiya* went as follows:

'Democracy is profoundly inimical to our national culture, it tramples down everything that it comes into contact with, in the name of some world order or the other. And in general all these phenomena – democracy, globalism, Zionism and cosmopolitanism – are identical twins.'[7]

In the new, more democratic political setting, where politicians competed more overtly for popularity, the 'plight' of the millions of Russians marooned in the former Soviet states was seen as one of the few foreign-policy issues which was likely to attract widespread interest. As the political struggle between Yeltsin and his rivals intensified in the summer of 1993, so nationalist and revanchist themes came more and more to the forefront. At the beginning of August, Vice-President Aleksandr Rutskoi, by then *de facto* figurehead of the opposition, declared his belief that the Soviet Union would be recreated and would 'again become a superpower that can guarantee peace on earth'. 'The Soviet people', he added, must reunite or 'be destroyed'. Ruslan Khasbulatov, the Parliament's Speaker, whose evolution to the right was even more precipitous, stated shortly afterwards that Yeltsin was acting 'in the strategic interests of the international intelligence community' and that he was 'deliberately destroying Russia's armed forces'.[8] In this climate of debate it was important for any modernising group to be very careful in choosing its rhetoric.

Amid all the political manoeuvring, and behind the rise of *lumpen* nationalism in the December 1993 election campaign, it is important, however, to distinguish an important underlying change in the nature of the foreign-policy debate. The trend away from unconditional Westernism in the content of what Russian specialists and officials are writing and saying about international affairs paradoxically marks a Westernisation of their style of thinking. In other words, Russians are focusing less on the old questions: 'Who are we? Are we Europeans? What is our mission in the world?', and so on, and focusing more on questions which are more familiar to us: 'What do we need? How can we get it? What will it cost?'

Foreign policy-making

Turning to the arena of foreign policy-making in Russia since 1991, we encounter a similar paradoxical pattern. The situation is at times extremely confused and even apparently chaotic, but here, too, there is an underlying Westernising trend.

When, at the beginning of 1991, Mikhail Gorbachev described Yeltsin and his democratic allies as 'neo-Bolsheviks', what he meant was that they showed a dangerous revolutionary impatience with other points of view, that they rejected his own cautious strategy and consensus-building tactics. Like the Bolsheviks, of course, they succeeded in winning power. But in the aftermath of revolution, intransigence may be less appropriate than those qualities of compromise and tolerance which Gorbachev – perhaps prematurely – was trying to bring to bear. In early 1992, as Yegor Gaidar led what he described as his 'cavalry charge' in economic policy, Yeltsin and his team were able to act virtually disregarding dissenting opinion. In foreign policy, Andrei Kozyrev seemed to be focusing almost exclusively on emphasising Russia's new solidarity with the West. As the 'Eurasians' pointed out, it appeared that relations with the new states of the Commonwealth of Independent States (CIS), where Russia had pressing concerns and vital interests, were being neglected. A Department for the CIS Countries was not formally established in the Foreign Ministry until March 1992, and it began to function only gradually: a decree setting up embassies in the 'near abroad' was published only in September.

By April 1992, however, when the Sixth Congress of People's Deputies met, it was becoming apparent that not even Boris Yeltsin could defy the laws of political gravity. He was openly challenged, and there was an increasingly sharp confrontation with the Parliament throughout the rest of the year which caused virtual paralysis in a number of key areas of policy. Yeltsin was brought to the realisation that in Russia, as elsewhere, the political leadership must accommodate the interests and views of powerful elites.

The compromise with the centre

After the disintegration of the Soviet system, the most powerful fragments of the old bureaucracy which remain intact are the military leaders and the state-sector industrial management. These groups have certain important political advantages. First of all, they have access to substantial organisational and material resources. Second, they are natural allies. They have a network of long-standing contacts from the Soviet period, during which they enjoyed high status, good access to the political leadership and substantial economic privileges. Large sections of them appear to have a common interest in slowing up marketisation and demilitarisation, and in preserving as much of the former Soviet economic and military space as can be preserved. Third, they can pose as protectors of the public against radical economic restructuring and unemployment, and as patrons of the Russians in the 'near abroad'. Fourth, in the political conditions of 1992 and 1993, this group and its 'centrist' political allies could occupy the crucial strategic ground between the radical Westernisers on the one hand – the less 'patriotic' democrats – and the irreconcilable nationalist and Communist wing. Finally, the army enjoys extra leverage because of the chaos, confusion and civil war on Russia's borders, and because of its role in resolving constitutional *impasses*.

Yeltsin's compromise with the centre, although it was talked about fairly openly from the Sixth Congress on, was not an easy one, especially in foreign policy. At times there seemed to be at least three Russian foreign policies: one promoted by the Ministry of Foreign Affairs, one by the Ministry of Defence and one by the Parliament. This created concern and confusion abroad. Long-prepared visits by the President to Tokyo were twice cancelled at the last minute. There were unheralded delays in troop withdrawals from the Baltic states, with different explanations being issued by different agencies in Moscow. Army generals supposedly engaged in CIS peacekeeping activities – in Moldova, for example – made partisan pro-Russian statements with impunity.[9] Controversial parliamentary declarations were issued relating to former Yugoslavia, to the Crimea, to the status of the Black Sea Fleet, quite at odds with the official diplomatic line. Some of the most alarming outbursts came from Vice-President Rutskoi, on visits to the Crimea and TransDnestria.

As for the President, he appeared unable or unwilling to impose discipline, giving his support first to one side then to the other, and casting the blame on Kozyrev and his friends.[10] Some of the worst confusion was evident inside the President's apparatus, which was constantly being reshuffled and reorganised, but which remained apparently incapable of harmonising policy. The establishment in May 1992 of a Security Council which appeared to afford extra leverage for military and military-industrial interests alarmed liberals, but neither it nor the Inter-departmental Foreign Policy Commission which it subsequently acquired seem to have played much of a coordinating role.

The stress showed in various ways. The Foreign Minister, Andrei Kozyrev, was himself clearly suffering. 'The party of war, the party of neo-Bolshevism, is rearing its head in our country,' he warned at the beginning of July. 'Wholesale transfers of arms are taking place in the Transcaucasus and Moldova. Under what agreement is this effected, I would like to ask? ... Why are the military leaders deciding the most important political issues?'[11] At the end of 1992 came the notorious speech in Helsinki, during which Kozyrev parodied the nationalistic posturing of his critics. The defence establishment, too, was unhappy. 'We do not have the procedure for inter-agency consultation prior to the taking of foreign-policy decisions. That is *prior to*, not *after* the decisions have been made,' complained the military newspaper *Krasnaya zvezda* in December 1992.[12]

Towards a foreign policy consensus

Contrary to all predictions, however, Kozyrev was still in the saddle at the end of 1993. Indeed, it was the Foreign Ministry which appeared to have taken up the burden of coordinating policy. Towards the end of 1992 and the beginning of 1993, there were signs of bridge-building going on between it, the Ministry of Defence and Parliament. Communications became more frequent and the tone of public remarks became more polite. Andrei Kozyrev, Pavel Grachev, the Defence Minister, and Evgeny Ambartsumov, Chairman of the Foreign Relations Committee in Parliament, all endorsed a compromise 'foreign policy concept', which was adopted by the Security Council in April 1993.

The importance of this document as a direct guide to Russian policy should not be exaggerated – it has never been published in full in any case. It was, however, important as a symptom of willingness on the part of different agencies involved in external relations to reach at least a paper accommodation over policy. The new concept reflected the established Foreign Ministry priority of rapprochement with the advanced industrial countries, but emphasised actual and potential conflicts of interest (for example, over technology trade), and envisaged a more active role for Russia in security and economic affairs in the 'near abroad'. If we compare it with the official and unofficial drafts which preceded it, we can build up a picture of the stages by which the compromise was reached.[13] It is also revealing to compare the 1992 draft Military Doctrine of the Russian Federation with the document adopted in November 1993, in which all remaining Cold War phraseology has been removed and in which threats and potential threats are seen overwhelmingly in areas closely bordering on Russia itself.[14]

More important, policy itself became much more coherent in 1993, as the Foreign Ministry sought to build on a wider domestic political base. As far as policy towards the West is concerned, the changes have been cautious, a matter of tone and detail. There has been a sharper focus on economic issues – arms exports, foreign investment in the energy sector and access to world markets, especially to the European Union.

The most striking changes have come in the politically sensitive sphere of policy towards the 'near abroad'. Already in the summer of 1992, the Deputy Foreign Minister in charge of this area began work on a new, more active strategy for the region, in response to harsh criticism from the Security Council, and indeed from the President himself. His report argued that Russia must win international recognition for its role as the leading force in ensuring 'stability and military security on the entire territory of the former Soviet Union'.[15]

By August, the Chairman of the Supreme Soviet's Foreign Affairs Committee, Yevgeny Ambartsumov, was promoting the idea of a 'Russian Monroe Doctrine' encompassing the former Soviet space. Finally, in February 1993, President Yeltsin chose the occasion of an address to an assembly of the industrialists' Civic Union to announce that Russia was going to push for greater integration in the CIS, and that it would not neglect its special peacekeeping responsibilities. 'I believe the time has come,' he declared, 'for distinguished international organisations, including the UN, to grant Russia special powers as a guarantor of peace and stability in the former regions of the Soviet Union.'[16]

Inside the CIS, economic leverage and sometimes overt military force have been used quite vigorously to gain political and strategic advantages for Russia. The most dramatic turnaround has come in regard to Ukraine. President Kravchuk, who had managed to seize the initiative in relations with Moscow in 1992, was reduced in September 1993 to agreeing to discuss handing over the entire Black Sea Fleet and Ukraine's remaining nuclear warheads to Russia in exchange for cancellation of its $2.8bn debt. The CIS has defied all predictions of its withering away, and new plans for economic and military cooperation are being discussed. Azerbaijan has agreed to reactivate its membership of the organisation and Georgia has joined for the first time. In public statements by officials in Moscow, justifications of interventions in the former Soviet area which refer to peacekeeping, to protecting the interests of Russians outside Russia, and to safeguarding Russia's interests are used more and more interchangeably.

Bringing to bear its military and economic advantages in a coordinated way, Russia has been able to drive hard bargains with its other CIS partners. During the summer of 1993, the former Soviet states in Central Asia were told bluntly that they must make a choice between closer involvement with the Turkey-Iran-Pakistan-sponsored Economic Cooperation Organisation, on the one hand, and with the CIS on the other. In November 1993, Kazakhstan and Uzbekistan were forced into deciding to introduce their own currencies after Moscow had set what they described as impossibly difficult conditions for participation in the rouble zone.

Of course, it is only in comparison to the conflict-ridden climate of 1992 that the atmosphere in which Russian foreign policy is made could be described as harmonious. The activities of the armed forces in Tajikistan and Abkhazia cause friction with the Foreign Ministry. Since the forceful resolution of Yeltsin's quarrel with the Supreme Soviet in October 1993 there are signs that the Ministry of Defence has sought to extract rewards for its assistance (for example, in the form of an upwardly revised manpower target for the armed services of 2.1m men). There is an important underlying conflict between those who perceive the health of the Russian economy as the primary goal, whatever the consequences for relations with the near-abroad states, and those who still think in terms of a former Soviet strategic and economic

space and see the need to make sacrifices (subsidised energy supplies, concessions on currency regulations) to preserve it.

It should also be emphasised that the Russian government has not simply capitulated to powerful interests. The hard line taken on currency issues vis-à-vis Kazakhstan and Uzbekistan provides an example of how it has been able to sustain consistent policies of its own in a number of areas. This is partly because the interests of Russian industrialists, even within particular sectors, are extremely diverse. There is a variety of views, too, among the army generals.

Amid all the confusion and ambiguity, what seems to be emerging, however, is a policy shaped as a constantly fought-over compromise between pragmatically conceived longer-term interests and the shorter-term interests of influential groups. In other words, something much more recognisable to Western eyes.

Conclusion

What does all this mean in practical terms? First of all, it means that, barring a large-scale domestic political upheaval, Russian foreign policy is more predictable than it has been since 1985. It appears to rest on a reasonably wide elite consensus, and its general direction is less vulnerable to personnel changes. If Kozyrev had been replaced by a more 'centrist' figure in mid-1992, for example, the effects could have been considerably more far-reaching than a similar shift in early 1994.

Second, Russia's international partners need to be sensitive about the effects of their actions on the country's concrete economic interests. Nationalist politicians claim to have uncovered a Western plot to cut Russia out of world markets and to undermine its high-technology competitive capacity. How exactly what remains of Russian advanced industry will be able to engage on a competitive basis in the world economy is by no means clear, but such concerns are going to continue to play an important part in the domestic politics of foreign policy in Moscow.

Third, it must be acknowledged that most Russians distinguish quite sharply between 'near abroad' and 'far abroad'.[17] They regard it as perfectly natural that Moscow should exercise special supervision over an area which lies next to Russia's borders and in which 25m Russians still live, and this attitude is now clearly reflected in government policy, alongside official recognition of the sovereignty of the former Soviet states. There is no simple or easy response to these uncomfortable facts. When it comes to peacekeeping (or peacemaking) in the Transcaucasus, say, or in Central Asia, the West will be tempted to allow the responsibility to slip by default into Moscow's hands. It would be more difficult but more constructive to take up the plan, backed by the Russian Foreign Ministry, that such operations should take place under the auspices of the United Nations or the Conference on Security and Cooperation in Europe (CSCE), and be subject to international sanction and monitoring.

The results of the Russian elections of December 1993 remind us, of course, that it is no longer sufficient to look at the foreign-policy preferences of the administrative elites. Social conditions, as is constantly pointed out, favour the rise of nationalist demagogues, and Serbia offers an ominous precedent. The government is clearly worried and has tactically hardened its tone in foreign policy. One of the outcomes of the election which is less frequently commented upon was that the parties representing the 'centre' did poorly and that the industry-backed Civic Union failed even to clear the 5-per-cent threshold needed to gain representation in Parliament. The possibility cannot be excluded that sections of disenfranchised industrialists will seek to form an alliance with extremist politicians such as Zhirinovsky and their numerous supporters in the military.

However, this is a concern for the future, and it is important not to allow alarm at the aggressive neo-imperialist rhetoric of the extreme right to colour our interpretation of the increased assertiveness which has been evident for at least the last 12 months. What we have seen so far is most likely not the 'evil empire' getting ready to strike back, but rather Russia feeling its way towards the role of a 'normal' regional power.

NOTES

1. W. Churchill, *The Gathering Storm* (Boston: Houghton-Mifflin, 1948), p.449.
2. V. Petrovsky, 'Priorities in a Disarming World', *International Affairs* (Moscow), 1991, No 3, p.4.
3. See for example, 'A Transformed Russia in a New World', *International Affairs* (Moscow), 1991, No 4/5, p.86; *Nezavisimaya gazeta*, 1 April 1992; *Interfax* release, 21 February 1992.
4. *Nezavisimaya gazeta*, 28 March 1992.
5. See P. Ferdinand, 'Russia and Russians after Communism: Western or Eurasian?', *The World Today*, December 1992.
6. S. Karaganov, *Russia - the New Foreign Policy and Security Agenda* (London: Centre for Defence Studies, University of London, 1992), p.31.
7. *Sovetskaya Rossiya*, 4 July 1992 (by V. Krupin). *Sovetskaya Rossiya* was not itself an organ of the extreme right.
8. A. Rahr, 'Yeltsin and the New Elections', *RFE/RL Research Report*, 27 August 1993, p.5.
9. One of the most scandalous was the one made by General Aleksandr Lebed, commander of the Fourteenth Army in TransDnestria, to the effect that this region of Moldova was 'a small part of Russia', and that Moldova was 'a fascist state'. Lebed was subsequently promoted. *Moskovskie novosti*, 1992, No 27, p.4; *Izvestiya*, 7 July 1992.
10. Radio Mayak, Moscow, 27 October 1992.
11. *Izvestiya*, 1 July 1992. These disputes are thoroughly analysed by Suzanne Crow, *The Making of Russian Foreign Policy* (Radio Free Europe/Radio Europe draft occasional paper, June 1993).
12. 23 December 1992.
13. One of the first attempts was the 'Strategy for Russia' produced by the Council on Foreign and Defence Policy, 'a non-government organisation containing 37 members, including politicians, entrepreneurs, members of the armed forces, diplomats and scholars'. *Nezavisimaya gazeta*, 19 August 1992. See also *Diplomaticheskii vestnik*, January 1993 (special issue); *Nezavisimaya gazeta*, 29 April 1993; *Moscow News*, 1993, No 20, p.9. The evolution of the 'concept' is analysed in Margot Light's 'Foreign Policy Thinking in Russia, Ukraine and Kazakhstan' (draft contribution to an RIIA research project on New Factors in the Foreign Policy of the Former Soviet States), pp.13-18.
14. *Rossiiskie vesti*, 18 November 1993, pp.1-2.
15. The minister, Fyodor Shelov-Kovedyaev, resigned in July 1992. He insisted that Russia should eschew the use of military force as an instrument in the region. J. Lough, 'Defining Russia's Relations with Neighboring States', *RFE/RL Research Report*, 14 May 1993. Criticisms by Yeltsin are in *Rossiiskaya gazeta*, 6 May and 24 October 1992.
16. *BBC Summary of World Broadcasts*, SU/1626, B1 (2 March 1993).
17. The Baltic states occupy an uneasy intermediate position.

Security issues
and the Eastern Slavic states

Susan L. Clark

Susan L. Clark is a member of the Research Staff at the Institute for Defence Analyses in Alexandria, Virginia, in the United States. She was a contributor to and the editor of *Soviet Military Power in a Changing World* (Boulder, CO: Westview Press, 1991) and *Gorbachev's Agenda: Changes in Soviet Domestic and Foreign Policy* (1989), as well as co-author (with Robbin Laird) of *The USSR and the Western Alliance* (1990).

With the rapidity of change in the former Soviet Union today, documenting specific events is best left to the newspapers, radio and television. This article looks instead at some of the general trends and security-related issues facing the Eastern Slavic states of Belarus, Ukraine and Russia.

In examining security issues today, it is necessary to look beyond the strictly military domain. Security matters must be understood in the context of their interconnections and interdependence with economic, political, social and other variables. This article begins with some general observations about developments within the Slavic states and follows with several more specific military-related issues, focusing on some of the more significant recent trends.

The reality of interdependence

One of the most important features of the present situation in much of the former Soviet Union, and among the Slavic states in particular, is the fact of interdependence. Such interdependence is certainly evident in the *economic* area, particularly in industry, where different elements of a given industry are located in what are now new and independent states.

One of the principal challenges in the wake of the disintegration of Soviet structures is the re-establishment of working relations among such enterprises in different states (and frequently even within one state). To date, many of these ties have not begun to work, though some enterprises have managed to forge ties on the basis of barter arrangements. Nevertheless, the question of how to handle transactions – deciding the value of goods, the form of payment (as many states set up their own national currencies), the methods of delivery and so on – remains largely dependent on ad hoc solutions and requires ingenuity on the part of managers who were used to having the central government take responsibility for such decisions.

Interdependence goes beyond economic relationships, however. For example, in the *military* sphere, too, there is currently a certain degree of interdependence between the Central Asian states and Russia. To date, the Central Asian states simply do not have the officer corps, the training or the military equipment to provide for their own defence. Collaboration with Russia affords them the opportunity to begin to develop their armed forces. Russian security assistance to the Central Asian states aims to prevent the spread of instability into the Russian Federation itself.

A third illustration of interdependence within the former Soviet Union is found in the *space programme*. Russia is the only country of the former Soviet Union that has the capability to have its own space programme. Nevertheless, at least at the present time it is still reliant on space components located in other states, most notably the Baikonur launch facility in Kazakhstan.

While the political declarations continue to stress the need for the new states to assert their independence, the reality of interdependence and a growing pragmatism in dealing with this reality has begun to shape certain government decisions. One example of this trend was the appointment in the autumn of 1992 of Leonid Kuchma as Prime Minister of Ukraine. He brought with him the experience of running the largest missile-production facility in the world. Almost literally the first thing he did after his appointment was to visit officials in Moscow, where he emphasised the absolute importance of developing and maintaining cooperation and economic ties with Russia. Another example was the decision by Belarus to remain in the rouble zone and join the collective security treaty spearheaded by

From *The World Today,* Vol. 49, No. 10, October 1993, pp. 189-193. *The World Today,* published by The Royal Institute of International Affairs. Reprinted by permission.

Russia. Belarus is heavily dependent on Russia for energy, industrial and other supplies; by staying within the rouble zone, it can purchase these goods at much cheaper prices. (It should be noted that Belarus' decision can also be partially attributed to the fact that it still lacks a real sense of nationhood and currently believes that accommodation with Russia is vital.)

The personnel gap

Another important feature of the current situation is the palpable need to develop professional cadres in much of the former Soviet Union. Under the Soviet system, officials outside Moscow simply were not responsible for making decisions or interacting with the international community. Their role was one of a bureaucratic administrative elite. Now that these former republics have become independent states, there is obviously a need for their governments to develop professional cadres in the areas of security policy, economics, diplomacy and so on. One of the urgent needs is to work more effectively with the international community. The other need is to set up governmental, legal and other structures to underpin the move towards political pluralism and the market economy.

One of the difficulties of developing new cadres is finding the personnel. Most of the talented young people prefer business opportunities (and money) to government service. As a result, there has been a reliance on the old cadres to fill the new positions. Indeed, in recent months emphasis has been placed on the experience that these old cadres can bring to the new governments, despite the fact that this experience is not relevant to efforts to create a market economy and institute other fundamental reforms. Nevertheless, in the case of Belarus, for example, it is argued that the experience of its leaders has provided the state with much greater stability than many of its neighbours. The same arguments were used in Ukraine in the case of Kuchma's appointment as Prime Minister. His industrial experience was touted as an important contributing factor in jump-starting the declining Ukrainian economy. In reality, however, the economy continues its downward spiral, partly because Kuchma has not been able to implement the painful reform measures necessary (although he is certainly not the only one to blame for this failure).

Within the context of cadres development, there is a role for the West to play, namely by providing technical assistance to help train personnel. Ukraine has indicated an interest in such assistance, and there are clearly many opportunities outside the Slavic states as well. Moreover, with the move towards greater decentralisation and regionalisation within Russia, there are regions in Russia itself – outside of Moscow – that also need to be able to develop professional cadres.

Despite the fact that the West Europeans, Koreans and others have been more involved in economic investment and are generally more visible, officials and the general public still perceive the United States as the leading player in virtually all areas of activity. But latterly the attitude towards the United States has reflected growing disillusionment. The United States has talked about large sums of money being made available to these new states, and the expectation was that this money would be quickly distributed. The blame for these dashed expectations can probably be laid on both sides. For its part, the United States certainly has not followed through on its promises expeditiously – if at all. Bureaucratic inertia

and uncertainty about the best way to use these funds has severely hampered its efforts. At the same time, it can be argued that the former Soviet states had unrealistic expectations of what could be accomplished, and how quickly. One obstacle here goes back to the previous point: the inexperience of these governments' elites in dealing with the international community and inadequate understanding of the functioning of other countries' bureaucracies.

More generally, in terms of increased anti-Americanism, this trend manifests itself most clearly and strongly in Moscow. This is partly attributable to the growing sense of disillusionment, but partly it is also due to the increased vociferousness of hardline nationalist forces which strongly oppose what they see as the Yeltsin government's overemphasis on relations with the West. Most troubling is that anti-Americanism and anti-Westernism are not limited to hardline elements. Thus, even among more moderate people, the argument can be heard that the West is taking advantage of Russia during its time of troubles and is trying to exploit its current weakness.

Looking to the future and possible constructive Western roles that will not necessarily require heavy financial investment, much can and needs to be done in the way of technical assistance. In the agricultural sector, assistance is needed in developing warehouses, preserving and storing food, developing transport networks to get the food to the consumers. In the industrial sector, assistance is needed in determining what industries can viably survive and what goods the market will actually support, and for developing supplier networks and infrastructure support in general. Perhaps most important, all forms of Western assistance and investment must look beyond the capitals of Moscow, Kiev and Minsk. It is only through greater regionalisation and decentralisation that the market economy and other fundamental reform can realistically take hold.

New decision-makers

A new feature of today's situation is the role of non-traditional actors. In other words, it is not necessarily government officials and policy analysts that are determining the course of events. The example of Lithuania's oil and gas supplies during the winter of 1992-93 provides a vivid illustration of this point. Although there are various versions of what happened and who is to blame – depending on whom one talks to – the facts are that Lithuania has been heavily dependent on Russia for its energy resources and deliveries of energy supplies largely ceased during this time. Many in Lithuania believed that Russia's actions were at least partly an attempt to influence Lithuania's elections, which were held 25 October 1992. The Russians rejected such accusations, explaining that they were simply demanding world prices, in hard currency, for their energy resources, and that Lithuania had not paid.

The Lithuanians, in turn, contended that they had paid the Russian government for some supplies that had still not been delivered, raising the question: if payments were made to the Russian government, did they reach the suppliers? One of the fundamental problems is that it is not the governments who are necessarily taking the decisions in such matters. Rather, it is, for example, energy suppliers and producers who ultimately set the policy, regardless of what agreements the governments may have reached.

This trend is also evident in the military security arena, particularly in the case of arms sales. Simply stated, there are a host of people and institutions involved in attempts to sell arms. There are official government agencies, including special groups set up within the ministries of defence, who have been entrusted with the responsibility of selling weapons abroad. Individual defence industries (both design and production facilities) have been trying to make their own deals.[1] Finally, there are also individual military personnel acting on their own, trying to sell anything from rifles to nuclear material.

Controversies over arms sales

It is the issue of arms sales and its vital role in the evolution of the former Soviet states (especially their conversion efforts) that can be singled out as the first specific military-related issue to be addressed. The troubling phenomenon of a multiplicity of actors involved in arms sales attempts, coupled with the questionable ability of the states to regulate the export of arms, presents serious challenges for the international community. Western criticism of, and concern about, these sales have provoked a certain amount of irritation on the part of the former Soviet states, as they question why the West has a right to sell weapons while they apparently do not.

In most cases, the argument can be made that the West has better regulatory mechanisms in place to prevent the proliferation of weapons, particularly to 'hot spots' in the world. To be fair, the new governments are trying to address this problem through new regulations and controls and have indicated that they do not aim to sell to renegade states, but it is not clear whether such intentions will always be observed. Indeed, the task of thwarting all individual attempts at illegal sales – in addition to regulating legal sales – remains a daunting one. Moreover, the increasingly strong military-industrial ties, especially between Russia and China, raise serious questions about overall international stability (particularly given the threat of China reselling technology and weapons to other countries).

On the question of the utility and appropriateness of arms sales, stated official positions differ, for example, between Russia and Ukraine. To date the Russian government has made no secret of the fact that it views arms sales as a legitimate means of financing efforts such as converting defence industries, providing money for social guarantees for military personnel and the like. One of the problems has been that the hard currency market for Russia's weapons has not necessarily proved as strong as Russian officials had hoped. Thus, whereas Mikhail Malei (the official in charge of Russia's conversion efforts) had originally projected $10bn worth of arms sales in 1992, which were specifically needed to fund the conversion process, actual sales were more in the range of $3bn.

Still, Russia has signed agreements totalling over $2bn with China, Iran and India, and the Foreign Economic Relations Minister, Sergei Glazev, expects arms sales to continue to account for 25 to 30 per cent of all Russia's industrial exports. Following President Yeltsin's visit to India in the spring of 1993, the question seems to be whether arms sales will now be pursued primarily as a way of maintaining weapons production at Russia's defence enterprises, and only secondarily as a source of income actually to convert many of these industries to civilian uses.[2]

In contrast to Russia's approach, Ukrainian officials assert that arms sales should not be the primary means of financing conversion; rather, they have established a conversion programme combining the use of market forces with government regulation. This is not to say, however, that Ukraine is not trying to pursue arms sales, and with some of the same countries as Russia. Both the shipbuilding and aircraft industries have been major components of Ukraine's economy. Yet according to the former Minister of Conversion, Viktor Antonov, the Ukrainian government has issued no production orders to the defence industries since January 1992.[3] Even with financial support from the government, success in arms sales abroad seems to be the only solution if these industries are to survive.

At this point, the fundamental problem for conversion to civilian production generally in the former Soviet Union is that these efforts are being determined by feasibility, not by market demands. To achieve significant advances in conversion, it will be necessary to determine what goods can actually be sold, rather than simply what the industries can produce. In terms of arms sales for the future, it should be anticipated that economics – above all the need for hard currency – will be the main driving force: political and ideological considerations will be of only secondary concern.

Who holds the nuclear key?

A second military-related issue is that of the continuing disputes over nuclear weapons. Statements by the Russian leadership and the military command of the Commonwealth of Independent States (CIS) have advocated that the Russian Ministry of Defence should be the one responsible for controlling strategic nuclear weapons, regardless of where they are located. Therefore, the Russian Ministry of Defence would have control even over those weapons that are still located in Kazakhstan, Ukraine and Belarus. There have been different reactions to this on the part of these three other states.

Belarus has already come to an agreement with Russia, whereby 30,000 troops stationed in Belarus – primarily strategic forces – have been placed directly under the control of the Russian Ministry of Defence. Furthermore, Belarus has sought to accelerate the process of nuclear withdrawal, and the Supreme Soviet Chairman, Stanislav Shushkevich, has announced that all nuclear weapons will be withdrawn from Belarus within two-and-a-half years rather then the seven years previously agreed to.

Ukraine, on the other hand, maintains that nuclear weapons control should remain under CIS command, as does Kazakhstan. Ukraine asserts administrative control over these forces (such as selecting the troops that serve in them), while operational control is to remain with the CIS. However, the dissolution of the CIS military command in June 1993 now appears to have given Russia de facto operational control. The Ukrainians regard Russia's attempts to exercise control over all nuclear weapons as yet another illustration of its intention to dominate the states of the former Soviet Union.

Ukraine's current tactic is to try to delay the removal of the 176 Intercontinental Ballistic Missiles (ICBMs) from its territory. To this effect it is seeking Western finance to dismantle the weapons itself. However, should the ICBMs eventually be moved to Russian soil, Ukraine stipulates that it must (a) receive at least some of the money from the sale of nuclear materials after the

ICBMs are destroyed, and that it must (b) receive security guarantees from the international community to protect it from future threats by another state, especially one holding nuclear weapons (namely, Russia).[4] It should also be noted that at least some Ukrainians see the continued possession of nuclear weapons as a means of asserting Ukraine's position in the world – that it is a country to be taken seriously.

In looking at future nuclear weapons issues, one question is whether Ukraine will become a non-nuclear state or whether it will retain some type of nuclear capability, even after it has eliminated the ICBMs. Indeed, as long as Ukraine defines its primary security threat as emanating from Russia, these ICBMs are of little use; rather, air-deliverable nuclear bombs would be much more in line with its requirements. The international community's pressure against Ukraine possessing a nuclear capability would, of course, be considerable; and while the current Ukrainian government appears to be using the nuclear weapons issue as a bargaining chip in its foreign and security policy, it has not rejected the idea of Ukraine ultimately becoming a non-nuclear state. The most likely near-outcome will be that Ukraine ratifies the Strategic Arms Reduction Treaty (START I) but not the Non-Proliferation Treaty.

In evaluating Ukraine's future prospects, however, at least two factors should be considered. First, among some of the more nationalistic forces – including those within the Ukrainian Parliament – an increasingly vocal minority has asserted the need for Ukraine to retain a nuclear deterrent, at least as long as Russia remains a nuclear power. Second, a great deal will depend on the future development of Ukrainian–Russian relations. What kind of political forces will be in power in each state? What kind of agreements might be reached, and what might be the level of accommodation between them?

A final consideration relates to the prospects for the ratification of the latest Strategic Arms Reduction Treaty (START II),which faces many obstacles before it can become a reality. First, of course, it will be necessary to implement START I, and so far it has not been ratified by Ukraine. Equally significant is the degree of opposition to START II within the Russian Supreme Soviet. Opponents argue that the Treaty is yet another example of the United States exploiting Russia's weakness; that it damages Russia's first-strike capability; and that it places Russia at a military disadvantage. Russian government officials themselves recognise that ratification will be a long and difficult process.

Levels of peacekeeping

The third military issue is the emerging role of the peacekeeping mission, especially for Russian military forces, and the rather ambiguous attitudes towards this mission.[5] Peacekeeping can be examined at three different levels of effort: within the international community, within the CIS, and within the Russian Federation itself.

International peacekeeping, under the auspices of the United Nations, the Conference on Security and Cooperation in Europe (CSCE) or some other multilateral institution, is commonly supported by security specialists and military officers. This is not to say that participation in a specific international peacekeeping mission – notably in former Yugoslavia – is not controversial.

Still, theoretically participation in peacekeeping missions is seen as an important vehicle for improving Russia's standing in the international community and for contributing to its integration into Europe. Furthermore, the armed forces have generally welcomed this role as providing them with a legitimate mission at a time when their purpose is being strongly debated.

The public's viewpoint is not necessarily so supportive. Some question the utility of Russia's involvement in areas that are perceived to be far from Russia's national interests (however they might be defined). There is also a general feeling that Russia's domestic concerns are so overwhelming and its finances so strained that additional duties along these lines are simply beyond its scope at this point.

Within the CIS, there have been agreements reached and certain procedures established for CIS peacekeeping. However, it is important to note that there has hardly been universal support within the CIS for a peacekeeping mission. In fact, one of the agreements reached in October 1992, outlining some of the procedures for peacekeeping, was signed only by Russia, Kazakhstan, Kyrgyzstan, Tajikistan, Armenia and Moldova.

Some of the key questions about CIS peacekeeping are, of course: who is be to protected, and what forces (namely, what nationality of forces) are going to be used to do this? The agreements stipulate that each of the signatories shall supply both military forces and military observers. However, in the case of the Tajik civil war, the Parliaments of Kyrgyzstan, Kazakhstan and Russia were reluctant to approve the dispatch of troops there. A peacekeeping force which was finally sent in March 1993 consisted only of Uzbek, Kazakh and Russian troops; Kyrgyzstan also sent troops, but President Akaev stressed that they were not to be considered part of the CIS peacekeeping mission, and they were actually deployed in Tajikistan less than one month before being withdrawn back to Kyrgyzstan.[6]

One broader question arising out of the CIS peacekeeping issue is Russia's motivations. It would be reasonable to suggest that at least some Russians see peacekeeping efforts as a way of preserving what empire they have (the Russian Federation as it currently exists) or, indeed, as a way of reconstructing some of what they have lost (the former Soviet Union). The difficulties of even what troops Russia would select for this purpose represent one of the dilemmas of this mission. For example, the participation of Russia's Fourteenth Army, stationed in Moldova as part of the peacekeeping force in the Moldova-Dniester conflict, raised considerable opposition among those trying to broker this conflict, since the Fourteenth Army has been actively supplying weapons to the Dniester insurgents and participating in some of the fighting. Moreover, the Fourteenth Army's commander, General Lebed, has recognised the 'Dniester Republic' as a legal entity and says his army belongs 'to the Dniester people'.[7]

This raises the more general issue of protection of the Russian diaspora throughout the former Soviet Union, which is frequently associated with the peacekeeping mission. The fact is that Yeltsin must seize and control the diaspora question because if he does not, it is the one issue that the hardline nationalists and reactionaries could exploit to gain more popularity with the Russian public at large. Some, such as the Presidential Council member, Sergei Karaganov, have suggested he can do so through advocating the protection of all human rights, not just those of the Russian diaspora.

The third level of 'peacekeeping' is within the Russian Federation itself. The key question here is what kind of forces Russia is going to use when Russia disintegrates, in which case the role would be one more of peacemaking than peacekeeping. With the creation of a specialised force for this mission, what will be the criteria for selecting personnel, what will be its national composition? It has already been determined that the basis for this force (as well as for meeting the greater demand for mobile forces in general) will be airborne troops; the peacekeeping troops will receive similar training to the airborne forces and they will both have their main base in the Volga Military District. The other important consideration is whether the Russian armed forces will actually be willing to act in this capacity within their own country's borders; to date they have done so in one region – North Ossetia.

A hierarchy of priorities

In conclusion, it is useful to highlight some of the security priorities for each of these three Slavic states and the vehicles they can use to pursue these priorities. Among all three Slavic states there are some overarching security concerns, such as the provision of social guarantees for the armed forces, the morale of the officer corps, budgetary constraints and continuing personnel problems (such as the unreliability of soldiers, draft evasion and hazing). While it may have been expected that at least some of the personnel difficulties would have subsided with the formation of national armies (thereby eliminating many of the ethnic problems associated with the Soviet military system), significant improvements have not been evident.

Looking at Ukraine, it is possible to identify two key priorities. First, it seeks to become accepted into the Western international community. Second, it wants to establish and consolidate relations with Russia on the basis of equality between two independent states (in other words, Russia must recognise that Ukraine is a distinct and separate entity, not an appendage of Russia or any structure that may emerge from the ashes of the old Soviet Union).

Ukraine is looking to several vehicles to implement these priorities. For integration with the West, a great deal of reliance is placed on collective security arrangements, although it is also generally appreciated that such arrangements will not be forthcoming unless Ukraine is able to manage its relations with Russia. Simply stated, Ukraine cannot afford to have a hostile relationship with Russia if it seeks integration with the West. Furthermore, some Ukrainians believe that their country has an important role to play as a bridge between Russia and the West, arguing that Ukraine is more of a Western nation than Russia and can therefore act as a link between the two. Ukraine seeks to manage its relationship with Russia largely through contacts with the West as well.

From its perspective, it is important for the United States to remain within Europe, in part because the United States is seen as the one country that can bring adequate pressure to bear on Russia when necessary, and a continued American presence in Europe indicates to Ukraine that the United States will remain involved (not retreating into isolationism).

More generally, there is a feeling that the international community must be prepared to play a role when Ukraine and Russia prove incapable of solving a problem on their own. Having identified these vehicles, one of the questions for Ukraine is whether its security interests might not be better served by emphasising bilateral relationships with various European and other countries, rather than by continuing its current emphasis on multilateral institutions.

In the case of Belarus, its paramount priority today is stability. A vital element of this stability is to ensure that the armed forces stationed in Belarus are provided with the necessary social guarantees. This is, in fact, a legitimate concern since the ratio of military personnel to civilians is much higher in Belarus than in any other former Soviet state. Particularly from the current leadership's perspective, the main vehicle for ensuring stability lies in accommodation with Russia, as evident in the decision to join the collective security treaty. At least for the moment, Belarus is not necessarily trying to assert its role as an independent state; it is more like an appendage of Russia.

Russia's top security concerns and priorities are to prevent the Russian Federation's own disintegration, to protect the rights of the Russian diaspora (and those of other minorities), to cope with instability on its own borders and in the 'near abroad', and to try to counter fears that the others in the former Soviet Union are trying to isolate Russia from the rest of the international community.

Peacekeeping is one of the key vehicles that Russia is likely to use in addressing these concerns. In some cases, it might seek peacekeeping with the international community, at other times it could be peacekeeping within the framework of the CIS, and sometimes Russia might undertake these efforts on its own. One of the key questions for Russia's future foreign and security policy is whether it will opt for an essentially Atlanticist orientation, a Eurasian orientation, or isolationism.

NOTES

1. Not all foreign sales efforts, of course, are focused on weapons sales. For example, the Milcoyan Design Bureau has reached an agreement with Dassault to manufacture horizontal tail sections for Dassault's Falcon business jets. The production of just one tail section per month is currently sufficient to meet the company's entire payroll for that month. This was discussed by Aleksandr Velovich at the Institute for Defence Analyses, 11 December 1992, in a presentation on the changes within the Russian defence industry. See 'IDA Seminar Series on Changes in the Former Soviet Union', December 1992 issue.
2. This point is discussed further in Stephen Foye, 'Russian Arms Exports after the Cold War', *RFE/RL Research Report*, Vol.2, No 13, 26 March 1993, p. 60.
3. As discussed at the Institute for Defence Analyses, 17 November 1992. See *ibid*, November 1992 issue.
4. In an attempt to assuage this concern, in January 1993 – and subsequently – Yeltsin offered President Kravchuk a guarantee to defend Ukraine from military attacks, including a nuclear one, if Ukraine eliminates nuclear weapons currently in Ukraine and becomes a non-nuclear state. See Margaret Shapiro, 'Ukraine Gets Defence Offer from Yeltsin', *Washington Post*, 16 January 1993, p. A14.
5. While Ukraine is participating in some international peacekeeping efforts, it is Russia that is dealt with here, since it really faces the greatest range of possible peacekeeping roles.
6. For more detail on the peacekeeping mission in the CIS, see Susan L. Clark, 'Russia in a Peacekeeping Role'. Paper presented at the United States Institute of Peace Conference on *The Emerging National Security Doctrine of a New Russia*, March 1993 (publication forthcoming).
7. For more detail on the Fourteenth Army in Moldova, see Vladimir Socor, 'Russia's Fourteenth Army and the Insurgency in Eastern Moldova', *RFE/IRL Research Report*, Vol. 1, No 36, 11 September 1992, pp. 41-48, at 46.

Will Russia disintegrate into Bantustans?

MAP OF THE RUSSIAN FEDERATION

Map supplied by Bogdan Szajkowski.

Bogdan Szajkowski

Bogdan Szajkowski is a Senior Lecturer in Politics at the University of Exeter specialising in social and political conflicts and in ethnic and nationality issues in the former Soviet Union and Central and Eastern Europe. He is the author of numerous books and articles on the former Communist countries. His most recent book, Encyclopedia of Conflicts and Flashpoints in the Former Soviet Union and Central and Eastern Europe, *will be published by Longman.*

Will the Soviet Union Survive until 1984? was the title of a somewhat prophetic book by Andrei Amalrik, published in 1970. Had he lived until 1991, he would have witnessed the final disintegration of the Soviet Union. Today, only two years later, paraphrasing Amalrik we must ask: Will Russia be fragmented into numerous smaller units, the equivalent of South Africa's old Bantustans? The signs are that the processes are set for the 'Bantustanisation' of the once-powerful Federation.

The past four years have seen the emergence of a multitude of conflicts and flashpoints in the former Soviet Union. A map prepared by the Office of the Geographer of the United States at the beginning of 1990 listed some 40 ethno-territorial conflicts in the Soviet Union. By March 1991, some 80 conflicts had been identified by a Russian academic, Vladimir A. Kolossov. By February 1992, Kolossov had listed 164 conflicts affecting 70 per cent of the territory of the former Soviet Union.[1] Today both publications are already substantially out of date. My own research suggests over 204 ethno-territorial conflicts in the former Soviet Union.[2]

The Soviet Union officially ceased to exist on 8 December 1991, when the leaders of Russia, Ukraine and Belarus unilater-

ally abrogated the Union Treaty of 1922 and created the amorphous Commonwealth of Independent States (CIS). This was the first stage in the disintegration of the Bolshevik empire.

Thereafter trends were set for the second stage – the disintegration of the former constituent republics. It is worth bearing in mind that, while the first stage of disintegration proceeded along the lines of existing borders and the titular majority of a particular republic, the second and subsequent stages are delineated along ethnic lines without clearly defined or indeed previously acknowledged (identifiable) borders.

The demands for independence of the so-called Transdniestr Republic and the Gagauz Republic fractured the territorial and political cohesion of the Moldovan Republic and set a precedent for future divisions accompanied by civil wars and militarisation of a number of areas. The disintegration of Georgia and, more recently, of Tajikistan, followed this route. To this list can also be added Karakalpakia, an autonomous republic on the territory of Uzbekistan, whose Supreme Soviet on 10 April 1993 approved a new Constitution under which the territory will become a sovereign parliamentary republic within Uzbekistan.

The third stage is the disintegration of the Russian Federation. The trend for the forth stage of further disintegration of the Federation's components into even smaller entities is already clearly detectable.

Ethno-territorial conflicts

Although the Soviet Union was a multinational state, only 67 nations out of the 103 recorded in the 1989 census had their own autonomous areas. As early as 1918, Lenin set out the framework for the ethno-territorial division of the Soviet state. According to him, there could be no norm which would ensure the right of all ethnic groups to their own autonomous territories. Rather, autonomous and ordinary districts should be united for economic

From *The World Today,* Vol. 49, Nos. 8-9, August/September 1993, pp. 172-176. *The World Today,* published by The Royal Institute of International Affairs. Reprinted by permission.

purposes in large autonomous regions (*krays*). Consequently, internal divisions of the former Soviet Union were purely administrative; ethnic demarcations seldom corresponded to the ethnic composition of a particular area. Frequent changes in the political-territorial organisation were used mainly for the centralised control and direction of the economy and society. The residues of this Leninist policy are still with us today.[3]

Between 1941 and 1957 repeated changes in the national-territorial organisation of the Soviet Union were made. In 1941-44, seven peoples accused of collaborating with the German occupiers were deprived of their autonomous status and deported to Siberia, Kazakhstan and Kyrgyzstan. The claims of the deported peoples (14 altogether) for the restoration of the boundaries of their states now have a legal basis in addition to their historical and moral foundations. In 1990, the Supreme Soviet of the Russian Federation adopted a special resolution on justice for deported peoples. One of the main points envisages the reconstitution of their national-territorial units with the boundaries which existed on the day of their deportation. But how, in practical terms, is that to be implemented, and what would be the political consequences? What rights do the titular peoples have to their designated territories if their boundaries are legitimised only by Soviet power, which no longer exists?[4]

The catastrophic decline of the Russian economy has had substantial negative consequences for Russia's state sovereignty. The recently published data on the socio-economic situation during the first quarter of 1993 make grim reading indeed.[5] The 19 per cent drop in industrial production during the first quarter, compared with the same period in 1992, has been accompanied by a 193 per cent inflation rate, compared with December last year. The percentage of unprofitable enterprises in all sectors of the national economy rose to 21, compared with 17 per cent last December. The highest proportional share of unprofitable enterprises (between 41-47 per cent) was recorded in the republics of Tuva and Sakha (Yakutia), the Magadan *oblast* and the Chukotka *okrug*. By the end of March 1993, one per cent (1.1m persons) of the total labour force of Russia had been registered as unemployed. Some 38 per cent of the unemployed are young people under 30 years of age. One in every three residents of Russia now has a per capita income below the minimum subsistence level. At the same time there has been a sharp increase in crime – 12 per cent up on the first quarter of 1992 – with only 45 per cent of reported crimes solved.

Communist collectivism and ethnicity

The common denominator for potentially the most explosive conflicts is the intertwining between Communist collectivism and ethnicity. One of the most important aspects of the operation of Communism was the collective nature of the system. Individual rights (including human, civil and property rights) were subjugated to the collective and controlled by the Communist party-state. The system not only negated the individual but, more important, used the oppressive apparatus in order to enforce compliance with collective (party-state) values, structures and procedures. Communist collectivism reinforced group rather than individual identity, but at the same time offered a comfortable net of social and political arrangements. There were few if any choices to be made, the answers were all but supplied, little

if any exercise of individual responsibility was required. The persistence of the political culture of collectivism remains one of the main obstacles to the effective transformation of the former Communist societies. It is also the main factor in the re-emergence of the ethnic conflicts.

There are both objective and subjective elements in the concept of ethnicity.[6] The objective elements cover characteristics which are actually held in common – kinship, physical appearance, culture, language, religion and so on. Some combination of these characteristics, but not necessarily all, would have to be present for a group of people to qualify as an ethnic grouping. The subjective elements rest on the feeling of community. What is important here is the representations which a group has of itself – regardless of whether those representations are actually correct or not. 'The myth can be potent, and it is the group's representations of itself that are important.'[7]

I should like to stress the importance of the subjective elements. Ethnic groups can only be understood in terms of boundary creation and maintenance. In such cases a common culture is not a defining characteristic of an ethnic grouping; it may, in fact, come into existence as a result of a particular grouping asserting its own position. Cultural features are used by ethnic groupings to mark the groupings' boundaries. Similarly, notions of kinship can be projected and/or constructed so as to give greater body to the feelings of commonality within the grouping. The retreat into ethnic socio-political boundaries and values offers safety at turbulent times. In post-Communist Russia, as elsewhere in the former Communist countries, it has become one of the most poignant socio-political forms of organisations and threats.

The decline of presidential authority

The continuous power struggle in the centre and, in particular, the confrontation between the Russian President on the one hand and the Supreme Soviet and the Congress of the People's Deputies on the other, has already had a very adverse effect on the regions.

One of the more recent examples comes from the Rostov *oblast*, where the local soviet abolished on 30 April 1993 the post of the representative of the Russian President. The representative and his staff were told to vacate their offices within a week and stop their activities. A serious conflict between the Supreme Soviet of Mordova and President Yeltsin (and thus the Russian Federation) erupted in April 1993 over the right of the Federation's President to interfere in the republic's power structure. On 2 April the republic's Supreme Soviet voted (by 116 votes to 37) to abolish the position of President of the Mordovan Soviet Socialist Republic. The deputies blamed the incumbent, Vasiliy Guslyannikov, for current economic hardships and accused him of abusing his position and attempting to create one-man rule. In turn, Boris Yeltsin on 8 April issued a decree confirming the powers of Guslyannikov. The decree has been seen in Mordova as a violation of Article 78 of the Constitution of the Russian Federation and Article 3 of the Federation Treaty which state that federal power may not intervene in the organisation of the republics' power structures. On 20 April Mordova's Supreme Soviet, ignoring the presidential decree, dismissed the government and created a new Council of Ministers.[8]

The growing disenchantment of the regions with the Russian

Federation and President Yeltsin's policies were also reflected in the voting figures during the referendum of 25 April 1993.[9] In 10 of the 19 republics – Adygeya, Bashkortostan, Altay, Dagestan, Ingushetia, Kabarda-Balkaria, Karachay-Cherkessia, Mari-El, Mordova and Chuvashia – Yeltsin failed to win a vote of confidence from the majority of voters.[10] It is interesting to note that several major *oblasts* and *okrugs* voted against the President. In the European part of Russia, voters in Belgorod, Bryansk, Kursk, Lipetsk, Orel, Penza, Pskov, Ryazan, Saratov, Smolensk, Tambov and Ulyanov *oblasts* expressed lack of confidence in Yeltsin. Beyond the Urals, voters in Altay *kray*, Admur and Chita *oblasts* and the Aga-Buryat and Ust-Orda Buryat autonomous *okrugs* also failed to deliver a vote of confidence.[11]

Crisis of statehood

The population's confidence in the authority of the state is extremely low. Laws that have been adopted are inoperative. There is increasingly evidence of a crisis of authority and of deepening antagonism between the executive and representative bodies.

As a consequence of the Russian Federation's inability to develop its own concept of state formation and bringing the federal mechanisms into operation, authorities in some of the republics and in *krays* and *oblasts* have been quite successful in building up their power structures based on the efficient interaction of local sources of power. Against the backdrop of the constant weakening of presidential and federal powers and the increasing turmoil in Moscow, local administrations have become guarantors of stability and formed the nuclei of state formation. There has been growing evidence that local soviets are slowly paralysing presidential power and breaking down the unity of executive power.

By now, many of Russia's regions have elected their own heads of administration. Previously, these had been appointed by President Yeltsin. The new heads have become responsible to the local electorate and are primarily influenced by local factors and conditions. Their legitimacy is based mainly on local constituencies rather than on central, federal authorities. If they are to survive in their posts they must above all respond to local demands for greater economic and political autonomy. The resolution of the local agenda – social/ethnical problems, border adjustments and so on – are often at variance with the interests of the Federation and its structures. The elected heads of local administration are unlikely to support the federal authorities (including the President) for long.

In many respects we are seeing the repetition of the 'Gorbachev delusion'. Here was a man confident that he was running *perestroika*, but his *perestroika* operated only in the centre and was executed through presidential decrees. Meanwhile, the peripheries and local party bosses strengthened their own powers and developed and slowly put into operation their own ideas reflecting local needs and aspirations.

The inoperability of the Federation Treaty

The Russian Federation technically consists of 18 union republics and 69 other subjects of the Federation (6 *krays*, 51 *oblasts*, 1 autonomous *oblast* and 11 autonomous *okrugs*). Eighteen of the 20 republics identified in the Federation Treaty[12] and invited to sign the Treaty did, in fact, put their signatures on the document on 31 March 1992.[13] Tatarstan and Checheno-Ingushetia refused to sign. Subsequently, Checheno-Ingushetia split into two separate entities. The Ingush Republic, created by the decision of the Russian Parliament on 4 June 1992, has so far not signed.

The Federation Treaty offered, at least in principle, the opportunity to conclude additional agreements on the re-allocation and mutual delegation of powers. More than a year after its signing, hardly any of the Treaty's provisions have been implemented.[14] The proclamation of norms has not been followed by appropriate additional legal provisions which would allow the exercise of rights granted in the Treaty. According to the Chairman of the Soviet of Nationalities of the Supreme Soviet, Ramazan Abdulatipov, a majority of the subjects of the Federation are dissatisfied with the way the Treaty is being executed.

The central and most contentious issue is that of the status of the components of the Federation and consequently the rights and obligations of the Union republics vis-à-vis the Federation, and similarly the rights of *krays*, *oblasts* and *okrugs* vis-à-vis the republics and the Federation.

The Treaty appears to hold the prospect for all the 87 subjects of the Federation to be given the rights and status of Union republics. Many of the *krays* and *oblasts* and several autonomous *okrugs* have been demanding political and economic rights equal to those of the republics. However, neither the federal nor the republican authorities are willing to accede to these demands, increasingly afraid of the loss of economic and political control and the possibility of demands for a greater degree of political independence.

After a year of confusion over the precise rights and obligations of the subjects of the Federation, President Yeltsin has only recently indicated his opposition to *krays* and *oblasts* acquiring the constitutional right to issue their own laws.[15] He has also spoken against the equality of all the subjects of the Federation as regards political rights. Not only do his pronouncements contradict the spirit of the Federation Treaty, but in many cases they come too late since many of the subjects of the Federation have already adopted a variety of their own legal provisions, which they see as being within their sphere of competence.

In the absence of any effective execution of the Treaty provisions, the republics and regions want to replace the federal authority, a demand which is fiercely opposed by the centre. The absence of a clear demarcation of powers between the centre and the regions is contributing to the weakening of state authority and the integrity of the Federation. For as long as the shape of the new federal structure and the prerogatives of its constituent parts remain unclear, problems of constitutional authority and delineation of prerogatives will, more likely than not, lead to a series of escalating conflicts.

The republics of Tatarstan and Yakutia-Sakha have drafted their own Constitutions. That of Tatarstan ignores the existence of the Russian Federation, while the Yakut version allots only defence and boundary protection to the federal level. There are numerous claims for the partition of 'double republics'. Given the incredibly complex pattern of ethnic distributions, no national and/or linguistic boundary can be wholly satisfactory to all parties. The Yakuts, for example, refer to the boundary of Yakutia as it was in the early nineteenth century, Tatarstan to that before 1552. They also express concern for their 'blood brothers living abroad', claiming the right to annex their settlement areas or at least to establish autonomous territories for them.[16]

On 30 April 1993, **Kalmykia** became a presidential republic within the Russian Federation, when deputies voted by an overwhelming majority to dissolve the Supreme Soviet and replace it with a 25-member 'professional' Parliament. They also abolished the local soviets throughout the country. The decision followed the election, on 11 April, of Kirsan Ilyumzhinov, a 30-year-old multimillionaire, as President of the republic. Subsequently, Ilyumzhinov imposed direct rule through a system of personal representatives in whom he vested special powers. The new President has emphasised the need for economic autonomy from Russia. It is, however, hard to imagine that such an autonomy can be achieved without the loosening and eventual severance of federal links with Russia.

The **Tuva** Supreme Soviet defied the Russian Federation on 11 May 1993 and amended the republican constitution to include the right to self-determination and the right to secede from Russia.[17] It was decided that a new constitution would be debated by the Parliament in June. Nationalists in the republic have long argued that Tuva's incorporation into the Soviet Union was no more legal than that of the Baltic states. Given that two-thirds of the population is Tuvin, secession has become an achievable option.

Bashkortostan has been in serious dispute with the Russian Federation for over 18 months now. In the spring of 1992, the republic's Supreme Soviet demanded of the Russian leadership that 30 per cent of Bashkortostan's industrial output should remain in the republic. The republic signed, albeit with serious reservations, the Federation Treaty establishing the Russian Federation. Bashkortostan insisted that a special appendix should be added to the Treaty. In it, the republic proclaimed that land minerals, natural and other resources (including oil, of which Bashkortostan is a major producer) on its territory are the property of its population and not of the Federation. It declared that issues related to the utilisation of its resources will be regulated by Bashkir law and agreements with the federal government. The republic has also proclaimed itself an 'independent participant in international law and foreign economic relations, except areas it has voluntarily delegated to the Russian Federation'.

In April 1993, Bashkortostan's Parliament approved a question to be put to a republic-wide referendum: 'Do you agree that the Republic of Bashkortostan must have economic independence and treaty-based relations with the Russian Federation and Appendix to it, in the interests of all the peoples of the Republic of Bashkortostan?' The wording of the question predetermines the outcome of the voting – few if any of the voters in the republic are likely to object to greater economic independence. In practice it means the freedom to export its products and maintain its own tax system, whereby Bashkortostan remits fixed payments to the Russian Federation budget, keeping the rest for itself. What is more significant, however, is that the republic's authorities intend to place any agreement with Russia on 'treaty-based relations', i.e., relations between states. By asserting at the referendum the

need for treaty-based relations, the Bashkir authorities have put pressure on Moscow to admit that Bashkortostan has a special status within the Federation. That precedent can now be followed by any of the Federation's units.

Tatarstan declared its sovereignty on 30 August 1990. On 21 February 1992 the Parliament of Tatarstan decided to hold a referendum on the status of the republic. Four million voters were asked: 'Do you agree that the Republic of Tatarstan is a sovereign state, a subject of international law, building its relations with the Russian Federation and other republics (states) on the basis of fair treaties?' The referendum took place on 21 March 1992, despite the ruling of Russia's Constitutional Court that it was unlawful. The results confirmed the earlier decision on the declaration of sovereignty of the Tatar state.

In November 1992, the Parliament of Tatarstan adopted a new Constitution which clearly defined the powers, sovereignty and independence of the republic. At the same time the deputies insisted on associated membership for Tatarstan of the Russian Federation – something that is not envisaged by the Federation Treaty. After the adoption of the Constitution, Moscow faced the dilemma of whether to sign a treaty with Tatarstan as an equal partner, thus creating a political precedent, or whether to treat the republic as an integral part of Russia, which Tatarstan refused to acknowledge. The second option could have far-reaching economic, military and political repercussions.

The nationalist and secessionist movement in Tatarstan continues to grow in strength. Eleven organisations and movements in the republic advocate the complete independence of Tatarstan. In an appeal issued on 13 April 1993 they called for a boycott of the all-Russia referendum on 25 April, arguing that Tatarstan had never voluntarily been a part of Russia and that the people of Tatarstan did not need a referendum into which the imperial forces wanted to drag them.[18]

On 11 May 1993, during President Mintimer Shaimiev's visit to Budapest, Tatarstan, in pursuit of its independent foreign and economic policy, signed an economic cooperation agreement with Hungary for 1993-98. Under the agreement Tatarstan will deliver 1.5m tons of crude oil per year to Hungary and in return receive industrial and agricultural products. It was the first such agreement negotiated between Tatarstan and a foreign country. In 1992 trade turnover between the two countries exceeded $235m.

The **Tyumen** region, rich in oil and natural gas, refused to sign the Federation Treaty in March 1992 and is now threatened with the secession of two of its autonomous *okrugs*: Khanty-Mansi and Yamalo-Nenets, both of which want to acquire the status of separate republics. Secession of the two *okrugs* would reduce the area of the Tyumen region from 1.4m sq km to a mere 161.000 sq km and deprive it of much of its resources and industry.

The division of the Magadan *oblast* and the creation of the **Chukot** Republic became a reality when, on 11 May 1993, the Constitutional Court of the Russian Federation decided that the separation of the Chukchee autonomous *okrug* from the Magadan *oblast* was in accordance with the Russian Constitution. In 1989 the Chukchee accounted for only 7.3 per cent of the *okrug*'s population, while Russians and Ukrainians made up 83 per cent. In September 1990, the *okrug*'s soviet proclaimed itself an autonomous republic, and in March 1991 it decided to separate from the *oblast*. Magadan's authorities contended that such a decision could be taken after a referendum had been held. The Court's decision opens the way for the secession of numerous other *okrugs* throughout the Russian Federation.

concept of the nation-state, sovereignty, self-determination, nation and borders.

Conclusions

The argument in this article is based on two broad assumptions. The first is that the residues of Communism will remain for a long time to come. It has proved relatively easy to carry out structural transformation in the former Soviet Union in order to achieve the edifices of liberal democracy. However, their functioning is more often than not at variance with liberal democratic principles and values. These will be able to take root only with generational change. The symbiotic relationship between Communist collectivism and ethnicity will continue to dominate the wider political agenda. It is the most difficult aspect to tackle because it reflects the basic, and in some sense perhaps irrational, feelings of individual and group insecurity.

At the same time, however, it has in political and strategic terms become the avenue for the expression of political, economic and social aspirations which had been denied so far. The substantial credibility gap which exists between the old structural (federal) arrangements and the demands of an essentially new post-Communist situation can only be bridged by drastic action: either by the dismantling of the old structure or through their fundamental modification. So far there has been little, if any, evidence of either.

Russia still wants to remain a federation rather than, for example, a confederation, a commonwealth or a community of nations. The old Tsarist slogan 'Russia is indivisible' is used as a rallying point by new democrats and old Communists alike. In one important respect the new Federation Treaty is even more reactionary than the 1922 Union Treaty, which contained at least a token provision for secession from the Union. The new Treaty does not. According to it, the territory of the Federation is integral and inalienable. The spectre of the disintegration of Russia is indeed threatening, but it is a progressive reality. The way this reality is dealt with in the long term will determine the stability of international relations.

The second assumption is that there are two incompatible processes taking place in Western Europe, on the one hand, and the former Soviet Union and Central and Eastern Europe, on the other. For four decades now the West European agenda has been dominated by integration in political, economic and strategic terms. This has been a long and arduous process based, first, on the clear identification of separate interests and, second, on the development of common strategies and goals. The East is now only at the stage of identifying separate interests. Integration may follow in due course, but if it is forced or artificially accelerated it will inevitably be full of cracks and consequent instabilities.

Perhaps one of the most important lessons to be learned from the historical experience of the former Soviet Union, and from the tragic events in former Yugoslavia, is that the federal organisation of the state and the multinational structure of its population are quite different things. There is an urgent need to re-examine our well-accepted analytical and methodological tools such as the

NOTES

1. Vladimir A. Kolossov, *Ethno-Territorial Conflicts and Boundaries in the Former Soviet Union* (University of Durham, International Boundaries Research Unit, 1992), p. 3.
2. Bogdan Szajkowski, *Encyclopedia of Conflicts and Flashpoints in the Former Soviet Union and Central and Eastern Europe* (London: Longman, December 1993).
3. Vladimir A. Kolossov, *op. cit.*, p. 10.
4. *Ibid.*, p. 12.
5. For details, see 'The socio-economic situation and the development of economic reforms in the Russian Federation in the first quarter of 1993', *Ekonomika i Zhizn*, No 17, May 1993.
6. Bogdan Szajkowski and Tim Niblock, 'Islam and Ethnicity in Eastern Europe'. Paper presented to the International Conference on Moslem Minorities/ Communities in Post-bipolar Europe' at the Saints Cyril and Metodij University, Skopje, Macedonia. April 1993, pp. 2-3.
7. Eliezer Ben-Rafael and Stephen Sharot, *Ethnicity, Religion and Class in Israeli Society* (Cambridge: Cambridge University Press, 1991), p. 6.
8. BBC SWB, SU/1676 B/5, 30 April 1993.
9. Of the 107.3m eligible voters in the Russian Federation, 69.2m participated in the referendum. Of them, 58.7 per cent had confidence in President Yeltsin; 53 per cent approved of his economic reforms; 31.7 per cent wanted early presidential elections; and 43.1 per cent favoured early parliamentary elections. Under the conditions set out by the Congress of People's Deputies and the Constitutional Court, the last two questions were not passed since they attracted less than half of the potential votes.
10. Only 2.7 per cent of voters in Ingushetia, 14.3 per cent in Dagestan, 25.9 per cent in Karachay-Cherkessia and 35.8 per cent in Kabarda-Balkaria voted 'yes' in answer to the question: 'Do you trust the President?'. BBC SWB, SU/1675 B/2, 29 April 1993; and BBC SWB, SU/1680 B/3, 5 May 1993.
11. BBC SWB, SU/1675 B/2, 29 April 1993. Interestingly, the referendum also showed considerable dissatisfaction with Yeltsin and his policies among the Russians living outside the Russian Federation. For example, of the eligible Russian citizens residing in Estonia, only 27.9 per cent of those voting expressed confidence in the President, with 71.3 per cent voting against. 72.6 per cent rejected the reforms; some 70.3 per cent supported early presidential elections, with 28.3 per cent against; and 50.3 per cent backed early parliamentary elections, with 48.7 per cent against. Of the 4,525 Russian citizens in Latvia who participated in the referendum, 21 per cent voted 'yes' and 78 per cent 'no' on the question of confidence in the President; 19.5 per cent voted 'yes' and 80 per cent 'no' in support of reform policy; 79 per cent voted 'yes' and 19 per cent 'no' on presidential elections; and 40 per cent voted 'yes' and 59 per cent 'no' on the question of fresh elections to the Russian Parliament. BBC SWB, SU/1674 C/5, 28 April 1993.
12. The Federation Treaty replaced the Union Treaty of 29 December 1922, which was abrogated by Russia, Belarus and Ukraine on 8 December 1991 when the three countries created the Commonwealth of Independent States (CIS).
13. The Treaty was signed by the Russian Federation, the Soviet Socialist Republic of Adygeva, the Republic of Bashkortostan, the Buryat Soviet Socialist Republic, the Republic of Gornyy Altay, the Republic of Dagestan, the Kabardin-Balkar Republic, the Republic of Kalmykia-Khalmg Tangch, the Republic of Karachay-Cherkessia, the Republic of Karelia, the Komi Soviet Socialist Republic, the Republic of Mari El, the Mordova Soviet Socialist Republic, the North Ossetian Soviet Socialist Republic, the Republic of Sakha (Yakutia), the Republic of Tuva, the Udmurt Republic, the Republic of Khakassia and the Chuvash Republic.
14. See, for example, an interview with the Chairman of the Soviet of Nationalities of the Supreme Soviet, Ramazan Abdulatipov. BBC SWB, SU/1656 B/5, 6 April 1993.
15. See Yeltsin's address to the Council of Heads of Administration of *Krays*, *Oblasts* and Autonomous *Okrugs* within Russia on 28 May 1993. BBC SWB, SU/1701 B/1, 29 May 1993.
16. Even in Kazakhstan, with its extremely mixed population and relative tolerance, the legislators wish to extend citizenship to all Kazakhs living 'abroad'.
17. Tuva enjoyed at least nominal independence between 12 August 1921 and 11 October 1944, when it was incorporated into the Soviet Union.
18. *Izvestia*, 13 April 1993.

Europe

- **Western Europe (Articles 13–16)**
- **Central Europe (Articles 17–20)**

Uncertainty in Europe is greater than at any time since World War II. There are conflicts over economic integration and expansion of the Economic Community (EC), conflicts with the United States on trade and security issues, disagreements over how best to cope with the dislocations created by the collapse of communism, developments in the former republics of the Soviet Union, and a continuing conflict in the Balkans. These disagreements affect relationships between the United States and Western European allies. Some states in Central and Southern Europe splinter into smaller units, while some attempt to consolidate into something larger. The opposing pressures create new problems and tensions for the Atlantic alliance and for the independent countries of Central Europe.

The lack of a coordinated European or NATO intervention in the former Yugoslavia painfully underscores the ambivalence on both sides of the Atlantic. The United States wonders about its role in Europe, while Europeans consider the painful fact that the idea of a common European defense is an illusion. NATO's identity crisis is highlighted by a lack of agreement about its purpose, the nature of future security threats, or future membership. European members of NATO reduced the number of forces assigned to NATO in many cases by more than 50 percent. The United States, with approximately 150,000 troops stationed in Europe, plans to make a 50 percent reduction by the mid-1990s. Budgetary or political pressures, however, could reduce the American military presence in Europe even more rapidly.

Instead of pursuing common defense and political policies, many members of the European Community attempt to disentangle their national and collective interests at the very time that countries in Central Europe and some of the former Soviet Union republics are trying to join NATO. The U.S. Partnership for Peace proposal, signed in early 1994, was one attempt to adapt NATO to current conditions in Europe, but as Henrik Bering-Jensen explains in "Redefined NATO Faces Growing Pains," this may be a difficult task for a cold war institution. While recent events in Russia cause former Warsaw pact nations to redouble their efforts to obtain NATO security guarantees, European and American leaders divide on the issue of an expanded NATO and, in 1994, Boris Yeltsin complicated this idea by declaring that Russia must be the first new member admitted to an enlarged NATO.

Progress toward a more integrated Europe was slowed by a number of events and trends in the 1990s. At the 1991 Maastricht Summit, the 12 members of the Economic Community agreed to an ambitious timetable for economic integration. Public opposition surfaced rapidly throughout Europe, tapping a widespread belief that the Maastricht Treaty attempted to do too much too soon.

Although EC member governments managed to secure domestic support for the creation of a single economic market and agreed to change the name of the organization to the European Union, meaningful progress towards integration was markedly slowed in 1993 by the collapse of the European currency system (EMS). In "Reinventing the Politics of Europe," Anthony Hartley discusses why the European community is at the beginning of a long but uncertain historical process. While progress toward an integrated European union may take a long time, the momentum toward further European integration is not exhausted. Instead, the focus has shifted to the pursuit of policies more suitable to a looser but larger confederation of 15 states with the incorporation of Australia, Sweden, and Finland by the end of 1994.

Historians may cite 1990 as the high point in the U.S.–German relationship, as these two key partners in the Atlantic alliance cooperated closely during the unification process, in negotiations with the former Soviet Union, and in multilateral arms control. However, disagreements among the two have repeatedly surfaced in recent years over appropriate coalition policies during the Gulf War, EC trading practices, the interest rate policy of the Bundesbank, and the future of international peacekeeping in the Balkans and in Somalia.

A redefinition of national interests by Germany and other Western European states is fueled by political realities and the costs of the collapse of communism in Eastern Europe, in the former USSR, and in the former Democratic Republic of Germany. Today, after several years' experience as a reunified state, Germany is still facing a tangle of questions about its identity and its capacity to change. As Marc Fisher notes in "Searching for Identity, Germany Struggles with Its History," Germany faces a choice in the coming years between right-wing nationalism, left-wing denial of nationhood, or a middle position. Answers to the identity question may be a long time coming.

One common response to changing conditions adopted by Germany and most Western European countries has been a distinct shift in immigration policies in an effort to keep out foreigners. In "Europe Slams the Door," Bruce W. Nelan describes recent policy changes designed to limit immigration. The United Nations estimates that between 5 and 10 million people plan to leave Eastern Europe and the former Soviet Union. Over half these migrants hope to head for Germany!

The high cost of German unification, the continuing surge of immigrants, global recession, and technological changes may have dashed hopes for economic growth and new jobs throughout Europe. Instead, xenophobia, nationalism, widespread disillusionment, and political alienation are fueling a sense of malaise across the continent. This atmosphere is compounded by the problems created in former Central European communist states from Poland to Russia, which are attempting to make a transformation without a conceptual model. In "The Great Transformation," Zbigniew Brzezinski summarizes some of the lessons learned since the collapse of communism, and relates these lessons to current Western aid policies and probable trends over the next decade.

While each of the former communist states of Eastern Europe—Poland, Czechoslovakia, and Hungary—took different pathways after the collapse of communism, they all experienced problems that suggested that the road back to the market will be longer than many reformers and Western economic experts anticipated. In the interim, some radical political adjustments have been made to cope with a dramatically changed environment. The separation of the Western two-thirds of Czechoslovakia, the Czech Republic, from Slovakia is perhaps the most dramatic recent occurrence in the region. Stephen Engelberg, in his article "In a New Slovakia, Fears Are Both New and Old," predicts that formal dissolution is likely to be the catalyst for a major realignment in the region.

There is a general consensus that the most serious threat to the stability of Europe is the conflict in the Balkans, but disagreements abound regarding the causes of this conflict. Many analysts claim that today's horrors are the product of deliberate misrepresentations of history—the legacy of conflicts created during the Ottoman Empire or the genocidal campaigns that took place during World War II. Economic hard times, however, and stumbling Western responses to the disintegration of Yugoslavia were also important factors at critical junctures in these conflicts. Steven Burg, in "Why Yugoslavia Fell Apart," describes how cold war principles and practices were unable to provide a stable framework to prevent the disintegration of the Yugoslav Federation or the descent into ethnic violence.

When the Bosnian conflict broke out in 1991, the Western European Union (WEU), foreseen as the nucleus of a common European defense, enforced naval sanctions against Serbia in the Adriatic Sea and later admitted Greece as the 10th member, but failed to mobilize an effective European military response. Instead, some NATO countries, such as France and England, who were also members of the WEU, provided troops and military equipment to the UN peacekeeping mission in the Balkans. U.S. participation was limited to such actions as helping to enforce the "no-fly zone" over Bosnia and deploying a small contingent of troops to neighboring Macedonia as part of a UN effort to prevent the conflict from spreading during 1993.

Until 1994, NATO ultimatums were routinely ignored by local militias. Serbian forces continued to seize territory, block UN humanitarian relief efforts, shell Bosnia's besieged capital of Sarajevo, and violate the no-fly zone imposed to enforce economic sanctions. The United States chose to downplay the conflict after the Clinton administration failed to obtain European support for a plan to aid Muslim forces with NATO air support. But in February 1994, a Serbian shell lobbed into the marketplace in Sarajevo that killed 68 civilians galvanized support for a series of U.S.–backed initiatives. NATO demanded and obtained the withdrawal of heavy artillery from around Sarajevo, and then moved quickly to implement cease-fires in several cities by threatening NATO air strikes. The first-ever military engagement by NATO occurred at the end of February when NATO F-16s shot down four Serb planes that had bombed a Muslim-held town, which was an unambiguous violation of the no-fly zone.

In a diplomatic initiative, the U.S. abandoned opposition to pressuring Muslims to accept Serb territorial gains by sponsoring an agreement to create a rump Muslim-Croat Federation from territories remaining outside Serbian control.

Whether the hiatus in the conflict will lead to an agreement acceptable to all parties is unknown. Progress toward a general agreement requires the active support of key players: Serbia, Russia, the United States, European allies, and a major UN peacekeeping operation. Recent events seem to correspond to an analysis outlined by John Mearsheimer and Robert Pape in "The Answer." While a new status quo built upon Serbian conquest of nearly 70 percent of the former state is not perfect or morally pure, these analysts predict that the partition will be viewed as the best answer by outside powers, since it can be done without spending much money or spilling additional blood.

Looking Ahead: Challenge Questions

Should the United States facilitate Europe integration?

Does downsizing of U.S. forces in Europe imply that the United States will disengage from Europe?

Is an expanded NATO a viable alliance structure for the United States in preparing for the next war? Would Western security guarantees strengthen the demands of democratic reformers or promote peace and stability in the region?

Should the United States continue its present policies in the Balkans? Why?

Does conflict in the Balkans have the potential to destabilize all of Europe and even lead to a more general war? Why or why not?

Redefined NATO Faces Growing Pains

Henrik Bering-Jensen

Summary: As NATO draws up its blueprint for the future, it must decide what to do about the former Warsaw Pact nations. Most are eager to join the alliance; Russia, however, has its own plans for Eastern Europe.

The original purpose of the North Atlantic Treaty Organization, as memorably expressed by its first secretary-general, Lord Ismay, was "to keep the Americans in, the Russians out and the Germans down." For four decades after World War II, the alliance lived up to its task admirably, facing down the Soviet menace without firing a shot, solidifying transatlantic relations and maintaining peace within Europe. NATO has earned a reputation, as one observer noted, as "the most successful military alliance in history."

But with the end of the Cold War and the demise of the Warsaw Pact, the future of NATO is in question. Without the Soviet threat, which provided NATO's focal point and cohesion, the alliance must carve out a new role for itself or perish. Some, such as NATO Secretary-General Manfred Woerner, argue that the alliance's primary goal must be to "project stability to the East." And others, such as Republican Sen. Richard Lugar of Indiana, argue that if NATO fails to take on the new challenges of militant nationalism and ethnic instability in Europe, it will become irrelevant. "Without a new mission that explicitly addresses these problems," says Lugar, "the importance of NATO will fade away." The choice today, he adds is not between the current NATO or a new NATO, but rather between a new NATO or no NATO at all.

A summit of the 16 NATO leaders will take place in Brussels on Jan. 10 and 11 to establish a blueprint for the future. As the representative of the most powerful member of the alliance, President Clinton is expected to take the lead, formally launching his much touted "partnership for peace" scheme for enhancing the security of Europe.

The meeting comes at a time when the transatlantic climate is less than cordial. Recent months have seen bitter disputes over trade, and Washington has suggested that U.S. foreign policy may be shifting directions, as indicated by Secretary of State Warren Christopher's recent comment that "Western Europe is no longer the dominant area of the world." Moreover, in the alliance's first great post-Cold War test — Bosnia — it has not exactly shown its best side; its inability to stop the "ethnic cleansing" has given rise to mutual recrimination between the U.S. and its European allies.

The key question on the summit agenda is what to do about the former Warsaw Pact nations—especially Poland, the Czech Republic and Hungary, which are lining up to join NATO as a shield against turmoil in the region and a possible political reversal in Moscow. But rather than being flattered, both NATO and the Clinton administration are in the middle of a sharp debate over the issue.

The main concern is how Moscow would react to a widening of NATO. Initially, the Russians seemed open to the idea of seeing their former client states join with the West. During President Boris Yeltsin's August visit to Poland, he stated that it was up to the Polish people, as citizens of a free and sovereign nation, to decide whether they wanted membership in NATO, a line he repeated in Prague. Only weeks later, however, the Russians changed their minds. In a letter to the main NATO governments, Moscow stated that expanding the alliance eastward would be viewed as a hostile act and an attempt to isolate Russia. As an alternative, Yeltsin has suggested joint Russian and NATO security guarantees for these countries.

All this puts the NATO allies in a rather uncomfortable position. As one British diplomat says, it is a question of being damned if you do and damned if you don't.

"On the one hand, if we do not reach out in some way and strengthen the nature of the security relationship with the countries of Eastern Europe, then we are going to be guilty of frustrating the publicly expressed wishes of the newly emerging democratic nations whose aspirations and wishes we claim to support," he says. "On the other hand, we are very concerned about the possible implications of admitting Poland, Hungary and the Czech Republic into NATO and the impact this might have on those forces in Russia which are opposed to President Yeltsin's reforms. We do not want inadvertently to end up creating the very insecurity we are trying to avoid."

The East Europeans have some compelling reasons for wanting membership. While it may be considered uncouth to state it publicly nowadays, Russia remains their main security concern. Two coup attempts within the past three years have demonstrated the frailty of Russian democracy. Whatever its present weakness, Russia remains the dominant nation on the European continent, and could someday begin to reassert itself. The Russian army is already active in the former Soviet republics, fanning the fires of ethnic conflict and collapsing the republics back into the Commonwealth of Independent States, dominated by Russia.

NATO membership for the East Europeans, by providing a security framework within which they could rebuild their political and economic lives, would keep them free from Russian dominance and help cement democratic and economic reforms, thereby shoring up the stable part of Europe against turbulence further east. This kind of stability was precisely what NATO provided for Western Europe when the alliance was formed in 1947. As Czech President Vaclav Havel once said, "We have always belonged to the Western sphere of civilization and share the values upon which NATO was founded and which it exists to defend."

Moreover, admitting East European countries to NATO would be relatively simple compared with letting them into the European Union, as the European Community is now known. Whereas EU membership (which the East Europeans

also want) involves profound changes in all areas of the life of a nation—its laws, trade practices and entire economic setup—membership in NATO involves only the area of national security.

Among the countries that have been most favorable to expanding NATO is Germany, which does not relish the idea of a power vacuum on its eastern border. "Germany does not want to be the Eastern border of the European zone of stability. Europe must not stop at the Oder-Neisse border," Manfred Weise, a member of the planning staff of the German Defense Ministry, has stated.

Referring to the mass of refugees who have come to Germany from the warring Balkans, German Defense Minister Volker Ruhe said, "If we

---

"We are concerned about the possible implications of admitting Poland, Hungary and the Czech Republic into NATO and the impact on those forces in Russia which are opposed to Yeltsin's reforms."

---

don't export stability, we are going to wind up importing instability."

During an early December meeting in Brussels of NATO foreign ministers preparing for the January summit, Britain, France and Canada were less keen on expanding NATO, believing it would constitute a direct challenge to the Russians.

West European opponents of expansion point to the dangers of diluting the alliance by making it too big and of making commitments that NATO would not be able to honor. They point to the Hungarian crisis of 1956, in which the Eisenhower administration raised expectations that it would support the revolt, then did nothing when the tanks rolled in. Most NATO officials want to keep the alliance's role manageable and specific and to avoid broad commitments. At the meeting in Brussels, British Foreign Secretary Douglas Hurd ruled out any new NATO responsibilities, stating, "Unless it is threatened itself, it is unlikely that NATO will intervene in the wars of other people."

Pointing to the chaos in Bosnia, opponents of expanding the alliance further argue that a NATO reaching to the Bug River on the Russo-Polish border and to Transylvania in the south would be involved in a host of intractable border and minority disputes; Hungary, for example, has minorities in Romania, Serbia and Slovenia. A European commentator in the *International Herald Tribune* compared the task facing NATO today to securing a house after an earthquake: The smart architect does not start by adding an extra floor to the shaken house — he first tries to secure the building's base.

While acknowledging the alliance's failure in Bosnia, NATO Secretary-General Woerner has compared the logic of calling for NATO's demise because of that failure to banning doctors for the persistence of illness or disbanding the police because of the proliferation of crime.

Those who support widening NATO also say that admitting new members might help prevent future Bosnias by embedding potential troublemakers within NATO, thereby circumscribing any violence that might flow from ethnic tensions or disputed borders. They point out that it is NATO membership, more than anything else, that has prevented Greece and Turkey from going to war over Cyprus.

The Clinton administration's "partnership for peace" proposal is an attempt to bridge some of these conflicting concerns. The partnership would be offered to all former Warsaw Pact members, including Russia, and four neutral European countries. The plan envisions joint military exercises, participation in NATO military planning, gradual standardization of equipment, help with defense conversion to civilian industry and "consultation" rights with NATO for members who feel their security is threatened. As a Clinton official describes it, the plan is "a way of beginning to pull Eastern countries into Western institutions' practices and norms."

What the proposal emphatically does not do is extend to the East Europeans the security guarantees detailed in Article 5 of the NATO treaty, which commits all members to come to the aid of any member that is attacked. Neither does it offer a concrete timetable or checklist of conditions for membership, which the East Europeans had sought.

"The basic problem with the partnership for peace proposal," notes Ken Myers, a foreign policy adviser to Indiana's Lugar, "is that it does not address any of the security concerns in contemporary Europe." Stephen Larrabee, a senior policy analyst at the Rand Corp. in Santa Monica, Calif., agrees. "It is somewhat of a nondecision," he says. "It holds up the prospect of membership, but it does not offer it. It seeks to buy time."

According to Larrabee, the partnership for peace idea is the result of an informal alliance between so-called Russia Firsters in the Clinton State Department (notably represented by Ambassador-at-Large Strobe Talbott, they tend to

give top priority to the U.S.-Russian relationship and the survival of Yeltsin) and elements in the Pentagon that oppose taking on any new commitments or extending the U.S. nuclear umbrella eastward at a time of declining resources.

The weakness of the Russia First approach, administration critics argue, is that it would give Russia veto power over NATO's actions and, rather than securing and consolidating what has been won from the collapse of communism, pin American hopes on the political fortunes of one man, thereby risking losing everything.

Former Secretary of State Henry Kissinger has characterized the plan as another instance of "muddleheaded internationalism" by the Clinton administration. Kissinger wrote in a recent column, "The partnership for peace would create a vacuum in Eastern Europe. If things turn out badly in Russia, it would lead to the emergence of a no-man's-land between Germany and Russia, which has caused so many European wars. And Poland would once again be defined as a potential victim."

Not surprisingly, the reaction has been even more negative in Eastern Europe. Rather than the "grand strat-

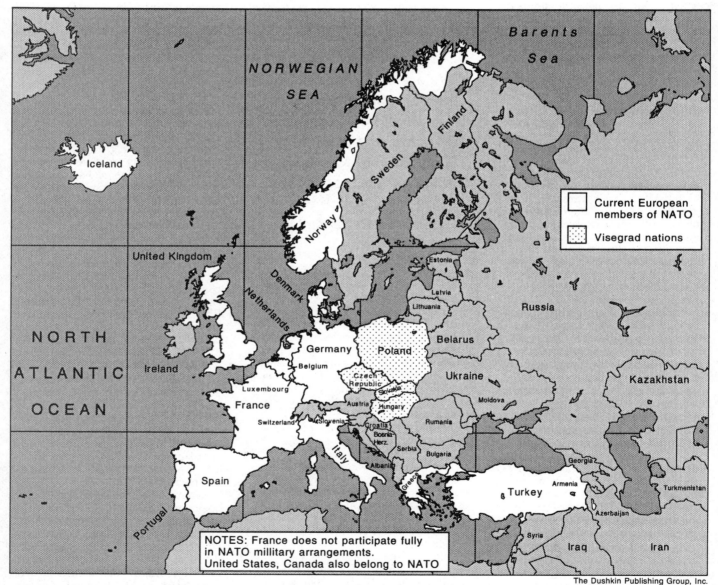

The Dushkin Publishing Group, Inc.

Through the "Partnership for Peace," NATO leaders may offer former Warsaw Pact foes membership in its organization. There would be an unprecedented cooperation between former Soviet bloc nations and the 16 allies of NATO. The invited nations will probably be Poland, Hungary, Slovakia, the Czech Republic, and the neutral nations of Sweden and Finland. Eastern Europeans want full membership and guarantees of protection if they are attacked. Moscow is against this idea, and the NATO members are somewhat wary of arousing Russian nationalism. It is expected that the cost of this "Partnership for Peace" would mostly be the responsibility of the Soviet bloc states, but the actual expenditures for the start-up are not clear due to the degree of military cooperation and responsibilities of the new members.

egy for the future" proclaimed by the Clinton administration, the East Europeans tend to see the partnership for peace plan as an exercise in casuistry, compromise and obfuscation, a diplomatic trick that attempts to pacify them without extending the security guarantees they desperately seek. Says Jacek Kalabinski of *Gazeta Wyborcza*, Poland's leading daily, "They see it is a deception."

By refusing to extend the security guarantees, East Europeans argue, America comes close to once again consigning Eastern Europe to the Russian sphere of influence, leading to accusations that Clinton is resurrecting the "ghost of Yalta," as Havel has called it, referring to the agreement among Franklin Roosevelt, Joseph Stalin and Winston Churchill in 1945 that conceded Eastern Europe to Russian hegemony. Whereas the Yalta accord could be rationalized by the fact that it merely reflected the situation on the ground at the end of World War II, yielding territory that Stalin's armies already occupied, no such excuses are valid today.

For most East Europeans, the partnership for peace plan makes a mockery of the idea of enhanced security by including the very power that they fear—Russia. Says a Polish diplomat, "How can you propose a partnership to the countries of Eastern and Central Europe with the same entity they are afraid of? It is not even funny."

The prospect of joint maneuvers with Russian troops is particularly distasteful to the East Europeans, who have just managed to rid themselves of Russian occupation forces. They are not alone. When the German government (which

> **"The partnership for peace would create a vacuum in Eastern Europe. If things turn out badly in Russia, it would lead to the emergence of a no-man's-land between Germany and Russia, which has caused so many European wars. And Poland would once again be defined as a potential victim."**

still has 32,000 Russian troops on its territory) recently found out that the Americans and Russians were planning joint "friendship" maneuvers on German soil, it immediately vetoed the idea.

By ducking the issue, critics of the Clinton administration say, the partnership for peace plan runs the risk of missing a critical moment for cementing these countries in the Western bloc.

According to Lugar's adviser Myers, there will never be an "ideal" point at which NATO membership for the East Europeans would not upset the Russians. However, one thing remains clear: Later, as Russia becomes stronger, doing so will become much more difficult.

As Kissinger wrote, "We resisted blackmail when Russia was strong; does it make sense to permit Moscow to blackmail us now with its domestic weakness?"

Says the Polish diplomat who rules out the idea of a partnership with Russia, "Time is acting against us."

Officially, however, there is not much the East Europeans can do but play along, choosing to interpret the partnership for peace plan as a first step toward membership, a kind of apprenticeship, rather than as a rebuff.

While a growing chorus of isolationism in the United States is calling for America to stay out of Europe entirely, history suggests that may be impossible.

The rationale for continued U.S. engagement in Europe has perhaps been best expressed by Havel: "I am convinced that the American presence in Europe is still necessary. In the 20th century, it was not just Europe that paid the price for American isolationism. America itself paid a price. The less it committed itself in the beginning of European conflagrations, the greater the sacrifices it had to make at the end of such conflicts."

Over the past 40 years, the United States has invested a great deal politically, economically and militarily in Europe to work out a stable security order there. As Kissinger has pointed out, NATO, for all its flaws and shortcomings, "remains America's sole institutional link with Europe and the most natural way for the United States to influence the political evolution in Europe."

Reinventing the politics of Europe

Anthony Hartley

Anthony Hartley, former Editor of *Encounter* and now Contributing Editor (Europe) for the *National Interest* in Washington, is a close student of European Community affairs and a former EC official. His previous contribution to *The World Today*, on the Clinton presidency, appeared in the February 1993 issue.

Once again the European Community has been ploughing through rough seas. No sooner had the Maastricht Treaty been ratified in Britain, by a process akin to Chinese water-torture, than a wave of speculation forced the devaluation of the French franc in circumstances that were as humiliating and politically uncomfortable as they were for John Major, Britain's Prime Minister, when the pound suffered a similar fate in October 1992. This time the European Monetary System (EMS) was altered to allow a fluctuation around the central rate of 15 per cent (instead of 2.5 per cent). Effectively the system itself was abolished, and the European currencies were left to float, apart from the continued link between the D-Mark and the Dutch florin. As the economic correspondent of *Le Monde* put it: 'The speculators have won. The EMS is badly damaged, Europe deeply weakened.'[1]

Since the crisis voices have not been lacking to proclaim that all may yet be well. For France's Prime Minister, Edouard Balladur, the Brussels agreement of 2 August has preserved the EMS and maintained the value of the franc through the mutual efforts of France and Germany. More recently Sir Leon Brittan, EC Commissioner for External Trade, has expressed his belief that the Maastricht timetable can still be kept. Yet these attempts to 'save the phenomena', a phrase used by the defenders of the Ptolemaic system of astronomy, are hardly convincing. The Editor of the *Rheinischer Merkur*, Thomas Kielinger, found a simpler and more artistic explanation: 'What we saw this week, however, was the triumph of Lancelot "Capability" Brown over Le Nôtre, the triumph of English landscape gardening over French geometrical rigidity.'[2]

The fact is that, at a time of falling European gnp, of heavy unemployment and of divergence between the principal European economies (most notably between Germany and the rest), any effort to set EC states on a forced march towards monetary union was bound to end in a debilitating failure. The monetary programme agreed at Maastricht was designed for another and more familiar world – a world of prosperity and full employment. At Maastricht neither the depth of the depression nor the results of German reunification were perceived. The link with the dominant and virtuous D-Mark, which had been intended to be the foundation-stone of the new system, turned out to be a link with pain – the measures adopted by the Bundesbank to counter post-reunification inflation. On 'Black Wednesday' this proved too much for Britain and Italy; on 30 July it proved too much for France.

But present European difficulties are wider spread than the obscuring of the monetary panel of the Maastricht diptych. The signing of that treaty almost coincided with the recognition by Germany of Croatia and Slovenia (23 December 1991). The announcement of future common foreign and security policies for a putative European Union saw the Yugoslav crisis well under way – a crisis which seemed to offer an opportunity for Europeans to show their mettle as peacekeepers and arbitrators. Indeed, some Community spokesmen seemed positively to welcome the occasion. Mr Jacques Poos, the Luxembourg Foreign Minister, led the euphoria with the rallying cry: 'This is the hour of Europe. Not the hour of the Americans.'[3]

What happened in Bosnia and elsewhere was rather different. World opinion and the United Nations have been seen to be powerless to prevent massacre and counter-massacre or to punish those who have used 'ethnic cleansing' as the instrument of a policy of expansion. By late 1993, much of Bosnia had been 'cleansed' of Moslems, despite the involvement of UN forces; a peace agreement still eludes Lord Owen; and UN sanctions do not seem to have discouraged President Slobodan Milosevic from pursuing a 'Greater Serbia'. The European Community, meanwhile, has distinguished itself neither by its unity nor by its efficiency. An original split between Britain and France, who wished to preserve a Yugoslav state, and Germany, which did not, was followed by the dispatch of small numbers of British, French and Spanish troops to Bosnia and Croatia on humanitarian missions. Britain and France have been united in resisting further military involvement in a civil war, while the German press has urged military intervention – though acknowledging that it would be constitutionally impossible and politically inappropriate for Germany to join any such operation.

Far from demonstrating the ability of a European Union to extinguish bush-fires kindled on its frontiers, the Yugoslav crisis has shown (1) that member states of the European Community are likely to have different interest and objectives when faced with trouble in Eastern Europe and elsewhere; and (2) that the laborious diplomatic negotiations, necessary to produce a carefully crafted formula to obscure such disagreements, delay the instant action required to seize even a fleeting opportunity of deterring aggression to a point where decisions always come too late. The stern test of Yugoslavia has undermined the European Community's claim to act effectively in a crisis involving European security and eroded the credibility of the new common foreign and security policies. The United States, on the other hand, remains the only credible intervener, an essential ingredient for effective resistance to aggression.[4]

Thus the two main provisions of the Maastricht Treaty have had discredit cast upon them, even before final ratification of the

From *The World Today*, Vol. 49, No. 11, November 1993, pp. 202-205. *The World Today*, published by The Royal Institute of International Affairs. Reprinted by permission.

agreement was permitted by Germany's Constitutional Court. Now the European Community has entered upon yet another internal conflict over the world trade negotiations in the framework of the so-called Uruguay Round of the General Agreement on Tariffs and Trade (GATT). France's refusal to accept the 1992 Blair House agreement between the United States and the EC on the agricultural sector of the GATT negotiation risks provoking a serious split in the Community and the failure of the negotiation, with the evil consequences that this would bring for world trade and the already depressed economies of Western Europe. At the time of writing it is impossible to tell how things will go and whether the Uruguay Round will be completed by mid-December 1993. The United States, in the person of its trade negotiator, Mr Mickey Kantor, has said that 'interpretation or clarification of Blair House cannot be a guise for modifying the terms of the agreement'.[5] Sir Leon Brittan's flying visit to Washington, to see whether some minor concessions on the American side were not possible, does not seem to have produced anything on the agricultural issue.

A concession, if it comes, will be left until the last moment. But France's Prime Minister, Edouard Balladur, is no De Gaulle. A small bone to fling to the farming lobby is certainly what he wants. For he must know that a French veto on a GATT agreement would not receive German support. On important issues Bonn has always supported the United States.

Can some of the devices that have been suggested – exemption of present EC agricultural stocks from the cuts in subsidised exports, 'back-loading' of such cuts – be used to reach a solution? The American negotiators also have their farmers to consider and, moreover, have been irritated by France's questioning of what, for the American side, is an agreed compromise. Mr Kantor's view is that French objections are not a matter for him but an internal EC dispute.

Mr Balladur is, therefore, faced by a choice between what will be, in effect, a retreat or causing a rupture that will damage France's industry and strain the working of the European Community. His difficulties illuminate the present confused state of European politics, where the twin pressures of unemployment and immigration have produced a disagreeably xenophobic brand of populism. The fall of the franc and the disappearance of the EMS were a humiliating setback for French policy, which had inflicted hardship on French citizens in order to sustain the parity with the D-Mark. French politicians and officials were disagreeably surprised by what happened. They had never believed that the Bundesbank would refuse to support the franc, and commentators found it hard to decide whom to blame most: 'Anglo-Saxon speculators' or 'egotistical German bankers'.[6]

The GATT issue provides another scenario where France can be seen as assailed by the United States and its European sympathisers. In addition, the presidential election is only 18 months off, new laws on immigration may require a referendum, unemployment stands at 3,215,800 (11.7 per cent) and seems likely to reach 12 per cent by the end of the year.[7] No wonder that the 'new policy' recommended by Philippe Séguin, Speaker of the National Assembly and an effective campaigner against the Maastricht Treaty, should find support, particularly with Mr Séguin's own Gaullist party, the *Rassemblement pour la République* (RPR), or that over 50 per cent of French citizens should now say that they would vote against the treaty in any new referendum.[8]

A nationalist and protectionist reaction to events since German reunification makes life more difficult for Mr Balladur, but also for the European Community. For, all over Europe, the apparent inability of governments to master unemployment and their own financial affairs is producing a confused populism that increasingly ignores established political parties and is sceptical of the remedies presented by politicians, bankers, trade union leaders and European officials. In Italy this cynicism takes the form of advocacy of a breakup of the present Italian state. In Britain, Mr Major's government has plunged in the polls, while the Labour opposition is felt to be boring. In France and Germany there have been outbreaks of xenophobia, attacks on Turkish or Arab immigrants or the burning of foreign produce in transit.

The tensions shared by European societies are producing a destabilisation of political institutions, not excluding those of the European Community. Blame for economic difficulties rubs off on to Community policies. High interest rates accompanying membership of the EMS can be held responsible for unemployment, as can Community social policies that increase labour costs and discourage employers from taking on new employees. The existence of the Community and its Brussels institutions has come to appear irrelevant to the problems created by economic depression, if not responsible for them, in that the drive to European Monetary Union (EMU) implied an attempt to impose deflationary policies on countries whose real economic situation required the opposite.

What should the European Community do to restore its credibility in the eyes of its citizens? Despite protestations to the contrary, it is clear that the Maastricht Treaty will require modification, to say the least, and that its timetable for monetary union is unlikely to be kept – if, indeed, its objectives can be realised at all in a time-span of under 20 years. After the recent experience of Britain, France and Italy, it is improbable that European political leaders will be willing once again to take the risk of trying to achieve 'convergence' by going against the grain of the world economic conjuncture. As for the common foreign and security policies, meetings of ministers will continue, and so will attempts to harmonise purely diplomatic activity or to pursue joint staff talks in the Western European Union (WEU). But the limits to this process are soon reached. Once it is a matter of intervention or 'peacekeeping', no government is going to allow the extent of its participation to be determined by anyone other that itself or its own parliament. It is impossible to imagine that, within any European organisation – never mind the name – Britain or France would allow the use of their armed forces to be decided by even qualified-majority voting on the part of countries, many of whom hardly possess any effective military capacity at all.

In the face of such considerations, should the European statesmen continue the struggle to 'help' history? Maastricht was an attempt to consummate in a few years processes which were bound to take far longer to achieve – if, indeed, success were possible in present-day Europe. If European leaders now decide to have another shot at EMU, will not the same fate await it? Can they accelerate common foreign and security policies which, if they are to be effective, must be the result of habit and use? Above all, should the Community constantly be setting itself deadlines which it then fails to keep, with the inevitable consequences for its credibility in the eyes of Europe's citizens?

'Time,' wrote Hugo von Hofmannsthal, 'is a strange thing.' It is also an essential ingredient in the preparation of lasting political change. Instead of the constant hurry and bustle of summits, ministers' meetings and complex timetables, accompanied by seemingly endless legislation coming off the production line, might it not be better to allow Europe to evolve at a pace and in a direction more adapted to the comprehension of its citizens? In retrospect it seems extraordinary that the Maastricht plan for Europe's future should have ignored the two principal matters of present concern to citizens of the European Community: unemployment and instability in Eastern Europe, to which recent events in Moscow have given an added urgency. It is strange that so strenuous a discussion on Europe in the year 2000 should have neglected the main features of its present political and economic conjuncture. The answer is, of course, that the ideas of Maastricht were gestated a decade or more back and were intended for a different world from the one that now exists after the collapse of Soviet power.

Meanwhile, as statesmen ponder the ruins of the EMS, political events are moving on. The future shape of the Community will depend on whether it is capable of catching up with these or whether it will lag behind change, offering the remedies of the 1970s and 1980s for the problems of the 1990s. A number of trends in European and international politics, while not bearing directly on the shape of European institutions, are nevertheless likely to influence the characteristics of the Community over the next decade:

● Increasing instability in Eastern Europe, particularly in Russia and Ukraine, will alarm other European states which, however, will be unequally affected and will, in any case, be unable to 'intervene', except by diplomatic means.

● Germany is likely, therefore, to become more and more preoccupied by such events as the West European country most exposed to their consequences in the shape of economic chaos and, possibly, a flow of refugees. This will not necessarily imply less support in Bonn or Berlin for the European Community, but it will mean more distraction from it and more urgency in its extension to the East. The German government's move to Berlin will play its part here.

● Over the next two years those European leaders most attached to the original 'Carolingian' Europe – Delors, Kohl, Mitterrand – seem likely to disappear. Their successors will probably see Europe's future in rather a different light from that of the immediate successors of the 'founding fathers'.

● There are already divergences in the way member states view foreign policy. Britain has a relationship with the United States which can be called 'special', provided that this is not taken to mean the possibility of invariably exercising influence in Washington. Germany is developing its own 'special relationship' with Russia and other East European countries. France and Italy are rivals for influence around the Mediterranean basin. The end of the Cold War has liberated such aspirations to more characteristically national policies on the part of Community member states.

● The logical conclusion of recurring GATT rounds will be a symbiosis between free-trade areas such as the EC and the North American Free Trade Area (NAFTA) – if it survives its passage through Congress. This will be good for the world's economy but will lessen Europe's sense of specificity.

Other trends could be added to these factors, which are helping to reinvent the politics of Europe. But even without taking into consideration, for instance, the evident weakening that is taking place in the Franco-German relationship, or the increasing impossibility of considering economic developments in any other than a global framework, those mentioned above are enough to encourage expectation of a Europe evolving on rather different lines from hitherto, casting aside some old orthodoxies to gestate a system that is less rigid and less ponderous.

In a recent *Economist* article, Mr Major correctly identified the real tasks facing Europe today.[9] If the European Community is to prosper, it must deal with unemployment and use its best endeavours to help the new democracies of Eastern Europe. To this Mr Delors has replied by an appeal to the European Community's 'founding fathers' who, he believes, aimed at the construction of a federal state.[10] This conception sees Europe as becoming a 'power' in the traditional sense of the word, an enlarged nation-state with a central bureaucracy, a single government and Parliament and single policies. It is a view that inclines easily to protectionism in that a Europe, with a trade policy sharply defined against competitors, would, it is thought, become more acutely conscious of its own identity. Moreover, European federalists usually present their model, not in terms of American federalism, about which they know little, but simply as a wider European state whose tendency is to draw power to the centre and impose a *Gleichschaltung* on laws and institutions.[11] Mr Major perceives a Community wider in its extent, less centralised in its machinery, and where there would be variations in what is required of each member state; a Community whose economic area would gradually blend into others to the East and West. It would be a Community which would pay more attention to the immediate problems of Europe and spend less time on constitutional changes which can prove divisive and destabilising in individual countries.

Which of these views of Europe's future is more likely to be realised? They both have their contradictions. Mr Major favours enlargement and less constitution-building. But enlargement, leading to a Community of some 20 states, will destroy the present system of decision-making, and something will have to be put in its place. Mr Delors looks to an eventual federation, but wishes to maintain the technocratic power of the European Commission. France and Germany advocate pushing ahead with integration, but wish to decrease the influence of the smaller countries. The argument on the future of the European Community is liable to become hopelessly embroiled, with little in the way of clear political principle about it.

The difficulty for the federalists is that theirs is an 'all-or-nothing' argument. But, since neither governments nor peoples seem prepared to move towards the 'all' of a European government, they are condemned to a series of fiercely contested compromises ending, all too often, in small symbolic gestures – a European passport or changes in nomenclature. The risk they run—and what now appears to have happened—is the neglect of real politics and an undue reliance on legal formulae. Political leaders, on the other hand, have their being in real politics. When their interests and their electorate require it, they will flout traditional European orthodoxy. They are happier with the European Council than with the European Parliament or the Commission, except when a small country believes that supranational bodies give it more of a hearing than it would otherwise receive. Maastricht, in any case, will probably be the last hurrah of federalism, a treaty pushed ahead by France's desire to restrain a newly unified Germany, and Germany's wish to start on its new course of untrammelled independence with European credentials to its credit.

It looks, therefore, as though the pragmatic, illogical view of a Community muddling through to some form of confederation for which there is no model – certainly not that of the nation-state – would correspond most nearly to events. There is, fortunately, much about Europe's future that we cannot foresee. For instance, will the peoples of the new candidate states – the Scandinavian countries and Austria – vote in favour of entry at their respective referendums? Not if the Community shows no signs of being able to cope with economic depression. Will the European Community emerge as something more like the Holy Roman Empire than the Roman Empire? Pragmatists are often accused of lacking idealism. But the Geneva of GATT has as much going for it in terms of human welfare as the Strasbourg of the European Parliament. The dimly perceived vision of a free-trade area extending halfway round the world does not lack ambition or daring. After Maastricht the European Community finds itself at the beginning of a long historical process whose final result remains uncertain. It is important not to confine it to the mould of theoretical assertions.

NOTES

1. *Le Monde*. 3 August 1993.
2. *The Times*, 7 August 1993.
3. *International Herald Tribune*, 30 June 1991.
4. On the limitations and dangers of peacekeeping, see Laurence Martin, 'Peacekeeping as a Growth Industry', *The National Interest*, No 32, Summer 1993.
5. *Financial Times*, 22 September 1993.
6. In the issue of *Le Monde* of 30 July 1993, that paper's Brussels Correspondent writes of the 'attacks of Anglo-Saxon speculation' which he sees as being encouraged by the *Financial Times*. On 3 August 1993, two days after the Brussels agreement, *Le Monde* speaks of the *'diktat* of Bonn and Frankfurt'.
7. See the *Wall Street Journal*, 30 September 1993. It should be remembered that, since France has conscription, some hundreds of thousands of young men are taken out of the labour market each year. France has never known unemployment at this level. Between the wars the highest figure was 374,000. See André de Lattre, *Politique économique de la France depuis 1945* (Paris: 1966), p. 437.
8. M. Séguin's views were presented in a speech on 16 June 1993 (*Le Monde*, 18 June 1993) and include attacks on free trade, high interest rates and the *franc fort*, the diminution of social benefits and the run-down of the public sector.
9. John Major, 'Raise your eyes, there is a land beyond', in *The Economist*, 25 September 1993.
10. This was hardly true of Konrad Adenauer. He was critical of supranational bureaucracy and commented that he was becoming somewhat tired of European Union, adding: 'If the birth pangs are already so difficult, one can hardly reckon on living children.' See Hans-Peter Schwarz, *Adenauer: Der Staatsmann 1953-1967* (Stuttgart: 1991), p. 737.
11. For instance, Brussels favours harmonised company law as essential to a Common Market. In the United States, this is left to the individual states, but these variations do not seem to affect adversely the operation of the internal market.

Searching for identity, Germany struggles with its history

Marc Fisher

Washington Post Foreign Service

BERLIN

Sometime before the century's end, most likely after he wins a fourth term next year, Chancellor Helmut Kohl will leave office, and the vital connection between a confused, insecure new Germany and the confident generation that rebuilt the country after World War II will slip into history.

Kohl's generation of Germans born toward the start of Nazi rule was "blessed by the mercy of late birth," as the 63-year-old chancellor often says. Scarred by fascism but too young to bear responsibility for its crimes, these people built a new society and will carry their pride to their graves.

Now, however, a new generation of politicians is taking over, people born toward the end of the war, people who know their parents started from nil but who never had to face hardship themselves. They include what many derisively tag the Tuscany Faction of the opposition Social Democratic Party—stylish, richly tanned politicians who spend their leisure months in Italy and have deeply ambivalent attitudes toward power and leadership.

"We lack the strong personalities with the will of leadership and the readiness to run a personal risk," says Norbert Gansel, 52, a senior Social Democratic legislator. "My party and my generation are not prepared to fight things through. The problem is, German politics cannot appeal to a national dream as [Americans] can. There is no German dream. There is only German nightmare. People talk about returning to normalcy now that the Wall is down. What does normalcy mean in German history? And what does return mean?

"The German capacity to adapt is a problem. Two world wars brought not only enormous territorial losses but millions of Germans who lost everything to bomb raids, like my family. The little pieces of jewelry, the china, all blown away by a bomb. And then, the terrible inflation at the end of the war. It all changed German society enormously. There is a German desire for security now. And we live in a time of insecurity. Insecurity never helps people live with insecurity. It only makes them more determined to maintain their security."

"There's a certain hedonism to my generation," says Claus Leggewie, 43, a political scientist. "We've had no terribly difficult challenges. The politicians of this generation act as if being German is unpleasant. The idea that Germany now has to take on new responsibilities is very uncomfortable for them because it means they must decide what Germany's interests are."

Almost four years after the fall of the Berlin Wall, reunified Germany finds itself in a tangle of questions about its identity and its capacity to change. A powerful country that has defined itself for a half century by economic success and political consensus now stands troubled and pessimistic at the edge of a generational transition.

The country Kohl has shepherded from the cocoon of U.S. and NATO protection into a new vulnerability as the major power in the continent's center is once again where it hoped never to be—at the heart of a volatile and struggling Central Europe.

The Wall's demise and the swift reunification—all accomplished in a historic instant of extraordinary happenstance and well-timed spurts of international leadership—forced a new beginning upon the Germans.

It is a painful time for a country unaccustomed to difficulty. Economists say Germany suffers structural woes that will produce long recession, high unemployment and continuing temptations for major companies to export jobs. "I see no light at the end of the tunnel," says Willi Liebfritz, director of the Ifo research institute in Munich.

A national poll by ZDF television in May found 96 percent of Germans surveyed unhappy with their country's plight. Although 4 percent said Germany was "all right," 46 percent saw "big problems," 38 percent worried about a "difficult crisis" and 12 percent were so morose as to say Germany "faces catastrophe."

Politicians and business leaders of all ideological stripes speak of a battle for resources pitting rich against poor, east against west, and even generation against generation.

Kohl has told aides he feels obliged to stay in office for several more years in part because of the ahistorical drift he

FACING A TROUBLED FUTURE?

DIVIDED NATION

Despite a common language and many shared traditions, eastern and western Germans remain far apart in attitudes and interests. Surveys indicate that, compared with their western counterparts, easterners are:

- more pacifistic;
- more optimistic about their own lives;
- more wary of international alliances;
- and more dependent on government,

ECONOMY

A recession and high unemployment created when East Germany's industrial base collapsed have been exacerbated by the strength of the German mark . . .

. . . which has made German exports more expensive and led to their decline in many foreign markets.

Officially, eastern Germany's jobless rate—including the unemployed and those on make-work projects and retraining programs—stands at 35 percent; unofficial estimates top 40 percent.

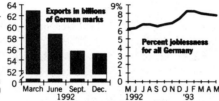

Number of German marks per U.S. dollar

Exports in billions of German marks

Percent joblessness for all Germany

M J S D M J S D M J
1991   '92   '93

March June Sept. Dec.
1992

M J J A S O N D J F M A M
1992   '93

COMPETITIVENESS

The World Competitiveness Report, released by the Geneva World Economic Forum, shows Germany slipping to fifth from second overall among 38 industrial nations, and to ninth from second in the quality of its business management. The report cited Germany's falling per capita income–a result of absorbing the poor east, rising inflation and struggle for national identity.

IMMIGRATION

Political asylum seekers

438,200

49,391

'81 '82 '83 '84 '85 '86 '87 '88 '89 '90 '91 '92

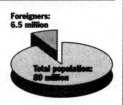

Foreigners: 6.5 million

Total population: 80 million

More than a million foreigners have moved to Germany since the country was reunited in 1990. In 1992, 440,000 entrants applied for political asylum, the only legal route for most foreigners. This year, 193,000 asylum-seekers arrived in the first five months. Germany has decided to turn away illegal migrants at its borders and deport asylum-seekers whose applications have been rejected.

Germany last year accepted 79 percent of all refugees seeking political asylum in the 12-country European Community. And Germany has accepted more than 300,000 refugees from the war in the Balkans, more than any other country.

RIGHT-WING VIOLENCE

Violent incidents with proven or suspected right-wing implication

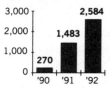

270
1,483
2,584

'90 '91 '92

In 1992, neo-Nazis and other right-wing radicals committed more than 2,500 violent incidents against foreigners in Germany. Seventeen people died in the violence. Anti-foreigner crimes have continued at a similar rate this year.

SOURCES:
Bloomberg Business News, German Embassy in Washington.

Compiled by The Washington Post's Berlin Bureau, Jeannette Belliveau, William Hifner.

---

sees in the postwar generation of politicians. The chancellor spelled out his fears in a recent television interview, saying that if Germany fails to complete its own unification and European integration in the next few years, "we will experience the same evil spirits that have reemerged in Yugoslavia and Central Europe. We are not invulnerable to nationalism, chauvinism and xenophobia, to all the evils that have found their way here often enough."

In a preview of one of his main campaign themes for next year's reelection effort, Kohl presented himself as a historical bridge to the "immeasurable suffering" of World War II and warned that Germany and Europe could once again "stand before the question of war or peace" next century.

"Kohl may recognize the problems, but what has he done about nationalism and its violent impact here?" asks Margarita Mathiopoulos, a Greek-German banker, political scientist and author of "The End of the Bonn Republic."

"What Germany needs," she says, "is leadership that does not succumb to the romantic, racially based nationalism" that raises the specter of fascist ideology. Without strong mainstream leadership and a healthy sense of nationhood, she says, Germany risks a dangerous vacuum filled by extremists offering simple solutions. "We must ask how much of our famous democratic stability is based on real democratic consciousness, and how much is a product only of economic prosperity?" she says.

Foreign Minister Klaus Kinkel's calls for "healthy patriotism" would be unremarkable almost anywhere else. But for many in Germany's postwar generation, the very ideas of patriotism and leadership are tainted, primitive reminders of Adolf Hitler and Joseph Goebbels and their manipulation of the populace. The word for leader, *Fuehrer,* was poisoned by Hitler. Even a casual use of the word in conversation causes many Germans to gulp.

Neither is suspicion of patriotism purely a reaction to the Nazis: German history is a long series of struggles within the nation. "I have no mind at all for the German nationality," Bismarck, a Prussian, wrote in 1862. "To me, a war against the king of Bavaria or Hanover is the same as a war against France."

"We Germans have a broken relationship with our nation," says Ben Grewing of the Federal Center for Political Education, a government agency charged with spreading the gospel of democracy. "In Germany, we are proud of what we have, not of who we are."

Since the 1950s, Germany has measured its stability and its adoption of democratic ideals largely through the success of its auto and machine tool industries and the solidity of the German mark. Now many are asking if the national foundation does not need something more.

A few weeks ago, 500 billboards with the slogan "Germany Is Becoming More German" sprouted around Berlin. The words are imposed over a masked or bandaged face of a woman staring through a half-dozen daggers that pierce the wall behind her.

The billboards are artist Katharina Sievering's attempt to confront Germans with their self-image. "The poster assumes Germans have a bad conscience and that Germans are feared," says Peter Herbstreuth, art critic of Berlin's Tagesspiegel newspaper. If Germans themselves associate Germanness with guilt and nativism, then Kinkel's appeals for a "healthy patriotism" will remain little more than rhetoric.

For the past 50 years, Germans have pursued a different ideal: the successful manager who aims for compromise and consensus, disdaining personal vision or charismatic appeal.

"The whole of modern Germany society is built on cooperation and continuity," says Leggewie, the political scientist. "Parties, newspapers, industry—none of them is used to competition or confrontation. Neither is the government: We spent half a century as the object of other countries' foreign policies. Even the '60s were not the national crisis for us that it was for the French."

But in an era of confrontation both within German society and in a Europe roiling with ethnic and economic conflict, that model may no longer suffice.

"Our society's greatest weakness is an engagement gap," says Werner Hoyer, 41, parliamentary leader of the Free Democrats, the junior partners in Kohl's coalition. "You don't get involved unless it immediately helps your business or family. We have no tradition of volunteerism as you [Americans] do. The generation of Kohl and [former longtime foreign minister Hans-Dietrich] Genscher had the will, the burning desire to build something new. They were historically minded and willing to forgo material things for a political career. My generation doesn't have that sense of mission that produces leadership. In my generation, politics is not very high-ranking in the social hierarchy."

In the face of rising social tensions and an influx of political and economic refugees, accompanied by a violent scapegoating of foreigners, Germans look toward their political leaders for a vision of the future. They come away empty-handed and frustrated. The country suffers from a deep disaffection with politics.

Many of Germany's troubles are similar to problems facing most major industrial nations. The need for structural economic change, the dangers of ethnic strife and the failure of politicians to provide answers have been dominant themes in the United States, Britain and France.

But as in so many of this century's most important issues, what sets Germany apart today is its struggle with history. Germans from all major parties watched Bill Clinton's presidential campaign with palpable jealousy, marveling at Americans' ability to generate hope in hard times. Kohl himself deeply admired Margaret Thatcher's knack for combining tough policies in Britain with hopeful, optimistic politics.

In Germany, however, pessimism reigns, a cultural tradition with deep roots and often unhappy consequences. "There is *Goetterdaemmerung* everywhere in Germany," Hoyer says. Finance Minister Theo Waigel speaks of "a national identity crisis" and the "sharpest economic crisis" since the Great Depression.

Germans have reacted to the strains of reunification and the collapse of its direct neighbor, the Communist East Bloc, with an endless reexamination of what it means to be German. We Germans, says Malte Lehming in a commentary in the Tagesspiegel, "find ourselves in a permanent condition of self-searching, a kind of eternal puberty."

An exasperated Kohl recently complained about "all this moaning and whining. No other country would have responded to its unification, a gift of history, with so much public brooding." Despite "unprecedented prosperity," Kohl said, Germans "react with excessive nervousness or even hysteria to the slightest fluctuations and changes."

Indeed, despite its problems, Germany has managed to use Europe's system of linked currencies to spread the cost of German reunification around the continent, and Germans continue to enjoy one of the highest standards of living—and the most generous vacation benefits and work conditions—in the world.

The chancellor has taken to regularly scolding his countrymen for taking their leisure as a birthright and for "spreading cultural pessimism," attitudes he says would have prevented West Germans of the 1950s from creating their economic miracle out of the ruins of World War II.

That admonition is one that Kohl's successors, whichever party they may represent, will not be able to make, if only because the miracle of the '50s was another generation's achievement.

A string of scandals resulting in the disgraced departure of four nationally known politicians so far this year has only reinforced the public impression that the new generation of politicians lacks the moral fiber of, for example, former chancellor Willy Brandt, who fled Nazi Germany and returned as an underground resistance fighter. The impact is considerable: Although 90 percent of Germans voted in 1990, one-third of Germans now tell pollsters they plan to boycott next year's elections.

Even as politician Hoyer and his colleagues warn that they must provide a vision of the new Germany or risk opening the door to nationalist extremists, many of these same Germans cannot bring themselves to champion Kinkel's "healthy patriotism." Among 14- to 27-year-old Germans, according to a new poll commissioned by the Ministry for Women and Youth, 47 percent of those polled in the west say they are proud to be German, while 68 percent of eastern youths express such pride.

"Why must I be a patriot?" says Egon Zeidler, a shopkeeper in east Berlin. "Somewhere in my head, I still think if we Germans aren't going to be a great military power, we should at least be a great economic power. And then comes national pride that someone smart can reawaken. And what's the next step? Kicking the next guy. And that's how it starts."

"It," of course, is the terrifying memory that lurks in the minds of older Germans and their children, if not in the youngest Germans. Even a generation removed, the memory is enough to render patriotism a soiled, suspicious concept.

"I always called myself a European," says Torsten Schramm, the son of an SS officer who responded to his father's life by becoming a director of Action Reconciliation, an organization that sends young Germans to perform public service work in Jewish institutions in Israel, the United States and elsewhere.

"This new 'I'm proud to be German' that you hear more and more now sounds macho to me," he says. "But I see that we need self-confidence to protect ourselves from the right-wing radicals. It's very hard for those of us who came up through the peace movement. We really don't know what to think."

Since the Persian Gulf War, Germany has struggled over its future military role, debating endlessly the clash between the country's postwar pacifism and its new, post-unification responsibility to share defense burdens with the United States and the United Nations. "Obviously, we need to show more solidarity to our friends who showed solidarity to us for all these years," Hoyer says. "But we should not simply give up this culture of reticence we have developed for very good historical reasons."

President Richard von Weizaecker—an elder statesman who has asked Germany's allies to be patient as the country seeks a middle ground between its historic extremes of pacifism and militarism—nonetheless has grown impatient with politicians who shy from recognizing that united Germany now has its own interests.

Weizsaecker says he dismisses the often-heard view that Germany "should hide itself in European integration to relieve foreign fears of a greater Germany. This is neither morally necessary nor a reasonable definition of our interests."

The dilemma Germany will face in the coming years is a choice between the extremes—whether right-wing nationalism or left-wing denial of nationhood—and the middle—Weizsaecker's honest balancing act of national interests with the postwar pledge to avoid going it alone.

Answers will be a long time coming, and they will be hard fought, but for politicians of the postwar generation—and for young Germans of the post-Wall generation—the only alternative to a dangerous flirtation with extremism is a rigorous attempt to find their own answer to the identity question.

EUROPE
SLAMS THE DOOR

Overwhelmed by migrants and too broke to support them, the nations of Western Europe are pushing the newcomers back home

BRUCE W. NELAN

THE GRASSY SQUARE IN THE MIDDLE of Slubice, a Polish town on the German border, is known locally as "the Bermuda Triangle." Most mornings, but particularly on Tuesdays and Thursdays when traffic across the frontier is heavy and the guards are busy, crowds of hopeful immigrants from Eastern Europe creep out of the woods and doorways where they have spent the night. Men, women and children straggle into the square to rendezvous with their "tour guides," the smugglers who will help them disappear into the West—for fees ranging from $50 to $200.

In another village 20 miles away, Polish entrepreneurs are carrying on a lively trade in rubber dinghies that will ferry migrants across the Oder River to Germany. Farther south, the activities of similar "travel agencies" directed or supervised by criminal gangs crowd the towns along the Czech-German border. Pilsen is so jammed with migrants from Bosnia and Croatia that its native Czech residents call it "Yugoslav City." That is partly a misnomer because while many of those in transit are from war-ravaged segments of the former Yugoslavia, other thousands are Bulgarians, Romanians, Turks and Russians. All of them, though, have something in common: they are desperate to get into Germany and to the other prosperous European Community countries they see as the promised land, and they are increasingly less likely to succeed.

West European governments are now more determined than ever to keep the foreigners out, and they are beginning to use regulations, deportations and gunboats to do so. The poor but eager migrants have become the main targets of murderous racial attacks on foreigners and xenophobic political movements in a dozen countries. With reception facilities overburdened, unemployment rates climbing to a national average of 10% and voters shouting in protest, Western governments are calling a halt. From Sweden in the north to Greece in the south, the Continent echoes with the sound of doors slamming shut.

Their fears are not unfounded. The U.N. Population Fund last week released its annual report, which confirms that illegal migration is rapidly increasing. "From 1980 to 1992 alone," the report estimates, "15 million people entered the West European countries as migrants." Other experts suggest that 5 million to 10 million people are planning to leave the states of Eastern Europe and the former Soviet Union. Half of them hope to head for Germany.

The U.N. report carefully observes that these migrants are not refugees, though there is considerable confusion on this issue. The word refugee is used regularly—but mistakenly—to describe anyone driven to leave home for any reason. But most national governments and international organizations recognize as refugees only those who live in "fear of political persecution if they return" to their homeland. As a result, many migrants who wish only to work and improve their life claim falsely to be refugees and ask for political asylum. Last year 700,000 of them applied to West European countries for asylum—438,000 in Germany alone. "I risked my life to get here," says Anton Lupu, a 33-year-old Romanian painter who made it across the border from Poland and has applied for asylum in Eisenhüttenstadt, Germany. "We didn't come to steal, only to work respectably. The difference between Germany and Romania is the difference between heaven and earth."

Though many will not say so in public, Europeans generally agree with French Interior Minister Charles Pasqua, who declares that France "no longer wants to be a country of immigration" but wants to move "toward zero immigration." France, a country of 57 million, is host to almost 4 million legal immigrants and as many as 500,000 illegals. The new conservative government in Paris has moved quickly in Pasqua's desired direction. Last month it increased the requirements foreigners must meet to acquire French citizenship. A second step, restricting the rights of legal immigrants, was approved in the first of two readings by both houses of parliament. A third measure gives police the power to stop foreigners and check for proper documentation. How would the police know for sure someone is a foreigner

From *Time*, July 19, 1993, pp. 38-41. © 1993 by Time Inc. Magazine Company. Reprinted by permission.

and thus susceptible to inspection? Suggested the bill's author, Alain Marsaud of the neo-Gaullist Rassemblement pour la République: "If you are reading the New York *Times* in the street, you may be presumed to be a foreigner." With classic logic, Pasqua argued, "How do you recognize a foreigner? By the fact that he is not French. How do you know he is not French? I answer: Ask him for his papers."

Germany, having taken in 887,000 asylum seekers during the past three years and 224,000 in the first six months of this year, has resolutely moved to stanch the flow. Without declaring it as such, Bonn has adopted a zero-immigration policy. The Bundestag has amended the Basic Law, Germany's constitution, to restrict the almost universal right of asylum it formerly—and proudly—provided. Effective July 1, economic migrants, who have made up about 95% of the more than 1 million who have arrived since 1990, are no longer to be treated as refugees. Border patrols have been beefed up, and the new law provides for the immediate expulsion of illegal migrants.

Under an agreement between Germany and Romania, deportation flights to Bucharest take off almost every day from Berlin. In the first five months of this year, 21,800 Romanians were returned. Germany has

ALIENS IN A LAND THEY CALL HOME

John Kohan
MOSCOW

An elderly couple, ethnic Russians afraid to identify themselves beyond their first names Ivan and Natalya, walk slowly across the bridge that links the Estonian city of Narva to the Russian community of Ivan-Gorod. They used to make the trip easily, before the break-up of the Soviet Union turned the Narva River into the official boundary between two independent countries. Above the huge medieval fortress that guards the west bank flies the Estonian flag. On the eastern shore, a rugged rampart displays the Russian tricolor. On the bridge below, lines of pedestrians and cars move slowly between customs posts set up at both ends. "We built this city," says Ivan, pointing back to Narva as he and his wife make their way to the Russian side, where bread and milk are cheaper. "Now they are tightening the noose around our neck to make us leave."

Since the collapse of the Soviet empire, about 24 million ethnic Russians have found themselves living in foreign countries, outside the boundaries of their historic homeland. The hundreds of thousands of Russian workers who flooded into the Baltic states of Estonia and Latvia after the 1940 Soviet annexation are viewed with suspicion now, as fifth columnists who are opposed to the nationalist aspirations of the new states. Many Russians have not helped matters any by refusing to learn local languages.

The problem has reached the boiling point in Estonia, where ethnic Russians and other Russian speakers make up 40% of the 1.6 million population. Worried about becoming a minority in their own homeland, Estonians in the State Assembly passed a package of laws that would deny citizenship—and hence employment—to anyone who had moved to Estonia after 1940 and who failed to pass a very complicated language test. Last month another law was passed requiring noncitizens to apply for either Estonian or Russian citizenship or to register as aliens and face possible deportation. "We want to determine where they stand," explains an Estonian Foreign Ministry official. "They cannot remain citizens of a nonexistent Soviet Union." But given the difficulties in obtaining Estonian citizenship, most Russians will be forced to become foreigners.

Reaction to the aliens act has been swift and shrill. In the northeast border region around Narva, where ethnic Russians constitute 95% of the population, local Russians plan to hold a plebiscite this week on the question of regional autonomy—a move the Estonians have denounced as "unconstitutional." Western governments have voiced concern about growing discrimination against minorities. But the harshest rebuke has come from Moscow, where Foreign Minister Andrei Kozyrev denounced the law as "quiet apartheid" and "ethnic cleansing in white gloves."

Under pressure from conservative opponents to take a tougher stand on the ethnic Russian question, Boris Yeltsin bluntly warned the Estonians not to misinterpret "Russia's goodwill." Moscow, he pointed out, had "ways of reminding them" of geopolitical realities. The Kremlin has already put the withdrawal of former Soviet forces from Estonia on hold to protest local mistreatment of Russians.

TIME Map by Paul J. Pugliese

Seeking to defuse the crisis, Estonian President Lennart Meri consulted with European legal experts. On their advice, Meri refused to sign the aliens act into law and last week called the Estonian parliament back into an emergency session, where more fuel was added to the fire when legislators proposed holding an emergency session to discuss suspending Narva's city council. Should this happen, tensions could get out of hand. As Vladimir Khomyakov, a Narva city-council member, brusquely put it, "This is our homeland; we have no other. The only way out now is autonomy. Otherwise, there will be war."

The irony is that few Russians living in Estonia want to secede completely from the Baltic state. Compared with the rest of the old Soviet empire, the economic reforms that Estonia has carried out in the brief period of independence are nothing short of miraculous. It is the only former Soviet republic with a stable, convertible currency, and the monthly rate of inflation has dropped in one year from 90% to 1.7%. Unless the rival ethnic communities can turn their present dialogue of the deaf into real cooperation, however, Estonia may yet succumb to the fever of nationalism that has so much of Europe in its grip.

—With reporting by Yuri Zarakhovich/Narva

EAST EUROPEANS THOUGHT THE COLLAPSE OF BARBED-WIRE BORDERS WOULD ALLOW THEM TO MOVE AROUND THE WORLD UNHINDERED

signed similar agreements with Bulgaria and Poland and most recently with the Czech Republic, which has taken back 18,000 people who entered Germany illegally in the first quarter of 1993. The treaties provide for cash payments from Germany to help countries absorb the returnees. Poland, for example, is to receive $71 million by the end of next year.

Germany's return policy follows guidelines agreed upon by E.C. immigration ministers last December, when the principle of "first safe country" was approved. That means that a bona fide refugee, fearing for his life, must seek asylum in the first safe country he reaches. If he does not and instead enters an E.C. state, he could be pushed back to the last safe country he was in before arriving inside the E.C.

The list of "safe countries" conveniently includes such eastern states as Poland, the Czech Republic, Slovakia, Romania, Bulgaria and Hungary. Thus not only can Germany send unwanted arrivals back to those states, but the "safe" countries will now be much more careful about letting migrants cross their borders lest they be stuck with them. Hungary, for example, turned back 1.3 million people from farther east over the past year because Austria and Germany will not accept them. Austria, in turn, has tried to stop Bosnians from using it as a route into Germany. Measures adopted in Vienna this year make it much harder for anyone entering Austria to live and work there, and this month new regulations go into effect that strictly monitor the length of time even legal workers may remain.

Italian officials insist they do not intend to go the way of France and Germany, but many of them are worried because the country is host to about 800,000 legal and at least 300,000 illegal foreign workers, even as unemployment heads toward 10%. Says Social Affairs Minister Fernanda Contri: "We need to work on the idea of a certain number of foreigners allowed in, a fixed number each year." To guard against a return of the Albanian boat people who were sent back two years ago, the Italian navy is patrolling the Adriatic. The powerful opposition group, the Northern League, calls unabashedly for zero immigration. "There should be an end to all this false pity," says Gianfranco Salmoiraghi, a League official in Milan. "Immigrants are caught in a form of slavery, exploited by unscrupulous employers to accept lower wages, thus depriving Italians of work."

The gates of Fortress Europe moved closer to the locked position last week when Sweden and Denmark announced new immigration restrictions that require Bosnians, as well as Croats, Macedonians and Serbs, to arrive with a valid visa. At the same time, Sweden has told 40,000 Bosnians now in residence that they can stay, but Denmark says its 14,000 Bosnians will be sent home when the civil war in the former Yugoslavia ends. The Danes should not hold their breath.

Greece, meanwhile, is rounding up and repatriating thousands of Albanians. Explains Foreign Minister Michalis Papakonstantinou: "Because of our tolerance, we have been swamped by Albanians." Officials in Athens estimate that the country now holds 200,000 illegal Albanians among 500,000 workers who have slipped in from other countries.

Britain's immigration laws have been tough for decades, but a bill now before Parliament would tighten the requirements for political asylum and take away the right of tourists and students to appeal when their request for an extension is refused. Under pressure from the E.C., Spain requires visas for arrivals from Morocco. The Spanish have persuaded Morocco to take back its own citizens as well as others who illegally enter their country across the mouth of the Mediterranean.

Residents of the poor countries and the former communist states are willing to do almost anything to reach the lands of opportunity in the West. Citizens of former Warsaw Pact countries thought that political freedom and the collapse of barbed-wire borders throughout Eastern Europe would bring them the opportunity to move around the world unhindered. Their expectation collides with the fact that many West Europeans simply do not want to encourage immigration into their ethnically homogeneous nation-states. The only foreigners who have a right to live in Germany today are those who have been granted refugee status or those who hold valid work permits, most of whom come in on "guest worker" programs. Germany has no immigration program in the sense that the U.S. or Canada or Australia has, with rules about moving in and becoming a citizen. Germany has only recently begun to consider ways to make it easier for thousands of ethnic Turks born and educated in the country to become German citizens.

Hopeful East Europeans may not be aware of that. On the grass of Slubice's Bermuda Triangle stands a group of well-dressed young Romanians—none really the victim of political persecution, discussing the newly erected barriers they face. "How exactly," one asks, "can you immigrate legally into Germany?" The frustrating answer: "As of now, you can't."—*Reported by Bruce Crumley/Paris, Leonora Dodsworth/Rome and Nomi Morris/ Berlin, with other bureaus*

The Great Transformation

Zbigniew Brzezinski

Zbigniew Brzezinski, U.S. national security adviser during 1977-1981, is the author of the recently published *Out of Control: Global Turmoil on the Eve of the 21st Century*. His previous work was titled *The Grand Failure: The Birth and Death of Communism in the Twentieth Century* (1989).

FOUR YEARS HAVE now passed since the implosion of the communist state in Poland set in train a process that led to the collapse of the other Central European communist states. Two years have now passed since the implosion of the Soviet system itself, following five years of agonizing "perestroika." It is, therefore, not too early to try to draw some lessons from the subsequent attempts to create, on the ruins of the communist systems, politically viable and economically successful democracies.

That on-going transformation poses intellectually challenging questions. When it began, there was no model, no guiding concept, with which to approach the task. Economic theory at least claimed some understanding of the allegedly inevitable transformation of capitalism into socialism. But there was no theoretical body of knowledge pertaining to the transformation of the statist systems into pluralistic democracies based on the free market. In addition to being daunting intellectually, the issue was and remains taxing politically, because the West, surprised by the rapid disintegration of communism, was not properly prepared for participation in the complex task of transforming the former Soviet-type systems. Consequently, it has had to improvise very hastily over the last several years.

It is in this context that I intend to address four important questions. First, what should we have learned by now regarding the processes of post-communist political and

Phases of Post-Communist Transformation

Phase One: 1-5 Years

Political Goal: Transformation
Economic Goal: Stabilization

Political	Legal/Regulatory	Economic	Western Aid
Basic democracy; Free press; End of one-party state and police system; Initial democratic coalition for change.	Elimination of arbitrary state controls.	Elimination of price controls and subsidies; End of collectivization; Haphazard privatization.	Currency stabilization; Emergency credits & aid.

Phase Two: 3-10 Years

Political Goal: From Transformation to Stabilization
Economic Goal: From Stabilization to Transformation

Political	Legal/Regulatory	Economic	Western Aid
New constitution & electoral law; Elections; Decentralized regional self-government; Stable democratic coalition = new political elite.	Legal/regulatory framework for property & business.	Banking system; Small & middle scale privatization; Demonopolization; New economic class appears.	Infrastructural credits; Technical/managerial assistance; Trade preferences & access; Initial foreign investment.

Phase Three: 5-15+ Years

Political Goal: Consolidation
Economic Goal: Sustained Take-Off

Political	Legal/Regulatory	Economic	Western Aid
Formation of stable democratic parties; Democratic political culture takes.	Independent judiciary & legal culture emerges.	Large-scale privatization; Capitalist lobbies; Entrepreneurial culture emerges.	Major foreign investment; Inclusion in key Western organs. (E.g. EC, NATO, etc.).

Duration of the phases above is influenced by the nature of the gestation *prior* to the final collapse of communism. Four basic types of positive and/or negative gestation impact on the pace of transformation: 1) both the political and the economic changes are positive; 2) political positive but economic negative; 3) political negative but economic positive and 4) both political and economic are negative. (Hungary and Poland both fall broadly in the first; Russia in the second; China in the third; Romania in the fourth.)

economic transformation? Second, what should we have learned regarding Western policies meant to aid and promote that transformation? Third, and in the light of the preceding two, what results can we expect to flow in the foreseeable future—over the next decade or so—from the ongoing efforts at the transformation? Fourth, and more specifically, what else should the United States now be doing in that context?

The Transformation Process

REGARDING the broad lessons of the transformation process, the first is that *expectations on both sides—in the old communist states and in the West—were much too high, and rather naive.* The liberated peoples of the former communist countries had truly exaggerated and simplistic notions of the kind of help that they would receive from the West. There was a generalized anticipation of manna from heaven, of some new "Marshall Plan" being applied on a vast scale, notwithstanding the actual historical and intellectual irrelevance to former communist countries of the Marshall Plan experience. And in the West, there was a general underestimation of the systemic complexity of the changes required, of the resistance of established and still-pervasive nomenklaturas, and of the duration of the process itself.

A striking example of the above is that the American aid programs which were initiated immediately after 1989-90 for Poland, and then for the other Central European countries, were based on the assumption that the transition process would last for about five years.[1] We now know that it will be much longer than that—ten years at a minimum for the Central European countries, probably in the range of fifteen to twenty years for the other countries—before it will be possible to say that the transformation has been completed. (One may also add, parenthetically, that the West was also rather over-optimistic as well as simplistic in its assessment of Gorbachev—of his intentions, as well as of his program—and that to some extent we currently display a similar tendency in our reactions to Yeltsin.)

A second and more complicated lesson is that *the transformation process itself is not a continuum, but a sequence of distinct phases.* Moreover, not all of the former communist states are in the same phase of the process of transformation, nor are they traversing the respective stages at the same pace. It is also noteworthy that the rapidity of the shift from phase to phase is heavily conditioned by what transpired politically and economically during the final (pre-implosion but also gestating) stage of the former communist systems.

The above requires some elaboration. The first critical phase, following immediately upon the fall of the communist system, involves a combined effort to achieve both the political transformation of the top structures of political power and the initial stabilization of the economy. The former typically means the imposition of top-down democracy; the latter typically requires stabilization of the currency while undertaking the initial unfreezing of economic controls. This initial stage is extremely difficult because it involves a fundamental change in established political and economic processes. It calls for boldness and toughness, being essentially a plunge into the unknown.

The first phase is also *the* critical one because its success is the necessary launch pad for the second stage, one in which the quest for broader political stabilization has to be combined with efforts at more pervasive economic transformation. The adoption of a new constitution, of a new electoral system, and the penetration of society by democratic processes are designed to institutionalize a functioning democracy. At the same time a broader economic transformation has to be launched, involving, for example, the establishment of a banking sector, de-monopoliza-

---

[1] See, for example, the U.S. General Accounting Office Report, "Poland and Hungary—Economic Transition and U.S. Assistance," May, 1992, pp.18-26, 30.

tion, as well as small and middle-scale privatization based on legally defined property rights.

Only when and if that phase has been successfully completed can the next—and third—phase be undertaken, in which comprehensive democratic institutions and processes truly begin to take hold in an enduring fashion, while economic growth becomes sustained as a consequence of the comprehensive unleashing of private initiative. A democratic political culture and an entrepreneurial tradition gradually become reality. This third phase can be described as involving political consolidation and sustained economic take-off. To make all this more concrete, one might hazard the judgment that Poland, the Czech Republic, and Hungary are now on the brink of entering that third phase. (See the attached chart on p. 92 for a schematic representation of the phases).

It is also important to note that the ability to embark on, and to traverse, particularly the first critical phase—the most important stage of decision—is heavily conditioned by the degree to which a particular fallen communist regime permitted both political relaxation and economic liberalization in its last years. The important fact to note is that, in effect, the final agony of communism also served simultaneously—at least, in several cases—as a period of political and economic gestation for the emergence of post-communism. The consequences of that gestation in the cases of Hungary (the Kadar regime in the 1970s and 1980s) and of Poland (the Gierek regime of the 1970s and the last 5 years of Jaruzelski in the second half of the 1980s) are self-evident.

The third lesson to be deduced from what we have seen of the transformation process involves *the primacy of political reform as the basis for effective economic reform. A democratic political consensus and effective political processes are* **essential** *for the successful initiation and consummation of the first critical stage of change.* One could theoretically postulate the need for an authoritarian system of discipline at this stage, because a great deal of social sacrifice is required—and generated—during its implementation. China obviously comes to mind here. However, in the wake of the collapse of the communist regimes in Central Europe and in the Soviet Union, an authoritarian approach does not seem feasible or desirable.

On the contrary, democratic consensus is imperative. But it must be organized and institutionalized. Initially, that typically calls for the presence of an effective, indeed of a charismatic popular leader—a Havel, Walesa, or perhaps Yeltsin—who can command popular support. It also requires the presence or rapid organization of a political movement that supports the leader in an institutionalized fashion, and is capable of sustaining popular support in the face of the social dislocations and deprivations that typically occur in this phase. But, above all, the initial phase, with its often euphoric post-communist enthusiasm, must be exploited promptly to build the foundations for legitimate and formal democratic procedures within which longer-term economic reforms are pursued. By the time the second phase is reached, public euphoria tends to have waned while disappointment with the transformation tends to escalate; thus much depends on the resilience and viability of the new democratic processes. Much of Russia's difficulties stem from Gorbachev's and then Yeltsin's failure to focus on the need for comprehensive political reform as an urgent priority.

The foregoing leads to a fourth lesson, which flows from the previous three: *the rapid and comprehensive transformation—the shock therapy of the so-called "big bang" approach—is only possible if both the necessary subjective and objective conditions exist.* The Polish case is a good example of the combination of the two. It involved the existence of a nation-wide counter-political elite, namely the Solidarity movement, which permeated society, was not crushed during the decade of the martial law, and could promptly serve as an effective counter-political elite on the national scale (rather than, as in some other cases, being confined to a few dissidents suddenly installed at the top of the national power hierarchy). That elite, moreover, was buttressed by the presence of a moral authority able to nourish the social will to sacrifice, namely the Catholic Church. In addition, a charismatic leader, who enjoyed special authority within the class likely to suffer the most from the social sacrifices, was able to personalize the political change. A free peasant class and a large underground economy provided economic responsiveness to the workings of the law of supply and demand, upon the lifting of price controls and the termination of subsidies. Finally, Poland benefitted from the support given to its surfacing entrepreneurial culture by an engaged diaspora comprised of some ten million Poles who live abroad.

The listing of these factors suggests that while the Polish "Big Bang" approach may be exemplary, it may also be, in many respects, exceptional. In the absence of some combination of political cohesion, commitment, and consensus with economic receptivity and responsiveness, the shock therapy is likely to produce political conflict and economic chaos, with well-positioned monopolies taking advantage of price liberalization simply to increase prices, thereby also stimulating inflation.

The fifth and last general lesson regarding post-communist reconstruction follows from this last point: *One should not rule out transformation strategies that involve slower motion through the needed several stages, and that are also reliant on continued governmental guidance rather than purely on the unleashing of independent and dynamic market forces.* Here the warnings of the very prominent Japanese development economist, the late Suburo Okita, come to mind. He argued cogently in several papers that governmental intervention is needed in countries in which the free market mechanisms lack tradition, experience, and appropriate social culture. He stressed that there are societies in which some combination of market mechanism and governmental planning is necessary for historical reasons, especially as the market mechanism is not always and of itself infallible.

The examples of both Japan and Korea are very pertinent to the case made by Okita. In the summer of 1993, the World Bank was completing an exhaustive analysis of what transpired in the Far East in the last three decades and what lessons may be derived from that experience. According to a preview in the *Financial Times*, one of the Bank's conclusions regarding the Korean experience was that "...from the early 1960s, the government carefully planned and orchestrated the country's development...[It] used the financial sector to steer credits to preferred sectors and promoted individual firms to achieve national objectives...[It] socialized risk, created large conglomerates, created state enterprises when necessary, and moulded a public-private partnership that rivalled Japan's."[2] Much the same could be said about Singapore as an example of successful directed growth. At the very least, such Asian experience should not be disregarded when contemplating the current political, economic and social dilemmas facing both Russia and Ukraine, countries without strong free market traditions and developed entrepreneurial cultures.[3]

The Western Response

LET US NOW turn to the second of the four major questions posed at the outset: the lessons to be learned concern-

[2] See Michael Prowse, "Miracles Beyond the Free Market," *Financial Times*, April 26, 1993.
[3] A useful compendium of Saburo Okita's writings on this subject is contained in "Steps to the 21st Century," *The Japan Times*, 1993. In addition to Saburo Okita's numerous writings, see also D.W. Nam (a former prime minister), "Korea's Economic Take-off in Retrospect," a paper presented at the Second Washington Conference of the Korean-American Association, Washington, D.C., Sept. 28-29, 1992; and N. Yonemura and H. Tsukamoto (both of MITI), "Japan's Postwar Experience: Its Meaning and Implications for the Economic Transformation of the former Soviet Republics," March 1992.

ing Western policy designed to aid and promote post-communist transformation.

First, Western aid is most critical during the first stage of transformation. In fact, significant Western aid is probably essential if that stage is to be traversed successfully. Later, after the first phase, Western aid ceases to be central, whereas access to Western markets and foreign investment become increasingly important. That access becomes the primary source of continued internal change and of export-driven economic dynamism. That is largely the case today in the relationship between post-communist Central Europe and the European Community, with the result that the issue of "access" has become much more controversial than the scale of "aid." In contrast, the former Soviet Union is still in the first phase of the transformation process, when direct Western aid for stabilization and initial political transformation is essential.

Second, and perhaps more controversially, after the critical first phase, the inflow of external capital is not decisive. If Western capital was the key to success, the former East Germany should be flourishing, Hungary should have taken off economically some time ago, followed by the Czech Republic, with Poland trailing behind. Moreover, Russia should be doing much better than China.

The former East Germany (GDR) has received monumental amounts of external capital over the last three years, at a rate of $100 billion per annum, for a population of a mere 16 million people. (Just calculate what anything comparable to such a per capita inflow would be required for Central Europe as a whole, or for Russia specifically!) But the crucial point is that the former GDR is still in a massive socio-economic crisis. Similarly, Hungary and Czechoslovakia (prior to its division into two states in early 1993) have been the beneficiaries of much larger capital inflows than Poland. Yet today, Poland has a larger private sector and is the first former communist country to have attained a positive economic growth rate.

China has been the beneficiary of relatively small amounts in terms of grants, loans, credits, and until recently, investments. Over the first twelve years after the start of the reforms in 1979, the total involved for China—a huge country with an enormous population—was less than $60 billion. This is much less than the Soviet Union/Russia has received since 1986—some $86 billion. Yet China has done extremely well in terms of its economic development, growing over the last decade at a rate of 6 percent per annum, last year at 9 percent, this year probably at 13 percent. Russia, in contrast, is still in an economic mess, with a negative growth rate.

In brief, after the conclusion of the first critical phase during which external assistance is central, the nature of domestic policies, social discipline and motivation cumulatively become more important than the inflow of external capital in determining success or failure in the pursuit of economic transformation.

A third lesson with respect to the inflow of external capital is that explicit preconditions and strict supervision of its utilization are imperative. In fact, if a choice is to be made between quite limited but tightly monitored financial assistance and large inflows of external and largely untargeted capital, the former is clearly more beneficial and, therefore, should be favored. This is especially true in the first phase, until trade and foreign investment replace the initial dependence on direct aid. Trade and investment almost automatically tend to be subject to more effective control by the directly interested and personally concerned parties. In the absence of close external supervision, as experience sadly shows, massive diversion and extensive theft of foreign aid is to be expected.

The West should have learned this from its experience with Poland under Gierek. In the 1970s, Poland borrowed about $30 billion, yet it is very difficult to account for what happened to these funds. Today, there are even more serious questions to be raised regarding the $86 billion that has flowed into the former Soviet Union since the second half of the 1980s. Some estimates made in the United States conclude that as much as $17 billion of it has been diverted away from intended purposes and recycled to Western banks. While recently in Moscow, I cited that estimate to Arkady Volskiy, the head of the Russian Union of Industrialists and Entrepreneurs. With a laugh he dismissed the estimate as absolutely wrong, insisting that the total diverted is at least $23 billion.

A recently concluded Japanese study, conducted on the eve of the July G-7 Summit in Tokyo by a private think tank, the Toray Corporate Business Research Inc., also addressed this issue. The study concluded that the Russian government has lost control over the capital flight phenomenon, with the consequence that large amounts of cash, gold, and diamonds have been stashed in Swiss and Hong Kong banks. "The scale of the capital flight has already exceeded 40 billion dollars," the study asserted.[4] Though this estimate may be too high, it is nonetheless clear that the problem of illicit diversion is a very serious one.

Accordingly, precise targeting and close monitoring by donors should be explicitly asserted, even if it offends the national pride of the recipients. Specific conditionality is also essential regarding the fundamentals of reform. Stabilization in the monetary area, depoliticization of the banking system, demonopolization, at least initial small-scale privatization, including in agriculture, and the decentralization of economic decision-making, are the minima that the West has the right to insist upon when granting aid, if the aid is to be helpful.

Fourth, the West ought to encourage the recipient countries to develop some longer-range mobilizing vision, one capable of sustaining

---

[4]As reported by KYODO, May 24, 1993. Further shocking details regarding the diversion of Western aid for illicit purposes are contained in Grigory Yavlinsky's op-ed article "Western Aid is No Help" in the July 28, 1993 *New York Times*.

domestic support for the needed painful reforms. Even with generous external aid, domestic sacrifices and a great deal of social pain are unavoidable. Therefore, the articulation of a more positive, hopeful, constructive perspective on the future is politically necessary. The public must perceive a sense of direction which justifies their transitional pain and sacrifice.

For the Central Europeans such a vision largely exists already. It involves the notion of united Europe, and of their eventual membership in it. That vision is very meaningful and tangible for an average Czech or a Hungarian or a Pole. It represents something to which they can relate personally. The issue becomes more difficult and elusive when one moves further east. What can provide such a constructive vision today for a Ukrainian who has experienced independence for two years and has found that it has brought mainly socio-economic deprivation? What is that vision for a Russian, who not only experiences similar socio-economic deprivation but also feels acutely humiliated by Russia's loss of the big power status? It is not easy in these circumstances to generate a positive vision of the future.

For the Ukrainians, perhaps it could be the notion of Ukraine eventually becoming, and being accepted by its Western neighbors as a Central European state, and thus part of a community that is already moving closer to the West. That vision certainly would be more tangible to the western Ukrainians than to the eastern Ukrainians, but it might have wider appeal to the Ukrainians who wish to define their nationhood in terms that differentiate Ukraine from Russia.

For the Russians, perhaps, the appropriate vision might be one of becoming a partner of the United States, given the fascination with America that is today so widespread in Russia. But if Russia is to be "a partner" of the United States, America will have to be explicit in insisting that such a Russia be truly a post-imperial Russia, because only such a Russia can become genuinely democratic. The fact is that Russia has still a considerable distance to go in the painful process of adjusting to its new post-imperial reality, a process that was consummated in the case of Britain with the loss of India, in the case of France with the loss of Algeria, in the case of Turkey under Attaturk who defined the concept of a new, would-be modern, would-be European, Turkey. The process of post-imperial self-redefinition is a complicated and difficult one. One can understand why opposition and confusion surround this subject in today's tormented Russia; but the issue must be addressed.

A Differentiated Future

IN THE LIGHT of the responses to the first two questions, what reasonable expectations regarding the post-communist transformation might be entertained in terms of the foreseeable future—say, the next decade or so? It follows from the analysis already offered that the transformation will be differentiated—in kind and time—as well as difficult. But what is likely to be the overall pattern? Are all of the former communist states safely on the way to becoming pluralistic, free market democracies?

Before I hazard some rather arbitrary, personal judgments in response to this question, let me suggest a fourfold predictive framework:

The first category includes countries with essentially positive futures, by which is meant countries in which it would take something altogether unforeseeable and, at the present time, rather improbable for them to be diverted from the process of becoming viable pluralistic democracies.

The second category includes countries whose prospects over the next ten years look somewhat better than even, but in which a reversal, indeed a political and/or economic failure, still cannot be excluded.

The third category involves countries whose political and economic futures, in my judgment, are likely to be still unresolved beyond this decade and into the next century.

Finally a fourth category, essentially an extension of the third, comprises countries whose futures currently, and into the foreseeable future, look distinctly unpromising.

In this classification, as already indicated, Poland, the Czech Republic, and Hungary fall into the first category, as do probably also Slovenia and Estonia. Of these, the first three are likely to be members of the European Community and of NATO within a decade, and even perhaps within this century. Without minimizing their internal difficulties, their futures appear largely predetermined, although Hungary or Estonia could be affected adversely by some external complications (notably, ethnic problems). In any case, the first three can be seen as about to enter, or as entering, Phase 3 on the table on p. 92, while the latter two are in Phase 2.

Even the likely success of the leading three, however, should not obscure the fact that it will take many years before the gap is significantly narrowed between the standards of living of the richer West and even its most promising post-communist neighbors. If one assumes, for example, that Germany and Austria will grow at 2 percent per annum, while Poland, Hungary, and the former Czechoslovakia will grow twice as fast, at 4 percent p/a, it would still take 30 years in the case of Czechoslovakia, 46 years of Hungary, and 63 years of Poland for the gap in the respective GNP per capita to be closed.[5] Even if the rates of growth were 2 percent and 8 percent respectively, the years required would still be 12, 17, and 23 for the respective Central European populations. Obviously the prospects are much dimmer still for the countries listed below in the second, third, and fourth categories.

The second category—countries whose futures are generally positive but which are

---

[5]Based on the CIA World Fact Book 1991, with the per capita GNP for Germany being $14,600; for Austria $14,500; for CSFR $7,700; for Hungary $5,800; for Poland $4,200.

politically and economically still vulnerable—includes Slovakia, Croatia (if it does not get entangled in a new war with Serbia), Bulgaria, perhaps Romania, Lithuania, Latvia, Kirgizikstan, and Turkmenistan (the latter two because of indigenous economic potential). Some of them—e.g. Latvia or Bulgaria—may be nearing Phase 2 but the others are still navigating through Phase 1.

The countries which fall into the third category—those whose political and economic futures are likely to be still unresolved for a decade or more—are, first and foremost Russia—and then Ukraine, Belarus, Georgia, Armenia, Azerbaijan, Kazakhstan, and Uzbekistan. Finally, those in the fourth category, whose futures for a variety of reasons look rather grim, are: Serbia, Albania, Macedonia, Bosnia, Moldova, and Tajikistan. None of the above can be said to be very advanced (or successful) in traversing Phase 1; some may not even have entered it; and most of them are, in fact, still governed by their former communist elites who masquerade under new labels, but whose commitment to a pluralist democracy and sensitivity to its nuances is still questionable.

Of those in the uncertain (third) category, Russia is, of course, the most important. One has to recognize some positive trends in ongoing Russian developments. The process of drafting the constitution has been moving forward, albeit with many difficulties. One can expect at least an initial formula regarding a new constitutional order to emerge from this exercise, and that in itself will be a step forward in the institutionalization of a democratic system. There has certainly been general democratization, particularly of the upper-metropolitan levels of Russian society. In a number of the large cities, democracy is an operational reality, though it lacks genuinely pervasive institutionalization. There has also been some privatization of the economy, and initial steps toward its stabilization. Also, at the top political levels, both President Boris Yeltsin and Foreign Minister Andrei Kozyrev have been willing to denounce—at least rhetorically—traditional imperial aspirations, thereby breaking with a past that would otherwise certainly inhibit genuine democratization.

But there are also contradictory trends: economic chaos is a reality; there is no effective monetary policy, inflation is still extraordinarily high, unemployment is rising; the writ of the government is effectively limited to a few metropolitan centers and does not run throughout the country; there is a lack of policy cohesion and consistency; the much hallowed privatization accounts for only about 50,000 of Russia's approximately 300,000 small shops, with most of those privatized located in Moscow, St. Petersburg, and Nizhny Novgorod;[6] there is massive diversion of Western funds and aid by the remnants of well-positioned nomenklatura and by the new class of middlemen; and many, probably most, of the new capitalists represent parasitic wealth, channeled mainly into consumption and not into productive investment.

Also complicating the economic picture is the evident renewal of imperial aspirations, which increases the likelihood of intensifying tensions with Ukraine and also generates problems with some of the other neighboring states. Most noteworthy here is the use of economic leverage and of military pressure to preserve informally the essential elements of the Kremlin's former imperial status. Quite symptomatic of Moscow's continued reluctance to accept Kiev's independence as an enduring fact was the contemptuous dismissal of it (in the words spoken to me in 1993 by a senior Russian policymaker) as "that conditional entity called Ukraine."

All of this justifies—and generates—some uncertainties regarding the future. One can expect, most probably, continued democratization, but in a context of inconsistent reforms that run the risk of producing peri-

---

[6]See also "Measuring Russia's Emerging Private Sector," Intelligence Research Paper, CIA, Washington, DC, November, 1992.

odic phases of intensifying anarchy—and thus the temptation to resort eventually to more authoritarian solutions. As a result, Russia does not fit either category one or category two, but has to be placed—reluctantly and regrettably—in category three. The same is true of Ukraine, whose independence is still in jeopardy and whose internal transformation has been lagging even more badly.

The foregoing cumulatively suggests that history is still open-ended as far as the final outcome of the post-communist transformation is concerned. *As of now, politically and economically successful liberal democracy is not a foreordained outcome, except perhaps for five out of the twenty-seven post-communist states.*

What Else Should the West Do?

IT IS TIME to turn to the last of the four questions posed at the onset; namely, what should be the posture of the West, and of the United States in particular?

The first need is still for a long-term and comprehensive strategy that integrates geopolitical and economic objectives. As yet, it simply does not exist. The needed strategy should be neither Russo-centric nor Russo-phobic. It must deal with the post-communist area as a whole, but recognize the significantly different stages of change within it. To develop and sustain such a comprehensive policy, the United States should press for the creation of a standing G-7 strategic planning board, one capable of monitoring changes and of advocating the needed division of labor among the principal Western powers, perhaps on a geographical basis. For example, Japan with its hesitations about aiding Russia, could be encouraged to be helpful by concentrating on some other formerly Soviet regions, such as Ukraine. Such a standing strategic board should also interact with pertinent representatives of the affected countries.

In addition, a more comprehensive strategy might involve, for example, Western credits for Central European exports of food and consumer goods to Russia. This would facilitate the Central European transformation while increasing the likelihood that aid for the Russian people will reach the designated recipients rather than being diverted into the black market by middlemen—as sadly has often been the case. In any case, some restoration of trade between Central Europe and the former Soviet Union is clearly in the interest of all of the parties concerned.

Second, the G-7 should now develop an aid package for Ukraine, paralleling the one adopted for Russia. Geopolitical pluralism in the space of the former Soviet Union should be viewed by the West as an objective of co-equal importance with systemic transformation. This point deserves repetition: geopolitical pluralism is as important as systemic transformation. The United States is beginning in a hesitant fashion to move in that direction, but its policy in this respect has been slow, marred by historical ignorance, beset by bureaucratic stalemates, and instinctively Russo-centric. An aid package for Ukraine, conditioned quite explicitly and specifically on a Ukrainian reform program, is justified on humanitarian and economic, as well as geopolitical, grounds.

Early in 1992, the head of the IMF, Michel Camdessus, publicly stated that Russia would need about $24 billion in external assistance, and that the other former Soviet republics would need an additional $20 billion.[7] A little over a year later, that total sum has been allocated for Russia but little or nothing has been designated for Ukraine and the other non-Russian republics. Yet chaos around Russia will either undermine Russia's own reforms or stimulate a revival of Russia's imperial ambitions, or both—with all of these outcomes being very detrimental to the cause of postcommunist transformation.

Third, facilitating access to Western markets and increased investment should now be the major focus of G-7 initiatives, especially as the EC has been slow in this regard. Some concessions

---

[7] *New York Times*, April 16, 1992.

were made by the EC at its June 1993 Copenhagen meeting, but they involved only a partial liberalization of the existing quota-based system limiting Central European access to Western markets. West European economic lobbies—for example, the European Chemical Industry Council or the European Largest Textile and Apparel Companies—as well as some key national ones—for example, the German Steel Association—have teamed up with European agricultural interests in agitating for continued discrimination against competitive Central European products.

The United States should press its allies on this score, because it has been somewhat more open than the EC, but it should also further liberalize its own policies, which have also been unduly restrictive toward Central European and Russian exports. The economies of Central Europe and Russia badly need trade-driven stimuli.

Fourth, the United States should de-emphasize some of the dogmatic elements in the advice that it offers to the former communist states. There has been a tendency in the West, and particularly in the United States, to make shibboleths of the free market and of the elimination of the role of the government in guiding economic development. Indeed, even advice on democracy should be offered with the historically humbling appreciation of the prolonged stages that were required to nurture and consolidate democracy in the West. Cultural conditioning and specific circumstances should be taken into account to a far greater degree than they have been in the rather dogmatic advice that has often been proffered.

Finally, it is not too early to start deliberations about the needed new security arrangements, designed progressively to encompass the former communist states. Geopolitical insecurity is rising in the former communist world and it is becoming as severe a political problem as socio-economic anxiety. There needs to be a response to it, developed and applied in stages, pointing toward the progressive acceptance into NATO of former communist states. Inclusion by stages of some of the former communist states will be more acceptable to Russia and to Ukraine if it is presented as part of a process, the end result of which should be the emergence of a broad Euro-Atlantic system of security that someday might also include Moscow and Kiev. In any case, as a practical matter, some former communist states should be able to enter NATO sooner than others, since it makes no sense to wait until all are ready to enter before letting the first one in. Accordingly, the admission of one (probably Poland) or more Central European states into NATO, roughly by 1996, should be a major goal of Western policy.

All of this represents a manageable agenda, provided the West has the needed political will and strategic direction. But will America address these issues? Will the West respond? Probably not quite as deliberately and as strategically as one might wish. The West is currently in a phase of internal preoccupation, with cultural hedonism dominating its value system. Cultural hedonism does not lend itself to an activist policy which entails commitment and also requires some measure of sacrifice. While it may be unfair to accuse the United States of embracing isolationism—for America is certainly not disengaging from its formal global obligations—it does appear that Washington is currently pursuing an essentially minimalist foreign policy. Though not deliberately isolating itself from the rest of the world, the United States at this stage seems inclined to define its obligations in the most narrow fashion, exercising its leadership responsibilities only in exceptional circumstances, when the necessity for action becomes overriding.

Hopefully, Western hedonism in general and American minimalism represent but a passing phase of what might be called "post-victory blues"—the inevitable let down after the sustained historical effort of the Cold War. One must hope so because if this phase does not end soon, the post-communist transformation will not only be much more painful and prolonged, but its outcome will be even more uncertain.

In a New Slovakia, Fears Are Both New and Old

Stephen Engelberg

Special to The New York Times

BRATISLAVA, Slovakia—Wedged into one of the most strategic corners in this unstable region, Eastern Europe's newest small nation has been gripped by uncertainty and foreboding in its first few weeks of independence.

Slovaks are frantically withdrawing their money from local banks, anticipating that the widely rumored end of the joint currency with the Czech Republic will mean a sharply devalued Slovak crown.

With the Government tightening its control over the press and television, opposition politicians and some journalists have stepped up their attacks on the democratic credentials of Prime Minister Vladimir Meciar.

Some even see a new era of "normalization," the euphemism for the purges that followed Moscow's invasion of Czechoslovakia in 1968.

Stirring the Stew

Slovakia's independence has added new complexities to a region already buffeted by ethnic conflict. Bounded by Ukraine, Poland, the Czech Republic, Austria and Hungary, this nation of 5.2 million stands at Eastern Europe's crossroads, and turmoil here can ricochet in myriad directions, including the direction of the 600,000 ethnic Hungarians in Slovakia.

From the first hours of the country's independence on Jan. 1, Mr. Meciar (pronounced METCH-yahr) has made clear his intentions to chart a new course. In his New Year's Day address, he pointedly rejected the twin pillars of politics in the Czech Republic: free-market economics and a ban on former Communists from top Government positions.

One of Mr. Meciar's chef economics ministers, for example, was a member of the paramilitary arm of the Communist Party; laws existing before the breakup of Czechoslovakia, would have barred him from such a post.

Separating People From Policy

"We refused socialism," Mr. Meciar said. "We also refuse the idea of capitalism of the last century. In November 1989 we rejected a system that was bad. But we cannot reject the work of those who toiled honestly under this bad system. It is necessary to draw a thick line between the past and the present."

Opposition politicians say Mr. Meciar's populist campaign last year, which demanded an easing of the "shock therapy" economic program favored by the Czechs, has stirred unrealistic hopes. They wonder how the mercurial Mr. Meciar, a former boxer, will react if he feels cornered by a public backlash that many sense is inevitable.

Under pressure from the International Monetary Fund, the Government adopted a frugal budget that cuts social programs, and members of Mr. Meciar's party, the Movement for a Democratic Slovakia, have been hard at work trying to lower expectations of an early end to the difficulties that have kept unemployment at 11 percent.

"The future of Slovakia has a huge question mark hanging over it," said Frantisek Miklosko, former president of the Slovak Parliament and a leader of the opposition Christian Democrats. "If social tension grows, and if Meciar strengthens an authoritarian regime, the situation could spin out of control. What is difficult to see is whether the target will be the opposition or the Hungarian minority."

Accusations of Propaganda

Mr. Meciar's allies dismiss such fears as propaganda that plays on biased Western views of Slovakia that have been spread by Prague and Budapest. Members of Mr. Meciar's inner circle are particularly incensed by frequent allusions to Slovakia's only previous period of independence, the World War II Nazi puppet state led by the Rev. Jozef Tiso.

"Because you had slavery 140 years ago in the United States, is it appropriate to speak of the United States as a slave state?" asked Roman Zelenay, senior member of the Movement for a Democratic Slovakia.

On Jan. 1, the editor in chief of Smena, the largest opposition paper, was dismissed by a managing board; among the seven board members were two legislators from Mr. Meciar's party, but Mr. Zelenay said that the dismissal was a business decision, and that Mr. Meciar learned of it later.

The separation of Czechs and Slovaks is closely linked to Mr. Meciar's political career. A Communist who was expelled from the party after 1968, he was an early member of the People Against Violence, an umbrella group for the anti-Communist opposition in Czechoslovakia's Velvet Revolution, in November 1989.

He became interior minister and later prime minister of the Slovak lands, but was ousted in March 1992. He then formed the Movement for a Democratic Slovakia and a center-left alliance that includes a large number of former Communists prominent in the Prague Spring, the 1968 attempt by the Czechoslovak Communist party to create "socialism with a human voice."

In his New Year's Day speech, Mr. Meciar went out of his way to assuage the fears of minorities, opening with greetings for Slovaks, Hungarians, Czechs, Poles, Ukrainians, Ruthenians and Gypsies.

But Hungarians remain uncertain about their role in the new state.

In the mostly Hungarian towns along the border between Slovakia and Hungary, the Government has been taking down signs with Hungarian place names and has banned their mention on state television.

Hungarians Are Nervous

Such steps, which seem trivial, have raised anxieties. Ethnic Hungarian politicians well remember a meeting several years ago in which Mr. Meciar wagged his finger at them and warned they would end up in jail if they played to nationalist sentiments. Government officials insist that their protection of minority rights meets or exceeds European norms.

The separation of the western two-thirds of Czechoslovakia, the Czech Republic, from Slovakia is likely to be the catalyst for a substantial realignment in the region. Although Slovak officials stress the Western roots of their nation's cultural history, they have great hopes for developing markets in Ukraine, Russia and other countries that once made up the Eastern bloc.

The answers that senior Slovak politicians give to the question of how the Czech and Slovak republics will develop over the long term are revealing.

Mr. Zelenay, for example, predicts with a half-smile that in 200 years, the Czechs will be speaking German and will need a revival of the 19th-century movement that restored the Czech language and culture.

Ivan Laluha, chairman of the foreign affairs committee in the Parliament and a member of Mr. Meciar's party, said Czechs would be more open to investment from abroad.

"Slovaks will be more oriented toward the homeland, still bound by classical vales like 'My home, for me and my children,' and still tied to the soil," said Mr. Laluha, a philosopher who was instrumental in rejecting the Government's initial proposals for a foreign policy that turned decidedly eastward.

He recalled with dismay Slovakia's reluctance to accept wealthy Hong Kong émigrés looking for a new home. "We can succeed, if we find enough courage to allow the entrance of capital in Slovakia," he said. "We have to be more daring, take more risks."

Mr. Laluha, a former Communist who belongs to the Movement for a Democratic Slovakia, acknowledged that Mr. Meciar is certain to suffer diminishing popular support over the next few years.

"We'll try to explain it to the voters," he said, "but I'm sure we'll lose a part of them. Come back and see us in a few years. See whether the voters put us on ice."

The disintegration of Yugoslavia has led to a reevaluation of the idea that a multi-ethnic state is a viable entity. The factors that led to the dismantling of such a state in Yugoslavia are many and are open to revision, but one of the lessons that can be drawn from the process is clear: "The wars in the former Yugoslavia [show] that the principles and practices that provided a stable framework for international security in the era of the cold war are no longer sufficient to preserve the peace."

Why Yugoslavia Fell Apart

STEVEN L. BURG

STEVEN L. BURG *is associate professor of politics at Brandeis University. This article is part of a larger project,* Nationalism and Democracy in Post-Communist Europe: Challenges to American Foreign Policy, *supported by The Twentieth Century Fund.*

The disintegration of the Yugoslav federation and its descent into atavistic interethnic violence cannot be attributed to any single factor. Internal political conflicts in the 1980s, and the effort by Serbian leader Slobodan Milosevic to mobilize Serb nationalism on behalf of a strengthened federation, destroyed the cohesion of the country's regional Communist leaderships and weakened their control over society. Deteriorating economic conditions—especially plummeting living standards—eroded the benefits of sustaining the Yugoslav state and stimulated the rise of mass nationalisms and interethnic hostilities. The conflicting nationalist aspirations of the Yugoslav peoples and their leaders' efforts to maximize power, led to conflict over the control of disputed territories.

The end of the cold war left both Soviet and Western policymakers believing that Yugoslavia no longer held the strategic significance, or merited the attention, it had enjoyed in a world divided between East and West. This mistaken belief, as well as the attention commanded by the Persian Gulf War, led to neglect of the brewing crisis in Yugoslavia until the cost of meaningful action had risen beyond the point acceptable to Western policymakers and their publics. Even when less costly but still effective action remained possible, Western policymakers were deterred from acting by the fear that the dissolution of Yugoslavia, even if achieved through peaceful negotiation, would hasten the disintegration of the Soviet Union.

The fall of Yugoslavia thus can be attributed to internal conflict and the international community's failure to respond to the crisis effectively. However, forceful action by either Yugoslav leaders or American and European administrations would have required innovative thinking about some of the most basic principles of the international system and the post–cold war security framework in the Euro-Atlantic community. No political leadership—Yugoslav, American, or European—was then ready to confront these tasks. The only positive outcome of the Yugoslav debacle, therefore, may be the stimulus it has provided for such new thinking.

THE DOMESTIC CONTEXT OF DISINTEGRATION

By the mid-1970s, Yugoslavia had become a highly decentralized federation in which the constituent republics dominated the central government. Regional leaderships carefully protected the interests of their territorial constituencies at the expense of other regions and the federation. The regional leaders shared a common interest in preserving the Communist political order that shielded them from responsibility and popular accountability but little else. Ethnic and political integration processes had only modest impact. The proportion of the population that declared itself to be "Yugoslav" rather than an ethnic identity in the national census, for example, increased from 1.3 percent in 1971 to 5.4 percent in 1981. For the vast majority of the population, distinct ethnic or national identities continued to command emotional loyalties and provide the most powerful bases for political mobilization.

The ethnically defined territorial structures of the Yugoslav system reinforced the political strength of ethnic identities and intensified political divisions in the leadership. Federal political bodies, including the collective state presidency and the Communist party leadership, were composed of representatives of the republics and provinces, selected by the regional leaderships. Individual positions in these bodies, including the country's prime ministership and presidency, rotated among the regions according to an explicit agreement. Only the army remained a unified, all-Yugoslav, organization.

While the political regions of Yugoslavia were defined in ethnic terms, in most cases they were not ethnically homogeneous. With the exception of Slovenia, their leaderships could not mobilize ethnic nationalism in support of political ambition or fulfill the nationalist aspirations of their ethnic majorities without alienating substantial minority populations and raising the prospect of severe ethnic conflict. The vast majority of ethnic Slovenes were concentrated in Slovenia and made up the majority of the population. Efforts by ethnically Slovene regional leaders to advance Slovene national-cultural interests and to strengthen Slovenian autonomy effectively encompassed all Slovenes. At the same time, these efforts neither threatened the status of a large minority inside Slovenia nor challenged the power of any other group over its own republic by encouraging a large Slovene minority population outside the republic to demand autonomy.

In Croatia, however, Serbs constituted a large minority or even a majority of the population in several areas of the republic. Croat leaders thus could not pursue exclusionary nationalist ambitions inside the Croatian state without risking the alienation of a large and territorially compact Serb minority that enjoyed strong links to Serbs outside the republic's borders. At the same time, a nationalistic Croatian government would stimulate unrest among the large, territorially compact population of ethnic Croats in adjacent areas of neighboring Bosnia and Herzegovina.

No single group could claim the overall majority in Bosnia and Herzegovina. While Muslims constituted the largest group (about 44 percent of the population in the 1991 census), they did not represent a majority. Serbs (over 31 percent) and Croats (more than 17 percent) constituted large minorities in the republic's

population. In many areas of Bosnia there was no single ethnic majority. In the larger cities, those who took the nonethnic "Yugoslav" identity constituted from 20 to 25 percent of the population. Thus the pattern of ethnic settlement in Bosnia was highly complex. No ethnic leadership could advance exclusionary nationalist ambitions on behalf of its ethnic constituency without alienating vast portions of the population—including substantial numbers of its own group who had adopted the multiethnic civic culture associated with "Yugoslavism."

By the mid-1980s, the collective leaderships of the country were divided between those who supported a looser association among the regions and those who continued to support a strengthened federal government. This division was reinforced by differences over the scope and pace of further economic and political reform. The Yugoslav economy had gone into sharp decline in the 1980s. Living standards fell and regional economic differences widened. In the 1960s and 1970s, for example, per capita national income in Slovenia had been about six times that in Kosovo province and about three times that in Macedonia and Bosnia and Herzegovina. Income in Croatia had been about four times that in Kosovo and about twice that in Macedonia and Bosnia. By 1988, income in Slovenia was more than eight times that in Kosovo and income in Croatia was approximately five times higher. The frictions introduced by these growing inequalities were intensified by the ethnic differences between the regions, and especially by the increasingly violent conflict between Serbs and ethnic Albanians in Kosovo.

THE NEW BALKAN STATES

⊗ National capitals
⊛ Yugoslav republic capitals
◉ Yugoslav autonomous regions capitals
• Other cities

0   25   50   75   100 Miles

© Current History, Inc.

KOSOVO AND MILOSEVIC

The 1980s began with the outbreak of nationalist demonstrations by the Albanian people in Kosovo.

THE BREAKUP OF YUGOSLAVIA

1990

Jan. 22—The Communist party votes to allow other parties to compete in a new system of "political pluralism."

Feb. 5—Slobodan Milosevic, president of the republic of Serbia, says he will send troops to take control of Kosovo, a province where ethnic violence has entered its 2d week.

April 8—The republic of Slovenia holds parliamentary elections—the 1st free elections since World War II.

April 22—The 1st free elections in more than 50 years are held in the republic of Croatia.

July 5—The parliament of the Serbian republic suspends the autonomous government of the Kosovo region. On July 2, ethnic Albanian members of the Kosovo legislature declared the region a separate territory within the Yugoslav federation.

July 6—The state president orders Slovenia's parliament to rescind its July 2 declaration that the republic's laws take precedence over those of the Yugoslav federation.

Sept. 3—In Kosovo, more than 100,000 ethnic Albanians strike, closing factories, offices, stores, and schools to protest Serbian takeovers of formerly Albanian-controlled enterprises and the dismissal of Albanian workers.

Sept 13—The Yugoslav press agency reports that ethnic Albanian members of the dissolved parliament of Kosovo have adopted an alternative constitution and have voted to extend the mandate of parliament until new elections are held. The Serbian government has called the alternative constitution illegal.

Nov. 11—The republic of Macedonia holds its 1st free elections since 1945.

Nov. 18—Parliamentary elections are held in the republic of Bosnia and Herzegovina.

Dec. 9—The 1st free parliamentary elections in Serbia since 1938 are held.

1991

Feb. 20—The Slovenian parliament approves laws allowing the republic to take over defense, banking, and other government functions from the central Yugoslav government; the parliament also approves a resolution to divide Yugoslavia into two separate states; Slovenia has warned that it will secede if the other republics do not approve the plan.

Feb. 21—The Croatian parliament adopts measures giving the republic government veto power over central government laws it considers threatening to the republic's sovereignty; the parliament also adopts resolutions that support the dissolution of the Yugoslav federation.

March 2—After reports of violent clashes between Serb villagers and Croatian security forces, Borisav Jovic, the leader of the collective presidency, orders federal army troops to the Croatian village of Pakrac.

March 16—Milosevic declares that he is refusing to recognize the authority of the collective presidency; with this act he effectively declares Serbia's secession from Yugoslavia.

March 17—Milosevic proclaims Krajina, an area in Croatia where 200,000 ethnic Serbs live, a "Serbian autonomous region."

June 25—The parliaments of Slovenia and Croatia pass declarations of independence. The federal parliament in Belgrade—the capital of Serbia as well as of Yugoslavia—asks the army to intervene to prevent the secessions.

June 27—Slovenian Defense Minister Janez Jansa says, "Slovenia is at war" with the federal government.

July 18—The federal presidency announces that it is ordering all federal army units to withdraw from Slovenia.

Sept. 8—Results of yesterday's referendum in Macedonia show that about 75% of voters favor independence; ethnic Albanians boycotted the referendum.

Oct. 1—Heavy fighting in Croatia between Croatian militia and rebel Serbs (aided by the federal army) continues near the Adriatic port city of Dubrovnik.

1992

March 1—A majority of voters approve a referendum on independence in Bosnia; Serb citizens, who comprise 32% of Bosnia's population but control 60% of the territory, have threatened to secede if the referendum is passed.

March 25—Fighting between Serb militias—backed by the federal army—and Bosnian government troops begins.

April 5—After the Bosnian government refuses to rescind a call-up of the national guard, Serb guerrillas shell Sarajevo, the Bosnian capital.

April 27—Serbia and Montenegro announce the establishment of a new Yugoslavia composed of the 2 republics.

May 19—At a news conference in Washington, D. C., Haris Silajdzic, the foreign minister of Bosnia, says his country is being subjected to "ethnic cleansing" by Serb forces.

May 24—In an election in Kosovo termed illegal by Belgrade, ethnic Albanians vote overwhelmingly to secede from the rump Yugoslav state.

July 2—Croat nationalists living in Bosnia declare an independent state that includes almost one-third of the territory of Bosnia; Mate Boban, head of the 30,000-strong Croatian Defense Council militia, says the name of the new republic is Herzeg-Bosna.

Nov. 3—*The New York Times* reports the Serbian-dominated Yugoslav army has quit the siege of Dubrovnik, Croatia, and has withdrawn its forces from the surrounding area.

1993

Jan. 22—Croatian army units attack Serb-held positions in Maslenica and the port city of Zadar; Ivan Milas, a Croatian vice president, says the attacks came after Serbs delayed returning the areas to Croatian control as called for in the January 1992 UN-sponsored cease-fire agreement; state radio in Belgrade says the self-declared Serbian Krajina Republic has declared war on Croatia.

April 7—The Security Council approves UN membership for Macedonia under the provisional name "the Former Yugoslav Republic of Macedonia" as a compromise with the Greek government; Greece has objected to the new country using the same name as Greece's northernmost province.

May 16—In the Bosnian town of Pale, Bosnian Serb leader Radovan Karadzic announces that in a 2-day referendum, at least 90% of Serb voters rejected the provisional peace plan put forward by UN mediator Cyrus Vance and EC mediator Lord Owen; the plan called for a UN-monitored cease-fire; the establishment of a central government composed of 3 Muslims, 3 Croats, and 3 Serbs; the creation of 10 partially autonomous provinces with proportional representation of ethnic groups in the provincial governments; and the return of forcibly transferred property. Karadzic says the world should now recognize that a new state—Republika Srpska—exists in the Serb-controlled territory in Bosnia.

Aug. 28—The mainly Muslim Bosnian parliament votes 65 to 0 to reject a peace plan devised by the UN and the EC that would divide the country into 3 separate republics based on ethnicity; in the mountain town of Grude, the parliament of the self-declared Croat state approves the plan and officially declares the Croat republic of Herzeg-Bosna; the self-declared Bosnian Serb parliament also accepts the plan.

Kosovo is viewed by Serbs as the "cradle" of their nation, but is populated by a demographically robust majority (over 80 percent in 1991) of ethnic Albanians. The demonstrations were initially suppressed by military force. But the decade saw almost continuous and often violent confrontations in the province between Serbs and Albanians. The Serbian leadership in Belgrade responded with increasingly repressive measures against the Albanians and their indigenous leaders.

Violence against Serbs in Kosovo contributed to the growth of nationalist sentiment among Serbs in Serbia and the other regions of Yugoslavia. But the movement received its most important support from Serbian Communist party President Slobodan Milosevic. Motivated at least in part by genuine personal outrage over the treatment of Serbs in Kosovo and by the failure of other Serbian leaders to defend them, Milosevic ousted a key proponent of interethnic accommodation with the Albanians of Kosovo and seized control of the Serbian leadership in September 1987. He then escalated his public defense of Serbian ethnic and political interests. He exploited the situation in Kosovo to further stimulate popular nationalism among Serbs all across Yugoslavia, and used that nationalism as leverage against the leaders of other republics and provinces. The intensity of popular emotions among Serbs was demonstrated by a series of large-scale, openly nationalist demonstrations across Vojvodina, Serbia, and Montenegro in the fall of 1988, and by a mass gathering of Serbs in Kosovo in June 1989.

The growing force of Serbian nationalism allowed Milosevic to oust independent leaders in Vojvodina and Montenegro, replacing them with more subservient ones, and to intensify repressive measures against the Albanians of Kosovo while placing that province, heretofore a relatively autonomous territory within the Serbian republic, under direct rule from Belgrade. These changes gave Milosevic effective control over four of the eight regional leaderships represented in the collective state presidency, the most authoritative executive body in the country. However, the disproportionate Serbian influence contributed to the de-legitimation of central authority and accelerated the political dissolution of the country.

Milosevic represented a powerful synthesis of Serbian nationalism, political conservatism, support for centralism, and resistance to meaningful economic reform. Developments in Serbia under his leadership stood in stark contrast to those in Slovenia, where the growth of popular nationalism took the form of demands for political democracy and rapid economic reform, the pluralization of group activity in the republic, and support for further confederalization of the Yugoslav regime. In Serbia the republic remained under the control of the unreformed Communist party. The Serbian Communists renamed themselves the Socialist party and co-opted some formerly dissident

intellectuals into their leadership, but remained under Milosevic's control. The Slovenian Communist leadership, in contrast, cooperated with emergent social and political forces in their republic to move rapidly toward a more pluralistic order. The Slovenian leadership, rather than seeing organized popular pressure only as a threat, also viewed it as an important and necessary asset in its struggle for economic and political reform in Belgrade.

THE DISINTEGRATION BEGINS

Relations between Serbia and Slovenia began to grow tense at both the elite and mass levels. In October 1988 the Slovenian representative to the central party presidium resigned because of increasingly acrimonious relations with Milosevic. In February 1989 the use of federal militia to suppress a general strike in Kosovo raised widespread concern among Slovenes that, if such force could be used against more than 1 million Albanians, it could also be used against the 2 million Slovenes. This fear was not entirely unfounded. A year earlier an independent Slovenian journal, *Mladina,* revealed that federal Yugoslav military leaders had met to discuss emergency plans for the takeover of the republic.

After the suppression of the strike, the president of the Slovenian Communist party, Milan Kucan, publicly condemned the repression in Kosovo. This marked the beginning of open conflict between the Ljubljana and Belgrade leaderships—the former having embarked on a secessionist strategy calling for internal democratization, and the latter having begun an effort to recentralize power and authority in the entire country while constructing a new, nationalist authoritarian regime in Serbia.

The escalation of conflict in Yugoslavia reached crisis proportions in the fall of 1989. The Slovenian leadership adopted constitutional amendments in September asserting the economic and political sovereignty of the republic, denying the right of the federation to intervene, and claiming the right to secede. In December it blocked an attempt by Serbian nationalists supported by Milosevic to pressure the Slovenian government into abandoning its strategy by bringing Serbs to Ljubljana for a mass demonstration. Milosevic responded to Slovene resistance by breaking off economic relations between the two republics. Democratic activist groups in Slovenia pressed for a complete break with Serbia. That move came the following month, at the January 1990 extraordinary congress of the ruling League of Communists of Yugoslavia.

Originally conceived by Milosevic and the Serbian leadership as a means of imposing greater central authority, the congress instead became the occasion for the collapse of the old regime. Unwilling and politically unable to support a draft platform calling for greater party unity, the Slovenian delegation walked out of the congress. The military and other regional party delegations, unwilling to surrender their own independence, refused to continue the congress. The congress then adjourned indefinitely, marking the de facto breakup of the nationwide party organization. This left each of the republic party organizations to respond independently to conditions in its own region. It also left the military (the Yugoslav People's Army, or JNA) the only organization still committed to, and dependent on, the continued survival of the federation.

The electoral victories of independence-oriented coalitions in Slovenia and Croatia in the spring of 1990, and the former Communists' victory in Serbia in December of that year, deepened political divisions among the regional leaderships of the Yugoslav federation. At the same time, political support for maintaining the federation evaporated almost completely. Federal Prime Minister Ante Markovic's attempt to create a countrywide political party committed to preserving the federation, for example, generated little support. And his effort to accelerate the holding of free elections for the federal parliament as a means of democratizing and legitimizing the federation failed completely.

In August 1990, Serbs in the central Dalmatian region of Croatia began an open insurrection against the Zagreb government. Already fearful of the nationalist campaign themes of the governing Croatian Democratic Community, and mindful of the violently anti-Serb character of the most recent episodes of extreme Croatian nationalism, the Serbs of Dalmatia viewed the government's effort to disarm ethnically Serb local police forces and replace them with special Croatian police units as a portent of further repression to come.

The Dalmatian Serbs declared their intention to remain part of a common Yugoslav state or, alternatively, to become an independent Serb republic. Their uprising should have been a clear warning to all concerned: the republic borders established by the Communist regime in the postwar period were extremely vulnerable to challenges from ethnic communities that did not share the identity on which new, nationalist post-Communist governments sought to legitimate themselves. Such communities were alienated or even threatened by the nationalistic legitimation of these new governments. If existing borders were to be preserved, substantial political guarantees had to be provided for the ethnic minority enclaves in the republics.

The overwhelming declaration of support for a sovereign and independent state by 88 percent of the Slovenian electorate in a December 23, 1990, referendum made the republic's secession look inevitable. The decision by Yugoslav leaders in February 1991 to begin determining how to divide the country's assets among the regions suggested still more clearly that the breakup of the country was at hand. But the threat by the Yugoslav minister of defense in December to use force to prevent Slovenia or Croatia from seceding signaled the possibility that a breakup of Yugoslavia would not be peaceful.

The most explosive conflict in Yugoslavia has been between the political aspirations of Croats and Serbs, whose historical and imagined national homelands and claims to sovereignty overlap. This is the conflict that destabilized the interwar regime and threatened to destabilize the Communist government in 1971. In December of that year, the Yugoslav leader, Josip Broz Tito, used the military to suppress the mass nationalist movement and to purge the leadership in Croatia. As a result, in the 1980s Croatian Communist leaders remained more conservative than their Slovenian counterparts. More important, because Croatian leaders traced their origins to the anti-nationalist purges of the early 1970s, they enjoyed little popular legitimacy. With the breakup of the Yugoslav Communist party in January 1990 and the onset of competitive elections in the republics, they were decisively defeated by the Croatian Democratic Union, a nationalist coalition led by Franjo Tudjman. The CDU's electoral victory polarized relations between Croats and Serbs in that republic and set the stage for a renewed confrontation between Croat and Serb nationalisms.

THE BATTLE OVER THE ETHNIC MAP

By 1990, definition of the emerging post-Communist order became the object of open conflict among several competing, and even mutually contradictory, nationalist visions. The Serbian vision allowed for two fundamentally different outcomes: either the federation would be sufficiently strengthened to assure the protection of Serb populations everywhere in the country, or the dissolution of the federation would be accompanied by the redrawing of boundaries to incorporate Serb populations in a single, independent Serb state. This did not preclude the accommodation of the Slovenian vision of an entirely independent Slovenian state, but it did contradict Croatian aspirations for an independent state defined by the borders inherited from the old regime.

Serb and Croat nationalist aspirations might both still have been accommodated by creating independent states that exercised sovereignty over their respective ethnic territories. But such a solution would have required the redrawing of existing borders that would call into question the continued existence of Bosnia as a multinational state of Muslims, Serbs, and Croats. Moreover, any agreement openly negotiated by Serbia that legitimated claims to self-determination based on the current ethnic composition of local populations would strengthen the Albanian case for an independent Kosovo, and raise the prospect for Serbia of either giving up that province peacefully or having to escalate the level of repression.

The increasing autonomy of the republics and the

growing interregional conflict stimulated fears among Serb nationalists that large portions of the Yugoslav Serb community might be "cut off" from Serbia. The repeated use of military force to suppress Albanian demonstrations in Kosovo in the 1980s, and changes in the Serbian constitution that revoked provincial autonomy, suggested that Milosevic and other Serb nationalists might take similar actions in retaliation for any effort to separate the Serb populations of either Croatia or Bosnia from Serbia. At the very least it suggested that any claim by Croats or Muslims to the right of national self-determination would lead to Serb demands for self-determination, and for the redrawing of internal borders to permit the consolidation of Serb-populated territories under the authority of a single Serbian national state.

Serbs, however, were not the only ethnic group in the former Yugoslavia that might exploit the redrawing of borders. Albanians in Kosovo had already declared their independence and adopted their own constitution in the summer and fall of 1990. Redrawing borders might lead them to claim several western counties of Macedonia where ethnic Albanians constituted the majority or a plurality of the local population. They might even lay claim to the bordering Serbian county of Presevo, where ethnic Albanians also constituted the majority. Radical nationalist elements in Kosovo had already called for the unification of all ethnically Albanian territories. Similarly, Muslim nationalists in Bosnia might lay claim to the several counties of the Sandzak region that lie across the Serbian-Montenegrin border in which Muslims make up the majority.

AN INEPT INTERNATIONAL RESPONSE

A narrow window of opportunity to negotiate a peaceful solution to the growing dispute among the republics and to address the demands raised by ethnic communities appeared to remain open until March 1991. The West's inaction in late 1990 and early 1991 can be partly attributed to preoccupation on the part of western European leaders with negotiations over European integration. Collective action through the European Community was further stymied by clear differences in perspective among the British, French, and Germans. United States policymakers, on the other hand, consciously chose to distance themselves from the issue. United States inaction may even have been due to a cynical calculation on the part of Secretary of State James Baker that this conflict should be left for the Europeans to handle, precisely because the difficulty of the issues and the internal divisions among them assured that they would fail, thus reaffirming the need for American leadership in Europe.

As noted earlier, the attention of Western policymakers was also diverted by two other issues: the military effort to reverse the Iraqi invasion of Kuwait, and the continuing political crisis in the Soviet Union. Any effort to facilitate the breakup of Yugoslavia appeared to have been precluded by fear that it might create an undesirable precedent for the Soviet Union. As a result, the political responses of the United States and other Western states to events in both the Soviet Union and Yugoslavia ignored the fundamental commitments to human rights for which they had pressed in meetings of the Commission on Security and Cooperation in Europe (CSCE) for more than a decade. Yugoslav policy was shaped almost entirely by the desire to preserve the territorial integrity of the Soviet Union.

Western states remained firmly committed to the status quo in Yugoslavia. No effort was made to encourage Yugoslav leaders to hold the federation together by devising new political arrangements that addressed the special interests and concerns of the territorially compact communities of ethnic minorities in the republics. Even more important, in an unprecedented and ill-advised extension of the Helsinki principles of territorial integrity and the inviolability of state borders, the West extended its political support to the borders between the republics of the Yugoslav federation. Neither the United States nor its European partners acknowledged that the growing nationalism of the various peoples of Yugoslavia not only called into question the survival of the federation—they also raised doubts about the political viability of multiethnic republics. The same principle of self-determination that the Slovenes and Croats might use to justify their independence could also be used to justify Dalmatian Serbs' demands for separation from Croatia. Moreover, any reference to the principles of sovereignty and territorial integrity to defend the Croats' claims to Croatia could be used just as easily by Serbs in Belgrade to justify defending the integrity of the former Yugoslavia. International actors made no attempt, however, to confront these issues. They failed to address the growing probability that the Serbian leadership in Belgrade and its Serb allies in the military would use the JNA either to prevent the secession of Slovenia and Croatia or to detach Serb-populated territories of Croatia and Bosnia and annex them to Serbia.

By taking a more comprehensive approach, the international community might have been able to mediate among the several contradictory values and goals of local actors. Extreme demands for the right to self-determination on the part of Serbs in Croatia and Bosnia might have been counterbalanced, for example, by Serbian concerns that adoption of the principle of the right to self-determination might lead to the loss of Kosovo. Croatian ambitions with respect to western Herzegovina might similarly have been moderated by the desire to hold on to the Krajina region.

Under these circumstances, it might have been possible to achieve an overall settlement based on trade-offs among the parties involved. But such an approach would have required the international community to place the peaceful settlement of conflicting demands for self-determination above the principle of territorial integrity of states. At the very least, it would have required the United States and the European Community to abandon their support for the borders of the republics as the basis for establishing new states within the boundaries of the former Yugoslavia. However, this approach stood the best chance of success before the cycle of interethnic violence had set in. By mid-1991 it already was too late.

THE LESSONS OF YUGOSLAVIA

The wars in the former Yugoslavia have made it clear that the principles and practices that provided a stable framework for international security in the era of the cold war are no longer sufficient to preserve the peace. The principles of state sovereignty, territorial integrity, human rights, and self-determination embedded in the United Nations Charter and other United Nations documents, and developed in detail in the documents of the CSCE, have proved contradictory, or at least subject to contradictory interpretation. Moreover, the mounting human tragedy in Bosnia has revealed the inadequacies of the decision-making principles, operational guidelines, and conflict-management capabilities of Euro-Atlantic institutions such as the CSCE, NATO, and the European Community, as well as the UN.

New diplomatic and political mechanisms must be developed to cope with demands for self-determination in ways that do not undermine the basic foundation of international stability—the system of sovereign states. The development of such mechanisms requires reconsideration of the meaning of self-determination in the contemporary era and the careful reconsideration of the indivisibility of state sovereignty. At the very least, it requires limiting the ability of states to use their claim to sovereignty to shield abuses from international inquiry. For any mechanisms to be effective, however, individual states and international organizations alike must become more proactive, undertaking preventive diplomatic and political efforts to solve interethnic and other conflicts before they threaten international peace.

International engagement in the Yugoslav crisis as early as 1990 would have remained futile if the Western states had continued to refuse to support the redrawing of borders as a possible path to a peacefully negotiated solution to the crisis. The declaration of independence by a territorially compact ethnic community, such as that of the Serbs in Croatia or any other group in Yugoslavia, could have been recognized as a legitimate demand for self-determination. By recognizing the equal rights of all peoples in the country to self-determination, international mediators might have been able to lead local actors toward mutual concessions. The key to such negotiations, however, lay in the recognition that international principles, and the rights derived from them, were equally applicable to all parties, as well as in a willingness to undertake the renegotiation of borders. This the international community failed to do.

Early insistence by outside powers on the democratic legitimation of existing borders might have encouraged greater concern for the protection of human rights and avoided the escalation of ethnic tensions in Croatia and Bosnia. The Communist order that held Yugoslavia together began to disintegrate as early as 1986. It entered into crisis in December 1989. This left sufficient opportunity for international actors to influence events. The importance in such a situation of clearly and forcefully articulating and enforcing the human rights standards to which states seeking recognition will be held cannot be overemphasized. By doing so international actors may affect popular perceptions and politics. In Yugoslavia, for example, the regional elections held in 1990 might have produced more moderate governments if the human rights standards of potential ruling parties had been at issue.

The existence of competing claims to territory complicated the Yugoslav crisis. But it does not by itself account for the magnitude of human destruction that has occurred. The extreme violence in Yugoslavia must also be attributed to the establishment of ethnically defined governments that failed to provide democratic safeguards for the human rights of minority communities. This reinforces the conclusion that if the international community is to facilitate the peaceful settlement of such conflicts elsewhere, it must devise the means to prevent ethnic domination and safeguard human rights. In short, the principles of sovereignty, territorial integrity, and national self-determination must be integrated into a single framework for determining the legitimacy of claims to political authority. And that framework must be based on the superiority of principles of human rights and democracy.

A partition plan for Bosnia.

THE ANSWER

John J. Mearsheimer and Robert A. Pape

JOHN J. MEARSHEIMER is professor of political science at the University of Chicago. ROBERT A. PAPE teaches at the School of Advanced Airpower Studies, Air University, Maxwell A.F.B., Alabama. These views are those of the authors alone.

Three ideas for peace in Bosnia are now conceivable: the fast-fading Vance-Owen plan; the new European proposal to create U.N.-protected "safe havens" for the Muslims; and the much less discussed concept of partitioning Bosnia into three independent states. There's only one constant: the Western powers want peace in the Balkans and don't want to spend much blood and treasure to achieve it. The debate is therefore governed by a judgment of what will work and how much force will be required to achieve it. Within these constraints, partition is the best option: it is the only plan that doesn't deny the reality of what has happened, does not acquiesce in the decimation of the Bosnian Muslims and has a chance of being enforced without a major military embroilment. The Clinton administration should look it over.

Vance-Owen, which is still the West's primary conception of postwar Bosnia, offers nothing but trouble. The plan would leave Bosnia's current external borders intact while ceding power to ten semiautonomous provinces whose borders would be drawn along ethnic lines. Croats, Muslims and Serbs would each dominate three provinces, while the province around Sarajevo would be jointly administered. No group's provinces would be fully contiguous; instead, each would control two contiguous provinces, with a third province geographically separated from the other two. Each province would rule itself, subject to a weak central government comprising representatives from each ethnic group, whose cooperation might well be impossible after the brutal past year.

Vance-Owen would require a two-step military operation: compelling Bosnian Serb withdrawals from seized territories (required because the Serbs now control some 70 percent of Bosnia, while Vance-Owen assigns them only 43 percent), and getting Bosnian Serbs and Bosnian Croats to submit to rule from Sarajevo. Otherwise, the intercommunal slaughter will continue. The first step seems feasible, as we describe later in discussing partition, which requires a similar military operation. But Vance-Owen's land mine lies in the near impossibility of the second step: bringing power to Sarajevo.

Several factors combine to make this difficult. First, the Bosnian Serb and Croat populations want to join Serbia and Croatia proper. Their submission to Sarajevo must be compelled by force—village by village, street by street, house by house. Whatever army is responsible for bringing about this submission would face endless guerrilla resistance. Second, all three sides are well-trained in guerrilla tactics and well-armed for guerrilla war. Indeed, the military doctrine of the former Yugoslavia stressed such tactics, and the Yugoslav army held large stocks of weapons appropriate for guerrilla war (mines, light machine guns and light mortars). The Serbs, who will resist Vance-Owen most fiercely, inherited the lion's share of these weapons.

Third, the mountainous and heavily wooded terrain of Bosnia is ideal for guerrilla resistance. An American military planner notes that Bosnia is "the most mountainous and inaccessible, fortress-like part of the country"—the region to which the former Yugoslavian army planned to withdraw and wage war against an invader. Those who cite the Gulf war as evidence that we can go into Bosnia with ease should remember that Bosnia resembles Vietnam far more than it does Kuwait. Finally, Vance-Owen would create a weak Bosnian central state that would be too feeble to impose rule with its own forces. Western forces would have to fill this power deficit.

What forces would the West need to overcome these obstacles? Public discussion suggests NATO would need 50,000 to 70,000 soldiers to police a post-Vance-Owen Bosnia, but these numbers are far too low. The Bosnian Serb and the Bosnian Croat populations made up 50 percent of Bosnia's pre-war population of 4.4 million and controlled territory about two-thirds the size of South Vietnam. Together they now field roughly 120,000 armed combatants, many of whom are free from central control. Furthermore, they would see NATO coming and fortify themselves in the most defensible terrain. Large infantry forces would be needed to deal with these indigenous fighters. The NATO troop requirement is difficult to estimate, but we can figure a rough minimum from similar counterinsurgency campaigns. A peak commitment of 550,000 American troops was insufficient to defeat Communist forces in Vietnam. German and Italian forces of roughly the same size failed to quell partisan resistance in Yugoslavia during World War II. Earlier, Austria-Hungary needed 200,000 troops to subdue a smaller and less organized Bosnian population in 1878. Thus, a NATO force of 400,000 troops seems reasonable.

Even so, NATO troops are poorly suited for the war they would face—they are best at waging armored war against other conventional armies—and the citizens of NATO countries would likely find the nature of a guerrilla war hard to stomach. Winning such wars depends on intelligence collection. Unfortunately, the best collection techniques violate the laws of war: reconcentration of populations, torture of insurgents. Guerrilla war can be waged without these methods, but civilized tactics impose a high military cost.

For these reasons NATO would be unwise to try to enforce Vance-Owen, even in the unlikely event that the Bosnian Serbs sign it. The price of putting this humpty-dumpty of a multiethnic state back together would be too great. If NATO takes a crack at the job, its Bosnian stay is likely to be painful and unsuccessful.

Safe havens are also a potential disaster. Under this concept the U.N. would send ground forces to protect six Muslim enclaves—Bihac, Srebrenica, Zepa, Sarajevo, Gorazde and Tuzla—that are now besieged by Bosnian Serb forces. Of the remaining 1.7 million Muslims in Bosnia, 1.2 million now live in the six havens, as residents or refugees. The U.N. forces would expand the perimeters of these areas and take "all necessary measures" to defend them from Serb or Croat attack. Reports say the current U.N. force of 9,500 British, French, Spanish and Canadian troops would be expanded by several thousand to accomplish these goals.

This plan violates a prime law of statecraft: the use of force should be married to a clearly defined political objective. Once the havens are secured, what next? The job of peace-making would be far from finished. Creating havens would leave Bosnia dotted with Muslim enclaves trapped in a hostile Serbian sea. Because they are geographically indefensible (Srebrenica and Zepa are less than ten miles in diameter) and economically unviable, the enclaves could never form the core of a new state, and maintaining them could impose a large military cost on the Western powers. Expanding their size would require costly offensive operations. A further risk is that the Serbs might move the war from the havens to undefended areas, where nearly 500,000 Muslims reside. This could lead the U.N. either to abandon some Muslims for the sake of others or to expand the havens progressively to include all of Muslim-held Bosnia. Doing the latter would mean raising Western troop levels as well. The plan does a bad job of dividing the responsibility for peace: the U.N. would do too

much, the Bosnian Muslims too little. What John Kennedy said of Vietnam should apply to the Muslims: "In the final analysis it is their war."

A clear partition of Bosnia, while not perfect, is clearly the most feasible solution. Bosnia would be divided into three ethnically homogeneous states. The Croatian and Serbian states would be free to join Greater Croatia and Greater Serbia, respectively; the Bosnian-Muslim state would stand alone as an independent entity. Minority populations trapped behind the new boundaries could move to their new homes under U.N. auspices.

A lasting solution requires that the Bosnian-Muslim state be militarily and economically viable. It must form a single, compact whole; it cannot be a tiny "leopard spot" state. It must be large enough to pose a substantial obstacle to an attacker and to meet the economic needs of its population. The Bosnian-Muslim state should be centered on Sarajevo and cover a large portion of the eastern half of what was pre-war Bosnia-Herzegovina. The northern border should run from Teslic to Tuzla to the western bank of the Drina River near Loznica, along the northernmost mountain ridge before the Pannonian plain. The western border should run from Teslic to Zenica to Konjic. This is mountainous terrain, and the Bosna River serves as a fallback line of defense. The southern border should run from Konjic along the Neretva River straight to the Serbian border. The Neretva Valley, with its high ridges, is a strong line of defense. The eastern border should run along the present border between Serbia and Bosnia up to Loznica. Most of this border follows the Drina River.

The remaining territory of Bosnia-Herzegovina would be divided among the Croats and Serbs. The Croats should get one large chunk of territory on the southwestern border of the new Bosnian-Muslim state. This would include most of the two major areas (provinces 8 and 10) awarded to them under Vance-Owen. The Serbs should be given the remainder of Bosnia-Herzegovina, which would include the Bihac and the Bosanska Posavina areas. The Muslims of Bihac (province 1 in Vance-Owen) would move to the new Bosnian-Muslim state, while the Croatians in the small area of Bosanska Posavina (province 3) would relocate to their new state.

The key territorial trade would be between the Muslims and the Serbs. The Serbs would give up much of their territory in eastern Bosnia (province 6) in return for Bihac (province 1), which the Muslims now control. But the Serbs would still control the southeast and northeast corners of present Bosnia-Herzegovina, and they would have a thirty-five-mile-wide east-west corridor running along its northern border, connecting Serbia proper to the Serbian regions of Western Bosnia and Croatia. Under this plan the Muslims would control about 35 percent (8,000 square miles) of former Bosnian territory; the Serbs, 45 percent (10,500 square miles); and the Croats, 20 percent (4,500 square miles). These percentages roughly reflect the amount of territory each ethnic group controlled in pre-war Bosnia.

How readily would the parties accept such a plan? We

cannot tell for sure, because partition has not been widely discussed in public by the rival groups, but we can determine something about their attitudes from their past statements and behavior.

The Bosnian Muslims have shown little interest in partition and have instead argued for maintaining the multiethnic Bosnian state that existed in April 1992, before fighting began. This position was perhaps reasonable in the war's early stages. But a multiethnic Bosnia must now have little appeal for the Muslims after their vast suffering at their neighbors' hands. The Croats are likely to accept partition along the lines we propose, as it would offer them much of the territory they were assigned by Vance-Owen, which they quickly accepted. The Serbs are more likely to balk. Though the plan would help them realize their dream of a Greater Serbia, they would also have to cede substantial territory in eastern Bosnia, including Sarajevo, to the Muslims. This they would likely resist. But if the world powers use enough force and provide sufficient incentives, the Serbs can, we believe, be compelled.

There are three main arguments against partition. First, some would argue that the military means it requires would escalate rather than dampen the violence in Bosnia. We would answer that violence is just as likely to endure. Greater Serbia, if allowed to preside over its conquests, may well be emboldened by its cost-free expansionism to move on elsewhere. Regrettably, there are times when lives can be saved only by threatening to take lives. Second, some would contend that the population transfer required by partition entails needless injury to innocents. Yet transfer is already occurring. Even Vance-Owen would produce its own population transfers, since minorities would doubtless be driven from areas designated for other groups. Transfer is a fact. The only question is whether it will be organized, as envisioned by partition, or left to the murderous methods of the ethnic cleansers.

Finally, some might complain that partition is incomplete because it fails to solve other related Balkan troubles that could produce future wars—most notably the conflict in Serbia's Kosovo region. There's merit to this. The Serbian government has already begun a slow-motion expulsion of Kosovo's 1.6 million Albanians, and signs abound that it plans a more dramatic and complete cleansing soon. Such a move could trigger a general Balkan war involving Albania, Macedonia and perhaps Bulgaria, Greece and Turkey. The West should reiterate that the cleansing of Kosovo will not be tolerated. It might also consider putting Kosovo on the table as it negotiates with Serbia over Bosnia. Freeing the region could be the price for full peace with the West.

But critical questions remain. How can this settlement be enforced if the Serbs resist? And can it be enforced with an acceptable military cost to the great powers, particularly the United States? We believe the answer to these questions is yes, and that the United States should prepare to lead the alliance into such a strategy.

Two basic military campaigns could be pursued. A "roll-back" strategy would use massive military force—supplied simultaneously by Western air forces and Bosnian Muslim ground forces—to win a decisive victory against the Bosnian Serbs and their Serbian supporters. They would be left with no choice but to accept Western demands. "Coercive bloodletting" is a less ambitious strategy. It would use similar means, but wouldn't depend on decisive victory. Instead, it would present the Serbs with the prospect of a costly war of attrition that would continue until they accepted partition.

In theory, air power can be used three different ways: to decapitate an opponent's leadership, to punish an opponent's population or to weaken an opponent's military forces. Of these, only the last stands a chance at being effective, but only if it is applied in conjunction with ground power.

Decapitation—an approach used in Desert Storm—would involve strikes against Serbian leadership in Bosnia and Serbia proper. The strategy has the advantage of requiring relatively few sorties over a few days by precision aircraft (mainly F-117s) against key leadership and telecommunication facilities. Decapitation raids would also cause little collateral damage, given accurate target intelligence. But finding and targeting the key Serb leaders from the air would be very difficult. U.S. troops took days to find Manuel Noriega after the Panama invasion, and they were hunting him on the ground. Furthermore, killing the key Serbian leaders (Radovan Karadzic and Slobodan Milosevic) probably wouldn't moderate Serb policies since extremist currents run strong in both communities. Cutting communication links is also impractical and would have little effect even if accomplished. Bosnian Serb forces simply have too many ways to communicate with their leaders; and this body can fight even without its head.

The second strategy, aerial punishment, would attempt to inflict enough damage on economic targets that Serbian civilians would compel their leaders to withdraw from their occupied lands. While most of Bosnia's economy is already in ruins, the Serbian standard of living could be substantially reduced by a short air campaign. Serbia's meager air defenses would be destroyed first; F-117s, F-111s, F-15Es, F-18s, F-16s, A-6s and Tomahawk cruise missiles would then knock out its electric power grids, oil refineries and food distribution system. In all, several hundred targets would be attacked. With good weather, the campaign might take less than two weeks.

But punishment is unlikely to cause the Serbs to abandon their Bosnian conquests. Air attacks generate more public anger against the attacker than the target. Air power slaughtered British, German and Japanese civilians in World War II; threatened Egyptian civilians in the 1970 "war of attrition" with Israel; and depopulated large parts of Afghanistan in the 1980s. In each case, the citizenry did not turn against its government. Moreover, Westerners concerned about the Balkan situation for mainly moral reasons would shrink from using such indiscriminate means against noncombatants. Finally, the opponent most vulnerable to aerial punishment—Serbia proper—is not the opponent the West most needs to coerce. Even if Belgrade agrees to press the Bosnian Serbs for withdrawals, it is not clear that they would obey.

The third strategy—weakening the Serbian army to the point where Bosnian Muslim ground troops can force its withdrawal—offers the best chance of success. This air campaign might include three sets of targets: the Serbian army in Serbia, the 35,000-man Bosnian Serb conventional army and the 35,000 Bosnian Serb irregulars. Of these three, the Serbian conventional army in Serbia proper is the easiest to track. It is concentrated in bases and armed with heavy weapons that can be found from the air. But destroying this army would only reduce Serbia's ability to *reinforce* its forces in Bosnia; it would do nothing to weaken them directly.

The Bosnian Serb conventional armies present a more important target, and they can be destroyed from the air if conditions are right. Since they seem to operate in small mobile units of about 500 men and are constantly on the move, they need to be forced into a concentration to be made vulnerable. (Air strikes could not destroy Iraqi Scuds in open desert. The odds of finding smaller artillery pieces that can be hidden in forests and mountains are even worse.) How do we do this? Engage them in ground action that forces them to gather in one place. If they fought a large, well-armed land army, they would have to mass in far larger numbers. They would then present a target that could be shattered from the air.

Bosnian Serb irregulars would be more difficult to strike from the air. These forces operate in tiny groups of 100 or fewer and rely on mortars and light arms to do their dirty work. This makes them hard to find and difficult to distinguish from Muslim and Croat fighters. On the other hand, these attributes make them a minor factor in the larger military equation.

Air power, in short, can help compel Serbian withdrawals by damaging the Bosnian Serb regular forces. But all this depends on the Bosnian Serbs facing a powerful, well-armed ground opponent. The Bosnian Muslims, *not* the Western powers, must supply these forces. To do this, the West is going to have to give them heavy weapons and provide training.

The Bosnian Muslims have been losing territory for lack of weapons, not troops. The total Bosnian Muslim population exceeds the Bosnian Serb population by at least 300,000. However, the Muslims can now arm only some 50,000 soldiers, while the Bosnian Serbs have 70,000 well-armed troops. What's more, the Serbs have 1,500 artillery pieces, tanks and other armored vehicles. The Bosnian Muslims have fewer than 50.

Western military assistance to the Bosnian Muslims would equalize the balance. Weapons could be delivered on C-130 transport aircraft; these can use short, primitive airstrips and can therefore operate from a number of fields and roads in Muslim-held Bosnia. The C-130s could deliver light infantry weapons—rifles, mortars, shoulder-launched anti-tank weapons, night vision devices, machine guns, mines—and also heavier weapons, including 105mm and 155mm artillery pieces. When airfields are not available, these weapons could be air-dropped. There's no need to use Croatian-held territory to transfer these goods. In a matter of months the Muslims would have 80,000 soldiers armed to the teeth and able to stop a Serbian offensive in its tracks.

Giving the Bosnian Muslims an offensive capability is more difficult for two reasons. First, the Muslims probably would need self-propelled artillery, tanks and armored personnel carriers, which require the giant C-5 transport aircraft, which in turn requires a long landing strip. Muslim-controlled Bosnia has only three such strips—Sarajevo, Bihac and Tuzla—and none is secure from Serbian anti-aircraft fire. So the heavy weapons would have to be brought into Bosnia over Croatian-controlled land routes, and it's likely the Croats would grant passage reluctantly. Second, the Bosnian Muslims have little experience using heavy weapons or conducting offensive operations. It would take a few hundred Western advisers and about two years after we begin arming them for them to become proficient.

This strategy would take time. The Muslims would require perhaps a year to halt further Serb gains and consolidate their defensive positions before they could move to compel Serb withdrawals. The West should therefore adopt a two-phase plan—protecting Muslim consolidation in the first, compelling Serb withdrawals in the second. The choice between rollback and coercive bloodletting could be deferred until the second phase. In the first phase the West would organize, train and equip the Muslim forces for defensive operations. A fleet of about 100 C-130s would ferry arms to the Muslims, while several hundred fighter and ground attack aircraft stand ready in Italy and on aircraft carriers in the Adriatic to destroy any large Serb offensives. The West would deploy 200 to 400 Special Operations Forces in Bosnia to assist its air operations by serving as ground spotters and to help the Muslims develop a command and intelligence aparatus.

In the second phase, the West would prepare the Muslims for offensive operations and support these from the air. The Serbs now have some 350 main battle tanks, 200 light armored vehicles and 1,000 artillery pieces. A coercive bloodletting strategy could be launched when the Bosnian Muslims have acquired a roughly equivalent ground force. A rollback strategy would have to wait until the Muslims assembled ground forces around twice the combat power of Serb ground forces.

Diplomatic and economic incentives should be joined to these military punishments. As its main reward, the West should offer to recognize Greater Serbia if the Serbs cooperate with the Western program. The Western powers should also promise to lift economic sanctions and perhaps even to help rebuild the Serbian economy.

Once a peace agreement is signed, populations would have to be moved in order to create homogeneous states. The international community should oversee and subsidize this population exchange. Specifically, the U.N. should establish a Balkan Population Exchange commission, modeled after the League of Nations-sponsored Refugee Settlement Commission, which managed the transfer of more than 1.5 million people between Greece and Turkey from 1923 to 1931. This commission should secure safe passage for immigrants, establish a bank to help them buy and sell property and administer a Balkan Marshall Fund to assist the development of new housing and industry in immigration zones. The commission should have a ten-year mandate: two years for resettlement, eight years for economic development.

How can the long-term survival of the Bosnian-Muslim state be guaranteed? It would inevitably be weaker than its neighbors. Population is a good indicator of latent military power. Allowing for the return of refugees, there are roughly 9 million Serbs, 4.5 million Croats and maybe 1.8 million Bosnian Muslims. There are also some 5.3 million Albanians in the region: of these, 1.6 million live in the Serbian region of Kosovo, 400,000 in Macedonia and 3.3 million in Albania proper. Thus, Serbia would be the strongest state in the region and the Bosnian-Muslim state would be among the weakest.

The NATO powers should therefore undertake to arm it well. They should also issue a security guarantee, promising to intervene with air power if its neighbors attack. NATO should also foster a defensive alliance between the Bosnian-Muslim state, Croatia and Albania. Those states are neither friends of Serbia nor strong enough to check it alone. They should have good reason to ally themselves with the Bosnian Muslims.

This partition plan isn't perfect; and it isn't morally pure. It means transferring hundreds of thousands of civilians from historic homes and countries. It means risking a small number of American lives. But it is the only plan that's realistic about what can be achieved in such a fraught area and idealistic about the principles at stake. And it can be done.

The Pacific Basin

Relations among the United States and countries in the Pacific Basin are characterized by change, as all parties readjust commitments and perceptions of security, political, and economic interests in light of the demise of the USSR. However, for the United States, Japan remains the primary relation; China is secondary.

A far-ranging policy debate was triggered in Japan by the U.S. demand for tangible contributions from all allies to the Persian Gulf coalition. After some delay, the Japanese agreed to make a significant financial contribution. Although the majority of the Japanese people were initially opposed to Japan's role in the coalition effort, opinion changed. Now the majority of the public favors a more activist role for Japan in international affairs.

The U.S.–Japan controversy during the Gulf War fueled preexisting resentments in both countries and triggered a major reassessment of Japan's strategic interests, role in the world, and relations with the United States. As Harry Harding and Edward Lincoln note in "Rivals or Partners? Prospects for U.S.–Japan Cooperation in the Asia-Pacific Region," economic competition and the end of the cold war have set this important bilateral relation adrift. While there is clearly a need for the two to create a new political architecture for the region, the task may be difficult because of divergent perspectives on a range of issues.

Reassessment of U.S.–Japan relations was also fueled by the economic recession and an unprecedented electoral upset in Japan. Public disclosures of political scandals involving leading figures in the ruling Liberal Democratic party resulted in the end of one-party rule in 1993 after 38 years in power. The new government is a coalition of disparate parties headed by a young, reform-minded prime minister, Morihiro Hosokawa. Much like President Clinton, Hosokawa promised to work for major political changes during the campaign. Stephen Anderson outlines some of the structural changes that are likely to occur in "Japan: The End of One-Party Dominance." He also predicts that the nation will adopt a more activist form of diplomacy, one more commensurate with Japan's economic and political status in the region and the world.

During his first year, Hosokawa moved quickly to implement a number of reforms, including a historic electoral reform bill designed to reduce political corruption by rewriting the electoral map. Moreover, Hosokawa used his initial popularity with the public to initiate changes in basic Japanese positions in foreign affairs. In an unprecedented move, Hosokawa acknowledged Japan's responsibility for atrocities committed in East Asia during World War II,

apologized for these atrocities, and raised the possibility of compensation for war victims. He also took steps to open long-closed rice markets and the construction business to foreign competitors. To reassure neighbors concerned with future Japanese security policy, he reiterated Japan's long-standing commitment not to develop nuclear weapons.

Hosokawa's more recent proposals for broader economic and political reforms met substantial resistance from members of his coalition government, opponents in the Diet, and from entrenched bureaucracies. He was forced to compromise on a number of initiatives to obtain an economic stimulus package. At the February 1994 biannual summit meeting on trade in Washington, D.C., Hosokawa adopted a position that seemed scripted by entrenched bureaucrats.

This summit meeting collapsed after the two sides failed to agree on specific measures to reduce Japan's trade surplus of over $60 billion with the United States. The two governments had agreed in principle to adopt an unprecedented results-oriented strategy for managing trade disputes in four key industrial sectors at a summit in Tokyo in July 1993. The new framework called for the use of objective criteria for measuring progress in opening Japanese markets and reducing the trade imbalance, but the two sides continued to differ on whether this meant that the Japanese had to agree to specific benchmarks or goals to measure progress in various industries.

After the collapse of the 1994 summit, the Clinton administration resurrected a trade regulation, Super 301, which might eventually lead to U.S. trade barriers against Japanese imports. In response, Prime Minister Hosokawa cautioned the United States against resorting to unilateral actions that might contravene General Agreement on Tariffs and Trade (GATT) principles governing world trade. Despite the potential seriousness of this breakdown in trade negotiation, the rupture was not viewed as a major crisis. Unlike earlier trade disagreements that stimulated new rounds of "Japan bashing" or "America bashing," most observers interpreted this breakdown as a temporary interruption in an ongoing effort to manage conflict in this highly important relationship.

The second most important issue for the United States in the Pacific Basin involves the current and future status of U.S.–China relations. The "most favored nation status" currently accorded China must be reviewed annually by Congress. This guarantees that China will be a focus of policy debates in the United States.

Since China's aging leadership survived a challenge by democratic forces during the spring of 1989, China has presented the United States with an ongoing dilemma over how to reconcile U.S. economic and political interests in China with the principle of promoting human rights. The importance of the dilemma was evident at the beginning of 1994 when the United States changed its China policy to focus more on increased contacts to improve human rights and less on threats of trade sanctions. Shortly after the policy shift, China released three political prisoners who had been jailed in connection with pro-democracy demonstrations in 1989. The timing of the releases appeared to reflect Chinese policy designed to affect U.S. decisions on China's trade status. Both sides tried to find a way to renew Beijing's trading privileges, as China is the world's biggest emerging market.

An increasing number of analysts are concerned about the potential threat to the peace and security of Asia in the medium term because of China's current military armament and arms sales programs. Nicholas Kristof reflects these concerns in "The Rise of China." Kristof concludes that the rise of China may have colossal economic, political, environmental, and military implications. However, a more immediate threat to U.S. security interests in Southeast Asia lies in recent actions of the hard-line communist regime of North Korea led by Kim Il Sung. A growing concern exists about whether North Korea will explode or implode during the final days of the dying communist dictatorship. North Korea's future is worrisome because of uncertainty about the regime's nuclear weapons program and widespread speculation that Kim Il Sung may be insane.

Although North Korea announced a decision to sign the Nuclear Non-Proliferation Treaty in the early 1990s, the regime has repeatedly reneged on agreements related to on-site inspections by international observers. The most recent round of this conflict occurred during 1993 when North Korea announced withdrawal from the treaty and unexpectedly blocked inspection by International Atomic Energy Agency inspectors of two of the most important sites. Perhaps America's agreement to cancel the annual military exercise with South Korea known as "Team Spirit" and North Korea's expressed intention to permit international inspection of all its declared nuclear facilities and resume international talks with South Korea in January 1994 averted a stalemate. However, as Keith Colquhoun concludes in "North Korea: The Dangerous Outsider," America may have to offer more than goodwill to find out whether North Korea has a homemade nuclear bomb. Meanwhile, uncertainty over North Korea's nuclear weapons programs delays planned American force reductions.

After two decades and a war in which 50,000 Americans lost their lives, the Clinton administration finalized a process started during the Bush administration to normalize relations between the United States and Vietnam. As President Clinton lifted the economic embargo against Vietnam in February 1994, the Vietnamese government vowed to continue cooperating fully to resolve issues related to missing American servicemen. American businesses had been pressuring the government since the late 1980s for access to this potentially lucrative market of 71 million hungry consumers, an educated and inexpensive labor force, and untapped oil and mineral resources. While the communist regime still does not tolerate political opposition, the country has embraced free-market economic reforms with a vengeance and has promised to become one of Asia's future economic "tigers."

At the regional level, perceptions of economic issues, rather than the need to strengthen existing political and military accords, dominate the concerns of key nation-state actors. James Fallows seeks to explain this preoccupation in "What Is an Economy For?" Fallows argues that underlying policy differences between America and Asian countries are fundamental differences in views of the purpose of an economic system. While Americans believe that economic development is needed to allow individual consumers to buy more, Fallows argues that Asians view economic growth as a means of keeping their country strong and efficient.

Looking Ahead: Challenge Questions

What are the key elements of the U.S.–Japan relationship?

Should the United States address the continuing trade imbalance with Japan and be concerned about Japanese investments in the United States?

Is the economic health of the United States tied to emerging economic prosperity spheres such as southern China? What should the United States do in the future to promote a peaceful transition in China?

Is a U.S. military presence critical for regional stability?

Can the United States prevent the Kim Il Sung regime in North Korea from becoming a nuclear producer and arms supplier?

Rivals or Partners?
Prospects for U.S.-Japan Cooperation in the Asia-Pacific Region

Harry Harding and Edward J. Lincoln

Harry Harding and Edward J. Lincoln are both senior fellows in the Brookings Foreign Policy Studies program. Harding is the author of A Fragile Relationship: The United States and China since 1972 *(Brookings, 1992). Lincoln is the author of* Japan's New Global Role *(Brookings, 1993). This article grew out of a paper prepared for the Japan Center for International Exchange and the Japan Center for Global Partnership.*

With the end of the Cold War, U.S.-Japan relations have been set adrift. Economic competition between the two countries is increasing, at a time when the disintegration of the Soviet Union has left them without a common enemy. Government officials and policy analysts in both nations are searching for a new foundation for Japanese-American relations. One candidate has been a "global partnership," in which the two countries would deploy their economic, diplomatic, and military resources toward managing and solving international problems.

The concept seems so attractive that it has become part of the conventional wisdom in most discussions of U.S.-Japan relations. It was embodied in the Tokyo Declaration, issued at the end of President George Bush's visit to Japan in February 1992. It has been endorsed by Winston Lord, the new assistant secretary of state for East Asian and Pacific affairs in the Clinton administration, who said during his confirmation hearings

that a "comprehensive, durable partnership with Japan" could help find solutions to "issues ranging from Korea to Somalia, Cambodia to Russia, technology to foreign aid, [and] the environment to democracy."

And yet, although the global partnership between Japan and the United States is unlikely to be as contentious as their bilateral economic relationship, neither is it likely to be characterized completely by cooperation and harmony. In fact, any realistic appraisal of the prospects for such partnership must begin with the frank admission that the two countries will approach many international issues from divergent perspectives. Nowhere are the implications of these differences more apparent, or more important, than in the Asia-Pacific region.

The most obvious differences between the two countries are rooted in economics. Though they are thoroughly intertwined by vast flows of goods, capital, and technology, Japan and the United States are highly competitive. Not only do the industrial and commercial sectors in each society compete for advantage in the world marketplace, but also the two governments try to advance their national economic interests as international economic integration proceeds.

The two countries also have different geopolitical interests. Japan, naturally, is immediately concerned by military and political developments on the Asian mainland. While both the U.S. and Japanese economies are dependent on imports of natural resources and raw materials from abroad, Japan's sense of vulnerability to the disruption of supply is palpably greater than that of the United States. And Japan, unlike the United States, has territorial disputes with both Russia and China.

Finally, differences in the history, culture, and structure of U.S. and Japanese society affect their outlook on international issues. The United States, a highly competitive form of multiparty democracy, is less tolerant than Japan of quasi-democratic alternatives. The United States also generally assigns a higher priority to promoting human rights abroad than does Japan. In theory, if not always in practice, Americans believe in relatively *laissez-faire* models of economic development, whereas Japanese are willing to give a greater role to government. In addition, the bitter legacy of Japanese military expansionism in Asia has made Japan far less willing to devote its own military resources to solving military problems than is the United States.

This blend of common and divergent perspectives is evident in the approaches that the two countries take to a wide range of regional and subregional issues in the Western Pacific.

The Dilemma over China

Both the United States and Japan want to see China stable, modernizing, liberalizing, and at peace with its neighbors. Both have been eager to cooperate with the ambitious program of economic reform that has been under way in China since 1978, through direct investment, technology transfer, and official development assistance. Immediately after the Tiananmen crisis of 1989, both imposed economic and diplomatic sanctions against Peking, delaying high-level contacts, reducing lending by international financial institutions, and suspending bilateral aid programs. More recently, both countries have been concerned by increases in China's defense budget, by China's interest in developing an offensive military capability, and by the reassertion of Chinese claims to the South China Seas.

But Japan's proximity to China makes it especially wary of political instability on the Chinese mainland for fear that it could produce an outpouring of refugees or weaken central control over China's armed forces. Tokyo has thus been eager to return to a supportive relationship with China and, indeed, has resumed bilateral aid and high-level official contacts. The United States, both less sure than the Japanese that a closer economic relationship promotes more rapid political and economic liberalization and more concerned about human rights, has maintained sanctions to punish China for continuing to repress dissent. Indeed, the Clinton administration could well adopt a tougher policy toward China, including restricting or withdrawing Peking's most-favored-nation status. Although Tokyo would prefer to maintain unity with Washington in formulating policy toward Peking, it is highly unlikely that Japan would join the United States in imposing such conditions on trade with China.

A final source of tension is Hong Kong. Both Japan and the United States have a growing economic stake in Hong Kong, both as a regional financial and commercial center and as an *entrepot* for the dynamic economy of southeastern China. Yet the two countries are not likely to see eye to eye on the demands of many Chinese professionals in Hong Kong for greater democracy as the territory moves back toward Chinese sovereignty in 1997. Americans will be sympathetic to efforts to expand the role of direct elections, organize competing political parties, and enlarge the role of the local legislature. But the Japanese may fear that such efforts will provoke Peking and thus jeopardize Hong Kong's longer-term autonomy, stability, and prosperity.

Russia's Democratic Experiment

Although both Japan and the United States want Russia's experiments with economic and political reform to succeed, differences in perspective have already impeded their cooperation. Japan, for example, has delayed providing foreign aid because of its dispute with Russia over the Northern Territories. Only after sustained American and European pressure did Tokyo reluctantly agree last April to extend economic assistance to Russia, and then only as part of a multilateral program rather than as a separate bilateral initiative. Moreover, whereas many Americans believe that aid is critical if Boris Yeltsin's program of economic and political reform is to succeed, many Japanese continue to doubt the efficacy of foreign aid given the chaotic conditions in much of Russia.

The different geostrategic locations of the two countries continue to influence their assessment of the consequences of the end of the Cold War. Americans tend to assume that the collapse of the Soviet Union and the emergence of a quasi-democratic system in Moscow have eliminated any significant strategic threat from Russia. In contrast, the Japanese, who fought one major war with Russia in 1904–05 and faced Russian troops at the end of World War II, nervously eye the huge military forces that the Kremlin maintains in nearby eastern Siberia.

On the other hand, Japanese and American perspectives have coincided in some areas. Russia's willingness to sell advanced military technology, seemingly at bargain prices, to regimes around the world, including China, may soon be a force for cooperation. Whatever the U.S. and Japanese views on the residual threat posed by Russia's own military forces, the two are likely to agree on the danger of the transfer of Russian military technology abroad and on the need to take common measures to control it. In addition, despite its reluctance to provide general economic assistance to Russia, Tokyo has been willing to join Washington in extending aid focused on such crucial issues as military conversion, denuclearization, and environmental protection.

The Korean Peninsula

Japanese and U.S. interests in the Korean peninsula have so far remained close. Above all, the two countries seek to prevent a reprise of the Korean conflict of 1950–53. They also want to keep North Korea from developing nuclear arms, to restrict the flow of advanced conventional weapons to Pyongyang, and to limit the export of Korean weapons to unreliable regimes in the third world. In addition, they want North Korea to move toward a market economy, rejoin the world economy, and relax political controls.

To that end, Japan and the United States have worked closely together. Japan was a major staging point for American forces in the Korean War, and the U.S. deterrent posture on the Korean peninsula requires access to bases in Japan. The United States has maintained strict economic sanctions on all transactions with North Korea, and Japan's commercial relationships with Pyongyang have been quite limited. The two countries have applied steady diplomatic and economic pressure to force Pyongyang to abandon its nuclear weapons program, accept International Atomic Energy Agency inspections of its nuclear facilities, and agree with Seoul on a supplementary system of bilateral inspections. At the same time Tokyo and Washington have also held out the prospect of diplomatic recognition, expanded trade and investment, and possibly economic assistance as incentives for more cooperative North Korean behavior.

In the years ahead, as progress is made toward normalizing relations with Pyongyang, the two countries' strategies may begin to diverge. The United States will be concerned with POW and MIA issues dating from the Korean War. Japan will have to address North Korean demands for reparations for its period of colonial rule. If one set of issues is easier to resolve, Tokyo and Washington will normalize relations with North Korea at different speeds. They may also differ on whether to secure Pyongyang's compliance with international nonproliferation regimes before normalizing diplomatic ties.

Japan's proximity to the Korean peninsula gives the issue of reunification particular salience there, whereas the United States, from afar, can view the prospect with equanimity. Both countries would presumably be concerned if reunification resulted from the sudden collapse of the North Korean regime (as in the case of Germany), but Japan would be much more immediately apprehensive about the dangers of instability in the north, the effect on the South Korean economy, and the prospect of a flood of refugees.

Easing Tensions in Indochina

Ever since Vietnam intervened in Cambodia at the end of 1978, Japan and the United States have worked together to resolve the conflict. Tokyo and Washington coordinated diplomatic and economic pressure on Hanoi, limiting trade, investment, and aid until Vietnamese troops left Cambodia and a peace settlement was reached. Since the Paris Accords were signed in October 1991, the United States and Japan have provided economic assistance to the interim government in Phnom Penh and financial support to the United Nations transitional authority in Cambodia. Tokyo has also, for the first time ever, provided troops for UN peacekeeping operations.

Japan, however, has stayed at least one step ahead of the United States in rebuilding ties with Vietnam. Unlike the United States, Japan has had full diplomatic relations for many years. Japan has also continued limited trade and investment with Vietnam and has even resumed economic aid, while the United States has maintained a tight economic embargo on Hanoi. The continuing U.S. resentment over the outcome of the Vietnam War, especially the treatment of American POWs and MIAs, that colors the U.S. approach could deepen the rift between U.S. and Japanese policy toward Vietnam, unless the Clinton administration moves quickly to complete the normalization of U.S.-Vietnam relations or to lift the American embargo.

The Taiwan Strait

Taiwan too could strain the U.S.-Japanese alliance. Both nations, of course, wish to ensure a peaceful future for Taiwan and to discourage China from using force to achieve reunification. And both presumably wish to see Taiwan have a greater role in international economic institutions, as befits its large and expanding gross national product, global trade flows, and foreign exchange reserves.

Since the early 1970s the United States and Japan have generally followed parallel policies toward Taiwan. Japan switched its diplomatic relations from Taipei to Peking in 1972, and the United States followed six years later. Both have unofficial offices in Taipei to manage extensive economic and cultural ties. And both have worked to ensure Taiwan's participation in the Asian Development Bank and the Asia-Pacific Economic Cooperation forum and to support Taiwan's application to join the GATT.

Differences in the history, culture, and structure of U.S. and Japanese society affect their outlook on international issues.

Still, several differences in perspective loom. First, the United States is committed to help preserve Taiwan's security by selling the island defensive weapons under guidelines established in the Taiwan Relations Act of 1979 and the Sino-U.S. communiqué of 1982. The arms sales may become increasingly contentious, however, especially as the mainland continues to modernize its armed forces and develop offensive capabilities. Japan, for example, fears that America's recent decision to sell

150 F-16s to Taiwan might be excessively provocative to Peking.

Second, Taiwanese demands for a more visible role in the world—and even for formal independence from the rest of China—are likely to gain a different reception in Washington than in Tokyo. Such demands could attract considerable sympathy in the United States, where there is a long tradition of supporting self-determination and where revulsion against the Tiananmen crisis remains strong. Conversely, many Japanese believe that their 50-year period of colonial rule over Taiwan—let alone their strong desire to maintain stable relations with China—makes it impossible to endorse any move toward Taiwanese independence. For similar reasons, Japan has already lagged far behind Western Europe and the United States in sending cabinet-level

Economic competition and policy differences need not lead to an environment of political rivalry and hostility.

officials to Taipei to discuss economic and commercial issues.

On the other hand, the United States would probably have substantially fewer reservations than Japan about the reunification of Taiwan and mainland China. Japan's reliance on the sea lines of communication that pass by Taiwan might make Tokyo apprehensive about Taiwan coming under the control of a mainland government. Japan might also be more concerned than the United States about the growth of Chinese economic and strategic power that could come with reunification.

South China Seas

The recent intensification of the disputes among China, Vietnam, and several other Southeast Asian nations over the islands in the South China Seas is of concern to both the United States and Japan. Both wish to prevent the controversies from setting off arms races among the claimants, let alone sparking open conflict. Both would presumably favor joint development of the rich natural resources that may lie beneath the islands, on terms equitable to all parties, while setting aside the issues of sovereignty for the time being.

Nonetheless, the issue could strain relations between the two. Japan has an immediate interest in the security of the sea lanes, but, given regional suspicions about Japan's long-term strategic intentions, Tokyo would be reluctant to deploy its own military forces to protect its interests. The outbreak of conflict over the islands could easily give rise to disputes about equitable sharing of burdens within the Japanese-American partnership.

Regional Security Issues

The Japanese-American alliance contributes much to peace and security in the Asia-Pacific region. Not only does it give the United States a military staging ground, it also obviates the need for Japan to undertake a military role that could alarm other nations in the region.

Yet burden sharing within the alliance remains a chronic problem. Although the collapse of the Soviet Union has reduced American pressure on Tokyo to increase military spending and although Japan's financial support for U.S. deployments is generally regarded as adequate, America may well insist that Japan assume a greater responsibility for its own conventional defense. But to do that, Tokyo will have to allay regional fears about the revival of Japanese militarism.

Until recently both Tokyo and Washington have been highly skeptical about forming a cooperative security regime in Asia. They summarily rejected Mikhail Gorbachev's proposals for naval arms control as efforts to prevent the United States from developing a counteroffensive capability in the Northwest Pacific. And they were cool to Australian and Canadian proposals for multilateral dialogue, regarding them as unpromising attempts to transplant European concepts in Asian soil.

The most recent batch of proposals for cooperative security, however, has been coming from the Association of Southeast Asian Nations (ASEAN), a group whose opinion must be treated with deference. And Tokyo and Washington appear to be beginning to realize on their own that preventing arms races, suppressing terrorism and piracy, and managing refugee flows can be achieved only through cooperative mechanisms.

At present, Tokyo and Washington appear to agree on a "multiplex" approach to cooperative security, consulting informally on subregional issues, particularly Indochina and Korea, but using the ASEAN post-ministerial conference and even Asia-Pacific Economic Cooperation (APEC), the principal government-level forum for regional economic discussions, for region-wide dialogue on force deployments, arms transfers, and security doctrines. And both insist that cooperative security regimes supplement, rather than replace, existing alliance structures. Maintaining that consensus will be important in the years ahead.

Economic Integration

The nations of East and Southeast Asia are now trading and investing with one another to the extent that one hears talk of the region taking shape as a distinct economic entity, as well as questions about ways to manage such a development. Much of the economic activity has been quite apart from relations with either Japan or the United States, but these two economic giants will inevitably play important roles in whatever arrangements emerge. And the two could take different approaches to the institutional issues raised by regional integration. The United States has shown some interest in APEC. Some Japanese, on the other hand, express unofficial interest in the more geographically restrictive East Asian Economic Caucus proposal of Malaysian Prime Minister Mahathir. As institutional evolution proceeds, Americans and Japanese will need to be aware of the extent to which their views on desirable arrangements converge or diverge.

At a subregional level, cross-border trade and investment are increasing rapidly between partners that were either separated by sharp political divisions or uninterested in each other in the past. These evolving economic ties are largely natural developments whose absence until now is a sad legacy of the Cold War and a sense of mutual exclusivity in economic structures. Most of these economic links do not affect the United States or Japan directly and are not particularly important as a matter of bilateral discussion, but their continued evolution should be encouraged by both countries.

Political and Economic Liberalization

The United States and Japan share democratic political institutions, and have a common interest in promoting human rights and political liberalization abroad. To this end, both countries have agreed that human rights should be one factor in determining the level of bilateral and multilateral aid to be given to developing countries. They have not only joined in criticizing China's suppression of anti-government protests in 1989, but have also worked in tandem to sanction the repressive behavior of the Burmese government.

But Japan and the United States also have clear differences about promoting human rights abroad. Not only do Americans tend to assign them a higher priority than do Japanese, but Tokyo appears to believe that the best way to promote human rights is to continue economic interaction, even economic aid, on the grounds that economic dynamism will eventually produce inexorable pressures for political liberalization. In contrast, many Americans regard normal commercial ties, let alone economic aid, as "rewarding" unsavory regimes, and therefore believe that human rights violations should be met by protracted sanction rather than continued engagement.

The differences in human rights policies evident in the way Japan and the United States have related to China since the Tiananmen crisis may affect the way the two countries deal with other Asian nations as well. One issue that may arise is whether it is more important to help consolidate democracy where it has already begun to take shape or to promote its emergence in the remaining authoritarian and totalitarian regimes. The first strategy would imply a focus on aiding the transition to democracy in nations like Mongolia and the central Asian republics; the latter, an emphasis on pressuring China, North Korea, Burma, and Vietnam to begin or resume political reform.

The United States and Japan also appear to favor different strategies for managing the transition to a market-oriented economy. Tokyo is increasingly willing to recommend that former Communist countries, in Asia and elsewhere, follow the path pursued so successfully by Japan and much of the rest of Asia in the 1960s and 1970s: extensive government involvement to build infrastructure, foster strategic industries, and promote exports, and gradual progress toward privatization of ownership and the decontrol of state-set prices. During two successive Republican administrations, especially during the Reagan years, Washington followed the principles of neoclassical economics in proposing quick and decisive progress toward privatizing and deregulating the economy. It remains to be seen whether the Clinton administration—more supportive of governmental intervention in the U.S. economy—will moderate the American position to bring it into greater conformity with that taken by the Japanese.

Environmental Protection

Although preserving the environment has become a pressing global concern, international policy approaches remain largely undeveloped. Many environmental issues should be debated at a global level, but that forum is often unwieldy, and particular problems may affect interests in one geographical region more than in others. Asia's rapid economic growth has worsened environmental problems and hastened consideration of policy responses. For example, deforestation in parts of Southeast Asia and extensive air pollution in China from the use of soft coal have serious implications both for the immediate locations involved and for the regional and global environment.

The United States and Japan, as the two advanced economies interacting closely with the region, share a concern about environmental degradation and have the financial and technical resources to make a difference. Neither country has a perfect domestic record in dealing with these problems, but both have gained considerable experience over the past two decades in tackling some of the worst problems.

The experiences of the United States and Japan, however, have been quite different. Japan's record on technical approaches to air and water pollution, pursued in a framework of considerable government-business cooperation, has been good, while its record on conservation issues such as fishing and deforestation has been weak. The United States has a better record on conservation, but government-business conflict has hampered some aspects of air and water pollution policymaking. More important, Japan has been far more willing over the past several years to commit foreign aid money to assist developing countries with environmental problems, while the U.S. government has been somewhat suspicious of the motives of developing countries in getting the developed nations to foot the bill.

If the United States and Japan approach environmental issues in the region individually, these divergent backgrounds and approaches could worsen the rivalry between the two.

A Realistic Partnership

U.S.-Japan relations must be based on reality, not on wishful thinking. It is naive to suppose that the intense economic competition between Japan and the United States would subside if the two countries could only agree to form a global partnership on international issues.

For one thing, cooperating on regional and global questions cannot compensate for a failure to manage bilateral economic issues. For another, although there are indeed many areas in which Tokyo and Washington can work together to achieve common purposes, they will approach other issues from divergent perspectives and with different objectives.

Recognition of the differences in attitude and approach by the United States and Japan has led some to see the emergence of a new global or regional rivalry between them. But economic competition and policy differences need not lead to an environment of political rivalry and hostility. It would be as foolish to ignore the common interests of the two countries as it would be to paper over the differences through appeals to vague concepts of partnership and harmony.

> "[M]erely changing the rules of the game will not create a Japanese government capable of moving forward in domestic and foreign policy. The structural changes at home mean a leaner economy and government austerity. The changes in the world at large force Japanese leaders to embrace their proclaimed activism. . . . The problem for politics and diplomacy is that the end of one-party dominance in 1993 has yet to reveal a new political order that provides leadership, reform, and international impact."

Japan: The End of One-Party Dominance

STEPHEN J. ANDERSON

STEPHEN J. ANDERSON *has been a research fellow in Tokyo at the Asian Forum. He is teaching at the University of Virginia and is the author of* Welfare Policy and Politics in Japan: Beyond the Developmental State *(New York: Paragon House, 1993), as well as articles on the public policy, politics, and international relations of Japan.*

This summer the Liberal Democratic party lost control of Japan's government. Between a June 18 no-confidence vote and the August 9 inauguration of a coalition cabinet, the party and the Diet were in upheaval. Scandal, internal splits, electoral stalemate, and an opposition coalition were the immediate causes of the ruling party's fall after 38 years in power.

Observers had not predicted rapid change in the LDP or the individuals who had governed since 1955. Analysts had pointed to structural weaknesses in the Japanese party system, while the media focused on the personalities of the leaders. The outcome took everyone by surprise. As the old leaders lost control, a new coalition unexpectedly began to pursue reforms.

THE OLD GUARD

From October 1991 until summer 1993, Kiichi Miyazawa led the government as prime minister and head of the Liberal Democratic party. Elected party president as a compromise candidate by the LDP factions that together held a majority of the seats in the Diet, Miyazawa, like many other recent leaders of the party who had ascended to the prime ministership, owed his position to and relied on funds from party vice president Shin Kanemaru.

Until overwhelmed by scandals in 1992, Kanemaru managed the party's largest faction, which had previously been headed by Kakuei Tanaka and was until this year led by Noboru Takeshita, both former prime ministers. The faction especially depended on Kanemaru to raise money—including, among other methods, stock deals revealed during the infamous Recruit scandal of the late 1980s. Kanemaru met his downfall because of a second scandal that began with the discovery of payments by a Sagawa package express company to more than 60 politicians. Though scandals come and go in Japan, all the established political parties were caught in the web of the Recruit and the Sagawa scandals. In mid-1992 Kanemaru turned up at the center of the web, under suspicion of accepting 500 million yen ($4.2 million) in illegal campaign funds.

The LDP power broker was forced to resign from the Diet. He was joined in disgrace by former faction leader Takeshita, and both were asked to resign from the party because of scrutiny of past contacts with right-wing groups. With these resignations, it appeared that the scandal might be managed. This January Kanemaru admitted his guilt; he was fined less than $2,000 by the public prosecutor's office.

The settlement, however, created an uproar throughout Japan. It was condemned in the media and in 130 resolutions by local assemblies; a man outraged by it was arrested after throwing paint on the prosecutors' offices. In a reversal, Kanemaru's offices and residence were then raided by the prosecutors, who seized gold ingots, art works, and stock certificates. By March Kanemaru himself had been arrested, held in a small jail cell, and shown on television in a wheelchair after being hospitalized for diabetes. The ruling party had survived huge scandals in the past and the system had continued basically unaltered, but the negative publicity from this one, kept alive by new revelations throughout 1993, played a large part in the major political changes that were to follow.

REFORM AT LAST?

Political reform dominated public debate in the media and the Diet, but different groups gave different definitions of it. Japanese citizens wanted to end the back room deals of campaign financing and the "money politics" represented by Kanemaru and Tanaka and Takeshita before him, but extending to all the major political parties. Related reforms included changes in campaign laws, controls on individual candidate groups known as *koenkai,* and more complete disclosure of political contributions. Yet these objectives became secondary to revising the electoral rules for the House of Representatives, the Diet's powerful lower house. Reform, for the politicians, was limited to the rules of election, rather than involving anything that would disturb the delicate area of political contributions. Political reform thus came to focus on revising the electoral laws.

Under the 1947 constitution, the House of Representatives is invested with the ultimate powers of deciding on legislation, passing the budget, and electing the prime minister. Yet the body's election districts predate the constitution, relying on boundaries largely set in 1925. Districts have multiple members, meaning that between two and six Diet members are elected for each district. Imbalance between districts' population and number of Diet members gives greater weight to voters from nonsuburban districts—more than six to one in some cases. The imbalances have brought only piecemeal changes by court order, and the electoral system is now seen as unfair, irrational, and antiquated.

Doing away with the multimember districts is a key electoral reform problem. An alternative is medium or small districts with single members; this would strike at the way *koenkai* individual support groups have organized small segments of a district to ensure victory for their candidate. In addition, a separate system of proportional representation would imitate that used by the upper house, the House of Councillors, and provide for nationwide candidate lists set by each party. Under proportional representation, votes for a given party are counted, and candidates are awarded seats on the basis of a ranked party list. This system would yield the broad representation seen in the House of Councillors and would protect the smaller parties threatened by changes in House of Representatives districts. By late 1993, the favored proposal for reform was to elect 250 representatives by district and 250 by a nationwide vote using proportional representation.

ARCHITECTS OF A REVOLT

Among leading politicians, Ichiro Ozawa seized on the issue of reform. Ironically, Ozawa was the Liberal Democrats' heir apparent to the indicted Kanemaru; although he had formerly served as secretary general of the ruling party, he had distanced himself from the charges of corruption and the surrounding turmoil. As

Kanemaru's career fell victim to corruption charges, Ozawa's political fortunes rose when he broke with his faction, ostensibly over the issue of reform but partly for reasons of internal rivalry. Ozawa joined with former party finance minister Tsutomu Hata in forming a rebel group they called Reform Forum 21, which called on the prime minister to push for passage of immediate reforms. Yet Ozawa, the ultimate Liberal Democratic insider, was linked by opponents to the crimes of Kanemaru.

Prime Minister Miyazawa faced tremendous pressure to pursue reform. The internal pressure from the Hata-Ozawa group was matched by broad public disapproval. By June, Miyazawa's cabinet had less than 10 percent support in public opinion polls. Politicians were blamed for scandals and the lack of progress on reform, particularly during popular Sunday morning and late night news shows. As on "Meet the Press" or "Nightline" in America, Japanese politicians were called on to respond to criticism, face their opponents, and answer probing questions from journalists before the television cameras.

After a taped interview, Miyazawa was charged with being a "liar" when it came to his commitment to political reform. The prime minister had promised reform during the June Diet session in a television interview with journalist Soichiro Tahara. This pledge was to prove fatal. Clips from the interview were replayed repeatedly on television as evidence of Miyazawa's lying about reform and his inability to lead the government.

The defection of Ozawa and Hata at the end of the Diet session was a major blow to the prime minister. Miyazawa lost an unprecedented no-confidence motion when the rebels of the group paraded in front of the LDP leadership to cast their votes with the opposition and against their party; the final count was 255 to 220 against the Miyazawa government. No longer able to command a majority, the prime minister decided on immediate elections after the dissolution of the Diet.

On June 18 Miyazawa faced the cameras in a late night press conference to explain his call for elections. No compromise was possible, with most of the Liberal Democratic politicians unwilling to have their multimember districts altered by the electoral reform sought by forces behind the leadership of the Hata-Ozawa splinter group.

Two days later Hata and Ozawa defected to form a new party, Shinseito. LDP leaders decided to call snap elections for July 18 with the hope that their resources and organization would prevail; their opponents, on the other hand, planned a reshaping of the political world.[1] Among Japanese journalists, the idea of the "great man" driving political history pointed to Ichiro Ozawa as the person to bring an end to long-term rule by one party. At the same time, structural changes in

---

[1]See "Time for a Change," *Far Eastern Economic Review,* May 6, 1993, for an interview with the magazine's Tokyo bureau chief that charts Ozawa's later strategy.

electoral competition and international relations that had set new parameters for Japanese politics had to be acknowledged.

ELECTION STALEMATE?

The 1993 election ended the arrangement known as the 1955 system, a term used to commemorate the merger that year of socialist and nonsocialist parties that had allowed the Liberal Democrats to first prevail in national elections. By itself, the 1993 balloting was not an utter defeat of the longtime ruling party; instead, the pre-election defection and the rise of several new parties because of popular movements and LDP defections drained away sufficient votes so that a majority was beyond the reach of any single party. The election signaled a structural change in Japanese politics: the long-term decline of a two-party system was being succeeded by a period in which multiple parties must join in coalitions to form governments. The July 18 results were actually ambiguous, and potentially pointed toward a stalemate.

The key result from the election was the defeat of the largest socialist party. The Nihon Shakaito had recently announced a change in the official English translation of its name from the "Japan Socialist party" (a direct translation, by which it had long been known) to the "Social Democratic Party of Japan." But this did little to help it among voters. Though it formed the largest opposition bloc in the Diet, the party could no longer be counted on to win or to champion an opposition point of view in a two-party system. In 1989 the party enjoyed a brief surge of support at the polls as the result of a tax protest by small businessmen and the middle class. The party leader at the time, Takako Doi, the first woman to head a major party in Japan, led the 1989 victory in elections for the House of Councillors. Doi later won a nonbinding vote for prime minister in the Diet's upper chamber. But the July defeat was bitter for her party: from 141 seats in the 511-seat lower chamber, the party fell to only 77.

The results were mixed for the Liberal Democrats. The *koenkai* groups were seen as successful in their support of most LDP candidates, and the party remained the largest bloc in the House of Representatives, winning 223 seats outright. By August the LDP had gained the support of independents and controlled 228 seats, one more than the number it held in June after the defection. Nonetheless, 228 is short of the 256 that constitute a majority. The party lost its majority because of defection rather than the election, but the loss of the majority was a harsh reality for the leadership.

Several parties other than the LDP came off as winners in the election. The candidates from the new parties capitalized on the protests against scandal and calls for reform, and the alternative parties also challenged the traditional parties. The newcomers benefited mostly from the decline of mainstream socialism, with the Democratic Socialist and Communist parties retaining 15 seats each. Among the established groups, the Buddhist-related Komeito used its neighborhood organization to gain a 7-seat increase, to 52 seats. But it was the new parties that had responded to and fueled the demand for political reform that won most of the redistributed Diet seats.

The media gave extensive coverage to the Japan New Party. In the July 1992 House of Councillors election, the party's first, it won 4 of the 126 upper chamber seats at stake. The party's leader, Morihiro Hosokawa, a former LDP governor of Kumamoto prefecture on the southern island of Kyushu, worked for the next year building a new party organization and recruiting candidates, including former television personalities, local leaders, and journalists to attract the support of younger and unaffiliated voters; the party won 36 seats in the House of Representatives in the July election. Hosokawa was joined by another former governor, Masayoshi Takemura, who had formed his own party in the Diet, the Sakigake party. With independents joining their bloc, the Japan New Party/Sakigake quickly reached the level of Komeito, controlling 52 seats.

Hata and Ozawa's Shinseito party was also successful. By August, Shinseito had gained a formidable 60 seats in the new Diet. Ozawa, hampered by people's association of him with scandal, decided not to attend the party's first press conference. Still, as secretary general he managed to raise funds, give candidates endorsements, and seek compromise on the creation of a non-LDP coalition. Shinseito benefits from having the most experience in national government among the new parties, as well as from its well-established candidates. In the new coalition, however, former ties by its members with the LDP meant trouble for the Shinseito candidate for prime minister, Tsutomu Hata.

None of the new parties had close to the LDP's plurality of seats in the House of Representatives. Commentators speculated that the Liberal Democrats might be able to form a new government, gathering some defectors back into the fold or even recruiting the Japan New Party to join a coalition. Such speculation died down only after internal debates revealed the depth of divisions within the LDP.

After the election results were in, the Liberal Democrats reorganized to prepare their response. In a vocal party meeting that was televised, subdued and shocked party elders listened to the loud and prolonged protests of younger members. In the race for party president, faction leader and Foreign Minister Michio Watanabe lost out to a reformed rebel, Yohei Kono. Kono had left the LDP in 1976 to act as a leader of the New Liberal Club, a splinter group, but had returned to serve as the chief cabinet secretary for the last Miyazawa cabinet. Now he was being elected party president so that he might become the reformer of the party that fell from power. In balloting that in previous years would have been to choose the new prime minister, Kono was selected as the party's first opposition leader.

The results of the national election showed a lack of confidence in the LDP government. All the other parties except the Communists took the opportunity to create a coalition. The shape of this coalition, with groups ranging from the left-wing socialists to right-wing conservative defectors, meant that political compromise was vital. But aside from the goal of ending LDP rule, observers saw little common ground among the coalition partners. Few prophesied success.

CREATING A COALITION THAT WORKS

The new parties avoided stalemate by agreeing about their cause: ending the long rule of the Liberal Democrats. Between July 18 and August 8 negotiators in intense sessions built a coalition without the Liberal Democrats, eventually backing a newcomer to the national scene. In Japan, explanations for the coalition's formation and choice of leaders range from the working-out of intensely personal politics to the changes facing the Japanese government and the issue of foreign relations after the cold war.

Speculation after the election was that compromise on the prime ministership and cabinet posts would give the jobs to experienced LDP rebels, at least. The rebels Hata and Ozawa were committed to forming a coalition government, with Hata emerging as a front-runner for prime minister. In the middle, between the LDP and the rebels, the newcomer, Morihiro Hosokawa of the Japan New Party—who had remained uncommitted throughout the campaign and after the election, fueling speculation he might join with the LDP—held the deciding vote.

The early negotiations were misleading to observers. At first the LDP defectors led by Tsutomu Hata remained the credible alternative for forming a coalition government headed by non-LDP politicians. But Hata, and Ozawa working on his behalf, proved unacceptable to the left-wing socialists of the coalition. Hata fell victim to longtime opponents, particularly the other established politicians who opposed these former LDP members because of their proximity to scandal. As negotiations continued only a newcomer such as Hosokawa remained an acceptable leader for the broad coalition.

Hosokawa agreed to join a coalition government only if he were named the new prime minister. He promised ministerial portfolios to Hata and his allies as well as to the socialists, including the post of speaker of the House for the Nihon Shakaito's former head, Takako Doi. Seven parties were awarded cabinet posts in the process of sealing the careful compromise. The broad coalition, including an additional party of 11 Diet members without portfolio in the upper house and two nonpoliticians in the cabinet, had created a government.

On August 8 new Prime Minister Hosokawa immediately staked his future on achieving electoral reform, implying, just as Miyazawa had before him, that he would resign if such reform did not pass. "I intend this cabinet not simply to lead the country for a brief interlude but rather to undertake the important mission of opening the way for a new era," Hosokawa proclaimed at his first news conference. In the first month of the new government, Hosokawa proved tremendously popular; public opinion polls showed him with a 70 percent approval rating. But by year's end the newcomer to national politics faced struggles over the electoral system and a budget bill that would test his political acumen.

The Japanese economy has been hurt by the worldwide recession. Analysts speak of a deflating "bubble economy" following from the high real estate and stock prices of the 1980s. Yet the finance ministry and cautious politicians have avoided further rapid expansion of the economy through public spending after three stimulus packages this year. But fiscal conservatism is not merely a matter of ideology, because Japan is also looking at rising entitlements. Japan has the most rapidly aging population of any advanced industrial society. While only 6 percent of the population was over the age of 65 in 1990, projections put the figure at 12 percent by the end of 1993 and show it doubling again in 30 years. By 2023, 24 percent of Japan's population will likely be over age 65, and of these, 15 percent will be over 75. The Hosokawa government pledged that it would stay the course for most LDP entitlements; it will probably not make major changes in other areas of public spending that might disturb the economy.

The problems of the new government were not wholly internal. Japan is sharing in the prolonged recession that in Europe and the United States has suppressed demand for Japanese exports. Japan faced adjustments for the appreciation of the yen, from 126 to the dollar in June 1992 to 105 or 106 to the dollar this October, that left businesses to cope with substantial instability for their international trade. Both these economic uncertainties and the political demands that Japan take on a larger international role meant that the coalition government had to move rapidly simply to keep up with world events.

THE QUEST FOR ACTIVIST DIPLOMACY

At the end of the cold war, Japan needs policies commensurate with its economic power and place in the world. Some of its leaders have called for an acti_ foreign policy, yet Japanese diplomacy has rem_ cautious. In August the Foreign Ministry removed responsibility for security matters from the North American Affairs Bureau and placed it in a new general policy bureau designed to separate such matters from the American alliance.

Two years ago, Prime Minister Miyazawa was regarded as highly qualified to lead Japan in the international community. The senior statesman had served in a lengthy and broad-ranging list of leadership posts and spoke fluent English in which he would be able to articulate Japanese views. But anticipated successes were not achieved and his initiatives suffered a series of mishaps. In January 1992, Miyazawa was embarrassed when United States President George Bush became ill and fainted during a formal dinner in Tokyo. The pair had plans to announce a "global partnership," but instead the leaders of the world's two largest economies parted in confusion.

The muddle in relations with America did little to advance Japan's role in global politics. The Persian Gulf War early in 1991 had left Japan with lingering doubts about its position. UN allies had criticized Tokyo's contribution of money without personnel. By the time the 1992 elections for the Diet's upper house rolled around, debate focused on Japanese roles in peacekeeping efforts. The LDP eventually won a majority of 69 of the 126 contested seats, but the opposition ran strong and hard-hitting campaigns against the creation of a Japanese peacekeeping organization (PKO). (The 1947 constitution limits the Japanese Self-Defense Forces, which currently consist of 249,000 troops, to noncombat roles, and the opposition questioned the constitutionality of LDP-sponsored bills sending troops overseas.)

In the Diet the opposition protested the bill establishing the PKO through four all-night sessions, using a filibuster tactic known as the "cow-walk." Vocal opponents demonstrated and left-wing guerrilla groups set off explosions to protest the bill's passage in June 1992. Foreign critics, especially in China, South Korea, and Singapore, also cautioned against sending troops overseas.

Public opinion was divided on Japanese involvement in the UN peacekeeping effort in Cambodia. To deflect international criticism, the ruling party used the peacekeeping bill to create a new initiative under the UN umbrella and to encourage democratic elections in Cambodia. The peacekeeping troops of the newly constituted PKO force and civilian Japanese volunteers who went to Indochina did so at considerable risk. Japanese fears were to some extent realized with the deaths of several members of the national contingent: an election watcher was killed by a disgruntled worker, and then a policemen was killed and several were wounded by Khmer Rouge guerrillas. The dispatch overseas of members of the Japanese armed forces had raised fears of remilitarization both inside and outside

the country. Yet on balance, the effort has been rated a success because of the Cambodian election, the return of King Norodom Sihanouk, and the establishment of a new government.

In Cambodia, Japan showed leadership. In particular, Yasushi Akashi has served as the special representative leading the United Nations Transitional Authority in Cambodia. Akashi, a career diplomat who rose in the Japanese foreign ministry through his pursuit of challenging assignments, faced daunting tasks in the Cambodian peacekeeping effort, including the separation and disarming of warring groups including the Khmer Rouge.

PKO troops entered the limelight back home when sent to Cambodia. After Diet approval of the peacekeeping organization, troops had gone immediately to Sweden to train at UN facilities. Once in Cambodia, engineers built bridges, health care workers supported activities of the UN transitional authority in the country, and several thousand more PKO forces joined in policing and election monitoring. During New Year celebrations this year, Japan's national broadcasting company, reflecting popular interest, featured live, nonstop, dusk-to-dawn coverage from Angor Wat, Cambodia. In 1993 Japanese citizens became increasingly aware of and gave growing approval to the efforts to support stability in Southeast Asia.

THE US AND UN CONNNECTIONS

Relations between Japan and the United States are based on a mutual security treaty and economic ties that remain a pillar of world order. In July Miyazawa hosted a reassuring Group of Seven summit meeting attended by President Bill Clinton and leaders of the world's five other leading industrial nations. Miyazawa stressed the theme of global partnership in security, political cooperation, cultural ties, and scientific exchanges. Many Japanese preferred the Republican administrations of Reagan and Bush, yet they accepted the coming of a new Democratic government. The switch to the Democrats raised hopes among those Japanese who had long urged America to lower its budget deficit, improve infrastructure, and increase competitiveness. By the meeting's end, the Japanese and American chief executives had agreed on a bilateral trade framework that created some anticipation of improved economic ties.

During his visit to Tokyo, Clinton met with the future leadership. A United States embassy reception for political leaders overcame the ruling party's criticism and gave the president a chance to meet future deputy prime minister Hata Tsutomu and future prime minister Hosokawa. With their message of change for their countries, Clinton and Hosokawa had common ground on which to begin their relationship during a meeting at the UN in New York in September.

Since Miyazawa had weathered criticism of UN initiatives, Hosokawa committed himself to continue such policies. Officials hoped that foreign policy actions would allow for Japanese leadership based on economic competitiveness and overseas development assistance. Unofficial flows of capital and investment more than double the $10.95 billion in official aid from Japan in 1992 and the record-setting levels topping $11 billion for 1993. The September visit to the UN by Hosokawa and Foreign Minister Hata would affirm earlier Japanese commitments to that organization and the world.

Japan became more prominent in the UN. The UN High Commissioner for Refugees, Sadako Ogata, flew frequently to Cambodia, Iraq, and other crisis spots to survey international problems with the migration and mass movement of peoples. Indochina especially elicited support among the Japanese citizenry for moving toward more prominent UN roles. Japan gave $1.9 million in humanitarian aid to the former Yugoslavia and $15 million for famine relief to Somalia. Further, Japan considered future commitments to the Middle East, Bosnia, Africa, Latin America, and Russia, where Japanese interests are not directly at stake.

This past year Japanese diplomats remained firm about their territorial disputes with Russia. With the cold war over, Japanese and Russians sought to settle the question of the Soviet-occupied islands below the Kurile archipelago, which Japan argues had long been Japanese territories. After Soviet President Mikhail Gorbachev's 1991 visit to Tokyo, observers wondered about a direct swap of aid packages in return for two of the four disputed islands. In July 1992, Miyazawa secured the backing of the Group of Seven at a summit in Munich for his position demanding that Russia give back the islands, as Japan lawfully had sovereignty over them.

Russian President Boris Yeltsin, bowing to Sakhalin politicians and Russian parliamentarians who argued that further loss of territory would be a blow to national pride, abruptly canceled a long-planned visit to Japan in September 1992 but went to Tokyo later. Yeltsin was only grudgingly invited to the Group of Seven summit in Tokyo this July, and was coldly received in October after his violent crackdown on the renegade Russian parliament. Despite contributions pledged at the G7 meeting, Japanese aid to Russia will be limited by the territorial dispute, if not the doubts Japan's business community harbors about the long-term prospects for the Russian economy, considering the political situation. Russo-Japanese relations remain in stalemate.

Japan is poised to play a leading part in the Pacific Basin. Starting with careful diplomacy toward the Association of Southeast Asian Nations (ASEAN), Japan has supported the common positions of Asian countries. The movement toward regional organiza-tions is a case in point. Since 1992 Japan has supported the government ministers meeting as the Asia-Pacific Economic Cooperation group, and the Pacific Economic Cooperation Conference, a forum for representatives from government, business, and academia; this year both groups established perma-nent secretariat offices in Singapore. Japanese back-ing for these seeks to increase economic cooperation in the region and initiate joint efforts to assure regional security; Japan is eager to move beyond bilateral relations with close neighbors and establish regional frameworks.

Japan supports the post-ministerial conferences of ASEAN to discuss security concerns. These talks after the meetings between ministers of the countries in the group are exploratory, and Japan remains com-mitted to a security relationship with the United States. But the ASEAN meetings provide a new setting for regional actors to discuss differences over prob-lems in Indochina and the Spratly Islands in the South China Sea, among other issues. In October Japan convened a meeting of ASEAN supported by the United States and Australia and attended by Hong Kong and South Korea on stopping the proliferation of weapons of mass destruction.

Toward China, Japan emphasizes favorable rela-tions with its most populous neighbor. Japan was China's second-largest trading partner after Hong Kong, and China for the past several years has received more than $100 million annually in Japa-nese foreign aid. Japan also anticipates a genera-tional shift in Chinese leadership. In October 1992 the Japanese emperor, Akihito, traveled to China in an effort to improve Sino-Japanese relations. Accom-panied by officials working on long-standing dis-putes about wartime responsibility, the China visit was criticized by a vocal right wing in Japan after the emperor expressed regret for the "Pacific War."

This June, a wedding in the imperial family focused attention on its members' roles in Japan. The family heard quite a lot, mainly from right-wing groups, about the partner chosen by Crown Prince Naruhito, the future national symbol of state. For his bride, Masako Owada, a 29-year-old diplomat edu-cated at Harvard and Oxford, the wedding celebra-tion continued a bureaucratic struggle, as well as marking a great personal change; in a struggle over influence, Owada's father, the top bureaucrat in the Ministry of Foreign Affairs, where his daughter also worked, had clashed with the tradition-bound Impe-rial Household Agency, particularly over the funeral of Emperor Hirohito. The celebration also saw a career woman accept traditional roles in her commit-ment to the crown prince, and her generation saw it as an acceptance of traditional roles by a modern career woman. Owada, in an intensely personal and controversial article in the May 24 *Newsweek,*[2] was said to have overcome her reluctance to accept the prince's proposal after assurances from the Empress Michiko that a comfortable private life was possible for the imperial family.

FUTURE POLITICS

At year's end the Diet was poised to debate political reform and annual budget priorities. Japan remained in the most severe economic downturn it had experienced since the 1973 oil crisis. Hosokawa pressed forward with his goals for reform while holding together his broad coalition.

Under one possible scenario, the twin legislative battles over electoral reform and the annual budget bring on a crisis. If there is a deadlock and the schedule in December becomes tight, the coalition government may be forced to compromise on reform in order to pass the budget before the deadline. The result could be an early election and a new government for Japan.

A scenario in which electoral reform is deferred also holds the potential for conflict. If Hosokawa, along

---

[2]Bill Powell, "The Reluctant Princess," *Newsweek,* May 24, 1993, pp. 28–31. Conservatives in Japan criticized the article because it applied a probing and revealing style of journalism to the imperial family.

with the influential Ichiro Ozawa, who engineered the coalition and now helps manage it, decide to defer reform, the government might last well into 1994. But citizens and opposing politicians will quickly remind leaders of the pledge to pass reform and of decisions on other critical matters that cannot be deferred. Ozawa may provoke crisis himself in order to pursue a second election and his vision of a new two-party system led by Shinseito and the Liberal Democrats.

Structural change encourages electoral reform. In domestic politics, a reformed system that combines new, medium-sized districts and proportional representation might restore public confidence. Yet merely changing the rules of the game will not create a Japanese government capable of moving forward in domestic and foreign policy. The structural changes at home mean a leaner economy and government austerity. The changes in the world at large force Japanese leaders to embrace their proclaimed activism. Countries throughout Asia, if not in Latin America, Africa, and elsewhere, expect that Japan will fulfill pledges to overcome the past and fulfill the promises that its diplomats suggest. The problem for politics and diplomacy is that the end of one-party dominance in 1993 has yet to reveal a new political order that provides leadership, reform, and international impact.

The Rise of China

Nicholas D. Kristof

Nicholas D. Kristof was Beijing Bureau Chief for The New York Times *from 1988 to 1993 and is currently writing a book about China with his wife, Sheryl WuDunn.*

THIS TIME IT IS REAL

The rise of China, if it continues, may be the most important trend in the world for the next century. When historians one hundred years hence write about our time, they may well conclude that the most significant development was the emergence of a vigorous market economy—and army—in the most populous country of the world. This is particularly likely if many of the globe's leading historians and pundits a century from now do not have names like Smith but rather ones like Wu.

China is the fastest growing economy in the world, with what may be the fastest growing military budget. It has nuclear weapons, border disputes with most of its neighbors, and a rapidly improving army that may—within a decade or so—be able to resolve old quarrels in its own favor. The United States has possessed the world's largest economy for more than a century, but at present trajectories China may displace it in the first half of the next century and become the number one economy in the world.

The only group that is paying serious attention to China's long-term prospects is the business community. Chief executives regularly whirl through Beijing and Guanzhou, and they are almost inevitably dizzied by the ubiquitous construction sites, the glitzy discos, the miniskirted prostitutes. They gush about how China's current economic revolution is the most important business trend they have ever seen and how they want to be a part of it, but they ignore the tectonic strains that can be expected in the years ahead. Almost nothing is so destabilizing as the arrival of a new industrial and military power on the international scene; consider Japan's history in this century or Germany's in the decades leading up to World War I.

There is still a significant possibility that China will never manage an economic takeoff. All kinds of things can go wrong, and economic trajectories are almost impossible to predict. Four decades ago, for example, the two countries in Asia that seemed to have the best economic prospects were the Philippines and Burma; ever since, they have been the laggards of the region. China must leap enormous hurdles, for its leaders face a crisis of legitimacy as well as a generational transition in the next few years (assuming that 89-year-old Deng Xiaoping is mortal). The central government rules territories—such as Tibet and Xinjiang—inhabited by ethnic minorities who yearn for independence. The government still has not dared to expose much of the huge state sector (accounting for about half of industrial production) to the cruelty of market forces, and when it does it could face strikes and revolts by disgruntled workers. Military coups, chaos and even civil war are all possibilities in China over the next dozen years. Yet there appears to be at least a realistic possibility that China will be able to sustain its boom for decades to come, and it would be foolish—and perhaps dangerous—to neglect this likelihood.[1]

Yet the international community is not giving adequate consideration to the colossal implications—economic, political, environmental and even military—of the rise of a powerful China. It is fashionable these days for people to express wonderment at how the changes underway in China are breathtaking, but there is very little specific analysis of the economic, environmental and military effects of China's growth.

---

1. It should also be noted that China has become sufficiently interconnected with the rest of the world that even if it falls apart it could have disastrous consequences. The last time China fragmented, in the years following the collapse of the Qing Dynasty in 1911–12, the local warlords did not have nuclear weapons. Next time, they may. Moreover, any major chaos in China could produce a wave of emigration such as the world has never seen. This deluge of up to tens of millions of boat people would impose a heavy burden on Japan, Southeast Asia and even the United States. In other words, even in failure China could be hugely important.

Reprinted with permission from *Foreign Affairs*, Vol. 72, No. 5, November/December 1993, pp. 59-74. © 1993 by The Council on Foreign Relations, Inc.

Nor is there much analysis of whether China's attempt to expand its influence reflects the hostile intentions of an aggressive regime or is simply the natural consequence of rising power. The answer is crucial to determining the world's response to China.

THE ECONOMIC GIANT

For most of recorded history, China has been more developed, prosperous, sophisticated and civilized than the West. It is only in the last 500 years that Europe managed to pull ahead, and yet since the early nineteenth century we have often seen China's backwardness as inevitable. This smug condescension was expressed most arrogantly by Ralph Waldo Emerson when he rather brutally described China as a "booby nation" that did not compare with the great civilizations of the world: "But China, reverend dulness! hoary ideot! all she can say at the convocation of nations must be—'I made the tea.'" The problem is that 500 years is the blink of an eye in the Chinese time frame. The Eastern Zhou Dynasty lasted almost that long, and who in the West has ever even heard of the Eastern Zhou Dynasty? A country's fortunes can change very quickly, as Japan and South Korea have shown, and China now is on a road that could restore it to its original greatness.

The conventional wisdom is that the world economy these days is tri-polar, revolving around the United States, Japan and the European Community (particularly Germany). This is true in terms of financial markets, such as stock investing and currency trading. But in terms of global trade, market size and sheer economic bulk, China is becoming a fourth pole in the international system. This is particularly true when one looks at "Greater China," consisting of the People's Republic, Hong Kong and Taiwan. According to World Bank projections, Greater China's net imports in the year 2002 will be $639 billion, compared to $521 billion for Japan. Likewise, using comparable international prices, Greater China in the year 2002 is projected to have a gross domestic product of $9.8 trillion, compared to $9.7 trillion for the United States. If those forecasts hold, in other words, Greater China would not just be another economic pole; it would be the biggest of them all.

Of course, this growth is a function of population increase alone, and we shouldn't get carried away by what it means. China is still a country of poor people; it just has a lot of them. During my five years in Beijing, I often encountered giddy American business executives passing through for their first date with the Middle Kingdom. Their tendency to extrapolate ("if every Chinese consumed as much of our product as the average Australian does now, we would double our global sales . . .") reminded me of the British indus-

trialists a century ago who calculated that if every Chinese added just one inch to his shirt tail, the mills of Lancashire could be kept busy for a generation.

One hundred years later the Chinese would come to afford longer shirt tails, but they would do so by manufacturing their own shirts—in sufficient quantities that they threaten to idle the West's great textile mills. China's present economic boom started in about 1978 and has since resulted in real annual growth averaging about 9 percent per year. It is not slowing down: in 1992, GNP grew by 12.8 percent, and this year 13 percent growth is predicted. Such a pace is dangerously overheated, but its sheer speed is staggering.

The economy will have to cool down for the next year or more, and in any case diminishing returns are likely to set in eventually as the economy becomes more efficient and sophisticated. But by and large the Chinese economy still has plenty of steam left in it. Some economists believe that if China enjoys political stability, and if the global trading system remains open to its exports, China could rack up 7 percent or 8 percent growth rates for at least another couple of decades. At an 8 percent clip, an economy quintuples in size every 21 years.

Already, China is much wealthier than statistics often show. Officially, per capita GNP is still only about $370 per year, but this figure is not very meaningful. The World Bank this year used two different approaches to purchasing power parity to derive GDP figures at internationally comparable prices. One method resulted in per capita GDP of $1,680, the other of $2,040. Because the data are of poor quality, the only thing that is certain is that the Chinese live much better than the official statistics would suggest.

GROWTH WITH CHINESE CHARACTERISTICS

One of the great uncertainties of China's economic takeoff, if it can be sustained, is what the environmental price will be and who will pay it. To the extent that China industrializes by dirtying its own air and fouling its own water, that is perhaps its right. But matters get a bit more complicated when China's economic miracle produces acid rain that destroys Siberian forests, or when it contributes to global warming that causes the seas to rise and inundate Bangladesh.

As it industrializes, China will require a dramatically larger share of world resources. In 1992, China unseated the United States as the leading buyer of gold, and the Chinese construction boom has caused a global scramble for certain kinds of steel. In coming years, China can be expected to use more of everything, especially energy. For now China uses relatively little energy, although it uses it inefficiently. In 1991, per capita consumption of energy in China was only 602 kilograms of oil equivalent, compared to 7,681 kilograms of oil equivalent in the United States. If, within a few decades, each Chinese uses as much energy as every South Korean does now, then China will use more energy than the United States.

In other words, a steady increase in China's industrialization would place a huge new strain on global energy supplies. This is particularly true because China is running out of oil—at least the kind that is easily exploited. Older oil fields, such as Daqing in the northeast, are running low, and it is unclear whether new fields are as promising as China says. China describes the Tarim Basin in the northwest as virtually another Saudi Arabia, and it has also brimmed with optimism about the South China Sea. But the Tarim Basin will require construction of a long and expensive pipeline through rugged terrain. In the meantime, Beijing is likely to become a net oil importer within a couple of years.

Most of China's energy comes from coal, particularly soft, high-sulfur, highly polluting coal. In 1991, Chinese polluters emitted 11 trillion cubic meters of waste gases and 16 million metric tons of soot. The sulfur in the coal also causes acid rain, which travels across international borders to attack forests far away in Siberia or Korea. Some experts believe that China will become the world's largest source of acid rain by the year 2010.

China has been using its economic boom to finance a far-reaching military buildup.

Perhaps the biggest worry of all, at least for Americans and Europeans, may be China's contributions to global warming. Chinese burning of coal releases carbon dioxide, the most important of the greenhouse gases that are suspected of trapping heat around the earth's surface. The greenhouse effect could, in turn, lead to climate changes, a rising of the oceans and inundation of coastal areas around the globe.

In 1950, China produced carbon dioxide amounting to less than 22 million metric tons of carbon. By 1986, that had risen to 554 million metric tons—and the figure was rising by more than 25 million metric tons a year. At last count, China ranked third in emissions of greenhouse gases, behind the United States and the former Soviet Union. But it is the fastest-growing emitter of greenhouse gases. The Stockholm Environment Institute calculated that if China's economy grows 8.5 percent a year for the next three decades, then by the year 2025 China will produce three times as much carbon dioxide as the United States. In one sense that is perfectly fair, since China will have far more than three times America's population. In fact, while China is the third-largest contributor of green-

house gases, it does not even rank among the top 50 countries in terms of per capita emissions. On a per person basis, every American churns out nine times as much greenhouse gas as every Chinese. And even if China eventually does become the largest emitter of such gases, that is understandable, since China has the largest population in the world. But it is discouraging for other countries, for while the West is making efforts to curb greenhouse gases China is blithely going ahead as it always has. Chinese officials make it clear that they will not sacrifice economic growth for the sake of the environment—their own or the world's.

KEEPING THE GUNPOWDER VERY DRY

While most countries have been cutting military budgets over the last five years, China has been using its economic boom to finance a far-reaching buildup. It seeks the influence of a great power, as well as its wallet. Thus the People's Liberation Army has purchased fighter aircraft and other equipment from the former Soviet Union, introduced new classes of naval vessels, and in some cases taken a more aggressive posture toward its border disputes with other nations.

The officially disclosed military budget is a bit of a joke, for it does not even include sums spent on weapons procurement or on research and development. Yet, however misleading the official figure is, it is worth noting that between 1988 and 1993 it leaped 98 percent, to $7.5 billion. In the same period, inflation rose only 32 percent. As a very crude benchmark, total military spending—including off-budget items—is around $18 billion this year. If that is adjusted to reflect equivalent purchasing power in the West, total military spending in international prices is much higher, perhaps as much as $90 billion. These figures are too imprecise for exact comparisons, but such a military budget would be one of the highest in the world. Just as important, it reflects a rising share of a rapidly rising GNP.[2]

China has used the money to bolster its ability to project power beyond its borders. Last year it purchased 26 SU-27 fighter jets from Russia, and it is

---

2. The figure was derived as follows. The World Bank official figure for 1991 per capita GNP in China is $370. The bank's two estimates of 1991 per capita GDP in international prices are $1,680 and $2,040. The average of these is $1,860, which is 5.03 times the official figure. If one takes this multiplier, 5.03, and uses it with the $18 billion estimate for military spending, the product is about $90.5 billion. But it should be emphasized that these numbers are shots in the dark. The multiplier for the military budget may be less than for GDP as a whole because services and labor cost—both very cheap in China—may account for a larger share of the overall economy than of military expenditures.

expected to buy another dozen or more. China has also reportedly bought SA-10s—a missile similar to the American Patriot, but perhaps not as sophisticated—from Moscow. By some accounts it is also negotiating for the purchase of up to 79 MiG-31 fighters, which would be built in China's Guizhou Province in a cooperative arrangement with Moscow. China has acquired air refueling technology apparently from Pakistan and Iran, and is believed to have converted some bombers into tanker aircraft. It is working on training pilots and crew so that by the year 2000 the air force may have a significant fleet of fighter planes and bombers that can be refueled.

Perhaps the biggest symbol of China's new interest in projecting power is its desire to have an aircraft carrier. After browsing at a Ukrainian carrier under construction, the *Varyag*, China has apparently decided to look elsewhere—either to build its own or to buy another. But last year then-President Yang Shang-kun confirmed in a secret speech to military officials that the leadership had already decided in principle to acquire an aircraft carrier. The aircraft carrier may reflect China's aspiration to develop a blue-water navy of ocean-going vessels, rather than just coastal ships. This naval expansion has attracted less attention than the air-force modernization but it is at least as significant. The new Jiangwei class of frigates, the Luhu class of destroyers and the newly upgraded version of the older Luda class destroyers are all formidable vessels, especially given the weaponry of the other powers in the region. A Jiangwei frigate might not intimidate an American admiral, but it looks quite unnerving to a Vietnamese.

One of China's most puzzling forays abroad is its apparent deal with Burma to develop two islands in the Indian Ocean as observation posts—and perhaps eventually as some kind of a naval base. China has no traditional interest in the Indian Ocean, but in 1985 it sent the navy on a cruise through the area, with port calls in Pakistan, Sri Lanka and Bangladesh. If China really is trying to acquire a naval base in Burma, that would be a major stride toward a blue-water navy, and a significant concern for other countries in the region.

This buildup has to be kept in perspective. Chinese military spending probably accounts for only about 4 percent of GNP, compared to 5 percent in the United States. Moreover, Chinese skills and technology start at such a low level that its army may not even be a match for Taiwan's, let alone the West's. An aircraft carrier and aerial refueling will help, but it may be a decade before China figures out how to use its new skills and equipment effectively.

CHINA'S NEXT WAR

The most likely site for a war is probably the South China Sea, which China claims as its own 1,000-mile long pond. This huge sea, encompassing the Paracel and Spratly Island groups, covers major international shipping routes, including those that carry oil from the gulf to Japan. The area is also claimed in part by Vietnam, Malaysia, Brunei, Taiwan and the Philippines.

China and Vietnam have fought naval battles in the area in 1974 and 1988, and the danger of a more decisive conflict may be growing for two reasons. First, some experts believe that there are extensive oil and natural gas deposits in the area, enhancing its appeal. China itself has estimated that the South China Sea floor contains 105 billion barrels of oil, an extravagant guess that it has since backed away from. But even vague hopes that the area is so bountiful will encourage Beijing to use force to control the sea. Second, China has always regarded the area as its own, but it is only now gaining the ability to enforce its view. The Chinese armed forces have extended a landing strip on Woody Island, the largest of the Paracels, so that it is now 2,600 meters long, thus creating a staging ground for any conflict. More ominously, China last year awarded exploration rights for a disputed part of the sea—an area that Vietnam insists is part of its continental shelf—to Crestone Energy Corporation, an American oil company. The head of the company told me he was promised the full backing of the Chinese navy in exploring the area.

Another possible flash point is the Taiwan Strait, particularly if Beijing grows more confident about its military capabilities. China has repeatedly promised that it will use military force if Taiwan declares itself an independent country, and I think we should take Beijing at its word. Moreover, Taiwan is now taking the first tentative steps toward what might be construed as de facto independence—such as campaigning for membership in the United Nations—and the ruling Nationalist Party in Taiwan may be beginning to crumble. Taiwan is expected to hold its first direct presidential elections in 1996, and it is remotely possible that the Nationalists will lose. If that were to happen, and if the new president were to favor independence, there would be great pressure in Beijing for intervention against Taiwan. Such a course of events is not likely because the consequences would be disastrous for both sides. But it is a reminder that there is a continuing risk, and perhaps a growing one, of a clash in the Taiwan Strait.

The other possibilities for war seem much more remote. China and Japan, for example, quarrel over ownership of a group of islands to the northeast of Taiwan. Indeed, there is not even agreement on what to call the islands. China calls them the Diaoyudao, Taiwan says they are the Diaoyutai, and Japan calls them the Senkakus. For now, cool heads are prevailing on all sides, but Japanese and Chinese nationalists may try to force the issue.

Map by Ib Ohlsson for FOREIGN AFFAIRS

WHOSE FAULT IS IT ANYWAY?

There is a tendency abroad to find fault with China for building up its army, bullying its neighbors and corroding the environment. This is unfair. What China is doing is in most cases perfectly natural, and even its territorial and military aspirations are reasonable. Any Chinese government, even a democratic one, might well follow similar policies, and any Chinese leader would be attacked at home for giving up claims to Taiwan, the South China Sea, the Diaoyudao or Hong Kong. China is not coveting territories with which it has no link, nor is it claiming some kind of Monroe Doctrine to police the region. The dispute over the South China Sea, for example, is enormously complex, and China can cite some historical ties to the area dating back hundreds of years.

Part of the problem is that China lost significant amounts of its territory over the last century and a half; in periods when it was weak. Any country in such a position would yearn to recover at least some of its land, and China by and large has been fairly reasonable in its demands. Since the end of the Cultural Revolution, for example, it has not demanded the return of the lands taken by Russia in the nineteenth century, nor has it sought the return of Mongolia. Even in the case of the South China Sea, the foreign ministry is making reasonable, cooperative noises at the same time that the navy is sounding more jingoistic. This divide between foreign ministry doves and military hawks may become more evident in coming years. The foreign ministry already has an important role,

namely building warm relations between China and the rest of the world. But the army is searching for a new role following the decline of the Russian threat, and so to maintain its own prestige and influence, it is forging for itself a new identity as protector of China's economic and political interests in the South China Sea and other disputed areas.

When they have been cheated, weak nations cite principles while powerful nations invoke artillery. This is as natural today as it was when the Athenians explained international relations to the Melians more than 2,400 years ago: "The strong do what they can and the weak suffer what they must." China is now in the process of transforming itself from a weakling to one of the strong. It will have the opportunity to do what it wants instead of what it must.

It is entirely understandable that China would want a blue-water navy, that it would seek a more powerful international role, because that is what great powers are supposed to do. China perceives a power vacuum in the Pacific as Russia and the United States retrench, and it wants to expand its interests there. For a nation that has always felt profoundly insecure, nothing makes more sense than a spanking new aircraft carrier as a symbol that it has made it. India already has two aircraft carriers—although they are not of much use—and China's leadership resents the fact that the West objects to it having even one. Likewise, for all the concern about China's military buildup, the People's Liberation Army is actually cutting the number of its troops from the present level of about three million. Such cuts will, however, improve the army's effectiveness, for they will free funds for much-needed equipment and training, and even after the cuts China will still have ten times as many soldiers as Japan.

The one area where China has been indisputably irresponsible is in arms sales. The evidence is overwhelming that it has sold M-11 missiles, or at least the technologies to make them, to Pakistan. The M-11 can carry nuclear warheads about 300 kilometers and adds to the risk of a war on the Indian-Pakistani border. China has also helped Algeria, in suspicious circumstances, build a nuclear power plant, and there are profound concerns about Chinese assistance to Iran's putative nuclear and chemical weapons program. On the other hand, China is not alone in being irresponsible. Almost all countries, including the United States, France and Japan, have engaged in dubious transfers of weapons and technologies. For its part, China sells far fewer weapons than does the United States or Russia.

GROWING PAINS

Growth is destabilizing. To understand the problems that erupt from the rise of a new power, we need not look only at Bismarck's Germany or Tojo's Japan. The rise of the United States a century ago is also a cautionary lesson, for, from the perspective of Latin America, the economic takeoff of the United States also led to a bullying of the neighborhood. It may well be, however, that dictatorial and insecure nations make the worst great powers. There was widespread suspicion, for example, of Germany's rise in the years before World War I, of Japan's rise before World War II, and of the Soviet Union's rise after 1945. In each case, the suspicions had a good basis, but these suspicions also reinforced the paranoia and hostility in Germany, Japan and the Soviet Union. Now, history may repeat itself, for there is a growing suspicion in Asia and abroad about China's intentions and aspirations.

For a reminder of the dangers, it is helpful to remember the experience of another great nation that possessed a great civilization and yet had been humbled in conflicts with its neighbors. Germany was humiliated by the Napoleonic invasion and by the way it was left behind in the scramble for colonies abroad. Under Bismarck, the country enjoyed the beginnings of an economic boom and industrial revolution that whetted its appetite for more power and prestige. Yet Bismarck himself had limited ambitions, wanting to maintain the "concert of Europe," not overturn it. It was only after Bismarck was ousted in 1890 that Germany, under Wilhelm II, became more greedy. Wilhelm pursued a rapid arms buildup, including the establishment of a blue-water navy, that gave Germany new opportunities to redress the injustices that it felt had been done to it. Feeling its new strength, Germany jockeyed for a place at the head table of nations. The result, to condense a long and complex saga, was World War I.

There are huge differences, of course, but China shares with turn-of-the-century Germany the sense of wounded pride, the annoyance of a giant that has been battered and cheated by the rest of the world. Beginning with its defeat in the Opium War 150 years ago, China lost chunks of territory to its neighbors, and it has never enjoyed the international respect that it craves. Yet now it is undergoing an industrial revolution and arms buildup that within a decade or two will allow it to avenge these wrongs. Deng Xiaoping is in many respects like Bismarck, seeking strength and modernization, but without trying to overturn the entire balance of power. The risk is that Deng's successor will be less talented and more aggressive—a Chinese version of Wilhelm II. Such a ruler unfortunately may be tempted to promote Chinese nationalism as a unifying force and ideology, to replace the carcass of communism. For all the differences between China and Germany, the latter's experience should remind us of the difficulty that the world has had accommodating newly powerful nations.

Internal Chinese documents, circulated among senior Chinese officials, underscore the paranoia and

sometimes irrationality at the highest levels of the Chinese government. "One cold war has ended; two more are beginning," one such document declared last year. "The Sino-Soviet Cold War has ended, but the confrontation and battle between the two systems and the two ideologies continues to rage." Another document explained that the fall of communism in Eastern Europe was nothing but the outcome of a careful plot by the United States. A classified analysis earlier this year warned: "The United States may be running out of energy, but it has never abandoned its ambition to rule the world, and its military interventionism is becoming more open." This sense that it is under assault from the West has caused China to make serious policy misjudgments, including its threats to seize Hong Kong before 1997. This feeling of encirclement also partly explains China's escalation of military spending.

China is not a villain. It is not a renegade country, but rather an ambitious nation.

Whoever is in power in China, Beijing will often seem to us to be prickly, mulish and fiercely independent—France cubed. China may sometimes appear to be thumbing its nose at the West, but such behavior in many cases reflects a profound insecurity that is unlikely to change any time soon. Insecure nations, like insecure people, get very touchy and resist guidance from others. Moreover, we must realize that the landscape looks very different in Beijing than in Washington. From the U.S. point of view China's leaders often seem like thugs in the way that they lock up dissidents, suppress Tibet, bully Hong Kong and peddle missiles. From Deng Xiaoping's perspective China is merely preserving stability and territorial integrity, as well as supplying relatively modest amounts of weaponry to friendly nations. From Deng's point of view the United States is the thug: inspiring "traitors" with Voice of America broadcasts, encouraging rebellion in Tibet, leading the way in weapons proliferation and even allowing plutonium to get into the hands of really dangerous countries like Japan. From Beijing's perspective, it is Washington that betrayed the bilateral relationship by abandoning a nonjudgmental friendship based on mutual interest and respect. Instead, the United States openly favored the Tiananmen "counterrevolutionaries" and then had the gall to complain when they were crushed. Of course, we do not need to agree with Beijing and we may still regard it as a brutal and self-deluded paranoiac. But the first step in dealing with China is to understand why it acts as its does and to recognize that the gulf between us is real—

in interests as well as perceptions. A less repressive regime would ease the problems in the Sino-U.S. relationship but it would not end them. China will continue to give us migraines.

Western hostility toward China encourages the paranoia and strengthens the domestic political position of the paranoiac. Consequently, such hostility is counterproductive, as well as wrong. We should be skeptical of Chinese intentions, without falling into hostility. We should maintain a dialogue with China, even if the tone is not always cordial. We should regard China as a complex and contradictory nation, one likely to be alternatingly partner and adversary.

China is not a villain. It is not a renegade country like Iraq or Libya, but rather an ambitious nation that is becoming the behemoth in the neighborhood. One of the oldest problems in international relations, ever since the rise of Assyria and Sparta, has been how the international community can accommodate the ambitions of newly powerful states. It is rarely a question of right or wrong, but rather of the instability that is inevitable as the previous military, economic and political balance must be recalibrated. If China is able to sustain its economic miracle, then this readjustment of the scales will be one of the most important—and perhaps dangerous—tasks in international relations in the coming decades. "The size of China's displacement of the world balance is such that the world must find a new balance in 30 to 40 years," Lee Kuan Yew, the former Singaporean prime minister, said earlier this year. "It's not possible to pretend that this is just another big player. This is the biggest player in the history of man."

North Korea: the dangerous outsider

Keith Colquhoun

Keith Colquhoun writes about Asian affairs for a number of publications and is the author of eight novels. His previous contribution to *The World Today*, in the April 1990 issue, was on the fate of Hong Kong.

The problem of North Korea is that the government is widely believed to be insane. A number of countries now have the bomb that probably should not, among them Pakistan, India and Israel. But although those countries make the world feel nervous at times of stress, it is assumed that the fingers on the triggers answer to rational minds. Not so North Korea. For a time this year it could be argued convincingly that the North was potentially the world's most dangerous country; that it could be the source of the first atomic explosion set off in anger since 1945 when Little Boy and Fat Man were dropped on Japan. Understandably, then, a sigh of relief was heard around the world when, on 11 June, it was announced that the United States had persuaded the North Koreans to stay, at least temporarily, in the Nuclear Non-Proliferation Treaty – the agreement that allows inspectors to poke about in possibly errant countries looking for evidence of nuclear mischief. The North may yet change its mind. Since June the nuclear inspectors have made some trips to the North, but say they have not been allowed to inspect all that they would like. However, for the moment the North seems to be going through one of those periods of calm that are granted even to the mentally afflicted.

North Korea has always been difficult to get into, not only for nuclear inspectors but for almost anyone. Not so long ago much of the world was like this, closed to the normally inquisitive foreigner. But now it is possible to roam freely in most of what was the Soviet Union. All China is open, except occasionally Tibet, and then only when noisy monks are making embarrassing demands for independence. Cuba, Myanmar (Burma) and Vietnam allow in journalists in the hope, usually misplaced, that they will write something polite about the government. Some Moslem countries, among them Saudi Arabia, are not keen on visits by Western women, but this is because they believe their own women will be encouraged to uncover their faces. North Korea, though, simply plays the hermit. What has it got to hide?

Lots, say the Korea-watchers. Not only the atomic bomb it is said to be making, the evidence for which will be examined later in this article; but dissent in the government over the dictatorship of its President, Kim Il Sung, and the supposed poverty of its people. Korea-watching is almost the last remnant of a vast profession of scholarly speculation that prospered in the Cold War. Kremlinologists deduced what seemed to be secrets of Soviet policy often aided by nothing more than old copies of *Izvestia* and their imaginations. The methods being applied to North Korea are just as circumspect.

Anyone seeking to solve the riddle of North Korea starts where Kremlin-watchers used to start: by applying for a visa to visit the place. At worst, the North can only say no. 'I confirm you are always welcome to our country,' replies a friendly Mr Youn, who works for North Korea's Trade Office in Neuilly-sur-Seine, near Paris, which acts as a kind of European Embassy. That's great. Now, how to get there? By way of Tokyo or Beijing? But not so fast. Another fax arrives from Mr Youn. 'We'd like to ask you to wait,' he writes. There are 'some technical problems'. Weeks later there are still 'technical problems'.

If you are really desperate to see North Korea, just to say you have actually seen it, take a bus from Seoul, the capital of South Korea, to Panmunjom, where the armistice was signed in 1953 at the end of the Korean war. The 38th parallel of longitude runs through Panmunjom, serving the purpose of a ceasefire line dividing the North from the South. From a viewing-stand on the south side you can look across the frontier to – well, not very much. If you are an imaginative sort of person it is not difficult to cast your mind back to the Korean war when on these hills hordes of Chinese, sent in to steady the retreating northerners, fought tooth and claw against the Americans, the backbone of the United Nations forces propping up the South. But, without the aid of history, it remains a rather dull landscape, from which, surreally, incomprehensible slogans are shouted from loudspeakers set in the northern hills. Right on the border itself is a building where representatives from North and South talk from time to time, sometimes quite rudely: the two countries are still formally at war. Here, anyone with a nostalgia for the Cold War might recall its *frissons*. The North's official news agency reported a recent meeting of the two sides thus: 'We sternly called the South side to account for its anti-national, anti-reunification attitude illustrated in its presentation of divisionist proposals.'

When the conference room is not in use it is possible actually to enter the North, by walking to the northern bit of the building.

From *The World Today*, Vol. 49, No. 11, November 1993, pp. 210-212. *The World Today*, published by The Royal Institute of International Affairs. Reprinted by permission.

Genuine North Koreans are there to gawp at. They look rather like South Koreans, although of course not as freedom-loving.

Go as a dustman

The trip to Panmunjom amounts to a peep over the Berlin Wall before Communism collapsed in East Germany. But what about a holiday in North Korea? From time to time the North gets the itch to show off a bit, to display at least the marvels of its capital, Pyongyang, to a wondering world. A number of travel agencies in Western countries are told that they can send approved groups on short stays to the North. Sometimes journalists manage to get on these trips by describing themselves as engineers, dustmen or even writers, but they are usually rumbled: officials in the North are as officious as officials elsewhere, and are rather more suspicious. Recently, in an inexplicable bout of panic, the North ordered all foreigners temporarily out of the country, even those with diplomatic status.

Pyongyang, like Seoul, was destroyed in the war. Both capitals have been rebuilt using lots of steel and concrete. Despite this, parts of Seoul are pleasant to walk through, with streets on a human scale and the bustle of a working town. Visitors to Pyongyang, though, are awed by its immensity and depressed by its bleakness. It has the cleanness of Singapore, but without a car in sight. Yet should you attempt to cross the empty road, a police-man may direct you to use one of the underground subways. Everyone remarks on the town's centrepiece, a hotel said to be the tallest building in Asia, presumably built for tourists, but almost empty.

This is interesting, says the tourist politely, and now what about a trip to the countryside? There are no such trips, not even for important people – for diplomats, say, representing the small number of countries that have relations with the North. The northerners are so proud of their capital that they appear to take the view, to paraphrase Dr Johnson, that anyone tired of Pyongyang must be tired of life.

There is one other place that the northerners are showing to selected visitors, and that is the site of a free-trade zone on the Tuman river, on the border with China and Russia. The zone is not yet in operation, and it is anyone's guess whether is will ever be. But possible investors are taken there, chiefly from South Korea and Japan. The government prefers that such journeys are made after dark, or, if this is not possible, that the curtains of the car or the train compartment should be drawn. As a result, strange stories have arisen about what goes on in rural North Korea. Someone catches a glimpse of a farm worker using what seems to a primitive plough, that in the South would be in a museum. Someone else spots a pile of coal being guarded by soldiers.

The common feature of these stories is that, outside Pyongyang, life is grim, and people are living on starvation rations. This may be true, but who would care to judge a country's economy on what can be gleaned by the view from a railway compartment? The people of Pyongyang seem well fed, and it seems unlikely that their country cousins are going short. There is plenty of fish in the sea around Korea, and the land is fertile. A month or two ago there was a story in an American newspaper of food riots in the North. The story was doubted, even by South Korea. It is known that the North has huge reserves of coal. This does not, of course, mean that there is not a coal shortage, but it cannot be assumed. Browsing around Pyongyang or taking an illicit look at the countryside is a way to spend perhaps a day, but pretty thin for someone wanting to understand the country. This was the sort of frustration felt by travellers to the Soviet Union in its rigid days. Even if you were important enough to be let in, you might be foisted off with a tour of the museums when what you really wanted was a chat with Stalin, or someone claiming to be close to him.

Ah, Stalin. The most common Western view of the North is that it is Stalinist in the way it is run. This is a plausible idea, although that does not make it true. The North's ruler, Kim Il Sung, probably did meet Stalin once on a trip to Moscow, although he was not a friend. Some historians believe that Stalin pushed Kim into invading the South in 1950, although others are equally sure that it was Kim's decision to try to 'reunify' the country. Kim did pick up some of Stalin's bad habits, notably orchestrating the people to make him feel like a god on earth.

A vast museum in Pyongyang aims to document his life from birth. Here are his gloves and his shoes, displayed like saintly relics. Throughout the country there are monuments to mark out some formative experience. This is where he liked to sit with his father, this is where he fished. Yet anyone trying to compile a life of Kim soon becomes baffled by a lack of verifiable facts. It is known that a man called Kim Il Sung was installed as leader when the Soviet Union occupied the North in 1945 after the defeat of Japan, and it is presumed that this is the same man who is President, making him by far the world's longest-lasting leader. His birthday is celebrated with some pomp on 15 April, with particularly extravagant celebrations in 1992, when he was said to be 80. Official accounts of Mr Kim's life are revised from time to time. The founding of the People's Korean Army has been backdated to 1932 to provide a background for Mr Kim's claimed guerrilla activities against the Japanese. The paucity of facts is no great problem for his acolytes. Their main difficulty is finding some new phrase to sing the praises of a man already called 'the supreme leader of the entire working people of the world'.

More succinctly, Kim Il Sung is known as the 'great leader'. His son, Kim Jong Il, is known as the 'dear leader'. It is in keeping with the general mystery of North Korea that no one is sure how power is divided between the Kims, senior and junior, or whether old Kim has surrendered any at all. One view is that young Kim now runs the army, that the army officers are deeply resentful of this and are just waiting for Dad to go so that they can get rid of his uppity son. This view may owe something to the general dislike felt for young Kim among Korea-watchers. Old Kim, they say, is a bit of a horror but he is a great survivor. Young Kim, though, is just a spoiled nothing. In line with this tenuous reasoning, Young Kim is said to be the author of all the beastly and irrational acts that North Korea has been blamed for over the past decades. These include the death of 17 South Korean officials when a bomb exploded in Yangon (Rangoon) in 1983; the blowing up of a South Korean airliner in 1987, killing all 115 people aboard; the use of the North's diplomats in Europe to smuggle drugs in the 1970s to earn hard currency. Most of the countries that matter, the United States particularly, accept that the North carried out these dirty deeds. If there is some shadow of a doubt it arises because much of the evidence against the North comes from the South which, in its time, has carried out dirty deeds of its own. Even today, the democratic South has political prisoners.

Government agencies in the South issue regular reports on the iniquities of the North. A recent one is entitled 'Political Prisoners' Camps in North Korea: Replicas of Stalinist Gulags'. It says 'intelligence experts' estimate that the North's concentration camps contain 200,000 people, or nearly 1 per cent of the population, and offers the view that the country is one immense prison. It is perfectly possible that every word in the report is true, but it may not be, or it may be that only part of it is true. It is one more example of the mystery of the North.

Tale of the bomb

For those who live in free countries, or even semi-free ones, it is tempting to believe that the 22m North Koreans are yearning to be free. No doubt some are. But it has to be said that, on the basis of the limited evidence available, the country is not seething with discontent. From time to time relations between the South and the North run sufficiently smoothly for a few southerners to be allowed to visit relatives who, at the end of the Korean war, found themselves stuck in the North. Some southerners have been surprised to find that their long-lost kin appeared to show no envy for the South's way of life. Rather, once embraces were out of the way and tea was on the table, the northerners set out to convince the southerners what a splendid place they lived in. Propaganda, perhaps? The northerners were specially selected? Quite possibly. But Koreans have no tradition of a liberal society. Living under Mr Kim's rule is undoubtedly preferable to living under the Japanese, who ran Korea as a colony until 1945. People can be awkwardly unpredictable. Many Taiwanese visitors to China return home expressing admiration for the mainlanders' stoic way of life, contrasting it with the greed of their own prosperous island. The admiration might not last if the Taiwanese had to live in China but, at least initially, they were not behaving as their government expected.

How much, in fact, do the northerners know about life outside? Some observers say, simply, they know nothing. A frequently offered 'fact' is that radios in the North are fixed to receive only the national station. This is probably nonsense, and even if it were true it is a simple matter to 'unfix' the tuning on a radio. However, enough has been broadcast on the national radio to make northerners aware that their country is having a quarrel with the outside world, and that it concerns the North's development of its nuclear industry. How dare the outsiders challenge the North's insistence that its intentions are entirely peaceful?

It was the North, though, that first hinted it was making a bomb. Back in 1991 a Japanese diplomat in Pyongyang reported to his government that, from what he had been told, the North might well be on the way to making a nuclear weapon. A northerner who had defected to the South said the same. Putting two and two together to make four-and-a-half, it was predicted that the North would have a bomb by January 1992. The North, as a signatory to the Nuclear Non-Proliferation Treaty, shrugged

its shoulders and allowed in inspectors from the International Atomic Agency in Vienna to look at its nuclear research plant in Yongbyon, 62 miles north of Pyongyang.

They found nothing alarming. However, a story circulated that, just before the inspectors arrived at Yongbyon, an American satellite had photographed many lorries leaving the plant. Had the bomb-making kit been moved elsewhere, perhaps underground? The plot thickened. In January this year the North refused to allow inspectors to visit two sites said to be used to store nuclear waste. What was in these waste tips? Could they contain evidence that the North had a bomb in the cellar?

This has been enough to alarm the North's neighbour, South Korea. Even Japan has had the jitters. When the North was reported to have test-fired a new missile said to have a range of 600 miles and capable of carrying a nuclear warhead, the Japanese got out their maps and said it could hit Osaka and other industrial cities. 'Just a rumour,' said the then Prime Minister, Kiichi Miyazawa, not very reassuringly. Most political news in Japan is based on rumour. China, the North's old friend, tried to persuade the inspectors to look at the waste tips, but was rebuffed. At the time this article went to press the waste tips have still not been inspected.

The evidence offered so far that North Korea has, or is making, a bomb, would hardly convince a jury, although that does not mean it is innocent. But what has really prompted the worries of the past months has been a fear of what the North might be capable of. Just as a hijacker has to be taken seriously when he threatens to blow up an aircraft, even though he may be bluffing, so the North has had to be calmed down, and, in the end, placated.

In getting the North to stay in the nuclear treaty, it seems likely that the Americans have agreed to end the military exercises carried out each year with South Korea, although this has not been announced. They will have assured the North that they no longer have nuclear weapons in the South, and will have invited the North to send their own inspectors to check. But the most important gain for the North is that, in the end, they got the Americans – not the South Koreans or the Japanese or the Chinese – to sit down with them. To keep them happy the Americans may now have to give substance, as well as goodwill. The North is looking for handouts, having lost its most generous friend, the Soviet Union. Japan was a prospect, but has lost interest. Israel may offer something, if only as a bribe to stop the North selling missiles to Iraq. But America is seen by the North as a crock of gold. The North is old-fashioned in some ways.

Back in 1991, when the North started to whisper about its nuclear plans, an Australian academic, Andrew Mack, hazarded the thought that the bomb scare could be a dummy to strengthen the North's hand in negotiations with the outside world. That could turn out to be a perceptive guess. On the other hand, the North at this very moment may be proudly tightening the final bolts on its own home-made version of Little Boy. With North Korea you never can tell.

What Is an Economy For?

We know the answer: to grow so that we can all buy more and keep the world economy spinning. Asians have a different answer: to grow so that a country can produce more—whoever buys the goods—and keep the country's, not the world's, economy spinning

JAMES FALLOWS

James Fallows is the Washington editor of The Atlantic Monthly *and the author of* National Defense *(1981) and* More Like Us *(1989). His article in this issue is the last of three to be drawn from his book* Looking at the Sun, *published by Pantheon.*

EVERY country and culture is unique, and the "Asian" economic system naturally is something different in Singapore from what it is in Thailand or Japan. There are comparable variations among European and North American styles of capitalism. In their emphasis on industrial guidance and national policy, France and Germany are more Asian than they are American. In their approach to leisure and the good life, the Europeans are less like the new Asian model than like Americans. Still, four main patterns distinguish the Asian system from the prevailing Western model. Some of them are descended from old clashes between the German and Anglo-American philosophies of economic competition which were outlined here last month. They involve:

■ The *purpose* of economic life. In the American-style model the basic reason for having an economy is to raise the consumer's standard of living. In the Asian model it is to increase the collective national strength. Ideally, the goal is to make the nation independent and self-sufficient, so that it does not rely on outsiders for its survival. The American-style goal is materialistic; the Asian-style goal is political, and comes from long experience of being oppressed by people with stronger economies and technologies.

■ The view of *power* in setting economic policies. Anglo-American ideology views concentrated power as an evil ("Power corrupts, and absolute power . . ."). Therefore it has developed elaborate schemes for dividing and breaking up power when it becomes concentrated. The Asian-style model views concentrated power as a fact of life. It has developed elaborate systems for ensuring that the power is used for the long-term national good.

■ The view of *surprise* and unpredictability. The Anglo-American model views surprise as the key to economic life. We believe that it is precisely because markets are fluid and unpredictable that they work. The Asian-style system deeply mistrusts markets. It sees competition as a useful tool for keeping companies on their toes, but not as a way to resolve any of the big questions of life—how a society should be run, in what direction its economy should unfold. This is, in Western terms, a military view of economics. Within the American military the Army competes with the Navy for funds, and competition within each branch keeps both the Army and the Navy sharp. But the services don't cast votes or place bids to decide where the nation should fight. Decisions like that are not left to a market.

■ The view of *national borders* and an us-versus-them concept of the world. People everywhere are xenophobic and exclusive, but in the Anglo-American model this is thought to be a lamentable, surmountable failing. The Asian-style model assumes that it is a natural and permanent condition. The world consists of us and them, and no one else will look out for us.

Consumers or Employees?

BY the tenets of post–Second World War Anglo-American economics, "What is an economy for?" isn't a very difficult question. In fact, it answers itself. Economic development means "more." If people have more choice, more leisure, more wealth, more opportunity to pursue happiness, society as a whole will be a success. In theory, any deal that the market permits will in the long run be good for society as a whole.

The Anglo-American system is long on theories. It is easy to pick up any English-language textbook and find theories proving that whatever gives more to the consumer is best for everyone. The Asian system is not so explicitly theoretical. Yet the fundamental purpose of the Asian model is evident from its performance. Its goal is to develop the productive base of the country—the industries either within the country or under the control of the country's citizens around the world. When it comes to a choice between the consumer's welfare and the producer's, it's really no choice at all.

In countless ways the most successful of today's Asian societies reveal their bias in favor of the producer. A few illustrations:

■ Japan and Korea are famous for protecting their rice markets. Even though the small plots, high land prices, and aged rural work force together make the cost of rice several times as high as it is elsewhere in the world, neither country gives its consumers the option of buying from overseas. In the Western world this is usually taken to be a quaint affectation. After all, Japanese and Korean spokesmen usually defend their policy in emotional terms ("our precious heritage"), and even if the markets were thrown wide open, there is a limit to how much foreign rice the Japanese or the Koreans could eat. (Because of crop failures following last year's wet summer, the Japanese government will allow emergency rice imports this year, but says it will close the market when the emergency has passed.)

In fact rice policy reveals a major, consequential pro-producer bias. Especially in Japan, but also in Korea and Taiwan, farm protectionism is the crux of sweeping anti-consumer social bargain. If there is a single factor limiting consumption in these countries, it is the extremely high price of land; and if there is a single force that keeps the price up, it is the system that sets aside so much land (one quarter of the nonmountainous land in Japan) for the production of very expensive crops. "High land prices have caused the Japanese to act in ways they would not have otherwise," Susan Hanley, of the University of Washington, wrote in 1992. "It is not Japan's Asian cultural heritage that sets it apart . . . so much as the result of its artificially high land prices."

■ The more successful the economy in Asia, the more likely it is to have a rigged, anti-consumer, high-priced retail system. Japan's is the most successful, and its retail economy is the most cartelized and expensive. It's not simply that imported goods are expensive; Japanese-made goods are too. According to a survey at the end of 1991, clothes cost twice as much in Tokyo as in New York, food about three times as much, gasoline about two and a half times as much, and so on.

Anglo-American economic theory can explain why Japanese prices are so high: the retail system is full of cartels and monopolies. A network of laws, contracts, and commercial agreements in Japan discourages discounting and price competition. Until it was relaxed in the early 1990s, Japan's famous *dai ten ho,* or "big store law," effectively outlawed supermarkets, since it required that small local merchants give their approval (or be bribed into doing so) before a big store could be built. It is hard for familiar economic theory to accept that such an inefficient and anti-consumer system might last for many decades, with the apparent approval even of the victimized population of consumers.

In the Asian model the goal is to develop the country's productive base. When it comes to a choice between the consumer's welfare and the producer's, it's really no choice at all.

The immediate reason the system lasts is the political power of small merchants, who—along with farmers and the construction industries—are big donors to the powerful Liberal Democratic Party in Japan. The more basic reason it lasts is that it helps producers, and in ways that offset the penalty to consumers. When competition in Europe or America pushes down the price of VCRs, cars, and semiconductor chips, Japanese producers can maintain high prices within Japan. In effect, producers wring monopoly profits out of their own people in order to build a war chest for competition overseas. When the yen doubled in value against the dollar from 1985 to 1988, retail prices in Japan should have fallen significantly—but they barely budged. Japanese corporations were taxing their own people with artificially high prices so that they could maintain artificially low prices in export markets in Europe and North America. In return for this tax the Japanese got strong organizations and full employment. This may not be an attractive bargain from the Western viewpoint, and no individual Japanese or Korean likes paying higher prices. But as a social bargain it is seen as keeping the nation's producers strong and thereby keeping the social fabric intact.

The closest counterpart in American experience is AT&T before its breakup. Ma Bell penalized consumers in many ways. Rates were higher than they might have been. All equipment had to be "authorized" by AT&T. At the same time, Bell used the money to fund its research labs and all its other operations. This is a version of everyday practice in Japanese business: consumers have fewer choices than they might ideally have, and corporations absorb and redeploy the money they save.

■ In their own role as consumers even corporations in Japan and Korea reveal the anti-consumer bias of the Asian system. Their workers have for several decades traded artificially low wages for the promise of full employment. The wages are artificially low because through much of the postwar era earnings have lagged behind the increase in corporate productivity. By Western economic logic wages should have been rising much more rapidly. Similarly, Japanese and Korean corporations have traded artificially low profits for their equivalent of full employment, which is an ever-growing market share. In 1991 a business survey listed the thirty most profitable large companies in the world. Twenty-three of them were American, four were British, and none were Japanese.

■ The parts of Japanese, Korean, and Taiwanese life that encourage consumption are made difficult. The parts that encourage savings, investment, and deferred gratification are made easy and attractive—the way it was in America during the Second World War. The automobile market in Japan, for instance, is dominated by the *shaken* racket. The word *shaken* (pronounced "shah-ken" rather than like the English word "shaken") literally means "car ticket." In effect a *shaken* is a reinspection certificate that each car in Japan must have in order to remain legally on the road. The *shaken* policy originated during the infancy of the Japanese auto industry, when domestic cars were such unreliable rattletraps that bureaucrats thought it would be dangerous to let them on the road without constant safety checks. The public-safety rationale for reinspections obviously no longer applies. Nonetheless, after three years and then every two years thereafter Japanese drivers must take their cars in for a new *shaken*, and every two years they are saddled with hugely expensive "necessary" repairs. By the time a car is three or five years old, it can cost so many thousands of dollars to meet *shaken* standards that it makes sense to buy a new car, even though new cars themselves cost much more than the same models outside Japan. It is a way to turn the population into a captive market for producers.

■ The experience of the past generation has taught most Asian countries one dramatically clear lesson. They can't really go wrong by giving consumers too little, but they can easily go wrong by giving consumers too much. During the collapse of Japan's bubble economy, in 1991 and 1992, government officials said privately that an atmosphere of hardship was useful. Consumerism had been getting out of hand, and the bubble's collapse would have a tonic effect—without imposing real hardship on Japan or endangering Japan's long-term prospects. (Business-failure rates among Japanese manufacturing and construction firms were actually lower during the "crash" years of the early 1990s than they had been on average during the booming 1980s.)

In Korea the late 1980s were heady, pro-consumer years. The 1988 Seoul Olympics did for the country what the 1964 Tokyo Olympics had done for Japan. Anything seemed possible. In the fashionable parts of Seoul young women wore miniskirts and young men hung out all night. By 1990 the trade surplus was heading for the cellar, and the government had to fight back with a huge "anti-luxury" campaign. With economic growth slipping, the national tax office announced that "extravagance beyond one's reported means" would invite tax scrutiny. In effect this meant that anyone who bought a Mercury Sable, Lincoln Continental, Mercedes, or BMW could expect to be put through the tax wringer—a more serious threat in Korea than in some other countries, because so much business is off the books. Tariffs and other barriers had already raised the price of these cars to more than twice what they would cost in the United States. That hadn't choked off sales, but the tax threat did; sales of the Sable virtually stopped after the tax men stepped in.

Beyond all these economic calculations is a question of human nature. Anglo-American economic theory boils people down to their roles as consumers. Life experience, even in America, tells us that people have more in mind than getting the cheapest possible price and the highest possible wage. In certain circumstances people *like* to work hard, and save, and sacrifice themselves. Even though lottery winners typically don't have society's most desirable jobs, many of them decide to keep working even after they have cashed in. For years and years studies have shown that people who own small businesses behave in a self-exploitative, economically irrational way. They typically work longer hours than normal employees and earn less money than they could if they sold off their assets and invested the proceeds. Decisions like these are oddities in the Anglo-American economic world, where they are explained away with little theories about the "utility" of work. They are central to the Asian model of individual and collective life.

The Emperor's Legacy

IN the United States the effort to break up political power and the attempt to prevent the concentration of economic power have been seen as parallel steps toward liberty. The United States has a three-branch government because of fear that any one branch will become too dominant. The great reformers in the American tradition have generally risen to strike down excessive concentrations of power, from Jefferson (in his battle with Hamilton) to Andrew Jackson to Teddy Roosevelt to Ralph Nader to Ronald Reagan, in their varying ways. The people who have argued for centralizing and exercising power have generally had the excuse of wartime: Abraham Lincoln, Woodrow Wilson, Franklin D. Roosevelt, John F. Kennedy, and Lyndon Johnson.

The deepest criticism of Japanese politics, made by the Dutch writer Karel van Wolferen, is that it lacks a definable center of political accountability. In the French or American system a President must finally make big choices, whereas in the Japanese system (as Van Wolferen explains it) the buck never stops anywhere.

The classic illustration of this problem is Japan's apparent paralysis during the first month after Iraq invaded Kuwait. The standard critique outside Japan was that the country was not doing its fair share. This entirely missed the point. Eventually Japan came up with quite a large sum of money, when it could have made the case for not contributing money at all. (The case would have been that it was foolish to go to war over this issue, and that if other countries had emulated Japan, by conserving their use of oil, they could have afforded to take a longer-term view.) Rather, the problem was that Japan seemed incapable of deciding what its position was. The Foreign Ministry announced one policy, the Finance Ministry disavowed it. The Prime Minister at the time, Toshiki Kaifu, was scheduled to go on a trip to the Middle East. Officials in the Foreign Ministry called the trip off. Feuding occurs in any government, but in this government not even the Prime Minister had the authority to resolve it.

Most other Asian societies do have a center of power. Indeed, this center has often been one dominant figure—a military strongman, as in Thailand, Indonesia, and often Korea; a statesman-leader, epitomized by Lee Kuan Yew, of Singapore; a sheer tyrant, as in North Korea and Burma; or a political boss, as in Malaysia and often Taiwan.

But whether the center of politics has been weak, as in Japan, or strong, as everywhere else, the political system as a whole has generally been authoritarian in Asia. Compared with any Western societies, and especially the Anglo-American system, Asian states have been less embarrassed and more explicit about the government's role in shaping society. The contrast is obviously sharper with America than with, say, France, which operates a Japanese-style *dirigiste* system without the social control. The Japanese system also resembles the most successful parts of government-business interaction in the United States, such as nuclear-weapons design and medical research. And it has analogues in many parts of Asia.

Some scholars contend that the heavy hand of government is the living legacy of Confucius. Anglo-American ideology warns against the abuse of power, and therefore tries to restrict Kings, Prime Ministers, and Presidents. The traditional Confucian "mandate of heaven" approach assumes that there will be an Emperor, asking only whether he exercises power well or poorly. Other scholars argue that such theories are merely cultural window-dressing, used by ruling groups to rationalize their hold on power.

Either way, the history of powerful governments in East Asia has made most governments both more competent and more legitimate when they work with businesses. They are more competent because the great prestige of the civil service continues to attract the best-educated people in the country. For a variety of historical and social-status reasons, jobs in the government bureaucracy are still among the most desirable ones in Korea, Japan, Taiwan, and other Confucian-influenced East Asian societies. Ambitious young graduates compete for positions in the Japanese Ministry of Finance or with the Korean Economic Planning Board the way ambitious young Americans compete for jobs at what we drolly call "investment" banks. (In 1990 Wasserstein Perella

& Company, the mergers-and-acquisition house that was spun off from First Boston, received more than 30,000 applications for eight positions for college graduates.)

Today's Asian bureaucrats always complain that the thrill is gone, that they're not paid enough, that the long hours are driving out the real talent, and so on. For instance, early in 1992 the *Yomiuri Shimbun*, Japan's largest paper, said that the bureaucrats were groaning because they were about to be switched to a mandatory work week of five (rather than six) days, as part of Japan's efforts not to work so hard. Their grievance was that it would just mean more overtime during the regular week. Still, by international standards the Asian governments attract very skillful people into their ministries, and the ministers have both personal and institutional legitimacy.

A Fundamental Mistrust of the Market

THE dynamic view of economics is connected to the main spirit of American culture. People's lives should change! The future should be full of surprise!

This is not the spirit of most Asian societies, least of all Japan. The more familiar you become with Japanese customs, the more you are impressed with the virtue of doing the expected thing. (Letters to friends in Japanese, for instance, are always supposed to begin with comments about the weather.) The ideal Japanese life is one from which uncertainty has been removed as early as possible—by getting into the right school, by joining the right corporation. In 1989 pollsters asked citizens in seven countries to react to the statement "It is boring to live like other people." In America 69 percent of respondents agreed with the statement. In Japan only 25 percent did.

In a much broader sense, the Asian systems mistrust the uncertainty the market brings. The Asian and Anglo-American models both trust the market to decide which products will succeed or fail, which companies will beat which others. The Anglo-American model trusts political and economic markets with larger decisions as well: what is a good society, what is the right course for economic growth. The Asian model shrinks in horror from this possibility—as American parents would shrink from the idea that "the market," in the form of music videos, TV shows, and shopping malls, should teach their children what is right and wrong.

"The peoples of China, North Korea, South Korea, Japan, and other Confucian cultures deeply believe that the state ought to provide not only material wherewithal for its peoples but moral guidance," the Korean scholar Jung-en Woo wrote in 1991. "By and large, Westerners have no way to understand this point except to assert that the Asian countries suffer from a series of absences: no individual rights, no civil society, no Enlightenment, and thus a weak or absent liberalism." The individual may sometimes feel these lacks, but what is more important is that the system roll on.

According to most Western political theory—displayed in America at its extreme—the state has no legitimate power to say what makes a good life or a healthy economy. Everyone makes such choices for every day; the choice for the society emerges naturally from these decisions. If everyone wants to avoid taxes, taxes stay low. If people want to buy computers—or guns, or X-rated videos—that industry flourishes. The genius of this system is that it can use people's hungers and jealousies as a tool. It perfectly melds political and economic theories: political liberalism and economic laissez-faire, each of which says to leave the individual alone.

The flaw is that the system suffers from "market failures," as economists and political scientists call them. Most people would be better off if the society invested more in schools or roads, but no one wants to vote for higher taxes. Everyone feels worse off when there are very wide social divisions, but no individual can make choices that narrow them.

In reality, the largest questions of right and wrong have been settled outside the market system—through religion, or family prejudice, or patriotism, or ethnic loyalty. But it is hard for the American-style system to argue that anything profitable is wrong if a willing seller and a willing buyer can agree on a price.

No government in Asia believes such things. Many individuals do, people being the same everywhere. But governments, with the possible exception of Hong Kong's, think that they, not individuals, should make the big decisions of right and wrong.

Time and again the visitor to Japan hears the phrases "confusion in the market" and "excessive competition." These are shorthand for the dangers of letting market forces get out of control. Each time these phrases come up, they raise intriguing translation problems. You can almost hear the interpreters saying the phrase as if it had quotation marks around it in English—"confusion in the market." There are no comparable terms in English, because the very concepts do not exist. What the Japanese and Koreans call "excessive" competition is what Western economics texts call "perfect" competition.

A deeper idea is the fundamental distinction between the market as a means and the market as an end in itself. Every healthy society knows that market incentives are necessary—real price competition, failure for products that don't make the grade, reward for innovation and enterprise. But only in the Western model is nothing besides the market necessary.

I N the early stages of their economic development, especially after the Second World War, Asian governments found it easy to set targets and plans. Above all else they had to catch up to the Western lead. Even now Asian systems reveal their faith that the goals should be chosen, rather than left to the market to decide. For example:

■ The Korean government has for decades divided up the work of national development among Korea's major companies. One group of companies must run the shipyards; another must collaborate with the Americans on semiconductor projects. In Taiwan the government requires companies to set aside a certain share of their sales revenue for research-and-development expenses. "Such measures would probably strike those South Koreans [and Taiwanese] who have absorbed the *political* ideals of the Anglo-Saxon model as flagrant violations of liberty," the economist Alice Amsden wrote in 1991.

> Yet this is a very Anglo-Saxon view of democracy, not a universal one. It could just as well be argued that to leave in private hands investment decisions that have the potential to make a major impact on the welfare of society is itself inherently undemocratic.

■ The Anglo-American system tries to permit as many deals to be made as possible. In general, anything that's profitable should be legal, unless there's a compelling argument against it. The only loyalties that are not supposed to be for sale are within a family and to the country. More generally, friendship is supposed to operate outside the market system. But in Asia, and especially in Japan, *business* relationships are also supposed to operate outside the market, with loyalty to one's employer being more important than whether the relationship is immediately profitable or not. A Japanese scholar named Michio Morishima pointed out, in *Why Has Japan "Succeeded"?*, that

> the "loyalty" market is opened only once in a lifetime to each individual, when he graduates from school or college. It is in this market that those who are able to provide loyalty meet those who are looking for it, their "lords."

■ During the Japanese stock market's long slide from 1989 to 1992, Japanese analysts contended that computer-program trading, introduced into the Tokyo stock market by American firms, was driving the market to daily lows. This strengthened the general feeling that the way to save the market was to restrict its flexibility—to make it more regulated again rather than to perfect its market forces. A Japanese report at the time said, "Deregulation of brokers' commissions in the US caused securities industry profits to fall and forced many firms into high-risk areas, such as aggressive mergers and acquisitions, a report by the Securities Industry Council charged." That is, letting too many decisions be made by the market created instability for all.

■ In the summer of 1991, when scandals were being revealed practically every day in the Japanese securities industry, a strange scandal was also unfolding in the earth-moving industry. Many of the competitors of the large Komatsu Corporation had been paying spies to provide secrets about Komatsu's master plan. The *Nihon Keizai Shimbun* reported, with a worried tone, that after the revelations "many [initially] thought confusion would reign in the construction industry." But, the paper said with relief, "it has been as calm as a lake in the morning—nary a ripple."

> One of the reasons for this camaraderie is the fact that the Japan Construction Equipment Manufacturers Association, the "club" of the construction machinery industry, has just been organized. Until the "club" was organized, the industry was one huge price war. And, if the war went on, no one would make a profit and all would lose. Sensing that they were cutting each other's throats, the industry finally got together. So Komatsu didn't want to ruin all that effort.

Once the industry had formed its cartel, everyone felt secure again.

In 1955 the American novelist Richard Wright, the author of *Black Boy* and *Native Son*, went to Bandung, in newly independent Indonesia, for the historic conference of the nonaligned countries. This was the first real postcolonial muscle-flexing by Asian and African countries, led by the likes of Jawaharlal Nehru, Gamal Abdel Nasser, and Sukarno. As a black American, Wright had gone expecting to feel fellowship with those who had been controlled by white colonialists. His book about the conference, *The Color Curtain*, reflected his increasing puzzlement over, and estrangement from, the nonaligned policies. Although he did not put it this way, mistrust of the market was one of the traits that struck him most.

> Still another and, to the Western mind, somewhat baffling trait emerged from these Asian responses. There seemed to be in their consciousness a kind of instinct (I can't find a better word!) toward hierarchy, toward social collectivities of an organic nature. In contrast to the Western feeling that education was an instrument to enable the individual to become free, to stand alone, the Asian felt that education was to bind men together.

The point for the moment is that one economic system assumes that it does not have to make the largest decisions about national purpose except when the system is being attacked from outside, in time of war. The other assumes that the state *always* has a role in guiding the nation. It is the clash between these visions, rather than the rightness or wrongness of either of them, that creates current problems.

Borders and Borderlessness

IN Western economics it's hard to come up with a theoretical reason for concentrating on national economic well-being. In the Asian model this is not a problem at all; it's taken for granted.

In daily life there is no shortage of nationalistic spirit in Western countries in general or the United States in particular. The flag waves constantly in American TV commercials. Crowds chant "USA" at international sporting events. But the principles that guide economic policy in the Anglo-American approach avoid the concept of national interest except in strictly military terms.

Most Anglo-American concepts in fact treat national economic interests as if they didn't really exist. Companies move their plants overseas, because that is what business logic says they should do. When it comes to politics, we're able to explain—but just barely—why one person should be inconvenienced for the good of all. I pay taxes because I'm part of a political community, even though in any given year I may pay more into the government than I directly get out. In the Anglo-American model there really isn't an economic community that justifies anyone's paying higher prices than he absolutely has to, or preferring to deal with someone from the same country rather than buying from overseas.

This outlook seems advanced and tolerant from the Western, liberal perspective. The world should be "borderless." In the summer of 1990 Roger Porter, who was then President Bush's chief domestic-policy adviser, gave a speech about America's outlook on world trade. Some people, he said, clung to the "old notion of nations, companies, and markets rigidly defined by national borders." But in this modern age, he concluded, such a notion was "outdated and dangerous." Porter was making a partisan argument in behalf of the Bush economic program, but his assumption that consciousness of nationality was "outdated and dangerous" reflected an educated Western view that has nothing to do with party.

In the United States discussions of corporate nationality have stuck mainly to the realm of theory. According to American assumptions, it is only natural for businesses to operate in rootless, global fashion. Therefore most Americans assume that denationalization has already occurred. American discussion on this point has been heavily influenced by the writings of Robert Reich, who was a lecturer at Harvard's John F. Kennedy School of Government before he became Secretary of Labor in the Clinton Administration. Since the mid-1970s Reich has been proposing solutions to America's long-term economic problems, and his ideas about industrial policy (some of which were published in *The Atlantic Monthly*) have attracted a broad following. During the Bush years Reich wrote several influential articles in the *Harvard Business Review* and a subsequent book called *The Work of Nations*, which argued that corporations had grown past the point where they could sensibly be considered American or German or Japanese. With headquarters in one country, research centers in another, factories in yet other countries, and customers all around the world, Reich said, big diversified corporations could be loyal only to their own economic interests. Though Chrysler had its headquarters in Detroit and Matsushita was based in Osaka, neither would necessarily care about the government or labor force of its home country. Each would go wherever the money, the market, and the skilled work force drew it. In an age of global corporations, Reich concluded, a nation's well-being rises or falls with the skills of its workers. Therefore he vigorously advocated plans for improving American education and retraining American workers.

In practical terms, Reich said in a 1990 article titled "Who Is Us?," published in the *Harvard Business Review*, this blurring of corporate nationality meant that the U.S. government should not try to help American-owned companies solely because they were American-owned. The government owed its loyalty to citizens and workers within its borders, and companies from Europe, Japan, Mexico, or anywhere else might have more to offer the American work force. When the U.S. government gave contracts to Boeing, provided bailouts to Chrysler, or negotiated on behalf of Motorola or Zenith, by Reich's analysis it might not have been helping American workers in any direct way. There was no telling where the companies would build the products that federal money was subsidizing. If Toyota was building plants in America and Chrysler was moving plants to Mexico, then Toyota should be considered at least as "American" as Chrysler.

As a theoretical matter, this proposition is sensible and appealing. Daily life abounds with cases that seem to confirm the point. American plants move to Mexico; Japanese and German plants open up in the United States. A large number of American commentators have embraced the "Who Is Us?" assumption, usually crediting Reich for having precisely defined the shift to a world in which corporations no longer have citizenship. Yet many of the specific illustrations on which this changed perspective is based turn out to be misleading. For instance:

■ In the summer of 1989 Reich published an article in *The New Republic* that provided a perfect illustration of the way a preference for home-based companies could backfire. U.S. trade negotiators, he said, had been hammering at the Japanese government to open the country's market to cellular phones made by Motorola. The irony, he said, was that in helping Motorola the government was doing little or nothing for American workers, because the phones Motorola wanted to sell were actually designed and made in Kuala Lumpur.

As a recent resident of Kuala Lumpur, I was surprised when I read this assertion, since I had known Motorola officials there and had never heard them say that they made cellular phones. As it turns out, they didn't. Motorola officials wrote immediately to *The New Republic* pointing out that the phones were made in the United States. James P. Caile, the director of marketing for Motorola's Cellular Subscriber Group, said in his letter that the telephones in question were designed and made in Arlington Heights, Illinois.

Half a year later Reich published his seminal article, "Who Is Us?" Once again he used Motorola as a main illustration of the difference between the welfare of American companies and the welfare of American workers. Motorola, he said this time, "designs and makes many of its cellular telephones in Kuala Lumpur, while most of the Americans who make cellular telephone equipment in the United States for export to Japan happen to work for Japanese-owned companies."

After this article appeared, Richard W. Heimlich, Motorola's director of international strategy, wrote to the *Harvard Business Review*, pointing out once more that the phones were made in America, not Malaysia. Heimlich's letter also questioned Reich's claim that some "Japanese-owned companies" were building cellular phones in America and exporting them to Japan. Heimlich's letter was published in the *Harvard Business Review*; Reich replied in the magazine about cellular telephones thus: "One of those [Motorola's] Southeast Asian plants, by the way, does make parts for cellular telephones, according to industry sources."

Heimlich also wrote directly to Reich, offering to discuss the issue further. Reich sent back an angry personal letter (which Motorola officials gave me when I asked for their side of the story), saying that he resented having his intellectual and academic integrity challenged. This letter referred Heimlich to a book by Edward Graham and Paul Krugman, which Reich said would substantiate his claims.

The book is called *Foreign Direct Investment in the United States.* I found when I looked at it that it says nothing at all about Motorola in Kuala Lumpur, and in a broader sense its argument is the opposite of Reich's. Its perspective is clearly internationalist, and one of its intentions is to rebut irrational American fears about the effects of foreign investment. Nevertheless the data Krugman and Graham examined show that corporate nationality does matter, and that it matters most for Japanese-owned firms.

At least in the United States, foreign-owned companies behave differently from American-owned firms in many ways. The biggest difference is that foreign-owned firms are far more likely to import their components from suppliers in the home country than to buy them locally. This difference is most pronounced for Japanese-owned firms. In December of 1991 Edward Graham published a comparison of Japanese-owned and American-owned manufacturing firms operating in the United States. He found that the Japanese-owned firms were less likely to produce goods for export from the United States, less likely to invest R&D funds in America—and four times as likely to import components, instead of manufacturing or buying them in the United States.

In the Winter, 1991, issue of *The American Prospect*, Reich once again used Motorola to illustrate the borderless nature of the new, integrated world, and Heimlich once again protested in a letter to the editor. Later that year Reich published *The Work of Nations*. It included a full-scale presentation of the borderless argument, including "one example" that summed up the folly of the U.S. government's working in behalf of U.S.-based corporations—the same example.

The power of the Motorola-in-Malaysia story depends on the assumption that it is one of many possible illustrations of a widespread trend. If there really were a large number of examples to choose from, it's hard to explain why an author would have stuck with such a troublesome case. After I made numerous calls to the Labor Department to ask Reich why he seemed so attached to this one story, he replied through a press representative at the department that he had "seen no evidence to change his mind" about the Motorola case.

■ Last year, after he became Labor Secretary, Reich presented another perfect example of the "coming irrelevance of corporate nationality." The example came in a memorandum he sent to President Bill Clinton on March 23, concerning trade and "competitiveness" strategies. "Our efforts should focus on opening foreign markets to American *exports*, rather than merely to U.S. products," he said, sensibly. American exports would employ workers in America; mere "U.S. products," for instance Coca-Cola sold overseas, might do little for America's work force. Then came the example:

> Japan's agreement to purchase 20 per cent of its semiconductors from non-Japanese firms, for example, does not necessarily promote high-wage production in the United States. Close to 75 per cent of the chips which Japan purchased last year from U.S. firms were fabricated in Japan.

If true, this illustration would be even more powerful than the Motorola story in showing that corporations had transcended nationality. It would also mean that the semiconductor agreement had completely backfired, "forcing" Japanese purchasers, Brer Rabbit–like, into buying more output from factories based in Japan. But this account of the agreement's effects also turns out to be inaccurate. According to figures collected by the U.S. Trade Representative's office, the percentage of such American-brand chips that were made in Japan was 30, not "close to 75." The semiconductor agreement had in fact achieved its stated purpose: most of the American chips sold in Japan were indeed designed and made in the United States.

■ In the same memorandum Reich gave another illustration of the borderless paradox. The U.S. government at that time was evaluating how to get involved in the emerging technologies of high-definition television. The main decisions lay with the Federal Communications Commission, which was to decide which transmission system, among several competing proposals, should be the standard for HDTV broadcasts within the United States. At the time Reich wrote his memo, three business consortia were vying to have their standards selected. One was led by the electronics makers Thomson, based in France, and Philips, based in Holland. The other two were all-American, in that the main partners in them were all U.S.-based institutions: an alliance between Zenith and AT&T, a group led by the Massachusetts Institute of

Technology and the Chicago firm General Instruments. (A fourth group, led by Japanese firms, dropped out of the competition when it became clear that its analog transmission system would lose in competition against the digital systems proposed by each of the other teams.)

In his memorandum to the President, Reich said that the government should look beyond strictly technical issues to see "which standard is likely to generate the greatest amount of high-wage production in the United States." He added,

> (Interestingly, the only consortium which has pledged to develop and manufacture its high-definition televisions in the United States is the Dutch-French group [Phillips-Thompson-Sarnoff] [*sic*]; the AT&T-Zenith group will not do so, because Zenith is moving all its television production to Mexico.)

Like the Motorola and semiconductor examples, this one seemed to show the folly of helping American corporations. But as with the other examples, the real facts of this case undercut the "Who Is Us?" argument.

The French-Dutch consortium did indeed plan to do the final assembly of its TV sets in America. Zenith planned to do its final assembly in Mexico. But this stage of the process boils down to "screwdriver jobs": final assembly is the bolting together of sophisticated, high-value components made somewhere else. Most of the value of an HDTV, which in turn means most of the sophisticated, high-wage jobs, would come from designing and producing those components. The most important and valuable components would be the many diverse semiconductors that would control the conversion and display of incoming digital signals. The high-resolution, large-scale picture tubes would be the next most valuable components. Where these specialized products were made, rather than where the sets were put together, would determine where the highest-value jobs from HDTV would end up.

If Thomson-Philips eventually leads the HDTV industry, the advanced semiconductors for its sets will almost certainly come from Thomson's factories in France. If the AT&T-Zenith group does, the semiconductors will come from AT&T in the United States. In a letter to Reich, Zenith's chairman, Jerry K. Pearlman, had emphasized that since the "American" consortium would make its advanced components in the United States, it would produce more highly skilled jobs for Americans than the European consortium would.

Pearlman is hardly an impartial observer, but his account of HDTV supply patterns conforms to most other accounts in the industry. It is "interesting," as Reich had said in his memorandum to the President, to speculate that the foreign-based consortium would create more high-value jobs within the United States, but this is probably not the reality. Most other evidence, both anecdotal and analytic, confirms the antique-seeming idea that corporations do their most valuable work in the country where they are based.

Them Against Us

ANGLO-AMERICAN theory instructs Westerners that economics is a "positive-sum game," from which all can emerge as winners. Asian history instructs many Koreans, Chinese, Japanese, and others that economic competition is a form of war. To be strong is much better than to be weak; to give orders is better than to take them. By this logic the way to be strong, to give orders, to have independence and control—to win—is to keep in mind the difference between us and them. This perspective comes naturally to Koreans when thinking about Japan, or to Canadians when thinking about the United States, or to Chinese or Japanese when thinking about what the Europeans did to their nations. It does not come naturally to Americans.

But, again, it comes naturally in the Asian system. There are more examples from Japan than from the other countries, because Japan got there first; Korea, for instance, would love to be just as nationalistic, but under the current balance of power in Asian economies it doesn't have a chance.

Here are a few ways in which Asian economies are more nationalistic than ours.

■ *Intra-industry trade.* Theory seems to call for international trade to become more specialized by region as time goes on. Wine and cheese will come from France, magazine editors from England, cars from Japan, wool from New Zealand, and vodka from the Russian potato lands. Each country will develop its own national skill.

In fact just the opposite occurs. Since the end of the Second World War the fastest-growing type of international trade has been "intra-industry" trade. German car companies like Mercedes, Audi, and BMW make cars that are attractive to customers in France, Japan, and America—but some people in Germany want non-German cars like Ferraris, Toyotas, Volvos, and Fords. Germany also has a very active auto-parts industry. It sells to other auto makers around the world, and its own auto makers buy parts from non-German makers, notably in the United States.

The result is that Germany actively sells automobiles and auto parts to the rest of the world—and actively buys the same things. This pattern, of sales *and* purchases within an industry, is intra-industry trade. It is measured on a scale that runs from zero to 100. An intra-industry trade rate of zero means that trade in a certain industry all runs one way: a country only sells or only buys a certain product. (For instance, Saudi Arabia's trade rate for oil sales would be zero.) A rate of 100 means that a country sells exactly as much of a certain product as it buys.

Countries that have very low intra-industry trade rates are typically Third World countries or others with unbalanced economies. The classic banana republic would sell only raw materials and would import nearly all the machinery it used. The intra-industry trade rate in most developed countries is high and steadily rising. Depending on the industry, countries in Western Europe have recently had intra-industry trade rates in the low 60s through the low 80s. The U.S. rates are slightly lower than the European ones, which is not surprising, since the U.S. economy is bigger and less influenced by foreign trade.

Japan does not fit this pattern. First, its overall rate has been unusually low. Edward Lincoln, of the Brookings Institution, in his 1990 book *Japan's Unequal Trade*, calculated that Japan's overall rate was 25, which was one third the overall rate for France and far below that of any other industrial power. This means in practice that the Japanese economy buys only the goods it simply cannot make: fuel, food, raw materials, and certain advanced products (notably airplanes) in which its industries cannot yet compete.

Second, Japan's rate has rarely risen. For the rest of the developed world intra-industry trade has been the main engine of trade growth during the postwar years. Countries started with different rates, but all the rates went up. Japan's stayed low through most of the postwar era and, according to Edward Lincoln, rose only modestly in the late 1980s, when Japanese manufacturers moved some of their plants overseas. It is not necessary to say that Japan's low rate is wise, unwise, or some mixture: its effect is to divide the world into "us" and "them" production zones, and to keep as many industries as possible in the hands of "us."

■ *Management.* The board members of U.S. companies are still mainly American white men, but there are exceptions. For instance, in May of 1992 *The Wall Street Journal* provided a long list of executives of major American corporations who were born outside the United States. The computer industry is full of people who started in other countries. The magazine world is full of the English.

Most Asian countries have a far more nationality-conscious policy. It would be inconceivable for a non-Korean to run one of the major Korean enterprises. Although it is difficult to find reliable figures for the number of non-Japanese who serve on the boards of directors of major Japanese companies (Japan's big-business federation, the Keidanren, says it has "no information" on this subject), the number, as best I can determine, is in the single digits. Japanese firms doing business around the world had a much higher proportion of Japanese managers than American firms had of Americans, or European firms had of their own nationalities. At the end of 1991 the *Nihon Keizai Shimbun* surveyed Japanese-owned companies in America. It concluded, "Only about 5 percent of executives are American and delegation of authority to local companies just isn't happening."

■ *Incoming investment.* During the late 1980s Americans debated about the higher levels of foreign investment coming into their country, and whether it was racist to be concerned about investment from Japan rather than, say, from Holland. One answer to this question is that there was more of it from

Japan. During the late 1980s Japanese investors overtook the Dutch to hold the second largest amount of U.S. assets. (The leading holders were the British.) In terms of new investments the Japanese were far ahead of everyone else in the late 1980s.

The real reason for the complaint about Japanese investment was that European investment did not seem profoundly foreign. European-owned companies in America were mainly run by Americans. Japanese-owned companies were to a much larger extent run by Japanese. During the 1988 campaign Michael Dukakis made a famous gaffe by denouncing foreign ownership at an auto-parts factory that turned out to be owned by Italian interests. The fact that on his visit he didn't notice that it was foreign-owned pointed up the underlying message: he would never have made that error with Mitsubishi.

Moreover, the British and Dutch economies were wide open for American investment. Japan's economy was not. Indeed, the share of Japan's economy that is owned by foreigners is the nation's most distinctive economic trait—because it is so tiny. Systems for measuring foreign ownership vary, but approximately 10 percent of the U.S. economy is now foreign-owned. For most European nations the foreign-owned share is higher, since the countries are smaller and their economies are more integrated. Yet for Japan the foreign-owned share is about one percent, and is virtually zero in certain crucial industries. The foreign-owned share of North American and European economies has been steadily rising. The foreign-owned share of Japan's economy has fallen for several years—despite the collapse of prices on the Japanese stock market in the early 1990s, which should theoretically have attracted bargain hunters from overseas.

For the first few decades after the Second World War, Japanese laws flatly prohibited foreigners from buying Japanese companies. The handful of foreign companies that are well established in Japan—Coca-Cola, IBM—are the exceptions that prove the rule. For various reasons they were able to grandfather themselves into the system. Their success is usually cited as proof that anyone who tries hard enough can find a way into the Japanese system. But most other companies were forbidden to do the same thing thirty or forty years ago, when it would have been cheap—and they can't afford to do it now.

Dennis Encarnation, of the Harvard Business School, has pointed out that when Japanese enterprises invest in plants in Europe or North America, they almost always buy a controlling interest—100 percent if possible, 51 percent at least. When foreigners have bought shares of Japanese firms, they have almost always ended up as minority owners, and often receive no seats on the board of directors.

■ *Technology.* There is a final point to emphasize about a nationality-conscious business policy: it goes with an aversion to relying on foreigners. This desire for autarky is completely understandable in historical and psychological terms, although it is considered irrational in the realm of economics.

When Japan suddenly became industrialized, in the opening decades of this century, it lost the ability to feed its own people from its own soil. When its leaders and generals considered making war on America, in the 1930s, what drove them was the fear that they would run out of oil. One nightmare they faced was that their shipping would be cut off and they could be starved out. Today is a very different time—supplier cartels can be broken, as with OPEC; people who have money, as Japan does, can find food to buy. Yet much the same mentality runs through many Japanese—and other Asian—approaches to technology. In ways that no economic theory can fully explain, the goal of national policy is to bring control of the technology into Japanese (or Korean, or Chinese) hands—even if this is irrational, even if it violates the spirit of the borderless world.

Asian history instructs many Koreans, Chinese, and Japanese that economic competition is a form of war. To be strong is much better than to be weak; to give orders is better than to take them.

Japanese corporations do practice a form of conventional economic competition, but all within their own borders. This is known as the "one-set" philosophy: each big company makes a set of products that includes one of each kind. Each beer maker produces a draft beer, a "dry" beer, a lager, and so on; each electronics company tries to produce a full range of radios, TVs, and fax machines. Successful Japanese students are expected to get top marks in every subject. Economists say that specializing in everything is in principle not possible. But in practice the urge to be on top in *every* field, rather than concentrating on some and leaving the rest to competitors, is a stronger impulse in Japanese society than in most others.

Americans may complain about the decline of their steel and semiconductor industries—that is, areas where the United States once enjoyed a lead and has had to watch factories shut their doors. But few Americans really think it is a problem if we have to buy our entire supply of CD players from overseas. The United States has no government project under way to create a domestic fax-machine industry, and when government guidance is proposed—for semiconductors, HDTVs, and superconductors—it is always controversial. The Japanese assumption is very different. In 1988, after an agricultural-trade conference in Montreal, a Japanese negotiator spoke to a Canadian colleague. "You know what really makes Japan unusual?" he said. "We are the only major industrial power that is not also a food exporter. If we could improve the productivity of our rice farming by fifteen percent a year, in eight years we would be competitive with California." Not even Japan's least competitive industry, agriculture, should be conceded to foreign competition.

The Japanese emphasis on the country's "unique" capacity for high-quality manufacturing provides an argument for national self-sufficiency. In 1985 the most disastrous crash in Japanese air history occurred outside Tokyo. A Boeing 747 owned by Japan Air Lines took off from Tokyo's Haneda Airport, bound for Osaka. Shortly afterward it crashed into a mountainside, killing 520 passengers. Officials from Japan Air Lines visited the bereaved families to express the company's contrition. On investigation it proved that the principal cause of the crash was a faulty repair job carried out by Boeing engineers, which had left one of the plane's pressure bulkheads in a weakened state.

Many lessons might be drawn from the catastrophe. The high death toll was in part an indictment of bureaucratic infighting within Japan's Self-Defense Force, which squabbled for hours over which branch would do what in going to aid the victims. Autopsies showed that many people had survived the crash but died later of exposure or injuries; they could have been saved with a faster response. Nonetheless the crash was taken in Japan as a symbol of the across-the-board shoddiness of American equipment; over the next few years I heard it mentioned in that context dozens of times.

I moved to Japan half a year after the JAL crash, and less than a month after the space shuttle *Challenger* blew up shortly after being launched. Several times during the next year I heard quite similar responses from Japanese: if we had done it, it wouldn't have happened. A Canadian friend was at the Japanese space center that day and recalls the air of schadenfreude. The unspoken mood was, what can you expect? This gloating was unwarranted on the part of Japanese quality-control experts, since their country's own H-2 rocket, usually described in the press as the first "pure" Japanese aerospace project, kept blowing up on the launch pad in the late 1980s and early 1990s.

But the general perception of shoddy American production perfectly reinforces the Japanese view of the JAL crash and the *Challenger* explosion. Early in 1992, when the speaker of the Japanese House complained about American work habits, a *Wall Street Journal* story quoted a Japanese pollster, Takayoshi Miyagawa, as saying that the comment "represents a general perception of Japanese people on the quality of American labor." The result of the JAL crash and similar U.S.-made catastrophes, he said, is that "the Japanese people think we should make by ourselves whatever concerns human life."

Sometimes the strategy of saving lives by restricting imports backfires. In 1988 Japan's Ministry of Health and Welfare coordinated a drive by the country's three largest vaccine-making companies to produce an alternative to an American vaccine that had not been approved for sale in Japan. The American vaccine, produced by the Merck Corporation, had the trademarked name of MMR and was used to protect children against measles, mumps, and rubella (German measles) with one inoculation. Merck's vaccine was extremely safe; after it had been used on more than 100 million children, no cases of serious side effects had been confirmed. Japanese doctors at the time administered three separate shots for the three diseases. To promote the growth of Japan's pharmaceutical industry, and to avoid using Merck's product, the Japanese government asked each of the three companies to produce its best vaccine for one of the diseases covered by MMR. These the government combined into a new vaccine, which it also called MMR. When the vaccine was ready, in early 1989, the Ministry of Health and Welfare began a mandatory nationwide inoculation program for children. "Rather than use foreign products, we wanted Japanese products because they are of better quality," an official of Japan's Association of Biologicals Manufacturers told Leslie Helm, who reported the story in the *Los Angeles Times*.

In fact Japan's MMR was of much worse quality than the foreign alternatives. Based on the safety record of Merck's MMR and similar foreign vaccines, the Ministry of Health and Welfare had expected that its vaccine would produce side effects in no more than one case per 100,000 inoculations—but the incidence of side effects was at least 100 times as great as predicted. The most serious side effects were meningitis and encephalitis, which killed some children and left others paralyzed or brain-damaged. By the end of 1989 the government had made the Japanese MMR vaccine optional rather than mandatory, but it left the vaccine on the market while the remaining stocks were used up and did not approve the safer Merck product for sale in Japan. (Japanese doctors have now returned to giving separate immunizations for the three diseases.)

The preferences of such a system cannot be explained by a desire to save lives—or to protect consumers. By modern Western standards such preferences seem illogical and self-defeating at best, brutally misguided at worst. Yet they are in keeping with the belief, widespread outside the English-speaking world, that inconvenience to consumers is less damaging in the long run than weakness of a nation's productive base. The fastest-growing modern economies, in East Asia, reflect this view. Like it or not, we live in the world that Asian success stories have shaped. We need to figure out how to compete in it.

The Middle East and Africa

- **The Middle East (Articles 26–28)**
- **Africa (Articles 29–32)**

With the end of both the cold war and the Gulf War, demands for political change dominate international and regional environments of the Middle East and Africa. At the same time that governments are adjusting to the collapse of the Soviet Empire and declining amounts of Western aid, attention to and involvement in regional conflicts grow. The Arab-Israeli conflict, increased grassroots demands for political change by Islamic fundamentalist and democratic reformers, concerns about the legitimacy of existing regimes, and a changing balance of economic and political power among the major players in the region—Iran, Iraq, Egypt, Saudi Arabia, and Syria—dominate relations.

While a lasting settlement to the Arab-Israeli conflict remains elusive, the participation of many Arab states against Iraq on the side of the coalition during the Gulf War had a major impact on inter-Arab relations. After the war, more Arab states were prepared to support the U.S.–sponsored negotiations between Israelis and Palestinians, and there was a generalized sense that conditions were ripe for a new negotiated status quo between Arabs and Israel. The U.S.–sponsored negotiation process made little progress and the intifada continued until September 1993, when both Israeli governmental and Palestinian Liberation Organization (PLO) negotiators reached agreement on a plan for Palestinian rule in Gaza and Jericho. Although scholars may eventually look back at the Middle East's tortuous road to peace and conclude that the 1993 Rabin-Arafat handshake initiated a process leading to lasting changes in the region, as the staff of *The Economist* describe in "Can It Really Be Peace?" there are fundamental differences about what the agreement means and there are a large number of potential spoilers capable of crippling the PLO-Israeli agreement.

The seriousness of these problems as obstacles to peace was evident almost immediately, as disagreements over the details for a phased withdrawal of the Israeli military and Palestinian rule stalled implementation of the plan in 1994. In February 1994, a Jewish settler opened fire on Arab worshippers in a crowded mosque in Hebron in the single bloodiest day in the conflict in the occupied territories since the 1967 Middle East war, when Israel captured the West Bank and Gaza. The PLO demanded international peacekeepers as a precondition to returning to the bargaining table, and riots in the aftermath of this incident spilled over into Israel for the first time.

In spite of the disruption of the Israeli-PLO peace process, a number of key powers in the region, including Syria, continue to signal their willingness to recognize Israel's right to exist once conditions are ripe. Changing

Arab-Israel relations are only one aspect of changes being made in the relationships among powerful Arab states as they adjust their policies to correspond to a changed regional environment. The Gulf War helped to reshape alliances, underscored the myth of Arab unity, permitted the United States to retain status as the major outside actor in the region, and increased the influence of key actors like Turkey and Iran.

In contrast, Saddam Hussein's regime, although it was able to survive the Gulf War, crush Kurdish uprisings in the south, and consolidate power by ruling by fear, was greatly weakened by the war. Iraq's ability to play a major role in the region diminished as Iran's oil industry was recovering from the Iran-Iraqi war. This recovery means that funds are now available to permit Iran to play a traditional role as a major regional power. While Iran remains very high on the U.S. "rogue countries" list, if not number one, Edward Shirley in "Not Fanatics, and Not Friends" asks Americans to consider when the United States might alter its approach to Iran. Shirley analyzes this question from the Iranian point of view in order to explain why anticlericalism is rampant in post-Khomeini Iran.

Iran's continuing status as a rogue state in the eyes of America is due in part to its efforts to undermine existing regimes in the region through support of radical Islam fundamentalists. The bombing of the World Trade Center in New York City reminded Americans once again of the existence of a new generation of Islamic terrorists who are capable of attacking governments from the Middle East to New York. Governments worldwide experience difficulties stopping the flow of money to loosely organized and highly dynamic groups of Islamic militants, in part because of the informal and complex network of support centers scattered from the Persian Gulf to the United States.

In the Middle East, authorities in Algeria and Egypt are unable to crush terrorist attacks by radical Islamic fundamentalist groups because these crusades are increasingly supported by large numbers of citizens who are alienated from political authorities. The appeal of Islamic fundamentalism in politics, in religion, and as a mode of living has spread dramatically in recent decades throughout much of the Middle East and Africa. As Jennifer Parmelee notes in "Radicals Gain Strength in Horn of Africa," the current violent antigovernment campaigns by Islamic fundamentalist groups in North Africa may be a precursor to increased political unrest by Islamic fundamentalists throughout the Horn of Africa. Fueled by domestic frustration and need, many of these groups are strengthened by aid from supporters in Sudan, Iran, and

Saudi Arabia. However, what is frequently lost in Western analyses of the growth of Islamic fundamentalism is the fact that much of the current unrest is rooted in historic discontent lingering from centuries of Ottoman and Western domination. This historic condition and alienation from corrupt ruling regimes has caused many millions of Africans to turn toward or return to Islam.

The growth of Islamic fundamentalism and increased demands for democracy throughout Africa are both reflections of widespread reactions to disastrous economic conditions and increased dictatorial tendencies of those executives who attempted to use repression to remain in power and to implement structural adjustment programs during the 1980s. The extent of human suffering caused by starvation in Somalia was the best-publicized of several cases where large-scale suffering by civilians is the by-product of conflicts. In "From Peace-keeping to Peace Enforcement," Patrick Gilkes explains that the disaster of Somalia grew out of the collapse of the moral authority of the elders and their replacement by the coercive powers of Siad Barre's state and the warlords who succeeded it. The pictures of the widespread starving played a key role in the U.S. decision to lead a military intervention in Somalia at the end of 1992 on a humanitarian mission. However, as the mission of United States troops changed, U.S. forces increasingly became involved in fighting. After several Americans were killed in clashes with supporters of General Aideed's faction in 1993, President Clinton announced the withdrawal of all U.S. troops by the spring of 1994. As Gilkes outlines, today many Somalis regard the UN as another faction and few view the UN or U.S. strategies as designed to "restore" Somalia.

The Somalia experience may accelerate a trend toward reduced Western involvement in future African conflicts. Declining Western interests and commitments in Africa come at the same time as a revival of demands for democratic reforms throughout Africa. Although Westerners tend to view the increased number of movements for democracy throughout Africa as the result of events in Eastern Europe, many of these movements, begun in the 1980s, are accelerated as more segments of civil society being radicalized by economic decline and the increased dictatorial tendencies of unaccountable executives attempting to implement structural adjustment programs through increased state repression. Coalitions of democratic forces have attempted to change the nature of the political system in nearly every country in Africa, with mixed results. In Mali, Benin, and Zambia these movements succeeded in driving long-entrenched political leaders from power. In other countries, such as the Congo and Angola, fighting accelerated after key partisans re-fused to accept the results of democratic elections. But democratic reform efforts persist in other countries such as Zaire, Malawi, and Kenya despite recent setbacks.

The most dramatic political changes in recent years have occurred in southern Africa, where signs indicate that peace may come to a region ravaged by decades of conflicts. Namibia won independence in 1990 after decades of rule by South Africa. Although fighting resumed in Angola after Jonah Savimbi's UNITA forces refused to accept the results of the UN–sponsored election in 1992, the peace agreement negotiated to end the 16-year war in Mozambique between the government and Renamo guerrilla forces still holds, despite delays in deploying a UN peace force. Moreover, broad, cooperative efforts helped prevent widespread suffering or starvation during the worst drought in 70 years.

After long and difficult negotiations, in 1993 the African National Congress (ANC) and the Nationalist Party (NP) finally agreed on the principles for a new constitution to govern a new South Africa after national elections in April 1994. These are historic elections, marking the first time that black South Africans have had the opportunity to vote. While threats to disrupt the new political order are made by followers of Inkatha and white extremists, or tied to more generalized violence and a depressed economy, Nelson Mandela, the leader of this new political order, is optimistic about the future. In "South Africa's Future Foreign Policy," Nelson Mandela outlines the contours of South Africa's future foreign policy based on the principles of human rights, promotion of democracy with guarantees for diversity worldwide, support for the UN, peaceful regional integration, and efforts to redress slow growth, severe poverty, and extreme inequalities in living standards, income, and opportunity domestically and throughout the region.

Looking Ahead: Challenge Questions

What actions can be undertaken by the international community to promote implementation of the peace plan between Israel and the PLO?

Explain why you agree or disagree with the thesis that the West should be willing to encourage democratic trends in the Islamic world even if it means that Islamic fundamentalists will gain power.

Explain why many Muslims in the Middle East and Africa today continue to link current political conflicts to old patterns of Western domination.

Why do some African analysts blame Western countries and institutions for the economic decline experienced by many African countries during the 1980s?

Can it really be peace?

Only if those who want it strive harder than those who don't

THE unlocking of the gateway to a Middle Eastern peace gave the ceremony on the White House lawn on September 13th exceptional importance. Old combatants, let alone those who still fight on, may choose not to walk through. But until now they did not have the choice; however well-intentioned, peace-seekers hit an impenetrable obstacle. Now that a start has been made on dividing a small patch of land between the peoples who separately claim it, the way is open. The aim must now be to prevent it, once again, from being closed.

Egypt was ahead of the game 15 years ago, when its decision to seek a separate peace with Israel changed history by eliminating the possibility of a fourth full-scale Arab-Israeli war: Egypt was the only Arab country with the strength, and the natural leadership, to pursue such a vendetta. But the bilateral peace did not discourage smaller wars, and it created no wider stability. On the contrary: the region was torn by political and ideological dissent; Israel felt empowered to invade Lebanon in 1982 and never to leave it altogether; Anwar Sadat was assassinated in 1981 and Egypt now hovers on the verge of turmoil; from 1987 the territories occupied by Israel in 1967 were shaken by the stones, and latterly the bullets, of the Palestinian *intifada*.

Scholars looking back at the Middle East's tortuous road to peace will, with luck and hard work, conclude that the 1993 Rabin-Arafat handshake set off far more lasting change than did the 1979 Israeli-Egyptian treaty. The luck could well turn sour; the hard work could falter. Yet with the Palestinians explicitly, and the Israelis tacitly, acknowledging each other's rights, there is a feeling abroad that the region may indeed be able, within a few years, to rid itself of the Arab-Israeli cancer at its centre. If Palestinians and Israelis find a way to live side by side—and eventually decide on sharing or dividing their capital city—the whole wretched business could be history.

It is a big "if". At best, the working out of an Israeli-Palestinian peace will be painful; at worst, a half-dozen, not improbable, things could cripple the process. If the arrangement crashes, the road would again be blocked.

Here is but a sample of the things that could go wrong. The Israelis, perhaps under a change of government, could narrow their horizons so that the symbolic deal becomes a be-all and end-all in itself. This would confirm the Palestinians' fear that they are being ensnared in a "Gaza and Jericho first . . . and last" trap. Palestinians, whose hunger for the best makes them the enemy of the good, may confirm Israeli fears that they are not to be trusted. Palestinians and their fellow-Arabs could be engulfed by the religious wave sweeping the Muslim world; practical efforts to move forward, step by sensible step, would then be overwhelmed by a new unleashing of old passions. Atrocities of one kind or another could destroy confidence; Yasser Arafat is one obvious target for assassination.

Plainly, it would be silly to be starry-eyed. The Middle East is at a turning point, but a long way from being safely turned. The excitement is that, for the first time in five decades, the turning is there to take. The question is whether Arabs and Israelis, with the outside world looking on, have the courage of their half-convictions.

Let the Palestinians build

Half a century ago, when Britain retreated from its Palestinian mandate, leaving the key under the mat for the most aggressive to snatch, the Israelis were not only better fighters than the Arabs but were also smart enough to recognise the advantages that accrue from saying "yes". Zionist policy was to agree to every offer, however inadequate—such as the United Nations 1947 partition plan, which allotted Israelis a non-viable slice of Palestine—and then to build on

From *The Economist*, September 18, 1993, pp. 23-25. © 1993 by The Economist, Ltd. Distributed by The New York Times Special Features. Reprinted by permission.

it, by force and by guile. The Arabs, who believed justice and numbers to be on their side, said "no" to compromise, went to war—and suffered.

Here lies a lesson for today's "rejectionist" Palestinians and their allies, not all of whom are either radical or fundamentalist. Many Palestinians, particularly among the hundreds of thousands who still live as refugees outside the old mandate, have their minds set on getting back the homes in Jaffa or Haifa that their families were driven from in the late 1940s; they refuse to accept the Jewish state and all that has happened since. More to the point are those who have long since come to recognise the reality of an Israeli state and the need for a truncated Palestinian one beside it, but are not prepared to accept the compromise now on offer; they stand out for a clear route to independence in all the territory seized by Israel in 1967, including East Jerusalem.

Instead, as they see it, they are expected to be satisfied with an unhappy little strip of territory (Gaza), so turbulent that it managed to defeat Israel's harshest efforts at control, plus a dusty outpost (Jericho) that nobody is much interested in. In addition, they will get a degree of autonomy so modest that they have been turning it down for years. And although they are being prom-

Total population, 1991, '000	
Jews	Arabs
4,203	2,696

Source: Israeli government statistics

Israeli security zone since 1985

GOLAN HEIGHTS
Occupied by Israel: 1967
annexed: 1981
| 10 | 18 |

GAZA STRIP
Occupied by Israel: 1967
| 1 | 700 |

WEST BANK
Occupied by Israel: 1967
| 102 | 1,100 |

ISRAEL
| 4,090 | 878 |

Sinai, occupied by Israel 1967-82

0   Km   40

Where they are now
Worldwide distribution of Palestinians
% of total, 1991

Total 5.8m

Rest of world 7.8
Israel 12.6
Jordan 31.6
Gaza 10.8
Lebanon 5.7
Syria 5.2
West Bank including East Jerusalem 18.6
Other Arab countries 7.7

Source: Centre for Policy Analysis on Palestine

ised that, after a two-year period of proving themselves, they will be empowered to negotiate a permanent solution, the promise contains no commitment whatsoever on what this final settlement will be.

Is the deal as unattractive as that? Yes, in a way. Gaza is a horror that from December, when the Israeli soldiers start to withdraw, will be the responsibility of the PLO's own policemen, drawn from its militia. The autonomy offered in the West Bank is small compensation. Control over education, health and welfare, which will come into effect next month, has long been on offer and regularly rejected. Full control over the dot that is Jericho sounds an absurdity.

But, if the Palestinians keep their heads and the Israelis their courage, it will not be like this at all. The Palestinians can build on

an inauspicious beginning no less surely, and a lot faster, than the Israelis built on their toehold in the British mandate. When Mr Arafat, with his PLO ministers, army chiefs and officials, set themselves up in Jericho, their presence could be the basis for genuine self-government.

How, in practice, can Mr Arafat and his men be confined to one West Bank town, travelling by a set route to Gaza? Boundaries within the West Bank are imaginary; the roads are open to cars and buses. The PLO will roam from city to city, town to town, taking care of its constituents. It will neither look nor feel like municipal government. By July 1994, when the Palestinians will have elected their new council, the Israelis will have withdrawn from the towns, and the military government will no longer be operative. What then will be the difference between Hebron or Nablus and Jericho?

The PLO accepted the deal it once scorned because it was running out of options and money, and had the hot breath of Hamas (the Islamic Resistance Movement) on its neck. But Yitzhak Rabin's recognition gives it the chance to turn what was originally designed as no more than a cautious twist in a long process into an imaginative leap. The chance will depend on restraint and confidence. Mr Arafat's decision to call a conference of all Palestinian groups is a wise start. But peace will work only if the Israelis are reassured that the PLO's horns and cloven feet are vanished for good.

Let Israel be bold
The Israeli government, no less than the PLO, lacked a workable alternative: it had to reach an accommodation with the enemy. Under the former Likud government, Israel's policy towards the Palestinians was set on a road to nightmare: oppression fol-

lowed by revolt followed by oppression stretched aridly ahead. When the Labour government took over last year, its policies were as harsh as Likud's but, unlike the Likud, it saw these policies as finite. The *intifada* was gathering a psychological toll from Israelis who recoiled from their fate as child-killers. The PLO's terrorist face faded as Hamas's grew ever more threatening. The principle of land for peace, buried since it was first propounded by the United Nations in 1967, was discovered alive and well.

Yet the speed with which the secret diplomacy unfolded caught the Israelis, like others, off-balance—with the nay-sayers recovering the quickest, and the most vociferously. Now the positive-minded are taking over; a poll shows the proportion of Israelis supporting the deal rising from 52% last week to 62% this week. But, not unreasonably, Israelis are clamouring for a say as history flashes past them. Many are demanding a new election or a referendum; Mr Rabin has no intention of going to the country until he is forced to do so, but he might favour a referendum if he fails to get parliamentary backing for the deal.

The prime minister's decision to return from Washington by way of a call on King Hassan of Morocco was a deft domestic manoeuvre—quite apart from "the domino effect" that the Israelis are happily chattering about. "Secret" talks with the Moroccan government are a permanent Israeli fixture. But the 200,000 or so Israelis of Moroccan descent—who unlike Iraqi Jews retain bonds of affection for the old country—tend to vote for the Likud. If Labour can woo them in the name of the king, the opposition's support will be eroded; already there is a temporary crumbling.

Israel's counterparts to the rejectionist Hamas are the militant ultra-religious movements that sponsor settlement in the lands of the Bible. Israeli soldiers will protect Israeli settlers, in Gaza as in the West Bank, and there has been no whisper of an intent to winkle them out. Indeed, the families that are there from religious conviction will be immovable, to the last moment and even beyond. The others, who traipsed into

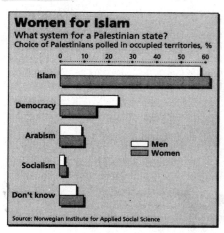

Women for Islam
What system for a Palestinian state?
Choice of Palestinians polled in occupied territories, %

0 10 20 30 40 50 60

Islam
Democracy
Arabism
Socialism
Don't know

Men
Women

Source: Norwegian Institute for Applied Social Science

occupied territory in search of space, clean air and cheap housing, are expected to follow the pattern in Sinai where, after the peace agreement, Israeli settlers held out grimly but only for as golden a handshake as they could get.

Mr Rabin has to have his people with him. Having recognised the PLO and accepted the outline of the deal, he, like Mr Arafat, can now either make or break a precarious peace. But while the Palestinians need to do something stupid to bring the process to grief, the Israelis can probably accomplish the same result by default.

If Israel is mean with the economic co-operation (read economic help) that the deal calls for, the Palestinians will never get going. Over the past quarter-century the occupied territories have been pulled and pushed into near-total dependency on Israel; no public-works programme in Gaza can begin to soak up a labour force which for years has worked in Israel or not at all. There is now talk of Israel allowing 100,000 Gazans back into Israel to work: this is about as many as worked there until the *intifada* first stopped the traffic altogether, and then halved it.

Political generosity is no less important. Peace depends on the confidence that the two sides can mutually create; at present there is none. Ever since the Labour government took power last year, the Palestinians have looked in vain for a sign, in particular the token release of a few of the 13,000 Palestinians in prison. Now, at last, there are reports that some of the internees will be freed, in batches.

Jordanian growls

Israel needs peace with the Palestinians for its own sake and, even more, for the sake of a wider reconciliation with the Arab world. Most Arab governments would be relieved to settle; the lack of a stable peace has done them no good and, to some of them, much harm. But, for all, there are gains and losses in recognising the Jewish state.

The initial reaction of Israel's Arab neighbours to the Oslo breakthrough was consternation. They were miffed at being bypassed and none more so than Jordan, which shared a delegation with the Palestinians but, like almost everybody else, was kept in the dark. Last week Shimon Peres, Israel's foreign minister, was talking of a double-coup, with Jordan as well as with the Palestinians. But the Jordanians dampened his enthusiasm, agreeing only to a low-key affair on September 14th at which Jordan's ambassador to Washington and the chief Israeli negotiator initialled an agenda of the items on which Israel and Jordan now agree. The aim is a peace treaty but this, the Jordanians said, was some years off.

Yet peace with Jordan is easier for Israel than with either Syria or Lebanon. The only bit of Jordan that Israel is sitting on consists of two small unoccupied strips that Israel has already said it is willing to give back. Harder to resolve are questions on water resources. And harder yet is the question of the possible return of Palestinian refugees living in Jordan, and enjoying Jordanian citizenship, most of whose families fled from the West Bank in 1967.

Jordan, which seized and ruled the West Bank and East Jerusalem between the 1948 and 1967 wars, grumbles that it has been getting the rough edge of the bargain ever since. Politically it is caught between two immense difficulties: more than half its population is Palestinian, which leaves it vulnerable to a takeover from an independent Palestinian state; its dominant political faction is the Muslim Brothers and their allies, which makes it cautious in moving towards an accommodation with Israel. The country's health depends on the health of its monarch, King Hussein, and that is precarious. Small wonder that Jordan steps back from risk-taking, over the Gulf war or over Israel.

But the country's rulers are now mildly outraged that Jordan could become the losing partner in what economists are beginning to see as an Israeli-Palestinian-Jordanian triangle. It suspects the Israelis of harbouring greedy plans to profit from the economic development help that may soon descend like manna on the West Bank and Gaza. Jordan, which has supported the Palestinians when it is not oppressing them—its latest gesture was to take in the 300,000 who were expelled from Kuwait after the Gulf war—is being elbowed aside. One source of Jordanian dismay is the suggested ceiling of $15m for annual exports to the West Bank; twice that amount is imported from the West Bank each year. Another is the exclusion of Jordan from the proposed new Palestinian police force.

Non-Jordanians tend to take Jordan's name in vain: the advantages and disadvantages of a Palestinian-Jordanian federation are discussed without much reference to its possibly disastrous effect on Jordan's own political balance. Crown Prince Hassan, King Hussein's outspoken brother, thinks it is time for Jordan to put itself first: as he told the London *Observer*: "The world is going to turn around and say 'bugger you' unless you get your act together."

Spoilers in waiting

The peace that Israel most craves is with Syria, which though it no longer has any desire to confront Israel head-on, does from time to time enjoy causing it intense grief. In theory this peace should not be hard: the basics have been in the open for months and both sides want it.

Israel would acknowledge Syria's sovereignty over the Golan Heights (somehow getting round the awkwardness caused by its foolish annexation in 1981) and start a phased withdrawal from all of it, except perhaps for one or two small salients directly overlooking Galilee settlements. The place would be demilitarised and monitored by outsiders; the United States this week repeated its offer to take part in this operation. The Jewish settlers in the Golan are Labour supporters who would leave, however reluctantly, under orders. It may be harder to re-educate an Israeli public which has been taught for so long, by Mr Rabin in particular, that Israel's occupation of the plateau is essential for its own security.

Yet the Israelis, expecting fresh miracles after the Palestinian breakthrough, wondered for a time whether Mr Rabin would go for broke, recognising the PLO and promising withdrawal from Golan in a single swoop. The prime minister's caution prevailed as he decided that Israel could absorb only one momentous event at a time. As a result, Syria's Hafez Assad was cool towards the Palestinian deal, reserving his right to allow the radical Palestinian groups based in Damascus to oppose it. Mr Assad, as a spoiler of plans he does not care for, is to be greatly feared. The counter to this is that he may well be held in check by his desire to get on with the Americans—and by his determination to get back the Golan.

It may be trickier for Israel to negotiate successfully with Lebanon which in effect, since Beirut is still not in control of its own destiny, means negotiating at one remove with Syria. Israel occupies a strip of southern Lebanon—its self-styled security zone—which it will leave only when it decides that northern Israel is safe from attack by Islamic guerrillas led by Hizbullah. Control of the Hizbullah could, in theory, be part of a several-sided deal with Syria: the Golan Heights, the Bekaa valley and southern Lebanon make up a single troubled area waiting to be pacified.

The trouble is that though Syria has a degree of physical control over the Hizbullah, the guerrillas' ideological loyalty is to Iran. And Iran, unlike Syria, is a wrecker unrestrained. Fundamental Islamists—in Iran, Lebanon, Egypt, Jordan and the occupied territories—cannot be placated with handshakes, better terms or economic aid. The anti-Israel battle-cry has been useful in their long-term war with secularism, providing them with a popular cause and recruits. They are not yet ready to give it up.

So, in a sense, battle-lines are joined. On one side is the Israeli government, a handful of Arab governments, the PLO and a majority of the Palestinians in the West Bank and Gaza: they all have, or should have, an overwhelming interest in making the peace work. Ranged against them are the cynical, the unhappy and the greedy backed by militant fundamentalists, some Jewish and many Muslim, who do not want any deal, good or bad. It is quite unclear at this stage which group will emerge the strongest.

Not Fanatics, and Not Friends

*The leaders of post-revolutionary Iran
may claim to be keeping the faith—but they know how
badly they need the West. What should we do when
they say it's time to let bygones be bygones?*

EDWARD G. SHIRLEY

*Edward G. Shirley is the pseudonym of a
former Iran specialist in the Central
Intelligence Agency. He is currently a
freelance writer covering the Middle
East.*

THE United States, mostly to its credit, has a tremendous capacity to forgive and forget. We forgave Britain for being a domineering mother and burning down the White House; we forgave Germany for its recurring bouts of megalomania and debasement of Western culture; we forgave Japan for bombing us on a Sunday morning and bringing us into the wickedness of the Second World War; and we have already forgiven Russia for twentieth-century totalitarianism and the very costly seventy-year war against communism.

One nation, however, has managed to engender an abiding distaste in the United States, even though the injury it has done us is comparatively minor. The antagonism derives in part from the especially durable and provocative images of the American-Iranian confrontation: the hostages, the aborted rescue mission Desert One, and yellow ribbons everywhere; Iranian women defeminized by black chadors and repressive Islamic laws; TV pictures of a sea of fervent believers, men, women, and children, shouting in frightening monotony "*Marg bar Amrika*" ("Death to America"); leaders referring repeatedly to the United States as the "Great Satan"; unforgettable photographs of the Ayatollah Ruhollah Khomeini, alive and dead. Iran's continuing system of government by the clergy is perhaps more disturbing and confusing to laical America than revolutionary socialism was.

For American politicians, Iran has been a booby trap ensnaring anyone foolish enough to touch it. When American politicians and their advisers attempt to deal with revolutionary Iran, they get caught in an unfair competition that pits the rational and straightforward American bureaucrat against the merchant Persian, a character defined in the Western imagination by his centuries-old genius for deception.

Nearly fifteen years have passed since the U.S. embassy in Tehran was closed and American official personnel were more or less denied access to Iran (the few days with Oliver North and company in Tehran do not really count). The U.S. foreign-affairs agencies, primarily the Department of State and the Central Intelligence Agency, grow noticeably, and naturally, more ignorant about Iran as fewer and fewer officers remain who have had meaningful contact with Iran, let alone sustained con-

From *The Atlantic Monthly*, December 1993, pp. 105-112. © 1993 by Edward G. Shirley. Reprinted by permission.

tact with Iranians of the Islamic Republic. Many American officials and journalists who must deal regularly with Iranian matters have probably never had an Iranian friend, and cannot read a Persian newspaper or talk to an Iranian in his native tongue.

This general ignorance fortifies the well-founded political fear of coping with Iran. With a few exceptions involving direct contact—the Iran-contra affair and the latter stages of the Iran-Iraq War, in which the U.S. Navy struck Iranian Revolutionary Guard units and (accidentally) Iran Air Flight 655—the American response to the Islamic Republic has been to embargo it, wound it through support of Iraq during the Iran-Iraq War, and hope that the Republic dies of exhaustion before the revolution can spread.

This response has not been without effect. Though Iranian revolutionaries can still draw worldwide attention through assassinations and support for other terrorist activities, which perpetuate the illusion of a continuing national revolutionary commitment, many of the Iranian people have grown nostalgic for the pre-revolutionary past. Inside Iran the revolution is moribund among its former standard-bearers: the young urban male poor, lower- and middle-class bureaucrats, lay Islamic intellectuals (many of whom are bitterly in exile), and even a significant portion of the younger clergy.

But should the U.S. government seriously alter its approach to Iran? Iran has intermittently been a strategic focal point of Western foreign policy since the early seventeenth century. Does it remain too important to ignore even now, after the collapse of the Soviet Union and the denouement of the "Great Game"? Could the U.S. government treat with Iran and avoid making unseemly moral compromises with a regime that has unquestionably had a hand in the killing and kidnapping of American and European citizens? The death edict against the novelist Salman Rushdie is a successful attack on and intimidation of Western civilization. Should the United States choose a policy of forbearance toward Iran, given that America's past actions in Persia have been of disputable benefit to either country?

It is hard to imagine the rise of Khomeini without Shah Mohammad Reza Pahlavi's decisions to make legal reforms that gave a limited franchise to women and Bahais in 1962, to redistribute agricultural land in 1963, and to grant extraterritorial status to U.S. military advisers in Iran (thus freeing them from complying with Iranian law) in 1964. The Shah's decisions were of American inspiration; Khomeini's reaction to them signaled the beginning of the Islamic Revolution, one of the great revolutionary movements of the twentieth century and one that, like the Russian, brought unimaginable suffering to millions who had expected a better world with the fall of the old regime.

Let us look at these questions from the Iranian side. Does the government of Iranian President Ali Akbar Hashemi Rafsanjani and Khomeini's clerical successor Ali Khameneh'i stand to gain or lose by pursuing more-normal relations with the United States, including the restoration of diplomatic relations? Is "*Marg bar Amrika,*" however rhetorical the incantation, indispensable to the legitimacy of clerical rule?

The Centrality of America

THOUGH American policymakers are often accused of wanting to remake the world in their own image, the accusation miscasts America's relations with the Third World, especially with the Islamic Middle East. Even under President George Bush, who was zealous in foreign affairs, the United States remained focused primarily on the sources of its culture, Europe, and of its economic anxieties, Japan. The rapid development and even more rapid conclusion of the Gulf War against Saddam Hussein demonstrates again the fickleness of U.S. foreign policy in the Islamic world. America has stood by Israel alone—the permanent exception in the Middle East, because Israel is a Western country inextricably bound to our history both modern and ancient.

It is impossible to frame the questions of American-Iranian relations properly until we appreciate the centrality of the United States in Iranian minds. Many Iranian clerics, Khomeini in particular, well understood the battle that was taking place in the hearts and minds of Iranians. Under the Shah, Americanized culture irrevocably alienated hundreds of thousands, perhaps millions, of Iranians from their roots. The old Westernized elites, who were educated in France or England in the latter part of the past century and the first half of this one, and who often took their Persian poetry tutors with them to Europe, were replaced by Americanized Iranians, overwhelmingly from the emerging middle class, whose understanding and appreciation of traditional Persian society was considerably less.

Though fueled by the dissatisfaction of Western-educated Iranians with the Shah's corrupt regime, Khomeini's revolution was also an attempt by traditional Iranian society to halt the destructive, vulgarizing process of Westernization. The war that Khomeini declared in 1964 when he announced that the Shah's regime was illegitimate and captive to American dictates, and which he perhaps thought had been won on his return to Iran in 1979, has continued unabated.

It is a war America will win. If word went out in the streets of southern Tehran—the populous city quarter most closely associated with revolutionary fervor and the oppressed poor—that everyone could choose either a prayer at Khomeini's tomb and imminent paradise or a U.S. immigrant visa and Los Angeles, we would once again see the U.S. embassy besieged, assuming it reopened (it is now a training center for the Revolutionary Guard Corps). Many might go to Khomeini's tomb, but few would do so without first ensuring that a close family member had made his or her way to the embassy. Contrary to Khomeini's most cherished intentions, the revolution connected the United States to a pre-revolutionary golden age.

Rafsanjani may know how popular a restoration of relations with the United States would be; he might even attempt a rapprochement with the United States as a means of shoring up his support. Today the militant Iranian expatriate and internal opposition—constitutionalists, monarchists, and the Mojahedin-e Khalq (the strongest and at least formerly one of the most anti-American of the opposition groups) alike—greatly fears that the U.S. government will restore diplomatic relations with clerical Tehran.

There are many reasons why Rafsanjani might not seek a restoration of diplomatic relations: what many observers believe is a personal dislike of the United States; fear of assassination attempts by hard-core xenophobes; concern that such a dramatic move would place him in bitter opposition to Khameneh'i, who appears to be much more deeply anti-American than Rafsanjani; and a real fear for the future of the revolutionary regime, which might be philosophically and, more important, physically threatened by the reopening of the U.S. embassy. (The embassy, after all, in 1953 participated with important members of the Iranian clergy in the successful coup d'etat against Prime Minister Mohammad Mosaddeq.) The Iranians ascribe tremendous power to covert enterprises. It is one thing for the clerical regime to deal with the U.S. government from a distance; it is an entirely different matter to allow it into downtown Tehran.

But a fascinating and confusing facet of Iranians is their ability to entertain and cajole the enemy if he appears implacable and insurmountable. The United States has, in Iranian eyes, shown itself to be both. Before almighty America the Soviet Union vanished and Iraq's army was crushed in hours. This latter point made an immense impression on the Iranian clergy and military, who for years had watched Iran's soldiers in the Iran-Iraq War gain and lose

ground with Somme-like slaughter and significance.

America's military performance reminded the Iranians of the incomparable differences in execution between First World (non-Muslim) and Third World (Muslim) wars. Saddam Hussein's survival, though troubling to a growing body of Western opinion which continues to worry about U.S. staying power and strategic insight, may well reinforce Iran's fear of America. As many Iranians see it, the decision to halt the Gulf War revealed not America's ignorance and weakness but its cunning and power: America chose only to chasten its errant proxy, leav-

> **Rafsanjani may know how popular among Iranians a restoration of relations with the United States would be; he might even attempt a rapprochement.**

ing Saddam Hussein in place so that he could once again threaten the Islamic Republic.

The efforts of those in Tehran who seek to replace the American presence and money in Iran with less-intimidating assistance have not been very successful. Though Japanese investment may total many millions of dollars, it has fallen far short of the much greater amounts that the Iranians had hoped for. The Europeans are back (the Germans never left), but the levels of their investment and assistance, relative to the immense task of reconstruction in Iran, are low. A primary reason for insufficient

foreign non-American investment in Iran has been reluctance on the part of investors, particularly the Japanese, to put their resources into an unstable country with a government that has been in an undeclared state of war with the world's premier power. Iran's rulers know this very well.

But Iranian officials and many Western commentators now no longer regard the Iranian economy as hostage to a rapprochement with the United States. According to them, an American green light on reinvestment in the Islamic Republic has been rendered superfluous by the changed nature of the Middle East. Iran is no longer at the gates of Baghdad, Saddam Hussein's villainy and the Gulf War have made Iranian Shi'ism seem less menacing, and Khomeini is dead. The Islamic Republic is not so disturbing as it once was to foreign investors.

Indeed, foreign investment, including American investment, is returning to Iran. But Iranians, like Arabs, love to reify fiction into fact through language. The consummated deals are probably far fewer and smaller in scale than Iranian officials and the press claim. Foreign businessmen do feel more comfortable in Iran since the death of Khomeini, but they also remain acutely conscious of the tension, disorder, moroseness, and continuing violence of post-Khomeini Iranian life. Elemental doubts remain among even the most optimistic foreign entrepreneurs and business executives about the reliability, creditworthiness, and true intentions of their Iranian counterparts—doubts that can recur sharply when a translator of *The Satanic Verses* and a former Prime Minister are stabbed to death, or when an Iranian city erupts in a huge riot after a canceled soccer game or a change in urban housing policy.

More than four years after the end of the Iran-Iraq War the Iranian economy remains in horrible shape, and the clerical government must deal with expectations, largely formed during the last years of the Shah's rule, that the revolution would bring a better existence, especially to the *mostazafin*, the oppressed poor. Though some Iranians would probably like Iran to become an autarkic state or to trade only with those countries that pose little cultural threat (the former Soviet Union, Japan, the Koreas), the majority in Iran—including the clergy—know that to improve the economy Iran must reach out to the West, the civilization with which Iranian businessmen and functionaries are most comfortable and best connected. And Iran must become more prosperous if the mullahs are to retain any loyalty among the poor, who died by the thousands for an undelivered victory in Iran's justified war against Iraq. After last summer's presidential elections—in which he was re-elected with the lowest percentage of the vote ever for an Iranian President—the pressure on Rafsanjani has been mounting to do something about the economy, which despite certain signs of growth and excitement remains drastically underdeveloped.

Anti-clericalism, the reverse side of Persia's historical devotion to its Shi'ite divines, is rampant in post-Khomeini Iran. This hostility toward politicized clerics remains the single greatest threat to clerical rule, and its intensity is tied directly to the health of the economy. Even among the traditional merchant allies of the clergy, who were a key element of the revolutionary success in 1978, the perception grows that the political clergy have changed state corruption, which under the Shah was notorious but historically comprehensible, into a Persian nightmare in which even the best connected cannot reliably obtain safe passage through government bureaucracies.

Strengthened by the political preeminence and economic ineptitude of the mullahs, anti-clericalism intertwines ever more tightly with the defining event of the Islamic Revolution: Iran's surrender in the Iran-Iraq War. For an Iranian who suffered and survived the eight-year war, the memory of that immense struggle is divided into two chapters. The first runs from September of 1980, when Iraq invaded Iran, to May of 1982, when the Iranian army recaptured the port of Khorramshahr. With the ejection of the Iraqis from Khorramshahr in a superbly fought battle, the Iranians regained their pride and almost all their territory. Popular memory in Tehran now views those first twenty-one months as an entirely different war, one that ended in a resounding victory for the Iranian nation and the regular, formerly imperial, Iranian army. The common man credits the regular Iranian army, not the Revolutionary Guard Corps, the clergy's shock troops, with the victorious role in the Khorramshahr fighting.

The second chapter, which followed Khomeini's decision on June 21, 1982, to take the war into Iraqi territory, is now seen as the "Clerics' War," six years of useless slaughter that left the nation impoverished. The more difficult daily economic life becomes in the Islamic Republic, the more the memories of war will work against the clerics and their praetorians, the Revolutionary Guard, who enthusiastically backed Khomeini's war *à outrance*. Few Iranians will care to remember that Rafsanjani counseled against taking the war into Iraq in the summer of 1982.

Clerical Politics

IN 1985 Khomeini authorized Rafsanjani to negotiate with his two most detested "Satans," the United States and Israel. The Iranians, desperate to find an effective means of combating the Iraqis' advantages in tanks and planes, compromised principle for the possibility of obtaining American TOW and HAWK missiles. Today Rafsanjani is once again nearly desperate, while the revolutionary passion inside the country, particularly among the clerics, has faded. Is it so unlikely that Rafsanjani will one day hear Khameneh'i declare that the Great Satan has been thoroughly humbled for fourteen years by the Islamic Republic, thus vouchsafing the return of the American embassy?

Khomeini's death has compelled the Iranian clerics to devise a system of government to replace the state and constitution that were essentially created by him, and it has thrown Iranian society into a search for another *rahbar*, or supreme leader. Though Rafsanjani has attempted to assume Khomeini's political mantle, he cannot possibly hope to achieve the unassailable political stature of the man who felled the Shah. As talented as Rafsanjani is (and he is *very* talented), he has been hard pressed to coerce or oblige others to go along with his decisions. So far he has gathered sufficient power to ensure that he will be held responsible for the fate of the country, but perhaps not sufficient power to ensure that he has the authority necessary to command reliably the fractious mullahs and their crisscrossing support networks.

Rafsanjani and Khameneh'i sit atop a clerical political system that is perhaps terminally headless. We should not forget that the Ayatollah Khomeini waged two simultaneous and to date successful revolutions in Iran. One was against the Shah and the West; the other was against traditional Twelver Shi'ism (the dominant form of Shi'ism in Iran and Lebanon), which had been more or less regnant in Iran since the middle of the sixteenth century and which had discouraged the superintending participation of Iranian clerics in affairs of state.

Iran's Islamic Revolution was made by the clerical second tier—the hojjat ol-Eslams, who rank below the ayatollahs. The senior ayatollahs, other than Ali Montazeri (whom Khomeini had at one point designated as his successor), were enthusiastic fans neither of Khomeini nor of his politico-theological construct, the *velayat-e faqih* (the "guardianship of the jurist"), which was both the idea and the office that ultimately provided Khomeini with unquestioned political and religious authority. Under Khomeini young clerics like Rafsanjani, Khameneh'i, Kho'einiha, Mahdavi-Kani, and Karrubi flourished and collected power, state offices, and titles. "Ayatollah" Khameneh'i has moved very far very fast—from being a juridically unimpressive hojjat ol-Eslam in 1978 to the presidency in 1981 and thence to his current position as the nation's revolutionary guardian upon Khomeini's death, in 1989.

This domination has been gained probably at considerable cost to the traditional clerical order with its centuries-old system of education, its pedagogic standards for promotion, exclusion, loyalty, and leadership, and, perhaps most important, its financial independence from state coffers. The state-sponsored demolition of the old order was practicable because Khomeini, a grand ayatollah with immense prestige even among his clerical enemies, was at the helm. And when it came to dealing with refractory clergy Khomeini could be tougher than any Pahlavi Shah.

Iran is currently experiencing a resurgence of traditionalism in the clergy, which calls for the clerical political role to be more advisory than participatory, and a corresponding rejection of the activist mullahs who helped to lead the revolution and much of the war effort against Iraq. Rafsanjani and Khameneh'i have forcibly brought about a compromise whereby junior mullahs, juridically mediocre and of fading revolutionary glory, give orders to their more knowledgeable elders. The compromise has been tense. The reigning clerical power, be it Rafsanjani or Khameneh'i or both, cannot help feeling that as Khomeini's shadow recedes, so does the legitimacy of his *velayat* system of clerical rule. And any system of clerical rule, if it is to pretend to legitimacy, must reflect with some plausibility Twelver Shi'ism's system of juridical seniority.

The Iranian government is now headed in the opposite direction, as Rafsanjani, a hojjat ol-Eslam, tries to eliminate or reduce centers of power other than his own. Khameneh'i continues in theory to hold considerable power (according to the constitution, immensely more than Rafsanjani), but caliphs in Islamic history have done far less well than sultans in the never-ending battle for power.

Rafsanjani will have to contend with Iran's peculiar form of democracy. Unlike the Arab Muslim countries of the Middle East, Iran has a pronounced democratic current running through its nineteenth- and twentieth-century history. But this current has repeatedly been diverted and drained by Persian shahs and clerics both, and there is little evidence to suggest that Rafsanjani will reject the Pahlavi tradition of arranging and rearranging Iran's parliament according to the ruler's needs.

However Rafsanjani tries to rearrange the Iranian political landscape, he is unlikely to abandon, in rhetoric or practice, certain elements and methods of the revolution. His use of terrorism and especially assassination abroad will probably continue, for such violent diplomacy enhances the fearful stature of the clerical government both abroad and internally. It has served as an effective means—indeed, the sole means—for revolutionary Iran to take revenge against those who have insulted or harmed the Islamic Revolution. Such violent diplomacy has been indispensable to maintaining a clerical pride severely wounded from without by Iran's near-total isolation, and from within by the post-revolutionary erosion of the nation's self-esteem.

Iranian Duality

THE Islamic Republic's simultaneous pride in and embarrassment about the revolution shape Iran's foreign policy. Most of Iran's clerics, whether traditional or radical, grew up on Pahlavi dreams of Iranian glory. They desperately want Iran to be a power to be reckoned with in the Gulf, in the Middle East, and now in Central Asia. Their pride and pragmatism have persuaded them of the need to reach out, at least for Western and expatriate Iranian capital and expertise.

At the same time, the clerics' pride and fear can send Iran's assassins to the very countries where its diplomats are working strenuously to encourage foreign and expatriate access to its markets. In all probability it is not one group of moderates in the Iranian government which designs diplomatic initiatives and a separate group of radicals which is responsible for terrorism. The same men conduct both policies. Rafsanjani may or may not have initiated the assassination of Salman Rushdie's Japanese translator and the killing of former Prime Minister Shahpur Bakhtiar in Paris, but he almost certainly approved or at least acquiesced in their executions. This pattern is a quite normal one in history. The Islamic Republic's Shi'ite antecedents—the medieval Fatimid dynasty of Egypt and its scions farther east, the Assassin city-states—all continued to send out lethal revolutionary missionaries long after the revolution had weakened, if not died, at home.

At home the Iranian government is likely to scale back its reliance on anti-American sloganeering; free up travel and currency exchange for the average Iranian; loosen restrictions on the press, which by Middle Eastern standards is already vibrant; allow women more choice in their dress; alter the arbitrary and decentralized nature of state-sanctioned violence, harassment, and prosecution (the clerical regime will nevertheless continue to brutalize those who seriously threaten clerical rule); encourage Iranians once again to show hospitality to Westerners; and send its representatives overseas with beards clipped.

The situation abroad, however, will be persistently contradictory, as Khomeini's successors struggle to define within an Islamic framework Iran's mission in a changed world. The collapse of the revolution at home could encourage even moderate Islamic revolutionaries—who still, after all, define themselves and hold power by virtue of their Islamic identities—to vaunt an "Islamic" foreign policy.

The Israeli-PLO accord could well force Tehran to rethink its policy toward the West and the Arab world. It will place further stress on the clerical regime's contradictory aspirations. Tehran will relish its position as the primary remaining hard-line opponent of Israel, and will dread the fact that it has also become the center of world attention—an easily spotted target for American, Israeli, Western European, and Russian displeasure if the accord is frayed by fundamentalist agitation or terror.

If the clerics can enact the "Islamic" policy cheaply and furtively, Iran will continue to strike at the West and, perhaps more important, at Saudi Arabia, which the Iranians despise for its rival religious (Arab Sunni-Wahhabi) hubris, missionary zeal, deep pockets, and hypocritical dependence on Western powers. But the threat that Iran will continue to export revolution—as opposed to simply striking at its own expatriates—should not be exaggerated. After an initial emotional rush Iran's Shi'ite revolution has won little admiration in the surrounding Sunni Muslim world. Though Sunni radicals were profoundly inspired by Khomeini's conquest, they have been far less sympathetic to the Shi'ite state since constructed. The Islamic world has for the most part been unresponsive to Iran's yearning to play a millenarian role. Iran still sits among Saddam Hussein to the west, a permanently decomposing Afghanistan to the east, a richer and ever-proselytizing Saudi Arabia to the south, and an array of Muslim republics to the north which show little more enthusiasm than Iran's other neighbors for easing its general isolation in the Sunni Muslim world.

A Flexibly Hard Approach

HOW should the United States deal with Iran? The short answer is, Be tough but be fair. In the Islamic Middle East, where political life is usually unforgiving, hard-line foreign policies are most likely to gain respect. The more the United States can consistently pressure Iran, the more Iran's rulers will take heed and avoid provocation. However, the U.S. government should choose its conflicts with the Islamic Republic carefully. As much as the United States may want to deny Iran access to certain markets, its ability to do so, particularly since the collapse of the Soviet threat, is limited. Fear of America is a very important psychological element in American-Iranian relations. That fear, or, as it is understood in Persian, *haybat*—awe of

insuperable authority—should not be squandered on public trade disputes with the Europeans or the Japanese unless the United States has the means and the will to win the argument.

America has reason to be indignant with the Islamic Republic. The U.S. government should state loudly and often that it will not tolerate Iranian support of terrorism and that if it discovers any evidence that Iran has engaged in terrorist activity, it will punish Iran financially and continue to impede in various ways Iran's commercial dealings with America's allies. It should resolutely stand behind Salman Rushdie, promoting his case at the United

> **Anti-clericalism, which is the reverse side of Persia's historical devotion to its Shi'ite divines, has become rampant in post-Khomeini Iran.**

Nations and attacking the Islamic basis of Khomeini's death warrant. In defense of free speech and to remind Iran's mullahs of America's undiminished psychological reach into their country, the U.S. government should provide sufficient funding to Voice of America for round-the-clock shortwave radio broadcasts in Persian and should announce its willingness to support expatriate Iranian television programming accessible in Iran by satellite dish. The U.S. Navy should frequently park its Indian Ocean fleet uncomfortably close to the Persian Gulf and send its submarines and fly its aircraft even closer.

Rafsanjani and the clerics in general

are not wild-eyed zealots. More often than not, the zealots eventually found martyrdom in the eight-year war with Iraq; their deaths are a significant reason for the present radical eclipse in Iran. Rafsanjani knows that the Iranian government can no longer call half a million young men onto the streets of Tehran to attack America. It could probably call barely 10,000. Rafsanjani has innumerable economic problems, and perhaps not much time to handle them; he knows that "*Marg bar Amrika*" will do him little good with his own citizens or with the foreign community he hopes to draw in for investment.

America should be firm with any ally that allows the Iranians to sidestep choices that they fear could cause them to make compromises in their revolutionary doctrine. America should also realize that Iran's contact with other Western countries, like its eventual contact with the United States, can have a corrosive effect on the revolutionary ethos and a moderating effect on the Iranians.

America should treat harshly those countries that sell weaponry to Iran's clerics. But it should perhaps do no more than grimace if a Western ally expands Iran's power grid, builds a dam, or supplies computer equipment to Iran's universities or telephone equipment to its cities. The U.S. government should be wary of depicting Iran as it once depicted the Soviet Union. Communist Russia was a threat to the entire free world; clerical Iran is not.

Despite the rhetoric of the Islamic Republic, Iran is a poor country with little continuing revolutionary appeal outside the Shi'ite world. Not Iran but Saudi Arabia, an American ally, has been the most troublesome missionary of Islamic fundamentalism throughout the subcontinent, the Middle East, and Central Asia. Clerical Iran has never been a totalitarian country, even in its darkest period in the early eighties. The contacts that have existed between its people and the West go far beyond what once existed between the West and the Soviet Union. Though Rafsanjani has decided that Western assistance is required to rebuild Iran, he probably made that decision with trepidation. He is well aware of the extensive contact that has persisted between Iran's citizens and their more prosperous relatives in the West. In addition, thousands of young Iranians are studying again in the West, primarily in the United States; a study of recent Iranian history shows the possible repercussions of a foreign education.

America should be careful not to obstruct through sanctions the flow of Western information and culture that continues to seduce Iran's youth away from the revolution. Lord Curzon believed that Iran's character has always oscillated between "the bigot's rage . . . and the agnostic's indifference." The revolutionary rage in Iran is well over. What has followed is probably not indifference.

The Iranian government has made its peace, at blinding speed, with France and Russia, the two primary suppliers of weapons to Saddam Hussein. Iran has legitimate reasons to want to re-arm, heavily. The United States has no reason to support Iran's plans to re-arm or to supply itself with nuclear or biological and chemical weapons, and is fully justified in preventing—or, more accurately, delaying—Iran's acquisition of weapons of mass destruction. But the U.S. government should admit, at least to itself, that such armament is understandable given the hell Iran endured in its war with Iraq. Theories of deterrence work just as well between Muslim states as they do between liberal democracies and communist dictatorships.

The Inevitable Contact

THE United States should probably not seek direct contact with Rafsanjani's government. There is little reason for it. Iran has several ways to reach the United States if it chooses to, and the United States has the same options. Any U.S. attempts to seek such contact explicitly, with the intention of holding further dialogue or resuming diplomatic relations, would probably seem to be either weakness (the Iranians would assume they had something the Americans wanted) or part of a larger effort to entrap or diminish Iran's clerical government.

Iran has always been at the forefront of the Islamic mind. The Islamic Republic's evolution has had and will have significant influence on Muslims throughout the world. In addition, Iran's ecumenical competition with Saudi Arabia may affect the price of oil. Rafsanjani may be aware that the United States might quickly make amends to Iran and restore, at a minimum, diplomatic relations if he were to initiate the process. Rafsanjani *will* begin the process one of these days, but not obviously. He will certainly explore the possibility through private emissaries, foreshadowing an inevitably more complicated and diffident public overture.

Though the U.S. government would do well to approach any such contact with considerable caution, the United States should not automatically assume that it will be hoodwinked by the crafty Persians. Iranians are an exceptionally clever, complicated people, but they do not view themselves as being particularly clever with Westerners. An Iranian will assume that the Westerner, certainly if he is English and probably if he is American, will get the better of any deal—just as Americans assume that Iranians will be dangerously wily. Iranians are not born crafty. They get there through the school of hard knocks, and most of them, clerics included, view their dealings with foreigners as an unending school of hard knocks.

The hard question for the United States will be what to say and do on the day when Rafsanjani declares America to be sufficiently chastened for a direct, unconditional American-Iranian dialogue. It would be ironic if the renewal of the United States' relationship with Iran signaled not the end of the Islamic Revolution but Iran's most astute compromise.

Khomeini and his successors have done a poor job of banishing America from the minds of the Iranian people. One of these days they will try to co-opt it by renewing contact. When the Revolutionary Guards move out of the former American embassy in Tehran and American diplomats move back in, American-Iranian diplomacy will once again become the pre-eminent topic of conversation in the Islamic Middle East. If the current Iranian government survives the encounter, Washington may bestow a new legitimacy, which the ruling clerics desperately need—an irony that neither Washington nor Tehran is likely to relish.

A Global Militant Network

Support for radical Islamic groups is far-flung

Steve Coll and Steve LeVine

Washington Post Foreign Service

The new generation of militant Islamic groups involved in bombings and attacks on governments from the Middle East to New York depends on an informal network of support centers scattered from the Persian Gulf to the United States, according to government officials and Islamic activists.

Sudan, Iran, Saudi Arabia, the smaller Persian Gulf kingdoms, Pakistan, Afghanistan, the former Yugoslav republics, Europe and the United States all today contain such informal support centers where Islamic radicals can find money, haven or ideological inspiration—despite efforts by some local governments during the past few months to clamp down.

Connections run between these scattered centers in the form of international charitable or evangelical institutions, charismatic personalities and informal financial transfers. The most common source of financial support is private donations or charitable contributions by wealthy Saudis or other rich Muslims, estimated by participants in the movements to amount to tens of millions of dollars each year.

"Islamic movement finances come through genuine people," says an activist in the London office of a pro-Iranian Islamic group. "That sort of money, even if it is from someone corrupted, he is given the money for Allah—it is not for show."

In any event, the activist concludes confidently, "When you're talking about the grass-roots movements, you don't need so much money."

The variety and complexity of the backing is typical of the problems that frustrate Middle East regimes struggling with dynamic, sometimes violent Islamic movements—Egypt, Israel, Algeria, Tunisia and, to a lesser degree, Saudi Arabia. In this world, participants say, hierarchy is rare, audited accounts are rarer, and the only truly unifying force is a broad, ideological commitment to political Islam.

The young radicals arrested in the recent terrorism cases in New York appear to have constituted one grouping in this broader sphere. The defendants came to New York from diverse parts of the Muslim world. Some had links to institutions involved in the galvanizing wars in Afghanistan and the Balkans. Some were drawn together by the charismatic preaching of the Egyptian radical Sheik Omar Abdel Rahman, spiritual adviser to Egypt's Islamic Group, who advocates borderless religious war against infidels.

Given the splintered, ideological and often voluntary character of external support for contemporary Islamic radicalism, can official efforts to disrupt the Islamic movement's centers of external support around the world succeed? And even if they did succeed, would such disruption make much difference to the progress of Islamic militancy in the Middle East and elsewhere?

Clearly, a number of prominent officials in Middle Eastern and Western governments involved think so. They and some independent analysts believe that violent elements in the Islamic movement make up a tiny, unpopular minority that can be marginalized by internal suppression and attacks on external sanctuaries and flows of financial support.

But activists in the movements, supported by other independent analysts, argue that this is just wishful thinking based on a profound misunderstanding of the Islamic movement's popular base. Those advocating violence may indeed be a minority, this argument goes, but attempts to repress them or to put pressure on the wide, essentially peaceful world of Islamic charity because some money reaches revolutionaries will only further radicalize the Muslim world.

"They're playing into their hands," says Rachid Ghannouchi, exiled leader of Tunisia's radical Nahda, or Renaissance, movement. "The people angry and divided will be enlarged. Such money and such help paid by individuals in the [Persian] Gulf has been used in relief and in solving indirectly the problems the governments face."

In part because of the recent terrorism cases in New York, one of the pan-Islamic revival's loose radical groupings most worrisome to secular or pro-Western governments in the Middle East is the multinational, itinerant circle of young Arab volunteers who have been directly involved in religiously inspired violence in Afghanistan, Bosnia or Middle East streets.

After the World Trade Center bombing in February, several regional governments attempted to clamp down in a coordinated fashion on centers of support for these radical war veterans, according to officials.

From *The Washington Post National Weekly Edition,* August 16-22, 1993, pp. 6-7. © 1993 by The Washington Post. Reprinted by permission.

BASES OF SUPPORT

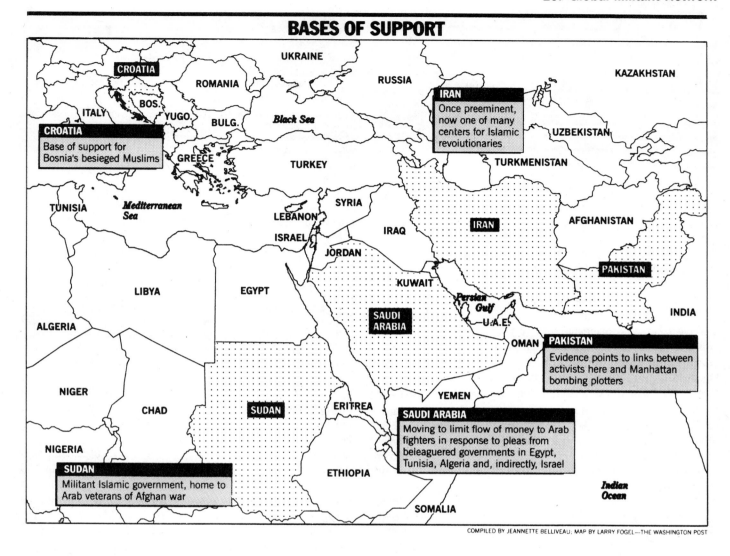

CROATIA
Base of support for Bosnia's besieged Muslims

IRAN
Once preeminent, now one of many centers for Islamic revolutionaries

PAKISTAN
Evidence points to links between activists here and Manhattan bombing plotters

SAUDI ARABIA
Moving to limit flow of money to Arab fighters in response to pleas from beleaguered governments in Egypt, Tunisia, Algeria and, indirectly, Israel

SUDAN
Militant Islamic government, home to Arab veterans of Afghan war

COMPILED BY JEANNETTE BELLIVEAU; MAP BY LARRY FOGEL—THE WASHINGTON POST

The moves followed pleas from Egypt, Tunisia, Algeria and, indirectly, Israel, they say. These governments believe that support provided to Arab fighters abroad, and related private charity funds, are leaking to the Islamic insurgencies they face at home.

The main centers of attention in this clampdown have been Pakistan, Sudan, Croatia and Saudi Arabia.

In April, Saudi Arabia announced a ban on private charitable contributions sent overseas without approval from Riyadh's generally pro-Western government.

The announcement marked a public reversal of Saudi policy during the 1980s. In those years the Saudi treasury poured at least $2 billion into the Afghan resistance against communism. Along with other gulf states, Riyadh sent what Western analysts estimate to have been several hundred million dollars annually to the secular Palestine Liberation Organization.

The kingdom also bankrolled Arab volunteer fighters in Afghanistan through its official evangelical charity, the Muslim World League, according to a charity official and others. In addition, the league, which has a reported government budget of about $30 million annually but also relies on private contribu-

tions, funded peaceful institutions associated with Algeria's Islamic movement and Islamic institutions in the Israeli-occupied West Bank.

Now such official funding has been stopped or drastically reduced in some cases, according to many Western and Middle East officials and Islamic activists interviewed, as well as published statements by members of the Saudi royal family. Those interviewed cite several reasons: Riyadh is troubled by vocal Islamic radicals at home; the Saudi royal family is unnerved by the recent wave of violent Islamic insurgency in Egypt and elsewhere; and Saudi Arabia is furious at Palestinians and Islamic radicals, past recipients of Saudi largess, who criticized Riyadh's handling of the Persian Gulf War.

"They realize they are contributing to the creation of a Muslim movement—training people," says one radical Islamic activist. Adds a Muslim World League official. "The government cannot have the same policy all the time for all places. Now it's a different time everywhere."

The April announcement marked an apparent attempt by Riyadh to extend this new outlook to private funding by wealthy Saudis whose activities were earlier encouraged or tolerated.

Some of these private Saudis have themselves become radicalized and support radical movements outside the kingdom, for a variety of reasons. Some oppose their government's undemocratic royal autocracy and see themselves as part of an international Islamic movement battling dictatorships. Others are motivated less by politics than by religious faith, responding in part to the Saudi government's longtime preaching about the righteous imperatives of pure Islamic law, which some Saudi theologians interpret to mean that injustice and secularism should be opposed by force, if necessary.

One wealthy Saudi businessman who evidently has adopted this outlook is Osama Binladen, offspring of one of the kingdom's best-known and most prosperous business families.

During the 1980s, Binladen answered the call for "holy war" against communism in Afghanistan, traveled to the front lines and bankrolled Egyptian, Saudi, Jordanian, Palestinian, Algerian and other Arab volunteer fighters, according to Arabs and Pakistanis involved in the war.

Today Binladen lives in exile in a posh neighborhood of Khartoum, Sudan, building roads and airports for Sudan's new radical Islamic government, financing a lavish guest house for itinerant Arab veterans of the Afghan conflict and lecturing at times on revolutionary Islam, according to Sudanese businessmen, officials and diplomats. Several hundred Arab veterans of the Afghan war are estimated to have sought haven in Sudan, diplomats say.

Widely described as unwelcome in his native Saudi Arabia, Binladen is seen by Egypt's authoritarian government as "the anti-Christ," as a Western official puts it. The Saudi financier is alleged by Egyptian and Western officials to provide funds to some Afghan war veterans accused of sponsoring anti-government violence in Egypt.

Binladen's aides deny this. Binladen himself declined to be interviewed. A Sudanese state security officer posted at his office in Khartoum says Binladen fears arrest or assassination by Egyptian, Saudi or Western government agents.

Arguably, the best way to think about Binladen's multistory Khartoum guest house is not as a centralized, string-pulling headquarters of Egyptian or other radicalism, but rather as one among many scattered centers of gravity where militant Islamic radicals may find haven, succor or support.

Binladen is a rich radical with a following. "They don't believe in organizations," says Hamza Hasan, an exiled Saudi who edits an anti-government magazine in London. "They think they are a *jamaa* (an Arabic word that means "group" or "society" and often connotes loose organization but firm commitment to religion)."

The vast majority of the 22 Islamic charities registered in Zagreb, Croatia's capital and a base of support for Bosnia's besieged Muslims, are apolitical humanitarian groups or evangelical societies based in Persian Gulf countries. There is no evidence that these groups support violence. Rather, many provide needed relief to Bosnian Muslims and other civilians amid dangerous conditions.

However, among the Islamic charities active in Zagreb are the state-run Iranian Red Crescent, which has been caught sending arms to Bosnian Muslims, as well as the Alkifah

Refugee Center of Brooklyn, N.Y., and its sister group, the Services Office, based in Peshawar, Pakistan. These last two have in the recent past sponsored Islamic volunteer fighters, according to Pakistani and Arab activists.

The Peshawar-based Services Office has been for a decade a principal gateway for Arab volunteers seeking to join the Afghan war, according to activists in Peshawar. Abdel Rahman, the Radical Egyptian cleric, has met with officials at both the Services Office and the Alkifah Center and has been described as close to them.

Indeed, there is evidence that some of Abdel Rahman's followers accused in the New York cases moved between these centers of support in the United States, Peshawar and Zagreb. One of the main figures accused in the alleged plot to bomb the U.N. headquarters and other targets, Sudanese-born Siddig Mohammed Siddig Ali, telephoned his sister from New York in May and told her that he was headed for the Bosnian conflict, according to the sister, Nur Ali, interviewed in Khartoum.

The Alkifah Center's Zagreb office is housed in a modern, two-story building staffed by Arabs who identified themselves as Algerians. The office contains booklets, audiotapes and videocassettes produced by Abdullah Azzam, the charismatic Palestinian who ran the Peshawar Services Office for almost a decade, recruited Arabs to the Afghan war with widely circulated sermons about the need for Islamic holy war, and helped those who answered the call to join the conflict. Azzam was murdered in Peshawar in 1989.

In Zagreb, the Alkifah deputy director, Hassan Hakim, says that his volunteers were engaged only in helping about 100 Bosnian refugee families and that the Azzam material he stocked reflected only an "ideological" affiliation. He says his center was connected only with the Brooklyn branch and received financial contributions from the United States. Hakim claims not to have heard about recent publicity concerning links between the Brooklyn center and some defendants in the New York terrorism cases.

Yet there is some evidence that the former Yugoslav republics have become a haven for some Egyptian radicals.

A European-based Islamic activist involved with the Zagreb charities said Egyptian Islamic radicals were among those involved with the Zagreb nexus and that Egypt's government "was concerned that Egyptian Islamists were being funded through the back door in Bosnia." A Cairo sympathizer with Egypt's Islamic violent radical groups says there were indeed members of those groups in Zabreg and Bosnia.

Egypt's interior minister, Alfi, says he had "no information" about the matter, characterizing such accounts as "a possibility" subject to the results of "many investigations . . . not yet completed."

Among all these centers of external support for Islamic radicalism today, one is distinct from the rest: Iran, where the Islamic revolutionary government is openly committed to the export of its radical ideas around the Middle East. Yet rather than a headquarters of pan-Islamic militancy, Iran is better understood as an active but in some respects handicapped competitor for influence in the resurgent Islamic revival.

That Tehran has both clients and ambitions in the ongoing Islamic revival is widely acknowledged.

Across from the Foreign Ministry in north Tehran is an old government building housing protocol offices for foreign diplomats and branch offices for two radical Islamic movements—Hezbollah, from Lebanon, and Hamas, from the Israeli-occupied West Bank and Gaza Strip.

As they enter, ambassadors from Western countries and moderate Arab regimes doing business with the protocol officers step to the right, while representatives of the Islamic movements step to the left.

The exact amounts of Tehran's financial transfers to these and other Islamic groups overseas are unknown. Iran's parliament has earmarked $20 million in aid for the Palestinian cause, according to Arab sources in Iran. But Israelis estimate that no more than several million dollars has been reaching Hamas annually from Iran, channeled through Tehran's overseas Islamic propagation organizations. Considerably larger sums, as well as training and logistical support, are thought to reach Hezbollah and its terrorist affiliate, Islamic Jihad, in Lebanon.

Broadly, Iran's strengths as a player in the pan-Islamic revival are seen to be the inspirational power of its original revolution, its track record in funding and supporting strikes against Western and Israeli interests, and its open rhetorical embrace of radical Islam in all its variations. "We do not have any centrally organized support structure for the revival of Islamic sentiment in the world," says Ahmed Javad Larijani, a member of the Iranian parliament and vice chairman of its foreign relations committee. "But we are putting a lot of effort to revive an idea, which we believe will be a stimulus."

Yet Iran's revolution remains infused with two elements that are anathemas to many radical Islamic Arabs: Iran's Shiite Islamic faith, predominant in Iran but a minority sect elsewhere, and its Persian nationalism, for centuries a bane to Middle Eastern Arabs. Moreover, Iran's overheated economy is bleeding cash, a problem seen by Western and regional officials as cramping Tehran's ability to fund clients and sympathizers abroad.

The most prominent of these clients are Hezbollah and Islamic Jihad, whose members share Iran's Shiite faith and revolutionary zeal. Among other things, Islamic Jihad has claimed credit for the March 1992 bombing of the Israeli Embassy in Buenos Aires, which killed 29 people.

Iran's many-faceted foundations, known as *bonyads,* are one key aspect of its institutional and financial support for these groups. At least a half-dozen such foundations established after the 1979 revolution operate in a nebulous twilight zone between the public and private sectors that is peculiar to Iran's post-revolutionary Islamic regime, according to diplomats, businessmen and Western analysts.

The foundations were established as charity organizations to help the downtrodden and to propagate the ideals of the revolution. Now they are multibillion-dollar conglomerates owning real estate and hundreds of companies, industries and hotels around the country. They say they need the money to keep caring for the needy and the families of war victims. Yet not all their work is charitable.

Foundation leaders often travel with diplomatic passports, and Western analysts see their overseas offices, particularly in Lebanon, as a vehicle for transferring money to groups such as Hezbollah. Their budgets are enormous. An official in the Bonyad Mustazaafan, the largest, says his foundation's budget amounts to one-quarter of Iran's gross national product. Few are in a position to check such an estimate, since the foundations are accountable to few and are seen as virtually ungovernable, diplomats and Iranians say.

The nominal line of authority for the foundations runs through structures devoted to Islamic propaganda worldwide that report ultimately to Iran's supreme spiritual leader, Ayatollah Ali Khamenei. Israeli analysts believe this is the structure that sends money to its radical Islamic movement, Hamas. Yet Western analysts say there is another line of command, running through the ministry of intelligence to the office of President Ali Akbar Hashemi Rafsanjani. This chain is seen as more directly responsible for state-sponsored terrorist strikes overseas.

Veteran diplomats in Tehran, for example, say that Islamic Jihad of Palestine, a small, cell-based, violence-prone group that operates mainly in the Israeli-occupied Gaza Strip, has links to the Iranian intelligence ministry.

What has been the recent effect of stepped-up diplomatic pressure on Iran and the coordinated clampdown against other, often Saudi-linked external support centers for radical Islam? Activists involved say that although the moves have had some impact, the effects have not been dramatic.

"No one can control the flow of money from Saudi Arabia," says one Saudi. "It is not one person—it is a thousand. . . . Money comes to us from inside Saudi Arabia. We have private talks with businessmen. Sometimes directly, sometimes indirectly. But it comes."

Radicals Gain Strength in Horn of Africa

Muslim Fundamentalist Groups Stepping Up Armed Attacks, Political Expansionism

Jennifer Parmelee

Special to The Washington Post

ADDIS ABABA, Ethiopia—Political activism and armed attacks by radical Islamic groups have been slowly but steadily on the rise in the Horn of Africa, increasing the potential for instability in a region already tormented by poverty and ethnic conflict.

Violent anti-government campaigns by Islamic fundamentalist groups in North Africa, particularly in Egypt and Algeria, as well as the presence of an activist, hard-line Islamic regime in Sudan, have raised fears that the stirrings in the Horn presage the region's emergence as the new battleground for Islamic radicals, according to dozens of sources around the region.

"The Horn so far has proven a barrier to hard-core Islamic fundamentalism like that in Sudan," said a senior Western diplomat with long regional experience. "If North Africa succumbs, [the Horn] could very well be the next front line."

The sources, from regional governments and aid and diplomatic communities, cite accumulating anecdotal evidence to portray a creeping threat in Somalia; the self-declared "republic" of Somaliland in northwestern Somalia; Ethiopia; Eritrea; and Djibouti; and Kenya. Yemen, across the Red Sea from the Horn, also has experienced a sharp rise in Islamic fundamentalist activity.

The sources cited organizations such as the Eritrean Jihad; the Ogaden National Liberation Front, in Ethiopia; and the Muslim Brotherhood Wahadiya in Somalia. They pointed to ambushes of gov-

BY JAY LIEBENOW FOR THE WASHINGTON POST

ernment troops in Ethiopia and Eritrea and to a striking increase in the number of Muslim women—whose traditional dress is modest but casual—now wearing Islamic head and body coverings as evidence of an increasingly assertive fundamentalist presence.

Some groups have recruited experienced preachers and fighters from *mujaheddin* and Muslim Brotherhood organizations in Egypt, Pakistan, Afghanistan, Yemen, Sudan and Saudi Arabia to press their agenda around the Horn, the sources said.

From *The Washington Post*, January 5, 1994, p. A26. © 1994 by The Washington Post. Reprinted by permission.

Most of the financial support for the radical groups, as well as some weapons, is traced to wealthy merchants in Saudi Arabia although there is no evidence the Saudi government is involved, according to local government sources and Western intelligence agencies. They said Sudan—the subject of close attention from the West since the implication of Sudanese suspects in the World Trade Center bombing—and its ally, Iran, also lend support but cannot match even private Saudi financial resources.

In addition to being home to millions of Muslims, the largely impoverished Horn in recent years has been repeatedly swept by hunger and violence. Somalia, without a government since early 1991, is considered particularly vulnerable to a hard-line Islamic movement seeming to offer security, structure and answers.

"It's a movement born of frustration and steeped in need," an Ethiopian government source said. "It will succeed only if we fail to address our social problems, which means our fight is not a military fight, it is an economic and political one."

The fundamentalist movement "is a colossus with feet of clay," the source added. "But unless it is handled well, it can hurt us all on the way down."

The latest alarm was sounded by the president of Africa's newest state, Eritrea, in a New Year message. Issaias Afwerki charged that the fundamentalist Eritrean Jihad had sought to attack Eritrea from base camps in Sudan. He said 20 Eritrean Jihad fighters were killed by his soldiers in the Dec. 16 attempt and several of the dead were Islamic mercenaries from other nations who fought beside Afghan mujaheddin rebels against Soviet forces.

Most cross-border incidents have been comparatively minor and their injuries minimal, Eritrean officials said. Eritrean Jihad reportedly commands only a few hundred members, but it recruits from Sudan's large Eritrean refugee population, so its potential strength is unknown.

Issaias said the source of the problem is Sudan. He said Eritrean officials had tried repeatedly to resolve the issue through diplomatic channels.

Sudan denied that an attack had been launched from its territory, the Associated Press reported Sunday from Khartoum, Sudan's capital. Foreign Minister Hussein Suleiman Abu Salih said his government would not tolerate any action that would hurt relations with Eritrea.

Eritrea's relationship with Sudan is highly sensitive, since the Khartoum government provided a base for the Eritrean rebels who won a 30-year war of independence in 1991 and now run the new country. Ethiopia's leaders, also victors in a war of rebellion, similarly relied on Sudanese support in their civil war.

But any surface friendliness between Sudan and its neighbors, especially Eritrea, has worn thin amid Khartoum's perceived meddling in other nations' affairs. Expulsions of Sudanese and other Arab nationals suspected of recruiting for fundamentalist causes have increased.

At least half of Ethiopia's and Eritrea's populations are Muslims, now experiencing their greatest religious advances in centuries; most of the rest are Christians. The governments of both nations are avowedly secular, have strong ties with the West and are outwardly committed to developing multi-party democracy—paths viewed as threatening by Sudan, observers say. Also anathema to Sudan are Eritrea's and Ethiopia's friendly relations with Israel.

Western diplomats and regional sources accuse Sudan's government, headed by Lt. Gen. Omar Bashir but dominated by the National Islamic Front, of providing weapons, food and money to radical Islamic groups in the region, some posing as charities, to promote the establishment of Islamic states.

Khartoum, which denies helping armed movements in the region, has expressed a desire to see its brand of Islam spread across the region and into sub-Saharan Africa.

Sudan's government sees itself as a new role model that "embodies the values of Islam and the tools of modernity," said Ghazi Atabani, influential state minister for political affairs. He said Sudan offers a viable alternative to what he calls "the likely failure" of Africa's democratic experiments. "It's not meant to destabilize others, of course," he said in an interview. "But we know that this is a model that erodes others as it grows. That's a natural phenomenon of life."

Sudan's alleged beneficiaries include the Islamic Front for the Liberation of Oromia in Ethiopia and the Islamic Union Party, known as Itihaad, a Somalia-based military group that has spread its influence from Djibouti through Somalia and eastern Ethiopia and into coastal Kenya. The bulk of Itihaad support, however, is said to be channeled through Saudi sources.

Itihaad, the largest and most active radical Islamic group known to be operating in the Horn, is run by Yusuf Ali Warsame of Burao, a town in northwestern Somalia. The group seeks to unite Somali-speaking populations separated by the Horn's colonial borders and forge them into an Islamic republic.

It has opened training camps for the many idle young men in Somalia and aided factional leader Mohamed Farah Aideed in his fight last summer against the U.S.-dominated U.N. force there.

In June 1992, more than 1,000 Itihaad fighters swept into Boosaaso, in northeastern Somalia, captured about 40 members of the Somali faction that controls the area and declared an Islamic republic. In the ensuing battle, up to 200 factional militiamen and 500 Itihaad fighters were killed.

In eastern Ethiopia along the Somali border, Itihaad has confronted Ethiopian government forces with increasing frequency. A month ago, near the town of Gode in the Ogaden desert, three Itihaad attacks killed four soldiers and wounded seven, officials said.

Last year, with the help of local elders, the government persuaded Itihaad to stay away from towns and from roads used by food convoys. Itihaad leaders later rejected any agreement and called for the government's overthrow.

"It seems they have gained confidence," said Kinfe Gebre-Mehdin, vice minister of internal affairs. "But we have not yet started operations against them. We are still trying the path of negotiation."

Ethiopian officials say Itihaad would be little without its Saudi benefactors, and they wonder why Washington does not press its Saudi allies to cut off assistance to the group. According to U.S. officials, the Saudi government denies supporting fundamentalist groups but says it cannot control all its wealthy citizens.

From Peace-Keeping to Peace Enforcement
The Somalia Precedent

US freedom of action appears to be the price the UN has paid for its Somalia operation. A year later, many Somalis regard the UN as another faction and Admiral Howe as another warlord.

Patrick Gilkes

Patrick Gilkes has worked for many years in the Horn of Africa as a journalist for the BBC and other media, and visited Somalia as a consultant for Save the Children.

The US decision to intervene in Somalia in December 1992 came well after the two-year-old crisis had finally hit the headlines. The power vacuum that followed the flight of Siad Barre from Mogadishu in January 1991, and the subsequent civil war in the capital, particularly the fighting between November 1991 and March 1992, attracted little attention despite the country's collapse into anarchy.[1]

UN Security Council Resolution 733 in January 1992 called for a cease-fire to allow for the distribution of food aid, shortly after an inept visit by UN envoy James Jonah had failed to halt the fighting in Mogadishu. UN Secretary-General Butros Butros-Ghali's appreciation of Somalia as a test case for the future of UN military intervention

Inspecting troops at the May 1993 transition from UNITAF to UNOSOM II are Lt. Gen. Cevik Bir of Turkey (second from left), and US Marine Lt. Gen. Robert Johnson (third from left).

UN Photo/M. Grant

From *Middle East Report*, No. 185, November/December 1993, pp. 21-24. © 1993 by MERIP/Middle East Report, 1500 Massachusetts Avenue, NW, #119, Washington, DC 20005. Reprinted by permission.

pushed the intervention decision forward. Muhammad Sahnoun, Butros-Ghali's special representative in Somalia from April to October 1992, accepted the need for intervention, but wanted it carefully prepared and agreed to at the local level. Sahnoun sharply criticized some UN agencies and officials, including Jonah, James Grant of UNICEF, and Jan Eliasson, Under Secretary for Humanitarian Affairs.

Sahnoun was forced to resign in October 1992, clearing the way for the appointment of Ismail Kittani whose main role was to prepare for intervention, though the worst of the dying had ended a couple of months earlier and the cease-fire in Mogadishu had been holding, if tenuously. The immediate problem of famine relief, in the area around Baidoa to the west of Mogadishu, had also eased; the ICRC had been quietly landing food south of the capital and sending it inland, if sometimes after extensive negotiations.

Setting Precedent

Sahnoun's fall, however, coincided with changes in US policy. In mid-1992, Senator Nancy Kassebaum's well-publicized visit to Somalia and her public call for the US to provide active support for UN operations led to a series of European ministerial and celebrity visits, putting Somalia firmly on the international circuit. Candidate Bill Clinton seized on the issue as evidence of President Bush's failures in foreign policy. Just before the Republican Convention in August, Bush announced an airlift of emergency food. After an embarrassing row with the Kenyan government, not informed in advance of the US decision to use Kenyan airfields, Operation Provide Relief eventually flew in some 28,000 tons of food.

Bush's decision for military intervention was announced just before Thanksgiving along with a press campaign carefully orchestrated to limit criticism. The President was reportedly appalled by accounts of banditry and theft of aid supplies, and the arrival of US forces did make food distribution in some areas easier.[2]

The decision came too late to influence the US election results, but it fit into Bush's idea of a world in which the US can and should intervene at will. The Pentagon saw it as a way to help protect the military budget, particularly as Clinton agreed to the intervention in advance, though he may not have realized just how high the price would be.[3] General Colin Powell, chairman of the Joint Chiefs of Staff, had some reservations, based on what he saw as the need to send sufficient numbers and on the necessity for US troops to be under US command. Command of the UN Transitional Assistance Force (UNITAF), came under the field commander, Marine Lt. General Robert Johnston, who was also given the freedom to take action without prior reference to the local UN authority. This set a significant precedent, which the US managed to continue after UNITAF metamorphosed into UNOSOM2 (UN Operation for Somalia) in May 1993. Now the US provides the deputy commander of UNOSOM2 forces (to which the US contributes less than 4,000 men, mainly in logistics), and Johnston in turn also has an entirely separate position as the commander of the 1,300-man Rapid Intervention Force that has carried out most of the active operations in Mogadishu. During the changeover from UNITAF to UNOSOM2, the new UN commander, Turkish Lt. General Cevik Bir, had an office only a few paces away from Johnston. Indeed, they largely shared a staff. Butros-Ghali also appointed retired US Admiral Jonathan Howe, who served in Bush's National Security Council and was involved in the original US decision to intervene, as the UN Special Representative. In New York, US representatives regularly attend the thrice-weekly meetings of the UN Policy Group on Somalia, and the daily Operational Task Force meetings.

US freedom of action appears to be the price the UN has had to pay for its expanded operations in Somalia. With Resolution 837, peacekeeping has become peace-enforcement under Chapter 7 of the UN Charter for the first time. (The Secretary-General is trying to create a Department of Peace Operations to cover all present aspects of peacekeeping, humanitarian operations, elections supervision and even quick reaction forces.)

The Islamist Dimension

One other factor seems to have been behind US policy. While Somalia has only a limited strategic value for the US, despite the air and sea facilities of Berbera in the north and Mogadishu in the south, and Islamism was never a substantial force in pre-1991 Somalia, the anarchy before and after the fall of Siad Barre gave it a considerable boost. The main Islamist proponent has been al-Itahad al-Islami, which first came to prominence in June 1992 when it temporarily seized control of a number of towns in the northeast and held the port of Bosasso for two weeks. Al-Itahad is believed to have links with the International Islamic Relief Organization and the Muslim World League, which organized schools and ran food distribution centers in Merca, Mogadishu and Lugh in the northwest.[4] Another group with links to al-Itahad is al-Da'wa al-Islamiyya of Sudan, which ran feeding centers and mother-and-child clinics in Mogadishu. Sudan, which sent relief aid to Somalia twice in the last year, was added in August to Washington's list of countries accused of sponsoring terrorism.

While the reality of al-Itahad's power is small, its influence has increased greatly in the last couple of years, partly as a response to clan conflicts. The US sees the possibility of "the infection" spreading to Kenya, where the growth of Islam in the coastal constituencies has been considerable, and Ethiopia, where the Islamic Unity Party (known to have close links with al-Itahad and with Sudan's Hassan Turabi) clashed with government forces in 1992.

The Required Villain

On arrival, US Special Envoy Robert Oakley made it clear that any move to disarm the "warlords" would be "too imperialistic."[5] This was a major disappointment for Somalis, who had expected and hoped for large-scale disarmament. Oakley also said the US wanted new Somali leaders to emerge naturally. Here again the US managed to disappoint, by concentrating on leaders of existing factions and warlords.

US administrations seem to have

difficulty understanding ethnic or territorial disputes, and usually look for the "wicked leader" whose removal would provide the simple solution. While Oakley remained the US representative, General Muhammad Siad "Morgan," a son-in-law of Siad Barre, played this role. He had been responsible for the destruction of the northern city of Hargeisa in 1988.[6] Today it is General Muhammad Farah Aideed, the warlord who had been most skeptical of the UN/US role and who is now blamed for the death of 350,000 Somalis last year (a figure plucked out of thin air).

Certainly Aideed bears responsibility for the situation in which famine conditions occurred, but so do Ali Mahdi and several of the other faction leaders and warlords currently negotiating with the US (including Generals Morgan, Gebiyu, Ahmed Warsame and Gani, all late of Siad Barre's armies). It is more than likely that Aideed was responsible for the attack on Pakistani troops on June 5, but the UN launched several days of bombing raids in reprisal on June 12, six days before it launched a formal investigation into the incident.

Aideed (who himself has called several times for an independent inquiry into that clash) has a lot to answer for. But it is difficult to escape the conclusion that his attempts to stand up to the UN and the US lie at the root of their opposition. Later UN responses, carried out by US Rapid Deployment Units, have included the June 17 attacks on the Digfer Hospital and the July 12 bombing of a house where dozens of clan elders, meeting to discuss peace moves, were killed. "Increasingly, Somalis regard UNOSOM as another faction and Admiral Howe as another warlord," concluded the London-based African Rights group in a July 1993 report.[7]

Clan Terms

Aideed and Morgan, as with all Somali leaders, can only be seen in clan terms.[8] Aideed is from the Habr Gidir, one of the main clans within the Hawiye, the clan family which controls Mogadishu and much of central Somalia. Morgan is from the Majerteen, one of the Darod clans, which include the Marehan, the clan of Siad Barre. The history of southern Somalia, and of the Somali state after 1960, can be seen in terms of the competition for power between the Darod, the Hawiye and the main northern clan, the Isaaq. The UN pressure on Aideed is clearly seen as meddling in Somali clan politics; it supports Aideed's great rival, Ali Mahdi, the self-proclaimed president of Somalia, who comes from the Abgal clan of the Hawiye. The largely nomadic, camel-herding Habr Gidir clans despise the more urban-based Abgal. Located in and around Mogadishu, the Abgal did not rise against Barre until near the end, and then seized the spoils. The Abgal, for their part, consider the Habr Gidir rough and uncivilized.

On a wider level, action against

*T*he disaster of Somalia grew out of the collapse of the moral authority of the elders, and their replacement by the coercive powers of Siad Barre's state and the warlords who succeeded it.

Aideed becomes support for the Darod clan, the main Hawiye rivals for control of Mogadishu. There is a widespread presumption that the US will put in a Darod as the next president. For the Hawiye and other southern clans, the Darod have been tainted by the events of recent years. The Darod themselves, who are hardly united, would argue that the problems lay with Siad Barre's Marehan sub-clan.[9]

Another concern is that the UN and the US have a hidden agenda: to reunify Somalia by reincorporating the republic of Somaliland, the area formerly under British control which proclaimed itself independent in May 1991. Somaliland has not yet received any international recognition, although its creation was very much the result of grassroots action from its people, who would certainly resist any attempt to reincorporate it.[10]

Colonial Concerns

The collapse of UN and US relations with Aideed have caused a serious deterioration in the relationship with Italy, the former colonial power of southern Somalia. Italy has been a generous benefactor to Somalia over the years, while doing remarkably well itself from the association. The largest single aid project was the Baardheere dam scheme, priced at over $750 million. The value lay not in the possibilities for irrigation or electrical generation, discounted respectively as temporary and excessive by most observers, but in the contracts awarded by the foreign donors. Even the World Bank objected to the scale and cost. Another major project was the northeast development, which included the rehabilitation of Bosasso port and road links to Garowe at a cost of up to $400 million. The EC, as late as 1989, granted another $54 million for a road into the Baardheere area. In its highly creative public investment program for 1987-89 the Somali government sought $1.025 billion in external aid; over 80 percent was pledged despite an impressively poor rate of debt repayment.

These projects provided lucrative contracts to Italian construction companies in particular, as well as payoffs to Somali government officials. The norm appears to have been 10 percent, though higher figures were often demanded and obtained. The spoils were carefully divided. The Christian Democrats had Ethiopia; the Socialist Party took over Somalia from the Communist Party in 1978, after Somalia broke with the Soviet Union. Between 1981 and 1990, Italy was Somalia's largest donor, providing over $1 billion for some 114 projects, most subsequently categorized as "absurd and wasteful."[11]

The fall of Siad Barre did not bring these contacts to an end. In the late 1980s, Italy extended links to the opposition, helping to organize the "Manifesto" group within the Hawiye clan in mid-1990. The group, which called for peaceful change to a democratic government, included Ali Mahdi, a prominent businessman and hotel owner, who was proclaimed president after Siad Barre fled. The Italians also backed the creation of the United Somali Congress (USC), a Hawiye group which opted for armed struggle, though it included a number of the "Manifesto" group.[12] The USC subsequently split; when these divisions turned into violence, the Italian and Egyptian governments cosponsored two unsuccessful reconciliation conferences in May and July of 1991.

Hence Italian irritation with the US assumption of control over UNITAF and UNOSOM2. Neither Italy (with 2,600 troops), nor France (1,090) has any representation on Admiral Howe's advisory group, or in the command structure. The Italians believed they could have achieved Aideed's disarmament through negotiations. The other side of this is the UN contingents which insisted on referring orders home, much to the anger of the US. Saudi Arabia, the United Arab Emirates, Kuwait and Italy are said to have been particular offenders in this respect. The UN's response, publicly ordering the Italian commander home, caused an international incident. Following suggestions that it was time to review the UN's tactics, David Shinn, US State Department Coordinator on Somalia, was sent to Mogadishu and Rome to smooth things over. As a compromise, it was agreed the Italian general would be replaced when his tour of duty ended September 1, and an Italian was posted to the operations center in New York. But no changes were made in current policy—summed up by Admiral Howe when he described the sound of a passing Cobra helicopter gunship as "the sound of freedom."

Unanswered Questions

The UN can take some credit for encouraging the return to agricultural activity and the renewal of market operations in some areas, but there remains the major query of how far humanitarian considerations have been lost in the fighting. UNOSOM2's costs for the first six months are estimated at $600 million, and at $1.6 billion for 18 months, to cover 20,000 troops and 8,000 support staff; in August the Secretary-General called

for another brigade. These sums are in sharp contrast with those pledged at the March conference on Humanitarian Assistance for an Action Program on Somalia. The UN requested $166 million, scaled down from the original $250 million. Pledges totalled $130 million.

Another question concerns Somali involvement in the whole process. UNOSOM seems reluctant to recruit Somalis. Few, if any, were consulted before the troops moved in, and efforts at reconciliation appear confined to those largely responsible for the present state of the country. There is an obvious need for local reconciliation as a prerequisite for regional and national debate; for any new administrative structures to be related to Somali clan balance; and for a sustained effort to involve women's groups, merchants, Somali NGOs, professionals, intellectuals, even poets (a political class of importance in Somalia). The reality of Somaliland has received no acknowledgment. The UN and the US appear prepared to ignore the parameters of the Somali economy, whose reconstruction is just as necessary as political change. It, too, has to start at the local level; large-scale development projects, like high-level reconciliation meetings of warlords and faction leaders, run the risk of repeating past problems. Siad Barre, and his manipulation of aid, left Somalia with no functional administration (and essentially no government income except aid flows). Major forms of economic activity were cross-border smuggling, extortion and protection rackets, looting and qat trading. These have provided the funds for the militia forces of the warlords. Aideed, for example, has benefited largely from his control of the qat trade from Kenya. Qat supplies from Ethiopia into Hargeisa in Somaliland in 1992 were running at an estimated value of $50 million per year; in Mogadishu the value is likely to have been twice as high.

The disaster of Somalia grew out of the collapse of the moral authority of the elders, and their replacement by the coercive powers of Siad Barre's state and the warlords who succeeded it.[13] Re-empowerment of the institution of elders at the local level would

go a long way towards resolving economic and political problems. There is, unfortunately, still little evidence of awareness at the UN or in the US of the need for appropriate tactics and strategies if Somalia is to be restored.

Footnotes

1 The institutions of the Somali state were in terminal decay long before 1991, largely because of Siad Barre's policies, although foreign aid preserved a façade. Cohesion in the armed forces broke down after defeat in 1978, the small civil service was undermined by low pay and overlapping spheres of authority which paralyzed it, the economy was dependent upon refugee aid and monetary assistance, and the end of aid in 1990 meant a total lack of resources to pay for state institutions.

2 Estimates that 80 percent of food aid failed to reach its target were grossly exaggerated (as was the 95 percent malnutrition figure). The ICRC estimated that its losses were about 20 percent. One senior UN figure was quoted as saying "this figure of 80 percent blasted about. That's crap. It was used by the US to justify intervention." Quoted in "Somalia. Operation Restore Hope: A Preliminary Assessment," *African Rights Report* (London), May 1993.

3 The US Special Envoy to Somalia, Robert Oakley, has estimated the total cost to the US from the period December 1992 to May 1993 (when the UN formally took over) at well over $2 billion.

4 The Director of Islamic Relief in Djibouti, Abdurahman al-Gaidy, responsible for Horn of Africa activity, denied in a November 1992 interview that his organization had any links with al-Itahad, emphasizing that his organization was purely an Arab humanitarian NGO. Al-Gaidy also denied that Islamic Relief had any contact with the al-Itahad training centers in Somaliland in 1992, near Boroma and Burao, where military and religious training was reportedly combined.

5 *United States Institute of Peace Journal* 6,3 (June 1993).

6 In May 1988, following a peace deal between President Mengistu in Ethiopia and Siad Barre, the main northern guerrilla opposition movement, the Somali National Movement, seized Burao and most of Hargeisa. The government response was horrific. For a devastating indictment of Somali government policy, and of the government commander, General Morgan, see Robert Gersony, "Why Somalis Flee," Report for the Bureau of Refugee Programs, August 1989.

7 "Somalia. Human Rights Abuses by the UN Forces," *African Rights Report* (London), July 1993, pp. 33-34.

8 The best introduction remains I.M. Lewis, *A Modern History of Somalia: Nation and State in the Horn of Africa* (New York, 1980). See also, S.S. Samatar, *Somalia: A Nation in Turmoil* (London: Minority Rights Group, 1991).

9 The main Darod clans are: Ogaden, Marehan (the clan of Siad Barre), Majerteen, Dolbuhunta and Warsengeli. These last three are sometimes referred to as Harti, particularly with reference to recent fighting in and around Kismayo in the south, though all three essentially live in the northeast or north.

10 Somaliland should provide a valuable example for the south of the way elders can solve problems and re-establish local control. The local council of elders of the Gadabursi in Boroma, for example, set up a permanent five-person committee last year which met daily to deal with local administrative issues. They also appointed their own executive commissioner. The UN has been trying to set up "neutral" local councils of elders, but most have been carefully arranged by the local power brokers to perpetuate existing local relationships. The core of the northern approach has been settlement of disputes at the local level and then trying to build up to the sub-clan, clan and inter-clan levels.

11 See Wolfgang Achtner, "The Italian Connection—How Rome Helped Ruin Somalia," *Washington Post*, January 24, 1993.

12 General Aideed's own connection with the Socialist Party broke down in 1989, when he sued Craxi and his brother-in-law for a promised commission and lost. See Achtner, op. cit.

13 Criticism of the extensive, degrading and superficial designation of Somalis as famine victims, bandits or warlords has considerable validity. Nevertheless, the term "warlord" can be defended as an accurate definition: "a military commander who had a regional power base and ruled independently of the central government." (Oxford English Dictionary).

Africa's 'New Wind of Change'

Stephen Riley

Stephen Riley, Senior Lecturer in Politics at Staffordshire Polytechnic, is co-author of *The African Debt Crisis* and author of a major study of the democratic transition in Africa, published in 1991. His article in this issue is an updated version of a talk he gave at Chatham House on 5 December 1991.

Euphoria surrounding the pace of change in contemporary Africa has led many to talk of a 'Second Liberation' or 'Second Independence'. The phrase 'New Wind of Change' has also been used to describe the dramatic political turbulence since 1990. But three recent events, all of which occurred at the end of April, illustrate just how serious the problems are facing states on the road to stable democratic rule in Africa.

● In Ghana, a referendum vote on 28 April 1992 overwhelmingly endorsed the planned return to multiparty constitutional rule, supervised by Flight-Lieutenant Jerry Rawlings who has been in power since 1982. But Rawlings is also expected to be a presidential candidate in the December elections.

● The return to Kenya of the veteran Kikuyu politician, Kenneth Matiba, also at the end of April, threatened to divide on ethnic grounds the major opposition group, the Forum for the Restoration of Democracy (FORD). Such a split in FORD would strengthen President Daniel arap Moi's chances of retaining power.

● In Sierra Leone, a coup on 30 April 1992 by a group of young officers, led by 25-year-old Captain Valentine Strasser, halted - at least temporarily - moves towards the expected multiparty parliamentary and presidential elections later this year. The coup exiled the former President, Joseph Momoh, who had at least initiated a return to pluralist politics.

Momoh's departure means that 11 African heads of state have been replaced since the beginning of 1990. Four of them - the Presidents of Benin, Cape Verde, São Tomé and Zambia - were voted out of office in competitive multiparty elections. Other heads of state - such as Siad Barre in Somalia or Mengistu Haile Mariam in Ethiopia - had to flee their countries when successful secessionist and often ethnically-based liberation movements took power. The autocratic President Samuel Doe was murdered in the Liberian civil war.

Meanwhile, existing authoritarian figures, such as Gnassingbé Eyadéma in Togo or Paul Biya in Cameroon, remain in office, but they have been undermined by popular protests and external pressures. In the capital of Togo in June 1991 crowds tore down the huge statues of Eyadéma, and a sovereign 'National Conference' subsequently revised the constitution to strip him of his formal powers. However, Eyadéma was able to regain his influence in November and December last year as a series of military interventions diminished the powers of the new Prime Minister, Kokou Koffigoh. Biya's regime in Cameroon was challenged in late 1991 by 'Opération Villes Mortes' (Operation Dead Towns), a series of widely supported strikes and urban protests which paralysed the country, but he still retains his position, and some influence, despite many such pressures.[1]

Optimists suggest that we are now witnessing the demise of the authoritarian model of politics which has underpinned most African states since independence.[2] This model has taken several forms, some more repressive than others. Its civilian form has been the shaky, often economically inefficient one-party state, with an ageing nationalist figure at the helm. In the 1960s many such one-party states were replaced by a military form of authoritarianism, but some have survived to the present day. Even one of the more benign civil one-party states - Tanzania - is now moving towards political pluralism. Ex-President Julius Nyerere has recanted his earlier advocacy and institutionalisation of 'one-party democracy'. Strong pressures and good arguments for a return to multiparty politics have emerged. In Tanzania it was said that 'even God permitted opposition by allowing Satan to live among his people'.[3]

The pressure for multiparty politics is equally strong in military regimes, as in Nigeria, or quasi-military regimes, as in Ghana. Some of these regimes are bowing to pluralist pressures, often at the behest of aid donors and creditors who have developed a remarkable consensus on the need for democracy, less corruption, greater respect for human rights and 'good governance' or 'good government' in Africa. There are also 'demonstration effects': the emergence of multiparty politics in Benin in March 1991 led to pressures for democratic change elsewhere in Francophone Africa, and the appearance of democratic politics in Cape Verde has influenced events across Lusophone Africa.

But others are quick to point out that the emergence of more democratic forms of government is patchy across the continent. Some regimes, such as Kenya's until recently, and Madagascar's, are resisting pro-democracy pressures both by local activists and by aid donors. Elsewhere the political changes have yet to be consolidated and democratic regimes legitimised. Democratic pressures are having an uneven impact, as some political leaders resist or deflect the demands of the primarily urban-based, pro-democratic groups while also trying to play off external creditors against each other.

Zaire is an interesting example. President Mobutu Sésé Séko cunningly seeks to maintain himself in power by dividing the domestic pro-democratic opposition. But he is becoming more of a liability to his external patrons. Military rioting in Kinshasa, after an unsuccessful 'National Conference' in August and September 1991, led to the deaths of over a hundred people and a combined French and Belgian military intervention - ostensibly to protect and evacuate nationals. Mobutu has continued to use his wiles to retain power. In February the National

From *The World Today*, July 1992, pp. 116-119. *The World Today,* published by The Royal Institute of International Affairs. Reprinted by permission.

Conference was suppressed, and further pro-democracy demonstrations were put down violently. The conference revived itself recently and declared itself a sovereign body. It may be that Mobutu's 27-year-old regime will finally collapse; a leaked cable from the Belgian Ambassador to Zaire is reported to have said: 'It is impossible to continue with Mobutu.'[4]

These developments and others across the continent raise a number of questions. Is a transition towards more democratic - and sustainable - forms of government in Africa now taking place? What external pressures and domestic social forces have led to the current political turbulence? What challenges will these emerging governments face? Are we merely seeing a brief revival of pluralist politics in Africa which will soon revert to authoritarianism ?

Pressures for change

The democratic revival in Africa is a product of several developments. Since the early 1980s democratic pressures have grown, both from within and without African societies. The crisis of the African state in the late 1970s and 1980s, beset by economic decline and unable to meet popular expectations, led many within African societies to criticise their often corrupt leaders and to argue for a more democratic polity. The growing external debt of many African states, their status in some cases as clients of the major powers, and the geopolitics of global power have increasingly undermined the notional, juridical sovereignty of many African states. At the same time the external pressure from Western governments, from institutions like the World Bank and from non-governmental organisations, for democratic changes has become much more overt and insistent.

The emergence of Mikhail Gorbachev in the Soviet Union and the 1989 revolution in Eastern Europe have fundamentally changed both the Soviet Union and its Eastern European allies. The 'Soviet Union' no longer exists. The former command economies have stopped being sources of aid and ideological inspiration to African states. Instead, they have become major, often successful, competitors for Western aid. The events of 1989 in Eastern Europe also demonstrated dramatically that single-party regimes could be toppled, even if they took a highly authoritarian form as in Romania.

Changes in the global order have meant that Western governments and international institutions influential in Africa have become more powerful.[5] They have also become more confident that their diagnoses of Africa's problems had been correct. Increasingly, in the late 1980s, Africa's problems were seen as political in character. Political reform has thus been added to a top-heavy reform agenda of economic structural adjustment, environmental conservation and population control policies.

Since early 1990, Western governments have indicated that political reform was a necessary condition for further assistance to Africa. Democratisers would be rewarded. President Mitterrand, at the La Baule Francophone African summit in 1990, said that France would in future link its aid contribution 'to efforts designed to lead to greater liberty and democracy'. A British version, 'Hurd's Doctrine', was also promulgated in 1990. Douglas Hurd, the British Foreign Secretary, argued that in future aid policy would favour democratisers: 'Countries tending towards pluralism, public accountability, respect for the rule of law, human rights and market principles should be encouraged.'

In June 1991 Lynda Chalker, the British Overseas Aid Minister, further elaborated the British position which tied future aid to 'good government'. She called for pluralism, accountability, democracy, respect for human rights and the rule of law (but not necessarily multiparty politics).

More recently the importance of political conditionality in aid disbursement was highlighted at the Harare Commonwealth summit in October 1991 and by the European Community in November 1991. The Community has signed a charter which links future aid to greater respect for human rights, less corruption, democratic politics and a free press in recipient states. Excessive military spending was also to be discouraged.[6] Such conditionalities are in accord with the new stance of both the American government and the World Bank. Both emphasise 'good governance'. From the World Bank's more modest perspective, 'good governance' simply involves accountability, openness and less corruption in government.

A key thrust of these policies is the removal of what is identified as political restrictions upon the economic reform of African states. It is believed that sustained economic reform, in a neo-liberal direction, will substantially improve the well-being of African peoples. Certainly economic decline, as well as economic reform, is a key issue in contemporary Africa. Africa's past economic failures, and its problems with the externally-approved structural adjustment measures of the 1980s, have contributed to the creation of what has come to be called a 'democracy movement' within African societies.

Many democratic protests within Africa were at first concerned with economic grievances. In Zambia in the mid-1980s protesters initially rioted in response to the rise in the price of maize meal, the food staple. But their grievances subsequently took on a political hue. A major complaint of the pro-democracy movement in the Ivory Coast in 1990 concerned a new 'solidarity tax' linked to an austerity programme. Food shortages and 1000-per-cent inflation sparked off the current crisis in Zaire. Protests in Somalia, Kenya and the Ivory Coast were also concerned with the corruption of the ruling elites.

The democracy movement which has emerged in many African states in the late 1980s resembles in some respect the nationalist coalitions which gained power in the late 1950s and early 1960s. A diverse group of people are involved. Lawyers, students, copper miners, public-sector workers, the unemployed, journalists and clergymen have all been active. In Benin and elsewhere in Francophone Africa, the Roman Catholic church plays an important role. It issued a pastoral letter which called for democratic change, described as 'conversion'. In Kenya and Sierra Leone, lawyers have been prominent in undermining the authoritarian regimes on human rights grounds. Student strikes or protests have contributed to change in the Ivory Coast and Zambia.

But the democracy movement has not been successful in every case. Ten African states may be regarded as liberal democratic, and at least a further 20 are moving in a liberal, pluralist direction. Five states are riven by civil wars.[7] The road to multiparty democracy remains a long, winding and sometimes tortuous one: witness Zaire, Madagascar, Cameroon and Gabon. Some African authoritarian leaders are trying to resist or accommodate domestic pro-democracy activism and external pressures. Kenya until recently and Madagascar are good examples of resistance, whilst the Ivory Coast is an example of accommodation.

In 1990 Daniel arap Moi described multiparty democracy as being part of a foreign ideology 'peddled by some unpatriotic people with borrowed brains'. His government in Kenya thus vehemently resisted pro-democracy pressures until December 1991, when it was announced that the Kenyan constitution would be revised to allow competitive multiparty politics. Earlier, pro-democratic protests and an embryonic democracy movement had been crushed. As a result, Kenya became a *cause célèbre* in the continuing debate on how aid could be used to promote 'good government'. Since December 1991 the ruling party has suffered extensive defections, and much ethnically-based violence has occurred. The principal opposition party, FORD, is badly divided. There are signs that some of Kenya's aid donors are drawing back from an insistence upon political pluralism, fearing greater conflict during the forthcoming elections.[8]

In Madagascar, President Didier Ratsiraka has also announced that 'even if I'm right I will bend', but little pro-democratic change has taken place as yet. The government responded to huge pro-democracy demonstrations by posting in public places pictures of the violence in Tiananmen Square in China in 1989. But the posters were presumably supposed to be deterrents: they were not pictures of the pro-democracy students but of the soldiers who killed them.[9] In Madagascar, however, it is likely that the authoritarian regime will have to bow to the prevailing external wind which now demands greater respect for human rights, less corruption and better governance.

In some regimes, such as that in the Ivory Coast, ageing authoritarian leaders have sought to retain power and accommodate political pluralism. The democracy movement in the Ivory Coast forced Félix Houphouët-Boigny to hold a multiparty election in October 1990, after the French had earlier refused to intervene militarily to help him quash an army and police mutiny. Houphouët-Boigny won the multiparty election with 82 per cent of the vote, although nearly 40 per cent abstained. He retains his grip on power, albeit tenuously - as he has been doing for 30 years past. Responding at a press conference to the calls for his retirement, the President said: 'I'm refusing to grow old so that I can serve my country. The Ivory Coast will have the best successor to Houphouët because God will help me to give him to you.'

The new democratic politics

The new democratic governments in Africa face a daunting array of challenges. They are surfacing in the poorest of all the world's continents. Benin, now a multiparty democracy, has a per-capita gnp of $380, with a literacy rate of 37 per cent for men and 16 per cent for women. The Gambia has managed to sustain multiparty politics since independence in 1965, despite having a per-capita gnp of $240 and an average life expectancy of 43 years. Life expectancy for black Africa as a whole averages just over 50 years. The United Nations has estimated that by the middle of the 1990s, 400m Africans will be living in poverty, 260m of them women. These are not encouraging conditions for the stability of the new democratic governments.

These new regimes have to balance the demands of their external creditors against the pressing needs of their newly enfranchised citizens. They also have to cope with the residue of the policy headaches of the 1980s: economic decline or stagnation, war, famine, refugees, environmental degradation, population pressures, food shortages, AIDS and other health problems, and policy reforms such as structural adjustment, privatisation and market liberalisation.

Some of the new political pressures they face will be old ones in a new guise. The armed forces remain a potent political actor, working behind the scenes to defend their own interests and those of their allies. They have acted in a positive way - for example, ousting Moussa Traore in Mali in March 1991. The continuing political instability in Togo illustrates some of the problems the soldiers represent. The new democratic governments will have to cut military budgets nevertheless. In Nigeria and Ethiopia, where the armed forces are far too large, they are being reduced. But there are still political dangers aplenty. There have, after all, already been over 80 successful military coups in independent Africa.

The new governments also face problems of intensified ethnic conflict and fears of 'Balkanisation'. In the 1960s the African 'solution' for ethnic conflict was the supposedly homogenising and unifying effect of single-party regimes. Freer, pluralistic politics will mean that ethnic divisions come to the fore with potentially divisive and destructive effects. Indeed, multiparty politics is simply one outcome of the breakdown of Africa's authoritarianism. An alternative is the collapse of the state into competing factions and disputed or dividing sovereignties. Liberia, Ethiopia and Somalia are illustrations of this.

It is also possible that the new democratic regimes could drift back into venality and authoritarian politics. It all depends on the sense of public purpose shown by the new leaders and on the political skills they deploy. Independent oppositions and a freer and less sycophantic press will help expose such potential weaknesses.

New leaders are unknown quantities. Frederick Chiluba, the new President of Zambia, has an unusual background in that he has emerged from the trade union movement, unlike the majority of the new democratic leaders. Some are lawyers or university lecturers; others are bankers or former officials with international institutions. The new President of Mali, Souman Sacko, used to work for the United Nations Development Programme, and President Nicephore Soglo of Benin was an international banker. These new leaders have appointed similar-minded and similarly trained people as advisers: politicians who have been described as 'techno-politicians' who are less concerned with the crudities of patronage or overt force than were the politicians of the 1960s and 1970s.[10] They will therefore be more adept at negotiating with external creditors and aid donors than at dealing with the political pressures from inside their own societies.

A further problem is that of party-political organisation. The old authoritarian politics afforded insufficient choice and too few political parties. The new democracies have many parties; perhaps too many for stable politics. At one count Angola had over 30 political parties, the Congo 71, and in Zaire over 200 parties are formed into a 'Sacred Union'.[11]

Democracies also need independent institutions, including an impartial civil services and a functioning parliament. Africa's bureaucracies were 'politicised' in the post-independence period of one-party regimes and military governments. Recruitment, postings and promotion were all affected by political criteria as the public sector swelled to satisfy the patronage demands of the political machine. In the 1990s attempts must be made to 'de-politicise' the civil service and recreate it along impartial, independent lines. Britain's 'good government' aid policy currently includes some fairly meagre help in this respect, with funding of £2m for civil service reform in Ghana and £5m for local government development in Zambia.[12]

The heavy hand of authoritarian politics has also had damaging effects on Africa's 'civil society' - that range of organised interests outside the state which are generally present in advanced industrial societies and can contain the excesses of state power or at least channel and express popular interests. Independent trade unions, local community associations, business groups and church associations are all a vital part of a functioning democratic system. Elements of a democratic civil society are now emerging and re-emerging in Africa, often helped by Western non-governmental organisations.

It is likely that new politics in democratic states will continue to be urban-based, as the pressures for democracy have come largely from city-dwelling, often professional groups: lawyers, students and public-sector workers. They will expect their interests to be defended, or improved, by the new regimes. This may mean that the needs of the rural majority, who produce most of Africa's exports and food, will continue to be neglected.

Much has been written about the social and economic conditions that are necessary for the appearance and survival of democratic forms of government. An educated population, with both political knowledge and the will to act, coupled with a modern industrial economy, a homogeneous society and a long-established set of democratic political values, are all identified as important conditions that enable democratic institutions to emerge and persist.[13] African states have few of these conditions. Many African states are socially heterogeneous, and political fissures follow social, religious and regional divisions. Their civic tradition as independent states goes back little more than a generation, and they did not inherit democratic traditions from the longer period of authoritarian colonial rule.

However, despite these deficiencies it would seem that Africa can nurture some forms of liberal democracy. The latest in The Gambia's long tradition of multiparty elections was held at the end of April. In addition, multiparty politics survives in Botswana and Senegal, although there is ethnic discontent in Senegal's Casamance region and the opposition criticises Abdou Diouf's government as a *de facto* one-party rule.[14] Yet across Africa more pluralist forms of politics are appearing. There are thus grounds for hope, despite the many challenges the new democracies face. But one of the major problems they confront is the simplistic approach adopted towards their difficulties, particularly from outside Africa. Simple political solutions are being insisted upon by external donors.

Sustained thinking about the implications of greater pluralism for African societies is rare. There is also an inconsistency in now requiring both democratic reform and continued economic adjustment and austerity. It is unlikely that the newly enfranchised citizens will actually vote for further austerity. For example, Frederick Chiluba's new democratic government in Zambia has soon run into economic and political difficulties, with 40 strikes in the last six months and growing criticism of Chiluba's political style and appointments.[15] As a result, the medium- to long-term prospect is one of instability in the newly democratised societies. Juggling the competing demands of external donors and an active citizenry is likely to remain difficult, despite the 'techno-politicians'. Some democratic states may thus fall to revived authoritarianism or at least military coups d'état as a consequence. Nevertheless, the democratic ideal - whether imported or not - is taking hold again in Africa. Ordinary people, as in Eastern Europe, are demonstrating that the 'New Wind of Change' is blowing.

NOTES

1. *The Independent*, 14 November 1991.

2. C. Legum, 'The Coming of Africa's Second Independence', *Washington Quarterly*, No 1, Winter 1990.

3. Cited in the *Bulletin of Tanzanian Affairs*, No 39, May-June 1991, pp. 11-12.

4. *Financial Times*, 27 September 1991; *The Economist*, 22 February 1992; *Africa Analysis*, 1 May 1992. Many of the other details in the text are from: S. P. Riley, 'The Democratic Transition in Africa', *Conflict Studies*, No 245, 1991.

5. M. Clough, *Free At Last? U.S. Policy Toward Africa and the End of the Cold War* (New York: Council on Foreign Relations Press, 1992).

6. *The Independent*, 29 November 1991. For an earlier discussion of the relationship between democracy, debt and structural adjustments, see: T. W. Parfitt and S. P. Riley, *The African Debt Crisis* (London: Routledge, 1989), Chapter 8.

7. This assessment is based upon the measures of democratisation in Africa developed by the African Governance Programme at the Carter Centre at Emory University, Atlanta. See their publication *African Demos*, published since 1990.

8. *Africa Analysis*, 3 April 1992.

9. H. Drysdale, *Dancing with the Dead: A Journey through Zanzibar and Madagascar* (London: Hamish Hamilton, 1991), p.121.

10. V. Britain, 'Plus ça change', *New Statesman and Society*, 14 June 1991, pp. 18-20.

11. *Africa Analysis*, 20 September 1991.

12. L. Chalker, 'Good Government and the Aid Programme', speech to the Overseas Development Institute/Chatham House, London, June 1991.

13. A fuller discussion of this can be found in, for example: J. A. Wiseman, *Democracy in Black Africa: Survival and Revival* (New York: Paragon House, 1990); and L. Diamond *et al.*, *Democracy in Developing Countries: Volume Two: Africa* (Boulder, CO: Lynne Reinner, 1988).

14. *Africa Confidential*, 3 April 1992.

15. G. Mills, 'Zambia and the Winds of Change', *The World Today*, January 1992; *The Guardian*, 4 May 1992.

South Africa's Future Foreign Policy

Nelson Mandela

Nelson Mandela is President of the African National Congress.

NEW PILLARS FOR A NEW WORLD

As the 1980s drew to a close I could not see much of the world from my prison cell, but I knew it was changing. There was little doubt in my mind that this would have a profound impact on my country, on the southern African region and the continent of which I am proud to be a citizen. Although this process of global change is far from complete, it is clear that all nations will have boldly to recast their nets if they are to reap any benefit from international affairs in the post–Cold War era.

The African National Congress (ANC) believes that the charting of a new foreign policy for South Africa is a key element in the creation of a peaceful and prosperous country. Apartheid corroded the very essence of life in South Africa. This is why the country's emerging political leaders are challenged to build a nation in which all people–irrespective of race, color, creed, religion or sex–can assert fully their human worth; after apartheid, our people deserve nothing less than the right to life, liberty and the pursuit of happiness.

This vision cannot be realized until South Africa can again participate fully in world affairs. For four decades South Africa's international relations were dog-ged by the apartheid issue. By the end of the 1980s, South Africa was one of the most isolated states on earth. Recovering from this will be no easy task. Conscious of this difficulty, the ANC is involved in developing those policies which will be necessary to take South Africa into the new world order as a responsible global citizen. Additionally, it is concerned with the need to forge a truly professional diplomatic service which will serve all of South Africa's peoples and represent their rich diversity. Fortunately, foreign governments have recognized the importance of this and are generously providing training for young South Africans who wish to make careers in foreign affairs.

Within the context of the current multiparty negotiations, preliminary discussions are also under way between political parties with an interest in foreign affairs in an effort to bridge the divides between them on important policy questions. The pillars upon which our foreign policy will rest are the following beliefs:

- that issues of human rights are central to international relations and an understanding that they extend beyond the political, embracing the economic, social and environmental;
- that just and lasting solutions to the problems of humankind can only come through the promotion of democracy worldwide;
- that considerations of justice and respect for international law should guide the relations between nations;
- that peace is the goal for which all nations should

strive, and where this breaks down, internationally agreed and nonviolent mechanisms, including effective arms-control regimes, must be employed;

- that the concerns and interests of the continent of Africa should be reflected in our foreign-policy choices;
- that economic development depends on growing regional and international economic cooperation in an interdependent world.

These convictions stand in stark contrast to how, for nearly five decades, apartheid South Africa disastrously conducted its international relations.

DEMOCRACY AND DIVERSITY

Because the world is a more dangerous place, the international community dare not relinquish its commitment to human rights. This appeal also has a special significance for South Africa. The antiapartheid campaign was the most important human-rights crusade of the post–World War II era. Its success was a demonstration, in my opinion, of the oneness of our common humanity: in these troubled times, its passion should not be lost. Consequently, South Africa will not be indifferent to the rights of others. Human rights will be the light that guides our foreign affairs.

Only true democracy can guarantee rights. This is why the ANC's decision to take up arms to secure the rights of South Africa's people will only be fulfilled in a government of the people, by the people and for the people. We have always embraced the cry for democracy across the world and South Africa will therefore be at the forefront of global efforts to promote and foster democratic systems of government. This is especially important in Africa, and our concerns will be fixed upon securing a spirit of tolerance and the ethos of governance throughout the continent. There cannot be one system for Africa and another for the rest of the world. If there is a single lesson to be drawn from Africa's postcolonial history, it is that accountable government is good government.

An international divide is emerging between countries that tolerate diversity and those that do not.

The growing violence of narrow "nationalism," which can lead to the Balkanization of states, is of particular concern to South Africans. Ancient and long-dormant animosities have been unlocked by the ending of the Cold War, and these now threaten the very existence of some countries. Some suggest that an international divide is emerging between countries that tolerate diversity and those that do not. The latter will fall prey to internecine strife, sapping, if not

destroying, the potential of their people. These countries will fall further and further behind the great technological advances being made elsewhere. As we witness in Yugoslavia, it is the young who will inherit the political and economic wasteland consigned to them by the archaic enmities of their fathers.

For many this fate beckons South Africa. Respect for diversity has been central to the ANC's political credo. As South Africa gears itself for its first democratic election, this tradition will guide our electoral campaign. But beyond our shores we will, as responsible international citizens, also honor this creed. A central goal of our foreign policy will, therefore, be to promote institutions and forces that, through democratic means, seek to make the world safe for diversity.

Around the globe, new conflicts and divides are surfacing. The chasm between the industrialized North and the underdeveloped South is deepening. If there is to be global harmony, the international community will have to discover mechanisms to bridge the divide between its rich and its poor. South Africa can play an important role in this regard because it is situated at a particular confluence of world affairs. But so too the United Nations has been freed from the straightjacket of the Cold War. South Africa's people look forward to our country's return as a full and active member of the United Nations family. It is the ANC's view that the United Nations has a pivotal role to play in fostering global security and order. But to achieve this, serious attention must be paid to a restructuring of the organization. South Africa intends to play a vigorous role in the debate on this issue. The United Nations should not be dominated by a single power or group of powers, or else its legitimacy will continuously be called into question. We hope a mechanism can be found so that the Security Council can reflect the full tapestry of humankind.

The United Nations and other international organizations have an important role to play in controlling the worldwide flow of arms. We know this from bitter experience. South Africa's transition to democracy has been unnecessarily violent; much of the blame lies in the proliferation of small arms throughout southern Africa. In addition to acceding to the major arms-control regimes, South Africa will actively support the United Nations' commitment to a general and complete disarmament under effective international control.

OUR AFRICAN DESTINY

South Africa cannot escape its African destiny. If we do not devote our energies to this continent, we too could fall victim to the forces that have brought ruin to its various parts. Like the United Nations, the Organization of African Unity needs to be attuned to the changes at work throughout the world. A democratic

South Africa will bring to an end an important chapter in Africa's efforts to achieve unity and closer cooperation, but it will not close the book.

Africa's international position has been acutely affected by global change. Some of this is positive. It has, for instance, become less likely that our continent will, as in the past, be treated as a battleground by contending forces in wider international conflicts. Economically the position appears less promising. The shift in international attention toward Eastern Europe has, in the view of some, increased Africa's marginalization and weakened the continent's economic position. Africa must respond to this by transforming its economic base. Greater economic cooperation between the countries of the continent and the reshaping of trading networks can make a significant contribution in this regard.

Southern Africa commands a special priority in our foreign policy. We are inextricably part of southern Africa and our destiny is linked to that of a region, which is much more than a mere geographical concept. The historical patterns of relations in southern Africa have, however, been highly uneven and inequitable. The regional economy that emerged under colonialism entrenched the domination of one country (South Africa) and incorporated other countries in subsidiary and dependent roles as labor reserves, markets for South African commodities, suppliers of certain services (such as transport) or providers of cheap and convenient resources (like water, electricity and some raw materials). South Africa's visible exports to the rest of the region exceed imports by more than five to one. This is a reflection not just of the stronger productive base of the South African economy, but of barriers of various kinds that have kept goods produced in regional states out of the South African market. Destructive apartheid policies have, moreover, caused further distortions. While South Africans experienced discrimination and repression at home, southern Africa fell victim to apartheid's destabilization strategy, which left two million dead and inflicted an estimated $62.45 billion of damage on the economies of our neighbors.

I share the view of many that the forging of closer economic relations can potentially be of great benefit both to a democratic South Africa and the rest of southern Africa. Increased trade with southern Africa and the wider continent could be of considerable significance for our manufacturing industries. Neighboring countries, too, could benefit by expanding their exports to South Africa. At present, only Zimbabwe and some of the Southern African Customs Union countries, foremost among them Swaziland, have more than a token presence in the South African market. This is in part a reflection of the strong underlying protectionist stance toward potential imports from the region. If this were to change, agricultural and industrial producers in several neighboring countries could receive an important boost. Cooperation in regional construction, infrastructure and resource development projects, as well as in virtually every sector and area, could also be of considerable benefit. In several cases, notably that of potential water and hydropower projects in several Southern African Development Community member states, projects will not be economically viable unless they can count on exports to South Africa. At the same time, South Africa would benefit in environmental terms by importing hydropower and could well become absolutely dependent on water imports from other countries in the years ahead.

Southern Africa will, however, only prosper if the principles of equity, mutual benefit and peaceful cooperation are the tenets that inform its future. Reconstruction cannot be imposed on the region by external forces or unilaterally by ourselves as the region's most powerful state. It must be the collective enterprise of southern Africa's people. Democratic South Africa will, therefore, resist any pressure or temptation to pursue its own interests at the expense of the subcontinent. Likewise, militaristic approaches to security and cooperation have no place in southern Africa. In partnership with its neighbors, a democratic South Africa will promote the creation of regional structures for crisis prevention and management. These should be augmented by institutions that offer facilitation, mediation and arbitration of interstate conflicts.

We are sensitive to the fact that any program that promotes greater cooperation and integration in southern Africa must be sensitive to the acute imbalances in existing regional economic relations. Any move toward a common market or economic community must ensure that industrial development in the entire region is not prejudiced. It is essential therefore that a program to restructure regional economic relations after apartheid be carefully calibrated to avoid exacerbating inequities. Similar principles will govern the transformation of such exploitative aspects of the regional economy as the migrant labor system. With many others, we believe this system is detrimental to development. It is, nevertheless, deeply entrenched, and a number of countries have become critically dependent on it for employment and foreign-exchange earnings.

Democratic South Africa will not adopt a narrow, chauvinistic approach to this issue and will not make unilateral changes to the system. Instead, it will seek an acceptable regional solution that takes account of the needs of the labor-supplying states.

In forging links with our neighbors, the ANC will draw on an African tradition, of which we are a part, of promoting greater continental unity. We are currently involved in consultations with the Southern African Development Community, and the Eastern and Southern African Preferential Trade Area. We look forward to a mutually beneficial association with both of these important vehicles for promoting regional prosperity. At the same time we recognize that southern Africa cannot afford a proliferation of institutions or a duplication of efforts and that the challenges of the future will require considerable institutional development. We likewise look forward to becoming involved in the process of reforming the Southern African Customs Union, linking our country to Botswana, Lesotho, Namibia and Swaziland (BLNS). Although SACU is the oldest integration arrangement in Africa, its current modus operandi is far from satisfactory. The old formula, in which "captive markets" for South African goods in the BLNS were bought by the allocation of a disproportionate share of customs revenue, has recently come under strain from both the South African Finance Ministry and neighboring countries. Our approach to the reform of SACU will be guided by broader considerations than the implications for the South African treasury. We will seek to democratize the

---

South Africa must strengthen those economic activities that are in international demand but that have failed to achieve their potential.

---

institutions of SACU, within the framework of a broader regional program, and to remove barriers in the existing arrangement to a more balanced location of industries.

THE ECONOMIC CRISIS

The primary motivation of the ANC's foreign economic policies as a whole will be to place South Africa on the path of rapid economic development with a view to addressing three key problem areas: slow growth, severe poverty, and extreme inequalities in living standards, income, and opportunity. The South African economy has grown very slowly since the early 1970s, with the exception of short periods of gold market booms. Annual GDP declined from almost six percent in the 1960s to less than four percent the following decade and to barely one percent during the 1980s. The economy contracted sharply during the recession-bound 1990s, and in 11 of the past 12 years, per capita income declined.

Poverty is manifested in extremely high levels of unemployment in South Africa, widely estimated to be above 40 percent, and by very poor social and economic indicators for the black population, particularly in the rural areas. These problems are compounded by the fact that inequalities remain entrenched on racial lines.

A recent World Bank report estimated that South African whites have a personal per capita income level that is 9.5 times higher than Africans, 4.5 times higher than people classified as colored (mixed race) by the apartheid system, and 3 times than Asians. Patterns of inequality extend beyond this to the provision of services, access to education, employment opportunities, and wealth generation—all still heavily inclined toward the white population.

As part of the global economy, South Africa has been deeply affected by the worldwide economic slowdown that began in the late 1980s, compounded in our case by the political uncertainties that face potential investors. There are many reasons for this state of affairs, the most important of which has been the political and economic policies of successive apartheid governments since 1948. These policies were destructive and wasteful but, more important, they conspired to prevent South Africa's economy from adapting to changing global conditions.

South Africa's staple exports—gold and other metals and minerals—have encountered deteriorating market conditions for many years, but the country has failed to develop more competitive alternatives. The ANC will inherit a relatively open economy, dependent on many imports from the outside world, but without the wherewithal to pay for them in the long term if the economy does not begin to grow rapidly. The key to South African recovery and growth is the strengthening of economic activities in which we have some potential and that are in international demand, but that have failed to achieve that potential in the past. Our manufacturing and service sectors will be critically important. South Africa does have potentially competitive manufacturing sectors such as metal engineering, pulp and paper, and some likely service sectors too, of which banking, insurance and tourism are the most important.

The ANC believes that the fundamental policies for achieving our potential in these and other sectors include: developing effective education and training programs; attracting foreign investment that strengthens our technological capacity and market access; engaging in a measured program of trade-policy reform that encourages competitive domestic sectors and lowers our import bill; a tough competition and antitrust policy that lowers prices and raises the efficiency of business as well as creates opportunities for black business development; and finally, the development of a range of initiatives to stimulate private sector investment and restructuring.

It is quite clear that the above policies are not a quick cure and that implementation will take some time. Given the inequalities in the South African economy it is equally clear that a number of short-term strategies are needed to help address immediate problems and to build the foundations of democracy. We must create jobs in urban and rural areas, partly through state intervention, assist small black business and micro-enterprises, improve access to housing and basic services, and restructure social-security programs for the very poor, the disabled, and the aged.

It is obvious to me that the primary components of our international economic relations, which must feed our development strategy, are the strengthening of our trade performance and our capacity to attract foreign investment. In addition we must examine the possibilities of obtaining technical and financial assistance from the developed industrial countries. We do not expect foreign investment to solve our economic problems, but we understand that it can play a very valuable role in our economic development. Though the inflow of direct and indirect investment will strengthen our reserves, most investment will have to be drawn from domestic sources. There are a number of institutions in our society with investment funds at hand, and more will grow.

These institutions will be expected to make a meaningful contribution to our economic development in a number of ways—some still under consideration—but including mechanisms such as prescribed investment. But foreign investors can open up new possibilities. They can bring new skills and technologies to a South Africa starved of innovation and technical know-how and can gain us access to new markets. Foreign investors can also provide competition for domestic monopolies and oligopolies, which have thrived on South Africa's isolation at the expense of ordinary people. They can establish partnerships with black South Africans who have deliberately been crippled, economically, by the apartheid system. The ANC believes the most important way to attract foreign investment is to create a stable and democratic political environment. Also important is the development of legitimate, transparent and consistent economic policies. Foreign companies should be treated as domestic companies, obeying our laws and gaining access to our incentives, and the ANC is committed to the principle of uniform treatment. And while we do not plan to provide exclusive incentives for all foreign investors, we realize that it might be necessary to make special arrangements to attract the kind of investment that will make a real difference in South Africa.

TRADE AND RECIPROCITY

The second primary component of our international economic relations that I referred to was our trade performance. Central to this concept, of course, is South Africa's full reintegration into the global trading regime. While we will strive to accommodate the concerns of the General Agreement on Tariffs and Trade (GATT) in regard to the high levels of protection of South African industry and to open our markets to global trade, we insist this is a two-way process. South Africa reserves the right to discriminate against the products of any country that will not open its market to South African goods. In short the concept of reciprocity will be paramount.

We cannot be expected to reintegrate our trade regime into the global system overnight, and we will resist any attempt by the GATT to force us to do so. While we will be enthusiastic supporters of free trade, we ask our trading partners and the GATT to understand that we cannot put thousands of jobs at risk by embarking on a speedy and uncoordinated revision of our total tariff regime. We shall undertake to reduce the number of tariff lines and to rationalize and simplify the tariff structure so that it begins to move closer to the rules and expectations of the GATT, but we are not prepared to place the demands of the global community ahead of the desires and needs of our people. We therefore envisage a considered program of trade policy reform that will address not only the levels of protection but also the development of effective export incentives that are internationally acceptable. The ANC remains concerned that, even if the Uruguay Round succeeds, the development of trading blocs (such as the European Community and NAFTA) might weaken the position of developing countries, particularly those—like South Africa—that are not members of any trading bloc. We remain concerned, too, that the Uruguay Round continues to neglect the interests of the South and that the negotiations seem disproportionately centered around the interests of farmers in the developed countries.

South Africa will resist any pressure or temptation to pursue its own interests at the expense of southern Africa.

A democratic South Africa will seek new avenues for its export products, including agricultural produce, and we reserve the right within the framework of the GATT to seek new export markets as aggressively as possible. At the same time we recognize the importance of the European Community, our largest trade and investment partner, and will actively seek to consolidate our long-standing relationship with the EC. As part of this process we are currently examining a number of options in regard to our future economic relations with the EC with a view to gaining preferential access to European markets. In addition we are examining methods of expanding and strengthening our relationship with North America, Japan, and the Pacific Rim economies.

We will seek assurances from members of the major trading blocs on the issue of market access, and we will strive to strengthen our South–South ties to help protect us against economic marginalization.

FRIEND TO THE WORLD

South Africa's future foreign relations will be based on our belief that human rights should be the core concern of international relations, and we are ready to play a role in fostering peace and prosperity in the world we share with the community of nations. We are well aware how important and how difficult the process of reintegration into the global political and economic system will be for South Africa. The ANC will be among the first in South Africa to take full responsibility for our own destiny, but we believe that as a developing country undergoing a difficult transition, we can expect the developed industrial nations of the world to assist us in this task. We are prepared, too, to shoulder our share of the responsibility for the whole southern African region, not in the spirit of paternalism or dominance but mutual cooperation and respect.

The time has come for South Africa to take up its rightful and responsible place in the community of nations. Though the delays in this process, forced upon us by apartheid, make it all the more difficult for us, we believe that we have the resources and the commitment that will allow us to begin to make our own positive contribution to peace, prosperity and goodwill in the world in the very near future.

International Political Economy

International economic issues occupy a central position in relations among international actors, including nation-states. The media reflect the growing importance of geo-economics by providing extensive coverage of annual summits of economic ministers, in addition to meetings of the heads of state of the Western nations comprising the Group of 7. The importance of economic issues is also illustrated by the coverage afforded such pure economic problems as the global recession, economic dislocations created by balance of payments deficits for developed and developing nations, worker dislocations, supranational capital flows created by the transition to an international economy, and the central role played by nongovernmental organizations (NGOs) such as multinational corporations in creating trade imbalances among nation-states. The political consequences of efforts by excommunist states to implement free market reforms is a preoccupation of major nation-states, as are efforts to establish regional free trade zones such as the North Atlantic Free Trade Agreement (NAFTA) among the United States, Canada, and Mexico. The difficulties being experienced by nearly all ex-communist states in their efforts to transform state-run economies into free market systems renew long-standing debates about how to forge such transitions in the less developed world.

Murray Weidenbaum's article, "The Business Response to the Global Marketplace," offers a useful outline of the more important trends in the international political economy: increased globalization of the marketplace and the growing importance of global corporate actors capable of influencing economic and political trends in international relations. Weidenbaum underscores how increasingly global in scope private enterprise has become and how parochial governmental policies remain. Contemporary political policymakers must be aware of how these trends may confuse corporate welfare with national well-being, especially in debates about economic competitiveness.

After seven years of negotiations, the United States and 116 other nations finally agreed in 1993 to revise the General Agreement on Tariffs and Trade (GATT) framework governing most international trade. While this agreement reflects certain important changes in the post–cold war era, Roger Cohen explains in "A Realignment Made Reluctantly" why the new GATT accord falls short of its target. Cohen, along with many other analysts, concluded that regional trade accords like NAFTA may provide a general model for the future.

Several regions of the world today were left out of the globalization of the world economy in terms of production and trade during the 1980s—most countries in Africa, some countries in Latin America and Asia, and former communist bloc nations. To cope with sliding economic conditions in developing countries, both bilateral and multilateral donors such as the International Monetary Fund (IMF) and World Bank have, in recent years, linked the granting of monetary credits, loans, and aid to a state's ability to implement economic and political reforms. Joan Nelson in "Beyond Conditionality" outlines some of the successes and limitations of such policies influencing economic reforms or in simultaneously promoting several goals on the new global agenda. Nelson concludes that truly multilateral arrangements that involve poorer nations in setting international standards and monitoring compliance might generate genuine commitments without the high costs of conditionality.

Although the global recession has slowed growth throughout the world, the most common vision of the global economy in the twenty-first century is one of increased economic exchanges in three dominant regions: North America, the Pacific Rim economies, and a reinvigorated European Community. Several trends suggest that by the late 1990s the integration of new capitalist nations and much of the developing world into this global economy will create a demand boom. Until then, industrial nations will probably continue to underperform the rest of the world's economies. Unfortunately, there is also a dark side to this vision, as the economies, and hence the people, of most developing countries may find it very difficult to compete and prosper in this worldwide economy. A host of interrelated economic, political, social, and ecological problems in these marginalized areas of the world may threaten the stability and prosperity of the new economic system.

This future vision underscores the importance of knowing which economic strategy is the best one to follow to transform from a centrally controlled to a free market system for ex-socialist and developing countries today. Unfortunately, there is no clear-cut answer to the funda-

mental debate about how to promote both economic and political reforms. On the surface, recent events in Russia and China suggest that gradualism rather than shock therapy may work best. This is an important issue in contemporary international relations, as it may contradict the basic premises undergirding the policies of the major international financial and lending agencies such as the World Bank and the IMF, and the foreign policies of major Western states, including the United States.

Looking Ahead: Challenge Questions

Provide examples of recent conflicts between the interests of corporations and U.S. national interests. Do the interests of major U.S. corporations usually overlap with U.S. national economic interests regarding how to increase the competitiveness of United States imports in international markets?

Should the United States develop a closer industrial partnership between government and corporations to more effectively compete with competitors in Japan, the Pacific Basin, and Europe?

Would you characterize the current economic trade system as based on precepts of free trade? Are there policies supported by the United States, Japan, and European governments or collective bodies like the European Community that conflict with the basic principles and goals of free trade? Will agreements between nation-states help or harm world trade objectives? For example, will a trend towards establishing regional free trade zones throughout the world hurt or help the current level of unemployment in the United States?

Do you agree or disagree with the World Bank's policy of making progress toward political and economic reforms a necessary condition for additional credit, loans, or aid? Are any of the experiences of developing countries who strove to implement World Bank structural adjustment programs during the 1980s relevant to current efforts by Eastern European countries and the republics of the former Soviet Union to implement similar adjustments? Why or why not?

Which strategy works best in developing societies—Chinese-style gradualism or Russian-style sudden change? Should the United States and major international organizations continue to make a country's ability to meet specified economic and political reforms a condition of economic and humanitarian aid? Why or why not?

The Business Response to the Global Marketplace

Murray Weidenbaum

Murray Weidenbaum is Mallinckrodt Distinguished University Professor and director of the Center for the Study of American Business at Washington University in St. Louis. He also serves as cochairman of the CSIS International Research Council.

THE GLOBAL MARKETPLACE had surely arrived when villagers in the Middle East followed the Gulf War on Cable News Network (CNN), via Soviet government satellite and through a private subsidiary of a local government enterprise. Both public and private businesses were involved, and they were located on three different continents. This increasing globalization of the marketplace is forcing individual enterprises to pay more attention to international developments and to adjust their structure and methods of operations to a broader and more rapidly shifting economic environment.

A number of other more quantitative indicators give a sense of the global marketplace. A rising share of the products manufactured in the United States (perhaps one-half or more) have one or more foreign components. Ford's Crown Victoria has a foreign content of 27 percent, while 25 percent of Honda's U.S.-manufactured Accord is made overseas.[1] This development was nicely summed up in a recent conversation. The customer asks the auto dealer, "Is this car made in the United States?" The salesman responds with another question, "Which part?"

A second way of looking at the global marketplace is to consider that one-half of all imports and exports—what governments label foreign trade—is transacted between domestic companies and their foreign affiliates or foreign parents. That is true in the United States, the European Community (EC), and Japan. From the viewpoint of political geography, the activity is classified as foreign commerce. But from an economic viewpoint, these international flows of goods and services are internal transfers within the same company.[2] That is the global enterprise in full operation.

One final indicator: Despite the massive and well-known U.S. trade deficit, U.S. companies sell to and in other nations as much as, if not more than, "foreign" companies sell in and to the United States.[3] This leads to a related set of questions on which experts answer differently: Is Honda USA part of the U.S. economy? What about IBM in Tokyo? What is clear is that the consequences of the internationalization of business are profound for many firms. Half of Xerox's 110,000 employees work on foreign soil. Less than one-half of Sony's employees are Japanese. More than half of Digital Equipment's revenues come from overseas operations. One-third of GE's profits arise from its international activities.[4]

Technology and economics are outpacing traditional ways of thinking about international politics. The standard geopolitical map is out of synchronization with the emerging business and economic map. Economic and technological forces are powerful agents for change.

A dramatic example is the Kuwaiti bank that was moved by facsimile machine. The day of the Iraqi invasion, the manager set up three open telephone lines with his office in Bahrain. Over two he transmitted all of the bank's key documents via fax. Over the third, he checked to make sure that each page was being received. From time to time, the shooting around him slowed the process. But, before the end of the day, the necessary transmissions were complete. The next morning the bank opened up as a Bahraini institution neither subject to the freeze on Kuwaiti assets nor to Iraqi control.[5]

On a more aggregate level, business planning must increasingly be geared to the fundamental shifts that are occurring in national positions in the international economy. There are likely to be three regions of dominant economic power far into the twenty-first century. One is North America, led by the United States. Another is Japan and the other vibrant Asian rim economies. The third is the reinvigorated European Community, where change is taking place on an unprecedented scale. Business support for a North American free trade area arises in good measure in response to the competitive developments in Europe and Asia.

From all indications, the countries along the Asian rim will continue to grow rapidly during the 1990s. Japan and the four "little dragons" (Hong Kong, Singapore, Taiwan, and South Korea) are being joined by Thailand, Malaysia, and Indonesia as the newest members of the club of industrialized

From *The Washington Quarterly*, Vol. 15, No. 1, Winter 1992, pp. 173-185. © 1992 by The Center for Strategic and International Studies and Massachusetts Institute of Technology. Reprinted by permission.

nations. Even so, radical changes in government policy toward business in the decade ahead will most likely occur, not across the Pacific Ocean, but across the Atlantic in Western Europe.

EC '92

The key structural shift in Western Europe is the economic integration of the 12 members of the European Community, scheduled to be completed in its essential elements by the end of 1992.[6] This phenomenon is usually referred to as EC '92 even though the actions being taken constitute an ongoing process that is likely to continue into 1993 and beyond. These governmental developments will have profound long-term effects on business productivity and international competitiveness.

Many discussions of EC '92 get mired in details and overlook the main points. The big positive about EC '92 is that the 12 countries are reducing restrictions on business, trade, and labor. People as well as goods and investments will be able to move readily from one of the Common Market nations to any other. That will tend to make industries more efficient as they achieve greater economies of scale and as standardization replaces 12 varieties of many products and services.

Not all of the changes will be beneficial to companies located outside of the community, however. A large negative, from the viewpoint of other nations, is that the trade wall around the EC is not coming down. Actually, the EC is toughening its external barriers to commerce. Enlightened economists are not supposed to use pejorative terms such as Fortress Europa, so let us cite some numbers instead. In 1960, before the Common Market gained momentum, more than 60 percent of the foreign trade of the 12 EC members was outside of the EC. Now over 60 percent of their trade stays in the EC—a complete reversal.[7] That ratio is bound to rise further as a result of EC '92.

This development toward a larger but more inward-looking community serves as a powerful reminder to companies headquartered elsewhere of the benefits of having strong European-based operations in order to take advantage of what is known as "national treatment." In effect, the EC is adopting the economic version of the U.S.

driver's license rule, under which each state honors the licenses issued by the other states no matter how great the variation in the rules of qualification. The results will be similar.

Some of the freedoms that will contribute to the integrated market of Europe may not, however, be extended fully to U.S. firms doing business in the EC, in part because of restrictions imposed by U.S. regulatory authorities themselves. An example is "mutual recognition," meaning that each member of the EC recognizes the laws of the other members. Under this concept, European banks whose home nation permits underwriting and dealing in securities (i.e., investment banking) can provide that service in other member nations, even those that prevent their own banks from doing so. As European banks begin to provide such services beyond the borders of their home countries, the more restrictive regulations of other member nations are likely to loosen.

This regulatory convergence, however, could prove to be a competitive stumbling block for many of the U.S. banks in Europe because of more restrictive U.S. regulatory standards. For example, the Federal Reserve System prevents foreign subsidiaries of U.S. banks from offering nonfinancial services "that could present undue financial risk or otherwise potentially harm the safety and soundness of the banking institution." As the Europe of the 1990s develops, the legal ability of large European banks to own nonfinancial companies and to provide more services than U.S. banks could substantially reduce the competitiveness of U.S. financial institutions operating in Europe.

The biggest negative coincident with the movement to EC '92 is that a more inward-looking Community is toughening its barriers to external commerce. The 1985 White Paper, which outlines the basic approach to the economic integration of the European Community, contains only a single sentence relating to the effects on relations with non-EC countries:

In addition, the Community's trading identity must be strengthened, so that other trading partners will not be offered the benefits from the enlarged Community market without themselves being forced to make concessions.[8]

The French government, for example, has announced new regulations on TV programming (an important service export for the United States and one of the relatively few favorable items in its balance of trade). In the guise of promoting EC-wide TV programming, the French are limiting non-EC programming to 40 percent of total air time.

In private conversations, the Europeans tell U.S. companies not to worry, that most of their trade restrictions, such as reciprocity and domestic content rules, are aimed at Japan. It is, however, far more than a mere riposte for the United States to say that it does not know how good their aim is. The same restrictions that adversely affect Japan can keep out U.S. goods. This may especially be the case for the automobile "transplants," which are built in the United States by Japanese-owned companies. Moreover, if the products of the Asian rim countries are kept out of Europe, the Western Hemisphere is their major alternate market.

EC '92 will produce winners and losers, on both sides of the Atlantic. Likely winners will include strong U.S. firms with an established presence in Western Europe. High-tech, well-capitalized U.S. companies are accustomed to competing on a continentwide basis. They can use one EC country as a base to sell to the other eleven. General Motors and Ford have more Europe-wide strength than such European automakers as Volkswagen, Fiat, Peugeot, and Renault. The same holds true for computer manufacturers such as IBM, Digital Equipment, Unisys, and Hewlett Packard compared to their European counterparts.

The winners will also include the stronger, high-skilled European companies that will be enjoying the economies of scale and growing domestic markets. They should emerge larger than ever.

One category of losers from EC '92 will be the high-cost European firms that have been sheltered within their national markets. These tradition-bound companies will be hurt by continentwide competition. Cheap labor and tax incentives will no longer be key competitive factors. The backward areas, such as Italy's Mezzogiorno, will fall further behind. Realistically, not all barriers to business will be down. The French are not going to make a stampede for German wine, no matter how great the reduction of formal obstacles to intra-European trade.

Finally, many U.S. businesses are likely to be losers from European economic unification. They will find it more difficult to export to Europe. They will also face tougher competition in their domestic markets from stronger EC enterprises. The losers will include many companies that have not yet awakened to developments across the Atlantic. One recent survey found that less than one-half of all U.S. corporations had even heard about Europe '92. Only a small fraction of U.S. firms are responding to that strategic change.[9]

Beyond 1992

By the end of 1992, the economic integration of the present members of the European Community will be far advanced. Of the 300 actions sanctioned in a general way by the EC in 1987, about 250 have been presented as formal proposals, and 130 of them have been adopted by the EC Council of Ministers. Thus far, many of the measures that have passed are difficult, major items. For example, German and Italian regulations covering ingredients of beer and pasta, respectively, have been outlawed as policies that impede imports from other member countries that abide by the EC regulations.[10]

Although the member nations of the EC are expected to be working in harmony much of the time, each will continue to have individual values, cultures, and needs. Despite the substantial amount of progress being made toward full integration, each of the 12 countries will still retain its own currency (at least for the next few years), its own tax system, and, of course, its ultimate sovereignty. Perhaps even more fundamental are the differing national traditions, especially the nine languages that are spoken in the Community.[11]

The EC is not a static concept. It started with 6 countries—Germany, France, Italy, Belgium, the Netherlands, and Luxembourg. Gradually, it has expanded to 12—adding the United Kingdom, Ireland, Denmark, Greece, Spain, and Portugal. That is not the end of the line. Many other European nations are seeking admission. They have been told to wait until 1993 or later.

Austria is a logical candidate for early entry into the EC. Although its economy is modest in size, its admission could be a strategic move, especially since Vienna often views itself as a gateway to Eastern Europe. Most likely, Hungary would then be close behind in the waiting line in Brussels. Czechoslovakia and Poland might be next or, at the least, they could apply to become "associate members."

With Denmark already a member, the other Scandinavian countries are prime candidates for EC membership—Iceland, Sweden, Finland, and especially Norway. With the end of the Cold War, the traditional neutrality of some of these nations should no longer be a barrier to entering into a formal relationship with the EC. In any event, the trade barriers between the EC and the European Free Trade Association or EFTA will be disappearing soon (EFTA includes Norway, Sweden, Finland, Iceland, Austria, and Switzerland). The EC and EFTA are joining forces to form a "European economic space" free of trade barriers.

Looking beyond the initial adjustment period, an economically united Europe will become a political and economic superpower early in the twenty-first century if not sooner. As Stanley Hoffmann, chairman of the Center for European Studies at Harvard, notes in his comment on the European Community:

> Clearly, the purpose of the whole effort is not merely to increase wealth by removing obstacles to production and technological progress, but also to increase Europe's power in a world in which economic and financial clout is as important as military might.[12]

Consider the implications if and when the EC expands from 12 members to 16 or 20. Adding all those gross national products (GNPs) together shows that, in the 1990s, Western (and Central) Europe will become the world's largest market area, with concomitant economic and political power. Despite all the protestations of openness and friendship, the nations in Asia, Africa, and the Americas—and many of their business firms—will be on the outside looking in. Nor is the economic unification of Western and Eastern Europe a foregone conclusion.

Business Potentials in Eastern Europe

Four decades of Communist rule have left the economies of Eastern Europe in extremely poor shape. They are experiencing great difficulty converting their inefficient nationalized industries into competitive private enterprises. Because of the Marxist cliché that unemployment does not exist under communism, East European enterprises are notoriously overstaffed. One steel mill in Poland employs 30,000 workers to make the same amount of steel a U.S. company would make with 7,000.[13]

To make matters worse, Eastern Europe lacks a business infrastructure, which is something so basic to the efficient functioning of a modern economy that Western nations take it for granted. These basic requisites for a private enterprise system include:

- a body of commercial law that is enforced;
- a credible accumulation of cost accounting data that can be used both for setting prices and making valuations of assets;
- personnel who can perform financial analyses;
- banks to provide credit on the basis of financial valuations rather than political determinations; and
- organizations to provide insurance for normal business risks.

In light of the criticism often hurled at these professions in the United States, it is fascinating to consider that Eastern Europe is a world with a shortage of lawyers, accountants, and insurance agents! From a positive viewpoint, that large area may provide a major new client base for many service enterprises headquartered in the more advanced economies.

Eastern Europe also needs generous supplies of capital from the United States and other capitalist nations. This is brought home by Lech Walesa's response to the numerous (and perhaps patronizing) statements by Americans that it is only proper for the United States to repay the moral debt it incurred when so many Poles—such as General Kazimierz Pulaski and General Tadeusz Kosciuszko—helped it during its critical formative period. Walesa on occasion has answered, "OK, so now send us General Electric, General Motors, and General Mills."

Attracting foreign capital in substantial amounts will not be easy. The recent credit history of the East European nations is abysmal. The East Europeans were brought up to hate greedy capitalists and their profiteering. But the move to capitalism (which seems to be an almost universal desire in those nations) will be difficult without capital and capitalists.

It also will be necessary for the rank-and-file employees of the East European nations to do a 180-degree turn in their attitude toward work. They must abandon their universal slogan, "They pretend to pay us and we pretend to work." Consider the thousands of East Germans who have been fired by their new West German employers because they were not in the habit of returning to work after lunch.

Not all East European nations are likely to make the transition to democratic capitalism; the most promising cases are Hungary, Czechoslovakia, and perhaps Poland. Some of the other countries, such as Bulgaria and Romania, may go the authoritarian route. Of course, it would be most heartening if several in fact demonstrate that a nation can return from communism to capitalism—a move that has yet to be accomplished anywhere.

Those countries that succeed could be tough competitors for the low-tech, high-labor-cost industries in the more advanced economies. They could, however, also become subcontractors and suppliers to established Western firms hard pressed by low-cost competitors. The high school education of East European workers is quite good as measured by standardized math and science tests.

The Soviet Union is conspicuously absent from this discussion of ascending economic powers. It is still very much a military superpower, but its economy—aside from the military sector—remains primitive, even if the current political and social instability can be overcome. According to the Soviet Academy of Sciences, Soviet computer capacity is less than one one-thousandth of that of the United States.[14]

Threats and Opportunities for Business

For the individual business firm, the rapid changes in the international economy offer both threat and opportunity. The opportunity arises as more of the developing countries enter the status of industrialized nations. Advanced economies are the best customers of other advanced economies. For example, Bangladesh is not an important customer of U.S. jet airplanes and grain, but Japan is. Yet at the same time home markets will become increasingly vulnerable to foreign competition.

Patterns of Business Adjustment. There is great similarity between the domestic threat of hostile takeovers and the loss of market position due to new foreign competition. In both cases, the firm is forced to review its strengths and weaknesses and to rethink its long-term strategy. Streamlining, downsizing, accelerating product development, and organizational restructuring are often responses to both internal takeover threats and foreign competition.

Stepping back and taking a longer-term perspective makes it clear that fundamental changes are occurring in the very nature of the private business enterprise. The most domestic-oriented firm is increasing its geographic reach as its suppliers and customers are, with increasing frequency, located on a variety of continents. Joint ventures are no longer an obscure legal form. To cite one example among many, over one-half of Corning Glass's profits come from joint ventures. Two-thirds of these cooperative endeavors are with a wide range of foreign companies, including Siemens and Ciba Geigy in Europe and Samsung and Asahi Glass in Asia.

Strategic alliances are no longer just a theoretical possibility; they, too, increasingly involve companies located on different continents. Philips N.V., the Dutch producer of consumer electronics, has cooperated extensively with Matsushita of Japan in developing new products such as compact discs and VCRs.[15]

Sweden's Volvo and France's Renault also have established a strategic alliance, with an explicit division of labor. Renault is doing diesel-engine development, while Volvo is handling advanced emissions controls. The two enterprises are also moving to coordinate parts purchasing, transportation and communication, and new-product strategy.[16] An interesting variation is the collaboration between the U.S.

firm Digital Equipment Corporation and Italy's Olivetti & Co. The two companies are funding and sharing the results from Olivetti's research laboratory in Cambridge, England.[17]

Mergers and acquisitions increasingly involve crossing national boundaries and dealing with two or more national governments, as well as a variety of state, provincial, and local authorities. In 1985, business mergers within the United States accounted for 85 percent of global merger activity. By 1990, U.S. domestic mergers accounted for less than half of the worldwide volume. Most of the U.S. companies operating in Europe do so through subsidiaries resulting from acquisitions.[18]

Partially owned subsidiaries, associated firms, licensing, and correspondent relationships are also on the rise. Often the same companies engage in joint ventures to develop new products, coproduce existing products, serve as sources of supply for each other, share output, and compete. There is no set pattern. Various companies—in the same nation and often in the same industry—are responding to the global marketplace differently.

United Technologies exemplifies the use of geographic diversification on a global scale in developing new products. For its new elevator, its French division worked on the door systems; the Spanish division handled the small-geared components; the German subsidiary was responsible for the electronics; the Japanese unit designed the special motor drives; and the Connecticut group handled the systems integration. International teamwork cut the development cycle in half.[19]

IBM is often cited as the role model for foreign firms focusing on high-technology markets. Potential imitators note that the corporation's basic research laboratories are in Switzerland and Japan, as well as the United States. Its 30-odd research divisions are located around the world. Thus, the process of international technology transfer at IBM is often internal to the firm. Xerox Corporation is another interesting example of global production. Xerox has introduced some 80 different office copying machines in the United States that were engineered and built by its Japanese joint venture, Fuji Xerox Company.

The automobile industry provides a

fascinating array of examples of inter-firm and intercontinental endeavors. General Motors has joint ventures with Japan's Toyota and Suzuki and partial ownership of Sweden's Saab, Korea's Daewoo, and Japan's Isuzu and Suzuki. Volkswagen reports joint ventures with America's Ford and Japan's Nissan and Toyota, and has a stake in Czechoslovakia's Skoda.[20] Virtually all of these companies compete with their partners and investors, at least to some degree.

The computer industry is not to be outdone in this regard. For example, Unisys is a customer of, a supplier to, and a competitor of IBM and Honeywell in North America, Fujitsu and Hitachi in Asia, and Phillips, Siemens, and BASF in Europe.[21] The trend is accelerating. In June 1991, AT&T, British Telecommunications, France Telecom, and Kokusai Denshin Denwa joined forces to provide large customers with a global communications network capability.[22]

Business Lessons for the Future. Some lessons can be learned from the experience of companies that do well in international markets. First, they change their basic corporate goals to conform to a global marketplace; for the most successful, top management leads that process of adjustment.[23]

Second, they translate a domestic advantage to create overseas opportunities by adapting their established home products to the local markets in other nations. Pall Filters, the major U.S. producers of wine filters, penetrated the sophisticated French market by designing a new French version of its filters. The company then went on to enter the Italian wine market with a second variation of its product.

In the service area, U.S. financial institutions compete internationally primarily by building on strengths developed in their domestic markets. Financial institutions in the United States and the United Kingdom have developed a high degree of technical expertise in constructing, managing, and marketing complex financial products and services used around the world. This expertise involves both the development of physical capital—primarily computer systems and software—and trained professionals and support staff with both technical and market knowledge.

For example, banks participate heavily in foreign exchange "swaps" related to balance sheet management because of their expertise in managing interest rate risks. U.S. investment bankers, in contrast, are more prevalent in the market for swaps related to new issues of securities. There is a broader sense in which financial institutions have sought competitive advantage in international markets through product specialization that mirrors their strength in domestic markets.[24]

Japanese banks, in contrast, initially penetrate an overseas market by serving the Japanese firms doing business there. Subsequently, they broaden their customer base (after learning more about the local market) to win local clients.[25]

The third lesson is that the successful global firms do not set up large international bureaucracies. One recent survey reported that the cost of the international staff rarely exceeds 1 percent of sales. Moreover, most overseas operations are run by foreign nationals who understand the local markets. Further, they start their foreign operations when the company is still of moderate size, contradicting the widespread notion that only giant companies can succeed overseas.

But it takes massive resources to provide a universal presence. Toyota, IBM, Phillips, DuPont, Bayer, Sony, and Unilever have expanded into almost all of the world's major markets.[26] A global economy, however, does not mean that every company should try to cater to every global market. Many small and medium-sized firms are learning the hard way to focus on specialty products and market niches where they have special advantages. For example, Sweden's L. M. Ericsson sells very specialized state-of-the-art components for communications equipment in approximately 70 countries.[27]

Local offices provide a company with a built-in laboratory for developing new programs and servicing techniques that can be adapted throughout the global network. Moreover, the power of modern communications means that Manchester, England, and Louisville, Kentucky, are as much a part of the international marketplace as London and New York. A mix of smaller and medium-sized locations is part of a pattern that gives the modern corporation diversification and stability during periods of rapid growth and recession alike.

Finally, global successes encourage foreign subsidiaries to make innovations that can also be used in the home market. Dunkin' Donuts established its reputation in the United States by always having fresh doughnuts and coffee prepared on the premises. In Tokyo, however, land was too expensive for that procedure, so the company started preparing the doughnuts and coffee on the trucks bringing in supplies. The company is now starting to follow this practice in some of its domestic sites in central cities.

Clearly, there will be winners and losers as business adjusts. Not every company is going to be a grand success in the global marketplace of the 1990s. All this illustrates an earlier point: In change, there is both threat and opportunity—and the global marketplace is surely changing rapidly.

Important Public Policy Implications

The current legislative battles over trade protectionism and foreign investment restrictions are only the most obvious manifestations of the rising tension between domestic political forces and transnational economic influences. Although private enterprise is increasingly global (in purchasing, financing, research, and production as well as marketing), government policy remains parochial. Understandably, voters still care about jobs in their country, province, state, and locality, and politicians react to those sentiments.

Business and National Governments. The tension between business and government is nothing new. It has traditionally existed between large private enterprises and the rulers of developing countries. In fact, most countries restrict foreign investments in defense, public utilities, and the media. Quite a few governments require that a majority of the capital of local firms be owned by their own nationals.[28]

The tension between governments generally (both those with developing and those with more advanced economies) and the business firm is being exacerbated by the rapid rate of economic, social, and technological change. Fortunately, there is another force involved that is ultimately likely to carry the day—the citizen as consumer. Consumers vote every day of the week—in dollars, yen, deutsche marks, pounds, francs, and lira. The same protectionist-oriented voters, as consumers, purchase products made anywhere in the world. They give far greater weight in spending their own money to price and quality than country of origin. And they increasingly travel to, and communicate with, people in virtually every land.

Thus, without thinking about it, consumers are adapting to the global economy. After all, if consumers were not so globally oriented, the pressures for restricting international trade would not arise in the first place. In the years ahead, the power of economic forces and technological change will increasingly force voters and government officials to adjust to the realities of the international economy.[29]

Meanwhile, some of the former *multinational* companies with large headquarters operations and a number of overseas subsidiaries are becoming *transnational* enterprises with activities and responsibilities spread more evenly around the world. For an increasing number of transnational companies, profits and revenues from abroad surpass those of the country of origin. Because the interests and stakeholders of these transnational businesses are located all over the globe, some of their leaders contend that they are losing their national identities and becoming "global citizens."[30]

Business and International Agencies. The transnational business firms also develop relationships with the international economic organizations established by governments. They participate actively in the business advisory committees of the Organization for Economic Cooperation and Development (OECD), the European Community, and the specialized agencies of the United Nations (UN), such as the Economic and Social Council and the International Labor Organization.

The rise of international regulatory agencies, in many ways, is an expected response of political forces to the global economy. Some types of supranational regulation are traditional, going back to the nineteenth century. For example, the forerunner of the International Telecommunications Union was established in 1865 as the International Telegraph Union. It dealt mainly with technical standards.

Some of the specialized agencies of the UN have moved ahead with the formulation of codes and guidelines. Examples range from the World Health Organization's Infant Formula Code, to the Food and Agricultural Organization's International Code of Conduct in the Distribution and Use of Pesticides, to the over 300 labor standards promulgated by the International Labor Organization. The latter in the aggregate have resulted in more than 5,000 government ratifications.

The UN's Economic and Social Council is developing a code governing multinational corporations. However, the effort has bogged down, given the complexities arising from the great variety of international business relationships (as described above). Also, the governments of the developing nations, in many cases, see a more activist role for the UN agencies than do the representatives of the more advanced economies, who are oriented to private-sector decision making in less regulated marketplaces.[31]

In a far more basic sense, the mobility of enterprises—of their people, capital, and information—is reducing the power of government at all levels. Some economists maintain that public-sector decision makers around the world are being forced to understand that in a very new way they have to become competitive in the economic policies they devise. Domestic policies that impose costs without compensating benefits or that reduce wealth substantially in the process of redistributing income undermine the competitive positions of domestic enterprises. The result is either the loss of business to firms located in other nations or the movement of the domestic company's resources to more hospitable locations.

Political scientists and economists have long since understood that people vote with their feet, leaving regions and nations with limited opportunity in favor of those that offer a more attractive future. In a day of computers, telephones, and facsimile machines, enterprises are far more mobile than that. Thus, the fear of losing economic activity to other parts of the world can be expected to reshape domestic political agendas in fundamental ways.[32] Moreover, more open economies characterized by governments that have less influence over private decision making will generate an unexpected side effect—the promotion of international harmony simply because of the growing economic incentives to avoid the devastation of war.

There is a positive role for government in dealing with the global marketplace and it is well known: Enhance the productivity and competitiveness of the enterprises located in the government's jurisdiction by reducing tax and regulatory burdens and lowering the real cost of capital through curbing deficit financing.

Also, antitrust laws need to be updated. It took decades for the U.S. Justice Department to acknowledge the role of imports in the domestic marketplace. Yet the "relevant market" (a key concept in antitrust enforcement) often now extends beyond the borders of the United States. Likewise, the geographic restrictions on U.S. banks, limiting them to a single state or region, prevent them from attaining the economies of scale and market positions that would match the now dominant power of Asian and European financial institutions.

Economic education at present faces the challenging task of helping citizens (consumers/taxpayers) to understand the increasingly global nature of economic life. It is true that it is easier to see the impact of foreign money in the domestic economy than it is to visualize the role of one country's investment in other nations. Yet the effects flow in both directions.

A quarter of a century ago, the citizens of Western Europe were complaining that the United States was making the world one big Coca-Cola franchise. The "American challenge" was a popular topic for public debates overseas. The U.S. reply was that U.S. investment benefited foreigners by creating employment, income, and tax collections in their countries. Although the shoe is now on the other foot, the results are very similar. Foreign investment is creating jobs, income, and tax revenue in the United States. Because the financing of outsized budget deficits drains off so much of U.S. domestic savings, that foreign money is a key factor in the continued prosperity of the United States.

In a positive way, U.S. public policy

should focus on the government's area of primary responsibility: the education of the future work force. Given the international economy in which the next generation will be competing, it is sad to report that, compared to the students of most other industrial nations, U.S. students know less biology, chemistry, and math, understand little of foreign cultures, and rarely speak or read foreign languages.

The low literacy rates and high dropout rates cannot be blamed on foreigners. Dealing with domestic educational shortcomings is the unique responsibility of Americans. A well-educated citizenry is vital to the future of a democracy; it is also the key to achieving greater productivity and global competitiveness.

Work for this paper was supported by a grant from the William H. Donner Foundation.

Notes

1. Alex Taylor III, "Do You Know Where Your Car Was Made?" *Fortune*, June 17, 1991, pp. 52–53.

2. "America and Japan: The Unhappy Alliance," *Economist*, February 17–23, 1990, pp. 21–24; Jane S. Little, "Intra-Firm Trade," *New England Economic Review*, May–June 1987, pp. 46–51.

3. De Anne Julius, *Global Companies and Public Policy* (Rotterdam: RIIA/Pinter, 1990); Kenichi Ohmae, "The Interlinked Economy," *Chief Executive*, October 1990, p. 50.

4. Jeff Shear, "Foreign Investment Is Making a Borderless Corporate World," *Insight*, July 1990, p. 40.

5. Sandra Feustel, "How a Fax Machine Saved GIC," *Institutional Investor* 24 (September 1990), p. 78.

6. This section draws on Murray Weidenbaum and Mark Jensen, *Threats and Opportunities in the International Economy* (St. Louis: Washington University, Center for the Study of American Business, 1990).

7. Wilhelm Nolling, *Fortress Europe? The External Trade Policy of the European Communities* (Frankfurt, 1988), p. 31; *Basic Statistics of the Community*, 26th ed. (Luxembourg: Eurostat, 1989).

8. Cited in Nolling, *Fortress Europe?* p. 31.

9. "Calls Japan the One to Beat in Europe After 1992," *Electronic News*, September 1989, p. 37; see also Kenneth Oehlkers, "Are Top U.S. Executives Slow to Develop a Global Outlook?" *A. Gary Shilling's Insight*, June 1990, p. 5.

10. Michael Emerson, "The Emergence of the New European Economy of 1992," *Business Economics* 24 (October 1989), pp. 5–9.

11. Nolling, *Fortress Europe?* p. 26. The EC nations are trying to move toward a common value added tax rate, such as 15 percent, to expedite trade across the Community.

12. Stanley Hoffmann, "The European Community and 1992," *Foreign Affairs* 68 (Fall 1989), p. 43.

13. Murray Weidenbaum, "Poland: Another Middle Way?" *Society* 28 (November/December 1990), pp. 51–55.

14. Yuri N. Maltsev, "When Reform Collides With Ideology," *American Enterprise* 1 (March/April 1990), p. 89.

15. David Lee, "Strategies for Global Competition," *Long Range Planning* 22, no. 1 (1989), p. 102.

16. Robert Simison and Stephen D. Moore, "Volvo Defends Alliance With Renault, Saying the Logic Will Soon Be Evident," *Wall Street Journal*, June 17, 1991, p. A–7.

17. Richard L. Hudson, "Digital and Olivetti Plan to Collaborate on Research Project at British Facility," *Wall Street Journal*, June 17, 1991, p. A5A.

18. Roy C. Smith and Ingo Walter, *The First European Merger Boom Has Begun* (St. Louis: Washington University, Center for the Study of American Business, 1991), p. 3.

19. "The Stateless Corporations," *Business Week*, May 14, 1990, p. 101.

20. Christopher Sawyer, "The Global Village," *Autoweek*, January 28, 1991, pp. 20–21.

21. Michael Blumenthal, "Macroeconomic Policy," in *International Economic Cooperation*, Martin Feldstein, ed. (Cambridge, Mass.: National Bureau of Economic Research, 1987), p. 16.

22. Robin Gareiss, "Carriers Set Global Plan," *Communications Week*, June 3, 1991, p. 1.

23. William Lilley, "How U.S. Companies Succeed in International Markets," *National Economists Club Summary*, December 1, 1987, pp. 1–3; Booz-Allen Hamilton survey reported by George Anders, "Role of Chief Is Seen Crucial in Going Global," *Wall Street Journal*, November 30, 1990, p. A–9.

24. Beverly Hirtle, "Factors Affecting the Competitiveness of Internationally Active Financial Institutions," *Federal Reserve Bank of New York Quarterly Review*, Spring 1991, pp. 38–51.

25. Rama Seth and Alicia Quijano, "Japanese Banks' Customers in the United States," *Federal Reserve Bank of New York Quarterly Review*, Spring 1991, pp. 79–82.

26. W. Chan Kim and R. A. Mauborgne, "Becoming an Effective Global Competitor," *Journal of Business Strategy* 9 (January/February 1988), p. 34.

27. Jordan D. Lewis, *Partnerships for Profit: Structuring and Managing Strategic Alliances* (New York: Free Press, 1990), p. 26.

28. Thomas N. Gladwin and Ingo Walter, *Multinationals Under Fire: Lessons in the Management of Conflict* (New York: John Wiley & Sons, 1980), p. 265.

29. Richard McKenzie and Dwight Lee, *Quicksilver Capital: How the Rapid Movement of Capital Has Changed the World* (New York: Free Press, 1991).

30. Wisse Dekker, "The Rise of the Stateless CEO," *CEO/International Strategies*, March/April 1991, p. 17.

31. Murray Weidenbaum, *Business, Government, and the Public*, 4th ed. (Englewood Cliffs, N.J.: Prentice-Hall, 1990), pp. 307–311.

32. Richard McKenzie, *The Global Economy and Government Power* (St. Louis: Washington University, Center for the Study of American Business, 1989), pp. 17–18.

A Realignment Made Reluctantly

Nations Warily Let Economics Displace the Cold War Issues

Roger Cohen

Special to The New York Times

GENEVA, Dec. 14—For all its arcane murkiness, the trade agreement struck today has traced important contours of the post–cold war era. The negotiations that began seven years ago in moderate obscurity have ended as a pivotal political event, engaging heads of state in discussions about rice and placing the likes of Steven Spielberg and Mario Vargas Llosa in heated debate about cultural values.

Most fundamentally, this unlikely transformation reflects the collapse of the Iron Curtain. In a world no longer defined by military and ideological conflict, what counts for politicians are economic success and the creation of jobs. That is why President Clinton and Chancellor Helmut Kohl of Germany have been as involved in the General Agreement on Tariffs and Trade talks as their predecessors were in negotiations to station new missiles in Western Europe.

For artists, the barricades are at a different place in a different ideological war, dividing those for and against a completely free market for their creations. That is why Hollywood and the Rive Gauche now talk GATT.

Beneath the Visions

But if the GATT discussions were supposed to be about the end of conflict and the laying out of a commercial framework for a new world—offering a vision of a planet without barriers enriched by freer trade and open to the invitations of an unfettered market—they came instead to reveal something more akin to unease rather than enthusiastic expectation.

Although failure was averted by an outline agreement today that will cut tariffs by about one-third and extend trade rules to a host of new areas including agriculture, what emerged from the 116-nation talks was a world suspicious of American economic and cultural domination and reluctant to accept an invitation to the global mall.

While, in the end, nobody was prepared to countenance a collapse of the talks—tantamount to inviting political and economic dislocation within the Western alliance and the emergence of regional economic blocs in the Americas, Asia and Europe—there was little evidence that nations felt sufficiently reassured by the demise of Communism to embrace a global economic opening that would transcend narrow self-interest and national traditions.

"The hope was that the GATT talks could be the centerpiece of a new era in which global institutions and opening would replace the old postwar alliances and provide a new sense of cohesion for the international system," said Robert D. Hormats, the vice chairman of Goldman Sachs International. "But there was resistance to that. If the global economy is a glue, it's a weak one."

Not Entirely Successful

Thus, although agreement was reached to establish a new Multilateral Trade Organization to symbolize the world's common interest in orderly commerce, the effort to extend GATT rules to the more than $1 trillion in annual worldwide trade in services had limited success.

Shipping was set aside, and the opening of markets to financial services like banking and securities trading was effectively postponed to a later date. Most significant, the world's, and particularly America's, booming trade in movies, music and other entertainment became a subject not for agreement but for unresolved and vitriolic conflict between the United States and Europe.

"Services, intellectual property and investment should have been the core of this round, because they are the core issues in the real world," said Alan Stoga, the managing director of Kissinger Associates. "In the end, these issues were put on the agenda, but not much more than that."

Even the appearance on the agenda of the movie question—part of the debate on trade in intellectual property—was enough to provoke an extraordinary European outcry, rooted in but not confined to France. The target was Hollywood, portrayed as a marauder as mindless as the dinosaurs of "Jurassic Park," intent on devouring the vestiges of European culture.

It was "Dallas" versus Dépardieu, culture as commerce versus culture as art—and the result was an impasse hailed by Jack Lang, the former Culture Minister of France, as "a victory for art and artists over the commercialization of culture."

The trade talks expose fears of a global mall run by the U.S.

In Washington, President Clinton told reporters that he was "disappointed" that the audio-visual portions of the agreement remained unresolved, but that no one "thought it was worth bringing the whole thing down over."

But, at a deeper level, it was Europe against the most visible symbol of the spread of American culture and economic influence in a world that is no longer bipolar. And for several French intellectuals and writers, the conflict assumed global dimensions.

Did the world, by endorsing the free-trade principles of GATT, really want to demolish national identities in favor of a blanket American-dominated culture and so encourage the emergence, in angry reaction, of the likes of the Russian nationalist Vladimir V. Zhirinovsky?

"Should we really convert the planet into a supermarket in order to leave people with a choice between Coca-Cola and the local ayatollah?" the French philosopher and writer Régis Debray asked.

Baseball Caps and Dinosaurs

That may sound like an extreme point of view—and there has been much relentless caricaturing of the United States in Europe in recent weeks. But it has become clear that GATT does raise the delicate political question of how far national traditions and policies are prepared to cede to the economic globalization symbolized by universal baseball caps and universal screen dinosaurs.

For example, in opening its market to imported rice for the first time, Japan was taking more than a small trade step. Rice cultivation is central to Japan's religion, culture and folklore and the bar on imports symbolized its sacredness. Each spring, the Emperor plants the first seedling on the grounds of the Imperial Palace. But in the end, the Japanese Government decided that access to markets outweighed these considerations.

Europe, however, balked, preserving its quotas and subsidies that penalize American films and limit the prospects in Europe of fast-expanding American services like pay-per-view and cable television channels.

As a result, the GATT accord emerged as a two-headed beast. On the one hand, said John Lipsky, chief economist for Salomon Brothers, "This is far better than no agreement, an encouragement to economic growth and a vital statement that the world still believes in trade liberalization."

On the other hand, the limits of that liberalization have been shown. By standing up for what they see as their threatened culture, European governments effectively said no to globalization. They also insured that the GATT accord will fall significantly short of its target, and suggested to many economists that regional agreements like the North American Free Trade Agreement may prove to be more of a model for the future than a much-vaunted, but somewhat hollow, multilateralism.

Beyond Conditionality

Foreign Aid and the Changing Global Agenda

Joan M. Nelson

Joan M. Nelson is a Senior Associate of the Overseas Development Council.

FOREIGN AID IS A FLEXIBLE TOOL, serving goals ranging from the most short-run and narrow diplomatic maneuvers, through broad medium-term geopolitical strategies, to long-run humanitarian and ethical objectives. By the late 1950s and early 1960s, foreign aid had emerged as a standard instrument of wealthy nations' foreign policies toward poorer nations and regions. Bilateral aid programs have reflected donors' varying international roles and priorities. For example, Scandinavian and Dutch programs have emphasized reducing poverty, while German and French programs have traditionally reflected stronger commercial and political concerns. US economic assistance has been strongly skewed toward Cold War and Middle Eastern security concerns since the 1950s. The World Bank, which has traditionally emphasized development infrastructure and (in the 1970s) more direct anti-poverty projects, has re-oriented its efforts to promote far-reaching reforms in economic policy and structure since the 1980s.

Western goals and priorities *vis-à-vis* poorer nations are now changing rapidly, and foreign aid policies will evolve accordingly. These shifts reflect not only the collapse of the Cold War and the disintegration of the Soviet Union, but also longer trends that have been building since at least the mid-1970s. These include:

• a growing understanding of global environmental threats and the emergence of international organizations and agreements to address them;

• a rising tide of legal and illegal immigrants from poorer countries into Western Europe, the United states, and Canada;

• the ominous growth of the international narcotics trade;

• the emergence of transnational groups monitoring and publicizing human rights abuses, and greatly heightened public disgust at these abuses;

• the weakening or replacement of authoritarian governments by more open political systems in most of Latin America, in parts of Asia and more recently in Africa.

The abrupt end of the Cold War has greatly reduced the security concerns that had informed much of US aid policy, but it has also added an immense new goal: the transformation and integration into the international system of the economies of Eastern Europe and the successor states of the Soviet Union. The same events have also opened the possibility of rapid progress toward global demilitarization.

Thus, the 1990s began with a greatly expanded Western agenda—both in terms of geographic scope and range of issues—with respect to the poorer nations of the world. All of these goals demand resources and require changes of policies and behavior within developing (as well as developed) nations. Therefore, all are being pursued in part through foreign aid. The tasks of foreign aid have multiplied dramatically.

Does Aid Work?

Paradoxically, while aid is viewed as a useful instrument for a daunting array of tasks, it is also widely regarded (particularly in the US) as ineffective and possibly even harmful. Perhaps influenced by images of starvation in Somalia and terrorism in Peru, many people assume that development has failed in the Third World and that development aid must therefore also have failed. Many believe that too much aid is misdirected to corrupt or repressive governments—that even where aid has promoted growth, it has not reached the very poor. Recently there has also been increased concern that specific aid projects, as well as the general pattern of development that is being promoted, pose unacceptable threats to the global or local environment.

The idea that development has failed and that aid must therefore be ineffective is both the broadest and the least well-founded of the various criticisms of foreign aid. Overall, despite major setbacks in the 1980s, Asia, Latin America and even much of Africa have made impressive progress in the past thirty years. The UN *Human Development Report* calculates that real per capita GDP tripled for all developing countries between 1960 and 1989, after correcting for differences in purchasing power. Even in the poorest nations, where progress tends to be slowest, incomes have grown by two-thirds (and by 84 percent in sub-Saharan Africa). Average life expectancy has increased by sixteen years, adult literacy by 40 percent and per capita nutritional levels by over 20 percent. Child mortality rates have been halved. Without question, bilateral and multilateral aid has contributed to this record. Particularly in the poorer countries, aid has provided a large portion of total investment, including funding for schools, clinics, roads and power—in short, the basic infrastructure of development. Some nations that experienced dramatic economic success, such as Korea and Taiwan, received extensive aid in the early stages of their development.

To argue that the contribution of foreign aid has been important is not to assert that it has been fully efficient. Bad judgment in design and execution, serious unanticipated side-effects, lack of coordination among donors and corruption within the system are ongoing problems. A good deal of aid has indeed been directed to corrupt and repressive governments. Support for some of the most blatant cases of abuse, such as those that occured in Zaire, reflected Cold War concerns and therefore has been virtually halted in the past few years. In many countries where aid has promoted growth, it has failed to benefit the very poor. The World Bank and many bilateral donors have reoriented parts of their programs, putting more pressure on recipient governments to adopt stronger measures to reduce poverty. Similarly, although the environmental implications of specific projects and broader development strategies have indeed been neglected, most aid agencies are currently working hard to correct that weakness.

To understand why development aid has been highly effective in some countries at some periods, and much less effective in other places or times, it is crucial to keep in mind two further points. First, the impact of aid is strongly influenced by the broader policies, programs and overall competence of the recipient country. The best-designed agricultural extension projects and irrigation investments may fail to make their expected contribution if overvalued exchange rates and inefficient government crop-purchasing monopolies erode farmers' incentives. In the 1980s, donors sharply increased their emphasis on policy reforms because they recognized that aid is most effective when it is combined with sound economic policies and competent government.

Second, growth and the effectiveness of development aid are also powerfully influenced by international economic trends and by the trade and financial policies of the industrial democracies. Smaller, highly trade-dependent economies are particularly vulnerable to shifts in international prices and demand. Industrial countries' tariff and non-tariff trade barriers cost developing countries roughly US$40 billion a year—almost as much as total aid from all the industrial democracies. During the mid-1980s, the combination of high indebtedness, increased interest rates and the abrupt cutoff of private investments and credits to much of the developing world resulted in net negative flows—from poor to wealthy nations—on the order of US$30 billion annually. Aid alone cannot secure growth, and its benefits may be undone by countervailing donor actions.

In short, the financial and technical resources of foreign aid are only part of a much larger and more complex set of forces that affect economic growth and social progress. Aid usually deserves neither the bulk of credit for progress nor the brunt of blame for stagnation or decay. Yet aid can play a major and occasionally determining role in particular sectors or circumstances. In more advanced developing nations, the role played by aid appropriately dwindles, though aid on harder terms may continue to contribute to the resolution of specialized problems or the support of specific reforms. In the poorest countries aid is a crucial, though not sufficient, ingredient for growth. And growth in turn is a necessary, though far from sufficient, condition for a range of major goals including environmental protection, the reduction of poverty and emigration and the consolidation of democratic openings. Growth also facilitates military downsizing and the conversion of military personnel and industries to civilian use.

Conditional Aid and Economic Reforms

Traditionally, aid has contributed to growth primarily by increasing the quantity and quality of physical and human capital. In the past dozen years, while retaining its traditional functions, aid has also increasingly been used as a lever to influence recipients' broad economic policies.

By the end of the 1970s, many development specialists were convinced that inappropriate economic policies were the primary cause of flagging growth in many countries, above all in sub-Saharan Africa. The debt crisis that broke out in August 1982 forced painful stabilization measures on much of Latin America and Africa, further spotlighting the need for more durable changes in their policies and economic structure. With this need in mind, the World Bank began to experiment with non-project aid conditioned on specific economic reforms. By the end of the decade, over 60 countries had received policy-

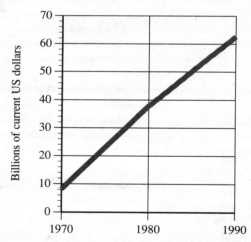

Trends in Levels of Development Assistance

Billions of current US dollars (vertical axis: 0–70)
Horizontal axis: 1970, 1980, 1990

Official development assistance includes all grants and loans on concessional financial terms, equivalent to at least a 25 percent element. Data are net disbursements; commitments and gross disbursements are somewhat larger. Figures include contributions to developing countries from both bilateral and multilateral sources. Multilateral aid accounts for approximately 20 percent of all aid flows.

Source: Development Cooperation 1984 *and* 1991, *OECD*

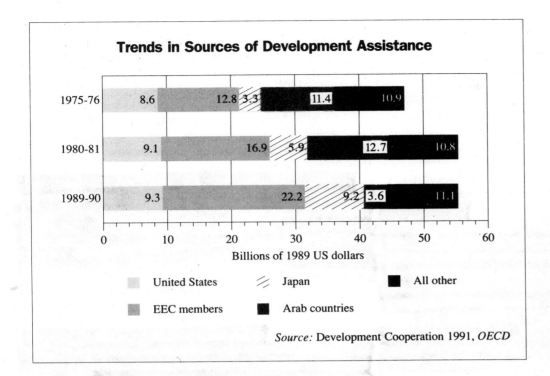

Trends in Sources of Development Assistance

	United States	EEC members	Japan	Arab countries	All other	
1975-76	8.6	12.8	3.3	11.4	10.9	
1980-81	9.1	16.9	5.9	12.7	10.8	
1989-90	9.3	22.2	9.2	3.6	11.1	

Billions of 1989 US dollars

Source: Development Cooperation 1991, *OECD*

based loans, accounting for 20 to 30 percent of World Bank assistance. The Agency for International Development also expanded its policy-based lending and, like other major bilateral lenders, coordinated at least part of its aid with World Bank and International Monetary Fund (IMF) programs and advice. Some of the conditions, like those long-required by the IMF, relate to the management of the economy as a whole. Others focus on more permanent structural reforms, including reduced government regulation of prices, reduced tariff and non-tariff barriers to trade, financial sector reforms and more efficient operation—even privatization—of loss-incurring public enterprises.

Have such conditions effectively altered policies? The experiences of the IMF and, in particular, the World Bank suggest that compliance with economic reform conditions is best for measures that: (1) can be put into effect by a small circle of officials; (2) are "single shot" (that is, do not require a series of implementation steps); (3) are readily monitored; and (4) on whose technical aspects there is a strong consensus. Such measures include reforms in price, interest and exchange rate policies and credit ceilings. Most IMF conditions, and a smaller proportion of World Bank conditions, focus on such actions.

In contrast, compliance is less likely with reforms that require the cooperation of many people and agencies, entail extensive follow-up measures or ancillary actions and are qualitative in nature and difficult to monitor objectively. Complex institutional reforms often prove particularly difficult.

Not surprisingly, governments in acute need of financing are more compliant with economic reform conditions than those with alternative sources of finance. But in general, compliance is best—particularly with more complex, extended reforms—when key officials are convinced that reforms are necessary, appropriate and have the backing of political leadership. When governments do not "own" the reforms, they tend to abandon

them under domestic political pressure (or less obviously, with slight improvements in the economic situation).

Since ownership or commitment by the government is the key to sustained reforms, the appropriate goal of reform-mongering aid agencies should not be short-run compliance but rather the achievement of a more lasting influence on a country's thinking about the nature of its problems and its search for workable solutions. Conditionality can further this goal. The negotiation of conditioned loans draws aid officials into intense ongoing dialogue with officials and politicians in recipient countries. Sometimes even non-compliance with conditions may have a long-run influence by defining specific policy options and prominently placing them on the agenda for national debate.

Indeed, the basic assumptions guiding economic policy debate and choices of development strategies in poorer countries have changed dramatically since 1980, and dialogue and conditionality have clearly contributed to that change. There is now substantial agreement regarding the importance of fiscal discipline (and its implications for both public expenditures and tax reform), price liberalization (including realistic interest and exchange rates) and open trading regimes, as well as consensus on the drawbacks of extensive direct government involvement in both production and detailed price and wage control. The parameters of debate about economic strategies between industrial and developing nations have thus narrowed substantially.

However, within those narrowed parameters urgent questions are being raised, in post-Communist as well as Third World countries, as to whether neo-classical prescriptions are sufficient to restart growth and address issues of poverty and equity. Even the most vigorous and sustained neo-classical reforms, such as those implemented by Chile, Mexico and Bolivia, incurred several years of painful damage to people and infrastructure before growth began. Can growth somehow be sped up? Or can transitional damage be contained by changing the phases and sequences of reforms? Granted that the state's direct economic role should be reduced, an effective state is nevertheless crucial for effective markets. What roles should the state now play in regulating the economy, providing social services and expanding infrastructure? How can poverty be reduced and the environment protected, given the necessity of economic adjustment?

Conditionality for Non–Economic Reforms?

Both the successes and the limitations of conditionality as a means of influencing economic reforms are relevant to other issues on the post-Cold War Western agenda. Environmental protection, increased respect for human rights, consolidation of democratic openings, reduced expenditures on arms, more vigorous efforts to reduce poverty and containment of the drug trade all entail changes in the policies, actions and underlying priorities of governments in poorer nations. Each of these goals is already the focus of specific aid projects and technical assistance, but should they also be targets of conditionality?

To some extent they already are. In 1990 and 1991, almost all major bilateral donors announced that they would begin to consider progress toward some or all of these objectives (as well

> **The wealthy nations' zeal for new, or newly elevated, goals on their agenda will be diluted by perennial diplomatic, commercial and residual security considerations.**

as economic reform) as criteria for providing aid. The charter of the newly-created European Bank for Reconstruction and Development makes competitive elections a precondition for its aid. Non-governmental organizations and legislative groups in North America and Western Europe (with backing from their counterparts in some poorer nations) are urging the World Bank to press political and environmental reforms on its borrowers.

The wealthy nations' zeal for new, or newly elevated, goals on their agenda will be diluted by perennial diplomatic, commercial and residual security considerations. Sanctions against blatant violations of international norms have already been eroded or abandoned—not only with regard to major countries such as China, but also in the case of far smaller ones like Haiti. However, more specific offers of assistance linked to requirements for policy reform are likely to be increasingly common in areas such as environmental reform, arms reductions and pro-poor measures.

As is the case with economic reforms, environmental, political and pro-poor conditions have a greater chance of success if they can be put into effect by a small circle of officials and do not entail extensive follow-on measures—for example, a condition requiring the release of political prisoners. By contrast, if

human rights were being widely violated by bands of marauding soldiers or warring ethnic groups, central government officials might lack the power to contain the offenders and end the violations. Similarly, specific legislation or regulations preventing the formation of civic associations might be an appropriate target for conditionality. But conditionality is probably not a useful way to press central governments to consult with citizens' committees on local projects—a goal that requires extensive institutional and procedural innovation, as well as cooperation from citizens' groups.

An even more important lesson from past experience with economic conditionality is the key role of government commitment. Where a government is committed, conditionality is largely redundant. Conversely, where a government remains indifferent or hostile to the goal—be it environmental protection, democracy or poverty reduction—conditionality will have little lasting effect.

I have argued that conditionality can often contribute to the domestic debate that is so crucial for commitment. However, conditionality's potential benefits must also be weighed against its probable costs. Conditionality is always resented on three grounds: it is regarded as an invasion of sovereignty; it is an explicit or implicit claim that the donor knows best what is good for the recipient; and it reflects power inequalities. At best, it runs the risks of diverting attention from substantive issues to procedure and bargaining, discrediting reforms by making them appear externally imposed and undermining officials' sense of responsibility for their own actions and their country's fate. Conditionality also carries costs for the donor: it consumes a great deal of staff time and energy and may sour the atmosphere for dialogue, thereby jeopardizing other foreign policy goals. At worst, conditionality degenerates into a ritual where recipients pretend to comply and aid agencies pretend to believe them.

Multiple conditionality—the simultaneous use of conditions attached to aid (or trade) to promote several or all of the goals on the new global agenda—carries additional risks. Perhaps most fundamentally, the goals themselves may conflict. Recent policy statements—for instance, those issued by both official and unofficial participants in the recent United Nations Conference on Environment and Development in Rio de Janeiro—emphasize the complementary nature of such goals as the improvement of human rights, broadened popular participation, competitive democracy, environmental protection, pro-poor policies and reduced expenditures on arms. But equally clear is the fact that these issues may interfere with each other, and with economic reform, under specific circumstances. The tension between market-oriented economic reforms and the consolidation of political liberalization in many fragile new democracies is only one example.

Moreover, priorities vary among bilateral and multilateral aid agencies, raising the likely prospect of competing pressures and demands. In addition, governments in many poorer nations are already severely overstrained and suffer from the consequences of prolonged fiscal crises and political discontinuities. If conditionality is to be productive rather than disruptive, donors will have to use it sparingly, keeping in mind the varying capabilities of individual poorer nations and the kinds of goals

Truly multilateral arrangements that involve poorer nations in setting international standards and monitoring compliance are more likely to generate genuine commitment without all of the costs of conventional conditionality.

that experience suggests are best suited to conditional approaches. Donors will also have to redouble efforts to coordinate among themselves.

Beyond Conditionality

Conditionality is only one of many approaches to influencing policies. The broadened global agenda of the 1990s portends considerably increased external intervention in what have traditionally been regarded as the sovereign affairs of individual nations. To be sustainable, such intervention may require modes of persuasion and pressure that move beyond the interaction between a single aid recipient and a single donor or a single recipient and multiple donors (as in aid consultative groups). Truly multilateral arrangements that involve poorer nations in setting international standards and monitoring compliance are more likely to generate genuine commitment without all of the costs of conventional conditionality.

Partial prototypes of such arrangements exist. In Central America, several overlapping channels for consultation among the governments of the region and between these governments and the donor community have evolved since the mid-1980s. These include the European Community-sponsored San Jose accords, the "Esquipulas process" among the five Central American presidents and the more recent US-sponsored Partnership for Democracy and Development. Without exaggerating their contribution, these arrangements have, with the support of a wide array of aid agencies, encouraged Central Americans to identify specific problems and targets for reform, to set goals and to monitor each other's progress to some degree. Other arrangements for mutual goal-setting and monitoring are emerging in the arena of environmental protection.

Such arrangements, in addition to avoiding some of the tensions and pitfalls of donor-recipient conditionality, have further advantages. They tap the growing expertise and experience in poorer nations more effectively and facilitate cooperation among neighboring countries in addressing mutual problems. Such cooperation may be crucial to successful reform within individual nations, most clearly with respect to arms reduction and aspects of environmental protection. Multilateral approaches will also generate pressure on wealthy nations to adopt essential complementary measures—for instance, curbing exports of arms or dangerous pesticides and reducing barriers to imports from developing nations.

In short, as genuinely multilateral goals take their place alongside more traditional foreign policy objectives, channels and modes of influencing policies and allocating aid will also change. Emerging multilateral channels of support and influence will neither replace bilateral programs nor supplant existing multilateral agencies such as the World Bank. They may, however, become key players with respect to some of the complex objectives on the new global agenda.

WHAT'S WRONG?

WHY THE INDUSTRIALIZED NATIONS ARE STALLED

This should be the best of times. After half a century of oppression, the peoples of eastern Europe and the former Soviet Union have buried communism. China's Communist mandarins are embracing free markets. The governments of Latin America are accelerating their turn toward capitalism and democracy. For the industrialized nations, the end of the cold war heralded prospects for peace. It also signaled something more: new markets and new economic opportunities.

With a spectacular surge of energy, the emerging capitalist countries have been building bridges of commerce with the richer countries and each other. The struggling economies of the former East bloc are selling more commodities and manufactured goods to their former enemies. Third World nations are welcoming foreign companies and investors, once the hated symbols of Western imperialism. The result: Their economies are booming. Since 1989, Malaysia's economy has grown at a 9% yearly rate, Indonesia's at a 6.8% pace, Chile's at 7%, and China has seen its per-capita income soar by 30%.

But hopes for a similar burst of economic activity in the industrial nations have been dashed. Canada, Britain, and the U.S. are stuck in low gear, Japan's economy is weaker than it has been in almost two decades, and Europe is in recession. Employment in the world's seven richest nations, the so-called Group of Seven, has fallen over the past two years. More than 25 million people are out of work, and the jobless count is rising.

No wonder many people share a sense of foreboding, a deep-rooted fear that the world's leading economies have lost their edge. Everywhere you look, that fear is pitting those profiting from the global economy against those losing jobs to overseas rivals. Stagnant wages are inflaming anti-immigrant passions in Europe and the U.S. Rising poverty is stirring worries about declining living standards.

What's wrong? Why is it that the U.S. and the other industrial nations can't grow faster? Why are unemployment high and job prospects bleak? The answer is that a new, brutally competitive world economic order is emerging with the demise of the cold war. The forces that are propelling this new order will persist for years and promise to make life tougher for almost everyone—from assembly-line workers to chief executives.

The fundamental force behind this new order is the integration into the global economy of the new capitalist nations and much of the developing world. With more than 3 billion inhabitants, many of them hungry for a better life, these new free-market adherents are competing as never before with the industrial world.

In just three years, the developing nations' share of world exports has jumped by some three percentage points, to 20%. As socialism fades from Russia to Vietnam and as borders open up from Mexico to Argentina to Indonesia, a new global trading system is emerging.

The world's richest countries are reeling from a "supply shock" of goods and people from the former East bloc and developing nations. To stay competitive, companies are locating more facilities abroad, eliminating jobs, and investing in technologies to boost productivity. "Integration of the world's economies, still in its adolescent stage, tends to eliminate differentials across countries," says David E. Bloom, an economist at Columbia University. "The industrial nations will underperform the rest of the world economy."

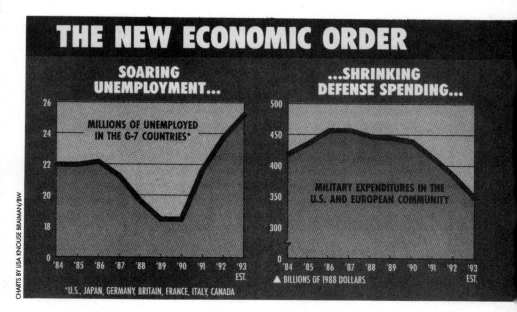

THE NEW ECONOMIC ORDER

SOARING UNEMPLOYMENT...

MILLIONS OF UNEMPLOYED IN THE G-7 COUNTRIES*

*U.S., JAPAN, GERMANY, BRITAIN, FRANCE, ITALY, CANADA

...SHRINKING DEFENSE SPENDING...

MILITARY EXPENDITURES IN THE U.S. AND EUROPEAN COMMUNITY

▲ BILLIONS OF 1988 DOLLARS

CHARTS BY LISA KNOUSE BRAIMAN/BW

"DEMAND BOOM." The cold war's end is hammering the industrial economies in another way. Now that the "evil empire" is no more, the world's most expensive arms race is over, and military demobilization is picking up steam. "The peace dividend, at least in the short run, is unemployment," says Michael D. Intriligator, economist at the University of California at Los Angeles.

Does the new economic order signal the end of prosperity for the industrial world, much like the contraction of the British Empire? To some, the answer is yes. The head of a major European steel producer hurting from foreign competition put it this way: "To the extent you raise the standard of living of developing countries, you must have a corresponding drop of the living standard in the West."

But history argues the opposite: Freer trade and broader markets create more growth, not less. The "supply shock" of cheap goods from the new capitalist countries will generate a "demand boom" for sophisticated goods and services, creating new jobs and economic wealth in the industrial countries. These countries have huge infrastructure needs, from power generators to air-traffic-control systems. They also will have billions of consumers with improving incomes.

The rub is that this demand boom will take time to develop. Several economies in Latin America and Asia, including Mexico and China, are cooling down as governments curb inflationary pressures. Political instability, especially in eastern Europe and Russia, could also damp demand from the emerging capitalist nations. "The economic revival for the industrialized world is two to three years away and, pessimistically, as much as 10 years away," says Albert M. Wojnilower, senior adviser at First Boston Asset Management.

More worrisome is that governments in the industrial countries will buckle under increasing pressure to shut out foreign trade. The lesson of the Great Depression is that beggar-thy-neighbor protectionism ends in an economic collapse. "There is a genuine risk that before too long a political backlash in the developed countries will lead to more protectionism, aborting development in many of the new regions and generating a depression," says Giles Keating, an economist at Credit Suisse First Boston Ltd. in London.

At the moment, the industrial economies are being deluged with raw materials and cheap manufactured goods. Coal, nickel, magnesium, and other commodities are coming out of Russia, sometimes smuggled through the newly independent Baltic countries into Western Europe. The talk in Moscow is that many of the young *nouveaux riches* tooling about town in Mercedes Benzes or BMWs got rich trading metals.

Last year, Russia's aluminum companies sold as much as 1 million tons in world markets. The Russian invasion is one reason why Aluminum Co. of America says it laid off 750 workers and idled a quarter of its manufacturing capacity on June 28. The Western aluminum industry has reduced its total output by 7.5% (1.2 million metric tons). The former East bloc countries are becoming more market-oriented, and, says Alcoa Chairman Paul H. O'Neill, "we believe the facts of [the aluminum] industry apply to several other basic-materials companies and industries. Looming on the horizon are the same circumstances for fabricated and finished goods, including such high-technology products as commercial aircraft."

Free markets have taken deep root in Southeast Asia and, more recently, in Latin America. Both regions are competing for markets and jobs with a plentiful work force and low wages. For example, a German production worker is five times more expensive than a Taiwanese worker and costs 10 times more than a Brazilian or Mexican competitor. No wonder manufacturing from the industrial nations is continuing to move to these low-wage areas.

It's not just cheap labor, though. Korea, Taiwan, Hong Kong, and Singapore, the so-called Four Tigers of Asia, are creating high-tech industries through technology transfers from the industrial world. Multinational corporations are building state-of-the-art manufacturing facilities in developing countries. Altogether, industrial production in the developing countries has grown at a 4.6% annual rate since 1989, compared with a mere 0.1% yearly pace in the richest countries, according to DRI/McGraw-Hill. Brazil is exporting everything from hydroelectric generators to sewing-machine motors. China accounted for 15% of total U.S. consumer-goods imports last year, up from 5% in 1987, figures Bruce Kasman, economist at Morgan Stanley & Co.

POLISH PROGRAMS. The industrial world's traditional lead in brain-power is eroding as well: Many of the new competitors are not wanting for skilled machinists, engineers, and even top-flight scientists. Texas Instruments Inc. has been designing integrated circuits and software in India since 1986. Sun Microsystems Inc. recently hired Russian scientists for software and microprocessor research.

Three years ago, Tadeusz Witkowicz chief executive of CrossComm Corp., a $30 million communications equipment maker, met a University of Gdánsk professor who sold him on the high skills and low wages of Polish computer programmers. Today, the Marlborough

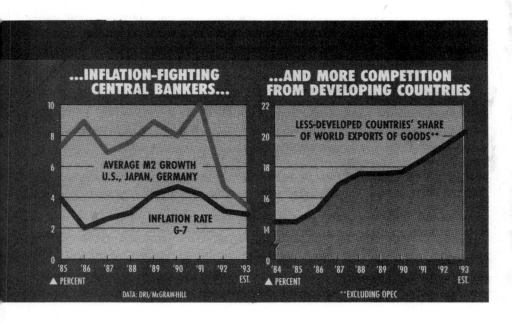

...INFLATION-FIGHTING CENTRAL BANKERS...

AVERAGE M2 GROWTH U.S., JAPAN, GERMANY

INFLATION RATE G-7

'85 '86 '87 '88 '89 '90 '91 '92 '93 EST.

▲ PERCENT

DATA: DRI/McGRAW-HILL

...AND MORE COMPETITION FROM DEVELOPING COUNTRIES

LESS-DEVELOPED COUNTRIES' SHARE OF WORLD EXPORTS OF GOODS**

'84 '85 '86 '87 '88 '89 '90 '91 '92 '93 EST.

▲ PERCENT

**EXCLUDING OPEC

(Mass.) company has 34 developers writing communications software from offices at the University of Gdánsk. The Polish workers make between $7,000 and $18,000 a year—a fraction of the pay for a comparable U.S. worker. Yet their skills are so good that the Gdánsk team wrote CrossComm's latest and most-advanced network software.

Stories like this show why investing in the developing countries has become so attractive. Foreign direct investment in these countries has doubled from an average of $23 billion from 1986 to 1990 to almost $50 billion in 1992. Foreign and domestic investors alike are pouring billions more into emerging-country stock markets like those of Mexico, India, and Korea.

Overseas investors are scrambling to buy into privatizations. The sale of state-run companies to private investors is picking up in eastern Europe, especially in Poland and the Czech Republic. Despite political opposition, Russia has moved swiftly to start privatizing its heavy industry.

"DERELICT." Rapid-fire privatizations from Peru to Argentina are driving Latin America's market revolution. On June 28, for instance, Argentina sold off shares in its state oil company, YPF. Together, Argentine and foreign investors snapped up 45% of the company, and the Argentine government pocketed $3 billion. "In the 1960s and 1970s, many poorer countries believed in self-sufficiency and closed themselves off to the world," says Paul Romer, economist at the University of California at Berkeley. "The biggest change in the developing world is that many countries now see the advantage of direct foreign investment and being attached to the world economy."

The new economic order is fast transforming the once inflation-prone industrial world. White-hot international competition is putting enormous downward pressure on prices, and disinflation is becoming the norm. Consumer prices in the G-7 countries are down from an average annual rate of 4.7% in 1990 to a 2.9% yearly pace this year. And in the U.S., the consumer price index rose at a 2.2% annual rate in the latest quarter. Since 1990, import prices of all goods from the developing countries have dropped by 12%.

Another way to measure the degree of disinflationary pressure is through the concept of the "output gap"—the difference between a country's potential and actual gross domestic product. The output gap of the six largest industrial nations, based on estimates of long-run productivity and labor-force growth, is 5% of GDP. It reflects huge excess capacity in both labor markets and product markets, says William Sterling, economist at Merrill Lynch & Co.

Even in Japan, joblessness is rising, as companies feel the pain

---

But these signs of disinflation seem to be ignored by the industrial world's central bankers. They are keeping monetary policy relatively tight, damping economic growth. "History has accused the central bankers of being derelict in fighting inflation in the 1970s and 1980s," says First Boston's Wojnilower. "It will accuse them of being derelict in the opposite direction in the 1990s."

Fiscal policy is also slowing growth in the industrial world. Social programs have become hugely expensive in all the industrial countries. Their budget deficits are approaching historic highs at an average 4% of GDP. The G-7 countries, with the exception of Japan, are trying to restrain spending. Fiscal constraint could reduce economic growth in the industrial world by over one percentage point during the 1993–94 period, according to economists at Morgan Stanley.

"LOW-COST GAME." Defense cuts are devastating an industrial infrastructure and skilled work force built up over the past half-century. The economic impact is greatest in the U.S. Military spending has dropped by 15% since 1989, after adjusting for inflation, and a million defense industry workers have lost their jobs. Real defense spending is projected to fall by an additional 25% over the next four years. And another million workers could get pink slips by 1996, according to William Sterling of Merrill Lynch. By the end of next year, for example, Lockheed Corp. says it plans on chopping 24% of its 19,000-person work force at its operations in Fort Worth. The layoffs mostly stem from cutbacks in the manufacture of F-16 fighter jets.

In Europe, real defense spending is down by 12% since 1989, with the biggest fallout in France and Britain. Europe's military expenditures are forecast to drop by as much as 5% a year in real terms for the rest of the decade. And employment in the European arms industry could fall by one-third to one-half over the next few years, according to the Stockholm International Peace Research Institute and others.

The industrial world is adapting to the new economic order, but it's a hard slog. The U.S. is ahead of the pack, largely because it has been traditionally a more open economy and has been fighting the battle for profits and markets with Japan, Germany, and the Four Tigers of Asia for more than a decade. Facing vicious competition at home and abroad, American companies have been investing in new technologies and overhauling the workplace. America has gone further than any other industrial country in deregulating its financial services, airlines, telecommunications, and trucking industries. The result: Even traditionally sheltered industries have been compelled to restructure to meet new price competition.

American companies have become a lot more competitive in recent years, and so has the American work force, even when up against stiff price competition from abroad. Take Xerox Corp. It imports low-cost copiers from a joint venture in Japan for sale in the U.S. But Xerox also makes high-priced copiers in Webster, N.Y., for export to Japan. For Xerox and many other American companies, labor costs are only one factor in a complex global equation. Quality matters, and so does worker productivity. In an interdependent global economy, "we don't want to get trapped in just the low-cost game," says A. Barry Rand, executive vice-president at Xerox.

OFFSHORE SHIFT. Europe is in the early stages of a similarly wrenching overhaul. France's new government, for example, has announced plans to privatize nearly two dozen state-owned companies, including Air France and Renault. Once in private hands, these former state-run companies will strive to become more efficient competitors and restructure their operations. Stung by global rivals, Germany's corporations are laying off workers and moving new plants overseas.

Corporate restructurings abroad are bound to take longer than in the U.S., though. Europe's unions are more powerful and their job protections far stronger. The European Community wants the steel industry to slash capacity, but Italy, Spain, and other governments are reluctant to reduce subsidies to their steel producers for fear of adding to the unemployment rolls. German steelmakers are lobbying for the EC to send jobless benefits to Eastern Europe and bar imports of East European steel. Social tensions are further exacerbated by ethnic conflicts, as a tide of immigrants from Western Europe's formerly communist neighbors and from North Africa pours in.

LESS THAN BLEAK. Even Japan is beginning to feel the force of the new economic order. True, Japan is running a huge trade surplus, and unlike the other industrial nation, it has a fiscal surplus. But economic growth is at its lowest level in almost two decades, and the Liberal Democratic Party must share the reins of power for the first time in four decades.

Japanese companies are being hurt by increased global competition, especially in overseas markets. In response, they are building more plants overseas, even as unemployment rises at home. Nissan Motor Co.'s $800 million expansion of its auto plant in Aguascalientes, Mexico, will make autos not only for the Mexican market but also for export to Japan, Canada, and the rest of Latin America. "We have to accelerate our shift to offshore production," says Michiyuki Uenohara, an executive adviser at NEC Corp. and a former senior executive and board member. "It's unavoidable."

The outlook may be rough, but it isn't bleak. Lower inflation rates are bringing down interest rates in all the rich countries. After a decade of debt profligacy during which they put up skyscrapers and leveraged balance sheets, companies throughout the industrial world today are eagerly refinancing high-cost debt at cheaper rates and raising billions in new equity.

In the longer term, freer trade is likely to spur faster economic growth. With many of their economies growing at a 5% to 9% annual rate, the emerging capitalist countries are beginning to spend more money on roads, sewers, environment, health care, and consumer goods. Over the next decade, Asia, excluding Japan, is expected to spend at least $1 trillion on telecommunications and power equipment alone. Westinghouse Electric Corp. recently announced an agreement to modernize 400 power plants in China.

THE FATAL MISTAKE. Consumer spending, too, is rising faster in the developing world than it is in the industrial countries, and the overseas markets for Coca-Cola, Procter & Gamble, McDonald's, and Citicorp are increasingly lucrative. "There are billions of new consumers coming into the marketplace. In the late '90s, there's going to be pretty dramatic growth," says William S. Stavropoulos, president of Dow Chemical Co.

These signs of improving trade and prospects for better growth ahead are still fragile. In every industrial nation, the combination of global competition and technological change is eliminating jobs and holding down wages. More and more people feel threatened by cheap labor in the emerging capitalist countries. Many industries are up in arms against "unfair" foreign competitors. The political leaders of the industrial world face mounting calls to shut out trade and immigrants. "Walling off thriving new industrializing economies would be a fatal economic error," says Lawrence H. Summers, Under Secretary for international affairs at the Treasury Dept.

These calls are becoming harder for heads of state to ignore, even though the recent G-7 meeting in Tokyo showed that world leaders are trying to move toward lower tariffs and more open markets. The free-trade system that America has championed since 1945 was designed with security concerns in mind, and for decades, fear of communism kept economic disputes from tearing the allies apart. With communism no longer a threat, trade issues are becoming far more contentious.

Still, freer markets and freer trade in the new global economic system are what will ultimately put an end to slow growth and high unemployment in the industrial world. "If a foreign country can supply us with a commodity cheaper than we ourselves can make it, better buy it of them with some part of our own industry," the Scottish political economist Adam Smith wrote more than 200 years ago. And that's what the new economic order is all about. The sooner the industrial countries learn to live with it, the sooner the global upturn will begin.

By Christopher Farrell and Michael J. Mantel in New York, with Bill Javetski in Paris, Stephen Baker in Pittsburgh, and bureau reports

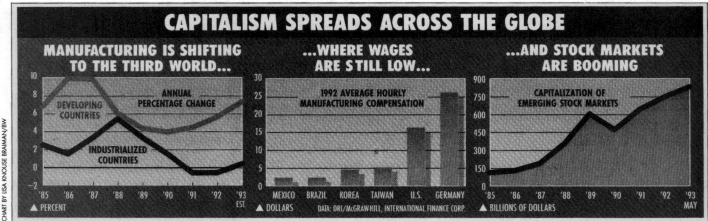

CHART BY LISA KNOUSE BRAIMAN/BW

CAPITALISM SPREADS ACROSS THE GLOBE

MANUFACTURING IS SHIFTING TO THE THIRD WORLD...
ANNUAL PERCENTAGE CHANGE
DEVELOPING COUNTRIES
INDUSTRIALIZED COUNTRIES
▲ PERCENT

...WHERE WAGES ARE STILL LOW...
1992 AVERAGE HOURLY MANUFACTURING COMPENSATION
MEXICO BRAZIL KOREA TAIWAN U.S. GERMANY
▲ DOLLARS   DATA: DRI/McGRAW-HILL, INTERNATIONAL FINANCE CORP.

...AND STOCK MARKETS ARE BOOMING
CAPITALIZATION OF EMERGING STOCK MARKETS
▲ BILLIONS OF DOLLARS

In Beijing and Moscow, Starkly Different Policies and Results

Clay Chandler

Washington Post Staff Writer

BEIJING—When Treasury Secretary Lloyd Bentsen prodded China's Vice Premier Zhu Rongji to open markets during their recent meeting here, the Chinese official kept repeating that he wanted to do things gradually, step by step, a little at a time.

The unspoken message was that China's policy of gradualism works. The Chinese believe that sudden economic and political changes, as have been seen in Russia over the past three years, can lead to chaos. Too much freedom, they suggest, may actually be the enemy of free markets.

Bentsen's recent trip to booming China and stagnant Russia offered some disturbing evidence to support the Chinese proposition. Chinese industrial production grew at the astounding annual rate of 29 percent last month. In Russia, by contrast, economic output contracted by nearly 15 percent last year.

For reporters traveling with Bentsen, the contrasts were arresting. Street vendors in Beijing were hawking fresh grapes in mid-winter at affordable prices, and nearby shops were selling fancy mountain bikes. On the streets of Moscow, however, a leading business seemed to be prostitution. Another robust industry was casino gambling. Foreign executives said they have taken to hiring bodyguards to protect themselves from gangsters.

The question of which strategy works best in developing societies—Chinese-style gradualism or Russian sudden change—is of more than academic interest. America's views about the proper mix of shock and therapy are instantly replayed in capitals around the world these days.

At the heart of the debate are two basic questions: Do economic reforms work best if introduced in a single "Big Bang," or should they be measured in tiny doses? And is instant political liberty the most effective means of promoting stable economic growth, or is it wiser to loosen up a little at a time?

On the surface, recent events in Russia and China appear to answer both queries simply—gradualism works best—and contradict some of the most basic premises of President Clinton's foreign policy.

In Russia, where Clinton urged more radical free-market reforms, economic "shock therapy" has been followed by plummeting growth rates and living standards. And democratic elections, though lauded in Washington, have produced a reactionary parliament dominated by interest groups out to roll back reforms.

In China, by contrast, the transition to free markets seems to have moved in deliberate stages from agriculture to light and medium industries. There have been no real elections; Communist Party leaders have crushed pro-democracy demonstrations, jailed political dissenters and kept tight restrictions on the press.

Still, even as Washington decries Beijing's disregard for human rights, China's living standards are rising swiftly and its economy is zipping ahead at an annual rate of 13 percent.

What lessons should be learned from Russia's obvious failure and China's apparent success?

"The notion that one can have all good things—democracy and all forms of economic liberalization—instantly and simultaneously [is] . . . a deeply held belief that has no grounding in practical historical experience," declared Hong Kong-based investment banker William Overholt in a recent book on economic development in China.

On the other side of the debate, many experts insist the performance of the two economies does not repudiate sudden liberalization as a strategy for development. The Russian and Chinese economies are so different, they argue, that meaningful comparisons are impossible.

Those who claim Russia should emulate China's go-slow development approach, fumed economists Jeffery Sachs and Wing Thye Woo in a recent essay, "might as well advise Russia to solve its agricultural problems by shifting from wheat to rice."

The case against rapid reform comes down to this: Shock therapy unleashes chaos. If firms are privatized too quickly, there is confusion about ownership, management responsibilities, product liability and production strategy. If prices are liberalized all at once, inflation is virtually certain. If the central bank clamps down on the money supply to keep inflation low, unproductive enterprises will go bankrupt, workers will be stripped of their livelihoods and social tumult will quickly follow.

A socialist economy without a plan, one Chinese leader has said, is like a bird without a cage—sure to fly away.

Granting political freedoms too quickly also can risk paralysis. "If men are to remain civilized or become so, the art of associating together must grow and improve in the same ratio in which the equality of conditions is increased," observed Alexis de Tocqueville in his study of American politics in the 19th century.

Clearly, the Russians are just learning that old art of associating—their battered parliament building attests to that—and in the meantime, their macroeconomic policies are in shambles.

Some U.S. analysts regard Beijing's heavy-handed rule as enlightened by comparison. By clamping down on dissenters, they contend, China's communist elites have kept pro-growth economic policies on track and spawned a middle class. Gradualists such as Overholt argue that, as in Asia's other high-growth economies, these new burghers will clamor most greedily for new freedoms.

"If true democracy comes to either of these countries, it will come to China first," predicts Marshall Goldman, professor of Russian economics at Wellesley College. "You have to have a middle class." Throughout his tour of Asia this month, Bentsen has emphasized that greater economic development and expanded trade are among the surest means of improving human rights.

Other observers, however, draw radically different conclusions from the Chinese and Russian experiences. Woo, an economist at the University of California, contends Chinese gradualism reflected deadlock among its political elites—reformers vs. old-time Stalinists—not any centrally coordinated theory. Indeed, Woo and many other China scholars attribute China's economic success to the very weakness of Beijing relative to rural provinces.

After the sweeping purges of the Cultural Revolution in 1978, he argues, China's central government was incapable of resisting Deng Xiaoping's effort to disperse economic policy-making responsibility among the officials in the countryside. The result was a sort of "Big Bang" in rural China that set the stage for explosive growth in agriculture and light industry.

"The success of China's export drive is based on economic forces that are only partially responsive to the central government," concurs Harvard China specialist Roderick MacFarquhar. Leaders in Beijing, he said, "haven't lost complete control, but in many ways they are just holding on."

Many scholars also caution that the different development strategies pursued by China and Russia reflect deep structural differences in the two economies. At the outset of Deng's reforms in the late 1970s, roughly 70 percent of the Chinese labor force was employed in agriculture, while less than 20 percent was engaged in industry. But when Gorbachev launched *perestroika* a decade later, more than 50 percent of the Russian work force was employed in industry and only 14 percent in agriculture.

Deng's development solution was comparatively simple: Do away with the agricultural collectives and turn the farmland over to peasant families. The challenge for Gorbachev—figuring out how to transform a tangle of rusting, inefficient, defense-oriented heavy industries supported by dirt-cheap credit from the state into lean, self-supporting manufacturers of consumer goods—was infinitely more complex.

Economists say China has been no more successful than Russia in killing off state-run manufacturers making products no one wants. The difference in China, many argue, is that the state concerns are tiny stones that are being submerged rapidly in the rising tide of the private sector. In Russia, however, such enterprises are hulking islands that can not be washed away easily.

The danger for China now is that it might choke on its own success. If the Chinese economy boils over, as some analysts expect, Beijing's leaders may have reason to discover the virtues of gradualism yet again.

The Politics of Arms, Arms Proliferation, and Arms Control

The potential horrors of future wars were suggested by Saddam Hussein's threats to use nuclear, biological, or chemical-tipped long-range missiles during the Persian Gulf War. The threat to use these weapons affected how both sides shaped their political and military strategies, including battle tactics. After the war, there was a rush to resupply depleted stocks of conventional weapons and to secure more sophisticated, high-tech weapons by combatants and historic rivals in the Middle East.

The idea that the proliferation of weapons increases threats to peace is the major theme of Tom Clancy and Russell Seitz's essay, "Five Minutes Past Midnight—and Welcome to the Age of Proliferation." Instead of accepting the belief that began with the Manhattan Project—that secrets can be kept—these authors argue that the assumption of secrecy to prevent arms proliferation is incompatible with scientific success. Given that the scientific knowledge, technical expertise, and materials needed to make weapons of mass destruction are dispersed throughout the world, it seems safe to say that the sociology of science and technology has changed drastically since World War II. Thus, Clancy and Seitz conclude that weapons of destruction will continue to spread.

Although the Gulf War underscored a host of new threats stemming from the proliferation of weapons, the collapse of communism and the promise of more cooperative East-West relations has transformed the world of arms control and led to the rapid culmination in the past few years of such major arms agreements as the Intermediate-range Nuclear Forces (INF) Treaty signed by countries in the former East and West blocs, the November 1990 European conventional forces treaty, and agreement on the Strategic Arms Reduction Talks (START) treaty signed during the summer of 1991. The dramatically changed negotiating environment among the nuclear superpowers was typified by the fact that the leaders of the United States and Russia were able to conclude the historic START II arms treaty with a handshake on December 29, 1992. This last-minute push came after months of stalling over several technical details.

Since the end of the cold war, the United States and Russia have continued to work closely in efforts to reduce, and where possible to eliminate, the former Soviet Union's nuclear weapons arsenal deployed outside the borders of the Russian federation. The ex-Soviet republics of Kazakhstan and Belarus agreed to eliminate nuclear weapons from their territories in the Lisbon Protocol signed in 1992. Russia and Ukraine are the only other ex-Soviet republics where nuclear warheads of the former Soviet Union are still deployed. An agreement to eliminate nuclear warheads from Ukraine required intensive three-way talks among the United States, Russia, and the Ukraine. Ukraine increasingly resisted the idea of removing nuclear warheads as tensions with Russia rose. After protracted negotiations, promises of increased western aid, and guarantees that Ukraine could consult with NATO and the United States in the event of future security threats, Ukraine signed an agreement that calls for the phased withdrawal of long-range, tactical, and cruise missile nuclear warheads from its territory and promised to sign the Nuclear Non-Proliferation Treaty in 1994. The fact that Ukrainian leaders warned only days after the agreement was signed that Ukraine would not implement it if Russia disrupted future fuel shipments was only one of many indications that difficulties lie ahead in efforts to implement all arms agreements in the chaotic post–cold war security environment.

In "Dismantling the Arsenals: Arms Control and the New World Agenda," Jack Mendelsohn identifies and describes the most immediate concerns of both the United States and Europe in terms of arms controls issues related to the future of nuclear weapons in a disintegrating Soviet empire. In addition, Mendelsohn describes how measures developed to counter East-West distrust may be aids in monitoring future agreements related to the deployment of short-range nuclear weapons and the spread of conventional weapons.

The dramatic progress achieved in recent years, with the completion of a number of treaty agreements by nuclear powers, was followed by unprecedented levels of cooperative measures and reciprocal monitoring at missile-production and missile-destruction sites. Yet, a host of problems related to the proliferation of nuclear weapons remain as one of the most serious threats to international arms control efforts. As Bruce Nelan notes in "Fighting Off Doomsday," with more than 25 countries processing or developing weapons of mass destruction and two dozen researching or stockpiling chemical weapons, it is now clear that proliferation cannot be stopped. By the next decade, many countries will have the delivery systems capable of carrying weapons of mass destruction, and some may use them if international controls fail.

Despite the visible concern and efforts in the international community to control nuclear weapons of mass destruction, the most immediate arms control challenges center on the need to control the sale of conventional arms. The success of advanced arms in the Persian Gulf—especially attack helicopters and air defense systems—increased demand for sophisticated conventional weapons. Government-sanctioned arms sales resumed almost immediately in the Middle East and elsewhere after the Gulf War. There was growing concern about the willingness of certain arms suppliers, such as China, to sell both high- and low-tech weapons. Finally, there was the general problem of economic conversions by the most developed counties. Private and public arms suppliers now scramble to find new markets for their products as governments in the industrialized world reduce their defense budgets. Robin Wright, in "Shifting Battle Lines in the Arms Race," reviews five of the most worrisome trends fueling conventional arms races worldwide: cascading, or the flow of arms from larger to smaller powers; surplus weapons sold at "junk" prices; widespread upgrading of existing conventional weapons; barter exchanges; and increases in domestic production.

The growing warning signs that the technology and materials necessary to produce chemical and biological weapons of mass warfare were spreading worldwide have stimulated several recent international efforts to thwart this spread. The first attempt to eliminate an entire category of weapons of mass destruction occurred in 1993 when more than 120 nations, including the United States and Russia, began the process of signing an agreement designed to ban the production, stockpiling, and use of chemical weapons. This recent treaty is notable among disarmament agreements because of the strictness of its verification regime. Countries refusing to sign the treaty may, after some years, face an embargo of sales of certain chemical products.

As the interlocking set of treaties and unilateral pressures now known as the nuclear nonproliferation regime slowed the spread of atomic weapons, the level of concern about proliferation declined. But it is instructive to remember that the highly advanced Iraqi nuclear program and more recent efforts in Iran and Libya suggest that the international distaste for nuclear weaponry is not shared by all. Jasjit Singh outlines the reasons why effective checks on nuclear proliferation ultimately require a reversal of the belief that nuclear weapons are usable and indispensable to international security. Effective nuclear controls also require a cooperative security framework. Singh offers the principles established in the Chemical Weapons Convention Treaty as a potentially useful model for future global denuclearization.

Looking Ahead: Challenge Questions

As a leader of a developing country with aspirations of becoming a regional military power, what lessons would you draw from the Gulf War about the usefulness of high-

tech weapons? Conventional arms? Chemical, biological, and nuclear (CBN) weapons of mass destruction?

What national, regional, or international actions or programs would be most effective in preventing the use of weapons of mass destruction in the next war in the Middle East? Should the United States do more to subsidize the conversion of state-owned weapons industries in the former republics of the USSR?

Do you support the joint proposal of former president Bush of the United States and President Yeltsin of Russia for a mutual reduction in nuclear weapons and greater cooperation in space for peaceful rather than military purposes? Explain.

Can the international community or national governments implement policies to stop proliferation of conventional and CBN weapons in the world's arms bazaar?

Five Minutes Past Midnight
and Welcome to the Age of Proliferation

Tom Clancy
and
Russell Seitz

Tom Clancy is the author most recently of *The Sum of All Fears*. Russell Seitz is an associate of Harvard University's John M. Olin Institute for Strategic Studies; this paper draws on a longer one written under the auspices of the Institute's Changing International Security Needs and America's National Interests Program.

AN H-BOMB in Iraq? Chinese uranium enrichment hardware in Iran? It's just not the same world as that in which the study of disarmament and proliferation began. Generations have passed since the completion of the Manhattan Project—generations not just of people but technologies. Progress, a concept that generally resolves us to endure the terrors that the future holds, is upon us, and with its arrival we find ourselves confronted with that most ancient and malevolent curse: "May you live in interesting times."

In the decade after Hiroshima, the yield of nuclear weapons increased a thousandfold, and today, seventeen years after India proved equal to the task of building a nuclear device using its own technical resources, the threat from weapons of mass destruction continues to grow. Nevertheless, there persists the naive belief that began with the Manhattan Project—that secrets can be kept. Secrecy, however, is incompatible with scientific success. Although a whole generation of world-class scientists—a traitor or two excepted—kept their oaths as to the technical details of the first generations of nuclear and thermonuclear weapons, they also helped raise up a new generation of graduate students and post-doctoral fellows who, by the time they matured, collectively knew more than their masters did. What took the Allies 40,000 man-years to do in the 1940s took India perhaps 2,500 in the 1970s.

A generation later still, much that is unspeakably classified in the context of weapons design and fabrication is merely the common knowledge of other disciplines that have undergone a separate evolution in the unclassified world of international scientific endeavor. And circulating today within the scientific commu-

Reprinted with permission from *The National Interest*, No. 26, Winter 1991/1992, pp. 3-12. © 1991 by The National Interest, Washington, DC.

nity is a wealth of expertise that dwarfs the amount of intellectual currency that existed in the 1940s and 1950s. The number of newly minted Ph.Ds and Sc.Ds entering the marketplace each year is transforming the global R&D scene in ways difficult to comprehend and impossible to reverse.

In the two generations that have grown to adulthood since World War II, the sociology of science and technology has been transformed. A once Eurocentric enterprise has become a global one. In 1939, German was the *lingua franca* of science—of physics in particular. Scientists were far fewer than today. Apart from America, Europe, Japan, and the USSR, few nations could boast of dozens, let alone hundreds, of Ph.Ds in the pure or applied sciences. Whenever individuals of scientific promise arose in the British or French colonies, they tended to be educated at those empires' hearts, there to spend their careers rather than return to the impoverished or nonexistent technical cultures of their homelands.

The intervening years have witnessed a transformation of the world of technology. What was extremely demanding then—building a few bombs stretched the "high technology" of World War II to its limits, and beyond—has ceased to be state-of-the-art or even demanding. In the 1940s, the Third Reich's atomic weapons program barely got off the drawing board. Its experimental program ended before a chain reaction was achieved. Yet today, little of the equipment, instruments, and materials (fissionables and explosives excepted) needed to develop the first generation of atomic weapons is alien to the research establishments of a large university or a Fortune 500 company. High technology has become a global enterprise and the scientific database that underlies it has become almost universally accessible.

With the advent of this burgeoning free trade in technical ideas and the people who think about them, we have entered a new era in the history of proliferation. It is cautionary to note that what the Germans could and did accomplish at the limits of their wartime high-technology binge—the V–2 rocket—has been successfully emulated by Iraq and North Korea. Perhaps the most fitting adjective to apply to the scientific and technical resources of most nations, with or without nuclear ambitions today, is "overqualified."

To be safely ignored in the establishment of an anti-proliferation regime, a nation needs to have rather fewer Ph.Ds and engineering diplomas than Venezuela or Bangladesh, and a technical economy incapable of building a diesel engine from scratch. So excellent an education is being afforded to so many from so far afield in the universities of the First World that technical sophistication has become an increasingly global phenomenon. There is little consolation in demography, for while a bare majority of all foreign graduate students stay on to seek their careers in the nations that educate them, thousands return home annually.[1]

Warm, Wet, and Gray

FOR FOUR decades, the United States and Europe have been engaged in exporting to the developing nations the most sensitive of nuclear materials. This uncontrolled trade has grown exponentially, increasing ninefold in the last thirty years and doubling in the last decade. The matter in question is warm, wet, and gray—a small tonnage of human brains freshly armed with doctorates in nuclear physics and all its related disciplines. Most of them go home.

A high-tech cadre of thousands has returned to the Third World with First World advanced degrees. For example, both India and Taiwan now have more than 2,500 American-educated Ph.Ds. Even more remarkable, South Korea is now acquiring more than 1,000 American doctorates *annually*. Similar numbers have stayed behind in the West to participate in state-of-the-art research in disciplines as varied as plasma physics, materials science, chemical engineering, and computer science. The percentage of the world's scientists and engineers resident in developing countries rose from 7.6 percent to 10.2 percent between 1970 and 1980 and today exceeds 13 percent.[2]

More than mere numbers is at issue. The strength of science has grown to a point where a comparative handful of scientists and engineers can successfully pursue tasks that once required the concerted effort of hordes of the best and brightest. Interdisciplinary areas of research are fertile ground for the rediscovery in the open literature of the technical factors that were originally cultivated in secret and kept thereafter in the well-guarded vaults of the superpowers' weapons establishments. Many, perhaps most, of the concepts, techniques, materials, and machines originally developed to enable the production of the first generation of thermonuclear devices have been reinvented, rediscovered, or spontaneously spun off into the world of civilian R&D and purely scientific endeavor.

A great deal of weapons-related information that is not labeled as such is hidden in plain sight within innocent-sounding subdisciplines that are both unclassified and so widely disseminated as to defy any attempt to return their sensitive content to effective regimes of security and compartmentalization. The realm of astrophysics, for example, includes all the intellectual underpinnings of nuclear weapons development, and indeed antedates it. The basic principles of how the sun works, set forth by Bethe and von Weiszacker in the 1930s, gave rise not just to the hydrogen bomb but to the epic task of harvesting fusion as a peaceful source of power.

On the more modest scale of planets, the extreme pressures common to their cores and the ignition of fusion bombs are described by one and the same set of Equations of State—the work of Fermi and Taylor. Static pressures in excess of three million atmospheres, fantasy in 1945, are now reached in diamond anvil cells that fit in a thimble. So today we have robust sub-disciplines of geophysics and astrophysics—the study of the dynamics of asteroid impacts and radiative transport in stars that utilize the liberated (or re-invented) expertise of the weapons laboratories on a daily basis—and those who use such weapons-derived computer codes have at their disposal vastly more computational power than Fermi or Bethe ever dreamed of.

In the aftermath of the information explosion, the component technologies of nuclear proliferation are no longer identifiably labeled as such. What is evolving spans the spectrum of scientific work—but with the advent of computerized databases a macroscope for visualizing such a 360 percent field of view is becoming available on line.

Second-Best Still Works

AS HIGH-technology ramifies, appropriate technologies multiply: the most engaging illusion of proliferation control arises from the temptation to believe that its central goal is to prevent the duplication of *existing* technology. Before the first prototype of a weapons system comes into existence at the level of conceptual design—before its component technologies have been fabricated—one cannot determine which alternate concept for each component will prevail in the long term. The initial selection between competing prototypes, with the winning concepts going on to participate in the inception of the first generation of fission bombs or ICBMs (or whatever), is a process that does not invalidate the concepts that are discarded at that point. It merely reflects the perceived practicality of a particular, infant technology. The fittest idea for such a time and place gets selected on the spot, on the basis of saving as much time as money can afford. But other concepts may prove as fit or fitter in other times and other places.

Rejecting a technique is not the same as falsifying an hypothesis. Thus, while uranium-isotope separation via gaseous-diffusion was the mainstay of the Manhattan Project, what was then an impractical technique of gas-centrifuge separation went on to become a practical source of weapons-grade fissionable materials in the Soviet Union in the 1950s.[3]

A current example involves the calutron, a bastardized descendant of a Depression-era atom smasher (the original Berkeley cyclotron). Relative inefficiency doomed the early calutrons, and the strength of existing materials limited gas centrifuges in the 1940s. But the Atomic Energy Commission and its successors blithely created a new discipline, materials science, and massively funded it for another half-century. The result: the materials science community naively solved those problems associated with the gas centrifuge and irremediably changed the context of separation technology. This is significant, because such initially dismissed branches of technology as the calutron can take root and flourish in the shadow of their "mature" competitors. Thus the western scientific community was taken by surprise when the calutron, a woefully inefficient device for electromagnetic uranium isotope separation, was reborn in Iraq. This second life testifies to the difference between the undoable and the merely obsolete. At ground zero it matters not if an H-Bomb has fallen from a B–2 or a Zeppelin.

Welcome to the Future

IN THE near future it will be possible to duplicate almost all past technology in all but the most forlorn of Third World backwaters, and much of the present state-of-the-art will be both intellectually and practically accessible. It is no longer safe to assume that looking for the paper trail of a nation attempting to emulate the work of the Manhattan Project will lead us to the laboratories of those with nuclear ambitions. The scope of technical enterprise in today's world prevents a rigid definition of what to look for. The motto of today's ambitious bomb-smiths might be, "These are our weapons technologies—if you don't like them, we have others." Teach a man to make microwave ovens and you've opened the door to radar and calutrons alike. COCOM (the Coordinating Committee on Exports Control) can list and monitor trade in "critical" components; but available tools and materials, and the ubiquity of iron, copper, sand, and vacuum, doom the exercise to futility in the not-very-long run.

This applies equally to other information of military value. Witness the publication in the Indian scientific journal *Current Topics* (April 25, 1991, Indian Academy of Sciences, New Delhi) of both low-and high-resolution satellite images of the Gulf War—despite their being withheld by the U.S. for security reasons. Those who did the withholding evidently overlooked India's possession of a downlink to an earthward-looking U.S. weather satellite, and its own high-resolution reconnaissance satellite to boot.[4]

This is not to suggest that the best efforts of the U.S. or NATO aerospace industries are at risk of obsolescence—India would be hard pressed to deliver a successor to the KH–11 reconnaissance satellite. It does, however, illustrate the already fragile nature of the assumptions that lead to the attempt to deny information to Iraq when satellite data flow unencrypted from orbit twenty-four hours a day. The satellite information could have been had for the asking by anyone on a computer network that, courtesy of DARPA (the Defense Advanced Research Projects Administration) and a host of other federal agencies, has come to span the globe. The new condition of entry to the orbital reconnaissance club is not the capacity to launch a satellite, but access to the Ethernet directory and the necessary subscription fee.

Similarly any effort to keep the microchips vital to *our* technology out of the hands of Iraq and Libya lacks relevance to the question of the evolution of a Third World bomb. The calutron, for example, is nothing more or less than the Mother of All Vacuum Tubes. Any "proliferation-control regime" for calutron-produced U–235 must encompass everything from traffic in vacuum pumps, and wire and sheet metal, to the interdiction of hydrofluoric-acid bootleggers and pick-axe miners of pitchblende. The prospects for such a regime are poor. Too much may be made out of mere copper, iron, and vacuum.

Centrifuge-enrichment technology is easy to inhibit by denying critical materials exports, but it is impossible to control. Steel is steel; any post-Bronze Age nation that possesses an iron foundry or steel mini-mill can produce a heat of martensitic high-strength metal as good as that embargoed. If high-strength composites—carbon fiber or kevlar—for centrifuge construction should be preferred to maraging steel, the raw material can be obtained by the ton from the stocks kept by any boatyard that builds competitive yachts.

As for the more sophisticated magnetic materials needed for the gas centrifuges levitated bearings, their embargo can only succeed if accompanied by a product recall encompassing all of the better sort of hi-fi loudspeakers of the last ten years. "Exotic" new materials, whose research is militarily subsidized, very often make their debut not as production-line aerospace components, but as up-scale sporting goods, such as boron fiber fly rods, and carbon fiber skis and tennis rackets. Examples could be multiplied. The point is that expensive materials developed for weapons applications can and do spin off into civilian markets that dwarf their military cousins.

The Russian Yard Sale

WE ARE partly to blame: consider the proliferation risks inherent in our emphasis on classifying data rather than protecting technology from exposure. It is edifying to attend the manufactures' displays that accompany many large technical meetings sponsored by engineering associations or the Department of Defense. There, proudly displayed, are the first fruit of Pentagon R&D—components whose exotic materials and advanced electronic, thermal, and optical performance seem unparalleled in the civilian sector, and which are very often offered before their end-use systems (the B–2 and SDI, for instance) have even been tested or publicly displayed. Silicon carbide laser mirrors or stealth carbon foam, it's all on offer in the West—albeit without reference to what it has been developed for. And now in the East, even more is on sale.

The Iron Curtain did more than isolate the citizens of the Warsaw Pact nations from the Free World. It also functioned as an impermeable barrier, a containment that kept in a mass of militarily important high technology often rivaling the best in the West. Now that containment has been breached, and the most secretive of military powers is spilling its technology into a new and multipolar world where nuclear ambitions have multiplied. Throughout the former Warsaw Pact, we are witnessing the Yard Sale at the End of History. The Soviet Union is selling jewels more precious than the Fabergé eggs of the Romanovs—at distress-sale prices.

To begin with, glasnost is having some curious results. In the course of celebrating the memory of the late Andrei Sakharov, his physicist-colleagues have explicitly revealed some (but not all) of the fundamental tricks of the weapons trade. In *Sakharov Remembered*, V.I. Ritus outlines the foremost of the early breakthroughs on two-stage fission-fusion bombs: the method of increasing the fusion reaction rate by incorporation of depleted uranium into a layered structure containing deuterium and a tritium precursor. When such a composite becomes fully ionized by the X-ray flux of a fast first-stage fission primary (contained in a *holraum* of appropriate geometry made of the right stuff), the radiation pressure is locally amplified by the abundant electrons liberated from the U–238. This increases the concentration of the deuterium nuclei, which increases the fusion reaction rate by an order of magnitude. "Such a method of reaction increase was called 'Sakharization' by our colleagues."

This is not the sort of hoary schematic speculation typical of Howard Morland's decade-old article "The H-Bomb Secret," but straightforward (albeit antique) thermonuclear bomb design information of a quality transcending the fission-bomb secrets that

sent the Rosenbergs to the electric chair. It has been on library shelves for over a year. In another paper, A.I. Pavlovski displays some X-ray flash photographs of how to overcome Rayleigh-Taylor instability by an iteration of implosion components. A third, by Yuri A. Romanov, further outlines the similarities and differences of early U.S. and USSR thermonuclear devices and bombs.

This level of candor may be a source of satisfaction to the curious, but while Drell, Teller, and Bethe remain close-lipped, and their protégés safely within the confines of Los Alamos and Lawrence-Livermore national laboratories, one wonders: what is going to become of the corresponding protégés of Sakharov and his contemporaries?

THE RESPONSE of Soviet laboratories to the outbreak of peace has been even more disturbing. Invoking glasnost and perestroika, they are ready and willing to sell off the fruits of decades of innovation and development for hard currency abroad, rather than seeking means of converting it to civilian use in a land where the ruble is despised. Despite the supposedly continuing vigilance of both the KGB and the military, a virtual sampler of military technology—some of it arising from nuclear weapons research—has been put on the table for Western entrepreneurs and Third World shoppers.

In the aftermath of Chernobyl, the Soviet nuclear power (and plutonium) industry found itself burdened with a generation of reactors no one wanted to operate and a corps of nuclear engineers and designers whose careers were suddenly jeopardized, (along with former counterparts in the defunct Warsaw Pact). In the summer of 1991, the USSR witnessed both a large reduction in the cash flow of many scientific and technical establishments *and* a contraction in many scientists' and engineers' prerogatives: no more cheap cafeterias, company food stores, and free childcare centers. Many institutions seeking to reverse this abrupt decline in the quality of life have established cooperatives to privatize the intellectual property of their researchers, and to seek its practice by joint ventures or licensing abroad. As a result, entities as diverse as national laboratories, military aerospace development centers, organs of the Soviet Academy, biomedical research facilities, and the City Council of St. Petersburg have suddenly circulated reams of abstracts of technical proposals by a variety of channels, ranging from individual scientists turned entrepreneurs to the Minister of Military Conversion.

The consequences of privatizing the component entities of the Soviet military-industrial complex, from basic metallurgical facilities to aerospace centers and nuclear R&D laboratories, may include the proliferation of ideas as well as artifacts and technologies. At one level of the game it is an intelligence windfall, but the de facto declassification of Soviet military high technology will have the effect of making many Western systems comprehensible to outsiders as well. Soviet high technology cannot be compromised without ours falling victim to some extent.

While there is some evidence of restraint concerning state-of-the-art technologies of C^3I (command, control, communications, and intelligence), a few of the systems offered are of a sophistication that have the capacity to change radically the correlation of forces among nations used to depending on the generations of technology available on the fringes of the global arms bazaar. These include a variety of dual-use services and information channels—such as image enhancement, and high-resolution satellite optical and radar imaging—that could seriously effect the outcome of conflicts between states otherwise without access to orbital reconnaissance. It would therefore seem prudent for analysts of low-intensity conflict to keep track of more than weapons systems as the 1990s evolve.

Today it costs roughly $100,000 a year, including support personnel and overheads, to employ an American or Japanese scientist. But the institutions employing tens of thousands of displaced Soviet military researchers are growing desperate. The asking price for their services ranges from $500 a month for a group leader with a Ph.D to $100 for a skilled technician. The liberalization of travel and emigration from Russia might allow weapons scientists, once denied any prospect of leaving, to sell their expertise to the highest bidder. One would expect the bids to be sizable. Pakistan, for example, having purchased a weapon design from China, would clearly benefit from the services of those familiar with the materials and techniques of

its manufacture. While a former employee of the now mothballed East German reactors should face a reasonable prospect of gainful employment in a reunited Germany that staunchly supports the International Atomic Energy Agency's anti-proliferation regime, he remains the lawful prey of headhunters in the family of states that seeks to circumvent that regime. One truly egregious example of the Soviet crack-up is the International Chetek Corporation—a would-be purveyor of "peaceful nuclear explosives" and *breeder reactors!* This enterprise is a spin-off from the Arzamas-16 nuclear weapons design center.

As glasnost mutates into an unbridled high-tech sell-off, we must revise our perception of how the technologies of mass destruction may soon spread across the globe. For what is on sale is not Manhattan Project surplus, but systems explicitly made for fighting the World War III that never was.

Traffic in Materials

SOME of the architects of the present regime of proliferation controls will protest that such speculations are moot. They will argue that, given iron-clad sanctions against trade in ^{235}uranium and ^{239}plutonium and vigilant monitoring of the technological basis for their enrichment and separation, traffic in weapons-building expertise is unlikely to result in anything being built, because of the sheer lack of the critical materials of construction. But such complacency is foolish.

The common wisdom is that, having been stripped of its uranium and plutonium, waste from spent nuclear reactor fuel assemblies poses only the problem of finding a safe means of long-term storage. However, the waste is still pregnant with elements like neptunium which, despite their never having been used in deployed American nuclear weapons, are every bit as fissionable as the better-known trans-uranic elements.[5]

Thus, by defining the problem exclusively in terms of uranium and plutonium—the historical basis of all past bombs—the IAEA has opened the door to a very curious future. There are no controls on neptunium, tons of which languish in waste repositories around the world. Those repositories are intended to keep humans safe from radiation, rather than radwaste safe from persons bent on mining it for fissionable elements—elements that were originally rejected for weapons use simply because they were uncompetitive with superior fissionable materials, *not* because they will not do the job.

In one of history's more unhappy ironies, those who have objected to international transport of spent fuel for recycling (for fear of putting plutonium at risk of hijacking, or the environment at risk of plutonium contamination) have in fact helped create convenient stockpiles of potentially recoverable weaponizable neptunium and plutonium at sites around the world. Given Iraq's enterprising revival of the uneconomical but viable calutron, perhaps it is time to contemplate anew the Rich Man's Atom Bomb.

Very often we forget how the imperatives of nuclear ambition can warp normative perceptions of safety and cost-effectiveness beyond recognition. Many a terrorist has made his own nitroglycerine. Some of the spent fuel residue is already four decades old and has decayed to a point where its once ferocious radioactivity has fallen nearly a thousandfold. Today, using technologies as diverse as robotics and zeolite ion exchange separation, a group bent on quarrying radwaste for weapons—a patently suicidal notion three decades ago—might live to tell the tale.[6]

Precisely

MORE ominous still is the risk of the qualitative escalation of proliferation, of nations following Iraq's example in proceeding directly to the H-bomb. The assumption that "strategic" yield devices are vastly more demanding technically has been undermined by two factors: first, numerically controlled machine tools of optical levels of precision and almost unlimited versatility; second, the availability of computers and attendant software that bridge the gap between the level of sheer genius needed to innovate thermonuclear devices and the less demanding task of getting them built once their operation is understood from its first principles. This hypothesis has been chillingly corroborated by the UN's recent discovery of Iraq's possession of precision machine tools as well as isotopically purified ^{6}lithium, with evident intent to develop a hydrogen bomb.

When the Einstein-Szilard letter brought the possibility of the atomic bomb to President Roosevelt's attention, the American Physical Society had just 4000 members. About half of this cadre of (mostly) Ph.Ds joined the Manhattan Project, which at its height employed roughly 10,000 scientists with advanced degrees, principally in chemistry and chemical engineering. Some of its veterans have reflected on the acceleration of their research efforts relative to the pace of their pre-war endeavors. They all concur that the program's relatively unlimited budget contributed mightily to its rapid progress. It took a great deal of money, some $2 billion in an era when the largest of industrial research establishments—General Electric or Du Pont, for example—had annual budgets on the order of $10 million. That acceleration has more modern examples, such as the Apollo program in the 1960s and the Iraqi nuclear program of the 1980s. It is a tacit principle of research management that money buys time, and having spent a billion dollars a year for a decade, Iraq's progress should surprise no one.

Technicians are as important to the problem as scientists. Building such devices requires exacting standards of mechanical precision and electronic performance, often reckoned in angstroms and nanoseconds. In the mechanical domain, the advent of digitally controlled machine tools with optical sensors and air bearings has effected a revolution in the quality of precision machining. This has largely trivialized the task of machining components for a first-generation nuclear device. The compatibility of these precision tools with computer-aided design (CAD) and computer-aided manufacture (CAM) software, as well as precision robotic manipulators, substantially lowers the demands on the proficiency and skill of their operators. It also reduces the need for prolonged proximity to potentially dangerous nuclear materials. One built-in deterrent to radwaste bombs—the presumed lethality of the starting material—must be re-examined in the light of machines that produce precision components untouched by human hands. Many Third World nations now produce artifacts as materially diverse as contact lenses and CDs, both of which rival the level of precision of the first generation of thermonuclear devices. Most required manufacturing technology can be had for the asking, and much is in place.

Issues of automation also involve informational components. Linking the output of a hydrodynamical model with the refinement of a mechanical design is a demanding computer-programming task. It has lately been simplified by the advent of sophisticated computer languages that are both mathematically explicit and increasingly user-friendly. Designs in turn must be interfaced with CAM software, but expertise in that area is becoming as widespread as robotics in the Pacific Rim.

While the role of computer science in weapons design led to the installation of formidable cryptographic safeguards to isolate the powerful computers of the weapons labs from the outside world, the advent of highly secure public-key safeguards in unclassified civilian computer networks has serious drawbacks. Provided with almost unbreakable computer security, the international dispersion of the people and hardware necessary to conduct the conceptual design, modelling, and CAD/CAM cycle becomes a possibility. While vigilance might detect the accrual of expertise necessary for realistic nuclear ambition in a single place, the same human assets scattered around the world might go undetected.

Green Hell

MANY Third World doctorates are in a discipline that did not even exist in 1945: molecular biology. With its advent, chemical and biological weapons (CBW) have become less the poor man's atom bombs than the lazy one's.

The major substantive advantage nuclear weapons possess as instruments of intimidation or defense arises from the universal realization of just how terrible their effects are. Hiroshima endowed nuclear weapons with status as emblems of national power and as the ultimate talisman of military ambition. It also created a powerful taboo against their further use. Yet the residue of repugnance that led even Adolf Hitler to refrain from risking the use of nerve gas, and a return to the chemical warfare of World War I, has decayed to the extent that Iraq has already ventured into the suburbs of the unthinkable.

Unfortunately, so low is the threshold of technical difficulty and so small the critical mass of men and material within the orbit of whatever fanaticism should find such a deed compelling, that it is hard to imagine a world not at risk once more from chemical and biological weapons. The political and military factors that spared the world a failure of CBW deterrence in the Gulf War and the relative success in interdicting trade in nerve gas precursors are of but little relevance. To build an A-bomb requires a cadre of at least a hundred scientists and a budget of many millions spent in exotic ways. But biotoxins can be obtained by a few, directing the labors of unskilled dozens at a task that might cost less than a pound of gold. As the drug war shows, attempts at interdiction are all but hopeless. Nor are complicated delivery systems necessary; think what Mathias Rust, the young West German who landed a plane in Red Square, could have accomplished with a crop-duster.

Nor is there any need for genetically engineered micro-organisms, produced in high-biotech laboratories. Plants and other organisms containing molecules of intimidating toxicity are both numerous and ubiquitous. For example, ricin, the lectin made infamous by an umbrella-gun wielding Bulgarian assassin in London, is a potentially abundant byproduct of the production of castor oil. Worse toxins exist. Even in Burundi or Vanuatu, appropriate technologies of mass destruction are at hand in the state of nature. In order not to be eaten, plants have evolved means of producing chemicals of unsurpassable toxicity—one molecule can kill an animal cell. These substances have legitimate uses in biomedical research, and those learning to manipulate them safely in the laboratory can learn to use them as weapons.

Death of the Illusion

PERHAPS students of proliferation should begin looking over the shoulders of those who study immunology and oncology, for they too are addressing problems of mutation and metastasis; of constantly changing threats and challenges; and of how to aid the human immune system in rising to meet them. The growth of technology can be as benign as that of any living tissue, or as malignant as the worst of cancers.

The hermetic secrecy of the Manhattan Project gave way in the 1950s to the public emergence of nuclear science and information technology. Half a century later, there are more secrets than ever inside the weapons laboratories, but few that remain novel to the unclassified realm of science and technology that has been burgeoning uncontrollably on the outside. The continuing inflation of an already sprawling high-technology sector that spans the globe is leading us into a future that may be beyond economic repair. It is one in which the growing similarity of civilian and military technologies may lead to the extinction of their meaningful difference.

Information is the universal solvent of secrecy. And secrecy is not to be regarded as a permanent thing. The more that is known, the less remains that can be kept unknown. With the exponential growth of the technologies of information, the pressure of the known can exceed the strength of a secret technology's containment, and secrets can implode into irrelevance. Two thousand years before Columbus, Heraclitus gave us fair warning: *He who does not expect the unexpected cannot detect it.* Contemplating the realm of science and technology today, and considering the prospect of what intelligence, human and artificial, can accomplish in the century to come, we arrive at the depressing conclusion that the present regime of proliferation control may be among that rare set of entities—a fit object for catastrophe theory.

Bibliography

Audouze, Jean, and Vauclair, Sylvie, *An Introduction to Nuclear Astrophysics* (D. Reidel Publishing, 1980).

Bethe, Hans A., *The Road from Los Alamos* (The American Institute of Physics, 1991).

Elton, Raymond C., *X-Ray Lasers* (Academic Press Inc., 1990).

Ginzburg, V.L., *Applications of Electrodynamics in Theoretical Physics and Astrophysics* (Gordon and Breach Science Publishers, 1987).

Herman, Robin, *Fusion* (Cambridge University, 1990).

Kapitza, Peter, *Kapitza in Cambridge and Moscow* (North-Holland, 1990).

Matsuyama, Takashi, and Hwang, Vincent, *SIGMA: A Knowledge-Based Aerial Image Understanding System* (Plenum Press, 1990).

Meyers, Robert A., *Encyclopedia of Lasers and Optical Technology* (Academic Press, 1990).

Miyamoto, Kenro, *Plasma Physics for Nuclear Fusion* (The MIT Press, 1976).

National Research Council, *Materials Science and Engineering for the 1990s* (National Academy Press, 1989).

Parker, Sybil P., *Spectroscopy Source Book* (McGraw-Hill, 1988).

Rosenblum, Arnold, *Relativity, Supersymmetry, and Strings* (Plenum Press, 1990).

Scheindlin, A.E., and Fortov, V.E., *Thermal Physics Review* (Harwood Academic Publishers, 1987).

Weinberg, Steven, *The Discovery of Subatomic Particles* (W.H. Freeman, 1983).

---

[1] The authors wish to thank Delores H. Thurgood of the Office of Science and Engineering Personnel of the National Research Council for providing *Summary Report 1990: Doctorate Recipients from United States Universities* (Washington: National Academy Press, 1991), as well as tabulations of Ph.Ds on a nation-by-nation basis for the physical sciences and engineering disciplines that have served as the database from which the statistics in this article are derived.

[2] Jacques Gaillard, *Scientists in the Third World* (University Press of Kentucky, 1991).

[3] The Soviet Union's seizure of German technical personnel after the collapse of the Third Reich led to major improvements in their nuclear program, just as the Manhattan Project benefited from the influx of German refugees in the 1930s. The Nobel laureate Gustav Hertz, who developed the gaseous diffusion process in the 1950s, was taken into custody by Soviet forces in 1945.

[4] India is an illustrative case of a nation whose high-tech sector is sufficiently sophisticated to host an indigenous upgrading of a demonstrated nuclear capability to a thermonuclear one.

[5] And popular too. The neptunium bomb was first theorized by German President von Weiszacker's brother, Carl-Friedrich, in a secret report dated July 17, 1940.

[6] Apart from not being, in Oppenheimer's phrase, "technically sweet" in their design philosophy, radwaste bombs repel the mind in terms of their potential fallout. Unfortunately, this may make them all the more attractive to the enthusiastic terrorist.

DISMANTLING THE ARSENALS
Arms Control and the New World Agenda

Jack Mendelsohn

Jack Mendelsohn, a former State Department official, was a member of the U.S. SALT II and START delegations and served at the U.S. Mission to NATO. He is currently Deputy Director of the Arms Control Association in Washington, D.C.

The collapse of communism and the promise of a more cooperative East–West relationship have transformed the world of arms control. Goals that were once unthinkable—making enormous cuts in strategic forces or actually destroying nuclear warheads—are now at the top of the agenda. Developments that were always dangerous but of only secondary concern because of the primary East–West confrontation—the widespread deployment of short-range nuclear weapons or the spread of conventional weapons to the developing world—have now become urgent issues. And verification measures, originally born of deep distrust between East and West and intended to inform adversaries about each other's military programs, are now available to help monitor agreements, build trust, and reduce tensions.

Nuclear Weapons

Understandably, the most immediate concern of both the United States and Europe is the future of nuclear weapons in a disintegrating Soviet empire. For now, at least, the goals of the United States and Russia seem to be congruent: to ensure the centralized command and control of the nuclear forces of the newly formed Commonwealth of Independent States (CIS), to encourage the safe and secure withdrawal of tactical (and, eventually, strategic) nuclear weapons from the outlying republics to Russia, and to prevent the spread of nuclear hardware and brainpower to third countries. Programs to address these problems are already under way or under consideration, although concern about their continued successful implementation will certainly persist.

In the longer term a different set of nuclear arms control issues will challenge policymakers. The end of the Cold War offers a unique opportunity to push the size of U.S. and Russian strategic nuclear forces down to considerably lower levels. As Soviet President Gorbachev suggested last October, and as President Bush proposed in his State of the Union speech in January, the United States and Russia could readily cut in half the number of strategic weapons permitted under the Strategic Arms Reduction Treaty (START).

How low strategic forces can ultimately be taken will depend on the actual role assigned to nuclear weapons. Most analysts agree that the United States can maintain its present "warfighting" strategy with as few as 3,000–4,000 nuclear weapons (see table 1). If, on the other hand, the United States were prepared to abandon its current warfighting strategy, which targets thousands of military, political, and economic sites, in favor of a purely deterrent one involving a very limited set of military-industrial targets, it would facilitate even steeper reductions in strategic warheads. This is apparently the strategy that underlies Russian President Boris Yeltsin's recent offer to reduce strategic arsenals to 2,000–2,500 warheads.

An essentially deterrent strategy would be based on the premise that relatively few warheads are required to dissuade an adversary from launching a deliberate nuclear attack. According to former Secretary of Defense Robert McNamara, during the 1962 Cuban missile crisis, when the United States had approximately 5,000 strategic warheads to the Soviet Union's 300, "President Kennedy and I were deterred from even considering a nuclear attack on the USSR by the knowledge that, although such a strike would destroy the Soviet Union, *tens* of their weapons would survive to be launched against the United States" (emphasis added). Nothing in the past 30 years has invalidated that conclusion or diminished the deterrent value of even a few nuclear weapons.

From *The Brookings Review*, Spring 1992, pp. 34-39. © 1992 by The Brookings Institute. Reprinted by permission.

Preventing Inadvertent Conflict

With the end of the adversarial relationship between the United States and Russia and the prospect of large-scale reductions in existing nuclear arsenals, longstanding fears of deliberate attack have yielded to a new concern about inadvertent conflict. To respond to this concern, the two nations will need to make it as difficult as possible to launch their nuclear weapons. They will have to ensure that all nuclear weapons are subject to both physical safeguards and chain-of-command arrangements that cannot be defeated or circumvented. To this end, all deployed and nondeployed nuclear weapons should have the latest technology electronic locks to prevent unauthorized use. Both arming and release codes for all nuclear weapons should be held by the national command authority (on-board commanders have access to the codes for U.S. ballistic missile submarines).

Another way to reduce the risk of inadvertent war is to increase the overall confidence of both sides in the survivability of their nuclear forces. This can be done by some relatively simple measures. For example, the president has proposed that land-based ballistic missile systems be limited by agreement to one warhead. That is one way to eliminate the concern that a small number of land-based multiple-warhead missiles on one side could be used early in a crisis and, in theory at least, destroy large numbers of similar systems on the other side. Alternatively, land-based systems could be made mobile or dispersed among multiple protective shelters. Finally, overall warhead reductions, on the scale discussed above, would by themselves decrease the number of multiple warhead systems and increase survivability by making it difficult, if not impossible, to undertake a disarming strike against the nuclear forces of the other side.

As one confidence-building measure, warheads could be removed from a portion of the land-based missile force and the systems taken off high state of alert. Ballistic missile submarines could patrol out of range of their targets, and aggressive anti-submarine warfare training activities could be strictly limited. Strategic bombers should remain off alert and their weapons stored away from operational bases. The sides could also limit the size and frequency of large-scale exercises and enhance confidence by exchanging data and giving advance notice of strategic force tests or practice alerts.

Finally, the United States, Russia, and the relevant CIS countries should agree to destroy the existing stockpile of retired and surplus nuclear weapons, perhaps 15,000 to 18,000 warheads on each side. As the two sides reduce their tactical and strategic arsenals, the number of warheads in storage will increase dramatically—as will concern over their possible theft, sale, misappropriation, or rapid redeployment. The destruction of redundant warheads should be coupled with a ban on the further production of fissile material for weapons purposes, a monitored limit on the production of new warheads to replace existing systems, and the storage, under international safeguards, of fissile material withdrawn from retired weapons.

Table 1. Selected Proposals for Strategic Arms Reductions below Warhead Levels in START

NUMBER OF WARHEADS	PROPOSAL
600	Andrei Kokoshin, *Bulletin of the Atomic Scientists*, September 1988
1,000	Carl Kaysen, Robert S. McNamara, and George W. Rathjens, *Foreign Affairs*, Fall 1991
1,000–2,000	Committee on International Security and Arms Control, National Academy of Science, 1991 (second-stage cuts)
1,000–2,000	Jonathan Dean and Kurt Gottfried, Union of Concerned Scientists, 1991
Below 2,000	Harold A. Feiveson and Frank N. von Hippel, *International Security*, Summer 1990
2,000–2,500	Boris Yeltsin, United Nations, 1992
Below 3,000	Harold Brown, *Arms Control Today*, May 1990
3,000	John D. Steinbruner, Michael M. May, and George F. Bing, *International Security*, Summer 1988*
3,000–4,000	Committee on International Security and Arms Control, National Academy of Science, 1991 (first-stage cuts)
4,700	George Bush, State of the Union Speech, 1992
4,000–6,000	Reed Report, Strategic Air Command, 1991
6,000	START Treaty, 1991**

*Most proposals consider 3,000 warheads to be the level beneath which current targeting strategy must be revised and 2,000 to be the level beneath which third-country forces (United Kingdom, France, China) must become involved in negotiations.

**START permits 6,000 "accountable" strategic warheads on each side. Because of lenient counting rules on air-launched weapons, each side may in reality deploy several thousand additional warheads.

Strategic Defenses

Closely related to the question of nuclear force reductions and to the shift from preparing for deliberate war to preventing inadvertent war is the issue of preserving the Anti-Ballistic Missile (ABM) Treaty's strict limits on strategic defensive systems. Despite the boost given anti-missile systems by the Scud-Patriot encounters during the Gulf war, the United States will have to tread carefully in its approach to tactical and strategic ballistic missile defenses. Strategic defenses, by their nature, undercut confidence in the retaliatory capability of strategic offensive forces and could therefore lessen the willingness of one side or another to make big cuts in strategic offensive forces. In some cases, such as those involving the relatively small national deterrent forces of France and Britain, deploying even a low level of strategic defenses may actually stimulate an increase in arsenals in order to overcome these anti-missile systems.

Thus the Bush administration's interest in rewriting the ABM Treaty to permit large-scale deployment of its newest version of Star Wars, known as Global

Protection against Limited Strikes (GPALS), runs contrary to a fundamental U.S. interest: to reduce nuclear arsenals in the CIS to as low a level as possible. Moreover, the goal cited by the administration in support of GPALS—to protect the United States against threats from third world "nondeterrables"—is questionable. CIA Director Robert Gates has predicted that it will be at least a decade before any country other than China or the CIS could strike the United States with long-range ballistic missiles. And most observers believe that long-range ballistic missiles would not be the delivery system of choice for any third world nation attempting to threaten the United States.

Although Yeltsin proposed a joint SDI program, it is unlikely, given the economic situation in the CIS, that in the long run Russia will really pursue such a costly defensive project. The same should be true for the United States. If the United States nonetheless persists in its efforts to deploy defenses, and if the Russians acquiesce to a similar program, then it will be critically important that any eventual strategic defensive deployments be limited to very few fixed land-based interceptors only. Anti–tactical ballistic missile systems, which are likely to be of interest to both sides and which are not prohibited by the ABM Treaty, should be designed so that neither their capability nor their widespread deployment will erode confidence in either side's strategic offensive retaliatory capabilities.

Conventional Weapons

In the short term, U.S., European, and CIS arms control goals regarding conventional weapons are likely to be similar: to encourage the prompt adherence to, and implementation of, past and pending arms control obligations, especially the recently concluded Conventional Armed Forces in Europe (CFE) agreement, and to complete the Open Skies and CFE follow-on talks (the former to create an aerial inspection regime and the latter to establish politically binding limits on troop levels). A third goal, to ensure the orderly transfer of conventional military forces from Union control to the newly formed states, is certainly shared by the West and Russia. But tensions among the states of the new CIS may make it difficult, or even impossible, to distribute conventional forces quickly or smoothly (see table 2).

In the longer term, now that the fear of a massive land war in Europe has become, in the words of the CIA director, "virtually nonexistent," the conventional weapons arms control agenda is likely to be occupied with four principal issues. The first is greater openness, or transparency, in military programs and activities. After several decades of relying primarily on satellites and sensors to monitor military activities, and as the infatuation with on-site inspection fades, we are just now beginning to recognize and exploit the potential of relatively straightforward cooperative measures to provide intelligence. Through extensive and intensive multilateral exchange, nations can increase

Table 2. CFE-Limited Conventional Weapons in the States of the Former Soviet Union (February 1991)

REPUBLIC	TANKS	ARMORED COMBAT VEHICLES	ARTILLERY	HELI-COPTERS	AIRCRAFT
Armenia	258	641	357	7	0
Azerbaijan	391	1,285	463	24	124
Belarus	2,263	2,776	1,384	82	650
Estonia	184	201	29	10	153
Georgia	850	1,054	363	48	245
Latvia	138	100	81	23	183
Lithuania	184	1,591	253	0	46
Moldova	155	402	248	0	0
Russia	5,017	6,279	3,480	570	2,750
Ukraine	6,204	6,394	3,052	285	1,431
TOTAL	15,644	20,723	9,710	1,049	5,582
Soviet forces in Germany*	5,081	9,167	4,228	432	1,029
TOTAL**	20,725	29,890	13,938	1,481	6,611
TOTAL PERMITTED UNDER CFE	13,150	20,000	13,175	1,500	5,150

Source: Arms Control Association.

* All Soviet forces in Germany are scheduled to be withdrawn by 1994.

** Under CFE, the states of the former Soviet Union west of the Urals (with the exception of Estonia, Latvia, and Lithuania) must agree to allocate among themselves the total equipment permitted the former Soviet Union. Surplus equipment must be destroyed.

the information available on budgets, force size, production levels, research, development and modernization programs, deployment plans, arms transfers, and operational practices. As such openness improves our ability to predict the evolution of the overall security environment, it will enhance stability and reduce the risk of overreaction.

A second objective regarding conventional arms is to defuse the dangers of localized or ethnic strife in Europe. While the threat of a general war in Europe is minimal, numerous potential regional flash points, such as Croatia-Serbia or Armenia-Azerbaijan, still exist. Even if the CFE treaty enters into force, a concentrated effort will still have to be made to deal with these problem areas by subregional arms control. Subregional constraints might involve lowering force levels in geographically restricted areas (force allotments in Hungary and Romania, for example, could be 25 percent beneath CFE levels); establishing disengagement zones (Hungary and Romania could both agree not to deploy military forces within 50 kilometers of their common border); or instituting special monitoring measures such as intensive aerial overflights or third-party inspections.

A third issue, how to integrate large numbers of demobilized soldiers into civilian life and forestall a "black market" in conventional military hardware, will be one of the most challenging, albeit nontraditional, new arms control tasks. But it may also be the one most amenable to direct economic intervention. The United States has already offered the CIS $400 million to help dismantle its nuclear and chemical warheads. The United States and its European allies may wish to consider establishing a similar Conference on Security and Cooperation in Europe (CSCE) fund to help destroy, securely store, or ultimately buy up surplus war material from Eastern Europe and the CIS states to keep it from leaking into the black market (as apparently happened during the Croatian-Serbian conflict).

We may also wish to use an international fund to help train, house, employ, or provide severance pay to demobilized CIS soldiers to keep them from becoming a disruptive social or political force. Germany did as much to speed the evacuation of Soviet soldiers from its territory, and the current Russian military budget has designated all its capital investment for housing. We may also wish to institute programs to train soldiers who remain in uniform to work on disaster relief, environmental clean-up, and other civil support missions.

Finally, with or without U.S. participation, the European states will need to work toward creating European-based peacekeeping, peacemaking (that is, interventionary), and conflict-resolution institutions to deal with continent-wide security issues. The U.S. government does not now favor such institutions because it fears that they would undercut U.S. influence in European security issues. But, at some point, the tensions created by Yugoslavian-type crises, where the United States adopted a hands-off policy and Europe had very limited tools to manage the conflict, will force the empowerment of one or another of the Euro-based organizations (the Conference on Security and Cooperation in Europe, the Western European Union, or the North Atlantic Cooperation Council), the United Nations, or another specially created body to deal directly and forcefully with subregional challenges to European security. Once some international institution is designated as the executive forum, it will have to earmark multinational forces for the peacekeeping task, and the member states will have to devise a decisionmaking process that keeps the parties to the problem from blocking action.

Stemming the Spread of Weapons

As the enormous changes in Europe have eased concerns about East-West conflict, the United States and other developed nations have turned their attention to the challenges to international security posed by the spread of weapons in the developing world. Ironically,

Table 3. U.S. Arms Transfers to the Middle East since the Iraqi Invasion of Kuwait

MILLIONS OF DOLLARS

COUNTRY	VALUE	EQUIPMENT
Bahrain	$ 37	Tanks
Egypt	2,170	Aircraft, munitions
Israel	467	Patriot, aircraft, helicopters
Kuwait	350	Air base upgrades
Morocco	250	Aircraft
Oman	150	Armored personnel carriers
Saudi Arabia	14,800	Aircraft, tanks, helicopters
United Arab Emirates	737	Helicopters
TOTAL	**$ 18,961**	

Source: Arms Control Association. The table lists transfers of major conventional weapons notified to Congress between August 2, 1990, and January 1, 1992.

the problem is largely the result of the developed world's own policies during the Cold War, when arming the enemy of one's enemy was considered to be the height of sophisticated geopolitics. Meeting the proliferation challenge will require of the developed world a full and rare measure of political will and self-restraint.

To be sure, regimes to control several types of proliferation already exist or are under negotiation. The nuclear Non-Proliferation Treaty, with some 140 members, has been a highly successful example of international cooperation and common perspective for a quarter of a century. Negotiations on a Chemical Weapons Convention are far advanced and likely to be concluded in the not-too-distant future. And major supplier groups (to control nuclear technology, chemical and biological weapons, missile technology, and conventional arms transfers to the Middle East) have already been established and are expanding their scope.

Building on the existing nonproliferation structures, arms control can make several useful contributions. The first is to encourage stronger supplier restraint. Supplier states first must resist domestic political or economic pressures to sell arms, and then they will have to demonstrate a high level of political skill to balance the concerns of the developed world with objections from less advanced countries that nonproliferation regimes will spark. The nuclear supplier group clearly increased the time and cost of Iraq's nuclear weapons program. Nonetheless, the extent of Iraq's program surprised almost everyone, a fact that underscores the need to strengthen and expand nuclear export guidelines to include limits on "dual use" items—an effort already under way.

The United States and the other major arms exporters will also have to make more explicit efforts to limit sales of conventional weapons to areas of tension. For example, in conjunction with a supplier regime, "caps" might be placed on the value of arms exports approved by the supplier group to any one country in any one year (see table 3). That would require an international register of arms transfer and agreement among at least the "big five" exporters (the United States, the United Kingdom, France, the former Soviet Union, and China, which accounted for nearly 90 percent of the arms trade in 1990) to declare transfers and respect the cap. Pressure could also be applied to potential arms recipients by linking, directly or informally, U.S. aid, as well as aid from international lending institutions, to military spending levels.

As important as supplier restraint may be, regional arms control will undoubtedly remain the best long-term way to slow proliferation. Models already exist: the Treaty of Tlatelolco (establishing a nuclear-free zone in Latin America) and the Conventional Forces in Europe treaty are examples. Rallying the political will and muscle to apply these models to regions of the world where the underlying tension has not been directly eased by the new cooperative spirit in Europe will be a challenge. But easing these regional concerns is the key to taking the pressure off the "demand" side of proliferation. In fact, supplier restraint should only be a tool to buy time for regional efforts to work.

Regional arms control in areas such as the Middle East, South Asia, and Korea will have to involve major outside players. The United States, Russia, France, or Britain, depending on the region involved, will have to take an active interest and leading role in bringing about even a modest reconciliation. This reconciliation process would involve, first, political dialogue (as between the two Koreas and at the Middle East peace talks), then transparency (as in the Sinai and on the Golan Heights), supplier restraint, confidence-building measures, and, eventually, explicit arms control measures to limit forces and disengage (or separate) threatening forces.

Improved verification and monitoring would also strengthen nonproliferation efforts. Confidence in arms control regimes and regional security arrangements can, in general, be buttressed by increased transparency and predictability. In the proliferation arena, where one is dealing, almost by definition, with countries trying to acquire military capabilities by clandestine means, comprehensive intelligence, monitoring, and verification regimes are critical. First, as the Iraq experience has demonstrated, all agreements dealing with weapons of mass destruction must permit the right to challenge inspections of suspect sites. Second, nations with sophisticated intelligence capabilities, the United States in particular, will have to begin to share intelligence more widely. Making information more generally accessible will increase the stake of other participating states in the nonproliferation regime, enhance their confidence in its viability, and strengthen any eventual case against violators.

Finally, arms control by example is an important adjunct to specific nonproliferation treaties and cooperative measures. Although it cannot by itself stop states or leaders determined to violate an international agreement or tacit understanding, it can enhance the moral authority of the major powers. Evidence of serious intent to implement supplier restraint, to pursue deeper nuclear force reductions, to destroy conventional weapons and nuclear warheads, to stop fissionable materials production, and to cease nuclear testing would bolster the case for "demand" reduction in the proliferation arena. It would also strengthen the hand of the major powers in making the case for taking collective action—whether export controls, political and economic sanctions, or military measures—against any state that violates international agreements or standards.

Fighting Off Doomsday

Whether the threat comes from North Korea or Ukraine, the world worries about more fingers on the nuclear trigger

By BRUCE W. NELAN

NORTH KOREA'S KIM JONG IL, 51, wears high-heeled shoes and a bouffant hairdo in an attempt to look taller. He is a poor speaker and worries whether he can match his father's commanding power. But even those who laugh loudest at his vanities take one of his indulgences quite seriously: Kim, who has taken over day-to-day dictatorial duties from his 81-year-old father, "Great Leader" Kim Il Sung, appears determined to build a secret arsenal of nuclear weapons. His government had threatened to quit the 150-nation Treaty on the Nonproliferation of Nuclear Weapons last Saturday; it had ordered all foreigners except diplomats to leave and barred international inspectors from the country. If the outside world resorted to military force, a senior official in Pyongyang had warned, it would mean "plunging the whole Korean peninsula into the flame of war."

But at the eleventh hour, North Korea agreed late on Friday to "suspend" its withdrawal from the pact, pulling Asia back from the start of a nuclear arms race. If Pyongyang will permanently rejoin the treaty and agree to inspections, the U.S. is ready to cancel its yearly military exercises with South Korea and make a "no first use" pledge not to initiate the use of nuclear weapons on the peninsula. While U.S. officials are still puzzled by North Korea's actions, they say they now realize how deeply inspections disturbed its closed society.

Even though the cold war is over, leaders like Kim are making the world a more, not less, dangerous place. The superpower standoff that exerted precarious control over the use and proliferation of weapons of mass destruction has vanished along with the Soviet empire. North Korea has not only embarked on the road to the bomb, but according to many analysts, it has actually arrived. It reportedly has enough plutonium for at least one nuclear bomb, and it has successfully test-fired a new missile, the 650-mile-range No-Dong I, that could reach beyond South Korea to Japan, China or eastern Russia. Kim's government is an eager peddler of missiles to other countries, and Western analysts fear that Pyongyang could assist other would-be nuclear powers like Iran.

"We are facing a sophisticated Hydra of suppliers," warns CIA Director James Woolsey. More than 25 countries have or may be developing weapons of mass destruction. More than two dozen conduct research in chemical weapons or already stockpile them. More than a dozen have ballistic missiles that could one day loft nuclear warheads far beyond their borders.

Ukraine, along with the former Soviet republics of Kazakhstan and Belarus, stumbled into the nuclear club when the empire crumbled. Although all three have promised to banish the weapons entirely, Ukraine has been wavering on its commitment. A growing number of its leaders regard their atomic arsenal as a bargaining chip to trade for Western aid and security guarantees—and increasingly as a safeguard against possible Russian aggression that they are loath to relinquish.

Once again, the post–cold war era is turning out to be more complicated than anyone expected as the West searches for ways to stop nuclear proliferation. There

is no obvious answer, and the Western dithering that has accompanied the rape of Bosnia does not inspire confidence that the international community will come up with a strong plan of action soon. The U.S. is juggling competing objectives that undercut its own commitment to nonproliferation—the desire to improve relations with China or to secure Syria's cooperation in the Mideast peace talks—and so far, Washington has not figured out how to galvanize its main allies around a tougher antiproliferation policy.

North Korea is currently the gravest concern. Pyongyang signed the nonproliferation treaty in 1985 but grudgingly agreed only last year to allow inspectors to examine what it insisted was its purely civilian nuclear-power industry. When the monitors showed up, they confirmed intelligence reports that the installation at Yongbyon, north of the capital, had been processing plutonium at least since 1987.

No U.S. blandishments will keep Pyongyang honest—even if it remains formally in the nonproliferation pact—if its real intent is to free itself from international oversight while it pursues its nuclear dream. North Korea may have temporized to forestall U.N. economic sanctions that loomed if it became the first member to quit the treaty. But most observers are pessimistic that Kim will really cave in to political or economic pressure. "We're not dealing with rational people but with an unreconstructedly Stalinist regime," says a top British diplomat. "They don't believe in compromise but in maximum advantage."

Though the Security Council could authorize military means to disarm or pun-

 From *Time*, June 21, 1993, pp. 36-38. © 1993 by Time Inc. Magazine Company. Reprinted by permission.

ish Pyongyang, any attempt to use force would be extremely tricky. Bombing a functioning nuclear facility could produce an instant Chernobyl and, probably, retaliation. "We might try to take out their nuclear capability with a scalpel," says a Western analyst in Seoul, "but they would respond with a chain saw."

Doing nothing about the North Korean bomb is a bad option too. South Korea was well along in the development of nuclear weapons in the 1970s until the U.S. pressured Seoul to cancel its program. It could quickly and easily change course again. A nuclear arsenal in North Korea "could result in the dissemination of nuclear weapons throughout the region," says Christophe Carle, research fellow at the Institut Français des Relations Internationales in Paris. "I can't imagine Japan and South Korea and Taiwan refraining from doing so short of extraordinary U.S. assurances." An East Asia in which six powers have nuclear arms would be perilously unstable.

China is not only a member of the nuclear club but also one of the world's leading proliferators of weapons of mass destruction. The Chinese have been selling ballistic missiles and nuclear equipment to all comers in the Third World. Its missile technology has gone to Pakistan, Saudi Arabia and Iran. CIA Director Woolsey has told Congress that China is getting new missile technology from Russia and Ukraine. This is ominous, he said, not only because the transfers improve China's military capabilities, but also because China could pass this more advanced technology to other states. So far, the U.S. has been unable to persuade China to curtail its sales.

The U.S. is struggling to find a lever to persuade Ukraine to give up the nuclear stockpile it inherited. A growing number of parliamentary deputies argue that Kiev should retain at least some of the 176 strategic missiles, 30 nuclear bombers and more than 1,600 warheads as a deterrent to any ultranationalist Russian government that might try to reimpose its rule on Ukraine. A more urgent fear is that Ukraine is close—12 to 18 months away—to cracking the Russian computer codes that prevent Kiev from retargeting or firing the nuclear missiles itself. If the Ukrainians succeed, they will gain operational control of the world's third largest stockpile of nuclear weapons. Moscow has not explicitly told the U.S. that it might attack Ukraine to prevent Kiev from obtaining control, but they have hinted at very high levels that this could happen. U.S. officials take these hints seriously.

Last week Defense Secretary Les Aspin proposed removing the nuclear warheads from the Ukraine missiles and placing them under international control; later they would be taken to Russia and

DECLARED NUCLEAR-WEAPON STATES		
KEY: 🐟 100 miles or more / 🐟 Less than 100 miles	Ballistic missiles (longest known range in miles)	Chemical or biological (Yes / Probably)
Britain*	2,900	
China*	9,300	Probably
France*	3,100	Probably
Russia*	8,100	Yes
Belarus†	6,500	
Kazakhstan†	6,800	
Ukraine†	6,200	
U.S.*	9,200	Yes
UNDECLARED NUCLEAR-WEAPON STATES		
India	1,550	Probably
Israel*	930	Probably
Pakistan	190	Probably
WORKING ON OBTAINING NUCLEAR WEAPONS		
Algeria	40	
Iran	300	Yes
Iraq	190	Yes
Libya	190	Probably
North Korea	300	Yes
Syria	300	Probably
CEASED DEVELOPING NUCLEAR WEAPONS		
Argentina	60	Probably
Brazil	190	
South Africa	930	Probably
South Korea	160	Probably
Taiwan	60	Probably

*Capable of delivering nuclear weapons †Committed to becoming nonnuclear states but currently possessing nuclear weapons under Russian control stationed in their territory. TIME Graphic by Steve Hart

dismantled, and Washington would purchase the fissile material inside. The U.S. Department of Energy has agreed to buy between $8 billion and $13 billion worth of the highly enriched uranium, which could net Ukraine a share reaching $2 billion. That might prove a powerful incentive for the cash-strapped country.

The West has even less leverage to prevent the further breakdown of administration all across the former Soviet Union that could lead to smuggling and illegal sales of some of the 27,000 nuclear warheads now under guard by various military units. "I do not believe the reports that one or more may have been sold already," says Harald Müller of the Hesse Institute for the Study of Peace and Conflict in Frankfurt. "But as discipline deteriorates we have to be afraid that the custodians will become ineffective."

Western officials have been worrying about nuclear proliferation for decades, but it took the Gulf War to focus everyone's attention. It startled the West to learn just how close Saddam Hussein had come to secretly acquiring an atomic arsenal. That made everyone realize the slow and massive military buildup to Operation Desert Storm would probably have been impossible if Iraq had had nuclear weapons, even mounted on inaccurate Scuds. And the high-tech efficiency of the victorious American forces telegraphed to all Third World countries that they should forget about tangling with the U.S. unless they had acquired nuclear weapons.

The problem, though, extends beyond nuclear to chemical and biological bombs and the means to deliver them to far-off targets. Ballistic missiles, with flight times of only a few minutes and an ability to penetrate most defenses, are the most psychologically destabilizing. High-performance jet aircraft can easily deliver nuclear, chemical or biological warheads. "Most countries have not yet equipped their delivery systems to carry weapons of mass destruction," said Robert Gates, former Director of Central Intelligence. But he warned that over the next decade many of them will do so if international controls fail.

THE SAD TRUTH IS THAT "PROLIFERation cannot be stopped," says Götz Neuneck, a physicist at the Institute for Peace Research and Security Policy in Hamburg. "If a country wants to develop these weapons, it can do it." Even slowing the spread is difficult. The nuclear nonproliferation treaty bars development by or transfer of the weapons to non-nuclear states. It has done some good, but it has not prevented additional states from acquiring the bomb. Several, including India, Pakistan and Israel, simply refused to sign. Iraq, on the other hand, signed the treaty but cheated. Iran and North Korea signed and have gone ahead with development.

Treaties also ban chemical and biological weapons but at least 18 countries stockpile either or both. An agreement among major supplying countries, most of them Western, limits the sale of ballistic missile systems. There are no enforcement provisions and North Korea pays no attention to it, while China promised Washington to obey the rules but continues to break them.

A major obstacle to controlling the spread of these weapons is that even medium-size countries can build them using domestic industries and imported "dual-use" equipment—high-tech items that have civilian as well as military applications. Last year, says Kenneth Timmerman, a specialist in Middle Eastern security issues, Germany sold a total of $5 billion worth of goods to Iran. Japan sold Tehran nearly $3 billion worth and the U.S. shipped almost $1 billion. Much of the trade involved "dual use" items.

In September 1991 the CIA established a center to keep track of weapons of mass destruction and stop the flow of dangerous technology to the Third World. To watch about 24 countries and more than 75 weapons programs, the center collects information from spies on the ground, satellite photos and electronic intercepts, which is used to apply pressure on importing and exporting nations. In some instances Washington quietly asks a friendly capital to stop certain exports because they are being diverted to a weapons program. In other cases the U.S. and its allies sometimes use covert action to halt the shipments.

President George Bush signed an intelligence finding authorizing covert CIA action to disrupt the supply of dangerous weapons or components. How that authority has been used is secret, but an official in Washington confirms that "it has been used. Things have been prevented from getting from one place to another." Even so, says another official, controls over exports "cannot prevent but can only make it more difficult to produce nuclear weapons."

The Clinton Administration says it is determined to strengthen international controls. But it has yet to settle on a plan of action, much less begin to persuade friends and foes to go along. In the end, to head off nuclear arms races in various regions of the world the U.S. might have to offer security guarantees to worried governments and threaten to intervene, if necessary, to keep the peace. But that would require an overhaul of its alliance system and a major expansion of its overseas commitments.

However firm its stance, the U.S. cannot entirely eliminate the ambitions and fears that prod nations to acquire weapons of mass destruction. Washington could not, even if it wanted to, guarantee Arab states against Israel, India against China, Pakistan against India or Iran against Iraq. Some of them have the bomb now, and the others will get it. In the years to come, the U.S. will have to choose very carefully where to engage its interests and its military forces. It may have its hands full just protecting itself.

—Reported by James Carney/ Moscow, Richard Hornik/Seoul, Jay Peterzell and Elaine Shannon/Washington with other bureaus

World View
Shifting Battle Lines in Arms Race

A shortage of cash has cut into global weapons purchases. But some individual nations and regions are surging ahead.

Robin Wright

Times Staff Writer

WASHINGTON—Four years after the fall of the Berlin Wall signaled the onset of global change, the race to acquire the world's deadliest and most destructive weapons is far from over.

Rather than open an era in which the world can convert swords into plowshares, the end of the Cold War instead finds nations devising ever more ingenious ways to improve their arsenals by upgrading arms rather than buying anew, to expand arsenals by tapping into a postwar weapons glut and to disguise big-buck spending on national security by playing financial shell games.

Even tangible progress heralded in a spate of new reports—a 15% cut in defense spending globally and a 20% decline in arms sales to the Third World last year—is so grossly uneven that it tends to obscure the military preparedness of several states and their potential threat.

Only a handful of countries, for example, now account for more than 75% of the world's major weapons sales.

"Man's quest for bigger and better weapons is not over," said Eva Marie Loofe, an expert on military spending at the Stockholm International Peace Research Institute (SIPRI). "For several reasons, the new (disarmament) trends do not look permanent. Many can and probably will be reversed."

Basic military doctrine and attitudes about the utility of nuclear weapons have undergone little fundamental change. And the progress so far does not herald any general commitment to a "new world order" in which countries proactively or altruistically disarm.

The biggest single cause of defense cutbacks is instead simple economics. Because of foreign debt and deep recessions, many Third World countries now lack sufficient cash reserves in hard currency to buy big guns, tanks and warplanes. Even some First World nations are financially strapped.

Meanwhile, former Soviet proxy states no longer have access to the grants and large discounts from Moscow that once gave them easy and relatively cheap access to sophisticated weaponry.

"No one's cutting willingly. If economies improve, arms sales will go up again," Loofe said.

Also, while the Cold War's end may have slowed the production and sale of new arms, it hasn't decreased the flow of older weapons. Indeed, it may even have facilitated arms transfers.

"Massive quantities of very lethal equipment have been released for practically nothing over the past four years," according to Edward J. Laurance, an arms specialist at the Monterey Institute of International Studies and a U.N. consultant.

"If you're a state or a sub-state, there's literally tons of materiel being offered on street corners, in catalogues and at bazaars. A lot of people are particularly taking advantage of the fact that new states don't have export-control laws in place yet," he added, referring to the 15 former Soviet republics and other nations undergoing major political transformations.

Five worrisome trends are running counter to the good news about post-Cold War arms cutbacks, according to European and U.S. experts.

CASCADING

The first is described by a key new buzzword within the trade: "Cascading," or the flow of arms from larger to smaller powers at minimal or no cost as a result of new arms pacts or the breakup of nations.

The 1990 Conventional Forces in Europe Treaty among the 53 members of the Conference on Security and Cooperation in Europe, for example, put limits on the number of tanks, warplanes and other war materiel the signers could keep in their arsenals.

But rather than destroy equipment—an expensive process in itself—several countries transferred some of their surplus to smaller or poorer allies. Among the thousands of transfers: Germany gave 11 tanks and 105 armored personnel carriers (APCs) to Turkey as aid, while the Netherlands transferred 100 tanks and 53 APCs to Greece.

And after the Soviet breakup, Moscow gave weapons from arsenals in Russia to other republics. Moldova, which didn't have its own army two years ago, is now receiving equipment that was in the hands of Soviet troops based there.

The ominous side of cascading is that arms are often transferred to hot spots—thus contributing to the prospect of conflict.

"The good news is that the levels of arms among the world's two major antagonists are down. The bad news is that there's lots more equipment in the hands of countries that didn't have them before. It's taking weapons out of the hands of people who are not fighting and giving them to people who are often in or near hot spots," Laurance said.

Once combatants over Cyprus, Turkey and Greece remain rivals, for example. Yet last year, Greece received 592 tanks and 206 APCs, while Turkey got 588 tanks and 335 APCs, all courtesy of cascading from Germany, the Netherlands and the United States.

And cascading among former Soviet republics has contributed to the increasingly bloody civil war in Tajikistan, fighting between Georgia and its Ossetian and Abkhazian minorities and the war between Azerbaijanis and Armenians.

SURPLUS

Other weapons are flooding the market because, with the Cold War over, they're now surplus. Many valued in the hundreds of thousands or millions of dollars in the 1980s are available in the 1990s for the price of junk.

In May, the Armed Forces Journal quoted the price of a Chieftain tank, which has normally sold in the range of $1 million, at around $4,000. The cost was based on its weight and the price of scrap per ton rather than the tank's military value.

The British have over 800 fully equipped and operational Chieftains for sale at that price, the magazine reported.

The Cold War's end has also shifted alliances and lifted restraints on doing business with the opposition. Several former rivals are now tapping into each other's arsenals.

The United Arab Emirates last year almost bought 400 U.S.-made Bradley APCs. Priced at $1 million apiece, the sale would have been a classic Cold War deal. In the end, however, the emirates instead bought more than 400 surplus APCs from Russia. Although brand-new, they were priced as surplus—about $20,000 apiece, Laurance said.

UPGRADE

Rather than buy new weapons, an increasing number of countries are now upgrading what they have, according to Steve Irwin, a senior analyst at Defense Forecasts Inc. The cost is usually 20% to 70% of buying new materiel.

One of the dominant trends for the 1990s, experts now predict, will be upgrading warplanes, since most countries can no longer afford new fleets of big-ticket combat aircraft.

"Upgrading means that although the amount of money being spent is going down, the sophistication of weaponry and the combat capability are increasing," Irwin said.

In one of the many ironic twists since the end to superpower rivalry, American companies are now offering upgrades on Soviet-made MIG-21 warplanes—as are the French, Israelis and, of course, Russians. All four, plus Britain and Canada, also offer upgrades on other equipment in one of the few growth industries in arms.

Fighter and bomber aircraft, helicopters, tanks and various warships can be upgraded, while artillery and missiles cannot, Irwin said. The key is often whether electronics can be improved—one of the reasons upgrading will for the near future be dominated by industrialized nations.

Some countries see opportunity in buying surplus equipment, then upgrading it. This year Pakistan has reportedly considered buying British Chieftains at $20,000 apiece and having them upgraded with advanced heat-seeking imaging devices. An alternative is to buy T-72 tanks—the Chieftain's East Bloc equivalent—from Poland for hundreds of thousands of dollars more.

BARTER

Third World countries are also getting around rising economic constraints by bartering for arms. Supplier countries, particularly in the old East Bloc, are often willing to accept payment in kind because of declining interest in their military wares.

Russia, for example, has agreed to sell weapons to Iran, in defiance of pressure from the West, in exchange for oil that can either be consumed domestically or resold.

After weighing the merits of U.S. and Russian warplanes, Malaysia this year bought 18 state-of-the-art MIG-29 warplanes from Moscow. Kuala Lumpur initially hesitated due to fears that political instability in Russia might jeopardize supplies of spare parts. The clincher was Russia's agreement to accept partial payment in Malaysian palm oil.

DOMESTIC PRODUCTION

Finally, an increasing number of countries are now producing their own arms in ever wider varieties, according to Michael Renner, a senior defense researcher at the Worldwatch Institute. The trend within the developing world started in the 1970s, accelerated in the 1980s and is now expanding widely.

In 1990, Pakistan began production of heavy artillery, while Chile launched the manufacture of propeller-driven aircraft. South Africa began manufacturing military helicopters and, the next year, production of its own main battle tanks, Renner said.

Since the Cold War's end, India has begun production or made plans to produce equipment it once imported, including main battle tanks, helicopters and guided missiles. Even the city-state of Singapore, once a producer only of small arms, is now producing large artillery.

Some countries are building up their independent capabilities because they no longer have a superpower shield and fear abandonment—a concern accentuated after the outside world's refusal to intervene in Bosnia-Herzegovina.

"For 95% of the world's conflicts in the post–Cold War world, it's reasonable to say that there probably won't be international intervention. So countries are looking to their own preparedness. They don't want to depend any more on external security guarantees," said Ian Anthony, a SIPRI arms specialist.

Other countries are simply expanding existing industries. Turkey, Greece and Spain, for example, are becoming arms producers through licenses from Western allies. Their current intent is to export mainly to cover initial costs, said Saadet Dager, also a SIPRI specialist.

Still other nations, notably China and Brazil, want to become Third World alternatives in the big-bucks world of arms sales—plans made possible by greater access to key technology. With the Cold War's end, for example, China has acquired technology and scientists from Russia, a former rival, to upgrade its arms industry.

China is now adapting Russian technology for new types of lighter aircraft and electronics for tanks. The world's most populous nation is also expected to be increasingly capable at sea with its own submarines and aircraft carriers, Dager predicted.

And Indonesia now makes helicopters based on German technology, while India and Pakistan both now produce their own missiles based on technology from, respectively, Russia and China.

The fact that most weapons produced in Third World countries are small or mid-size doesn't diminish international concern.

"We still need to worry, because weapons don't have to be expensive to be deadly or worrisome," said Richard F. Grimmett, author of a new Congressional Research Service report on arms sales to the Third World.

"China sold only $100 million (worth of arms) in 1992 and was ranked a distant 10th," Grimmett explained. "It's way down from the time it sold to both Iran and Iraq during their war. But the fact is that China has the capacity to sell various forms of missiles which don't have to cost a lot. So the dollar value is not the key. The issue is what's being sold to whom—not necessarily how much—that defines whether there's a problem."

The enormous volume of lower- and middle-level weaponry—from machine guns to antitank weapons and artillery—already on the world market and the knowledge of how to produce them will also make them increasingly difficult to track or accurately monitor, the experts said.

Like the international arms trade, positive trends in defense spending since 1989 have also been overshadowed by countertrends.

One of the most worrisome is the way several countries cutting back on military budgets turn around and increase spending on internal security.

"We're seeing a hidden reverse twist to military spending" that reflects the shift in threats from wars between countries to conflicts within states, said Dager of the Stockholm peace institute.

Of the five major new armed conflicts in 1992, in which more than 1,000 people died, four were internal: Azerbaijan, Tajikistan, Bosnia and Laos. (The Kashmir crisis involving both India and Pakistan was the fifth.)

"Because countries are afraid of internal breakup or fighting, they're trying to accumulate small arms, sometimes even illegally, which may not register in the arms data. They're also increasing paramilitary and police," Dager added.

The level of cutbacks in military spending worldwide is also far from even. The global decline of 15% is largely due to the halving of spending in one year by the 15 former Soviet republics.

But the North Atlantic Treaty Organization's military spending, of which the United States accounted for the largest percentage, actually rose, according to the 1993 SIPRI survey due out this month. U.S. military spending went up by 3.5% in real terms between 1991 and 1992, SIPRI figures show.

Even within the developing world, where spending generally has been falling for a decade, defense budgets are rising in the Far East and Mideast. Saudi Arabia, with $36 billion worth of weaponry bought in the 1989–1992 period, has accounted for fully one-third of all Third World arms purchases since the end of the Cold War.

And the cutbacks, as in Latin America and Africa, can be deceiving, since the long-term debt to pay for earlier arms acquisitions now stands at $1.06 trillion.

Cuts within individual countries also belie a growing collective expense.

The number of international peacekeepers, for example, has soared from a steady level of 10,000 to 15,000 in the late 1980s to 62,000 by the end of 1992, due largely to the rising number of internal wars. Accordingly, SIPRI reported, the costs of international peacekeeping quadrupled last year to $1.4 billion—an expense absorbed by the international community.

The bottom line on both decreased defense spending and cutbacks in arms sales is that neither necessarily bears any relation to diminished prospects for conflict.

"The most pessimistic aspect of the arms sale story is that most of the budding conflicts today are the result of the weapons scattered around the world during the Cold War, mainly the lower-end arms with which the world has become awash courtesy of the past half-century," said William Durch, an international security specialist at the Henry L. Stimson Center in Washington.

"The breadth and depth of armament in general is already such that you can't expect to dampen or avoid conflict because people don't have guns, which might have been true of the first half of the century."

The bomb or peace

To check the spread of nuclear weapons, we must stop thinking that they are synonymous with security

Jasjit Singh

JASJIT SINGH,
of India, is director of the Institute for Defence Studies and Analyses in New Delhi. A member of India's National Security Advisory Board, he is the author of several works on defence, including *Air Power in Modern Warfare*.

CHANGES in the global political architecture during the past few years have led to a number of agreements to reduce nuclear weapons. The threat of a nuclear war and global holocaust has receded. On the other hand, the unmasking of the nuclear weapon programme pursued by Iraq for many years, unknown and undetected in spite of regular inspections by the International Atomic Energy Authority, has generated renewed concern about nuclear proliferation.

Proliferation means different things to different people. The five acknowledged nuclear weapon states—the United States, the former USSR, China, France and the United Kingdom, see the problem essentially as one arising out of the spread of nuclear weapons to other states: in other words, "horizontal" proliferation. Most other states see the problem as far more complex, although no consensus view exists. The fact that 157 states are now parties to the Treaty on the Non-Proliferation of Nuclear Weapons (NPT) which was signed in 1968 is an indication of this widespread concern. It also highlights the commitment of the five nuclear weapon states to total nuclear disarmament and reflects the expectations of the non-nuclear weapon states that this commitment will be honoured at an early date.

The real problem is that for more than forty-five years the world has been led to believe that nuclear weapons have kept the peace in Europe. The United States and NATO justified their nuclear weapons strategy as necessary for their security against the perceived threat of the Soviet Union's massive conventional forces and, later, the combination of nuclear and conventional forces. There is no way of testing this proposition, but its logic has appealed to many other states and their decision-makers.

A very large number of states do not have the means to acquire nuclear capability, or lack sufficiently strong security incentives to do so. Others have been coupled in the past to the nuclear weapons of the two superpowers. But a powerful logic in favour of acquiring nuclear weapons for their own security has been operating in many states, which have been swayed by the rationale of nuclear deterrence. In such situations a "ripple effect" takes place as other, neighbouring countries feel obliged to acquire nuclear weapons in their turn.

Besides the security incentive, nuclear weapons have acquired a certain aura in the international system. The five permanent members of the United Nations Security Council are nuclear weapon states, and there have been many incidents in which a state has used nuclear weapons as an instrument of policy to coerce others. These and other factors create incentives for proliferation, which is a source of instability.

There is no intrinsic reason to suggest that

Courtesy of *The UNESCO Courier*, October 1993, pp. 35-39.

only the states of the North can act in a responsible manner, although unfortunately the debate normally implies this. China, a major state of the South, has possessed nuclear weapons for the past twenty-five years. But an increase in the numbers of those who control nuclear weapons inevitably carries serious risks, not least those arising from miscalculation and accident. There is thus no reason to disagree with the prevalent view in the North that any increase in the number of nuclear weapon states is destabilizing. However the problem cannot be resolved by addressing the question of horizontal proliferation alone.

FLAWS IN THE NON-PROLIFERATION TREATY

The NPT is the only non-proliferation regime that has so far been established. The general view, especially in the South, is that the Treaty is discriminatory, but this is only a small part of the problem. NPT has failed to meet its own stated objectives, especially when judged against three critical yardsticks—sound principles, efficiency, and security interests. The number of warheads proliferated from less than 12,000 in 1968 to 55,000 twenty years later. The twin objectives of non-proliferation and disarmament set out in the NPT have not been met. This makes it necessary to establish a more viable non-proliferation regime for the twenty-first century.

The NPT has also given nuclear weapons a certain legitimacy, while at the same time tending to provide a false sense of security. States which adhere to the Treaty as non-nuclear weapon states are believed to be such, although the reality may be different, as Iraq's example shows. South Africa clandestinely built up a stockpile of at least six nuclear weapons. It joined the NPT in July 1991; its denuclearization will remain under question. North Korea signed the NPT in 1985 but is pursuing a weapon-related programme. Iran is a party to the Treaty but is suspected by some of having a weapon-related programme.

THE COLLAPSE OF THE USSR

The disintegration of the USSR has led to unprecedented risks of nuclear proliferation, opening three major areas of concern.

Firstly, there is widespread uncertainty about the extent of control being exercised over nuclear weapons. On 21 December 1991 the leaders of eleven former Soviet republics signed the Alma Ata Accord in which it was agreed that decisions about the use of the strategic nuclear forces of the Commonwealth of Independent States (CIS) would be made by the Russian president "with the agreement" of the leaders of Ukraine, Belarus and Kazakhstan—and after "consultation" with other Commonwealth leaders. Actual control of the "nuclear button" is believed to rest with Marshal E. Shaposhnikov, the commander of CIS Strategic Deterrence Forces, and President Boris Yeltsin. The system does not have the reliability of NATO in the sense that there are no institutionalized political controls between Russia, Ukraine, Belarus and Kazakhstan. Nor can the stability of these states be taken for granted. Russia has been resisting multilateral controls even on the processes of dismantling nuclear weapons.

Secondly, it is hard to predict the effects of Russia's domestic crisis on the mechanisms for controlling nuclear weapons within the country. In the former Soviet Union, control over nuclear weapons was maintained through a balance of tensions between three mutually reinforcing pillars of the power structure—the Communist Party, the KGB and the military. Today the Communist Party is disbanded, and a stable political framework has yet to be firmly established. The KGB, which traditionally controlled the nuclear warheads, has undergone a fundamental transformation. The military has been severely affected by the dissolution of the USSR and the social and economic problems this has caused. It was generally believed that Soviet theatre military commanders possessed delegated authority to use nuclear weapons in their jurisdiction. There is little to suggest that this has changed. In the West concern has focussed essentially on the fate of strategic weapons in the former Soviet Union, but nearly 17,000 non-strategic nuclear warheads constitute a more serious danger. Control over these weapons has inevitably been far more diffused and uncertain.

Thirdly, the continuing social and economic crisis in the former USSR has increased the risk of leakage of nuclear weapon technology and know-how. A nuclear brain drain could reinforce clandestine weapons programmes. New trends in ethno-religious nationalism may provide further incentives to nuclear proliferation.

THE DANGERS OF PROLIFERATION

It was the transformation of political relations between the United States and the Soviet Union that made real progress possible in nuclear arms reductions, rendering START itself obsolete even before it was signed. Political relations, rather than weapons *per se*, are the critical factor in international security.

The biggest problem with nuclear weapons may be described as one of asymmetry of capabilities. Asymmetry creates greater complexities and uncertainties in multi-polar situations where nuclear weapons of one state have implications for a number of others. Inevitably asymmetry increases with the increase in the number of nuclear weapon states, creating instability and providing a powerful incentive for proliferation.

Instability and proliferation, therefore, are closely linked. Broadly speaking, stability can be enhanced only through one of two diametrically opposite methods—global nuclearization by extensive horizontal proliferation which could keep the peace on the so-called European model of nuclear deterrence, or denuclearization through complete and global nuclear disarmament. It is obvious which one would be the better option.

Denuclearization has traditionally been considered too idealistic on the grounds that nuclear weapons cannot be disinvented, and in theory the problem of the rogue state and violations would always remain. However, the Chemical Weapons Convention now awaiting approval by the United Nations General Assembly is quite relevant here and could be taken as a model for dealing with the threat of nuclear weapons. One of the most positive results of the end of the Cold War, this Convention is based on the principles of universality and comprehensiveness and includes provisions for extensive verification and routine inspection. This is particularly important since chemical weapons are easier to manufacture than nuclear weapons, and even the less developed states of the South have some access to technology and resources to develop them because of the extensive and expanding chemical industry. Violations of non-proliferation agreements concerning nuclear weapons would thus be far easier to check than those concerning chemical weapons.

It is becoming feasible to construct a world without chemical weapons, and to go from there to a nuclear-weapon-free world is only a few steps down the same path. Denuclearization,

Glossary

CFE Treaty: The Conventional Armed Forces in Europe Treaty, signed on 19 November 1990, came into force on 9 November 1992. Sets ceilings on treaty-limited ("conventional" or non-nuclear) equipment in the Atlantic-to-the Urals zone. 29 states parties, including the former Soviet republics since 1992.

CSCE: Conference on Security and Co-operation in Europe. Began to meet in 1973 as a forum for matters relating to security, human rights and economic and scientific co-operation in Europe. 51 member states (all the European states plus the United States and Canada and the former Soviet republics).

IAEA: International Atomic Energy Agency. Established in 1957 by the UN to promote the peaceful uses of atomic energy and to ensure that nuclear activities are not used to further any military purpose, it has 113 member states.

ICBM: Intercontinental ballistic missile (range in excess of 5,500 km). **IRBM:** Intermediate-range ballistic missile (range of from 1,000 up to and including 5,500 km).

NATO: North Atlantic Treaty Organization. Established by a Treaty signed by 12 states in Washington on 4 April 1949, it now has 16 members: Belgium, Canada, Denmark, France, Germany, Greece, Iceland, Italy, Luxembourg, the Netherlands, Norway, Portugal, Spain, turkey, the United Kingdom and the United States. (France and Spain are not in the integrated military structures of NATO.)

NPT: Treaty on the non-proliferation of nuclear weapons, signed on 1 July 1968; came into force on 5 March 1970. It prohibits nuclear weapon states from transferring to other states nuclear weapons or the means of manufacturing or acquiring them. 156 states are parties to the Treaty.

SALT: Strategic Arms Limitation Talks. Negotiations between the United States and the USSR which sought to limit the strategic nuclear forces of both sides and resulted in two treaties. The SALT I Agreements and the ABM Treaty limiting the development, testing and deployment of Anti-Ballistic Missile Systems were signed in 1972. The SALT II Treaty was signed in 1979 but never ratified.

START: Strategic Arms Reduction Talks. US-Soviet treaty, signed on 31 July 1991, which reduces US and Soviet offensive strategic nuclear weapons. In view of the new political situation in Eastern Europe, a protocol was signed at Lisbon on 23 May 1992 by the United States, Belarus, Kazakhstan, Russia and Ukraine.

TNF: Theatre or tactical nuclear forces (also called non-strategic nuclear forces).

Nuclear weapons with ranges of up to and including 5,500 km. The US-Soviet Intermediate-range nuclear forces (INF) Treaty of 1987 obliged the United States and the USSR to destroy all land-based missiles with a range of 500–5,500 km (intermediate range and shorter-range) and their launchers by June 1991.

UN: United Nations Organization. International organization established in June 1945 by the San Francisco Treaty in succession to the League of Nations, which was officially dissolved in July 1947. It seeks to maintain world security and peace and works on behalf of international co-operation for economic and social progress and respect for human rights. Its principal organs are the General Assembly (where each of the 183 member states has one vote), the Security Council (five permanent members: China, France, Russia, the United Kingdom and the United States, plus ten members elected for two years), the Secretariat, the Economic and Social Council (54 members elected by the General Assembly for three years), and the International Court of Justice.

WTO: The Warsaw Treaty Organization, or Warsaw Pact, was established in 1955 by a treaty of friendship and mutual assistance between 8 countries: Albania, Bulgaria, Czechoslovakia, the German Democratic Republic, Hungary, Poland, Rumania and the USSR. Dissolved on 1 July 1991.

Sources: United Nations, Stockholm International Peace Research Institute (SIPRI)

however, will have to be dealt with on the conceptual as well as the physical level. The problem with nuclear weapons is that belief systems have been built up to support the idea that they are usable and indeed almost indispensable to international security. If the dangers of proliferation are to be addressed on a durable basis, steps must be taken to counter these ideas. The real dangers of nuclear proliferation stem from nuclear fundamentalism.

Nuclear fundamentalism needs to be tackled at the conceptual level. This is why 138 states, mostly of the South, have been regularly voting at the UN since 1978 for a convention to outlaw the use and threat of use of nuclear weapons. This would be the most powerful method of delegitimizing nuclear weapons and eroding the concept of their utility. At the same time, methods of maintaining national security need re-examination.

In defence of their sovereignty nation-states have traditionally sought to enhance their own security at the cost of the security of other states. Nuclear weapons, of course, represent an extreme example of this process. The result is a *competitive security* framework that seeks to create and exploit vulnerability in other states. This approach should be replaced by a move towards a *co-operative security* framework in which the security of each side becomes of equal importance, the two sides make allowances for each other's minimum needs, and co-operate not to raise each other's levels of insecurity. This would represent a comprehensive model of collective security.

Collective Security and Emerging Global Issues in the New World Order

Trends like globalism fueled by internationalization of the world economy blend with nationalistic, religious, and political ideologies to confuse the New World Order. Benjamin Barber describes two of the dominant tendencies today—economic globalism and Islamic fundamentalism—as "the forces of Jihad and the forces of McWorld." Although currently the tendencies seem equal in strength, Barber claims that their impact on international relations is in opposite directions with the one driven by parochial hatreds and the other by universalizing markets. Barber concludes that these axial principles of our age clash at every point except one: They may both be threatening to democracy.

The criticality of basic assumptions about future security threats is illustrated in "Defence in the 21st Century," an analysis compiled by *The Economist* staff. Beginning with the premise that the Western democracies will not be faced with an armed power with global reach for another 20 years, this analysis concludes that only seven "perfect divisions," under the coordinated control of the democracies and organized within a new multinational system built upon existing NATO arrangements, will be needed to cope with future military threats. The appro-

priateness of such a military doctrine is the subject of intense debates both at home and among NATO allies.

Since the Gulf War, the UN has overseen the enforcement of economic sanctions against Iraq and in the Balkans, helped free the last of Beirut's American hostages, challenged Libya's terrorism, sent UN peacekeeping forces to former Yugoslavia and Somalia, and received authorization to monitor elections or cease-fire agreements or play an active peacekeeping role in conflicts in almost every region of the world. The current secretary general of the UN, Boutros Boutros-Ghali, anticipated this rapid expansion in the demand for UN services and has been a tireless advocate for a more activist role for the UN in international security affairs.

In "Empowering the United Nations," Boutros Boutros-Ghali reviews the challenges and lessons learned during recent UN peacekeeping operations, the problems posed by unpaid bills, and the need to maintain development programs while also meeting new peacekeeping responsibilities. Ever the optimist about the capacity of this organization, Boutros-Ghali predicts that the UN will continue to take on larger responsibilities and play a greater role in keeping the peace throughout the post–cold war period.

Boutros-Ghali is both the chief official spokesperson for the UN and one of the most famous advocates for the school of thought that supports an increased UN role in a world characterized by changing ideas of sovereignty. He is also the architect of an ambitious plan, "An Agenda for Peace," which proposes major reforms in the organizational structure of the UN and the development of a standby peacekeeping army that would allow UN units to move into conflict zones before fighting begins. Supporters of the Agenda for Peace plan usually view an enhanced international peacekeeping force under the authority of the UN as a credible alternative to interstate warfare.

Currently, as Lucia Mouat describes in "Can the UN Be the World's Cop?" the organization's most visible peacekeeping operations are facing major problems, bogged down, or on hold. In major trouble spots such as Angola, the presence of UN personnel failed to prevent fighting among rival factions. In Somalia, the UN's mission shifted from neutral observer to active participant in armed conflicts before the withdrawal of the U.S. and other major

Western countries' forces in 1994. Mouat outlines some of the issues and lessons learned from past UN missions in Southern Africa, El Salvador, former Yugoslavia, Cambodia, and Somalia.

The expanding scope of UN programs, the current tasks assigned UN personnel, and the still unfulfilled requests for additional UN peacekeeping services have overwhelmed the resources and capacities of this international organization. The UN is currently too financially strapped to carry out all its mandates. The recent problems experienced by the commander of UN forces on the ground in Bosnia in 1994 in obtaining additional troops to help police the temporary cease-fire illustrate what may be a recurring lesson of UN efforts at peacekeeping: no major UN international peacekeeping operation can succeed without the active support and participation of the major world powers.

Today, it remains an open question whether the major powers, including the United States, will agree to underwrite the costs of additional international peacekeeping until major organizational reforms are agreed to and implemented. Many observers have concluded that substantial changes may be required in the operating procedures and organizational structure of the UN, in addition to new commitments on the part of major world powers to this international organization, before the UN can play an effective, expanded role in international relations.

Success in managing interstate warfare will ultimately rest on the ability of the world community to cope with the conditions in world society that cause or aggravate conflicts. In "Poverty, Population, and Pollution," Nafis Sadik, executive director of the UN Population Fund, addresses the overpopulation-poverty argument advanced by some. While the conventional thesis suggests that poverty is created by overpopulation, Sadik argues that the relationship is more in the nature of a cycle: poverty both breeds unchecked population growth and results from it. According to Sadik, many economic development plans are incomplete and ineffective, particularly in their failure to address family planning.

This volume begins and ends with topics related to the cultural basis of world conflicts. Samuel Huntington's introductory article, "The Clash of Civilizations?" outlines a provocative thesis about the development of a fault line between the West and non-Western civilizations as the principal basis for future conflicts. Increasing ethnic conflicts are a central feature of the post–cold war international order. The volume concludes with a note that care must be exercised when analyzing contemporary conflicts that the label "ethnic conflicts" does not serve as an excuse for highly simplistic or prejudicial analyses and conclusions. As Neil Whitehead and R. Brian Ferguson explain in "Deceptive Stereotypes about 'Tribal Warfare,' " the analysis of ethnic conflicts as tribal warfare tends to confound discussion of the need for humanitarian intervention and promotes deceptive and static stereotypes. Rather than view local wars as eruptions of primitive tribal animosities, Whitehead and Ferguson argue that we should try to understand the interplay of local and external forces that causes violence to emerge as international conflicts.

Looking Ahead: Challenge Questions

Where might the "forces of Jihad and the forces of McWorld" most threaten recent efforts to establish a more democratic order? What, if anything, should the United States do to support the democratic movement in this particular conflict situation?

Do you support current efforts to increase the role of UN peacekeeping forces in such places as Bosnia, or should UN peacekeeping activities be limited to more modest operations such as monitoring elections and referendums?

Should U.S. military personnel, such as the forces deployed during Operation Restore Hope in Somalia, be required to serve under the command structure of the UN in future peacekeeping operations? Why or why not? Will troops from developing countries who are replacing U.S. and Western countries' forces be more effective in fulfilling the peacekeeping function in Somalia?

Do you support long-term involvement of U.S. troops to implement a future agreement in Bosnia? Why or why not?

Explain how poverty could lead to higher population growth. What do you think is the relationship between the two variables of poverty and pollution that creates problems for population planning? Can the UN, the U.S., or other outside actors play a more effective role in breaking the overpopulation-poverty cycle? Why or why not?

Jihad vs. McWorld

The two axial principles of our age—tribalism and globalism—clash at every point except one: they may both be threatening to democracy

Benjamin R. Barber

Benjamin R. Barber is the Whitman Professor of Political Science at Rutgers University. Barber's most recent books are Strong Democracy *(1984),* The Conquest of Politics *(1988), and* An Aristocracy of Everyone.

Just beyond the horizon of current events lie two possible political figures—both bleak, neither democratic. The first is a retribalization of large swaths of humankind by war and bloodshed: a threatened Lebanonization of national states in which culture is pitted against culture, people against people, tribe against tribe—a Jihad in the name of a hundred narrowly conceived faiths against every kind of interdependence, every kind of artificial social cooperation and civic mutuality. The second is being borne in on us by the onrush of economic and ecological forces that demand integration and uniformity and that mesmerize the world with fast music, fast computers, and fast food—with MTV, Macintosh, and McDonald's, pressing nations into one commercially homogeneous global network: one McWorld tied together by technology, ecology, communications, and commerce. The planet is falling precipitantly apart and coming reluctantly together at the very same moment.

These two tendencies are sometimes visible in the same countries at the same instant: thus Yugoslavia, clamoring just recently to join the New Europe, is exploding into fragments; India is trying to live up to its reputation as the world's largest integral democracy while powerful new fundamentalist parties like the Hindu nationalist Bharatiya Janata Party, along with nationalist assassins, are imperiling its hard-won unity. States are breaking up or joining up: the Soviet Union has disappeared almost overnight, its parts forming new unions with one another or with like-minded nationalities in neighboring states. The old interwar national state based on territory and political sovereignty looks to be a mere transitional development.

The tendencies of what I am here calling the forces of Jihad and the forces of McWorld operate with equal strength in opposite directions, the one driven by parochial hatreds, the other by universalizing markets, the one re-creating ancient subnational and ethnic borders from within, the other making national borders porous from without. They have one thing in common: neither offers much hope to citizens looking for practical ways to govern themselves democratically. If the global future is to put Jihad's centrifugal whirlwind against McWorld's centripetal black hole, the outcome is unlikely to be democratic—or so I will argue.

MCWORLD, OR THE GLOBALIZATION OF POLITICS

Four imperatives make up the dynamic of McWorld: a market imperative, a resource imperative, an information-technology imperative, and an ecological imperative. By shrinking the world and diminishing the salience of national borders, these imperatives have in combination achieved a considerable victory over factiousness and particularism, and not least of all over their most virulent traditional form—nationalism. It is the realists who are now Europeans, the utopians who dream nostalgically of a resurgent England or Germany, perhaps even a resurgent Wales or Saxony. Yesterday's wishful cry for one world has yielded to the reality of McWorld.

The market imperative. Marxist and Leninist theories of imperialism assumed that the quest for ever-expanding markets would in time compel nation-based capitalist economies to push against national boundaries in search of an international economic imperium. Whatever else has happened to the scientist predictions of Marxism, in this domain they have proved farsighted. All national economies are now vulnerable to the inroads of larger, transnational markets within which trade is free, currencies are convertible, access to banking is open, and contracts are enforceable under law. In Europe, Asia, Africa, the South Pacific, and the Americas such markets are eroding national sovereignty and giving rise to entities—international banks, trade associations, transnational lobbies like OPEC and Greenpeace, world news services like CNN and the BBC, and multinational corporations that increasingly lack a meaningful national identity—that neither reflect nor respect nationhood as an organizing or regulative principle.

The market imperative has also reinforced the quest for international peace and stability, requisites of an efficient international economy. Markets are enemies of parochialism, isolation, fractiousness, war. Market psychology attenuates the psychology of ideological and religious cleavages and assumes a concord among producers and consumers—categories that ill fit narrowly conceived national or religious cultures. Shopping has little tolerance for blue laws, whether dictated by pub-closing British paternalism, Sabbath-observing Jewish Orthodox fundamentalism, or no-Sunday-liquor-sales Massachusetts puritanism. In the context of common markets, international law ceases to be a vision of justice and be-

From *The Atlantic Monthly*, March 1992, pp. 53-55, 58-63. © 1992 by Benjamin R. Barber. Reprinted by permission.

comes a workaday framework for getting things done—enforcing contracts, ensuring that governments abide by deals, regulating trade and currency relations, and so forth.

Common markets demand a common language, as well as a common currency, and they produce common behaviors of the kind bred by cosmopolitan city life everywhere. Commercial pilots, computer programmers, international bankers, media specialists, oil riggers, entertainment celebrities, ecology experts, demographers, accountants, professors, athletes—these compose a new breed of men and women for whom religion, culture, and nationality can seem only marginal elements in a working identity. Although sociologists of everyday life will no doubt continue to distinguish a Japanese from an American mode, shopping has a common signature throughout the world. Cynics might even say that some of the recent revolutions in Eastern Europe have had as their true goal not liberty and the right to vote but well-paying jobs and the right to shop (although the vote is proving easier to acquire than consumer goods). The market imperative is, then, plenty powerful; but, notwithstanding some of the claims made for "democratic capitalism," it is not identical with the democratic imperative.

The resource imperative. Democrats once dreamed of societies whose political autonomy rested firmly on economic independence. The Athenians idealized what they called autarky, and tried for a while to create a way of life simple and austere enough to make the polis genuinely self-sufficient. To be free meant to be independent of any other community or polis. Not even the Athenians were able to achieve autarky, however: human nature, it turns out, is dependency. By the time of Pericles, Athenian politics was inextricably bound up with a flowering empire held together by naval power and commerce—an empire that, even as it appeared to enhance Athenian might, ate away at Athenian independence and autarky. Master and slave, it turned out, were bound together by mutual insufficiency.

The dream of autarky briefly engrossed nineteenth-century America as well, for the underpopulated, endlessly bountiful land, the cornucopia of natural resources, and the natural barriers of a continent walled in by two great seas led many to believe that America could be a world unto itself. Given this past, it has been harder for Americans than for most to accept the inevitability of interdependence. But the rapid depletion of resources even in a country like ours, where they once seemed inexhaustible, and the maldistribution of arable soil and mineral resources on the planet, leave even the wealthiest societies ever more resource-dependent and many other nations in permanently desperate straits.

Every nation, it turns out, needs something another nation has; some nations have almost nothing they need.

The information-technology imperative. Enlightenment science and the technologies derived from it are inherently universalizing. They entail a quest for descriptive principles of general application, a search for universal solutions to particular problems, and an unswerving embrace of objectivity and impartiality.

Scientific progress embodies and depends on open communication, a common discourse rooted in rationality, collaboration, and an easy and regular flow and exchange of information. Such ideals can be hypocritical covers for power-mongering by elites, and they may be shown to be wanting in many other ways, but they are entailed by the very idea of science and they make science and globalization practical allies.

Business, banking, and commerce all depend on information flow and are facilitated by new communication technologies. The hardware of these technologies tends to be systemic and integrated—computer, television, cable, satellite, laser, fiber-optic, and microchip technologies combining to create a vast interactive communications and information network that can potentially give every person on earth access to every other person, and make every datum, every byte, available to every set of eyes. If the automobile was, as George Ball once said (when he gave his blessing to a Fiat factory in the Soviet Union during the Cold War), "an ideology on four wheels," then electronic telecommunication and information systems are an ideology at 186,000 miles per second—which makes for a very small planet in a very big hurry. Individual cultures speak particular languages; commerce and science increasingly speak English; the whole world speaks logarithms and binary mathematics.

Moreover, the pursuit of science and technology asks for, even compels, open societies. Satellite footprints do not respect national borders; telephone wires penetrate the most closed societies. With photocopying and then fax machines having infiltrated Soviet universities and *samizdat* literary circles in the eighties, and computer modems having multiplied like rabbits in communism's bureaucratic warrens thereafter, *glasnost* could not be far behind. In their social requisites, secrecy and science are enemies.

The new technology's software is perhaps even more globalizing than its hardware. The information arm of international commerce's sprawling body reaches out and touches distinct nations and parochial cultures, and gives them a common face chiseled in Hollywood, on Madison Avenue, and in Silicon Valley. Throughout the 1980s one of the most-watched television programs in South Africa was *The Cosby Show.* The demise of apartheid was already in production. Exhibitors at the 1991 Cannes film festival expressed growing anxiety over the "homogenization" and "Americanization" of the global film industry when, for the third year running, American films dominated the awards ceremonies. America has dominated the world's popular culture for much longer, and much more decisively. In November of 1991 Switzerland's once insular culture boasted best-seller lists featuring *Terminator 2* as the No. 1 movie, *Scarlett* as the No. 1 book, and Prince's *Diamonds and Pearls* as the No. 1 record album. No wonder the Japanese are buying Hollywood film studios even faster than Americans are buying Japanese television sets. This kind of software supremacy may in the long term be far more important than hardware superiority, because culture has become more potent than armaments. What is the power of the Pentagon compared with Disneyland? Can the Sixth Fleet keep up with CNN? McDonald's in Moscow and Coke in China will do more to create a global culture than military colonization ever could. It is less the goods than the brand names that do the work, for they convey life-style images that alter perception and challenge behavior. They make up the seductive software of McWorld's common (at times much too common) soul.

Yet in all this high-tech commercial world there is nothing that looks particularly democratic. It lends itself to surveillance as well as liberty, to new forms of manipulation and covert control as well as new kinds of participation, to skewed, unjust market outcomes as well as greater productivity. The consumer society and the open society are not quite synonymous. Capitalism and democracy have a relationship, but it is something less than a marriage. An efficient free market after all requires that consumers be free to vote their dollars on competing goods, not that citizens be free to vote their values and beliefs on competing political candidates and programs. The free market flourished in junta-run Chile, in military-governed Taiwan and Korea, and, earlier, in a variety of autocratic European empires as well as their colonial possessions.

The ecological imperative. The impact of globalization on ecology is a cliché even to world leaders who ignore it. We know well enough that the German forests can be destroyed by Swiss and Italians driving gas-guzzlers fueled by leaded gas. We also know that the planet can be asphyxiated by greenhouse gases because Brazilian farmers want to be part of the twentieth century and are burning down tropical rain forests to clear a little land to plough, and because Indonesians make a living out of converting their lush jungle into toothpicks for fastidious Japanese diners, upsetting the delicate oxygen balance and in effect puncturing our global lungs. Yet this ecological consciousness has meant not only greater awareness but also greater inequality, as modernized nations try to slam the door behind them, saying to developing nations, "The world cannot afford *your* modernization; ours has wrung it dry!"

Each of the four imperatives just cited is transnational, transideological, and transcultural. Each applies impartially to Catholics, Jews, Muslims, Hindus, and Buddhists; to democrats and totalitarians; to capitalists and socialists. The Enlightenment dream of a universal rational society has to a remarkable degree been realized—but in a form that is commercialized, homogenized, depoliticized, bureaucratized, and, of course, radically incomplete, for the movement toward McWorld is in competition with forces of global breakdown, national dissolution, and centrifugal corruption. These forces, working in the opposite direction, are the essence of what I call Jihad.

JIHAD, OR THE LEBANONIZATION OF THE WORLD

OPEC, the World Bank, the United Nations, the International Red Cross, the multinational corporation . . . there are scores of institutions that reflect globalization. But they often appear as ineffective reactors to the world's real actors: national states and, to an ever greater degree, subnational factions in permanent rebellion against uniformity and integration—even the kind represented by universal law and justice. The headlines feature these players regularly: they are cultures, not countries; parts, not wholes; sects, not religions; rebellious factions and dissenting minorities at war not just with globalism but with the traditional nation-state. Kurds, Basques, Puerto Ricans, Ossetians, East Timoreans, Quebecois, the Catholics of Northern Ireland, Abkhasians, Kurile Islander Japanese, the Zulus of Inkatha, Catalonians, Tamils, and, of course, Palestinians—people without countries, inhabiting nations not their own, seeking smaller worlds within borders that will seal them off from modernity.

A powerful irony is at work here. Nationalism was once a force of integration and unification, a movement aimed at bringing together disparate clans, tribes, and cultural fragments under new, assimilationist flags. But as Ortega y Gasset noted more than sixty years ago, having won its victories, nationalism changed its strategy. In the 1920s, and again today, it is more often a reactionary and divisive force, pulverizing the very nations it once helped cement together. The force that creates nations is "inclusive," Ortega wrote in *The Revolt of the Masses.* "In periods of consolidation, nationalism has a positive value, and is a lofty standard. But in Europe everything is more than consolidated, and nationalism is nothing but a mania. . . ."

This mania has left the post-Cold War world smoldering with hot wars; the international scene is little more unified than it was at the end of the Great War, in Ortega's own time. There were more than thirty wars in progress last year, most of them ethnic, racial, tribal, or religious in character, and the list of unsafe regions doesn't seem to be getting any shorter. Some new world order!

The aim of many of these small-scale wars is to redraw boundaries, to implode states and resecure parochial identities: to escape McWorld's dully insistent imperatives. The mood is that of Jihad: war not as an instrument of policy but as an emblem of identity, an expression of community, an end in itself. Even where there is no shooting war, there is fractiousness, secession, and the quest for ever smaller communities. Add to the list of dangerous countries those at risk: In Switzerland and Spain, Jurassian and Basque separatists still argue the virtues of ancient identities, sometimes in the language of bombs. Hyperdisintegration in the former Soviet Union may well continue unabated—not just a Ukraine independent from the Soviet Union but a Bessarabian Ukraine independent from the Ukrainian republic; not just Russia severed from the defunct union but Tatarstan severed from Russia. Yugoslavia makes even the disunited, ex-Soviet, nonsocialist republics that were once the Soviet Union look integrated, its sectarian fatherlands springing up within factional motherlands like weeds within weeds within weeds. Kurdish independence would threaten the territorial integrity of four Middle Eastern nations. Well before the current cataclysm Soviet Georgia made a claim for autonomy from the Soviet Union, only to be faced with its Ossetians (164,000 in a republic of 5.5 million) demanding their own self-determination within Georgia. The Abkhasian minority in Georgia has followed suit. Even the good will established by Canada's once promising Meech Lake protocols is in danger, with Francophone Quebec again threatening the dissolution of the federation. In South Africa the emergence from apartheid was hardly achieved when friction between Inkatha's Zulus and the African National Congress's tribally identified members threatened to replace Europeans' racism with an indigenous tribal war after thirty years of attempted integration using the colonial language (English) as a unifier, Nigeria is now playing with the idea of linguistic multiculturalism—which could mean the cultural breakup of the nation into hundreds of tribal fragments. Even Saddam Hussein has benefited from the threat of internal Jihad, having used renewed tribal and religious warfare to turn last season's mortal enemies into reluctant allies of an Iraqi nationhood that he nearly destroyed.

The passing of communism has torn away the thin veneer of internationalism (workers of the world unite!) to reveal ethnic prejudices that are not only ugly and deep-seated but increasingly murderous. Europe's old scourge, anti-Semitism, is back with a vengeance, but it is only one of many antagonisms. It appears all too easy to throw the historical gears into reverse and pass from a Communist dictatorship back into a tribal state.

Among the tribes, religion is also a battlefield. ("Jihad" is a rich word whose generic meaning is "struggle"—usually the struggle of the soul to avert evil. Strictly applied to religious war, it is used only in reference to battles where the faith is under assault, or battles against a government that denies the practice of Islam. My use here is rhetorical, but does follow both journalistic practice and history.) Remember the Thirty Years War? Whatever forms of Enlightenment universalism might once have come to grace such historically related forms of monotheism as Judaism, Christianity, and Islam, in many of their modern incarnations they are parochial rather than cosmopolitan, angry rather than loving, proselytizing rather than ecumenical, zealous rather than rationalist, sectarian rather than deistic, ethnocentric rather than universalizing. As a result, like the new forms of hypernationalism, the new expressions of religious fundamentalism are fractious and pulverizing, never integrating. This is religion as the Crusaders knew it: a battle to the death for souls that if not saved will be forever lost.

The atmospherics of Jihad have resulted in a breakdown of civility in the name of identity, of comity in the name of community. International relations have sometimes taken on the aspect of gang war—cultural turf battles featuring tribal factions that were supposed to be sublimated as integral parts of large national, economic, postcolonial, and constitutional entities.

THE DARKENING FUTURE OF DEMOCRACY

These rather melodramatic tableaux vivants do not tell the whole story, however. For all their defects, Jihad and McWorld have their attractions. Yet, to repeat and insist, the attractions are unrelated to democracy. Neither McWorld nor Jihad is remotely democratic in impulse. Neither needs democracy; neither promotes democracy.

McWorld does manage to look pretty seductive in a world obsessed with Jihad. It delivers peace, prosperity, and relative unity—if at the cost of independence, community, and identity (which is generally based on difference). The primary political values required by the global market are order and tranquillity, and freedom—as in the phrases "free trade,"

"free press," and "free love." Human rights are needed to a degree, but not citizenship or participation—and no more social justice and equality than are necessary to promote efficient economic production and consumption. Multinational corporations sometimes seem to prefer doing business with local oligarchs, inasmuch as they can take confidence from dealing with the boss on all crucial matters. Despots who slaughter their own populations are no problem, so long as they leave markets in place and refrain from making war on their neighbors (Saddam Hussein's fatal mistake). In trading partners, predictability is of more value than justice.

The Eastern European revolutions that seemed to arise out of concern for global democratic values quickly deteriorated into a stampede in the general direction of free markets and their ubiquitous, television-promoted shopping malls. East Germany's Neues Forum, that courageous gathering of intellectuals, students, and workers which overturned the Stalinist regime in Berlin in 1989, lasted only six months in Germany's mini-version of McWorld. Then it gave way to money and markets and monopolies from the West. By the time of the first all-German elections, it could scarcely manage to secure three percent of the vote. Elsewhere there is growing evidence that *glasnost* will go and *perestroika*—defined as privatization and an opening of markets to Western bidders—will stay. So understandably anxious are the new rulers of Eastern Europe and whatever entities are forged from the residues of the Soviet Union to gain access to credit and markets and technology—McWorld's flourishing new currencies—that they have shown themselves willing to trade away democratic prospects in pursuit of them: not just old totalitarian ideologies and command-economy production models but some possible indigenous experiments with a third way between capitalism and socialism, such as economic cooperatives and employee stock-ownership plans, both of which have their ardent supporters in the East.

Jihad delivers a different set of virtues: a vibrant local identity, a sense of community, solidarity among kinsmen, neighbors, and countrymen, narrowly conceived. But it also guarantees parochialism and is grounded in exclusion. Solidarity is secured through war against outsiders. And solidarity often means obedience to a hierarchy in governance,

fanaticism in beliefs, and the obliteration of individual selves in the name of the group. Deference to leaders and intolerance toward outsiders (and toward "enemies within") are hallmarks of tribalism—hardly the attitudes required for the cultivation of new democratic women and men capable of governing themselves. Where new democratic experiments have been conducted in retribalizing societies, in both Europe and the Third World, the result has often been anarchy, repression, persecution, and the coming of new, noncommunist forms of very old kinds of despotism. During the past year, Havel's velvet revolution in Czechoslovakia was imperiled by partisans of "Czechland" and of Slovakia as independent entities. India seemed little less rent by Sikh, Hindu, Muslim, and Tamil infighting than it was immediately after the British pulled out, more than forty years ago.

To the extent that either McWorld or Jihad has a *natural* politics, it has turned out to be more of an antipolitics. For McWorld, it is the antipolitics of globalism: bureaucratic, technocratic, and meritocratic, focused (as Marx predicted it would be) on the administration of things—with people, however, among the chief things to be administered. In its politico-economic imperatives McWorld has been guided by laissez-faire market principles that privilege efficiency, productivity, and beneficence at the expense of civic liberty and self-government.

For Jihad, the antipolitics of tribalization has been explicitly antidemocratic: one-party dictatorship, government by military junta, theocratic fundamentalism—often associated with a version of the *Führerprinzip* that empowers an individual to rule on behalf of a people. Even the government of India, struggling for decades to model democracy for a people who will soon number a billion, longs for great leaders; and for every Mahatma Gandhi, Indira Gandhi, or Rajiv Gandhi taken from them by zealous assassins, the Indians appear to seek a replacement who will deliver them from the lengthy travail of their freedom.

THE CONFEDERAL OPTION

How can democracy be secured and spread in a world whose primary tendencies are at best indifferent to it (McWorld) and at worst deeply antithetical to it (Jihad)? My guess is that globalization will eventually vanquish retribalization.

The ethos of material "civilization" has not yet encountered an obstacle it has been unable to thrust aside. Ortega may have grasped in the 1920s a clue to our own future in the coming millennium.

Everyone sees the need of a new principle of life. But as always happens in similar crises—some people attempt to save the situation by an artificial intensification of the very principle which has led to decay. This is the meaning of the "nationalist" outburst of recent years. . . . things have always gone that way. The last flare, the longest; the last sigh, the deepest. On the very eve of their disappearance there is an intensification of frontiers—military and economic.

Jihad may be a last deep sigh before the eternal yawn of McWorld. On the other hand, Ortega was not exactly prescient; his prophecy of peace and internationalism came just before blitzkrieg, world war, and the Holocaust tore the old order to bits. Yet democracy is how we remonstrate with reality, the rebuke our aspirations offer to history. And if retribalization is inhospitable to democracy, there is nonetheless a form of democratic government that can accommodate parochialism and communitarianism, one that can even save them from their defects and make them more tolerant and participatory: decentralized participatory democracy. And if McWorld is indifferent to democracy, there is nonetheless a form of democratic government that suits global markets passably well—representative government in its federal or, better still, confederal variation.

With its concern for accountability, the protection of minorities, and the universal rule of law, a confederalized representative system would serve the political needs of McWorld as well as oligarchic bureaucratism or meritocratic elitism is currently doing. As we are already beginning to see, many nations may survive in the long term only as confederations that afford local regions smaller than "nations" extensive jurisdiction. Recommended reading for democrats of the twenty-first century is not the U.S. Constitution or the French Declaration of Rights of Man and Citizen but the Articles of Confederation, that suddenly pertinent document that stitched together the thirteen American colonies into what then seemed a too loose confederation of independent states but now appears a new form of political realism, as veterans of Yeltsin's new Russia and the new Europe created at Maastricht will attest.

By the same token, the participatory and direct form of democracy that engages citizens in civic activity and civic judgment and goes well beyond just voting and accountability—the system I have called "strong democracy"—suits the political needs of decentralized communities as well as theocratic and nationalist party dictatorships have done. Local neighborhoods need not be democratic, but they can be. Real democracy has flourished in diminutive settings: the spirit of liberty, Tocqueville said, is local. Participatory democracy, if not naturally apposite to tribalism, has an undeniable attractiveness under conditions of parochialism.

Democracy in any of these variations will, however, continue to be obstructed by the undemocratic and antidemocratic trends toward uniformitarian globalism and intolerant retribalization which I have portrayed here. For democracy to persist in our brave new McWorld, we will have to commit acts of conscious political will—a possibility, but hardly a probability, under these conditions. Political will requires much more than the quick fix of the transfer of institutions. Like technology transfer, institution transfer rests on foolish assumptions about a uniform world of the kind that once fired the imagination of colonial administrators. Spread English justice to the colonies by exporting wigs. Let an East Indian trading company act as the vanguard to Britain's free parliamentary institutions. Today's well-intentioned quick-fixers in the National Endowment for Democracy and the Kennedy School of Government, in the unions and foundations and universities zealously nurturing contacts in Eastern Europe and the Third World, are hoping to democratize by long distance. Post Bulgaria a parliament by first-class mail. Fed Ex the Bill of Rights to Sri Lanka. Cable Cambodia some common law.

Yet Eastern Europe has already demonstrated that importing free political parties, parliaments, and presses cannot establish a democratic civil society; imposing a free market may even have the opposite effect. Democracy grows from the bottom up and cannot be imposed from the top down. Civil society has to be built from the inside out. The institutional superstructure comes last. Poland may become democratic, but then again it may heed the Pope, and prefer to found its politics on its Catholicism, with uncertain consequences for democracy. Bulgaria may become democratic, but it may prefer tribal war. The former Soviet Union may become a democratic confederation, or it may just grow into an anarchic and weak conglomeration of markets for other nations' goods and services.

Democrats need to seek out indigenous democratic impulses. There is always a desire for self-government, always some expression of participation, accountability, consent, and representation, even in traditional hierarchical societies. These need to be identified, tapped, modified, and incorporated into new democratic practices with an indigenous flavor. The tortoises among the democratizers may ultimately outlive or outpace the hares, for they will have the time and patience to explore conditions along the way, and to adapt their gait to changing circumstances. Tragically, democracy in a hurry often looks something like France in 1794 or China in 1989.

It certainly seems possible that the most attractive democratic ideal in the face of the brutal realities of Jihad and the dull realities of McWorld will be a confederal union of semi-autonomous communities smaller than nation-states, tied together into regional economic associations and markets larger than nation-states—participatory and self-determining in local matters at the bottom, representative and accountable at the top. The nation-state would play a diminished role, and sovereignty would lose some of its political potency. The Green movement adage "Think globally, act locally" would actually come to describe the conduct of politics.

This vision reflects only an ideal, however—one that is not terribly likely to be realized. Freedom, Jean-Jacques Rousseau once wrote, is a food easy to eat but hard to digest. Still, democracy has always played itself out against the odds. And democracy remains both a form of coherence as binding as McWorld and a secular faith potentially as inspiriting as Jihad.

DEFENCE IN THE 21ST CENTURY

Meet your unbrave new world

START by drawing a military map of the world as it is in September 1992. The Soviet Union is not there; the Warsaw pact is a non-phrase; you can safely omit the vanishing Confederation of Independent States. Expunge half a century of memories; the world is changed. But not utterly. Take care to mark on the map all the exploding countries, surly religio-historical culture zones and chip-on-shoulder dictatorships around the globe that can still cause military trouble for the democracies even though the cold war is a fading memory.

This is the world as it is. There are some pattern-breaking events that could change it greatly for the worse in the next 15 or 20 years. But concentrate for the time being on things as they are.

The end of the Soviet Union means that in 1992 there is nobody who can cause military trouble for the democracies on a global scale. No power now exists whose soldiers might imaginably occupy Western Europe, whose nuclear warheads could devastate America, whose navy reaches into all of the world's oceans, whose guns and money support local friends on every continent. The disappearance of this huge adversary is excellent, but not quite as excellent as had been expected. The collapse of communism has not had the effect, as many people thought it would, of reducing the number of smaller, less-than-global causes of trouble. On the contrary, it is producing more of them.

The sergeant-major retires

This is because the cold war had one claim to merit: it was a system of discipline. Most countries, in most parts of the world, belonged in some degree to one or the other of a pair of teams. If a member of one team got into an argument with a member of the other team, he could appeal to his team leader for help. Since the team leaders did not wish to fight each other, unless the issue was vital, they would generally urge restraint. Wars did happen—a whole series between India and Pakistan, for instance—but usually in parts of the world where the cold-war team system was loosest.

This was a powerful preserver of stability: not only stability between countries, but stability inside them as well. A dictator under pressure from opponents within his own country could tell his team leader that these people were backers of the other team (which was often true), and in would flow the cash, the arms and the military advisers he needed to keep himself in power. There were exceptions here too—coups in South America (because in that part of the world most coup-makers and coup-victims were plainly on the same cold-war side) and civil carnage in middle Africa (where cold-war loyalties hardly mattered)—but a lot fewer than there might otherwise have been.

It was a mixed blessing, but it did mean less bloodshed. It has now gone. Without the cold war, a country threatened by invasion can turn for outside help in only one direction, to the cold war's victorious alliance of democracies. But the democracies may not help. They no longer have to worry about the expansion of communist power, and they are reluctant to get mixed up in foreign fights that could kill their voters' sons. They raised a warning finger in the Gulf war, but then the finger wobbled. The democracies are not eager to realise that they are the only stabilisers left.

This has worrying consequences. A country that is thinking of bullying another country—in order to get a slice of its territory, or a share of its oil profits, or whatever—may justifiably think that its chances of getting away with it are better than they have been for half a century. The bully may indeed conclude that it would be sensible to get on with the job without delay, before those powerful democracies start to realise that they cannot let this sort of thing go on unreproved for ever.

A dictator under challenge, from within or from abroad, may react in an equally dangerous way. Since he can no longer turn to the other superpower for protection, because the other superpower has vanished, he may try to prolong his existence by equipping himself with the most brutal weapons he can lay his hands on—nuclear missiles, gas, the doomsday devices of biological warfare.

The prospect is not improved by the other depressing post-cold-war discovery. The utter defeat of communism is not turning out to be an utter victory for its adversary, pluralism. The world is not on the threshold of ideological uniformity. The rationalists of the right—the late 20th century's equivalent of the 18th-century Age of Reason's believers in swift human perfectibility—had thought it was. They are discovering that life is more complicated. The Last Man will not be inhabiting the same smoothly running pluralist machine all over the globe for a long time yet.

It is true that nobody but a handful of Fidel Castros is now prepared to argue the virtues of the command economy. There is, it is agreed, no serious alternative to the free market as the basis of economic life. But a lot of would-be capitalists have found that the creation of an efficient free-market economy is much harder than they had expected. It needs capital, which is not easy to organise. It needs workers willing to work more enthusiastically than they had to in the old communist days. Above all, it needs men who understand how capitalism operates. If even places like Hungary and Bohemia are finding it difficult to do all this, it is going to be far tougher for scores of countries in Asia and Africa.

It is also being realised that the economic side of

pluralism is not automatically linked to the political side; a capitalist country does not smoothly and inevitably become a democratic one too. The advance of democracy will be slow, patchy and interruptible. There should be no surprise in this. History has seen plenty of capitalist dictatorships; Hitler's Germany was one of them.

Wars of interest, wars of conscience

Today's world is a scruffily untidy place, in which successful new patches of pluralism will gradually take root alongside stubbornly resistant patches of the old order. It is a world in which countries that fail to make a quick jump to capitalist prosperity may disappointedly fall back on the politics of nationalism, or religion, or the murky area where the two overlap. It is a world in which the two-team system of the cold war, the simplest form of international life, has ceased to apply. It is, in short, a rather explosive world.

The democracies that find themselves face to face with this new reality do not need to respond to every explosion it produces. But they will have to be ready to act when an eruption seems likely to do them serious harm. They will want to make sure that they can keep on getting the raw materials their economies need. They will wish to protect the farther-flung members of the democratic club. They may think it necessary to take some pretty rapid action if what had at first seemed to be a minor quarrel with a missile-armed power looks like blowing up into a major confrontation.

These are wars of interest. But in this new world the military policy of the democracies may also have to be prepared for a different kind of fight.

As people have lately been discovering, things can happen outside the borders of the democracies that pose no direct threat to democrats' interests and yet are so horrifying that it seems almost impossible to ignore them. As the television screens keep on flickering out their messages of shock, it is increasingly unlikely that all of these horror stories will be ignored; and the business of stopping the horror will sometimes include military action. These are wars of conscience.

The break-up of Yugoslavia has been the first real test of how the democracies will cope with wars of conscience. It has produced all the predictable symptoms: first the official flinching away from the dangers of intervention; next the public demand that something be done; then the agonised attempt to find a more or less cost-free way of doing something. What has been happening in ex-Yugoslavia will happen—is already happening—in other parts of the ex-communist world. Similar things have long been going on in Africa and parts of Asia. The crises of conscience will multiply. The more of them there are, the likelier it is that a decision will eventually be taken to go and rescue the poor devils, and pay the price of doing the right thing.

Otherwise the democracies could wake up one morning to realise that they have let the world break into two parts. Their own part will be an archipelago of comfortable civility. Outside this comfortable archipelago other people will be suffering awful things. In Europe, the awfulness could be going on not far from the gates of Rome, Vienna, Warsaw and Budapest. The new world, democrats will discover to their dismay, has no order; it is even more anarchically brutal than the old one.

It is now possible to fill in some of the details on that military map of the coming 20 years. With any luck, wars of interest require the placing of only two big question-marks.

Latin America seems unlikely to present any large danger to other people's interests. The same is true of Africa south of the Sahara, unless some wild dictator improbably tries to make a monopoly of the mineral mines at the southern end of the continent. The great triangle south of the Himalayas—the Subcontinent—comes near the top of the list for explosiveness, but is hideously complicated and not of great economic importance; unless events there look like upsetting the global balance of power—for instance, by creating a Chinese-Indian alliance with designs on ex-Soviet Asia—this is a region to be treated with circumspection.

As things stand in 1992, only two obvious areas need to be marked red for immediate danger under the wars-of-interest heading. One is the Korean peninsula, where North Korea's acquisition of nuclear arms could upset the whole Asian applecart. The other is the Muslim crescent running through south-west Asia and north Africa, with its powerful combination of oil, Islam and a long history of anti-western resentment.

The potential wars of conscience need a broader shading of the map. Such wars can have various causes. A dictator may be trying to exterminate part of his own people. He may be set on making himself the neighbourhood boss. But the commonest appeal to conscience is likely to be the sort that has been coming from ex-Yugoslavia. The area capable of producing future Sarajevos is not confined to the ex-communist world. It also includes large sections of Africa and Asia, and perhaps parts of Latin America too.

The group-against-group savagery that plucks at the conscience in ex-Yugoslavia happens wherever state boundaries and the sense of racial or religious identity do not more or less coincide. Where "we" and "they" feel angrily different from each other, but live within the same country, it takes a clever and sensitive government—or a brutally repressive one—to stop trouble breaking out.

That is why the democracies' television sets will be showing more civil-war horror pictures of women shoppers dead in the street, and their governments will be getting more desperate appeals for help. Many of those appeals will fall on deaf ears; but in the end some will be listened to.

Provided the below do not apply

And now remember the warning in the second paragraph of this article. Everything so far said applies to the pattern of the world that the eye sees in 1992. But several things could break that pattern, and produce a much worse one:

•A failure to stop the proliferation of weapons of mass destruction would make nonsense of all this. If anything up to a dozen extra countries, most of them with unpleasant governments, get hold of missiles with nuclear or biological warheads, the calculations about both wars of interest and wars of conscience are nullified. This is, alas, the most plausible of the pattern-breaking possibilities.

•A decision by China to try to make itself a power in the world would also mess things up considerably. At the very least, it would end the attempt to use the United Nations as an instrument of the new world order. This sort of China could not go on siding with the other four permanent members of the Security Council, and would use its veto to show its opposition. Worse, the new China would probably set out to make itself the leader of the countries that oppose an American-European-Japanese setting of world rules—partly by providing these countries with the missile and nuclear technologies it possesses and they, so far, do not.

•The rearmament of Japan, which might be caused either by this new sort of China or by a nuclear North Korea, would arouse deep hostility in America and Europe. This could destroy the hope of keeping the world's three main economic groups within a single set of trade rules. And that would certainly kill the idea that America, Europe and Japan can be the co-shapers of the 21st century.

•A reversion by Russia to anti-western policies may seem the least likely of these calculation-wreckers, if only because Russia's economy so obviously needs friendly democracies. But irrationality in Moscow can never be ruled out. Russia is still the world's second-biggest nuclear power. It shares a long European border with the democracies. They had better know what to do if it does go wrong.

If these four things can be prevented from happening, the soldiers can look squarely at the new world's military agenda. This requires some radical thinking about the wars the soldiers may have to fight, and the kind of armed forces and weapons they need to fight them with. But first one tempting distraction has to be got out of the way.

• • •

Two kinds of war, two kinds of army?

ONE way of describing how much the soldiers have to change their ways is to point out that the military history of the 20th century has been essentially a history of battles won and lost in Europe. The two world wars began with European quarrels, and their outcome was settled by a clash of armies on Europe's northern plain. The cold war was won, almost bloodlessly, by a 40-year confrontation of armed willpower in the centre of that plain.

The 21st century, it seems, will be different. The soldiers will for a time need to keep an eye cocked in Russia's direction, in case embittered nationalism makes that country an enemy again. They may have to play their part in sorting out the worst of the post-communist mess in Europe. But for the most part their attention will be turned farther afield, southwards and eastwards, to wars they may have to fight in more distant places.

This will be a shock for Germans and Russians, whose military experience is overwhelmingly European. It will be a little easier for France, which knows something about wars outside Europe, and perhaps for Holland and Spain, though their extra-European military memories are more distant. It will call for some mind-clearing by the Americans, most of whose military man-hours in the 20th century have been spent in Europe. The one country to which it will be no surprise at all is Britain, whose armed forces spent the 19th century largely on non-European business.

The British therefore have a special interest in an awkward question that emerges from the previous article. If you talk to soldiers and foreign ministry officials and think-tank people in America and Europe, you find that many of them think the world now faces two entirely different sorts of war, which require two different sorts of armed force.

In one kind of war, the adversary will be a large, ordinary army and air force. In the other, it will be a baffling mixture of trained soldiers and wild-eyed irregulars, equipped with anything from smallish amounts of good modern weapons to shotguns and pitchforks. Wars of interest will usually fall into the first category, because attacks on the material interests of the democracies will generally be organised by governments that command orthodox armies. Wars of conscience will tend to fall into the second category, being mostly the result of explosions of ethnic or tribal hatred. Dealing with tanks, goes the new theory, is utterly unlike dealing with shotguns and pitchforks with the odd artillery piece thrown in. So one may need two separate, specialist armies.

Britain's 19th-century army would have sympathised. It thought it existed to re-fight the battle of Waterloo. Yet in fact it spent most of the century fighting enemies who ranged from the Sikhs—armed and trained almost up to European standards—to Afghan guerrillas, Zulu impis and Sudanese religious zealots.

The answer to the question is almost certainly No, two different sorts of army are not necessary. But this is not because the British got through the 19th century with only one sort; what the 21st century will need cannot be deduced from what the 19th century stumbled along with. Nor is it because the treasury ministers of the democracies will not pay for a double-decker army. If a double-decker were needed, they would have to find the money. It is because when you look more closely at the second sort of warfare—"sub-conventional" to some, "the war without fronts" to others—you see that armies designed to fight high-technology wars can probably cope with most of the difficulties of this second sort too.

In the end, you have to pay the price

That bland phrase, "sub-conventional warfare", conceals three separate varieties of military operation. One is the familiar peace-keeping business. The enemies have grown more or less tired of fighting each other, but do not quite trust themselves to stay that way, so they invite a party of outsiders to come and keep them peaceful. This can usually be done by a few battalions of lightly armed soldiers.

The rescue missions that have taken food and medicine to civilians in Bosnia and Somalia this year are variations of this. They need medical specialists—and a smooth-tongued commander—but they rest on the same basis. The combatants may not have stopped fighting each other but they are prepared to hold their fire just long enough to let the food and medicine through to the civilians huddled in shelters.

The next sort of sub-war is tougher. Here no truce exists; triggers are going to get pulled. But the number of people causing the trouble is small enough for something like ordinary life to be restored if you deploy large enough quantities of armed supervision. This is what the British have done in Northern Ireland, the Spaniards in the Basque country, and the Syrians in Lebanon. It needs good intelligence work, inquisitive patrolling, a lot of men—up to 18 battalions in Northern Ireland, all included—and a willingness to accept a steady trickle of horrors and casualties. But it can be done, without creating a special army to do it.

The other variety is the one that has got people in two minds. This happens when the peace-breakers are too numerous and too well-armed and too bloody-minded to be kept more or less under control by flooding the place with your own troops. If they are to be stopped, there has to be a serious fight. This is where a choice must be made. But the choice is not what kind of armed force to use. It is whether to accept the price of going into a fight, whatever means you employ.

In fact, the means employed by the army that won the Gulf war are just as useful in this worst kind of sub-conventional warfare. Eagle-eyed aerial reconnaissance is essential; the more cleverly the other side has got its guns and home-made armoured cars tucked away in the trees, the handier it is to be able to spot them from the air. The more accurately you can aim bombs from aircraft and projectiles from launchers on the ground, and the farther away you can do the aiming from, the fewer civilians you will kill and the fewer casualties you will suffer yourself. When closer-quarter action is unavoidable, tanks can give the men involved a fair degree of protection; even in the shambles of Vietnam, not one American tank base ever got overrun.

Satellites, airborne radar, armour-plating and precision-aiming are as helpful in this sort of fighting as they were in the Gulf. The well-protected but nimble and hit-them-from-a-distance army that is right for modern conventional wars is good for unconventional ones too.

If the democracies will expand their research-and-development budgets, their technological advantage can be made even bigger. Eyes gleam in the design departments of the arms industry. Reconnaissance aircraft that do not need pilots can bring you pictures of your targets without risking a single airman's life. Robot gun-carriers can lurch up the hills of future Sarajevos and do the close-quarter work without a human finger on the trigger.

But technological gee-whizzery misses the point. Such novelties can cut their owners' casualty rates in any kind of war, but they will make no conceivable war casualty-free.

In America, a buttoned-up section of the Pentagon is looking into the whole range of modern sub-conventional warfare, and the generals do not seem to relish what it tells them. The Europeans have barely started to think about the subject. But in the end the important question is not technical. It is political: whether governments are prepared to send their soldiers to be killed in such wars.

They are not always unbearably bloody. The Vietnamese pushed the Khmers Rouges back to the fringes of Cambodia in 1979 without great difficulty; the American operations in Grenada and Panama, admittedly small, were easily done. Provided the soldiers are trained for this sort of fighting, these wars can be won. But there will always be a price, and sometimes the price will be high.

As they weigh it up, the politicians can at least tell themselves that one species of sub-conventional warfare, perhaps the most frightening of all, is now part of history. The communist guerrilla movement, the model for all sub-conventional warriors after it beat the Americans in Vietnam, combined great tactical skill with the right kind of weapons and stunning morale. But the ideology that created it has collapsed, and Russia no longer gives it arms. Except in a few corners of the world such as Peru—and even there Shining Path is not quite the real thing—the communist guerrilla movement is extinct. The democracies, inspecting the ethnic and religious battle-lines that still crisscross the map, have that much to be thankful for.

What it will take

HOW big an armed force will be needed to get safely through the next couple of decades? The question of who exactly needs this force—America and Europe separately, or together?—and the further questions of how far Europeans can combine their military efforts, and where Japan fits in, will be evaded in this article, since they raise economic and geopolitical issues to be discussed later. For the moment, assume a High Command of the Democracies that can make military calculations on behalf of all the above.

The high command will operate on the building-block principle. The first block, the essential starting-point, is an expeditionary force big enough and swiftly deployable enough to win the largest war of interest that can reasonably be foreseen anywhere in the world in the coming 20 years.

That could be quite large. The cold war has left a lot of countries, rich and poor, with muscular armed forces handsomely equipped with modern weapons from the two alliances' arms-makers; on one count, 23 countries currently have 1,000 or more tanks apiece. More than one of these countries is in a position to do something the democracies would think they ought to stop. North Korea might try to take over South Korea if Kim Il Sung got desperate. Iran could have another go at becoming the godfather of the Gulf. An Arab country gone fundamentalist might try to go expansionist too. Trevor Dupuy, a voluble American ex-colonel, has written a book about ten possible wars between now and 1996, killing in all 265,000 people. That is melodrama, but wars there will be.

The kernel

There is something near unanimity on what this calls for. This writer has talked to military men in Washington, London, Paris, Bonn and Brussels, and almost all of them say the largest foreseeable fight could be coped with by an expeditionary force of seven solid divisions, with about 15,000 men apiece, plus the necessary back-up.

That is, not coincidentally, about the size of the American-British core of the force that won the Gulf war, not counting the fairly marginal American marines and paratroops. No potential adversary of the next few years is likely to have a much bigger army than Saddam Hussein had at the start of 1991. True, the next man may use his army better than Mr Hussein did. But then Mr Hussein could probably, as it turns out, have been beaten by a smaller force than the one the allies actually sent against him. So the seven-division calculation still seems about right. On the same Gulf-war precedent, most generals think that most of the seven divisions should be "heavy", meaning with plenty of tanks, though that could change if helicopters seem to be ousting tanks from the battlefield; see the article on page 14.

Seven divisions are not a lot. Between them, the United States, Germany, France and Britain still have five or six times that number; Japan, Italy, Turkey, Spain and the smaller countries of democratic Europe could together put up at least as many again. And the number needed may fall below seven as the years go by, if the armies they might have to fight grow rusty in the changed circumstances of the post-cold-war world. That will happen if the main arms-making powers—America, Russia and Western Europe, but also increasingly places like China, Japan and Brazil—can agree on a tighter set of rules to limit the supply of weapons to suspect countries and the training of their soldiers.

However, the seven divisions now needed are not the end of the story. The men on the ground require air cover: say, 200 fighters to keep off the other side's air force, and 400 ground-attack aircraft to help with the fighting down below. If the air support can include some big, global-reach bombers, B-52s or stealthy sons-of-B-52s, able to obliterate a Maginot line of fortifications, so much the better.

The divisions also have to be got to the crisis area, and faster than most of the Gulf army managed to get there. This needs, to start with, a fleet of 150 or so big transport aircraft. But aircraft can basically fly in only the men, not their tanks and other heavy gear; even the Future Large Aircraft now being contemplated in both America and Europe would not make it possible to move more than about a brigade of tanks (of the ten or more such brigades that might be needed), and that not until 2005 or so. So better arrangements than anybody now has for moving the heavy stuff quickly by sea are the next item on the list.

The aim should be to get two or three divisions to the trouble spot within a month, and the rest of the force in a month or so after that. This cannot be done solely by hiring or commandeering merchant ships. They take too long to load, they are generally too slow, and their crews will sometimes be of doubtful loyalty. The starting-point of the sealift for a seven-division operation should be a score or so of big, fast, custom-built ships like the ones the American navy plans for the later 1990s. All this assumes that there will be friendly ports in the region where the ships can unload. There probably will be, given that the expedition will usually be aimed at a local bully whom most of his neighbours detest. Failing that, a port will have to be captured.

Most important of all, if those seven divisions are to fight with anything like Desert Storm efficiency, is the panoply of help that floats in the sky above them and stands comfortably behind them on the ground. This includes the satellites that tell them what the enemy is doing; the reconnaissance aircraft that supplement the satellites' information; many of the army's gunners, signalmen, engineers and doctors; a lot of its helicopters and its trucks; and the computerised command-and-control system that, with the occasional hiccup, moves the men the right way and guides their guns.

These things were the key to success in the Gulf, and they are expensive. In round terms, for every dollar you spend on the divisions themselves (not counting the sealift and airlift to get them there), you may have to spend three or more dollars extra on this back-up of technological brain and muscle. . . .

The extras

That was the first building block. The democracies' high command then has to decide whether it will take the risk of being able to mount only one such expedition at a time.

It seems unlikely that two big crises, the seven-division sort, are going to happen simultaneously, unless one of those pattern-changing events—an outbreak of nuclear proliferation, or a bid by China to make itself global leader of the opposition—sharply worsens the prospects for the 21st century. The number of possible big crises may actually diminish. It should be clear by the mid-1990s, for instance, whether or not the world has to go on feeling nervous about the Korean peninsula. But it will be sensible to make allowance for the fact that an unexpected minor crisis, or an irresistible call for a peace-making war of conscience, could overlap with a big fight. Put down a couple more divisions, plus trimmings.

So far the high command has been able to make its calculations as if the countries it represented were a single unit. It now has to think about their separate requirements.

None of these countries wants to be left without a soldier on its soil when its contribution to the expeditionary corps has gone abroad. Some already have little local difficulties to attend to. Britain uses well over a division's worth of men in Northern Ireland. Italy has nearly a division's worth trying to deal with a Mafia insurrection in Sicily. The Spanish army has the Basque separatists. Everybody suspects that this sort of thing could happen to him one day. How much armed force each country will wish to keep in reserve against that rainy day will vary with the size of the country, and its degree of nervousness; but it need not be much bigger than its hypothetical slice of the expeditionary force.

The one special case is what to do about the risk of Russia going wrong again, and bringing back a new version of the cold war. This would be bad news for everybody, but particularly for Europe, which sits on the same stretch of land as Russia.

The reaction of conservative European soldiers is to want to keep a large army sitting in Europe, gazing anxiously towards Moscow even when the real action is elsewhere. This would be a mistake. If Russia does go wrong, it will not become a serious danger again overnight. Its economy is in too much of a mess. Its non-nuclear armed forces are probably incapable of offensive action for some time to come. Short of doing a nuclear Samson in the temple, which seems un-Russian, this country is currently out of action. Provided politicians in the democracies read the warning signs correctly, they should have several years to get ready to meet any new challenge. What they need now is therefore only the bare bones of the counter-Russian defences they will need if the worst happens.

In terms of men, bare bones means "mixed-readiness" units, each of which consists, say, one-third of full-timers and two-thirds of reservists. This would suit the continental Europeans well. They still like to believe that conscription is a social virtue. Of course, the expeditionary force for dealing with sudden crises elsewhere in the world will have to consist of highly trained, ready-to-go professionals. But if France, Germany and others still insist on calling up their youngsters, their conscripts could do a fairly short period of full-time service followed by two or three weeks a year of reserve training. That is how the Swiss run their army, and other Europeans might like to organise their watch on Russia on these lines.

For the weapons these men would need, "force-reconstitution" is required. The world might have, with luck, five years' warning of a Russian return to bad old ways. Unfortunately, it can take 10-15 years to design and build a new tank like America's Abrams or a new fighting aeroplane like Britain's Tornado. Force-reconstitution is the technique of getting a country rearmed faster than that.

It includes putting undiminished amounts of money into research and development, so that new weapons are ready for production without delay.

For some of those weapons it will be useful to start up the production lines, and keep them ticking over gently; that is miserably expensive in cost per unit produced, but it can save valuable time if production has to be suddenly accelerated. For humdrum items such as light arms and armoured troop-carriers it may make sense to order the machine-tools needed to produce them, but then to take the process no further until and unless the crisis arrives. All this costs money, and may prove unnecessary; but, while the shape of the new world is still in doubt, it is a precaution worth taking.

This is broadly what is needed to cope with the clear dangers and the misty uncertainties of the coming period. There are other possibilities. Special forces—the tough, secretive units that go for the adversary's jugular—plainly have a large future. And Congressman Stephen Solarz, a Democrat from New York, has another suggestion.

Mr Solarz thinks that the problem of finding troops to fight the messy wars of peace-making, the future Bosnias, could be eased if the United Nations was authorised to raise its own version of France's Foreign Legion, a fighting force of international volunteers. This force would not be sent into action unless the governments of the countries that sit on the UN Security Council gave it their approval. But those governments would not be sending their own armies into battle, which makes them nervous; they would be sending tough young men who knew what they had enlisted for, and whose mothers would be unlikely to complain.

How much would it all cost? That depends on how it was organised. If everything except the purely national requirements were done by America and Europe as a shared venture, the bill would certainly be much smaller than the combined figure to which the various governments are now trying to reduce their defence budgets. The peace dividend would be that much bigger. Even with less than total cohesion, it could be done on defence budgets of well under 3% of GNP for almost everybody. The more Europeans and Americans insist on doing things separately, the larger the bill they will all have to pay.

● ● ●

EMPOWERING THE UNITED NATIONS

Historic Opportunities to Strengthen World Body

Boutros Boutros-Ghali

Boutros Boutros-Ghali is Secretary General of the United Nations.

A new chapter in the history of the United Nations has begun. With newfound appeal the world organization is being utilized with greater frequency and growing urgency. The machinery of the United Nations, which had often been rendered inoperative by the dynamics of the Cold War, is suddenly at the center of international efforts to deal with unresolved problems of the past decades as well as an emerging array of present and future issues.

The new era has brought new credibility to the United Nations. Along with it have come rising expectations that the United Nations will take on larger responsibilities and a greater role in overcoming pervasive and interrelated obstacles to peace and development. Together the international community and the U.N. Secretariat need to seize this extraordinary opportunity to expand, adapt and reinvigorate the work of the United Nations so that the lofty goals as originally envisioned by the charter can begin to be realized.

PEACEKEEPING IS A GROWTH INDUSTRY

Peacekeeping is the most prominent U.N. activity. The "blue helmets" on the front lines of conflict on four continents are a symbol of the United Nations' commitment to international peace and security. They come from some 65 countries, representing more than 35 percent of the membership.

Peacekeeping is a U.N. invention. It was not specifically defined in the charter but evolved as a noncoercive instrument of conflict control at a time when Cold War constraints prevented the Security Council from taking the more forceful steps permitted by the charter. Thirteen peacekeeping operations were established between 1948 and 1978. Five of them remain in existence, and are between 14 and 44 years old. Peacekeeping has sometimes proved easier than the complementary function of peacemaking. This shows that peacekeeping, by itself cannot provide the permanent solution to a conflict. Only political negotiation can do that.

"The former Yugoslavia has become the United Nations' largest peacekeeping commitment ever."

During the Cold War years the basic principles of peacekeeping were gradually established and gained acceptance: the consent of the parties; troops provided by member states serving under the command of the secretary general; minimum use of force; collective financing. It was also learned, often the hard way, that peacekeeping success requires the cooperation of the parties, a clear and practicable mandate, the continuing support of the Security Council and adequate financial arrangements.

The end of the Cold War has led to a dramatic expansion in demand for the United Nations' peacekeeping services. Since 1988 14 new operations have been established, five of which have already completed their mandates and been disbanded. In the first half of 1992 the number of U.N. soldiers and police officers increased fourfold; by the end of the year they will exceed 50,000.

Some of these new operations have been of the traditional, largely military type, deployed to control unresolved conflicts between states. Examples are the military observers who monitored the ceasefire between Iran and Iraq from 1988 to 1991 and those who currently patrol the demilitarized zone between Iraq and Kuwait.

But most of the new operations have been set up to help implement negotiated settlements of long-standing conflicts, as in Namibia, Angola, Cambodia, El Salvador and Mozambique. Namibia was a colonial situation but each of the other four has been an internal conflict, albeit with significant external dimensions, within a sovereign member state of the United Nations.

There is another aspect to the end of the Cold War. The thawing of its frozen political geography has led to the eruption of savage conflicts in, and sometimes between, newly emerging independent states. The former Yugoslavia has become the United Nations' largest peacekeeping commitment ever. Ethnic conflict across political borders and the brutal killing of civilians there are reminiscent of the ordeal that U.N. peacekeeping forces faced in the 1960s in the then Congo. U.N. forces again are taking an unacceptable level of casualties. It is difficult to avoid wondering whether the conditions yet exist for successful peacekeeping in what was Yugoslavia.

The 1990s have given peacekeeping another new task: the protection of the delivery of humanitarian supplies to civilians caught up in a continuing conflict. This is currently underway in Bosnia-Herzegovina and Somalia, member states whose institutions have been largely destroyed in a confused and cruel web of civil conflicts. This task tests the established practices of peacekeeping, especially the circumstances in which U.N. soldiers may open fire. Existing rules of engagement allow them to do so if armed persons attempt by force to prevent them from carrying out their orders. This license, used sparingly in the past, may be resorted to more frequently if the United Nations is to assert the Security Council's authority over those who, for personal gain or war objectives, try to rob or destroy humanitarian supplies destined for suffering civilian populations.

BEYOND PEACEKEEPING

All these new modes of peacekeeping have had far-reaching implications for the way in which U.N. operations are organized and conducted.

In internal conflicts, or indeed in interstate conflicts where one or other of the governments is not in a position to exercise full authority over territory nominally under its control, not all the parties are governments. As a result the peacekeepers have had to learn how to deal with a multiplicity of "authorities." The leaders of such groups are often inaccessible and their identity even unknown; chains of command are shadowy; armed persons who offend against agreements signed by their supposed leaders are disowned; discipline is nonexistent or brutal. And everywhere there is an evil and uncontrolled proliferation of arms.

Peacekeeping operations still invariably include military personnel. But now the civilian elements often have an even more important role. This is especially true when the task is to help implement comprehensive and complex settlements, as was or is the case in Namibia, El Salvador, Cambodia and Mozambique. Political action is required to resolve disputes between the parties and persuade them to implement the agreed arrangements. Information programs must explain the United Nations' role and advise the people of the opportunities the settlement gives them. Refugees must be brought home and resettled. Elections must be observed and verified or even, in Cambodia, organized and conducted by the United Nations.

Local police must be monitored to ensure that they carry out their duties in the spirit of the new order and not the old. Respect for human rights must be verified, an especially important task in El Salvador and Cambodia. In the latter country the United Nations also has responsibility for controlling the key parts of the existing administrative structures.

All of these tasks, some of them very intrusive, must be carried out with complete impartiality by civilian peacekeepers. Staff members of the U.N. system, with policy and election observers made available by member states, have risen to these new civilian challenges.

The involvement of such a variety of civilian personnel, alongside their military colleagues, creates a need for tight coordination of all aspects of an operation. As a result it has become normal for the overall direction of a multifaceted peacekeeping operation to be entrusted to a senior civilian official as special representative of the secretary general, to whom the force commander, the police commissioner, the director of elections and other directors report.

RESPONSES MUST BE QUICK

One of the lessons learned during the recent headlong expansion of U.N. peacekeeping is the need to accelerate the deployment of new operations. Under current procedures three or four months can elapse between the Security Council's authorization of a mission and its becoming operational in the field. Action is required on three fronts: finance, personnel and equipment.

On finance, the member states should provide the secretary general with a working capital fund for the start-up of new operations, so that cash is immediately available. They should also revise existing financial procedures so that the secretary general has authority to spend that cash, within reasonable limits, as soon as the new operation is authorized.

The question of personnel is more complicated. Procedures for the transfer of U.N. staff to new operations in the field are being simplified for more rapid reaction. But most peacekeeping personnel (troops, police, election observers) are made available by governments. The answer is not to create a U.N. standing force, which would be impractical and inappropriate, but to extend and make more systematic standby arrangements by which governments commit themselves to hold ready, at an agreed period of notice, specially trained units for peacekeeping service.

A handful of governments already do this. A recent invitation to all member states to volunteer information about what personnel and equipment they would in principle be ready to contribute, if asked, produced disappointing results. I have now decided to take the initiative and put specific proposals to governments, in order to identify with reasonable certainty sources of military and police personnel and equipment that governments would undertake to make available at very short notice. These commitments would constitute building blocks that could be used, when the moment came, to construct peacekeeping operations in various sizes and configurations, ranging from a small group of military observers to a full division, as required.

Allied with this effort will be the provision of more extensive guidance to governments on training troops and police who they may contribute to the United Nations for peacekeeping duties.

"U.N. troops would be authorized to use force to ensure respect for the ceasefire."

Equipment can cause even greater bottlenecks than personnel. There are two complementary ways in which this problem can be eased. First, member states should make it possible for the United Nations to establish a reserve stock of basic items (vehicles, radios, generators, prefabricated buildings) that are always required for a new peacekeeping operation. Second, member states could agree to hold ready, at various locations around the world, reserves of such equipment. These would remain their property but could be made immediately available to the United Nations when the need arose.

An even more radical development can now be envisaged. It happens all too often that the parties to a conflict sign a ceasefire agreement but then fail to respect it. In such situations it is felt that the United Nations should "do something." This is a reasonable expectation if the United Nations is to be an effective system of collective security. The purpose of peace enforcement units (perhaps they should be called "ceasefire enforcement units") would be to enable the United Nations to deploy troops quickly to enforce a ceasefire by taking coercive action against either party, or both, if they violate it.

This concept retains many of the features of peacekeeping: the operation would be authorized by the Security Council; the troops would be provided voluntarily by member states; they would be under the command of the secretary general; and they would be impartial between the two sides, taking action only if one or other of them violated the agreed ceasefire. But the concept goes beyond peacekeeping to the extent that the operation would be deployed without the express consent of the two parties (though its basis would be a ceasefire agreement previously reached between them). U.N. troops would be authorized to use force to ensure respect for the ceasefire. They would be trained, armed and equipped accordingly; a very rapid response would be essential.

This is a novel idea that involves some obvious difficulties. But it should be carefully considered by the international community as the next step in the development of the United Nations' capability to take effective action on the ground to maintain international peace and security.

UNPAID BILLS

There have been prolonged delays by member states in meeting their financial obligations regarding peacekeeping operations. For instance, four months into one of the largest and most complex U.N. operations ever, only nine member states had fully paid their obligations to the U.N. Transitional Authority in Cambodia. Delays in payment add to the fragility of an already delicate mission by hampering the United Nations' capacity to deploy and causing delays in the schedule. These in turn threaten the agreed timetable and jeopardize the entire peace process. At a time when the United Nations is being asked to do more than ever, it is being shortchanged by the member states who have breached their legal obligations and deprived the United Nations of necessary resources.[1]

These difficulties occur against a background of dramatically increasing costs for establishing and maintaining peacekeeping operations. During the first half of 1992 there was a fourfold increase in peacekeeping costs—from some $700 million to about $2.8 billion. Expenses are likely to rise even higher with new and expanded operations that could be launched in the coming months. Meanwhile the continued failure of most member states to meet their financial commitments to peacekeeping operations and to the United Nations in general is a most serious problem. The continued viability of these missions, as well as the credibility of the United Nations itself, is threatened.

---

1. *Editor's Note:* The five member states with the largest arrears, in both regular budget and peacekeeping assessments as of October 1992, are the United States, Russia, South Africa, Japan and Ukraine.

MOUNTING DEVELOPMENT NEEDS

Political stability is not an end in itself; it is a condition of durable economic and social development and the fulfillment of the human potential. At the same time inseparable links between peace and development need to be acknowledged and understood. The world has seen the deterioration of economic and social conditions give rise to political strife and military conflict. The activities of the United Nations for peace and security should not be carried out at the expense of its responsibilities for development. It is essential that peace and development be pursued in an integrated, mutually supporting way.

> *"The activities of the United Nations for peace and security should not be carried out at the expense of its responsibilities for development."*

One can point to a number of situations where the United Nations has kept the peace, or at least prevented conflicts from escalating, but the balance sheet on the development side is less than encouraging. A billion people live on less than one dollar a day; children in many parts of the world are dying unnecessarily of diseases that could easily be cured; women are striving to be both breadwinners and homemakers in situations of intolerable strain; and there are too few jobs. The crisis is deeper than merely another manifestation of the familiar disparity between the developed nations of the North and the developing South.

No such clear-cut pattern offers itself to our eyes today. East European countries and the former Soviet Union are struggling in their transition toward democracy and market-based economies. Even the nations of the Organization for Economic Cooperation and Development are not immune to economic and social ills. Poverty, unemployment, inequity and growing insecurity exist in virtually every part of the globe. Even rich nations are tempted to turn inward to attend to their own agendas. But today there is no longer any such thing as "someone else's problem"; the globalization of economies and communications deepens our interdependence.

The responsibilities of the United Nations in the field of social and economic development are central to the purposes and principles of the charter: first, because the maintenance of international peace and security is inextricably entwined with economic and social progress and stability; and second, because the promotion of social and economic progress is a specific task given to the United Nations by the charter.

Development policy was significantly shaped by the Cold War and the process of decolonization. When the charter was being framed at San Francisco in 1945, and when most of our current world economic institutions were being created, most of today's states were either colonies, semi-colonies or parts of extensive empires. The notion of "development" was unformed; the concept of the "Third World" had not emerged. The idea that the United Nations should be concerned with economic and social issues sprang from what has been called "welfare internationalism," which evolved in wartime planning for the peace and was a formative influence on the Bretton Woods institutions dating from that period.

As demands for independence gathered momentum in African and Asian lands, programs of assistance and economic cooperation were initiated by former colonial powers. These were joined by assistance programs established by states with no recent colonial past, such as the Nordic countries. Meanwhile the World Bank was becoming the lead institution in the channeling of multilateral development finance to developing countries.

Provision of development assistance to newly independent nations became part of the foreign policies of the industrialized countries, intricately bound up with the global contest for power and influence. The United States, through its Agency for International Development, became a major provider of development finance and technical assistance in Africa, Asia and Latin America. The Soviet Union was deeply involved with a relatively small number of states considered potentially significant in its ideological sphere, and provided substantial technical support for them. In both cases development assistance was often interwoven with military aid.

Just as the Cold War distorted the vision of collective security set forth in the U.N. Charter, it also impaired cooperation for development. Bilateral foreign aid programs were often an instrument of the Cold War, and remain deeply affected by considerations of political power and national policy. Multilateral development programs, even when managed well and with admirable ethical purpose, derived from ideas and ideologies that proved inadequate at best and in some cases ruinous.

At this time of change in world affairs, when restructuring the institutions of international relations is high on the agenda, there are increasing demands for action in the field of economic and social development. The call for a new unity and clarity of purpose from the United Nations in the field of development—which is now commonly understood to include social and economic development and environmental protection as well—has come from developing and developed countries alike.

Traditionally U.N. social development activities have concentrated on the most vulnerable groups of populations. Increasingly in developing countries efforts at modernization tug at institutions that hold the social fabric together. Declining social cohesion, in turn, can undermine economic progress. The organization is beginning to take a closer look at specific phenomena affecting social cohesion and to view the social and economic dimensions of development in a more integrated way. Issues of demography and cultural, religious, ethnic and linguistic diversity are so closely related today to prospects for political stability and economic advancement that the involvement of the United Nations in issues of social development is acquiring a qualitatively different nature.

If the process of decolonization is over and the Cold War has ended, and now that there is no "struggle" or bipolar competition to dramatize and distract development efforts, how can the United Nations seek consensus on the need for a fairer, more just, world and focus on the long-standing needs of the poor?

Today a consensus is emerging around a fundamental perception that the unfettered talents of individual human beings are the greatest resource a society can bring to bear on the task of national development. But the troubled state of the global economy indicates that we are still far from achieving universal economic prosperity, social justice and environmental balance. Cooperation for development will require the greatest intellectual effort in the period ahead because, as understood and applied until now, it has not resolved the urgent problem of the development of the planet. The need is comprehensive. Issues once approached separately, or sequentially, now may be seen as essentially indivisible.

CHANGED VIEW OF SOVEREIGNTY

The transition from one international era to another is symbolized today, as it has been at earlier turning points in the history of the United Nations, by a new group of member states taking their seats in the General Assembly. (Armenia, Azerbaijan, Bosnia-Herzegovina, Croatia, Georgia, Kazakhstan, Kyrgyzstan, Moldova, San Marino, Slovenia, Tajikistan, Turkmenistan and Uzbekistan all joined in 1992.) Their entrance reaffirms the concept of the state as the basic entity of international relations and the means by which peoples find a unity and a voice in the world community.

While respect for the fundamental sovereignty and integrity of the state remains central, it is undeniable that the centuries-old doctrine of absolute and exclusive sovereignty no longer stands, and was in fact never so absolute as it was conceived to be in theory. A major intellectual requirement of our time is to rethink the question of sovereignty—not to weaken its essence, which is crucial to international security and cooperation, but to recognize that it may take more than one form and perform more than one function. This perception could help solve problems both within and among states. And underlying the rights of the individual and the rights of peoples is a dimension of universal sovereignty that resides in all humanity and provides all peoples with legitimate involvement in issues affecting the world as a whole. It is a sense that increasingly finds expression in the gradual expansion of international law.

Related to this is the widening recognition that states and their governments cannot face or solve today's problems alone. International cooperation is unavoidable and indispensable. The quality, extent and timeliness of such cooperation will make the difference between advancement or frustration and despair. In this setting the significance of the United Nations should be evident and accepted. Nothing can match the United Nations' global network of information-gathering and constructive activity, which reaches from modern world centers of power down to the villages and families where people carry out the irreducible responsibilities of their lives.

At the other end of the scale only the United Nations can convene global-scale meetings of ministers and heads of states or governments to examine complex issues and propose integrated approaches. Such gatherings can have enormous implications for the world's good. At the Conference on Environment and Development in Rio de Janeiro in June 1992, for example, states obligated themselves to take global consequences into consideration in their domestic decisions. This is a fundamental philosophic undertaking by the world's nations, adding one more pillar to the gradually growing array of internationally accepted principles of national conduct.

REFORMING THE U.N.

Renewing the promise of an effective and cooperative United Nations means, in the first instance, reform of the organization and the broader system of specialized agencies from within. There is much that can be done now, but it must be understood that this will be an evolutionary process. The world is still in some ways in its "Middle Ages" when it comes to international organizations and cooperation. Centuries were required before the struggle among monarchical and baronial forces was transformed into states capable of carrying out responsibilities in the fields of security, economy and justice. There is no doubt that the institutions of the U.N. system must travel such a path if chaos is to be avoided.

Given firm leadership and a common resolve by member states I am confident that major achievements can be made by the end of this century.

To initiate reform from within I launched, soon after taking office a year ago, a process of restructuring the U.N. Secretariat. My first short-term aim was to eliminate duplication, redundancy and excessive layering of offices and duties at headquarters. This process has brought some results and must continue toward a coherent institutional strategy.

The Administrative Committee on Coordination is the highest body bringing together the executive heads of all the specialized agencies and organizations of the U.N. system. This committee must act more definitively to guide and harness the work of the various organizations of the system.

Similarly, the Economic and Social Council, despite its preeminence in the charter, has proved too weak to provide coherence and form to the work of the specialized agencies, the Bretton Woods institutions, the regional economic commissions and the array of U.N. programs. Duplication is widespread; coordination is often nominal; bureaucratic battles aimed at monopolizing a particular subject are rife, and organizational objectives are sometimes in conflict.

The proliferation of institutions that characterize U.N. work in the economic, social and environment fields has been another product of previous decades. Member states often pressed for measures on a piecemeal basis. Bureaucracies were sometimes set up as substitutes for problem-solving and served, in some cases, to camouflage problems rather than expose them to serious attention.

I have recommended the introduction of a flexible high-level intersessional mechanism to enable the council to respond in a continuous and timely way to new developments in the economic and social sphere. It should possess an early-warning function encompassing threats to security and well-being: from energy crisis to the burden of debt, from the risk of famine to the spread of disease. As the Security Council can envision new possibilities in the cause of peace, so the Economic and Social Council's role can be significantly strengthened. At this time when old conceptions of development are fading and new departures are required, each element of the U.N. system will need to reexamine and justify anew its mission and the human and financial resources it employs.

THE INTERACTION OF PEOPLES

New possibilities exist for shared, delegated and interactive contributions to the world organization from the burgeoning number of regional associations and agencies and the huge network of nongovernmental organizations that in the past largely operated from North America and Europe but increasingly are a feature in countries all over the world. More than a thousand NGOS are active in the United Nations, working through and with people everywhere.

There is an even deeper level to this trend: relationships among nations are increasingly shaped by continuous interaction among entire bodies politic and economic. Such activity almost resembles a force of nature, and indeed may be just that. Political borders and geographic boundaries pose slight barriers to this process. Governments increasingly prove ineffective in efforts to guide or even keep track of these flows of ideas, influences and

transactions. The challenge for the foreseeable future will be to make sense of these evolving relationships between and among peoples.

As one area for such efforts, I have put forward the concept of "post-conflict peace-building." In the aftermath of warfare, concrete cooperative projects that link two or more countries and peoples in a mutually beneficial undertaking can not only contribute to economic and social development but also enhance the confidence that is so essential to peace. Freer travel, cultural exchanges, youth projects and changes in educational practices all could serve to forestall a reemergence of cultural and national tensions that could spark renewed hostilities. Post-conflict peace-building will be needed not only in cases of international conflict, but also for the increasing number of intrastate, internal conflicts arising today.

CHANGING U.N. CULTURE

The spirit of the U.N. Charter was kept alive for decades under very difficult circumstances. Hope has been crucial; achievement is now required. Beyond declarations, beyond position-taking, the time is here to look at ideas as plans for action. Beyond restructuring, the culture of the United Nations must undergo a transformation.

The bipolar contest relegated the United Nations to a status far removed from its original design. A propensity to rhetoric, to protocol and a delight in maneuvering for marginal advantage or national prestige came to characterize many delegations' activities. Committees and commissions have been assigned important duties only to find governments participating through assignment of lower level officials, unauthorized to engage seriously. Time is too precious and the tasks too urgent today to permit these indulgences.

In the Cold War era a fundamental split was taken for granted on virtually every issue. We have been relieved of that burden. But we cannot expect to be free of controversy, dispute or debate. The problems before us are complex and the solutions not at all obvious. If we work seriously on them, we must expect serious differences of opinion. Rather than be deterred by this we should be grateful and eager to engage in the intellectual struggle that is needed. Sharp differences are inevitable, but consensus is possible. I am committed to a broad dialogue between the member states and the secretary general. Preserving the world authority of the United Nations requires the fullest consultation, participation and engagement of all states, large and small. This in turn requires the empowerment of people in civil society and a hearing for their voices at all levels of international society and institutions.

Can the UN Be the World's Cop?

Called on to intervene in civil wars and shepherd states toward democracy, the blue helmets are caught between increased dangers and faltering support

Lucia Mouat

Special to The Christian Science Monitor

UNITED NATIONS, N.Y.

When the fighting gets fierce and innocent victims appear on TV screens, the world increasingly looks to the United Nations for help. Often more by default than design, UN peacekeepers have been taking on the role of world cop.

The UN now operates 17 peacekeeping missions at an annual cost of more than $3.5 billion. Two new missions were launched in September. UN Secretary-General Boutros Boutros-Ghali says as many as 100,000 troops may be involved in UN missions by the end of the year.

Yet the UN's most visible and, until recently, most widely praised activity faces major problems. The newer missions often take peacekeeping forces into uncharted territory, where more ambitious but ambiguous mandates increase expectations without always giving those on the ground the authority, resources, or training needed to carry them out.

Traditionally, peacekeepers were sent only after a cease-fire was signed and both sides accepted their presence. Their job was to monitor the accord with minimal personnel and weapons. Today, they often must intervene in civil wars, where they are expected to disarm combatants. It has become a risky job involving peacemaking, peace enforcement, and nation-building.

In some new operations, the traditionally neutral UN is accused of being partisan or of not being tough enough on recalcitrant parties. In Somalia, a maverick clan leader who initially agreed to arms and cease-fire accords now wages virtual war on UN troops. Dozens have been killed. The struggle to contain Gen.

Mohamed Farah Aideed has become one of the UN's most controversial actions.

As the conflict escalates, the US ad-

ministration has urged the UN place more emphasis on restoring a political structure. Some in the US Congress have

---

Salvador: Success Flows From 'Thirst for Peace'

Secretary-General Boutros Boutros-Ghali has called the United Nations Observer Mission in El Salvador (ONUSAL) "a prime example of the need for a fully integrated approach to peace-building." It ranks as one of the most successful UN peacekeeping programs.

It was UN-mediated talks that brought an official end to the country's 12-year civil war in January 1992. The peace pact, dubbed a "negotiated revolution," called for sweeping military, judicial, electoral, and constitutional reforms. But the UN didn't walk away after the pact was signed. It stayed not only to verify compliance but also to "facilitate the consolidation of peace, democracy, and justice."

For the first time ever, the UN set up human rights offices in a country six months before a cease-fire was established. The UN remains deeply involved, with its members wearing the *cascos azules* (blue helmets) as mediators, cops, human rights monitors, and economic advisers. The UN brought in over 600 civilian police from various countries to keep a watchful eye on the military-trained Salvadoran National police while a new, civilian police force was being trained at a new police academy. By July 1994, there should be 3,500–5,000 new officers in place.

On Sept. 13, the UN began a new role, establishing an electoral division of 37 specialists to oversee preparations for the March 1994 presidential elections. Voter registration has been slow,

but at UN urging the Salvadoran government is implementing a plan to speed up the process with an emphasis on reaching women and rural voters. (On election day, the UN will have 800 observers (two per voting booth) in the country.

The cease-fire has been "impeccably observed," the UN says.

But there have been hitches. Army officers accused of human rights abuses and corruption refused to step down for eight months. The rebel Farabundo Martí National Liberation Front failed to declare and destroy all of their weapons. Human rights violations continue, albeit far fewer than during the war. Creation of the new civilian police force—a crucial element in demilitarizing society—was delayed. And distribution of land to former combatants as stipulated in the accords has fallen well behind schedule. The UN attributes the delays to a shortfall in international aid.

Given the uncertain chemistry of peacekeeping, the Salvadoran formula has worked remarkably well. ONUSAL officials say a critical element has been the public demand that feuding factions put the past behind them. When necessary, UN officials have waded in and acted as "catalyzers" to break an impasse. But primarily, says ONUSAL spokesman Jorge Ulate-Segura, the mission's success is due to Salvadorans' own "thirst for peace."

—David Clark Scott

Former Yugoslavia: Mission Caught in a Maelstrom

The United Nations operation in former Yugoslavia involves 25,000 soldiers, police, and civilians from several countries. The effort is one of the UN's most problem-bound, controversial, and costly, and illustrates the difficulties the UN faces in its new brand of mission.

An original force of 14,700 was deployed in the spring of 1992 in Croatia. Known as the UN Protection Force or UNPROFOR, it was sent to oversee implementation of the 1991 Vance ceasefire, which required the Yugoslav Army, which backed rebel Serbs, to withdraw and disarm. Provisions of the plan have either not been implemented or have been reversed. And after 18 months of fighting in neighboring Bosnia-Herzegovina, Croatia and its rebel Serbs are on the verge of a new war.

When war erupted in Bosnia in April 1992, the European Community was in charge of negotiations there. Its personnel withdrew from the capital of Sarajevo because of the fighting, leaving UN personnel as the only international media-tors. This, in effect, forced expansion of the UN mission to Bosnia. Later, a small contingent was placed in Macedonia to prevent further Serb actions.

Senior UNPROFOR officials express misgivings about the overall operation, which has seen about 56 men killed and hundreds injured. They complain privately about lack of a clear mission, mismanagement, stifling bureaucracy, political interference, and open hostility from the parties they are asked to assist.

Individual units are often guided by their governments, which for domestic political reasons restrict their actions. The Western powers sometimes seem more concerned with protecting their own personnel than the civilians UNPROFOR is supposed to help.

The UN has reinforced that impression itself by approving resolutions that it declines to enforce, such as the creation and protection of "safe havens" for Bosnian Muslims and the use of "any means" to ensure the delivery of aid to war-torn areas.

Some of the warring factions have exploited UNPROFOR. UN troops have been attacked, UN headquarters shelled, Security Council directives flauted, and UN relief convoys blocked. Croatian President Franjo Tudjman blames the UN for the continued rebel Serb occupation of 22 percent of his country and claims the UN has failed to implement the Vance peace plan.

This is not to detract from the sacrifices made by individuals and UNPROFOR units. The British units, for instance, have taken enormous risks in trying to keep open aid routes and assist civilians trapped by fighting.

And the former UN commander for Bosnia, French Lt. Gen. Philippe Morillon, took perhaps the most dramatic step of the operation when on his own initiative, he helped save the besieged eastern Muslim Slav enclave of Srebrenica from a Bosnian Serb assault.

—Jonathan Landay

Cambodia: Victory at the Ballot Box, but Threat of War Lingers

As UN forces in Cambodia wind down their most ambitious peacekeeping mission in history—to demobilize Cambodian armed forces and organize free and fair elections to choose a new government—hopes that democracy and peace will prevail are mixed with fears that the operation will fail to achieve its promise.

Norodom Sihanouk was again named king on Sept. 24, and a new government was installed in keeping with a constitution approved by lawmakers elected in May.

The restoration of the monarchy and inauguration of a new leadership officially ended the 18-month UN operation that brought Cambodia back into the international community, but was marred by setbacks that offer important lessons for future peacekeeping operations.

After the UN spent $2 billion on a mission that involved more than 22,000 people, including 20 killed in warfare, Cambodia remains rife with political elitism, lawlessness, and violence by Khmer Rouge guerrillas who still control about 20 percent of the country.

The UN mission in Cambodia suffered several setbacks, the most serious being the failure to disarm and demobilize the combatants. That has allowed the Khmer Rouge to remain a threat to the peace process.

At times, the UN operation appeared near collapse. Then came the elections, the first multiparty voting in 83 years and cornerstone of the peace agreement signed in 1991 by the four warring factions—the Vietnamese-installed government and three opposition groups.

The Khmer Rouge originally signed the accord, but later pulled out of the peace process and threatened to sabotage the ballot with violence. A voter turnout of 90 percent in the face of such threats underscored Cambodians' desire to build a better future and led to swift international recognition of the new government.

But the country is a long way from being an open, democratic society. The Constitution, which gives broad, undefined powers to King Sihanouk, was drawn up in secret by a small group of politicians and rubber-stamped by the 120-member constituent assembly.

Although economic development fell outside the scope of the UN mission, one senior UN official recommends steps be taken in future operations to guarantee economic development to bolster political reforms.

Michael Williams, director of human rights and information for the UN mission in Cambodia, said most Cambodians assumed the operation would bring improved infrastructure to attract foreign investment and economic development.

"If economic development does not take place in Cambodia, then there's no doubt that political gains of the last year will be undermined and that the country will probably descend into another spiral of violence," Mr. Williams says.

—Kathy Chenault

called for a reassessment of US involvement and for setting a deadline for troops to come home.

In another crucible, Muslims in Bosnia-Herzegovina criticize UN troops for not dealing more forcefully with Bosnian Serbs who block aid deliveries, and blame UN mediators for not helping wrest back at the peace table lands taken by ethnic cleansing.

The difficulties encountered in new operations are damaging UN credibility. Analysts warn that the UN is in danger if consensus decisions are not backed by deep commitment by member states.

Some analysts view the Council's efforts to protect Muslim safe havens, for example, as tough talk that was largely symbolic from the start. Without political will, they say, the Council becomes a convenient vehicle for nations to show heart without taking national action and with no real intent to follow through. The UN then becomes the scapegoat.

"The UN is being used as a repository for conflicts that can't be resolved in any other way and as a way of distancing [members] from difficult situations in which they don't want to get involved," says Hurst Hannum, a UN expert at Fletcher School of Law and Diplomacy in Medford, Mass.

"You can't just cast a couple of votes, make some pious statements, throw a few troops in the field, and think it's done—this is a serious, difficult business," says Edward Luck, president of the United Nations Association of the US. "The failures count a lot. They undermine financial and political support for the organization and bring into question its credibility."

Many now agree the UN must decline some requests for help. In President Clinton's Sept. 27 speech to the General Assembly, he warned that UN money may depend on it: "If the American people are to say 'yes' to UN peacekeeping, the UN must learn how to say 'no.' "

UN members should think seriously about what kinds of interventions are in their national interest, analysts say. Lawmakers and the public should be involved in the debate. The Council can try to set some general guidelines.

Mr. Boutros-Ghali insists that the success of UN peacekeeping depends chiefly on the political will of the parties to the dispute. UN experience in El Salvador and Namibia are cited as examples. Yet in new peacekeeping efforts, consent has sometimes been given and later been withdrawn.

In Angola, rebel forces agreed to the UN role, but after the election returned to war to achieve their aims. Croatia now wants UN troops out by Nov. 30 unless firm deadlines are set for disarming Serb units in occupied territory.

Ending missions can be difficult, as the 29-year-old Cyprus operation illustrates. But Gareth Evans, Australia's foreign minister and author of "Cooperating for Peace," says the UN should give thought to pulling out of some missions if local support wanes or goals cannot be fulfilled. The UN, he says, should clarify conditions for an exit early on.

Council mandates should be more specific, experts say. Vague and limited initial mandates, though easier for the Council to agree on, can lead to an incremental commitment of forces and an ineffective mission, according to a new US Institute of Peace report on peacekeeping.

The UN has been criticized, too, for bureaucratic delays. Improvements have recently been made in operational capacity: A 24-hour operations room to deal with Somalia and Bosnia missions is in place, and governments are lending mili-

---

Somalia: Use of Force Shakes UN Credibility

Somalia is the UN peacekeepers' first venture into peacemaking, in which troops were mandated to use force to establish a secure environment for humanitarian efforts and for rebuilding the country.

The anarchy that cost some 300,000 lives through starvation and war has largely been quelled outside the capital, but the mission has stumbled over efforts to disarm the militia of Gen. Mohamed Farah Aideed in Mogadishu. Although General Aideed's men are thought to number only about 1,000, they are equipped with Soviet and American arms and are engaged in urban guerrilla warfare aimed at discrediting the UN presence. Aideed's militia is blamed for the deaths of about 66 UN personnel since last May.

The battle with Aideed has stirred controversy among Somalis, within the UN force itself, and in the United States Congress. While some Somalis accuse the UN of taking sides, contributing nations have had second thoughts about suffering casualties for the sake of a stable Somalia.

The Italians, according to UN and Somali sources, apparently struck a deal with Aideed's militia to go easy on weapons searches in exchange for not targeting their soldiers. The Germans sought to place their first post–World War II troops abroad in Belet Huen, where things are relatively quiet. And US congressmen, as casualties mount, have called for a reassessment and a date for US troops to come home. The UN secretary-general has warned that the mission could collapse if nations pull back from commitments.

The heavy military action in Mogadishu (also causing many Somali casualties) and the failure to capture Aideed have led to calls for shifting the emphasis to rebuilding the political structure. The issue of the mission's focus has caused tensions at several stages, which some attribute to the involvement of many nations.

Indeed, coordination of the forces of 30 nations is "the most difficult problem," says US Ret. Adm. Jonathan Howe, head of the UN mission. Admiral Howe notes differences of language, culture, and military styles. For example, Pakistani troops are accused by some relief and UN officials of using too much force, the Italians of using too little. Not all nations are willing to follow UN commands, Howe says. "You have to have unity of command. You can't have 30 different policies and go your own way." Even US troops, who have carried out most major offensives, are not technically under UN command, but answer to the Pentagon.

Yet should the nation-building part of the UN mandate take precedence, Howe cautions there are not sufficient resources for an effective effort. Rebuilding a nation's police, court, and political system from the ground up takes more money than has so far been given, he says. Donors have provided only "a token amount."

—Robert M. Press

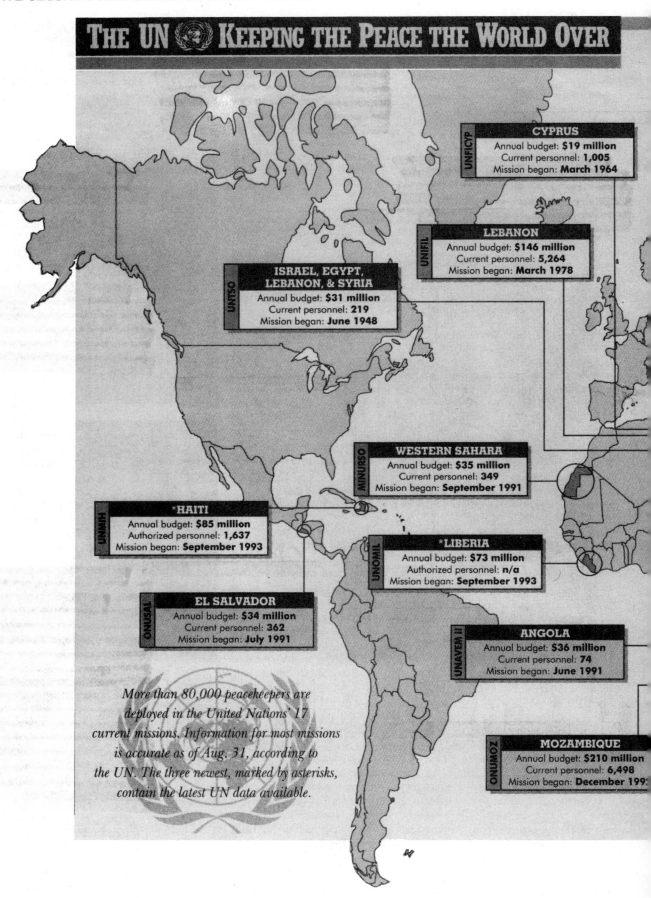

THE UN KEEPING THE PEACE THE WORLD OVER

CYPRUS (UNFICYP)
Annual budget: **$19 million**
Current personnel: **1,005**
Mission began: **March 1964**

LEBANON (UNIFIL)
Annual budget: **$146 million**
Current personnel: **5,264**
Mission began: **March 1978**

ISRAEL, EGYPT, LEBANON, & SYRIA (UNTSO)
Annual budget: **$31 million**
Current personnel: **219**
Mission began: **June 1948**

WESTERN SAHARA (MINURSO)
Annual budget: **$35 million**
Current personnel: **349**
Mission began: **September 1991**

*HAITI (UNMIH)
Annual budget: **$85 million**
Authorized personnel: **1,637**
Mission began: **September 1993**

*LIBERIA (UNOMIL)
Annual budget: **$73 million**
Authorized personnel: **n/a**
Mission began: **September 1993**

EL SALVADOR (ONUSAL)
Annual budget: **$34 million**
Current personnel: **362**
Mission began: **July 1991**

ANGOLA (UNAVEM II)
Annual budget: **$36 million**
Current personnel: **74**
Mission began: **June 1991**

More than 80,000 peacekeepers are deployed in the United Nations' 17 current missions. Information for most missions is accurate as of Aug. 31, according to the UN. The three newest, marked by asterisks, contain the latest UN data available.

MOZAMBIQUE (ONUMOZ)
Annual budget: **$210 million**
Current personnel: **6,498**
Mission began: **December 199**

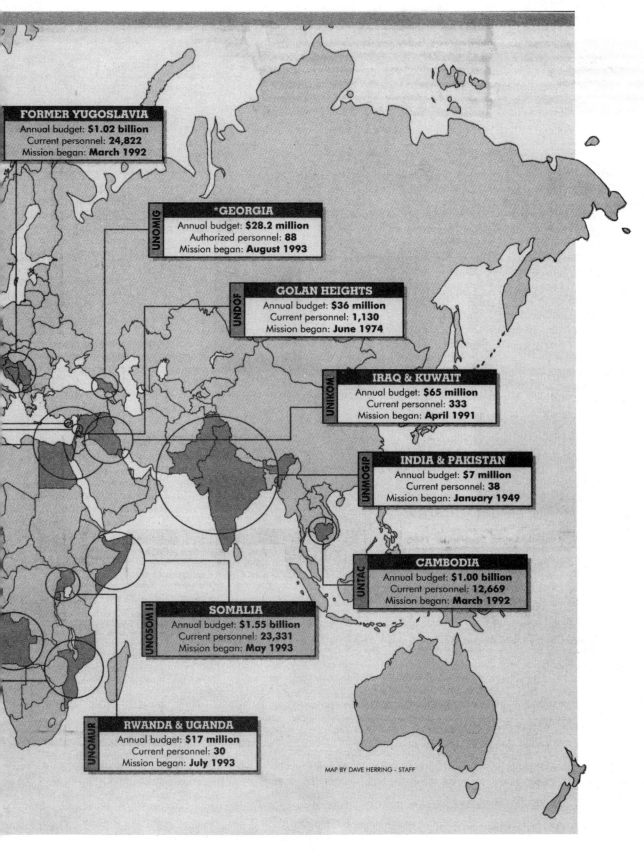

FORMER YUGOSLAVIA
Annual budget: **$1.02 billion**
Current personnel: **24,822**
Mission began: **March 1992**

UNOMIG
GEORGIA
Annual budget: **$28.2 million**
Authorized personnel: **88**
Mission began: **August 1993**

UNDOF
GOLAN HEIGHTS
Annual budget: **$36 million**
Current personnel: **1,130**
Mission began: **June 1974**

UNIKOM
IRAQ & KUWAIT
Annual budget: **$65 million**
Current personnel: **333**
Mission began: **April 1991**

UNMOGIP
INDIA & PAKISTAN
Annual budget: **$7 million**
Current personnel: **38**
Mission began: **January 1949**

UNTAC
CAMBODIA
Annual budget: **$1.00 billion**
Current personnel: **12,669**
Mission began: **March 1992**

UNOSOM II
SOMALIA
Annual budget: **$1.55 billion**
Current personnel: **23,331**
Mission began: **May 1993**

UNOMUR
RWANDA & UGANDA
Annual budget: **$17 million**
Current personnel: **30**
Mission began: **July 1993**

MAP BY DAVE HERRING - STAFF

tary experts to the UN for short-term stints.

Yet, given the new peacemaking role, better coordination and planning are still needed, many experts say.

Military professionalism is far more crucial in current peacekeeping operations than in the past, says Maj. Gen. Indar Jit Rikhye, leader of five previous peacekeeping operations, military adviser to two former UN secretaries-general, and a co-author of the Institute study. The UN's ability to coordinate and conduct military operations in the field still falls far short, he says. "There can be no military operation without teamwork."

Boutros-Ghali has been pushing for a standby army of trained reserves that could be assembled quickly as needs arise.

Southern Africa: Lessons Learned From Three UN Missions

Namibia's peaceful transition to independence in March 1990 remains one of the UN's major peacekeeping triumphs. The 9,000-strong United Nations Transitional Assistance Group (UNTAG), provided a model for UN intervention during a major transition in the nation's history. UNTAG was charged with monitoring the demobilization of all armies, restricting guerrilla forces and the South African armed forces to bases, and supervising and controlling the whole electoral process.

It was the next phase of the interlinking Namibian independence settlement and Angolan peace accords that turned out to be one of the UN's greatest disasters in Africa.

Angola's first multiparty elections on Sept. 30, 1992, turned sour when rebel leader Jonas Savimbi rejected the results and returned to the bush, plunging the country back into a bitter civil war. The UN Angola Verification Mission (UN-AVEM II) was charged with monitoring and verifying a cease-fire, confinement and demobilization of troops, formation of a new defense force, disposal of weapons, and monitoring and verifying the electoral process.

In Mozambique, a UN peacekeeping force of about 7,500 is trying to learn from the mistakes of Angola and ensure that the implementation of a peace accord in Mozambique does not trigger renewed hostilities.

In retrospect, the reasons for both the success of the Namibian operation and the failure of its Angolan counterpart, UNAVEM II, are clear.

In Namibia, the ratio between UN personnel and inhabitants was 1 to 200; in Angola, that figure was 1 to 12,000. Perhaps the most important factors however, revolve around political will, the extent to which contending factions respect the election process, and the demobilization of opposing forces.

In Namibia, the political settlement was the outcome of more than a decade of painstaking negotiations and experiments in self-rule. This period in which South Africa equivocated on relinquishing its authority over its neighbor served as a prolonged transition to independence.

Once Pretoria made its decision, however, UN Special Representative Martii Ahtisaari quickly developed a relationship of trust with the South African administrator-general, despite Pretoria's contention of UN bias toward the former guerrilla movement, the South West Africa Peoples' Organization (SWAPO). South Africa's role in delivering the internal parties, which feared a SWAPO victory, was crucial and perhaps the most vital element missing in the Angolan equation.

'Unless the political will is there, the UN operations will inevitably become tangled up. . . .'
—a Western diplomat

The numbers of the UN mission in Angola were far too small and its resources hopelessly inadequate to demobilize the parties. The mission failed to ensure neutrality of the police, so it was easy for the rebel National Union for the Liberation of Angola (UNITA) to wage war in pursuit of their goal of political power. The UN failed to gain any meaningful rapprochement between the parties.

Some question the appointment, within the cultural context, of a refined British woman, though an able diplomat, as the director responsible for gaining the respect of hardened UNITA generals. Margaret Anstee herself points to the limited UN mandate to merely "verify and observe" the implementation of the Angolan accords and electoral process as "woefully inadequate."

There is little doubt, too, that the limited numbers and resources of UNAVEM II made it impossible to establish whether a proper demobilization of the opposing armies in Angola was taking place.

Ms. Anstee insists that the parties might have reached agreement on a cease-fire at talks in Abidjan in April if she had been able to commit the UN to providing a "small, symbolic force" of blue helmets to oversee an accord.

"I still believe that the only hope of achieving a peaceful solution in Angola is for the international community to break this vicious circle by providing such a symbolic presence," she wrote in a recent letter to The Daily Telegraph of London.

The UN Special Envoy in Mozambique, Aldo Ajello, insisted from the start of his term in December last year that he will not countenance embarking on the electoral process until demilitarization has been successfully completed.

He has already sanctioned a 12-month delay in the proposed date for the country's first multiparty elections now scheduled for October next year.

He also ensured that the UN operation, ONUMOZ, had a broader mandate and that ONUMOZ had the powers to disarm combatants and organize elections.

By coaxing the two Mozambican leaders into an eight-day meeting in August, Mr. Ajello acknowledged that only trust at the leadership level can lay the foundations for a positive UN intervention.

"Unless the political will is already there, the UN operations will inevitably become tangled up in internal conflicts," said a Western diplomat. "That's always a no-win situation."

—John Battersby

Apart from problems of defining missions and providing resources to carry them out, the UN has learned that root causes of conflicts can never be ignored. The lesson is clear that it is often impossible to accomplish one objective in isolation—whether it is supervising elections in Angola and Cambodia or feeding the starving in Somalia.

In Cambodia, a successful election was carried out, but the Khmer Rouge remains armed and in control of one-fifth of the country. The Angolan civil war has reached new levels of intensity since the vote. And while the hungry have been successfully fed in Somalia, UN officials say they must also deal with the political and social collapse that caused the problem or history may repeat itself.

UN diplomats now point to the need for more vigorous efforts in preventative diplomacy to halt potential conflicts at an earlier stage. The peacekeeping mission in Macedonia, aimed at curbing the spread of the Balkan conflict, is the first deployment of troops for that purpose.

Much still depends on increasing UN military professionalism and on being sure that real political commitment lies behind each Council threat.

"If the UN is seen as a paper tiger, full of Council resolutions with no teeth, it's going to be in big trouble," says Mr. Luck. "It's not going to be an effective instrument when we need it and want it most."

Poverty, population, pollution

One person in five lives in absolute poverty

Nafis Sadik

Nafis Sadik is Executive Director of the United Nations Population Fund (UNFPA), the world's largest source of multilateral assistance to population programmes. On her appointment in 1987, she became the first woman to head a major voluntary-funded UN programme. A physician of Pakistani nationality, she is the author of many articles in the field of family planning and health, and has edited a book Population: The UNFPA Experience *(New York University Press, 1984).*

The elimination of poverty is first and foremost a moral imperative; but it is also essential for the protection of the global environment and for the health of the global economy. On all these grounds, we can no longer tolerate a situation in which one in five human beings—a total of 1 billion people—lives in absolute poverty.

Protection of the environment is a requirement for ending poverty—a ruined and plundered resource base could not support our current and future numbers—and slower, more balanced population growth is both a precondition for, and an outcome of, finding solutions to the twin problems of the environment and poverty.

In the past, economic development was seen as the solution to poverty, and demographic transition as the eventual solution to population growth. Some damage to the environment was accepted as a necessary, but only marginally important, cost of development. These assumptions are no longer justified.

In many cases development has not only failed to eliminate poverty but has actually increased it, with deadly effects on population growth and environmental damage. For when development efforts are ineffective, they disrupt existing social and economic systems without providing compensating benefits. Even when development is effective it vastly increases human sources of pollution and environmental destruction. The industrial technology in use in most of the world was developed without thought for its environmental effects.

An unwanted side-effect of incomplete development has been to encourage rapid population growth. Mortality has fallen and life expectancy has risen, but there has been much less effect on birth rates. Increasing income and improving child survival leads in the first place to larger families. Only when development programmes include a family-planning element does family size fall significantly.

Another unintended side-effect of incomplete development has been massive and sustained urban growth. Classic development theory relies on the city as the engine of economic growth and therefore encourages urbanization. However, no one foresaw rates of urban growth of between 4 and 7 per cent such as are being seen now in many developing countries where urban growth has spiralled beyond control.

The crisis is produced as much by numbers and concentrations as by technologies and structures. This is a peculiarly difficult dilemma. If development is simply the replication of world experience to date, it condemns the environment, and therefore itself.

The keys to modern development

Education, health care and balanced population growth, with special attention to the status of women, are the keys to modern development. They also form a basis for the elimination of poverty and protection of the environment.

Developing countries' own resources of food and raw materials—and above all their human resources—are sufficient for balanced development, if they are exploited in a thoughtful way rather than for short-term gain. The aim of all who are committed to development must be to work towards the marriage of public policy with private interest and a full sense of community combined with respect for human rights and dignity.

There are many reasons why so many people are and remain so poor. One is the sheer scale of the problem; the poor are the fastest-growing segment of the population in any country and in the world as a whole. Another reason is that the

Courtesy of *The UNESCO Courier,* January 1992, 18-21.

poor are trapped in a vicious cycle where poverty, lack of education, lack of earning power, poor nutrition and poor health feed on each other. However the main reason for continuing, large-scale poverty is quite simple—the lack of a concerted will, nationally or internationally, to do something about it. Many promises have been made, but few have been kept. Many development theorists have pointed out that poverty can kill us all, but they have not been heeded. Ending poverty has simply not rated a high priority in most countries, whether industrialized or developing.

The poor themselves certainly have the will and the motivation to defeat their poverty. Anyone who has ever set foot in a slum, a poor village or a shanty-town knows what ingenuity, skill and effort go into the daily struggle to survive. We in government and the development business must learn not to get in the way. This is not the same as abdicating responsibility; consider how many ready-made anti-poverty programmes have come to grief because the poor were not involved in their design and execution; consider how many more have failed because they ran foul of some contradictory policy.

Consider in particular how women have been excluded and how their contribution to the national and local economy and society has been undermined by schemes with the word "development" in their titles. The pattern is so consistent across continents and levels of development that it is difficult not to conclude that the intention was to exclude women from the new society and to keep them safely at home with the children.

Community involvement

Experience shows that the successful grass-roots development programmes are those which respond to national needs through local action and involve both men and women, rich and poor. For national policy to succeed, effective and appropriate services must be delivered locally and at the family level. Even more important, families and communities must be involved in the policy-making and management process.

There is considerable scepticism today about the ability of governments to deliver development services to the poor and even more about governments' ability to involve communities in decision-making, although in most countries this has scarcely been given a fair trial. Where governments are committed—

as, for example, in Sri Lanka, or in Costa Rica—the experience has certainly been that services such as education, health care, family planning, agricultural extension and even housing can be delivered with community co-operation. Recent reports say that the State of Kerala, in India, has achieved universal literacy—largely through a combination of official and community action.

The other aspect of service delivery is, of course, self-help. The poor are almost completely self-reliant, because they have no one else to rely on. Considering what they achieve with so few resources, it should come as no surprise that they can do a great deal when resources are more plentiful. With small amounts of outside help and organization, shanty communities in Sri Lanka have made themselves the model for a national self-help housing programme. The Grameen Bank in Bangladesh is a famous example of success in extending credit to the poor.

Can successful community-based experience be transferred to productive areas of the economy, for example to industry or agricultural policy? A growing number of economists and other analysts of the development process now think so. If, for example, the supply of water for irrigation is controlled and paid for by user groups, the result is that less water is used and it is used more effectively.

The mix depends upon the country and the community. Flexibility is the key to a successful approach. Above all, understanding that improving services to the poor is an important development goal must be inculcated at all levels. The banking industry in Indonesia was very sceptical about making loans to women's groups, but it has been shown that with outside funding women's groups will both repay on time and make profitable investments. Commercial banks are now much more enthusiastic about such business.

If the global importance of small-scale development is to be recognized, the big organizations—inter-governmental groups, multilateral agencies, international policy-making institutions—must give it their seal of approval. It is very difficult for the very big to see the very small, but it is important for them to learn. There are too many examples of massive, internationally-funded development projects that have ended in expensive, environmentally dangerous and socially catastrophic failure.

A role for the United Nations

The United Nations system is being given more work to do in the post-

–cold war era. The system has already proved its value as a neutral forum for discussion of different approaches to development. It has proved its value as a channel for development assistance which is not tied to one ideology or approach. Greater resources are now needed so that the system can work towards a new international consensus on the shape of development.

Even more important, perhaps, than resources for the future effectiveness of the United Nations system will be a clearer sense of direction. The United Nations is an inter-governmental system and, in the end, governments decide how effective they want it to be. It is quite clear that the various parts of the system need better co-ordination. It is equally clear that our agencies and their mandates, their political direction and their management, are fragmented and need to be reviewed and revised so as to meet the needs of the next century. After three development decades, the best we can say—and it is a considerable boast—is that we have survived. We are supporting the largest number of humans ever to have inhabited the planet at one time. We have escaped nuclear war and we seem to have reassessed the risks of nuclear meltdown. The United Nations has not collapsed, blown apart or withered away. Some of our institutions are stronger than before and some of them have learned how to work effectively. There is international consensus on the need for action to protect the environment, even if there is disagreement as to what that action should be. There is a very strong and practical consensus on the need for slower, more balanced population growth worldwide.

There seems to be an even chance that the female half of the population will get its share of development investment in the future and be allowed to make a full contribution to development work. The international community may come to understand that enabling the poor to escape poverty may be the key to survival for the rest of us.

Deceptive Stereotypes About "Tribal Warfare"

Neil L. Whitehead and R. Brian Ferguson

Neil L. Whitehead is assistant professor of anthropology at the University of Wisconsin at Madison, and R. Brian Ferguson is associate professor of sociology, anthropology, and criminal justice at Rutgers University in Newark.

Who would have imagined the current nostalgia for the cold war? We lived with the threat of imminent nuclear destruction for decades, but at least the battle lines seemed clear. East versus West, Communism versus capitalism. Any brushfire war, anywhere in the world, could be forced into this mold. To be sure, this interpretation blinded us to many realities, but at least it was tidy.

That sense of order is missing today. The great polarity has evaporated, and we are left with proliferating local conflicts that seem to be getting more savage all the time. Groping for a framework to make sense of the carnage, pundits and politicians are tapping into old ideological currents about "tribal warfare." These explanations, however, are contradicted by much recent research. Rather than illuminating the wellsprings of violence, they only muddy the waters.

The human species is held to be inherently tribalistic. We are said to cleave to others like "us" and to react with unreasoned fear and hostility to "them." Humans form tribes, it is said, and the relations between tribes are hostile. Applied to recent outbreaks of violence around the world, the concept of tribalism suggests that a weakening of control by central governments allows an upsurge of primal antagonisms. The violence seems to erupt from the people themselves.

These views are based on mistaken, but deeply ingrained, ideas about the origin and nature of tribes. "Tribe" itself is a loaded term. In the rhetoric of European expansionism during the heyday of colonialism, it was used as a disparaging label for indigenous peoples whose political organization did not exhibit the hierarchical, centralized authority of a state. In this pejorative sense, *tribal* was contrasted with *civilized*.

But tribe also refers to a genuine kind of polity, a group that anthropologists describe as being bounded and distinct from its neighbors to some degree, capable of a measure of coordinated political action, yet lacking a stratified central structure. Many indigenous people do not exhibit this cohesion, their highest sovereign units being families or more extended groups of kin.

But true tribes often were created in the areas that European colonialists governed, in response to a gradual process of colonial expansion during the past 500 years. For example, the Mohegans emerged out of Algonquian populations in New England to become a distinctive tribe by taking sides in 17th-century colonial wars.

Frequently, tribal peoples have engaged in brutal, horribly destructive wars, a direct inspiration for Hobbes's "war of all against all." The loudly trumpeted mission of Europe's colonialists was to put a stop to such carnage, to "pacify the savages."

The problem with this interpretation is that, in cases from all over the world, comparing the *earliest* reports of European contact with indigenous peoples to later reports shows that tribal warfare sometimes was absent when the Europeans first arrived, or a least was much less intensive than it was after they appeared. Perhaps more astonishing, the tribes that are so prominent in later accounts often were unrecognizable as tribes when the Europeans initially arrived.

The central point in the volume that we recently edited, *War in the Tribal Zone* (School of American Research Press, 1992), is that both the transformation and intensification of war, as well as the formation of tribes, result from complex interactions in an area that we call "the tribal zone." The zone begins at the points where centralized authority makes contact with peoples it does not rule. In tribal zones, newly introduced plants, animals, diseases, and technologies often spread widely, long before the colonizers appear. These and other changes disrupt existing sociopolitical relationship, fostering new alliances and creating new kinds of conflicts.

Thus, life and war on the American Great Plains took on an entirely new cast when smallpox, horses, guns, and displaced peoples arrived from distant frontiers. The arrival of priests, traders, soldiers, and settlers in a tribal zone always complicated circumstances and often encouraged new kinds of wars (for example, as various tribes took different sides against rival colonial powers), along with new patterns of trade and political alliances. The new people who arrived had trouble dealing with the lack of boundaries and the independence of the native peoples that they encountered, so they encouraged the formation of politically unified groups–tribes. Even without such direct encouragement, the extreme conflict frequently generated by the arrival of colonialists promoted tribalization, as local people were compelled to band together just to survive.

To be sure, both warfare and tribes have existed for a very long time in human history. But the often-horrifying tribal bloodshed that was, and continues to be, used to justify the expansion of European control in most cases was a reaction to a colonial presence. Thus, research done by one of us shows that the formation of a distinctive Carib people in northern South America, and the devastating warfare reported in the region, was a response to the initial bloody colonization by rival Spanish and Dutch powers from the 16th through the 18th centuries.

Research by the other author on the Yanomani of the remote borderlands of Brazil and Venezuela, who often are said to be one of the most violent peoples on earth, shows that their violence is tightly connected in timing, targets, and intensity to changes in the presence of Westerners stretching back for centuries.

How is this relevant to contemporary conflicts? We are in danger of allowing our misunderstanding of tribal conflict, a misunderstanding that is a product of our own cultural history, to prevent us from grasping the real causes of contemporary violence in various countries.

To speak of "ancient tribal hatreds," as many observers of conflicts in Somalia and in the former Yugoslavia have done, invokes an image of timeless, unchangeable political oppositions. In fact, tribal boundaries are highly changeable; they can arise, dissolve, or shift as a result of diverse circumstances. Labeling current conflicts as tribal also promotes the idea that violent conflict is a predictable outgrowth of cultural differences between groups. In fact, tribes often are from identical cultures, and cultural difference itself is a very poor predictor of violent conflict–just as cultural homogeneity is not necessarily a predictor of peace. Consider the fact that Somalia is one of the most culturally homogeneous states in all of sub-Saharan Africa.

To invoke tribal warfare in areas such as the former Yugoslavia is especially misleading. The essence of tribal political organization and of real tribal warfare is that it is based on extensive discussion and consensus among local leaders. In the Balkans, authoritarian leaders give the orders. If the fighting has become increasingly polarized along cultural lines, it is because self-aggrandizing heads of state have deliberately played on existing cultural differences. When soldiers who have been encouraged to think of themselves as defenders of one ethnic group are ordered to rape women of another, ethnic hatred will grow. It is clear that ancient animosities do exist in the culture of the region, but these seeds of violence only blossom when they are cultivated by politicians.

Another danger is that we may accept the stereotypical assumption that tribal warfare is irrational, perhaps even an expression of atavistic biological impulses. In contrast, close study of the decision making involved in genuine tribal warfare usually reveals canny strategizing about very tangible interests. Moreover, the main circumstances shaping tribal military decisions are rarely purely local, as is often claimed, but instead involve the connections between local groups and the outside world. Very frequently, the fighting is about who will benefit more or suffer less from ties to colonial power centers. Thus, from the 17th-century Mohawk Indians to the 20th-century Yanomani, wars have been fought to gain monopolistic control over the physical space around Western colonial outposts and missions.

These observations suggest how we should understand war in places such as Somalia. A variety of power bases exist, growing out of the local organization of subsistence and exchange, but also shaped by a long history of political interactions with foreign governments. The ruling groups in Somalia were supported by the superpowers during the cold war, the abandoned. United Nations forces now have become entangled in this political web, becoming identified with one side against another in a conflict where the sides themselves are defined largely by the nature of their relationship with outside powers. For example, in this complex political field, Ali Mahdi Mohammed has been the most prominent leader aligned with United Nations forces, and Mohammed Farah Aidid has been painted as the U.N.'s foe, even though earlier he had also cooperated with and benefited from the U.N. presence.

A broad-ranging debate over the newly elevated principle of "humanitarian intervention" is just beginning. The issue will be with us for years, if not in Somalia or Bosnia, then somewhere else. It is a confounding issue, and each case will be disquietingly unique. But our understanding will always be clouded if we view local wars as eruptions of primitive tribal animosities. A better conception is that violence emerges and is structured by the intersection of local and external forces. Any act of humanitarian intervention will itself become a part of the interplay. If such interventions continue in Somalia or elsewhere, we must recognize and continually monitor their effects— and that means avoiding deceptive stereotypes about tribal wars.

Abbreviations

ABM: Antiballistic Missile
ACC: Arab Cooperation Council
ADP: African Development Bank
ALCM: Air-Launched Cruise Missile
ANC: African National Congress (South Africa)
APEC: Asia-Pacific Economic Cooperation
ASAT: Anti-Satellite
ASEAN: Association of Southeast Asian Nations
ASW: Anti-Submarine Warfare (DOD)
AWACS: Airborne Warning and Control Systems
bbl: Barrel
BMD: Ballistic Missile Defense
C³ (C-cubed): Command, Control, Communications
CAP: Common Agricultural Policy (EC's)
CARICOM: Caribbean Community
CBN: Chemical, biological, or nuclear weapons
CDU: Christian Democratic Union
CENTO: Central Treaty Organization
CFCs: Chlorofluorocarbons
CFE: Conventional Forces in Europe
CFE: Conventional Forces in Europe
CIA: Central Intelligence Agency (U.S.)
CIS: Commonwealth of Independent States
CMEA: Council on Mutual Economic Assistance
CNN: Cable News Network
COCOM: Coordinating Committee for Multilateral Export Control
COMINT: Communication Intelligence
CSCE: Conference on Security and Cooperation in Europe
CSU: Christian Social Union
CTB: Comprehensive Nuclear Test Ban Treaty
CWC: Chemical Weapons Convention
DARPA: Defense Advanced Research Projects Administration
DOD: Department of Defense
DPRK: Democratic People's Republic of Korea
EBRDEE: European Bank for Reconstruction and Development in Eastern Europe
EC: European Community; renamed EU in 1993
ECOSOC: Economic and Social Council (UN)
ECU: European Currency Unit
EEC: European Economic Community
EFTA: European Free Trade Association
EMS: European Monetary System
EMU: European Monetary Unification
ERM: Exchange-Rate Mechanism
ERP: European Recovery Plan (Marshall Plan)
EU: European Union
FAO: Food and Agricultural Organization (UN)
FDP: Free Democratic Party
FIS: Islamic Salvation Front
FLN: National Liberation Front
FMLN: Farabundo Marti National Liberation Front
FTA: Free Trade Agreement
FUNCINPEK: National United Front for an Independent, Neutral, Peaceful, and Cooperative Cambodia
G-77: Group of 77
GATT: General Agreement on Tariffs and Trade
GCC: Gulf Cooperation Council
GDP: Gross Domestic Product
GNP: Gross National Product
GPALS: Global Protection Against Limited Strikes
IAEA: International Atomic Energy Agency
IAS: Inter-American System
ICJ: International Court of Justice
ICBM: Intercontinental Ballistic Missile
IDA: International Development Association (World Bank)
IDB: Inter-American Development Bank
IFC: International Finance Corporation (World Bank)
IFP: Inkatha Freedom Party (South Africa)
IGO: Intergovernmental Organization
IMF: International Monetary Fund
INF: Intermediate-Range Nuclear Forces

IRP: Islamic Renaissance Party
ITO: International Trade Organization
KPNLF: Khmer People's National Liberation Front (Cambodia)
LDC: Less Developed Country
LDP: Liberal Democratic Party
LLDC: Least Developed Countries
MERCOSUR: Southern Cone Common Market
MFN: Most Favored Nation
MIRV: Multiple Independently Targetable Re-Entry Vehicle
MNC: Multinational Corporation
MTCR: Missile Technology Control Regime
NAFTA: North American Free Trade Agreement
NATO: North Atlantic Treaty Organization
NES: National Energy Strategy
NGO: Nongovernmental Organization
NIEO: New International Economic Order
NORAD: North American Aerospace Defense Command
NP: Nationalist Party (South Africa)
NPT: Non-Proliferation Treaty
NSA: National Security Agency
NSC: National Security Council
NTM: National Technical Means
NWFZ: Nuclear Weapons-Free Zone (Middle East)
NWO: New World Order
OAS: Organization of American States
OAPEC: Organization of Arab Petroleum Exporting Countries
OAU: Organization of African Unity
OECD: Organization for Economic Cooperation and Development
OPEC: Organization of Petroleum Exporting Countries
OSIA: On-Site Inspection Agency
PDS: Party of Democratic Socialism
PLA: People's Liberation Army
PLO: Palestine Liberation Organization
PRC: People's Republic of China
PSI: Project Services International
SAC: Strategic Air Command (DOD)
SACEUR: Supreme Allied Commander in Europe (NATO)
SACP: South African Communist Party
SACU: Southern Africa Customs Union
SALT: Strategic Arms Limitation Talks
SAP: Structural Adjustment Program
SDI: Strategic Defense Initiative
SEATO: Southeast Asia Treaty Organization
SELA: Latin American Economic System
SEZ: Special Economic Zone (China)
SOP: Standard Operating Procedures
SPD: Social Democratic Party
SSBN: Submersible Ballistic Nuclear (Nuclear Ballistic Missile Submarine)
START: Strategic Arms Reduction Treaty
SWAPO: South West Africa Peoples' Organization
UNAMIC: UN Advance Mission in Cambodia
UN: United Nations
UNAVEM II: UN Angola Verification Mission
UNCTAD: United Nations Conference on Trade and Development
UNESCO: UN Educational, Scientific, and Cultural Organization
UNICEF: UN Children's Fund
UNIDO: UN Industrial Development Programme
UNITAR: UN Institute for Training and Research
UNO: United Nations Organization (the whole UN system)
UNOSOM: UN Operation for Somalia
UNPAAERD: United Nations Programme of Action for African Economic Recovery and Development
UNPROFOR: UN Protection Force
UNSC: United Nations Security Council
UNTAK: UN Transitional Authority in Cambodia
WEU: Western European Union
WHO: World Health Organization
WFC: World Food Council
ZPG: Zero Population Growth

This glossary contains primarily technical, economic, financial, and military terminology not usually defined in most World Politics textbooks.

— A —

Absolute poverty: The condition of people whose incomes are insufficient to keep them at a subsistence level.

Adjudication: The legal process of deciding an issue through the courts.

African, Caribbean, and Pacific Countries (ACP): Fifty-eight countries associated with the European Community.

African National Congress (ANC): South African organization founded in 1912 in response to the taking of land from Africans and the restrictions on their employment and movement. Following attempts at peaceful resistance, its leaders were tried for treason and imprisoned. In 1990, ANC de facto leader Nelson Mandela was released from prison, and a continued resistance against the apartheid state grew. The ANC was legalized in 1991.

Airborne Warning and Control System (AWACS): Flying radar stations that instantaneously identify all devices in the air within a radius of 240 miles and detect movement of land vehicles.

Air-Launched Cruise Missile (ALCM): A cruise missile carried by and launched from an aircraft.

Antiballistic missile (ABM): A missile that seeks out and destroys an incoming enemy missile in flight before the latter reaches its target. It is not effective against MIRVs.

Apartheid: A system of laws in the Republic of South Africa that segregates and politically and economically discriminates against non-European groups.

Appropriate technology: Also known as intermediate technology. It aims at using existing resources by making their usage more efficient or productive but adaptable to the local population.

Arms control: Any measure limiting or reducing forces, regulating armaments, and/or restricting the deployment of troops or weapons.

Arms race: The competitive or cumulative improvement of weapons stocks (qualitatively or quantitatively), or the buildup of armed forces based on the conviction of two or more actors that only by trying to stay ahead in military power can they avoid falling behind.

Association of Southeast Asian Nations (ASEAN): A regional regrouping made up of Indonesia, the Philippines, Singapore, and Thailand.

Atomic bomb: A weapon based on the rapid splitting of fissionable materials, thereby inducing an explosion with three deadly results: blast, heat, and radiation.

Autarky: Establishing economic independence.

— B —

Balance of payments: A figure that represents the net flow of money into and out of a country due to trade, tourist expenditures, sale of services (such as consulting), foreign aid, profits, and so forth.

Balance of trade: The relationship between imports and exports.

Ballistic missile: A payload propelled by a rocket, which assumes a free-fall trajectory when thrust is terminated. Ballistic missiles could be of short range (SRBM), intermediate range (IRBM), medium range (MRBM), and intercontinental (ICBM).

Bantustans: Ten designated geographical areas or "homelands" for each African ethnic group created under the apartheid government of South Africa. Beginning in the late 1970s, South Africa instituted a policy offering "independence" to the tribal leaders of these homelands. The leaders of four homeland governments accepted independent status, but no outside actors recognized these artificial entities as independent nation-states. Under the terms of the new constitution, all homeland citizens are now considered to be citizens of South Africa.

Barrel: A standard measure for petroleum, equivalent to 42 gallons or 158.86 liters.

Basic human needs: Adequate food intake (in terms of calories, proteins, and vitamins), drinking water free of disease-carrying organisms and toxins, minimum clothing and shelter, literacy, sanitation, health care, employment, and dignity.

Bilateral diplomacy: Negotiations between two countries.

Bilateral (foreign) aid: Foreign aid given by one country directly to another.

Binary (chemical) munitions/weapons: Nerve gas canisters composed of two separate chambers containing chemicals that become lethal when mixed. The mixing is done when the canister is fired. Binary gas is preferred for its relative safety in storage and transportation.

Biosphere: The environment of life and living processes at or near Earth's surface, extending from the ocean floors to about 75 kilometers into the atmosphere. It is being endangered by consequences of human activities such as air and water pollution, acid rain, radioactive fallout, desertification, toxic and nuclear wastes, and the depletion of nonrenewable resources.

Bipolar system: A world political system in which power is primarily held by two international actors.

Buffer Stocks: Reserves of commodities that are either increased or decreased whenever necessary to maintain relative stability of supply and prices.

— C —

Camp David Agreements/Accords: Agreements signed on September 17, 1978, at Camp David—a mountain retreat for the U.S. president in Maryland—by President Anwar al-Sadat of Egypt and Prime Minister Menachem Begin of Israel, and witnessed by President Jimmy Carter.

Capitalism: An economic system based on the private ownership of real property and commercial enterprise, competition for profits, and limited government interference in the marketplace.

Cartel: An international agreement among producers of a commodity that attempts to control the production and pricing of that commodity.

CBN weapons: Chemical, biological, and nuclear weapons.

Chemical Weapons Convention Treaty: Signed in 1993, the treaty requires its 130 signatories to eliminate all chemical weapons by the year 2005 and to submit to rigorous inspection.

Cold war: A condition of hostility that existed between the U.S. and the Soviet Union in their struggle to dominate the world scene following World War II. It ended with the collapse of the Soviet Union in 1991.

Collective security: The original theory behind UN peacekeeping. It holds that aggression against one state is aggression against all and should be defeated by the collective action of all.

Commodity: The unprocessed products of mining and agriculture.

Common Heritage of Mankind: A 1970 UN declaration that states that the "seabed and ocean floor, and the subsoil thereof, beyond the limits of national jurisdiction . . . , as well as the resources of the area, are the common heritage of mankind."

Common Market: A customs union that eliminates trade barriers within a group and establishes a common external tariff on imports from nonmember countries.

Commonwealth of Independent States (CIS): In December 1991 the Soviet Union was dissolved and fifteen independent countries were formed: Armenia, Azerbaijan, Byelorussia (Belarus), Estonia, Georgia, Kazakhstan, Kirghizia (Kyrgyzstan), Latvia, Lithuania, Moldavia (Moldova), Russia, Tadzhikistan (Tajikistan), Turkmenistan, Ukraine, and Uzbekistan. Some of the republics have since changed their names. CIS represents a collective term for the group of republics.

Compensatory Financing Facility: An IMF program established in 1963 to finance temporary export shortfalls, as in coffee, sugar, or other cyclically prone export items.

Concessional loans: Loans given to LLDCs by MBDs that can be repaid in soft (nonconvertible) currencies and with nominal or no interest over a long period of time.

Conditionality: A series of measures that must be taken by a country before it could qualify for loans from the International Monetary Fund.

Conference on International Economic Cooperation (CIEC): A conference of 8 industrial nations, 7 oil-producing nations, and 12 developing countries held in several sessions between December 1975 and June 1977. It is composed of four separate commissions (energy, raw materials, development, and financing). It is the forum of the North-South dialogue between rich and poor countries.

Conference on Security and Cooperation in Europe (CSCE): Series of conferences among 34 NATO, former Soviet bloc, and neutral European countries. Established by 1976 Helsinki Accords. There are plans to establish a small, permanent CSCE headquarters and staff.

Consensus: In conference diplomacy, a way of reacing agreements by negotiations and without a formal vote.

Counterforce: The use of strategic nuclear weapons for strikes on selected military capabilities of an enemy force.

Countervalue: The use of strategic nuclear weapons for strikes on an enemy's population centers.

Cruise missile: A small, highly maneuverable, low-flying, pilotless aircraft equipped with accurate guidance systems that periodically readjusts its trajectory. It can carry conventional or nuclear warheads, can be short-range or long-range, and can be launched from the air (ALLUM), the ground (GLCM), or the sea (SLCM).

Cultural imperialism: The attempt to impose your own value systems on others, including judging others by how closely they conform to your norms.

Current dollars: The value of the dollar in the year for which it is being reported. Sometimes called inflated dollars. Any currency can be expressed in current value. *See* **Real dollars.**

— D —

Decision making: The process by which humans choose which policy to pursue and which actions to take in support of policy goals. The study of decision making seeks to identify patterns in the way that humans make decisions. This includes gathering information, analyzing information, and making choices. Decision making is a complex process that relates to personality and other human traits, to the sociopolitical setting in which decision makers function, and to the organizational structures involved.

Declaration of Talloires: A statement issued in 1981 by Western journalists who opposed the UNESCO-sponsored New World Information and Communication Order, at a meeting in Talloires, France.

Delivery systems or Vehicles or Launchers: Land-Based Missiles (ICBMs), Submarine-Launched Missiles (SLBMs), and long-range bombers capable of delivering nuclear weapons.

Dependencia model: The belief that the industrialized North has created a neocolonial relationship with the South in which the LDCs are dependent on and disadvantaged by their economic relations with the capitalist industrial countries.

Deployment: The actual positioning of weapons systems in a combat-ready status.

Détente: A relaxation of tensions or a decrease in the level of hostility between opponents on the world scene.

Deterrence: Persuading an opponent not to attack by having enough forces to disable the attack and/or launch a punishing counterattack.

Developed Countries (DCs): Countries with relatively high per capita GNP, education, levels of industrial development and production, health and welfare, and agricultural productivity.

Developing Countries (also called Less Developed Countries): These countries are mainly raw materials producers for export with high growth rates and inadequate infrastructures in transportation, educational systems, and the like. There is, however, a wide variation in living standards, GNPs, and per capita incomes among LCDs.

Development: The process through which a society becomes increasingly able to meet basic human needs and ensure the physical quality of life of its people.

Direct investment: Buying stock, real estate, and other assets in another country with the aim of gaining a controlling interest in foreign economic enterprises. Different from portfolio investment, which involves investment solely to gain capital appreciation through market fluctuations.

Disinformation: The spreading of false propaganda and forged documents to confuse counterintelligence or to create political confusion, unrest, and scandal.

Dumping: A special case of price discrimination, selling to foreign buyers at a lower price than that charged to buyers in the home market.

Duty: Special tax applied to imported goods, based on tariff rates and schedules.

— E —

East (as in the East-West Struggle): A shorthand, nongeographic term that included nonmarket, centrally planned (communist) countries.

East-West Axis: The cold war conflict between the former Soviet Union and its allies and the United States and its allies.

Economic Cooperation among Developing Countries (ECDC): Also referred to as intra-South, or South-South cooperation, it is a way for LCDs to help each other with appropriate technology.

Economic statecraft: The practice of states utilizing economic instruments, such as sanctions, to gain their political ends. Economic statecraft is closely related to "mercantilism," or the use of political power to advance a country's economic fortunes.

Economically Developing Countries (EDCs): The relatively wealthy and industrialized countries that lie mainly in the Northern Hemisphere (the North).

Escalation: Increasing the level of fighting.

Essential equivalence: Comparing military capabilities of two would-be belligerents, not in terms of identical mix of forces, but in terms of how well two dissimilarly organized forces could achieve a strategic stalemate.

Eurodollars: U.S. dollar holdings of European banks; a liability for the U.S. Treasury.

Euromissiles: Shorthand for long-range theatre nuclear forces stationed in Europe or aimed at targets in Europe.

Europe 1992: A term that represents the European Community's decision to eliminate by the end of 1992 all internal barriers (between member countries) to the movement of trade, financial resources, workers, and services (banking, insurance, etc.).

European Community (EC): The Western European regional organization established in 1967 that includes the European Coal and Steel Community (ECSC), the European Economic Community (EEC), and the European Atomic Energy Community (EURATOM).

European Currency Unit (ECU): The common unit of valuation among the eight members of the European Monetary System (EMS).

European Economic Community (EEC): The regional trade and economic organizaiton established in Western Europe by the Treaty of Rome in 1958; also known as the Common Market. Founded in 1957 by France, West Germany, Italy, Belgium, the Netherlands, and Luxembourg for the purpose of economic integration. It was joined in 1973 by the United Kingdom, Ireland, and Denmark, and in 1981 by Greece. Spain and Portugal have also applied for membership. Its main features include a common external tariff, a customs union on industrial goods, and a Common Agricultural Policy. Full economic and monetary union remains an objective.

European Free Trade Association (EFTA): Austria, Finland, Iceland, Liechtenstein, Norway, Portugal, Sweden, and Switzerland. Each member keeps its own external tariff schedule, but free trade prevails among the members.

European Monetary System (EMS): Established in 1979 as a preliminary stage toward an economic and monetary union in the European Community. Fluctuations in the exchange rate value of the currencies of the participating countries are kept with a $2^{1}/_{4}$ percent limit of divergence from the strongest currency among them. The system collapsed in 1993, thus slowing progress toward monetary integration in Europe.

European Union. *See* **European Economic Community.**

Exchange rate: The values of two currencies relative to each other—for example, how many yen equal a dollar or how many lira equal a pound.

Export subsidies: Special incentives, including direct payments to exporters, to encourage increased foreign sales.

Exports: Products shipped to foreign countries.

— F —

Finlandization: A condition of nominal neutrality, but one of actual subservience to the former Soviet Union in foreign and security policies, as is the case with Finland.

First strike: The first offensive move of a general nuclear war. It implies an intention to knock out the opponent's ability to retaliate.

Fissionable or nuclear materials: Isotopes of certain elements, such as plutonium, thorium, and uranium, that emit neutrons in such large numbers that a sufficient concentration will be self-sustaining until it explodes.

Foreign policy: The sum of a country's goals and actions on the world stage. The study of foreign policy is synonymous with state-level analysis and examines how countries define their interests, establish goals, decide on specific policies, and attempt to implement those policies.

Forward based system (FBS or FoBS): A military installation, maintained on foreign soil or in international waters, and conveniently located near a theatre of war.

Fourth World: An expression arising from the world economic crisis that began in 1973–74 with the quadrupling in price of petroleum. It encompasses the least developed countries (LLDCs) and the most seriously affected countries (MSAs).

Free trade: The international movement of goods unrestricted by tariffs or nontariff barriers.

Functionalism: International cooperation in specific areas such as communications, trade, travel, health, or environmental protection activity. Often symbolized by the specialized agencies, such as the World Health Organization, associated with the United Nations.

— G —

General Agreement on Tariffs and Trade (GATT): Created in 1947, this organizaiton is the major global forum for negotiations of tariff reductions and other measures to expand world trade. Its members account for four-fifths of the world's trade.

General Assembly: The main representative body of the United Nations, composed of all member states.

Generalized System of Preferences (GSP): A system approved by GATT in 1971, which authorizes DCs to give preferential traiff treatment to LCDs.

Global: Pertaining to the world as a whole; worldwide.

Global commons: The Antarctic, the ocean floor under international waters, and celestial bodies within reach of planet Earth. All of these areas and bodies are considered the common heritage of mankind.

Global Negotiations: A new round of international economic negotiations started in 1980 over raw materials, energy, trade, development, money, and finance.

Golan Heights: Syrian territory adjacent to Israel that occupied it since the 1967 war and that annexed it unilaterally in 1981 in the UN demilitarized zone.

Gross Domestic Product (GDP): A measure of income within a country that excludes foreign earnings.

Gross National Product (GNP): A measure of the sum of all goods and services produced by a country's nationals, whether they are in the country or abroad.

Group of Seven (G-7): The seven economically largest free market countries: Canada, France, Great Britain, Italy, Japan, the United States, and Germany.

Group of 77: Group of 77 Third World countries that cosponsored the Joint Declaration of Developing Countries in 1963 calling for greater equity in North-South trade. This group has come to include more than 120 members and represents the interests of the less developed countries of the South.

— H —

Hegemonism: Any attempt by a larger power to interfere, threaten, intervene against, and dominate a smaller power or a region of the world.

Hegemony: Domination by a major power over smaller, subordinate ones within its sphere of influence.

Helsinki Agreement. *See* **Conference on Security and Cooperation in Europe.**

Horn of Africa: The northeast corner of Africa that includes Ethiopia, Djibouti, and Somalia. It is separated from the Arabian peninsula by the Gulf of Aden and the Red Sea. It is plagued with tribal conflicts between Ethiopia and Eritrea, and between Ethiopia and Somalia over the Ogaden desert. These conflicts have generated a large number of refugees who have been facing mass starvation.

Human rights: Rights inherent to human beings, including but not limited to the right of dignity; the integrity of the person; the inviolability of the person's body and mind; civil and political rights (freedom of religion, speech, press, assembly, association, the right to privacy, habeas corpus, due process of law, the right to vote or not to vote, the right to run for election, and the right to be protected from reprisals for acts of peaceful dissent); social, economic, and cultural rights. The most glaring violations of human rights are torture, disappearance, and the general phenomenon of state terrorism.

— I —

Imports: Products brought into a country from abroad.

Inkatha Freedom Party (IFP): A Zulu-based political and cultural movement led by Mangosuthu Buthelezi. It is a main rival of the African National Congress in South Africa.

Innocent passage: In a nation's territorial sea, passage by a foreign ship is innocent so long as it is not prejudicial to the peace, good order, or security of the coastal state. Submarines must surface and show their flag.

Intercontinental Ballistic Missile (ICBM): A land-based, rocket-propelled vehicle capable of delivering a warhead to targets at 6,000 or more nautical miles.

Interdependence (economic): The close interrelationship and mutual dependence of two or more domestic economies on each other.

Intergovernmental organizations (IGOs): International/transnational actors composed of member countries.

Intermediate-range Ballistic Missile (IRBM): A missile with a range from 1,500 to 4,000 nautical miles.

Intermediate-range Nuclear Forces: Nuclear arms that are based in Europe with a deployment range that easily encompasses the former USSR.

Intermediate-range Nuclear Forces Treaty (INF): The treaty between the former USSR and the United States that limits the dispersion of nuclear warheads in Europe.

International: Between or among sovereign states.

International Atomic Energy Agency (IAEA): An agency created in 1946 by the UN to limit the use of nuclear technology to peaceful purposes.

International Court of Justice (ICJ): The World Court, which sits in The Hague with 15 judges and which is associated with the United Nations.

International Development Association (IDA): An affiliate of the World Bank that provides interest-free, long-term loans to developing countries.

International Energy Agency (IEA): An arm of OECD that attempts to coordinate member countries' oil imports and reallocate stocks among members in case of disruptions in the world's oil supply.

International Finance Corporation: Created in 1956 to finance overseas investments by private companies without necessarily requiring government guarantees. The IFC borrows from the World Bank, provides loans, and invests directly in private industry in the development of capital projects.

International Monetary Fund (IMF): The world's primary organization devoted to maintaining monetary stability by helping countries fund balance-of-payments deficits. Established in 1947, it now has 170 members.

International political economy (IPE): A term that encapsulates the totality of international economic interdependence and exchange in the political setting of the international system. Trade, investment, monetary relations, transnational business activities, aid, loans, and other aspects of international economic interchange (and the reciprocal impacts between these activities and politics) are all part of the study of IPE.

Interstate: International, intergovernmental.

Intifada (literally, resurgence): A series of minor clashes between Palestinian youths and Israeli security forces that escalated into a full-scale revolt in December 1987.

Intra-South. *See* **Economic Cooperation among Developing Countries.**

Islamic fundamentalism: Early nineteenth-century movements of fundamentalism sought to revitalize Islam through internal reform, thus enabling Islamic societies to resist foreign control. Some of these movements sought peaceful change, while other were more militant. The common ground of twentieth-century reform movements and groups is their fundamental opposition to the onslaught of materialistic Western culture and their desire to reassert a distinct Islamic identity for the societies they claim to represent.

— K —

Kampuchea: The new name for Cambodia since April 1975.

KGB: Security police and intelligence apparatus in the former Soviet Union, engaged in espionage, counterespionage, antisubversion, and control of political dissidents.

Khmer Rouge: Literally "Red Cambodians," the communist organization ruling Kampuchea between April 1975 and January 1979 under Pol Pot and Leng Saray.

Kiloton: A thousand tons of explosive force. A measure of the yield of a nuclear weapon equivalent to 1,000 tons of TNT (trinitrotoluene). The bomb detonated at Hiroshima in World War II had an approximate yield of 14 kilotons.

— L —

Launcher. *See* **Delivery Systems.**

League of Nations: The first true general international organization. It existed between the end of World War I and the beginning of World War II and was the immediate predecessor of the United Nations.

Least Developed Countries: Those countries in the poorest of economic circumstances. Frequently it includes those countries with a per capita GNP of less than $400 in 1985 dollars.

Less Developed Countries (LDCs): Countries, located mainly in Africa, Asia, and Latin America, with economies that rely heavily on the production of agriculture and raw material and whose per capita GNP and standard of living are substantially below Western standards.

Linkage diplomacy: The practice of considering another country's general international behavior as well as the specifics of the question when deciding whether or not to reach an agreement on an issue.

Lisbon Protocal: Signed in 1992, it is an agreement between ex-Soviet republics Kazakhstan and Belarus to eliminate nuclear weapons from their territories.

Lome Convention: An agreement concluded between the European Community and 58 African, Caribbean, and Pacific countries (ACP), allowing the latter preferential trade relations and greater economic and technical assistance.

Long-Range Theatre Nuclear Forces (LRTNF): Nuclear weapon systems with a range greater than 1,000 kilometers (or 600 miles), such as the U.S. Persing II missile or the Soviet SS-20.

— M —

Maastricht Treaty: Signed by the European Community's 12-member countries in December 1991, the Maastricht Treaty outlines steps toward further political/economic integration. At this time, following several narrow ratification votes and monetary crises, it is too early to foretell the future evolution of EC political integration.

Medium-range Ballistic Missile (MRBM): A missle with a range from 500 to 1,500 nautical miles.

Megaton: The yield of a nuclear weapon equivalent to 1 million tons of TNT (approximately equivalent to 79 Hiroshima bombs).

Microstates: Very small countries, usually with a population of less than one million.

Missile experimental (MX): A mobile, land-based missile that is shuttled among different launching sites, making it more difficult to locate and destroy.

Most Favored Nation (MFN): In international trade agreements, a country granting most-favored-nation status to another country in regard to tariffs and other trade regulations.

Multilateral: Involving many nations.

Multinational: Doing business in many nations.

Multinational corporations (MNCs): Private enterprises doing business in more than one country.

Multiple Independently Targetable Reentry Vehicle (MIRV): Two or more warheads carried by a single missile and capable of being guided to separate targets on reentry.

Munich syndrome: A lesson that was drawn by post–World War II leaders that one should not compromise with aggression.

Mutual and Balanced Force Reductions (MBFR): The 19-nation Conference on Mutual Reduction of Forces and Armaments and Associated Measures in Central Europe that has been held intermittently from 1973 to the end of the 1980s.

Mutural Assured Destruction (MAD): The basic ingredient of the doctrine of strategic deterrence that no country can escape destruction in a nuclear exchange even if it engages in a preemptive strike.

— N —

Namibia: African name for South-West Africa.

National Intelligence Estimate (NIE): The final assessment of global problems and capabilities by the intelligence community for use by the National Security Council and the president in making foreign and military decisions.

Nation-State: A political unit that is sovereign and has a population that supports and identifies with it politically.

Nautical mile: 1,853 meters.

Neocolonialism: A perjorative term describing the economic exploitation of Third World countries by the industrialized countries, in particular through the activities of multinational corporations.

Neutron bomb: Enhanced radiation bomb giving out lower blast and heat but concentrated radiaiton, thus killing people and living things while reducing damage to physical structures.

New International Economic Order (NIEO): The statement of development policies and objectives adopted at the Sixth Special Session of the UN General Assembly in 1974. NIEO calls for equal participation of LDCs in the international economic policy making process, better known as the North-South dialogue.

New world order: A term that refers to the structure and operation of the post–cold war world. Following the Persian Gulf War, President George Bush referred to a world order based on nonaggression and on international law and organization.

Nonaligned Movement (NAM): A group of Third World countries interested in promoting economic cooperation and development.

Nongovernmental organizations (NGOs or INGOs): Transnational (international) organizations made up of private organizations and individuals instead of member states.

Nonproliferation of Nuclear Weapons Treaty (NPT): Nuclear weapon states, party to the NPT, pledge not to transfer nuclear explosive devices to any recipient and not to assist any non–nuclear weapon state in the manufacture of nuclear explosive devices.

Nontariff barriers (NTB): Subtle, informal impediments to free trade desinged for the purpose of making importation of foreign goods into a country very difficult on such grounds as health and safety regulations.

Normalization of relations: The reestablishment of full diplomatic relations, including de jure recognition and the exchange of ambassadors between two countries that either did not have diplomatic relations or had broken them.

North: (as in North-South dialogue): (a) A shorthand, non-geographic term for the industrialized countries of high income, both East and West; (b) Often means only the industrialized, high-income countries of the West.

North Atlantic Treaty Organization (NATO): Also known as the Atlantic Alliance, NATO was formed in 1949 to provide collective defense against the perceived Soviet threat to Western Europe. It consists of the United States, Canada, 13 Western European countries, and Turkey.

North-South Axis: A growing tension that is developing between the North (economically developed countries) and the South (economically deprived countries). The South is insisting that the North share part of its wealth and terminate economic and political domination.

Nuclear free zone: A stretch of territory from which all nuclear weapons are banned.

Nuclear Nonproliferation Treaty (NPT): A treaty that prohibits the sale, acquisition, or production of nuclear weapons.

Nuclear proliferation: The process by which one country after another comes into possession of some form of nuclear weaponry, and with it develops the potential of launching a nuclear attack on other countries.

Nuclear reprocessing: The separation of radioactive waste (spent fuel) from a nuclear-powered plant into its fissile constituent materials. One such material is plutonium, which can then be used in the production of atomic bombs.

Nuclear terrorism: The use (or threatened use) of nuclear weapons or radioactive materials as a means of coercion.

NUT (Nuclear Utilization Theory): Advocates of this nuclear strategy position want to destroy enemy weapons before the weapons explode on one's own territory and forces. The best way to do this, according to this theory, is to destroy an enemy's weapons before they are launched.

— O —

Official Development Aid (ODA): Government contributions to projects and programs aimed at developing the productivity of poorer countries. This is to be distinguished from private, voluntary assistance, humanitarian assistance for disasters, and, most importantly, from military assistance.

Ogaden: A piece of Ethiopian desert populated by ethnic Somalis. It was a bone of contention between Ethiopia and Somalia that continued until 1988 when a peace agreement was reached.

Organization of Economic Cooperation and Development (OECD): An organization of 24 members that serves to promote economic coordination among the Western industrialized countries.

Organization of Arab Petroleum Exporting Countries (OAPEC): A component of OPEC, with Saudi Arabia, Kuwait, the United Arab Emirates, Qatar, Iraq, Algeria, and Libya as members.

Organization of Petroleum Exporting Countries (OPEC): A producers' cartel setting price floors and production ceilings of crude petroleum. It consists of Venezuela and others such as Ecuador, Gabon, Nigeria, and Indonesia.

— P —

Palestine: "Palestine" does not exist today as an entity. It refers to the historical and geographical entity administered by the British under the League of Nations mandate from 1918 to 1947. It also refers to a future entity in the aspirations of Palestinians who, as was the case of the Jews before the founding of the State of Israel, are stateless nationalists. Whether Palestinians will have an autonomous or independent homeland is an ongoing issue.

Palestine Liberation Organization (PLO): A coalition of Palestinian groups united by the goal of a Palestinian state through the destruction of Israel as a state.

Partnership for Peace Program: A U.S.–backed policy initiative for NATO formulated by the Clinton administration in 1994. The proposal was designed to rejuvenate the Atlantic Alliance and contribute to the stability of recent independent countries in Eastern Europe and the former Soviet Union. No NATO security guarantees or eventual membership in the alliance are specifically mentioned.

Payload: Warheads attached to delivery vehicles.

Peacekeeping: When an international organization such as the United Nations uses military means to prevent hostilities—usually by serving as a buffer between combatants. This international force will remain neutral between the opposing forces and must be invited by at least one of the combatants. *See* **Collective security**.

People's Republic of China (PRC): Communist or mainland China.

Petrodollars: U.S. dollar holdings of capital-surplus OPEC countries; a liability for the U.S. Treasury.

Physical Quality of Life Index (PQLI): Developed by the Overseas Development Council, the PQLI is presented as a more significant measurement of the well-being of inhabitants of a geographic entity than the solely monetary measurement of per capita income. It consists of the following measurements: life expectancy, infant mortality, and literacy figures that are each rated on an index of 1–100, within which each country is ranked according to its performance. A composite index is obtained by averaging these three measures, giving the PQLI.

Polisario: The liberation front of Western Sahara (formerly Spanish Sahara). After years of bitter fighting over Western Sahara, Polisario guerrillas signed a cease-fire agreement with Morocco in 1990. The UN will conduct a referendum in Western Sahara on whether the territory should become independent or remain part of Morocco.

Postindustrial: Characteristic of a society where a large portion of the workforce is directed to nonagricultural and nonmanufacturing tasks such as servicing and processing.

Precision-Guided Munitions (PGM): Popularly known as "smart bombs." Electronically programmed and controlled weapons that can accurately hit a moving or stationary target.

Proliferation: Quick spread, as in the case of nuclear weapons.

Protectionism: Using tariffs and nontariff barriers to control or restrict the flow of imports into a country.

Protocol: A preliminary memorandum often signed by diplomatic negotiators as a basis for a final convention or treaty.

— Q —

Quota: Quantitative limits, usually imposed on imports or immigrants.

— R —

Rapprochement: The coming together of two countries that had been hostile to each other.

Real Dollars (uninflated dollars): The report of currency in terms of what it would have been worth in a stated year.

Regionalism: A concept of cooperation among geographically adjacent states to foster region-wide political, military, and economic interests.

Reprocessing of nuclear waste: A process of recovery of fissionable materials among which is weapons-grade plutonium.

Resolution: Formal decisions of UN bodies; they may simply register an opinion or may recommend action to be taken by a UN body or agency.

Resolution 242: Passed by the UN Security Council on November 22, 1967, calling for the withdrawal of Israeli troops from territories they captured from Egypt (Sinai), Jordan (West Bank and East Jerusalem), and Syria (Golan Heights) in the 1967 war, and for the right of all nations in the Middle East to live in peace in secure and recognized borders.

Resolution 435: Passed by the UN Security Council in 1978, it called for a cease-fire between belligerents in the Namibian conflict (namely SWAPO, Angola and other front-line states on the one side, and South Africa on the other) and an internationally supervised transition process to independence and free elections.

Resolution 678: Passed by the UN in November 1990 demanding that Iraq withdraw from Kuwait. It authorized the use of all necessary force to restore Kuwait's sovereignty after January 15, 1991.

— S —

SALT I: The Strategic Arms Limitation Treaty that was signed in 1972 between the U.S. and the former Soviet Union on the limitation of strategic armaments.

SALT II: The Strategic Arms Limitation Treaty was signed in 1979. SALT II was to limit the number and types of former Soviet Union and U.S. strategic weapons. It never went into effect, as it was not ratified by the U.S. Senate.

Second strike: A nuclear attack in response to an adversary's first strike. A second-strike capability is the ability to absorb the full force of a first strike and still inflict heavy damage in retaliation.

Secretariat: (a) The administrative organ of the United Nations, headed by the secretary-general; (b) An administrative element of any IGO; this is headed by a secretary-general.

Short-range Ballistic Missiles (SRBM): A missile with a range up to 500 nautical miles.

Solidarity: Independent self-governing trade union movement started in Poland in 1980. It was terminated in December 1981 after radical members of its Presidium passed a resolution calling for a national referendum to determine if the communist government of Poland should continue to govern.

South (as in North-South axis): A shorthand, nongeographic term that includes economically less developed countries, often represented by the Group of 77.

Sovereignty: The ability to carry out laws and policies within national borders without interference from outside.

Special Drawing Rights (SDRs): Also known as paper gold. A new form of international liquid reserves to be used in the settlement of international payments among member governments of the International Monetary Fund.

State: Regarding international relations, it means a country having territory, population, government, and sovereignty, e.g., the United States is a state, while California is not a state in this sense.

State terrorism: The use of state power, including the police, the armed forces, and the secret police to throw fear among the population against any act of dissent or protest against a political regime.

"Stealth": A code name for a proposed "invisible" aircraft, supposedly not detectable by hostile forces, that would be the main U.S. strategic fighter-bomber of the 1990s.

Strategic Arms Limitation Talks. See **SALT I** and **SALT II.**

Strategic Defense Initiative (SDI): A space-based defense system designed to destroy incoming missiles. It is highly criticized because the technological possibility of such a system is questionable, not to mention the enormous cost.

Strategic minerals: Minerals needed in the fabrication of advanced military and industrial equipment. Examples are uranium, platinum, titanium, vanadium, tungsten, nickel, chromium, etc.

Strategic nuclear weapons: Long-range weapons carried on either intercontinental ballistic missiles (ICBMs) or Submarine-Launched Ballistic Missiles (SLBMs) or long-range bombers.

Strategic stockpile: Reserves of certain commodities established to ensure that in time of national emergency such commodities are readily available.

Structural Adjustment Program. See **Conditionality.**

Submarine-Launched Ballistic Missile (SLBM): A ballistic missile carried in and launched from a submarine.

Superpowers: Countries so powerful militarily (the United States and Russia), demographically (Pacific Rim countries), or economically (Japan) as to be in a class by themselves.

Supranational: Above nation-states.

— T —

Tactical nuclear weapons: Kiloton-range weapons for theatre use. The bomb dropped on Hiroshima would be in this category today.

Tariff: A tax levied on imports.

Technetronic: Shorthand for technological-electronic.

Territorial sea: The territorial sea, air space above, seabed, and subsoil are part of sovereign territory of coastal state except that ships (not aircraft) enjoy right of innocent passage. As proposed, a coastal state's sovereignty would extend 12 nautical miles beyond its land territory.

Terrorism: The systematic use of terror as a means of coercion.

Theatre: In nuclear strategy, it refers to a localized combat area such as Europe, as opposed to global warfare that would have involved the United States and the former Soviet Union in a nuclear exchange.

Theatre Nuclear Forces (TNF): Nuclear weapons systems for operations in a region such as Europe, including artillery, cruise missiles, SRBMs, IRBMs, and MRBMs.

Third World: Often used interchangeably with the terms less developed countries, developing countries, or the South, its two main institutions are the nonaligned movement (which acts primarily as the political caucus of the Third World) and the Group of 77 (which functions as the economic voice of the Third World).

Tokyo Round: The sixth round of GATT trade negotiations, begun in 1973 and ended in 1979. About 100 nations, including nonmembers of the GATT, participated.

Torture: The deliberate inflicting of pain, whether physical or psychological, to degrade, intimidate, and induce submission of its victims to the will of the torturer. It is a heinous practice used frequently in most dictatorial regimes in the world, irrespective of their ideological leanings.

Transnational: An adjective indicating that a nongovernmental movement, organization, or ideology transcends national borders and is operative in dissimilar political, economic, and social systems.

Transnational Enterprise (TNE) or Corporation (TNC). See **Multinational Corporation.**

Triad (nuclear): The three-pronged U.S. strategic weapons arsenal, composed of land-based ICBMs, underwater SLBMs, and long-range manned bombers.

Trilateral: Between three countries or groups of countries, e.g., United States, Western Europe, and Japan; United States, Russia, and China.

— U —

Unilateral: One-sided, as opposed to bilateral or multilateral.

United Nations Conference on Trade and Development (UNCTAD): A coalition of disadvantaged countries that met in 1964 in response to their effort to bridge the standard-of-living gap between themselves and DCs.

— V —

Verification: The process of determining that the other side is complying with an agreement.

Vietnam syndrome: An aversion to foreign armed intervention, especially in Third World conflicts involving guerrillas. This is an attitude that is especially common among those who were opposed to U.S. participation in the Vietnam War.

Visegrad Group: Term used to refer to Poland, Hungary, Slovakia, and the Czech Republic. These countries were subject to the same conditions and status in their recent application to participate in NATO's Partnership for Peace initiative.

— W —

Walesa, Lech: Leader of the independent trade union movement known as Solidarity, which came into existence in August 1980 and was dissolved in December 1981 by martial law decree. He was elected president of Poland in December 1990.

Warhead: That part of a missile, projectile, or torpedo that contains the explosive intended to inflict damage.

Warsaw Pact or Warsaw Treaty Organization: Established in 1955 by the Soviet Union to promote mutual defense. It was dissolved in July 1991. Member countries at time of dissolution were: the Soviet Union, Bulgaria, Czechoslovakia, Hungary, Poland, and Romania.

West (as in the East-West conflict): Basically the market-economy, industrialized, and high-income countries that are committed to a political system of representative democracy. The three main anchors of the West today are North America, Western Europe, and Japan, also known as the Trilateral countries. Australia and New Zealand are also parts of the West.

"Window of vulnerability": An expression often used, but not consistently defined, by President Ronald Reagan and his administration during the 1980s. Military specialists used the word to refer to a period of time in the late 1980s when it was predicted that the United States silo-based ICBMs could be accurately hit by Soviet missiles while the mobile MX system (now scrapped) would not yet be operational, and when the aging B-52 bombers would no longer be serviceable while the Stealth aircraft would not yet be operational. President Reagan planned to close this "window" by MIRVing the silo-based ICBMs, by hardening their concrete covers, by building B-1 bombers, and by the "Star Wars" initiative.

World Bank (International Bank for Reconstruction and Development [IBRD]): Makes loans, either directly to governments or with governments as the guarantors, and through its affiliates, the International Finance Corporation and the International Development Association.

— X — Y — Z—

Xenophobia: A dislike, fear, or suspicion of other nationalities.

Yield: The explosive force, in terms of TNT equivalence, of a warhead.

Zimbabwe: Formerly Rhodesia.

Zionism: An international movement for the establishment of a Jewish nation or religious community in Palestine and later for the support of modern Israel.

SOURCES

International Politics on the World Stage, Fourth Edition, 1993, The Dushkin Publishing Group.

Global Studies: Africa, Fifth Edition, 1993, The Dushkin Publishing Group.

Global Studies: Commonwealth of Independent States, Fourth Edition, 1992, The Dushkin Publishing Group.

Global Studies: The Middle East, Fourth Edition, 1992, The Dushkin Publishing Group.

Credits/Acknowledgments

Cover design by Charles Vitelli

1. The Western Hemisphere
Facing overview—United Nations photo by Maggie Steber.

2. The Former Soviet Union
Facing overview—Novosti photo.

3. Europe
Facing overview—United Nations photo by Philip Teuscher.

4. The Pacific Basin
Facing overview—United Nations photo by John Isaac.

5. Middle East and Africa
Facing overview—United Nations photo.

6. International Political Economy
Facing overview—United Nations photo.

7. The Politics of Arms, Arms Proliferation, and Arms Control
Facing overview—United Nations photo.

8. Collective Security and Emerging Global Issues in the New World Order
Facing overview—United Nations photo by John Isaac. 259—United Nations photo by John Isaac. 260—United Nations photo.

ANNUAL EDITIONS ARTICLE REVIEW FORM

■ NAME: _____ DATE: _____

■ TITLE AND NUMBER OF ARTICLE: _____

■ BRIEFLY STATE THE MAIN IDEA OF THIS ARTICLE: _____

_____

_____

_____

_____

■ LIST THREE IMPORTANT FACTS THAT THE AUTHOR USES TO SUPPORT THE MAIN IDEA:

_____

_____

_____

_____

_____

_____

■ WHAT INFORMATION OR IDEAS DISCUSSED IN THIS ARTICLE ARE ALSO DISCUSSED IN YOUR TEXTBOOK OR OTHER READING YOU HAVE DONE? LIST THE TEXTBOOK CHAPTERS AND PAGE NUMBERS:

_____

_____

_____

_____

_____

_____

■ LIST ANY EXAMPLES OF BIAS OR FAULTY REASONING THAT YOU FOUND IN THE ARTICLE:

_____

_____

_____

_____

_____

■ LIST ANY NEW TERMS/CONCEPTS THAT WERE DISCUSSED IN THE ARTICLE AND WRITE A SHORT DEFINITION:

_____

_____

_____

_____

_____

_____

We Want Your Advice

ANNUAL EDITIONS:
WORLD POLITICS 94/95
Article Rating Form

Here is an opportunity for you to have direct input into the next revision of this volume. We would like you to rate each of the 48 articles listed below, using the following scale:

1. **Excellent: should definitely be retained**
2. **Above average: should probably be retained**
3. **Below average: should probably be deleted**
4. **Poor: should definitely be deleted**

Your ratings will play a vital part in the next revision. So please mail this prepaid form to us just as soon as you complete it.
Thanks for your help!

Annual Editions revisions depend on two major opinion sources: one is our Advisory Board, listed in the front of this volume, which works with us in scanning the thousands of articles published in the public press each year; the other is you—the person actually using the book. Please help us and the users of the next edition by completing the prepaid article rating form on this page and returning it to us. Thank you.

Rating	Article	Rating	Article
1	1. The Clash of Civilizations?		22. Japan: The End of One-Party Dominance
4	2. The Conceptual Poverty of U.S. Foreign Policy		23. The Rise of China
	3. Evaluating Foreign Policy Relationships: America and Post–Cold War Asia		24. North Korea: The Dangerous Outsider
	4. A Renewed Security Partnership? The United States and the European Community in the 1990s		25. What Is an Economy For?
			26. Can It Really Be Peace?
			27. Not Fanatics, and Not Friends
			28. A Global Militant Network
	5. Ten Issues in Search of a Policy: America's Failed Approach to the Post-Soviet States		29. Radicals Gain Strength in Horn of Africa
			30. From Peace-keeping to Peace Enforcement: The Somalia Precedent
	6. Islam in the West's Sights: The Wrong Crusade?		31. Africa's 'New Wind of Change'
	7. Latin America's International Relations in the Post–Cold War Era		32. South Africa's Future Foreign Policy
		1	33. The Business Response to the Global Marketplace
	8. Global Village or Global Pillage?		34. A Realignment Made Reluctantly
	9. The Real Coup		35. Beyond Conditionality
	10. The New Russian Foreign Policy		36. What's Wrong? Why the Industrialized Nations Are Stalled
	11. Security Issues and the Eastern Slavic States		37. In Beijing and Moscow, Starkly Different Policies and Results
	12. Will Russia Disintegrate into Bantustans?		
	13. Redefined NATO Faces Growing Pains		38. Five Minutes Past Midnight—and Welcome to the Age of Proliferation
	14. Reinventing the Politics of Europe		
	15. Searching for Identity, Germany Struggles with Its History		39. Dismantling the Arsenals: Arms Control and the New World Agenda
	16. Europe Slams the Door		40. Fighting Off Doomsday
	17. The Great Transformation		41. Shifting Battle Lines in Arms Race
	18. In a New Slovakia, Fears Are Both New and Old		42. The Bomb or Peace
			43. Jihad vs. McWorld
	19. Why Yugoslavia Fell Apart		44. Defence in the 21st Century
	20. The Answer		45. Empowering the United Nations
	21. Rivals or Partners? Prospects for U.S.–Japan Cooperation in the Asia-Pacific Region		46. Can the UN Be the World's Cop?
			47. Poverty, Population, Pollution
			48. Deceptive Stereotypes about 'Tribal Warfare'

(Continued on next page)

ABOUT YOU

Name_____ Date_____

Are you a teacher? ☐   Or student? ☐

Your School Name _____

Department _____

Address _____

City _____ State _____ Zip _____

School Telephone # _____

YOUR COMMENTS ARE IMPORTANT TO US!

Please fill in the following information:

For which course did you use this book? _____

Did you use a text with this Annual Edition?   ☐ yes   ☐ no

The title of the text? _____

What are your general reactions to the Annual Editions concept?

Have you read any particular articles recently that you think should be included in the next edition?

Are there any articles you feel should be replaced in the next edition? Why?

Are there other areas that you feel would utilize an Annual Edition?

May we contact you for editorial input?

May we quote you from above?

ANNUAL EDITIONS: WORLD POLITICS 94/95

BUSINESS REPLY MAIL

First Class   Permit No. 84   Guilford, CT

Postage will be paid by addressee

The Dushkin Publishing Group, Inc.
Sluice Dock
DPG **Guilford, Connecticut 06437**